WILLIAM PITT
THE YOUNGER

WILLIAM PITT
THE YOUNGER
by
Robin Reilly

G. P. PUTNAM'S SONS • NEW YORK

FIRST AMERICAN EDITION 1979

Library of Congress Cataloging in Publication Data

Reilly, Robin.
William Pitt the Younger.

Bibliography: p.
Includes index.
1. Pitt, William, 1759–1806. 2. Great Britain—
Politics and government—1760–1820. 3. Prime ministers
—Great Britain—Bibliography.   I. Title.
DA522.P6R44   1979   941.07′3′0924   [B]   78-13050
ISBN 0-399-12130-7
PRINTED IN THE UNITED STATES OF AMERICA

Contents

Acknowledgements

THE SOURCES of all quotations from manuscript and printed material are listed in the text under Notes and References. I am grateful, in particular, to the Trustees of the British Museum, and to Captain G. M. T. Pretyman and the authorities of the County Record Office, Ipswich, for permission to quote from manuscripts in their possession. Transcripts of Crown-copyright records in the Public Record Office appear by permission of the Controller of HM Stationery Office.

The portrait of George III by Zoffany is reproduced by gracious permission of Her Majesty the Queen. Permission to reproduce paintings and engravings, or to use copyright photographs, was kindly granted by the Marquis of Lansdowne, the Earl Fitzwilliam, the Earl of Rosebery, the Viscount Cowdray, the Viscount FitzHarris, the Trustees of the British Museum, the Administrative Trustees of the Chevening Estate, Christ Church Oxford, The City of Kingston-upon-Hull, the Courtauld Institute, The Leger Galleries Ltd, the Benchers of Lincoln's Inn, The National Portrait Gallery, London, the National Gallery of Art, Washington, D.C., the Royal Marine Corps, and the Scottish National Portrait Gallery.

I offer my sincere thanks to all those who have generously given practical help towards the preparation of this book, and particularly to Dierdre Guy, who typed the manuscript and drew my attention to numerous careless omissions and faults of woolly description, and to Dr. P. Cole.

Introduction

IT IS THE COMMON DILEMMA of those who choose to write biography that their subjects, often characters of minor significance in comparison with their contemporaries, must be made to stand out in relief from the social and political background without assuming an importance that is neither merited nor justifiable in history. No such dilemma faces the biographer of the younger Pitt. For twenty-two years, which included three when he was out of office and rarely attended the House of Commons, he exercised a supremacy over British politics that remains unique in the story of parliament. His reputation as 'The Pilot that weathered the Storm' has survived untarnished the most prejudiced labours of historians. It is not even possible to deny his greatness by depreciating his opponents: he dominated a House of Commons that included Fox, Burke, Sheridan, Wilberforce, Windham and Grey. He brought to the office of Prime Minister new standards of integrity that made the behaviour of all his predecessors, and a fair number of his successors, appear shabby or criminal. He worked as few ministers have ever worked. His private life was unblemished. He died, at the age of forty-six, 'The Saviour of Europe'. The portrait that has been handed down the years is immaculate, and bloodless.

The dilemma of Pitt's biographers is both different and unusual. His lifetime spanned a period of extraordinary change, brought about rapidly by revolution and war, and more gradually by the development of forces that were then unidentified or scarcely understood. Britain faced a bewildering succession of crises—financial, commercial and military—in all of which Pitt played a central part. The wealth of relevant material for a political biography is so great that it seems to dictate the structure of the work: either it must extend to the equivalent of at least two weighty volumes, containing a comprehensive account of Pitt's public career, accepting that the man will be buried by the events; or it must be unashamedly an outline, a brief life, attempting neither detail nor characterization. Both alternatives provide a disguise for the lack of material for a study of his private life.

Pitt was a poor correspondent, even when he had time to spare, and he revealed little of himself in those letters that have survived. Two of his closest associates during his years of greatest power, Dundas and Addington, destroyed the greater part of his correspondence with them; and Bishop Pretyman Tomline, to whom Pitt's private papers were entrusted, indulged in an orgy of devastation which ensured that nothing of the slightest personal significance that came into his possession remained to posterity. Not content with the role of incendiary, Tomline appointed himself official biographer. The result combines uncritical devotion with a suffocating pomposity of style, and is most notable for containing 'the whole contents of the Annual Register and Parliamentary Debates'.* Tomline's work is, nevertheless, important. No less than his destruction of Pitt's private papers, it was dedicated to the preservation of his friend's reputation, and, interred among the platitudes, there is a portrait, however sanctified, by one of the few men who ever shared Pitt's confidence.

The search for Pitt's private character leads naturally to the letters, the journals and the memoirs of his friends, his associates, and his enemies. These cast valuable, if often biased, light upon his thoughts and motives. The search leads, also, to an examination of his speeches in the House of Commons. Made almost without notes, and often under considerable pressure, they might be expected to yield

* Thomas Moore: *Memoirs of the Right Honourable Richard Brinsley Sheridan* (London 1825) Vol. II, p. 35.

useful clues to the character of the man who made them; but Pitt's iron self-restraint prevented any spontaneous display of emotion, and the restrictions imposed on the reporting of parliamentary debates rob his speeches of much of their power. Parliamentary proceedings seldom make good reading. The art of oratory is part language and part histrionics, and its style requires repetition, emphasis and dramatic delivery, effective in the atmosphere of the moment but often sterile or even absurd in print. The speeches of eighteenth-century politicians abound in classical allusions and quotations which were the equipment of educated Englishmen but now appear as affectation. Stripped of the voices, the gestures, the dramatic pauses, or even the original words or phrasing, the speeches of Pitt, Fox, Burke and Sheridan are sadly unimpressive. In an age when verbiage and quotation were often mistaken for eloquence, and grandiloquence substituted for style, brevity and clarity were rarities little esteemed among orators.

It is not possible in a single volume to describe in detail the events of Pitt's lifetime or the intricacies of his policies. Those details may be found elsewhere, in the histories of the period, the political studies by Sir Lewis Namier and Richard Pares, and the monumental biographies by Stanhope, Holland Rose, and John Ehrman (whose second volume is still to be published). I have therefore given little more than an outline of the events, selecting for special attention those episodes which seem to shed light on Pitt's character and personality, and giving some weight to three important influences in his life: his health, his alcoholism and his sexuality. This is not a work of deep original research. It is an attempt to assemble and interpret material, much of it already published, which may help towards a better understanding of the man who was Britain's youngest, and perhaps greatest, Prime Minister.

I

'The Cleverest Child'
1759-1776

THE BRILLIANT SUMMER OF 1759 lasted late into October. It was, as always in England, just cause for celebration. 'Can one,' asked Horace Walpole, 'easily leave the remains of such a year as this? . . . One would think we had plundered the East and West Indies of sunshine.' It was not, however, for sunshine that the church bells were 'worn threadbare with ringing'. After twenty years of expensive and bloody war, briefly interrupted by the futile and often disregarded Treaty of Aix-la-Chapelle, the bells were rung for victories. At Minden, at Quebec, and at Quiberon Bay, the British and their allies had triumphed. The heroes of the people were Major-General James Wolfe and Admiral Sir Edward Hawke. Wolfe, in death, achieved immortality in history, and Hawke the thanks of parliament and a handsome pension, but much of the credit was due to the man who, as Secretary of State for the Southern Department and Chief Minister of the Crown in the House of Commons, was responsible for the conduct of the war. For William Pitt, who had taken office in strained harness with the Duke of Newcastle in June 1757, these victories were the first ripened fruit of his strategy. His satisfaction in these public successes enhanced his pleasure in an event of some importance in his private life: on 28 May his wife, Hester, had given birth to their second son. The year was, indeed, as a London newspaper described it, 'glorious and ever memorable'.

The Pitt family was established and, overlooking certain curiosities common to English pedigrees, respectable. The descendants of Sir William Pitt, a substantial landowner and Commissioner of the Navy early in the seventeenth century, could claim connection through marriage to the Earls of Londonderry, Ligonier, and Stanhope, and by elopement to a trooper in the Horse Guards named Smith. They had acquired land, position, and the patronage of parliamentary seats; and they had served their country, providing two governors of Fort St George, Madras, a consul at Masulipatam and more domestically, a colonel who had been aide-de-camp to the King.

William Pitt, the architect of British victories in the Seven Years' War with France, was descended from Thomas, a physician of Blandford, Dorset, and younger brother of Charles I's Commissioner of the Navy. William's grandfather had achieved some notoriety as governor of Fort St George, and more for his purchase of an exceptionally large diamond. 'Governor' or 'Diamond' Pitt was a man of considerable ability, extreme irascibility, and few scruples. In September 1709, when the directors of the East India Company recalled him, he returned to England with a substantial fortune which was augmented eight years later by the sale of the great diamond to the Regent of France. Both the Governor and his eldest son, Robert, were returned to parliament as members for the rotten borough of Old Sarum, which boasted only seven electors, and they were joined in 1715 by Robert's two younger brothers as members for Wilton and Hindon in Wiltshire. The Pitts were already forming one of those family parties in the House of Commons whose votes were solicited by political leaders. They were also forming influential connections by marriage. Robert's wife, Harriet Villiers, was descended from the great Dukes of Buckingham, and his brothers and sisters had married into the Lyttelton, Londonderry, Fauconberg, Cholmondeley, and Stanhope families.

Little of the Governor's fortune was inherited by his grandchildren. His wife, and his children, of whom four survived him, were enthusiastic spenders, and he had lived in some style. He left a legacy richer in squalid family disputes and litigation than in possessions, and he was remembered with gratitude only by the lawyers. When Robert, his spendthrift, quarrelsome, and devious eldest son, died a year after him in 1727, the residue of both estates was seized by William's elder brother Thomas.

William Pitt, the Governor's favourite grandchild among what he called 'the cockatrice brood', was born in 1708. He was educated at Eton, an experience which he said later cowed boys for life, and at Oxford. In parliament he chose to oppose the government led by Sir Robert Walpole, joining those members who, grouped around the heir to the throne, looked for office on the death of the King. Pitt's oratory, a powerful blending of a remarkable command of language, disdainful self-confidence, and hypnotic personality, won him few friends and, so long as he chose to remain in opposition, ensured the active disfavour of George II; but his supremacy in the House of Commons was undeniable. The sane and painstaking efforts of Robert Walpole to preserve peace with Spain appeared perverse and faint-hearted beside Pitt's trumpet blasts to arms in defence of British trade. Walpole's hastily concocted Convention of Pardo in 1739, his last bid for peace, was denounced by Pitt, with some justice, as an 'illusory expedient'. On 8 October war was declared. It was a victory for commercial interests and for Pitt, and the war was greeted by the London crowds with uncomprehending joy. Almost alone among those concerned with national policy Walpole understood that war with Spain could not be confined to the high seas and the Spanish colonies in America: 'They may ring their bells now, but soon they will be wringing their hands.'

Within three years Walpole's worst fears were realized and Europe was in turmoil. The British became involved in the scramble for possession of the Habsburg dominions following the death of the Emperor Charles VI, and the King's beloved Electorate of Hanover, tactlessly described by Pitt as 'despicable', was threatened. Walpole resigned, narrowly escaping impeachment. Engaged by treaty* as allies of Queen Maria Theresa, the British, though not at war with France, found themselves fighting the French as well as the Spanish. A brave display was made at the battle of Dettingen on 16 June 1743, when George II personally presided over a victory which was but scarcely deserved and sadly mismanaged, but the glory was short-lived. The army was crushed at Fontenoy in the following year and

* The Pragmatic Sanction (1713), confirmed by the Treaty of Vienna (1731), guaranteeing the inheritance by Maria Theresa of the Habsburg possessions ruled by her father, the Emperor Charles VI.

by the winter it had been withdrawn from the Continent to deal with the urgent menace of invasion. The Jacobite rebellion of 1745, following the landing of Prince Charles Edward Stuart in Scotland, lacked the massive French support promised earlier, but nevertheless offered a sufficiently serious threat to the Hanoverian monarchy to require the full strength of the small British army to destroy it at Culloden in April 1746. Strong detachments of soldiers were quartered in Scotland for several years afterwards to suppress the Highlanders.

The evident weakness of the administration, the panic produced in London by the advance of the Jacobite army as far as Derby, and the demands of a Continental war, at last brought Pitt into government. The King, who had declined to appoint him Secretary at War, was induced to accept him as Paymaster of the Forces. An army was again sent to Holland, where the Duke of Cumberland*, attempting to gild the laurels he had won at Culloden, led his mixed force of Austrian, Dutch, Hanoverian, Hessian, and British troops to decisive defeat at the hands of the French. This battle, at Laffeldt on 21 June 1747, was the last of the war. Preliminaries of peace were signed in April 1748 and six months later these were expanded into the Treaty of Aix-la-Chapelle. The terms, which failed to determine the main issues between Britain and France in their commercial rivalry and conflicting colonial ambitions, ensured that peace would be temporary.

As Paymaster, Pitt had been able for the first time to demonstrate his abilities in office. He suppressed his unstable temperament sufficiently to avoid unnecessary conflict with his colleagues in government, and his work to improve conditions in the army pleased the King. By refusing the traditional and highly lucrative perquisites of Paymaster he also gained a reputation for unusual integrity and great popularity in the City. There was good reason to suppose, as he did, that he would soon be promoted to high office and that, on the death of Henry Pelham in 1754, he would succeed him as leader of the House of Commons. He was to be disappointed. In the reshuffle of ministers no suitable place was found for him and he retired. Two years later the patchwork peace disintegrated and, after a year of political manoeuvring, Pitt was recalled to office, the leadership of

* William Augustus, Duke of Cumberland (1721-65), third son of George II.

4

the House, and what was to be in effect the direction of British strategy.

Pitt's design was based upon the supremacy of trade. As he had said in the House of Commons eighteen years earlier, 'When trade is at stake it is your last retrenchment, you must defend it or perish.' From 1757 he was concerned less with the defence of British interests than with the systematic destruction of those of the French. The blockade of the enemy fleets in port made possible the conquest of Canada, the capture of Guadeloupe, the attack on Manila, and the victories of Robert Clive and Eyre Coote in India. The territorial acquisition and expansion inseparable from these military adventures laid the foundations of a vast empire for which Pitt has been both credited and blamed; but territorial gains were incidental to his strategic plan. Under his direction the French were deprived of their trade in fish, furs, sugar, spices, gum, and slaves, and lost control of the China tea trade. Attempts to break out from the harbours of Brest and Toulon resulted in the destruction of both French fleets. In 1759, the year of victories when his second son was born, Pitt reached the zenith of his power and popular acclaim. Within two years he was once more out of office, and in 1763 a peace was signed which abandoned his most cherished hopes and, so he believed, his most important achievements.

The younger William Pitt was born at Hayes, Kent, on 28 May 1759. His elder brother, John, was three years his senior, and a third son, James, was born two years later. Their sisters, Hester and Harriot, were born in 1755 and 1758. Their mother, Hester, was a Grenville, and thus a member of one of the most important political families in England. She was also a woman of considerable beauty and respectable intellect, and one who, despite her husband's uncertain temper, and finally paranoia, was able to offer him untiring devotion and care. Married at the comparatively late age of thirty-three, and thirteen years younger than her husband, she was deeply in love with him and ready to make any sacrifice for his welfare. Her sweetness of temper was essential to the comfort of her husband and the happiness of her children, and it was her resolution and passionate loyalty that secured the fabric of their family life.

The part played by heredity in the formation of character may be

5

overestimated, but it would be unrealistic to ignore it. If the influence of the elder Pitt is evident in the political capacities and behaviour of his son, it is also clear that their characters were dissimilar. Young William inherited more from the Grenvilles than a striking physical resemblance. Patience, optimism, pertinacity, and the concentration of both interest and ability in administration and finance were not noticeable in the elder Pitt or his ancestors, but they were characteristics of the best of the Grenvilles. The Pitts were unstable*, sometimes to the extent of derangement, and their brilliance was wayward. Fearless individualists, both in their public and their private lives, they neither cared for nor understood their fellow men, and were aloof and tactless in their dealings with them. In this at least, the Pitts and the Grenvilles had something in common.

The Pitt children were brought up in that atmosphere which envelops the families of the famous. Their father, after the King the most important man in the land, was the object of attention, respect, and curiosity wherever he went. Their journeys, on family holidays to the Devon or Dorset coasts, became progresses which were almost royal in quality: church bells were rung, flowers were strewn in their path, petitions and addresses presented. While at Hayes Place, their house in Kent, they were accustomed to frequent visits of men who were often members both of the government and of the family. In 1761, two years after young William's birth, his father was rewarded for his services by the creation of a peerage for his wife, who became Baroness Chatham. This device enabled Pitt to remain in the House of Commons. Five years later, however, Pitt accepted the earldom of Chatham for himself, abandoning the arena of his power, whether in office or out, and sacrificing much of his popularity. It was an error of judgement so elementary and clumsy as to cast doubts upon his fitness for office.

Hayes Place, which Pitt seems to have considered as little more than a cottage, was a substantial house containing twenty-four bedrooms and standing in an estate of several hundred acres of pasture, woodland 'scattered with Pleasing Negligence', and gardens elegantly 'adorned with Seats, Alcoves, etc.' [1] In 1765 Pitt inherited,

* Of the elder Pitt's brothers and sisters, one died in an asylum, and at least two more were mentally disturbed. The strain reappeared in the second Lord Camelford and Lady Hester Stanhope.

unexpectedly, the property of Burton Pynsent in Somerset. This extraordinary bequest from Sir William Pynsent, an admirer unknown to Pitt, gave him an opportunity for ruinous extravagance denied to him, in spite of alterations, improvements and purchases of land, at Hayes. He embarked upon an orgy of road-building, landscaping, deforestation and afforestation, experimental farming, and architectural adventure. A large new wing was added to the already unmanageable house, furniture was acquired, portraits commissioned, including a series by the fashionable and expensive Sir Joshua Reynolds, and a column 140 feet high erected as a memorial to Pynsent. While his wife made determined but futile economies, Pitt continued to spend. When his debts became insupportable, he borrowed from his friends, respecting the excellence of their desire to help him and apparently unconscious of his improvidence. It seems probable from his behaviour that he considered the balancing of income and expenditure trivial, irrelevant, and vulgar. It is certain that he never made any attempt to create such a balance.

Pitt's experience of life at Eton had determined him to have his sons educated at home, and in 1765 he engaged the Reverend Edward Wilson, a graduate of Pembroke Hall *, Cambridge, as tutor. The eldest son, John, who would in due course inherit the earldom, was destined for the army. Though amiable he exhibited signs of a natural lethargy which proved incurable. James, who could not expect to inherit title or estates and must therefore earn his living, was to be sent into the navy, the profession traditionally preferred for younger sons who might hope to found their family fortunes upon prize money. For William—'Eager Mr. William', 'impetuous William', 'little Secretary'—Pitt reserved the palm of parliament. He was, almost from the first, his father's favourite. Alert, precocious, patient and industrious, William seemed, even in childhood, to possess to an astonishing degree the finest qualities of both Pitt and Grenville. Though Pitt doted on all his sons, referring to his eldest optimistically as 'the young Vauban', and to the youngest as 'dear little tar', it was 'our dear William' who engaged his time and attention during his years of retirement.

William was a fragile child. Short, thin, and pallid, he was subject

* Now Pembroke College.

7

to frequent and debilitating colds and coughs, accompanied by swollen glands and fevers. The little evidence available seems to indicate that these were the symptoms of infected tonsils and adenoids, and he appears to have outgrown them, as might be expected, when he reached puberty. There is nothing to suggest that these early illnesses, which caused so much concern to his parents, had anything to do with his ill health later in life, unless the treatment prescribed by the family doctors weakened his already delicate constitution. Dr Anthony Addington, Pitt's physician, believed that William had inherited from his father a tendency to gout and that soot bark, blistering, and a 'cordial confection' would 'root out . . . something morbid that had long lurk'd' in the boy's body.[2] It would be unwise to dismiss the diagnosis without further evidence. Gout was one of the few ailments which eighteenth-century physicians were fully competent to recognize, and, however unlikely it may appear, it is possible that Addington's diagnosis was not as fatuous as the prescribed treatment.

In addition to the boy's tutor, a nurse, Mrs 'Pam' Sparry, looked after the Pitt children and it is evident that William was her special charge. In spite of his delicacy he took part in the pursuits of his brothers, learning to ride well and to shoot, but his interests lay naturally more in his books. At the age of seven he was able to write a letter to his father in passable Latin and his letters to him in English show so odd an imitation of the elder Pitt's style at its most pompous that one might be tempted to accuse him of deliberate parody. To his father, who described wasps as 'an ambuscade of Pandours' and his horses as 'these coursers of spirit not inferior to Xanthus and Podarges',[3] the eleven-year-old William wrote on 31 July 1770, 'I flatter myself that the sun shone on your expedition and that the views were enough enlivened thereby to prevent the drowsy Morpheus from taking the opportunity of the heat to diffuse his poppies upon the eyes of the travellers'.[4] It is a relief to find him addressing his elder brother in terms of affectionate banter which might have been used by any educated boy of his period.

All the children inherited, in part at least, their mother's looks and much of her charm, but it seems again to have been William who was most fortunate. Lady Caroline Holland, mother of Charles James Fox, described him as 'really the cleverest child I ever saw *and brought up so strictly and so proper in his behaviour*.'[5] She added,

8

with remarkable prescience, '*Mark my words*, that little boy will be a thorn in Charles's side as long as he lives.' The poet, William Hayley, introduced by Captain Alexander Hood * to the two elder Pitt boys while they were on holiday in Dorset in June 1773, found that William 'eclipsed his brother in conversation'. He also endeared himself to Hayley by riding to show him several places of historical interest in the neighbourhood of Lyme Regis and particularly the spot 'where the shake of an earthquake, in some preceding centuries, was supposed to have produced a wild and beautiful irregularity of appearance in the face of nature'.[6]

William's early education seems to have taken the form of lessons, with his brothers and sisters, under Edward Wilson, augmented by personal tuition from his father. Pitt certainly read the classics with his son and expected from him a high standard of expression in written and spoken language. Though frequent illness interrupted his studies, the boy's quick mind and extraordinarily retentive memory enabled him to digest and accumulate learning without apparent effort. In Wilson's phrase, he 'seemed never to learn but merely to recollect'.[7] The letters written in his childhood to his mother and brothers and sisters show an attractive light touch and well-developed powers of observation and description. They contrast a little sadly with the high-flown and unsuitable strivings after eloquence directed to his father and senior relations. He also wrote some verse. A long effusion, *On the Genius of Poetry*, in William's hand but perhaps composed with his sister Harriot and dated 1771, shows some precocity of phrasing and a fair neatness of expression in fashionable imitation of Pope.[8] More interesting in terms of his future is the play, which appears to have been his unaided work and in which he acted with his brothers and sisters at Burton Pynsent on 30 May 1772. Though William's performance was wooden and awkward [9], the plot and his role in it show his youthful interest in political intrigue and give some indication of his enduring ideal of loyalty. The part he had written for himself, that of a statesman who risked everything to serve his king in time of treason and conspiracy, was one which he came close to playing again, but in earnest, seventeen years later.

After Eton, Pitt had been educated at Oxford, and it is surprising

* Later Admiral Lord Bridport.

9

that he chose to send his younger son to Cambridge, so much further away from Burton Pynsent. The deciding factor was probably his wish that Edward Wilson should continue to tutor the boy. Wilson, who had recommended his own college, wrote to his wife in December 1772.

I could not have acted with more prudence than I have done in the affair of Pembroke Hall. Mr Pitt is not the child his years bespeak him to be. He has now all the understanding of a man. . . . He has sound principles, a grateful and liberal heart, *and talents une-qual'd*. He will go to Pembroke, not a weak boy to be made a property of, but to be admired as a prodigy; not to hear lectures but to spread light. His parts are most astonishing and universal. He will be perfectly qualified for a wrangler *before he goes*, and will be an accomplished classick, mathematician, historian and poet. This is no exaggeration, believe me. . . .[10]

Chatham, less dazzled by his son's abilities, believed him 'too young for the irregularities of a man, [but] . . . he will not, on the other hand, prove troublesome by the Puerile sallies of a Boy'.[11]

William Pitt arrived at Pembroke Hall on 8 October 1773 *, aged fourteen. As the son of a peer he was not obliged to sit any examinations in order to obtain his degree, but Cambridge enjoyed a reputation for industry rather greater than Oxford's, and Pembroke was, as Pitt wrote to his father, a 'sober' college with 'nothing but solid study there'.[12] His attendance was intermittent and, during his first year, he spent little time in his spacious set of rooms over the college gate. Within two weeks of his taking up residence he suffered a recurrence of his old illness. The attack was severe, and Dr Robert Glynn, called in immediately by Wilson, expressed doubts that his patient would survive to manhood.[13] 'Pam' Sparry was sent post-haste to Cambridge to nurse him and, in December, he was pronounced fit to be moved to Burton Pynsent.† The crisis passed, and William regained his strength, but his parents remained anxious and, between December 1773 and the summer term of 1776, he spent only seven months at Cambridge. Addington was again called on to

* His name had been entered in the college books in April.
  † This incident accounts for Thomas Moore's story that Pitt was accompanied to the University by his nurse.

examine the boy and was more than ever persuaded that the cause of his illness was gout. He prescribed as treatment a bottle a day of the most toxic of all wines, port.[14] That his patient made a good recovery and never again showed symptoms of any similar trouble convinced Addington that his diagnosis was correct and his prescription effective, but it was strange treatment for a boy who, two years earlier, had not been allowed by his father to taste ale. In the short term Pitt probably owed his recovery to rest, care, fresh air, and healthy exercise; in the long term the medical advice he followed was to prove fatal.

At home William rode with Wilson, hunted with the local hounds (his mother and sisters following in 'the little Chaise') and continued his studies. At Cambridge his studies were entrusted to the special care of Joseph Turner and George Pretyman, two college lecturers, and Edward Wilson remained with him until 1775 when he was appointed rector of Binfield, Berkshire. Pretyman then became William's sole tutor. He was eight years older than his pupil and was to become his private secretary and lifelong friend. His influence might therefore be expected to be significant, but there is no evidence that this was so. Dr George Pretyman was a cleric of more than ordinary insipidity and his prime distinction lies in his use of his close association with the younger Pitt to write one of the most vapid and unreadable biographies in the English language. In all other respects his reputation remains unblemished. It is plain that William found him, at times, intensely irritating, but he remained loyal to him under the most trying circumstances and did his utmost to further Pretyman's career. Though prim and pedantic, Pretyman was a considerable classical scholar and mathematician, the two disciplines in which his pupil excelled, and he was later elected Fellow of the Royal Society. To the young Pitt, accustomed to the grandiose and declamatory form of his father's speech, Pretyman's style may not have seemed unduly sententious or ornate.

William took his M.A. degree, by right and without examination, in 1776, but remained at the University for a further three years, keeping regular terms and studying hard. As he wrote to his mother, 'This place has so many Advantages for Study, and I have unavoidably lost so much Time lately, and can spare so little for the Future.'[15] He seems to have been aware that his years at Cambridge represented the single opportunity he would ever have to cultivate his

11

mind, and it is clear that he was never again able to find time to add significantly to his formal education. He attended few lectures but applied his remarkable intellect and phenomenal memory to the classics, mathematics, English history, and political philosophy. To the end of his life he was able to discuss, in learned company, the etymology and comparative merits of the classical authors, and illustrate his argument with long, accurate, and relevant quotations from Thucydides or Pliny, Plutarch or Cicero, Quintilian or Sallust. He was fascinated by Newton's *Principia* *, as much for the detailed concentration required for its understanding as for its intrinsic merit, and was familiar with the most important works on English civil law and political thought. His understanding of written French was adequate and he had made some study of French literature, but of the contemporary English authors he knew little. He had a poor opinion of them which he did not change in later life. His interest in theology was slight, and his regular attendance at chapel was more from duty than devotion. Pretyman prayed for him.

From 1776 William was able to take some part in the social life of the University. His circle of friends, drawn mostly from other colleges, was sober for the times, and almost all of them were later to be associated with him in politics. His closest friend, later to be also his brother-in-law, and the only one of William's intimate circle from his own college, was Edward James Eliot. Others included John Pratt (later Lord Camden), Lord Westmorland, Lord Althorp, Lord Euston (heir to the Duke of Grafton), Lord Granby (later Duke of Rutland), William Lowther, Henry Bankes, J.C. Villiers, St Andrew St John, Charles Long, and William Meeke. All were what the watchful Dr Pretyman approvingly described as 'young men of his own age and station in life'.[16] Young Pitt's conversation, if Pretyman may be believed, was 'abounding in playful wit and quick repartee' and 'his society was universally sought'.[17] A rather less infatuated opinion, from William Wilberforce, who went up to St John's College in October 1776, confirmed that in company William was 'remarkably cheerful and pleasant, full of wit and playfulness'.[18] Wilberforce, destined to be one of Pitt's most intimate friends, scarcely knew him at Cambridge. Their groups of friends were very different. De-

* Sir Isaac Newton's *Philosophiae Naturalis Principia Mathematica*, written in 1685-6 and first published complete in 1687.

12

scribed as 'by far the most agreeable and popular man amongst the undergraduates at Cambridge',[19] Wilberforce wrote of his set, 'They drank hard, and their conversation was even worse than their lives.'[20]

As early as January 1775 William began to visit Westminster to hear Chatham speak and to listen to debates. His letters to his mother show that he listened critically while paying particular attention to the effect of speeches upon ministers and members. Chatham's electrifying presence and extraordinary authority were founded upon unrivalled use of language and brilliant delivery. His speeches were great artistic performances which even his friend David Garrick might have envied. William Pitt watched with care. He was consciously preparing himself for the stage from which his father was soon to make his last dramatic exit.

II

'Only Earl of Chatham'
1760-1767

IN 1760, after a reign lasting thirty-three years, George II died. He was succeeded in October by his grandson, an earnest, stubborn and rather dull twenty-one-year-old, who had inherited but not digested his father's * mass of prejudices. The first of the Hanoverian Kings to consider himself British, he had made his declaration of this belief in his speech from the throne in 1761: 'Born and educated in this country, I glory in the name of Britain',[21] and this profession was sincere. He cared little for Europe and even less for the Electorate of Hanover, so dear to his grandfather, which he referred to in terms scarcely less offensive than Pitt's. Contrary to his historical reputation, he was neither stupid nor ill-educated; and it is now accepted that he was not, until the last few years of his life, insane.[22] That he was bluntly honest, courageous, tactless, often inept, and in his early years as King disastrously advised, is seldom questioned.

It was a convention throughout the eighteenth century that opposition to the government grouped itself round the heir to the throne. Since the King chose his ministers, the monarch and his

---

* Frederick Louis, Prince of Wales, eldest son and heir to George II, had died in 1751. 'Poor Fred' had married, in 1736, Princess Augusta of Saxe-Gotha.

eldest son were brought into political conflict which might develop into personal loathing. Opposition to George II's administrations had been led by Frederick, Prince of Wales, but at the time of his death the new heir apparent was twelve years old. This lack of a centre of opposition, which also robbed it of much of its reason for existing, created a political instability which worsened with the death of Henry Pelham in 1754. The crisis of war had made possible a contrived and temporary alliance between Pitt and the Duke of Newcastle but, although their abilities were so complementary as to make their combined power almost unassailable, their temperaments were so ill-matched as to make any co-operation between them a matter for astonishment. Newcastle was a nervous, fussy, indecisive hypochondriac, obsessed by detail, and one of the most successful political manipulators in the history of parliament. The elder Pitt was shrewd, opinionated, arrogant, bold and domineering. He enjoyed the grand gesture as much as the grand design, cared nothing for electioneering, and retained his popularity by his ardent patriotism and evident integrity. Newcastle was mocked by his contemporaries, and underrated. Pitt was trusted and feared.

Newcastle, as First Lord of the Treasury, was nominal head of the government, but its true leader was Pitt, before his ennoblement, dominating the House of Commons with his oratory. The rest of the administration inherited by the new King were of little account except for Lord Anson at the Admiralty, and Henry Fox who was busy lining his pockets as Paymaster of the Forces. George III viewed them all with suspicion. All had served his grandfather, and some, including Pitt, had deserted his father in order to do so; but it was necessary to retain a stable and powerful ministry at least until the war should be won. The King prudently contented himself with minor replacements and the appointment of Lord Bute as Secretary of State for the North.

John Stuart, 3rd Earl of Bute, was then forty-eight years old. A connection of the Dukes of Argyll, he had been befriended by Frederick, Prince of Wales * and after the Prince's death, had become the mentor, confidant, and most intimate companion of the heir to the throne. Suspected, unjustly, of being the lover of the

---

* Frederick unkindly described him as 'a fine showy man, and would make an excellent Ambassador at any court where there was no business'.

widowed Princess of Wales, Bute had engaged the affections of the young Prince to a degree which, in other circumstances, might have been considered unhealthy. There were, indeed, many who believed that his political influence was far from benign, and the extent of his power was regarded with growing apprehension. Bute had assumed command of the forty-five members of parliament and sixteen peers returned for Scotland, had control of his wife's life interest in a vast fortune,* and had married his daughter to Sir James Lowther, an avid collector of parliamentary boroughs. The addition of the King's devotion and support should have made Bute invincible, but he had neither ability nor the sense to cultivate a personal following, and his opponents thought him contemptible. He was, as Lord Shelburne wrote of him, 'proud, aristocratical, pompous, imposing . . . rash and timid, accustomed to ask advice of different persons, but had not the sense and sagacity to distinguish and digest, with a perpetual apprehension of being governed, which made him, when he followed any advice, always add something of his own in point of matter or manner, which sometimes took away the little good which was in it or changed the whole nature of it. He was always upon stilts and never natural'.[23] His slow and ponderous method of speech was described by a contemporary as much like the firing of minute guns.

On 5 October 1761, less than a month after the King's marriage to Princess Sophia Charlotte of Mecklenburg-Strelitz, Pitt resigned from the government. Although the King disliked him, and unwisely made no serious attempt to retain his services, Pitt's departure from office was of his own doing. His plans for the more vigorous prosecution of the war, which included an attack on Spain and ever increasing expenditure from an already bankrupt exchequer, were not approved by his colleagues in Cabinet, and Pitt could never brook contradiction. His attitude was made clear in his resignation speech: 'Without ever having asked any one single employment in my life, I was called by my Sovereign and by the voice of the people to assist the State when others had abdicated the service of it. That being so no one can be surprised that I will go on no longer since my advice is not taken. Being responsible I *will* direct, and will be responsible for nothing that I do not direct.'

* Bute had married Mary, only daughter of Edward and Lady Mary Wortley Montagu, who inherited £1 ½ million from her miserly father.

Of Pitt's family connections and friends in government, his brother-in-law, Earl Temple, alone resigned with him. For the next five years, little consoled by the barony conferred upon his wife, and a pension of £3,000 a year with remainder for two lives, Pitt retired to the country and waited, with perfect confidence, for the call to return. A year later the Duke of Newcastle also resigned and, though the King did not at first appreciate the gravity of his predicament, he was left without any possibility of choosing a lasting administration. Bute became First Lord of the Treasury, and George Grenville, Hester Chatham's brother, Secretary of State. Discord in the Cabinet became acrimonious and open, the cause once more being differences over foreign policy in general and the negotiations for peace with France in particular. The two factions within the government made abortive approaches to Newcastle and to Chatham. The terms of peace, negotiated towards the end of 1762 and signed in March 1763, resulted in a few ministerial resignations and disappointed many who had hoped for greater recognition of Britain's victory, but the gains were not derisory. Canada, Cape Breton and the islands in the St Lawrence, and Louisiana east of the Mississippi; Tobago, St Vincent, and the Grenadines in the West Indies; Senegal on the African coast; and Minorca, exchanged for Bell Isle; all came under British rule; and in return for the restoration of their trading stations, the French recognized the supremacy of the East India Company, undertaking also not to interfere with the authority of rulers in the Carnatic and Deccan who were supported by the British.

Many of those who criticized these terms did so on the ground that even those few conquests which had been returned to France, and particularly the island of Guadeloupe, should have been retained. This was an unrealistic position to adopt when both public opinion and the country's critical financial crisis demanded peace at almost any price. Pitt was the leader around whom such criticism rallied, but the basis of his censure was different. Bute, he believed, had sacrificed the friendship of Prussia without either replacing it with an alliance with Austria or tempering the hostility of France and Spain. Such a situation left Britain helpless in Europe while the great acquisitions overseas would require protection in any future war. Others argued that the fur trade of Canada, and the expense of governing such a territory, were a poor reward for returning the profitable sugar plantations of Guadeloupe. It was the Duke of Bedford who alone foresaw the true danger arising from the conquest of Canada. The destruction of French power to the north of the New England colonies removed the one threat to their security which ensured their adherence to Britain. The most celebrated conquest of Pitt's administration, won in glory and applauded in public emotion, had laid the foundation for revolution and the loss of the American colonies.

Confronted by the financial problems of war, Bute had concluded peace. Faced with the financial problems of peace, Bute resigned. His public life was under severe attack and his personal life was the target of malicious and unfounded slander.* Never distinguished for his courage or tenacity, he had mismanaged his political fellows by lack of attention, and irritated his sovereign. The King let him go apparently without a twinge of regret and replaced him as First Lord of the Treasury by George Grenville. During the next two years George III learnt much about constitutional monarchy that would be useful to him later in his reign. Most essentially he discovered that a Chief Minister of the Crown, though chosen by the King, might not be dislodged unless there was already available a replacement who could command the support of the House of Commons.

If George Grenville was a sore trial to the King, the Queen had presented him with another which was to prove even worse, and more lasting. On 12 August 1762 she had given birth to a son, George Augustus Frederick, a 'strong large and pretty boy . . . as ever was seen'. [25] As Prince of Wales he was to become the King's, and his country's, most constant and wearying distemper.

A more immediate problem existed in the person of John Wilkes. The son of a wealthy distiller, educated at Leyden, Wilkes was a cross-eyed, ugly charmer whose reckless pursuit of debauchery had gained him influential friends. Having purchased the parliamentary seat for Aylesbury he was a member of the House of Commons. He was also a member of the notorious Hell Fire Club, whose obscene and blasphemous activities at Medmenham Abbey were presided over by Sir Francis Dashwood, Chancellor of the Exchequer. A protégé of Lord Temple's, Wilkes had started, in 1762, a newspaper,

*Reproached for her own scandalous conduct, Elizabeth Chudleigh, (soi disant Duchess of Kingston) replied to the Princess Dowager of Wales, 'votre altesse royale sait que chacune a son But.' [24]

18

the *North Briton*, in which he made violent attacks upon the Crown and its ministers and indulged his taste for venomous scandal. When Madame de Pompadour asked him, 'How far does the liberty of the Press extend in England?', Wilkes replied, 'That is what I am trying to find out.'[26] His libels against the King's mother were serious enough, but his accusation that the King's speech contained falsehood bordered on treason. The ministers felt obliged to act and did so with singular lack of sense or discretion. Instructions were given for the arrest of everyone involved in the production of the *North Briton*. These instructions were embodied in a 'general warrant' which empowered the authorities to seize any persons, unspecified in number or by name, and their papers without detailing any charges against them. Wilkes was thrown into the Tower of London. Lord Temple, as Lord-Lieutenant of Buckinghamshire, was ordered to remove Wilkes from his colonelcy of the county militia. When he refused to do so, he was dismissed from his own appointment.

Wilkes was brought before Sir Charles Pratt, Chief Justice of Common Pleas and a close friend of Pitt's, early in May 1763. Pratt ruled that Wilkes, as a sitting member of parliament, could not be held for any but those offences outside parliamentary privilege: treason, felony, or a breach of the peace; and he was not charged with any one of these. Wilkes was released. It was characteristic of him that he was not content to have escaped from justice by reason of the ineptitude of his prosecutors. He cried out against tyranny and affected to be the victim of a plot against the liberty of the citizen. Heaping insult upon invention he accused the Secretaries of State of theft and applied for a search warrant against them to recover his stolen possessions. During the legal actions that followed, Sir Charles Pratt ruled general warrants to be illegal, and both Wilkes and his printer were awarded damages. This victory in the courts, a fine example of impartial judgement, further emboldened Wilkes but frightened many of his supporters. Wilkes set up his own press, conveniently giving proof of his sole responsibility for publication and opening the way for his effective prosecution. On 15 November the House of Commons voted by a majority of more than two to one that issue number 45 of the *North Briton* was a seditious libel. Following the production in the House of Lords of a copy of an obscene poem entitled *The Essay on Woman*, printed by Wilkes on his private press, he was charged with publishing pornography.

Wilkes fled to France. Tried in his absence, he was outlawed. It seemed a fitting end to a tawdry career; but the career was not ended.

The ministry had behaved with clumsiness but, under pressure, had shown resilience. A motion in the House of Commons to declare general warrants illegal was lost by a small majority and, as the popular feeling of outrage cooled, so support for Wilkes, in the country as in parliament, melted away.

Grenville turned his attention to the national economy, avoiding unpopular taxation by ruthless reductions in the army and, a more serious blunder, in the maintenance of the navy. Warships were allowed to rot and the dockyards were run down. Having introduced these economies best designed to ensure that Britain would be in no position to fight, Grenville then took the first unwitting steps towards creating a situation which must lead to war. The East India Company was self-financing, using the profits from trade to pay for its own civil administration and armed forces; and the great fortunes made by Englishmen in India generally returned to England with them when they retired. The American colonies, on the other hand, made no such sensible and useful contribution. Emigrants to America rarely returned to their home country, and Britain paid the heavy costs of security and the maintenance of bases for trade. Against these arguments might be set the American adverse trade balance with Britain *, the severe shortage of bullion, and the crippling burden imposed on the colonies by the regulation of their trade with other countries. Such regulation was, in effect, ignored: the duties upon imported molasses were seldom paid, and great fortunes were made out of goods smuggled to France and Spain, Britain's enemies in the Seven Years' War. Grenville was determined that such taxes as might be imposed should be collected. He reduced the duty on molasses by half and employed the navy to help enforce the collections of customs dues. The manoeuvre was subtle. Even in New England it would appear perverse to condemn the reduction of a tax or the enforcement of a law more than thirty years old. Encouraged by the lack of opposition to these moderate measures, Grenville introduced, in March 1765, his Stamp Act

* In 1760 the adverse balance was £9,000,000.

imposing duty on all documents required for legal transactions and upon newspapers.

On the face of it this form of taxation was logical and proper. Already applied in Britain, it yielded valuable revenue with minimal costs of collection, and fell, fairly it was thought, on those best able to pay. Alternatives, such as the suggested tax on ownership of black slaves which would have fallen almost exclusively on the southern states, were both more costly and less equitable. Stamp duties, unlike customs revenues, were cheap to gather and difficult to evade. The extension of this tax to America had been considered earlier by Pitt, but he had thought it imprudent to try to introduce it in time of war and the decision had been deferred. In parliament it met with little serious opposition, Pitt being absent, though several fine speeches were made against it, notably by Colonel Isaac Barré, the one-eyed veteran of the siege of Quebec. It was anticipated that the revenue to be raised would amount to some £60,000, barely one-sixth of the cost of maintaining an adequate army in North America and about a shilling a year for every man, woman, and child in the colonies. Such was the moderation of the demand that even Benjamin Franklin, after token hesitation, accepted the Act and secured the appointment of at least two of his friends as collectors, or 'Stamp Masters', at a salary of £300[27] a year. To the colonists, however, this innovation of a direct tax appeared as the last, and worst, of a series of repressive measures which combined with commercial restrictions to endanger their prosperity. The dire economic state of the colonies was not appreciated in England. Ample evidence of this existed in the bankruptcies of commercial concerns and individuals, the precipitate decline in real estate values, and in the reports of the governors; but it was ignored. Grenville's obscurantist determination to restore the nation's economy made him blind and deaf to the ominous signs of revolt. At this critical moment George III, heartily sickened by Grenville's hectoring manner, called on the Marquess of Rockingham to form a new administration. Assured of the active support of the King's uncle, the Duke of Cumberland, who became head of the ministry in all but name, Rockingham accepted.

Handed a poisoned chalice, Rockingham swiftly poured it away. The Stamp Tax injured principally the prosperous American middle class whose support was most needed and who were best qualified to organize revolution. Although the crucial importance of the professional, propertied, and merchant classes in the development of revolution was not then understood, the inflammatory activities of Patrick Henry in Virginia provided sufficient cause for apprehension. By August it had become clear that the Act would not be implemented without the use of force. The British government retreated, Pitt, consulted by Rockingham, refused to give advice to anyone but the King, who in turn declined to ask him for it; but on 18 January 1776 Rockingham and the Duke of Grafton were authorized to find out if Pitt would take office. Pitt's rigmarole of a reply proved incomprehensible to his plain-spoken sovereign, and Rockingham was instructed to continue at the head of the administration. Rockingham pressed for repeal of the Stamp Act, the King for its modification; but faced with the disagreeable prospect of Grenville's return George III deferred to the advice of his ministers. The Act was repealed by parliament, by an overwhelming majority, on 7 February. This success, however, could not save Rockingham's tottering ministry from other frequent and humiliating defeats. In desperation the King at last turned to Pitt who accepted the task of forming a government on his own terms. He accepted, also, the earldom of Chatham. In so doing he robbed his administration of its greatest potential strength, his own voice in the House of Commons.

Chatham, by his refusal to work with any recognized parliamentary group, had obtained power in isolation. To retain it he must acquire vigorous support which could come only from the adherents of the factions led by Rockingham, the Duke of Bedford, and the Grenvilles. His first task therefore was to shatter these groups and gather up those fragments he selected as suitable for use. The Duke of Grafton was easily persuaded to accept the office of First Lord of the Treasury, a post commonly held by the leader of the government, and General Henry Seymour Conway agreed to remain as Secretary of State. Lord Shelburne, in his admiration for Chatham, had long deserted Bute, and became Secretary of State for the South. Chatham's old friend, Sir Charles Pratt, created Baron Camden in 1765, became Lord Chancellor, and Lord Granby, Commander-in-Chief. Chatham, as Lord Privy Seal, had no departmental responsibilities and was thus free to initiate, supervise, and inspire. This was all very well, but leadership of the government in the great

22

forum of the House of Commons was shared between General Conway and the political shuttlecock, Charles Townshend. Neither was by any measure equal to the task.

The consequence of Chatham's lack of judgement in accepting a peerage, a decision which had also cost much in loss of popularity, was now apparent. Deprived of his authoritarian voice in the House of Commons, his government suffered a series of defeats, some of which were due to Chatham's gratuitously insulting behaviour towards certain of Rockingham's adherents, and others to his failure to draw to his side any of the Bedford group. Further afield, he found the European powers unwilling to realign themselves to suit his purpose. In particular, Frederick the Great of Prussia, for long an ardent admirer of William Pitt, refused to risk conflict with Britain's enemies by allying himself with the Earl of Chatham. In America, where Chatham's return to office had been greeted with expressions of delight suitable to the long-awaited arrival of a liberator, the colonists' victory in obtaining repeal of the Stamp Act had encouraged them to discover another source of discontent. Under the Mutiny Act passed in 1766, authority was vested in British military commanders to obtain accommodation and food for their troops from the local inhabitants on demand. Both Massachusetts and New York refused to comply with the Act. Finally, the East India Company's victories and conquests had persuaded Chatham that the time had come when all territory under Company control should be brought under the sovereignty of the Crown, and thus the regulation of parliament, reducing the Company to the status of leaseholder. In this he was opposed by both Townshend and Conway, who favoured negotiation. Chatham, as always infuriated by obstruction or the questioning of his authority, found himself thwarted at every turn. In December, complaining of gout and 'the infelicity which ferments and sours the councils of His Majesty's servants', he withdrew to Bath to nurse his failing health and assaulted vanity.

He left behind him at Westminster a ministry which was both divided and disordered. Accustomed always to making decisions of policy without consultation with his colleagues, whom he considered, not always unjustly, unworthy of his confidence, Chatham neither bequeathed them a clear policy nor communicated his intentions.[28] On 28 February, some fifteen weeks before he was summoned to office, Chatham had written to Shelburne, 'I am fitter for a lonely hill in Somersetshire than for the affairs of State.' [29] By the end of the year there were many who would have agreed that his modesty, however false, was justified; Lord Chesterfield, writing of Chatham's peerage, observed acidly, '. . . he has had a *fall upstairs*, and has done himself so much hurt, that he will never be able to stand upon his legs again . . . he is now, certainly, only Earl of Chatham; and no longer Mr Pitt in any respect whatever.' [30] Like others, he found Chatham's acceptance of a place in 'that Hospital of Incurables, the House of Lords' incomprehensible. Though many chose to believe that Chatham's withdrawal was due to pique and frustration, his illness was genuine. He had long suffered from crippling gout, and there were sombre indications that his illness was not only physical. He remained at Bath, unable to attend the opening session of parliament in the new year, until the end of February, when news of the defeat of Townshend's budget brought him, an exhausted invalid, to London. On 4 March he wrote to Grafton indicating his intention to dismiss Townshend. Eight days later he had an audience of the King. He was not to see him again for more than two years.

In Chatham's absence Townshend had committed the government to policies for India and America that were the direct reversal of those pursued by his leader. To the East India Company he had offered negotiation of a contract, abandoning Chatham's intention to add the conquered territory to the empire. His solution for America, which he claimed in the House of Commons on 20 January would raise revenue without creating unrest in the colonies, consisted of new customs duties on a quantity of goods, including paper and tea, imported from Britain. This further regulation of trade, introduced in May, yielded the predictable result: American opposition to direct taxation was extended to embrace all forms of tax imposed by the British parliament. Under Chatham's direction, even from the House of Lords, the government would have rejected any proposal to increase indirect taxation. Lacking his leadership, ministers were content to follow Townshend. Their failure to make any attempt to resist him was understandable: his measures were approved by the King and popular among the majority in both houses of parliament; but the consequences, of which clear warning had been received, were more remarkable and more lasting than any could have foreseen. Alone among Chatham's ministers, Lord Shelburne, the

24

ablest of them all, applied himself to the shaping of policy inspired by his master. His work at this period constructed the framework for the settlement of Canada by the Quebec Act of 1774.

'This situation, I think, cannot last much longer', wrote Lord Chesterfield in April, 'and if Lord Chatham should either quit his post or the world, neither of which is very improbable, I conjecture that what is called the Rockingham Connection stands the fairest for the Ministry.' [31] But three months later Chatham was lying in a darkened room in Hampstead, seeing no one and attending to no official business. It was Charles Townshend who died that summer. He was succeeded as Chancellor of the Exchequer briefly by Lord Mansfield and, in December, by Lord North.

The continuing absence of his first minister, and the weakness of the government without him, was a source of acute anxiety to the King. He wrote regularly to Chatham expressing, in turn, patient concern, increasingly urgent persuasion and extreme irritability. To these exhortations Chatham replied in his customary convoluted style, baffling the King by his genuflections. He was grateful for His Majesty's 'transcendant goodness'; he entreated 'most humbly to renew the tender of his devoted services'; he begged permission 'to lay himself with all duty and submission at the King's feet'; but he gave no indication of his ability to return to work, nor indeed of any intention to do so. In May he had been persuaded to see the Duke of Grafton, who had told him that the ministry could not continue without assistance from either the Bedford or the Rockingham group. It was a melancholy meeting as Grafton recalled: 'his nerves and spirits were affected to a dreadful degree . . . and it appeared like cruelty in me to have been urged by any necessity to put a man I valued, to so great suffering as it was evident that my commission exacted. The interview was truly painful.' [32] In August Chatham gave his wife, Hester, a general power of attorney. Grafton had already asked for permission to resign, but the King was determined not to throw the government open to bidding among political factions. He authorized Grafton to enter into negotiations to form a new administration, but, for the time being, both Chatham and Grafton must remain.

The end of the year brought no comfort to the government or the people. Chatham, still unable, or unwilling, to take any part in public affairs, was at Hayes, which he had recently repurchased.

25

Nursed and protected by his devoted Hester he had withdrawn into a private world which none but his immediate family was permitted to approach. Disquieting rumours that he was mad, already current in April, began to spread. The country lay under a deep covering of snow.

III

Chatham in Opposition 1768-1773

IN JANUARY 1768 the ministry, which had ceased to be Chatham's in anything but name, was strengthened by the addition of Lord Gower, Lord Weymouth, and Richard Rigby, all experienced members of the Bedford group. Chatham's loyal disciples were outnumbered in Cabinet and it was not long before his policies were as far removed from the government's as he was from ministerial deliberations. The strength of the Bedfords was shown immediately in the creation of a new office, that of Secretary of State for the American Colonies. This removed responsibility for colonial affairs from Shelburne and put it into the harsh and clumsy hands of Lord Hillsborough, for whom Chatham had little regard. It was clear that Shelburne, brilliant but distrusted, was to be levered from office, and nothing but Chatham's return could have saved him.

In September the King, conscious of Shelburne's opposition to the foreign and colonial policies approved and pursued by the senior ministers of the Crown, decided to dismiss him. Such a move was possible without Chatham's concurrence, but he must be consulted and it was feared that he might use the dismissal of Shelburne as the cause of his own resignation. Willing as George III might be to lose his absentee Prime Minister, Chatham's resignation on these grounds would be damaging to the government's reputation both in parliament and in the country. The Duke of Grafton was dispatched to Hayes to probe Chatham's reactions.

As he had anticipated, Grafton was not permitted to see his ailing chief but conducted his business with Hester, who handled a difficult interview with her customary tact and made a note of their conversation.[33] She reported Chatham's opinion that the removal of Shelburne would be 'quite contrary to the King's service' and would 'never have his consent', but she was unable to disguise the gravity of her husband's illness or her belief that there was 'but a small prospect of his ever being able to enter much again into business'. A second proposal, to dismiss Sir Jeffrey Amherst, commander of the army that had completed the conquest of Canada in 1760, from his post as absentee Governor of Virginia, was considered by Chatham 'most unhappy and very unfortunate'. Grafton had obtained the information he needed. In the absence of any possibility of Chatham's early return to lead the government, or a clear threat of resignation, both Shelburne and Amherst could be dismissed. He had delivered to Hester the King's message that he could not see 'any reason to fear that Lord Chatham would act improperly' and was confident that it had been understood.

On 12 October Grafton received a letter from Chatham deploring 'the removal of Sir Jeffrey Amherst and that of Lord Shelburne' and asking the King's permission to resign.[34] It was clear, as Grafton was quick to realize, that Chatham was under the misapprehension that both dismissals had already taken place. George III and Grafton both wrote at once imploring Chatham to reconsider and were rewarded by a second letter in which he declared 'all chance of recovery will be entirely precluded by my continuing longer to hold the Privy Seal'.[35] The King seized the opportunity: 'I think myself', he wrote to Grafton, 'amply repaid the having wrote to him, as it [Chatham's reply] contains an open avowal that his illness is alone the cause of his retiring.' [36] Chatham's resignation was accepted with professions of regret; Shelburne's followed a few days later; and Amherst was dismissed. The way had been cleared for the systematic mismanagement of colonial affairs which drove the Americans through resentment and resistance into rebellion and independence.

Chatham's resignation and the removal of Shelburne and Amherst caused less stir than had been anticipated. The awful consequences were not yet evident even to Horace Walpole, who wrote on 20 December, 'the times wear a very tempestuous aspect, and while there is a singular want both of abilities and prudence, there is no want of mischievous intentions . . . luckily America is quiet.' The 'very tempestuous aspect' of the situation at home was attributable to the reappearance of John Wilkes. In the election held in the spring of 1768, Wilkes, who had returned from France for the occasion and had himself admitted into a city company as qualification, stood as parliamentary candidate for the City of London. Defeated, he offered himself for Middlesex, where he used land given to him by Lord Temple to qualify him as a county freeholder. His campaign, organized by John Horne * and Serjeant Glynn, relied upon the popularity of his rebellion against authority and his dramatic appearance as a fugitive risking arrest among the voters. He was welcomed as a new champion of liberty and elected on 28 March amid scenes of jubilation which deteriorated into riots. † At his own instigation he was arrested on 20 April. It might have been wiser to have allowed Wilkes to take his seat in the Commons and employ his undoubted talents in relatively harmless opposition, but the law must be upheld and the King was determined that the insolent and outlawed progenitor of the *North Briton* should be crushed. To Lord North he insisted that 'the expulsion of Mr Wilkes appears to be very essential and must be effected.' Wilkes appeared, on 27 April, before Lord Mansfield, who cancelled his outlawry on a legal technicality but fined him £1,000 and sentenced him to a total of twenty-two months' imprisonment on the charges of publishing the *North Briton* and the *Essay on Woman*. Wilkes remained, however, member of parliament for Middlesex.

On 10 May, the day of the opening of parliament, a great crowd,

---

* Later known as Horne Tooke.

† The *Annual Register* [37] reported that '. . . the rabble was very tumultuous. . . . The mob paraded the whole town from east to west obliging everybody to illuminate, and breaking the windows of such as did not do it immediately. The windows of the Mansion House, in particular, were demolished all to pieces, together with a large chandelier and some pier glasses, to the amount of many hundred pounds. They demolished all the windows of Lord Bute, Lord Egmont, Sir Sampson Gideon, Sir William Mayne, and many other gentlemen and tradesmen in most of the public streets of both cities, London and Westminster. . . . At Charing Cross, at the Duke of Northumberland's, the mob also broke a few panes; but his Grace had the address to get rid of them by ordering up lights immediately into his windows and opening the Ship alehouse, which soon drew them to that side.'

mostly 'of young persons who appeared to be apprentices and journeymen', assembled from all parts of the City with the apparent intention of releasing Wilkes from prison and escorting him to the House of Commons. The rioters, who were estimated to number between 20,000 and 40,000, broke through the ranks of the Foot Guards sent to guard the prison and, after the Riot Act had been read twice by a magistrate in warning, the troops fired into the crowd. Eleven people were killed and more wounded before the crowd was dispersed to spread violence through other parts of London. The cries of 'Wilkes and Liberty' and 'Damn the King, damn the government, damn the Justices' were heard that night from Southwark to Westminster, and the damage to public and private property was extensive. The affair became known as the 'Massacre of St George's Fields' and provided Wilkes's cause with its first martyrs.

Further riots accompanied the election of Serjeant Glynn, Wilkes's friend in Middlesex, to replace a fellow member who had died, and fights broke out between weavers from Spitalfields employed by Wilkes, and Irish chairmen organized by supporters of the government. The disorders, which spread over a period of three months [38] and continued sporadically throughout the year, both inflamed and were stoked by a series of strikes among discontented weavers, sailors, Thames watermen, and coal-heavers. They roamed the streets in their thousands, shouting for higher wages and cheering for Wilkes. Grafton and his Cabinet, fearing the 'spirit of riot which . . . threatened to bring on a disrespect to all government and lawful authority' [39], determined that Wilkes must be expelled from parliament. A motion to this effect was passed by the House of Commons in February 1769. In the subsequent elections for Middlesex in February and March, Wilkes was re-elected unopposed, and on both occasions re-expelled. In April, in a fourth election, he was opposed and again re-elected, polling nearly four times as many votes as Colonel Henry Luttrell, his nearest rival. Early in May the House of Commons, in a last and as it proved vain attempt to put an end to this political farce, declared Wilkes ineligible and Luttrell elected. This decision raised complex constitutional issues which divided parliament and the country, and which have remained the subject of argument. The violent controversy was not resolved for Wilkes until fourteen years later, when the motion declaring his 'incapacity' to serve as a member of parliament was at last deleted from the Journals of the House.

On 9 May parliament was prorogued. The government's problems were severe. The decision to nominate Luttrell in the place of Wilkes, who had been elected no less than four times, was openly denounced as a violation of electoral liberty. The attitude of the ministry may be summarized as an acknowledgement of the right of the King and the people to influence the decisions of the House of Commons, but a resolute defence of parliamentary independence of action. It was legitimate to respect the King's wishes or to take proper note of popular agitation; but it would be dereliction of duty and an abrogation of constitutional balance if members yielded their powers of decision to coercion or violence. The young Charles James Fox, who had entered parliament in 1769 and was later to appoint himself champion and guardian of the people, supported the view of parliamentary privilege and independence. It was an essential ingredient of the mixed constitution, founded upon the authority of the Crown, parliament, and the people, none of which was to be allowed to rule alone. The troubles of the government were soon to be intensified: the Earl of Chatham was preparing to return to political life.

Chatham's breakdown, 'the product of years of overwork and declining health, had been both physical and mental. From the summer of 1767 he had given up any attempt to deal with either public or private business, delegating everything to Hester, to whom Cabinet ministers and friends alike addressed their letters. The doctors had been adamant that her husband must not be troubled with or allowed to take any part in affairs of state, and she exerted all her considerable authority to make sure that their advice was followed. It is a measure of her strength, and her love, that she was able to withstand the strain of this period when the health of her husband and of her younger son, William, were the subject of continuous and intense anxiety. She seems never to have lost her composure, tired in her devotion, or failed in her common sense and discreet handling of affairs. Dr Anthony Addington was convinced that Chatham would not be well until he had suffered 'a fit' of gout. This happy event occurred in November 1768, when the patient was already showing signs of recovery. By January, whether as a result of this fit or by one of those fortunate coincidences which appear so often to have brightened Addington's life and enhanced his reputation is not clear, Chatham was strong enough to resume control of his own business and amused himself by purchasing another estate adjoining his land at Hayes. In April he went out in his carriage for the first time since his collapse. Three months later he attended the King's levee, where George III received him with great kindness and consideration. Chatham had returned, but in opposition. He was not invited to return in any other capacity.

He found his world much changed. Grafton, weak and indolent, had allowed power to slip from his grasp into the hands of the King, who had found, to his surprise and satisfaction, that his views on almost all matters of policy were shared by the Bedford group. In Europe Britain was isolated, the French had been permitted to attack and conquer Corsica, and an important overture from Frederick the Great had been rebuffed. The American colonies, though temporarily quiet, had been grossly mishandled. New York's refusal to comply with the Mutiny Act had been summarily punished by the suspension of assent to all Acts of the Assembly. Though this had been lifted by Shelburne at the earliest opportunity, the fact that New York had been forced to submit, and the threat to their legislative powers, hung over the colonies as a constant reminder of repressive rule from Britain. As Secretary of State for the Colonies, Hillsborough was harshly inept. Opposition to Townshend's taxes was led by Massachusetts. A circular, drafted by Samuel Adams, called on the other colonies to join in common resistance to the new duties. Hillsborough, applying the principle of isolation and punishment successfully employed against New York, issued a crude reply instructing the colonies to ignore the circular and suspending the Massachusetts Assembly. The colonies, which had found New York's opposition to the Mutiny Act insufficient cause for united action, rallied behind the resistance of Massachusetts against taxation, and signed non-importation agreements to exclude British goods from America.

On 1 May 1769 the Cabinet decided by five votes to four to remove all taxes except that applied to tea. This extraordinary manoeuvre must be assumed to have been intended to mollify the people of Massachusetts, while simultaneously reassuring the British that their right to tax the Americans was unimpaired. The effect was somewhat different: the people of Massachusetts, and of all the American colonies, were made aware that taxation was to continue but that rebellion reduced it; the British were made to understand that the government was weak, vacillating, and vulnerable to pressure.

Seeking to retain the right to impose duties to produce revenue or control trade, the government had succeeded only in maintaining an irrelevance.

Chatham was determined to bring down the ministry. During his prolonged illness, Hester had made up his quarrel with her brothers, Lord Temple and George Grenville. This nucleus of a powerful party in opposition might be further strengthened by an alliance with Rockingham and the defection from the government of some of Chatham's followers. He busied himself with overtures to Rockingham, who received them coldly, and in reasserting his dominance over his disciples. On 30 July he went to stay with Temple at Stowe. Edmund Burke, always watchful for movements of political significance, reported to Rockingham: 'lord Chatham passed by my door on Friday morning in a jimwhiskee drawn by two horses, one before the other,—he drove himself. His train was two coaches-and-six, with twenty servants, male and female. He was proceeding with his whole family (Lady Chatham, two sons and two daughters) to Stowe. He lay at Beaconsfield, and was well and cheerful, and walked up and down stairs at the inn without help.' [40] This evidence of Chatham's renewed strength, coupled with knowledge of his intense activity in other circles, cannot have reassured the government.

In January 1770 Chatham was ready to launch his assault. When parliament met on the 9th, he rose to denounce the expulsion of Wilkes, accusing the House of Commons of tyranny and urging the Lords to exercise their powers on behalf of the people. 'Unlimited power', he declared, 'is apt to corrupt the minds of those who posses it . . . where the law ends, there tyranny begins.' His speech was full of his old vigour and persuasion. When he finished he had won over Lord Camden who, in a speech which caused his dismissal, admitted that he, as Lord Chancellor, had countenanced the unconstitutional action of the Commons. Seven members of the government, including Lord Granby, resigned. On 22 January Chatham supported Rockingham's motion of censure of the government in a crushing speech which castigated Grafton's ministry for its handling of affairs at home and abroad and ended with a strong argument in favour of the reform of parliament. That evening Grafton told the King he must resign. It appeared that Chatham's first object had been achieved. His second, his own return to power, seemed certain to follow. He had, however, underestimated the personal loathing

33

the King felt for him. On 30 January Grafton was succeeded as first minister by Lord North.

Much has been written to North's discredit. It is true that the consequences of his long tenure of office were, in the main, disastrous to Britain, but the portrayal of him as a fumbling incompetent is false and unjust. He lacked the vision of the statesman, but he possessed most of the qualities required in a political leader. He was hard-working, shrewd, imperturbable, witty, well-read, a master of language and repartee, and impervious to defeat. His appearance was not engaging. His heavy-lidded, protuberant eyes and bulging cheeks gave him, as Horace Walpole remarked, 'the air of a blind trumpeter'. He was awkward, ungraceful, and sadly short-sighted. He was also incurably somnolent, falling asleep on the Treasury bench, and even more often pretending to do so, during debates. On one occasion, waking from his slumbers, he rose with his customary clumsiness and left his seat, carrying away the wig of the Treasurer of the Navy, which he had dislodged with the hilt of his sword. Wilberforce described him as 'that fat old fellow': Samuel Johnson said more succinctly, 'He fills a chair.' His tongue, according to Nathaniel Wraxhall, who had plenty of opportunity for studying him, was 'rather too large for his mouth', which 'rendered his articulation somewhat thick, though not at all indistinct'. It was Wraxhall, too, who remarked in him one of the most valuable attributes of the complete parliamentarian: 'Lord North rarely rose to sublimity, though he possessed vast facility and command of language. If necessary he could speak for a long time, apparently with great pathos, and yet disclose no important fact.' [41]

During the years when he was opposed by Chatham, North had one inestimable advantage: he led the government from the House of Commons *. Walpole believed that North's ability and 'the goodness of his character would have raised him much higher in the opinion of mankind, if he had cared either for power or applause.' [42] Whatever his faults, and his poses, he cannot be dismissed as a buffoon. It is well to remember that he led the government for twelve years in a House of Commons whose members had known Chatham in the full vigour of his powers, and against the opposition of the younger Pitt, Charles James Fox, Edmund Burke, and Richard Brinsley Sheridan.

* Frederick, Lord North, was the eldest son of Francis, 1st Earl of Guilford, and thus eligible to sit in the House of Commons until his father's death, at the age of eighty-six, in 1790.

Chatham was enraged by North's appointment. He had expected that the King would send for him to form an administration. Not only had the government survived, and accepted a new leader, but Grafton gave it his active support and encouraged his own followers to do the same during its early days of instability. The King had come to detest Chatham, though he respected his authority, patriotism, and integrity. As he made clear in his letter urging Lord North to accept the leadership, he was not prepared to consider either Chatham's return or a change of government.[43] No champion of Wilkes, or of electoral reform, was acceptable to George III. In anger and disappointment, Chatham armed himself for his last long campaign. Launched at first against the tyranny of the House of Commons, his attack was increasingly directed against the excessive influence of the Crown.

Chatham had the support of the City of London. In March 1769 a 'loyal' merchants' petition had been presented to the King at St James's, but the petitioners were unrepresentative and, of the 130 who set out, only about a dozen arrived, mud-caked, at the Palace. They were 'interrupted by a desperate mob . . . who insulted, pelted and maltreated the principal conductors, so that several coaches were obliged to withdraw. . . . and those who arrived at St James's were so daubed with dirt, and shattered, that both members and drivers were in the utmost peril of their lives.'[44] Three weeks later the City presented an official petition, enumerating the iniquities of the government and asking for redress. To this George III made no reply. Under William Beckford *, the newly elected Lord Mayor, who was both a friend of Chatham's and an enthusiastic supporter of Wilkes, the City presented yet another petition on 14 March 1770. This took the form of a remonstrance, informing the King in plain language that previous complaints remained unanswered, 'their injuries confirmed; and the only judge [Lord Camden] removable at the pleasure of the crown has been dismissed from his high office for defending, in Parliament, the Law and the Constitution.'[45] They called for the dissolution of parliament and the dismissal of the ministers responsible for the nomination of Luttrell in place of Wilkes. The King replied curtly that the petition was 'disrespectful to me, injurious to my Parliament, and irreconcilable to the

* Twice Lord Mayor of London (1762 and 1769) and father of the author of *Vathek*.

principles of the Constitution'. The problem might be brushed aside but it did not go away. The agitation continued and grew, and petitions poured in from all parts of the country. Samuel Johnson described them as 'a tempest of outrage'. On 17 April Wilkes was released from prison.

For all his efforts, Chatham was unable to attract the support of any political group large enough to upset the government. The Rockinghams were lukewarm and even the fiery Burke was advocating moderation. Chatham determined to make himself 'a *scarecrow of violence* to the gentle warblers of the grove, the moderate Whigs and temperate statesmen'.[46] In June Beckford's death left the City without a strong and unifying leader and its influence declined, for a time, in factional quarrels. Parliament rose, and Chatham withdrew to Hayes, and then to Burton Pynsent, there to occupy himself with his family and his property. The summer was warm and he spent long days in the fields. 'I am', he wrote to Hester, who had remained with the younger children at Hayes, 'now at peace.' He was preparing himself for the next assault.

His opportunity occurred soon after parliament reassembled on 13 November. A serious dispute had arisen between Britain and Spain about their respective rights to the Falkland Islands. The small British garrison at Port Egmont had been expelled. In spite of the efforts of the twenty-four-year-old James Harris, temporarily in charge of the embassy at Madrid until the arrival of a new ambassador it seemed that war was inevitable. The French were implicated, and intelligence from France indicated that 'great military preparations' were being made, including the mass movement of troops towards the coast.[47] Chatham's speech on 22 November was a fine demonstration of his extraordinary powers: the mastery of language, the breadth of understanding, the wisdom and authority of long experience combined with vitality of vision, the authentic voice of the patriot, which proclaimed his supremacy as statesman and orator over members of both Houses. He castigated the government for ignoring national security, for the destruction of 'all content and unanimity at home', while the deplorable neglect of the navy and army, and the failure to attract a single ally in Europe, left the country defenceless at a time of immediate danger. He demanded reform, in government, in the civil administration, and in parliamentary representation. The crisis required the formation of a national government. 'I mean', he declared, 'to alarm the whole nation—to rouse the Ministry if possible . . . to awaken the King.' He did not achieve all his objects, but his speech produced startling effects. The response to what Johnson described as Chatham's 'feudal gabble' took the form of a sudden activity in naval, military, and diplomatic affairs. Meanwhile, to protect the public from Chatham's incendiary patriotism the House of Lords closed its doors to strangers. The crisis passed. On Christmas Eve Louis XV dismissed his Minister for War and Foreign Affairs, the duc de Choiseul, and on 22 January 1771 the Spanish ambassador signed a declaration restoring Port Egmont to Britain.

Throughout the first half of 1771 Chatham persevered in his attacks upon the government, denouncing ministers as 'ignorant, futile, and incapable' and pressing for electoral reform, but the opposition was lethargic and divided, and the voice that might have provided energy and unity was no longer to be heard in the Commons. By accepting a peerage Chatham had sacrificed his contact with the people, and his exhortations to the Lords as 'grand hereditary counsellors of the Crown' and defenders of the Constitution against the exercise of arbitrary power were unheeded. In the summer he again retired, withdrawing to Burton Pynsent. During the following three years he attended parliament only once, and that in response to an urgent appeal for help from a minority group seeking justice and freedom. When he returned it was to speak for reason and moderation in British dealings with America. These, and above all the welfare of his country, were the causes which could still rouse him. His passionate concern for Britain, and for liberty, remained undiminished, but the fire of ambition had grown cold.

At Burton Pynsent Chatham found rest and recreation. He had made himself a substantial landowner. He imagined himself the complete farmer. He had, it is clear, little idea of farming, but he was not short of plans, all of which involved enormous expense. Towering over the extensions to the house, the increased acreage, the plantations, and the prize cattle, 'the most beautiful of sows', and a profusion of peacocks, dogs, and brood mares, loomed the 140-foot-high pile erected in memory of his benefactor, Sir William Pynsent. Chatham spent hours on horseback superintending work on the estate, but his descriptions of himself as 'tending the flocks or following the plough' or, indeed, as occupying his 'farmer's chimney-corner'[48] were a little too fanciful even for the devoted Shelburne to accept. The simple bucolic life which he imagined himself to be leading was ruinously extravagant, and his financial position was further complicated by the fees and duties to which his pension was liable and the fact that it was often as much as a year in arrears. When Lord North, who was sincerely troubled by Chatham's difficulties, asked George III to increase the annuity to provide the full £3,000 which had been awarded, the King replied that he would not do so until 'decrepitude or death puts an end to him as a trumpet of sedition'.[49] Chatham was obliged to fall back on the generosity of his friends.

Although he had told Shelburne that he did not 'see that the smallest good can result to the public from my coming up to the meeting of parliament',[50] Chatham made a brief appearance in May 1772. 'Far from well and extremely lame', he returned to support a Bill to relieve religious nonconformists of some of their disabilities under the law and give them greater social freedom. Passed by the House of Commons, many of whose members owed their seats to dissenters' votes, the Bill was, as the King made clear to Lord North, to be thrown out by the Lords. To the charge that the dissenters were men of close ambition, Chatham replied, from his knowledge and conviction, with acerbity: 'They are so, and their ambition is to keep close to the college of Fishermen, not of cardinals, and to the doctrines of inspired apostles, not the decrees of interested and aspiring bishops.' To the claims of the established Church he answered, 'we have a Calvinist creed, a Popish liturgy, and an Arminian clergy.'* His efforts were in vain and he returned to the peaceful contemplation of his acres.

During his absence the political scene was overshadowed by the affairs of the royal family. Two of George III's brothers, the Dukes of Gloucester and Cumberland, had contracted marriages which the King considered undesirable. Gloucester had married Maria, Dowager Countess of Waldegrave, a widow of unblemished reputation and great beauty, but unfortunately the illegitimate daughter of Sir Edward Walpole. Cumberland, even less discreet, had chosen

---

* Followers of James Arminian (Harmensen) the sixteenth-century Protestant who preferred the theory of conditional predestination in opposition to Calvin's doctrine of absolute predestination.

Mrs Anne Horton, also a widow, a woman of social ambition and sister to Colonel Henry Luttrell. The King, to avoid future mis-alliances, required the passage of the Royal Marriage Act. This declared marriages by members of the royal family, as defined in the Act, invalid without the prior consent of the monarch, unless the royal party to the contract was more than twenty-five years of age and had notified the Privy Council twelve months in advance. Charles Fox chose this opportunity to attack the government, of which he was a junior member, and to provoke the King, but the Bill was passed with little other opposition. George III had written to North on 26 February, 'I have a right to expect a hearty support from everyone in my Service, and shall remember Defaulters.'[51] So far as Fox was concerned he was as good as his word.

Later in the year the King suffered also the death of his mother, the Princess Dowager of Wales, and the disgrace and humiliation of his sister, Caroline Matilda. Married at the age of fifteen to the profligate and incipiently imbecile Christian VII, King of Denmark, she had been brutally treated by her husband and in 1772 was found guilty of finding consolation in the arms of John Frederick Struensee, an influential German physician at the Danish Court. Struensee was executed, and Caroline Matilda, after imprisonment at Kronberg, was divorced and exiled to Celle, in Hanover, where she died three years later.

North pursued a slow, methodical consolidation of the national economy and his own political position. He had acquired the confidence, and was gaining the affection, of the King, who found him honest, loyal, and in the absence of any other suitable candidate for leadership of the government, indispensable. In spite of the war scare in 1770, North's economies continued to effect a deterioration in the armed services, though the Earl of Sandwich, who succeeded Sir Edward Hawke as First Lord of the Admiralty in 1772, made heroic efforts to check the decay of the fleet. In 1773, Chatham's youngest son, James, was sent to join the navy. To Captain Alexander Hood, Chatham wrote on 28 April: 'When I hear you have hoisted your Flag, poor Lady Chatham and I will call a Council of heavy hearts; About our loved little Boy, as things come near, I confess, I tremble, twelve years old is a very tender age for Action.'[52] His fears were real. The previous June a British revenue cutter had run aground off Rhode Island. The inhabitants burned the ship and manhandled its commander, who had been engaged in frustrating the activities of the smugglers of Narragansett Bay. In December 1773 an incident at Boston lighted an explosive train which was to draw Chatham out of retirement.

IV

'Let Us Fall Like Men'
1774-1778

MASSACHUSETTS had been an area of particular disaffection for some years, and there had been a serious incident, to be known as the 'Boston Massacre' in March 1770, when five rioters had been killed and the British troops sent to defend the customs house stoned by the mob. American reaction to this affray had been unsympathetic to the Bostonians. The *New York Gazette* declared it was 'high time to put a stop to mobbing'. In the summer New York broke the non-importation agreement and opened its port to British goods. Other States followed suit and normal trade was resumed, though the continued duty on tea contained the seed of further discontent. For three years the hostility towards Britain festered beneath the surface while the colonies bickered among themselves. When the break came it was the immediate result of an ingenious scheme to help the East India Company out of financial difficulty. The large surplus stocks of the Company were to be permitted to be sent direct to America, without incurring either handling charges in England or British duties, enabling it to be sold at about half its previous price. Tea, regarded by many in America as the drink of traitors, would thus, it was thought, come to be popular and satisfactory profits accrue to the ailing East India Company. The theory was not without

41

logic, but it ignored evident and disabling obstacles. It held no charm for Bostonians, and in the great centres of smuggling, at New York and Philadelphia, there was furious indignation. The colonies might have agreed among themselves not to buy tea: instead, the radical leaders chose to prevent its being landed. At New York and Philadelphia landing was refused and the ships loaded with tea were obliged to turn back to England; at Charleston it was dumped in damp cellars where it was soon ruined; at Boston, on 16 December 1773, 340 of the East India Company's tea-chests were seized by a party of 'Mohawk Indians' and thrown into the sea.

Governor Thomas Hutchinson's report of this 'Tea Party' reached London in January 1774. Hutchinson, loathed by the people of Massachusetts who had petitioned the King six months earlier for his removal, was replaced. To make sure that the prescribed punishment would be meted out with suitable severity General Thomas Gage was named as his successor. The matter was not put before parliament until March, by which time the King and Lord North had digested the advice of the new Governor. 'If', Gage had reported, 'we take the resolute part they will undoubtedly prove very meek.' North, urged on by George III, proposed the closure of the port of Boston until the ruined tea should have been paid for; changes in the Massachusetts constitution, including nomination of the upper house by the Crown to replace election by the house of representatives; the transfer, at the whim of the Governor, of trials for capital offences to England; and the quartering of troops in Boston in barracks to be provided by the city. The parliamentary Bills necessary to give effect to these proposals were passed with ease. Opinions differed among members as to the most suitable measures required to meet the situation, but scarcely any disputed the right, however abstract, of Britain to tax the American colonies, or the necessity to maintain law and order in America. There was also a more widespread feeling that the Americans had been too troublesome for too long. It was essential that the colonies should be settled in prosperous tranquillity, and if necessary by force. General Gage warned the government not to underestimate the crisis, or the number of troops that would be required to put down a general rebellion. Chatham, almost alone, understood the wider dangers. When, on 6 March 1774, he wrote to Shelburne, 'where our strength lay, and our happiest resources presented themselves, it is all changed into danger, weakness, distraction and vulnerability',[53] he was thinking as much of the old enemy, France, as of America.

In spite of his opposition to the government's policies, Chatham believed Lord North to be the best Chief Minister then available. As he explained to Shelburne, 'He serves the Crown more successfully and more sufficiently upon the whole, than any other man now to be found could do.'[54] This was not false modesty, and genuine humility was not among Chatham's virtues; it was a statement of opinion that took account of his own infirmities. His retirement had given him rest, but there was no cure for his recurrent and crippling gout. He struggled to Hayes, where he was laid up for a month, and at last appeared for the debate on 26 May, too late to influence the passage of any but the last of the four punitive Bills introduced by the government. By then news had been received of the death of Louis XV, an event which, Chatham believed, greatly reduced the possibility of France's refraining from intervention in case of war with America. Chatham came to the Lords, 'his legs wrapped in black velvet boots, and as if in mourning for the King of France he leaned on a crutch covered with black likewise'.[55] Two days later Thomas Walpole found him in bed at Hayes wearing, as his cousin Horace gleefully reported, 'a duffil coat without arms, bordered with a broad purple lace. On his head he had a nightcap, and over that a hat with a broad rim flapped all round.' He 'affected fatigue or gout'.[56] Horace Walpole's wasp's eye view of all but his dearest friends fails to disguise the pathos of the bizarre spectacle which he attributed to Chatham's love of drama.

American distrust and anger were aggravated by the passage of the Quebec Act. Originally outlined by Shelburne, the purpose of the Act was to provide for the settlement of Canada after ten years of British rule. This settlement included the definition of boundaries and the construction of an administration that would both admit and welcome the Catholic majority to a just place in the country's affairs. The territorial adjustments, which extended the Canadian frontier to the Ohio, reserving to Canada the fur-hunters' grounds in the north-west and creating a barrier against the western expansion of the colonies, aroused outraged opposition in America and effectually bankrupted a Philadelphia company in which both George Washington and Patrick Henry held interests. The proposed administration was also considered a threat, through the Church of Rome, to religious freedom in the colonies. The Quebec Act, intended, and accepted for twenty years by Canadians, as a realistic expression of tolerance and justice towards an alien and divided nation, appeared to the Americans as yet another attempt to strangle and enslave the colonies. Where the British government sought for trade, the colonists looked for expansion. The two aims were not incompatible but they could not be achieved in the poisoned atmosphere of distrust and incipient rebellion which then prevailed. Moreover, to a people who regarded the established Church of England as dangerously close to Rome, the creation of frontiers to the north and west, dominated by a Catholic majority supported by Britain, appeared as the re-creation of the old French threat to their security which they had thought destroyed in 1760.

Chatham opposed the Quebec Act. He did not believe that the concessions to the French Catholic majority would make any difference to their loyalty to Britain; he feared that Canada would continue to act as a magnet to France and thus as a threat to America; and he was rightly convinced that the Act, disastrously timed, would be seen as part of 'the whole system of American oppression'.[57] Even while Benjamin Franklin was advocating payment for the tea destroyed at Boston,[58] radicals clamoured for a solemn league and covenant of the colonies against Britain. The compromise, a congress in Philadelphia, was dominated by radical delegates. Resolutions were passed to restrict all trade with Britain, making exception for exports considered essential to the survival of the southern territories, to refuse all payment of taxes to Britain, and to make military preparations for defence.

North's government wavered between a desire to punish and the need to conciliate, between the protection of prestige and the dilution of dogma, between the determination to govern and a realization of the impracticability of government at such a distance without consent. In January and February 1775 Chatham made appeals for the withdrawal of British troops from America and presented to the Lords a provisional Act for the settlement of the colonies. In essence his plan reasserted the legislative supremacy of Britain in all matters of trade and navigation, but recognized Congress and freed the colonies to assess and raise revenues by their own methods. A hope was expressed that Congress would consider making a grant towards British costs. The proposals were shelved without discussion. In the Commons, Edmund Burke, in a speech of great eloquence, enunciated the principle, held by the Rockinghams, of authority without the exercise of power. It was a cloak of compromise, never used but already shop-soiled from frequent display to doubtful customers. From it Burke succeeded in drawing a thread of genuine policy. In his insistence that freedom and prosperity were the essential ingredients of imperial unity and strength he was anticipating the ideals of commonwealth. His contemporaries were, as ever, impressed by his language, but they remained unmoved by his argument. North, like a fussy nurse unable to decide whether to administer a spoonful of medicine or of syrup, characteristically mixed them together. He proposed that the colonies should acknowledge British sovereignty and the right to levy taxes, but that they should devise their own means of raising revenue to contribute to common costs. Before this plan could be considered, the first shots of revolution were fired at Lexington.

The Massachusetts militia had been armed to provide a defence against any attack that might be made by General Gage's troops, and a quantity of arms had been stored at Concord, some twenty miles from Boston. On 19 April a strong British detachment, sent to confiscate the rebel arms, was fired upon by the militia. In the brief engagement that followed, about sixty Americans and 273 British were killed or wounded. The jubilant colonists rushed to take up arms. The British government, alarmed but confident, hastily dispatched strong reinforcements and three generals to America. Sir Jeffrey Amherst having refused to return to Canada as Commander-in-Chief, Gage * was continued in command at Boston, and three major-generals—William Howe, John Burgoyne, and Henry Clinton—were sent to serve under him. Walpole, as usual subordinating truth to wit, wrote: 'Howe was one of those silent brothers, † and was reckoned sensible, though so silent that nobody knew whether he was or not. Burgoyne . . . was a vain, ambitious man, with a half understanding that was worse than none; Clinton had not that fault,

---

* His wife was American and suspected of betraying his orders to her countrymen.

† The eldest, George Augustus, 3rd Viscount Howe, one of the ablest soldiers of his time, was killed at Ticonderoga in 1758. He was succeeded in the title by Richard (later Earl Howe), a brilliant naval commander and victor of the battle of the 'Glorious First of June', 1794. William, the youngest, had served under James Wolfe at Quebec in 1759. He succeeded as 5th Viscount in 1799.

for he had no sense at all.' [59] In the first major engagement of the war, at Bunker Hill on 17 June, the British were victorious, but at a loss of more than a thousand casualties. As Burgoyne reported to Lord Palmerston, 'our victory has been bought by an uncommon loss of officers, some of them irreparable, and I fear the consequences will not answer the expectations that will be raised in England.' [60]

North's conciliatory proposals were rejected, and George Washington was appointed Commander-in-Chief of the American forces. At this stage there was widespread sympathy in Britain for the colonists. 'A FRIENDLY ADDRESS to *Lord* NORTH', published in *Gentleman's Magazine* in July 1775, contained more sense and a clearer warning than any speech heard in parliament during the previous twelve months: 'Let me entreat thee,' wrote the anonymous author, 'if thou hast any regard for trade, for the peace of thy own mind, and for the prosperity of Great Britain and the colonies, immediately to repeal all the repressive acts that have been passed, and to make such overtures as will secure a speedy accommodation. God knows, this is no time to quarrel with our best friends, and to give up three millions a year by suspending their trade, and contending for an unjust tax; for however pacific France and Spain may appear at present, be assured, that, when we have enervated ourselves by the unnatural contest, we shall be attacked by the united force of both.' This opinion was shaken by the American invasion of Canada in August. The attack failed on 31 December at Quebec, when Richard Montgomery was killed and Benedict Arnold severely wounded, but its effect on public opinion, and thus on parliamentary opposition, was decisive.

The appointment of Lord George Germain *, a bellicose ex-general anxious to redeem in office the reputation he had forfeited in the field, to be Secretary of State for the American Colonies did nothing to improve the climate for negotiation. There might still have been time for a peaceful settlement. The American colonies were not united in rebellion. Even when America declared its independence on 4 July 1776, the States of New York, Maryland,

---

* As Lord George Sackville, he was accused of cowardice and disobedience for his conduct as commander of the British contingent at the battle of Minden in 1759. He was tried by court martial, dismissed from the army, and declared unfit to serve in any military appointment. He was restored to public life through the influence of George III, assuming the name of Germain in 1770.

Pennsylvania, and New Jersey were reluctant to sever their ties with Britain, and the scattered and ill-organized resistance by loyalists indicated a minority opposition which might have grown under proper care. This minority misled the British into a belief that there was a general feeling of loyalty that would be expressed in active support of British arms. This reliance upon a serious division in the American ranks was perhaps the greatest error, in both political and strategic terms, made by the British government during the war.

For more than two years Chatham took no part in public affairs. By the middle of 1775 he had again sunk into a state of manic depression from which he drifted into temporary insanity broken by infrequent and fugitive moments of lucidity. Hester Chatham was left to deal alone with the urgent problems of their debts. The Alexander Hoods had advanced them £10,000, and more loans had been obtained from other friends, and from Thomas Coutts, the banker. It was Hester, too, who was obliged to advise her eldest son about his return from the army in Canada. John Pitt, whose conscientious scruples had persuaded him to resign rather than take an active part in a war against the American colonies, was sent home with dispatches in November. At Chatham's personal wish he did not return. In a letter to Benedict Arnold in September 1775, Washington had written, 'If Lord Chatham's son should be in Canada, and in any way fall into your power, you are enjoined to treat him with all possible deference and respect. You cannot err in paying too much honour to the son of so illustrious a character and so true a friend to America.' [61] The elder Pitt daughter, Hester, had married in 1774 Charles, Viscount Mahon, son and heir of Earl Stanhope. The second daughter, Harriot, was still at home, and young William's illness kept him there, also, until the summer of 1776. William, at his mother's request, wrote to Captain Alexander Hood to inform him, in his stilted, formal style, of James's safe arrival at Portsmouth: 'I need hardly tell you, and it is scarcely more necessary to express the Sensibility to the Kind Friendship of those who sent him on his first Voyage in so satisfactory a manner, which his prosperous return naturally revives in the minds of all who are interested for Him . . . My Father still continuing in the same mortifying state.' [62]

Lady Chatham succeeded in selling the house in Bath, and also disposed of parts of the Somerset estate to local farmers, but her attempts to let either Hayes or Burton Pynsent failed. Without the support of Alexander and Molly Hood, and of Thomas Coutts, the Chathams must have foundered in their sea of obligations. To add to their troubles, the young James had also incurred heavy debts in Gibraltar. Chatham believed himself to be dying and wrote a memorandum to his friend and doctor, Addington, restating his views about the American war and asking him to preserve it to bear 'testimony that he persevered unshaken in the same opinions'.[63]

By the spring of 1777 Chatham was showing signs of recovery, and on 30 May he appeared again in the House of Lords, muffled to the neck in flannel and leaning heavily on a crutch. In his absence the war in America had taken the generally negative course he had feared. Gage had been replaced as Commander-in-Chief by Howe, and, in spite of reinforcements of both British and hired Hessian troops, which could ill be spared or paid for, the army had failed to achieve conclusive victory. It was already clear that the country was too large to be conquered by any army that Britain could assemble, and the time had passed when a few isolated defeats might have persuaded the loyalists into action or the less enthusiastic to defect. Howe's successes in the capture of Long Island and New York, Clinton's capture of Rhode Island, and Washington's almost continuous series of retreats to avoid battle, had done much to demoralize the Americans, and the militia began to return to their homes; but Washington's surprise attack across the Delaware at Trenton on 26 December 1776, resulting in the surrender of nearly a thousand Hessians, had given new hope to the revolutionaries. At home, North's government faced rapidly increasing expenditure and the ruin of his economic policy. The position was not improved by the King's admission that he was £600,000 in debt on the civil list, a sum settled by parliament which also voted to increase the civil list to £900,000 a year.

In Chatham's speech on 30 May 1777 members of the House of Lords heard the authentic voice of statesmanship. The voice was feeble, often scarcely audible, but the wisdom of long experience and penetrating understanding of affairs commanded attention. Even his enemies, who saw him as a figure of fun, a valetudinarian performer, heard him with respect for his patriotism and in the uncomfortable knowledge that his forebodings were well-founded. He appealed for the redress of grievances, the repeal of vexatious laws, for reconcilia-

48

tion while there might yet be time. He informed the House of his reason to believe that the Americans were receiving financial help from France, that the presence of American revolutionary representatives in Paris could be for one purpose only, and that French recognition of American independence must result in war with France and, inevitably, with Spain. America, he believed, could not be conquered. The defence of inalienable rights was not to be regarded as rebellion. By insisting upon submission Britain would be casting away the greatest benefits of colonization: trade in time of peace, and support in time of war. Where Britain might look for friendship in prosperity, the government's policy would produce hostility in war. 'My father's speech', wrote William, who was in the gallery to hear it, 'took up half an hour, and was full of all his usual force and vivacity . . . I only regretted that he did not always raise his voice enough for all the House to hear everything he said. . . . He spoke a second time . . . in a flow of eloquence and with a beauty of expression, animated and striking beyond conception.' [64]

Chatham's appeal elicited little support. The King in particular rejected his speech as 'highly unseasonable'. It contained, he told Lord North, 'nothing but specious words and malevolence'.[65] The 'too great lenity' to the Americans had, he decided, 'increased their pride and encouraged them to rebel'. While the King saw successful rebellion in America as a dangerous incitement to disobedience at home, Chatham was, as always, watching Europe. Even as he spoke, British armies in America were putting into execution a strategic plan designed to finish the war before the year's end. This plan, the keystone of which was the separation of the New England colonies from the rest by a conjunction of Howe's army from New York with Burgoyne's moving south from the St Lawrence through the Hudson gap, provided the first British disaster of the war. It began well with Burgoyne's capture of Ticonderoga in July, but Howe had departed from the original design by diverting his force to take Philadelphia. By the time this was accomplished it was too late to return to the Hudson. Burgoyne, unaware of Howe's diversion, was cornered, outnumbered by three to one, by an American force under General Horatio Gates and obliged to surrender his entire army at Saratoga on 17 October.

The news of Saratoga was received with jubilation in France. The playwright Beaumarchais * was in such haste to be first with the news in Paris that he was thrown from his horse and dislocated his shoulder. The reaction of the Rockingham opposition was scarcely less cheerful or precipitate. Their pleasure in the vindication of their judgement was short-lived. The French had been waiting for just such a sign that Britain would be engaged in a long and wasting war three thousand miles away. In February 1778 France signed a treaty of friendship with the American revolutionary States and, as Chatham had predicted, Britain was again at war with France and Spain.

Even before the war had spread to Europe, the government, informed that a further 80,000 troops would be required to suppress the American rebellion, had decided upon a change of strategy. At the end of January George III had warned North of the danger of a French declaration of war and, in this event, had advocated the wisdom of withdrawing the army from America to strengthen Canada, Nova Scotia, and the Floridas. He also recommended attacks upon French possessions in the West Indies, and on New Orleans, while using the navy to destroy American trade. He repeated this advice on 3 February reminding North that Britain's part in a land war in Europe and America simultaneously would be 'feeble in all parts and consequently unsuccessful'.[66] Convinced of the necessity of suppressing the revolution in America, the King was nevertheless far from sure that the army would be the best instrument of this policy. Sir Henry Clinton, who had succeeded Howe as Commander-in-Chief, was ordered to concentrate on a naval war, blockading ports and destroying shipping, while his efforts on land should be devoted to drawing Washington and his army into a decisive action. After the outbreak of war with France, he was ordered also to attack and capture the island of St Lucia.

Conscious of his inadequacy as a war minister, North asked to be allowed to resign. He continued to make the same request, at frequent intervals and with mounting urgency, for the next five years.

The Rockingham group, assured of the futility and inherent dangers of the war, urged the recognition of American independence. In March the King yielded to North's anxious plea that

---

* Pierre Auguste Caronde, author of *Le Barbier de Seville* and *Le Mariage de Figaro*.

Chatham be asked to state his terms for forming a government, but added the crippling condition that Chatham should not be allowed a personal interview with his sovereign. Chatham insisted that he could not agree to take office without such discussion, provoking George III to describe the greatest statesman of the age as 'that perfidious man'.[67] North, rightly declaring that the country was 'totally unequal to a war with Spain, France and America',[68] and that 'peace with America, and a change in the Ministry are the only steps which can save this country', was refused permission to resign.

Early in April the Duke of Richmond informed Chatham of his intention to move that the colonies be granted independence. The old statesman could not stand aside and watch the liquidation of the empire he had shaped. Ignoring the protests of his physicians, he insisted upon going to the House of Lords 'before this bad grows worse'. On 7 April the whole House rose to greet him as he entered the chamber, supported by William, and his son-in-law, Lord Mahon, and remained standing while he bowed and was assisted to his place. As soon as Richmond had spoken, Chatham rose to reply. He was scarcely able to stand, his voice was so weak that his words were often inaudible, and his mind wandered so that he lost the thread of his argument ànd was unable to find words to express it; and yet, amid the confusion of thought, there were moments, all the more moving in their contrast and in the memories they revived, of the old eloquence and authority. When he was master of his mind, he was still master of his audience, and the crippled, emaciated figure excited admiration as much as pity. 'My Lords,' he said, 'his Majesty succeeded to an Empire as great in extent as its reputation was unsullied. Shall we tarnish the lustre of this nation by an ignominious surrender of its rights and fairest possessions? Shall this great Kingdom fall prostrate before the House of Bourbon? . . . Shall a people that fifteen years ago was the terror of the world now stoop so low as to tell its ancient inveterate enemy, "Take away all we have; only give us peace." It is impossible. . . . In God's name . . . Let us make one effort; and if we must fall, let us fall like men.' [69]

It was his last heroic effort and the strain was too great for his enfeebled body. He sank back exhausted into the arms of his supporters. Richmond replied to him 'with great tenderness and respect', but repeated his own arguments in favour of independence for the colonies. Chatham struggled to rise again but collapsed unconscious and was carried into the adjoining Prince's Chamber, where, attended by Dr Richard Brocklesby, he recovered sufficiently after about twenty minutes to be moved to a house in Downing Street. Two days later he was taken to Hayes. The House of Lords adjourned the debate immediately as a mark of respect. Chatham had left the House for the last time.

From Staffordshire, Josiah Wedgwood, successful potter and enthusiastic supporter of the American revolution, wrote to his partner, Thomas Bentley, in London: 'Poor Ld. Chatham! How are the mighty fallen! . . . It was almost a pity to call him into life again he made his exit so much in his own way. He certainly will never again die so much to his own satisfaction.' [70]

Chatham lingered for four weeks, nursed as always by his devoted Hester, and surrounded by his family. On 11 May, Dr Addington wrote to his son Henry: 'You will be grieved to hear that Lord Chatham is no more. It pleased Providence to take him away this morning, as if it were in mercy, that he might not be a spectator of the total ruin of a country which he was not permitted to save.' [71] Sir Philip Francis, thought to have been the author of the celebrated *Letters of Junius* *, wrote of him: 'He is dead; and the sense and honour, and character, and understanding of the nation are dead with him.' [72]

The executors named in Chatham's will were his widow, his brother-in-law, Lord Temple, and his old friend Lord Camden. John, Viscount Pitt, Chatham's heir, having been summoned to join his regiment in Gibraltar, much of the burden of the funeral and family mourning fell on the nineteen-year-old William. To Dr Pretyman he wrote from Hayes on 16 May: 'I am truly obliged to you for your friendly and affectionate concern for me on this distressful occasion. The loss I have sustained is indeed irreparable, and my feelings in consequence are what no words can convey. At the same time, the shock was the less dreadful as I had so long been prepared to expect it.' [73]

---

* These letters appeared in the press between 1767 and 1772, savagely attacking those in authority (the Duke of Grafton was one of the unfortunate targets) in prose thought by Burke to exceed even Wilkes's *North Briton* in wit and venom. The identity of the author remains a mystery, though Burke, Grenville, Edward Gibbon, and Chatham himself have been among those suspected. The author, evidently moving in the inner circles of society and parliamentary life, is now believed to have been either Shelburne or Francis.

Parliament, informed by Colonel Isaac Barré of Chatham's death, voted unanimously for a state funeral and a monument in Westminster Abbey. George III alone sounded a discordant note, informing Lord North that the inscription on Chatham's monument should be confined to commenting upon his influence in 'rouzing the nation at the beginning of the last war'.[74] Any other form of compliment would be considered 'rather an offensive measure' to the King personally.

Chatham's body lay in state in the Painted Chamber at Westminster for two days. At two o'clock on Tuesday 9 June the great funeral procession made its way through Westminster Hall, New Palace Yard, and Broad Sanctuary to the west door of the Abbey. The cortège was led by the High Constable of Westminster and the Messenger to the College of Arms, followed by 'six men conductors in cloaks, with black staves headed with Earl's coronets, Seventy poor men, in cloaks, with badges of the crest of Pitt on their shoulders and black staves in their hands.'[75] After these came the standards; servants, physicians, chaplains, and divines; and the banner, borne by Colonel Barré and attended by the Dukes of Northumberland, Manchester, and Richmond, and the Marquess of Rockingham. There followed the great banner with helmet and crest, sword and shield, surcoat and coronet, borne by Somerset, Windsor, and Richmond Heralds and Norroy King of Arms. The coffin, covered with black velvet adorned with eight escutcheons of the Earl's arms under a canopy of black velvet, was accompanied by four pall-bearers from the House of Commons: Edmund Burke, Sir George Savile, John Dunning, and Thomas Townshend. Behind 'the picture of Britannia weeping over the arms of Chatham, painted on sarsenet,' * and Clarenceux King of Arms, William Pitt walked, as chief mourner, flanked by his cousins, William Needham † and Thomas Pitt. ‡ Eight noblemen 'assistant mourners', members of the family, and friends followed. A great crowd had assembled.

George III was not represented at the funeral. Of the royal family, only the Duke and Duchess of Gloucester, already disgraced at Court, risked his displeasure by attending. 'The Court', as William wrote, 'do everything with an ill grace.'[76]

---

* Sarsenet or Sarcenet: a fine silk material sometimes known as 'Saracen'.
† Second son of Chatham's sister, Catherine.
‡ Eldest son of Chatham's eldest brother, Thomas; created 1st Baron Camelford, 1784.

The Gordon Riots
1779-1780

HESTER, COUNTESS OF CHATHAM, did not attend her husband's state funeral. Throughout their lives together she had shown a devotion as genuine as it was total, and she was prostrated by his death. William wrote to her from the Mahons' house in Harley Street soon after he returned from the Abbey, where he had sat through the long service at the head of the coffin, sending a short and reassuring account of the ceremony by servants returning to Hayes that evening. He joined his mother there the following morning and, some days later, accompanied her and his younger sister, Harriot, to Burton Pynsent, remaining with them until October. The return of Chatham's favourite sister, Anne Pitt, known as 'the Virgin', from her travels in Europe, was not consoling. Always unbalanced, she had become dottier than ever and had to be confined in a mental home, where she died two years later.

The settlement of Chatham's estate revealed the full extent of his financial incompetence. The largest of the loans provided by his friends had been repaid, but at the cost of mortgages of more than £23,000 on Burton Pynsent and Hayes. Parliament came to the rescue by voting £20,000 towards the settlement of outstanding debts, and a perpetual annuity of £4,000 to the earldom of Chatham.

These grants paid the most pressing of the many creditors and enabled John, who had succeeded to the title as 2nd Earl, to maintain his dignity; but there was little left for the rest of the family. Lady Chatham's annuity, producing little more than £2,000 a year after deduction of duties, was barely enough to keep her at Burton Pynsent, and much of William's time was spent in trying to obtain the arrears and some guarantee of regular payment for the future. His own situation was one of some embarrassment. At Cambridge he had been studying for the law, and in January 1777 had been admitted to Lincoln's Inn. The time was fast approaching when he must give up his rooms at Pembroke Hall and move to London. Meanwhile, the £3,500 bequeathed to him could not be paid, and he had no expectations beyond a mortgage of £1,500 on the Burton Pynsent property, assigned to him in 1774, to which he would not become entitled until his twenty-first birthday. For the next few years he lived on £600 a year, of which half came from his elder brother and half from his mother, who paid it from an allowance also made to her by the new Lord Chatham.

In November Pitt found a suitable set of rooms in Lincoln's Inn. The price of the lease was £1,100. He considered this 'a frightful sum' but, as he wrote to his mother, the rooms were 'in an exceeding good situation' and he had heard of none cheaper.[77] Lady Chatham's eldest brother, Lord Temple, advanced £1,000 against the security of Pitt's slender expectations and the lease was acquired. Pitt took possession of his rooms in Stone Buildings in late December 1779. Within twelve months he and his brother mortgaged this lease, with that of another set of rooms in Lincoln's Inn, in return for a loan of £1,500 at interest of five per cent. Thus, at the age of twenty-one, Pitt had obtained a loan on property bought with an earlier loan (from Temple) which in turn was secured by a mortgage. For the rest of his life the state of his personal finances, which he ignored with a cool indifference worthy of his father, continued to be as complicated and to display the results of the same imprudence as this first transaction.

Pitt remained in residence at Pembroke Hall until the end of 1779, but he spent much of his time in London, staying often at Nerot's hotel in King Street, St James's. During these visits he was able to conduct family business with the loyal and generous banker, Thomas Coutts, and also attended both houses of parliament to listen to debates. His younger brother was in London on leave from the navy

55

during the spring. Pitt reported, 'James is gone with my sisters to the ball as a professed dancer, which stands in the place of an invitation; a character which I do not assume, and have therefore stayed away.' [78] He occasionally accompanied his sisters to private balls and to the fashionable gatherings at Ranelagh but he was already showing signs of preferring male company. Lord Chatham took his seat in the House of Lords in June and both he and Pitt were frequent visitors at the house of their elder sister, Hester, Lady Mahon.

In January 1779 England's greatest eighteenth-century actor, David Garrick, died. Walpole noted the 'most extravagant pomp' of the funeral procession to Westminster Abbey. [79] 'The Court', he added, 'was delighted to see a more noble and splendid appearance at the interment of a comedian than had waited on the remains of the great Earl of Chatham, though *his* funeral was appointed by the orders of the House of Commons.' Next month London witnessed another spectacle that attracted even greater public participation. It arose from a dispute between two distinguished seamen, Admiral Augustus Keppel and Vice-Admiral Sir Hugh Palliser. In March 1778, Keppel took command of the home fleet, reputed to be twenty ships, at Portsmouth. Contrary to the repeated boasts of the First Lord of the Admiralty, Lord Sandwich, the fleet consisted of but six ships fit to put to sea. In July, after much rebuilding and refitting, and some reinforcement, Keppel sailed with thirty ships. His second-in-command was Sir Hugh Palliser. Following an indecisive engagement with a slightly superior French fleet off Ushant, Palliser ignored Keppel's order to renew the action and the French escaped. Both men held seats in the House of Commons. Palliser charged Keppel with misconduct and neglect of duty, and the Admiralty Board ordered a court martial. Keppel was tried in January aboard the *Britannia* and acquitted after proceedings lasting more than a month. He became a national hero. Palliser, tried for insubordination and also acquitted, was pilloried by the people and resigned his commission. Public reaction to the two acquittals was largely political. Palliser was a government supporter; Keppel was not. In this dispute, and in the revelation of government incompetence, the opposition scented victory.

The news of Keppel's acquittal reached London on 11 February 1779. Late that night, 'as the people grew drunk, an empty house in Pall Mall, lately inhabited by Sir Hugh Palliser, and still supposed to belong to him, was attacked, the windows were broken, and at last, though some guards had been sent for, the mob forced their way into it, and demolished whatever remained. The windows of Lord Mulgrave and Captain Hood were likewise broken and some few others accidentally that were not illuminated . . . Lord Sandwich, exceedingly terrified, escaped through the garden with his mistress, Miss Reay *, to the Horse Guards, and there betrayed a most manifest panic.' [80] Pitt was in London, having an unsightly cyst removed from his face, when Keppel arrived in the City on the 15th. He wrote to Edward Eliot in the light ironic tone that he reserved for intimate friends.

I am just come from behind the Throne in the House of Lords, and preparing to take my station in Fop Alley. The short Interval between the duties of a Statesman and a Beau, allows me just Time to perform that of a good Correspondent. . . . I am almost disabled . . . by the bodily Pain of the operation I am undergoing, and from my Mental Faculties being completely stupified [sic] by the Soporific Scene I have just left; which presented nothing but Motions carried Nemine Dissentiente, or what is Ten Times worse, earnest debates upon Points of order. . . . I rejoice to hear that the good People of England have so universally exerted their natural Right of Breaking Windows, Picking Pockets etc. etc., and that these Constitutional demonstrations of Joy, are not confined to the Metropolis. . . . The Conquering Hero himself has this evening made his Entry, and every Window in London (a Metaphor I learnt in the House of Lords) is by this time acquainted with his Arrival. . . . I begin to fear that the Clamour may subside, and the King still be blest with his present faithful Servants. [81]

He signed himself 'Most sincerely and illegibly Yours'.

As Pitt had forecast, the government did not fall, but it was brought close to defeat when, on 3 March, Fox proposed a motion of censure on the Admiralty. North saved himself by taking the motion as one of censure against the entire ministry. This rallied sufficient

* Martha Ray, a singer, was murdered outside Covent Garden Theatre a few months later by Lieutenant James Hackman, a rejected suitor.

support to snatch victory when the division was taken at one o'clock next morning; but the majority was small. It provided an early hint that North's government was again vulnerable to organized opposition.

While qualifying himself for the law, Pitt was already making preparations to enter parliament. In July he began to canvass support for his candidature for Cambridge University in the next general election. He wrote to his uncle Lord Temple, to Lord Palmerston, and also to John Townshend, one of the two sitting members. Cambridge, as he told his mother, had become 'doubly interesting' to him. Temple replied with friendly assurances of 'best good wishes and readiness to serve' in any way in his power, but cautioned Pitt against embarking on a parliamentary career before he was fully prepared for either politics or the law.[82] There seemed, however, to be some prospect of standing without being disgraced at the polls, and Pitt determined to make the attempt whenever parliament should be dissolved. The possibility of success was diminished by the death, in September, of Lord Temple.

Early in 1780, having come down from Cambridge after six years' interrupted study at the University, Pitt took up residence at his Lincoln's Inn rooms. During the next six months he was a regular visitor to the gallery of the House of Commons where he often found himself sitting with William Wilberforce. The friendship forged then became one of the closest of Pitt's life and, though shaken, survived the heavy demands made upon it by political differences. Pitt was in the gallery to hear the debates on economical reform, following Burke's introduction of his plan to thin the Civil List and decimate the profitable sinecure offices attached to the royal household. Though narrowly defeated on his major proposals, Burke succeeded in defeating the government on his motion, on 14 March, to abolish the Board of Trade. This was, Pitt reminded his mother, 'a scene which I never saw before'[83] and he was impressed, as he admitted he had not been earlier, by Burke's ability and style. Though familiar with the published reports of speeches, he had not previously had many opportunities to hear Burke in debate. He told Eliot, 'Burke's Extempores have both Times exceeded his corrected Publication, which (entre nous) is in my Opinion much the worse for revision. I had no Idea till now of his Excellence.'[84] He also admired Lord Shelburne's performance from the opposition benches in the Lords.

Burke's plan was a symptom of growing pressure upon the government to reduce the power and influence of the Crown. In a speech to the freeholders of Westminster in February, Fox had warned them against falling 'a sacrifice to that corruption which has given the crown an influence unknown to any former period of our history. Permit this influence to increase, and the country is enslaved, freedom destroyed, and the English constitution completely overthrown.' [85] Supporting Burke's Bill in the Commons, he had declared: 'The King, it was true, was the sovereign of the people, but the King was to hold the crown only as long as the people should choose.' [86] On 6 April this pressure reached its peak in the House of Commons when John Dunning, who had been Solicitor-General during the final two years of Grafton's administration, moved that 'The influence of the Crown has increased, is increasing, and ought to be diminished.' This provoked uproar, and one of the rare occasions when Lord North was sufficiently stirred to lose his temper. When the House divided at midnight, a stunned government heard the Speaker, Sir Fletcher Norton, announce that Dunning's extraordinary motion had been carried by a majority of eighteen votes. But Dunning was not finished with his butchery. Two further resolutions, declaring the competence of the House to correct abuses in the Civil List and urging immediate redress of the economic and electoral abuses detailed in petitions signed by thousands and received from all parts of the country, were passed without division. At two o'clock on the morning of the 7th, immediately after he left the House, Lord North wrote to the King asking to be allowed to retire at the end of the session. Though he did not say so to his Chief Minister, George III thought 'It would be madness not to call a new parliament as soon as we have hobbled through the present session.' [87]

The government had been shaken, but those who believed that it would fall immediately underrated North's composure and resilience. When, on 24 April, Dunning moved that parliament should not be dissolved until the resolutions passed on 6 April should have been implemented, the House rejected the motion by 254 votes to 203. Fox who had again spoken against the government, declared himself 'hurt, mortified and filled with indignant resentment'. He had not yet learned the ways of the House and was, indeed, never fully to understand them. The 'independent' members, mostly representatives of county constituencies and less interested in faction than in what they conceived at any time to be their duty to the country, might vote for reform in abstraction; but measures overtly impugning the prerogative of the Crown smelt to them of treason and would never have their votes. This lesson, obscure to Fox, was not lost upon Pitt. As an educated observer, who was not required to declare his opinion, he was in an excellent position to estimate the relative strengths of the Crown, parliament, and the people, and to assess those loyalties upon which a minister might rely. He learnt that a defeated government might remain in office and recover its majority in the House; that intemperate speech and behaviour seldom achieved their aims; and that, for all his apparent inattention, Lord North knew more about survival than any of his contemporaries.

Two months later Pitt was able to see for himself the development and effects of mob violence. He had already had some experience of this during the demonstrations in support of Keppel in February 1779, but the Gordon riots were on a scale that made previous disturbances seem trivial. Since the Quebec Act of 1774 acknowledging the establishment of the Roman Catholic Church in Canada, much thought had been given to proposals for the relaxation of some of the prohibitions against Catholics in England. In particular, it was considered necessary for military recruitment that the oath of supremacy * should be replaced for the army by a simple oath of allegiance. A relief Act to this effect was passed by parliament in 1778. Next year it was proposed that this act of toleration should be extended to Scotland. In England the small measure of relaxation had passed almost unnoticed; in Scotland it provoked riots. Everywhere in Britain the Roman Catholic faith was associated with Jacobitism, but nowhere in the country was prejudice greater than in the Presbyterian lowlands of Scotland.

Lord George Gordon, third son of the Duke of Gordon, was twenty-nine years old. He was ambitious, mentally unstable, and impatient. For six years he had been a member of parliament, but his speeches against the government and the royal family had not

* The oath of supremacy, required by the various Test and Corporation Acts passed in the reigns of Charles II and George I, denied the supremacy of the Pope but did not assert the supremacy of the Crown.

60

brought him the esteem he thought his due. By the summer of 1780, taking advantage of petitions against Catholic influence which were pouring into parliament, Gordon had become the leader of the anti-Catholic movement to be known as the Protestant Association.

On Friday 2 June, Gordon headed a procession to parliament where he was to present a petition, said to contain 120,000 signatures, praying for the repeal of the relief Act passed in the previous year. He was followed by a crowd later estimated to number about 60,000 which had assembled in St George's Fields.* The original procession had been peaceable, the petitioners marching eight abreast behind large 'No Popery' banners and following Gordon's repeated instructions to maintain order and avoid excessive noise; but as they marched they were joined by the most violent, disreputable, and drunken elements of the London streets. By two o'clock, when the first coaches carrying members of parliament began to arrive, the crowd had become a disorderly mob, among whom orders had been circulated to stop unpopular peers and not to allow them to enter the House until they agreed to wear the blue cockades sported by the petitioners and to cry 'No Popery'. Several members of the House of Lords, including the Lord Chief Justice, Lord Mansfield, Lord Hillsborough, and the Bishops of Lincoln and Lichfield, were assaulted and pelted with mud, and those who succeeded in entering the House were besieged there by a mob which threatened to break down the doors. Lord Sandwich was one of many who preferred discretion to duty and turned their coaches for home without venturing near the parliament buildings. Members of the Commons were met with less violence, though two were severely injured and others had their coaches smashed. Appalled by this turn of events, many of the original petitioners had left. A mob numbering about 18,000 remained, all the more dangerous for being largely made up of the ignorant, the unthinking, the bigoted, and the professionally criminal, inflamed by hatred and excited by violence, beyond the control of any leader.

While this menacing rabble battered on the doors of the House of Lords, Gordon presented his petition in the Commons. During the angry debate that followed, he made frequent excursions onto the gallery overlooking the lobby and shouted inflammatory information

* A site on the south bank of the Thames now partly occupied by Waterloo Station.

61

to the crowd below. Those who saw him were left in little doubt that his religious fervor had developed into unreasoning fanaticism. One hundred and ninety-eight members had reached the House of Commons that day. In the division, Gordon's motion for the immediate consideration of the petition received only eight votes including his own. When this news was relayed to the crowd outside it seemed that the members of parliament, many of whom had already drawn their swords, might have to fight their way to safety. A pitched battle was averted by the arrival of a mixed contingent of Horse and Foot Guards, accompanied by two Justices who, with considerable good sense and subtlety, succeeded in persuading the mob to disperse.

Most of those genuinely interested in the petition went home: the rest went on the rampage that night in the streets of London. Armed with axes, spades and hammers, they destroyed the Sardinian Chapel in Lincoln's Inn Fields and pillaged a Catholic chapel in Golden Square. On Saturday it seemed that the violence had spent itself, but that evening riots broke out again with renewed fury. They continued for five days and nights. At first directed against Catholic property and meeting-places, the destruction was soon spread to include the houses of the great, and commercial and public build-ings. Newgate prison, and the adjacent gaols of Bridewell and the New Prison in Clerkenwell, were attacked and the prisoners released; distilleries were sacked and burnt; the streets ran with raw spirits, and drunken rioters were cremated alive in the fires they had lighted. Among the houses destroyed was that of the Lord Chief Justice, whose magnificent library of books was burnt in the street. Later, when giving judgement in a trial, Lord Mansfield remarked ruefully, 'I have not consulted books; indeed I have no books to consult.'

By the night of Tuesday 6 June it was clear that no effective action to restore order was being taken by the City authorities. Brackley Kennett, who had started life as a waiter in a notorious brothel, but risen to become a city alderman and Lord Mayor of London, was both a politician and a coward. He had no wish to offend the City, where, although the outrages were deplored, there was much sympathy for the aims of the Protestant Association; and, like most of his fellow aldermen and many of the city magistrates, he was afraid that any firm action against the mob would provoke reprisals against his own person and property. Kennett's craven behaviour was sustained by the abject failure of the magistrates, who were careful to avoid the scenes of rioting, and by an interpretation of the law restricting the use of troops which reduced the army to impotence. This interpretation was founded upon an opinion given by Philip Yorke, 1st Earl of Hardwicke, one of the most respected legal authorities of the eighteenth century, which declared that troops might not be ordered to fire on the mob until the Riot Act had been read to the rioters by a magistrate. When magistrates could not be found or, when found, could not be persuaded to act, the troops were obliged to be passive spectators, as more than three hundred had been when Lord Mansfield's house was looted and burnt. Lord Amherst, as Commander-in-Chief, received urgent calls for help, some signed by Kennett, from all parts of the city, but had insufficient troops to answer every call. The collapse of the civil authority made the use of troops futile, and their passive presence often acted as a further incitement to the rioters.

The King, who throughout the emergency had acted with exemplary coolness, sense, and courage, determined to have the law re-examined. At a Privy Council on Wednesday 7th, the Attorney-General, Alexander Wedderburn*, gave it as his opinion that officers might use their discretion in the use of whatever force might be required to prevent illegal acts. A royal proclamation giving effect to this change in the interpretation of the law was published the same day, and Amherst acted upon it without delay. By nightfall the army in London, reinforced by militia regiments called in from the counties, numbered more than 15,000. The King's shrewd and resolute action marked the turning point in the crisis. The night of the 7th was the worst of a series of nights of horror, but the effective use of troops was decisive. The rioters had broken into gunsmiths' shops and stolen quantities of muskets from the Artillery Ground. Troops were rushed to guard the royal palaces, the Bank of England, the Guildhall, and other public buildings. Property owners barricaded their doors, armed their families and servants, and prepared to defend themselves. In Downing Street, Lord North found himself besieged while entertaining Sir John Macpherson, William Eden, and three others to dinner. 'You see, Macpherson,' he said,

* Later 1st Baron Loughborough.

unruffled, 'here is much confusion.' The King, who spent the night touring the defences of Buckingham House and the royal stables, decided if necessary to take personal command of his Guards regiments to put down the riots.

That night there were several serious clashes between the military and the mob. Four more prisons were attacked and set on fire. At the Fleet prison the Riot Act was read without effect and the Light Dragoons charged the crowd. The force commander estimated that about a hundred rioters were killed. Langdale's distillery, one of the largest in the country, was looted and burnt. The streets around flowed with unrefined gin which the rioters drank from the gutters. Many died in agony. The Northumberland Militia, arriving too late to do more than scatter those who were not too drunk to move, marched on to the Bank of England where John Wilkes, respectable as the champion of liberty against licence, was taking a leading part in its defence. In the midst of the shooting Lord George Gordon appeared. For the past two days he had risked his life many times in the thick of the confusion, trying to persuade the crowds to disperse; but the riots had long since ceased to have any connection with the movement he had led. There was also an unexplained and sinister aspect to the rioting: many observers had noticed the presence among the crowds of well-dressed men, some in the uniforms of officers in the army or navy, who were inciting the mob to further outrage and directing the assaults on property. What had begun as a peaceful demonstration by people who, however illiberal in their attitudes, were sincere in their extreme loyalty to the established Church, had developed into an insurrection dominated by lust for violence and destruction. Lord George Gordon no longer had any authority over the crowd. Sir Nathaniel Wraxhall, who had been in the city throughout the riots, wrote that 'London offered on every side the picture of a city sacked and abandoned to a ferocious enemy.' [88]

As the crowds were gradually dispersed or driven across the Thames, Lord Amherst stationed strong contingents of troops on the bridges across the river, denying Westminster and the City to the mob. By Thursday afternoon the insurrection had been brought under control. On Friday it was over. Pitt, who had spent much of the period at his rooms at Lincoln's Inn, wrote that the building had been 'surrounded with flames on all sides, but itself perfectly free

64

from danger.' [89] Many of the young lawyers had banded together to defend their chambers. A party of four hundred, of whom Pitt was one, with their servants, protected the area of Lincoln's Inn. Making light of the dangerous situation, Pitt told his mother: 'Several very respectable lawyers have appeared with muskets on their shoulders to the no small diversion of all spectators. Unluckily the appearance of danger ended just as we embodied, and our military ardour has been thrown away.' [90]

London was the scene of many violent disturbances in the eighteenth century but none compared in destruction, savagery, terror, and loss of life with the Gordon riots of June 1780. No record exists of the numbers killed. According to government reports 285 rioters were killed and a further 173 wounded in skirmishes with troops, but this took no account of those who had drunk themselves to death or burned in the many fires. Wraxhall believed that more than 700 had lost their lives, and even that was probably an underestimate. The damage, which included the total destruction of more than thirty great houses, is said to have been more than ten times that caused in Paris during the entire period of the Revolution.[91] On the night of the 7th alone, Walpole had counted thirty-six fires on both sides of the river. More than 450 people were arrested. At the end of June trials began at the Old Bailey, and others followed in the borough courts. In the south ward of London fifty-eight were found guilty, twenty-five executed, and seventy-six acquitted. Of those hanged seventeen were under eighteen years old and three under fifteen. Two were young women.

Lord George Gordon was arrested and sent to the Tower of London. He was tried in February 1781 on charges of high treason and entrusted his defence to his cousin, Thomas Erskine, and Lloyd Kenyon.* The prosecution, led by the Attorney-General, employed seven other learned counsel. The case was tried by the Lord Chief Justice, Lord Mansfield, whose house and library had been destroyed in June. The outcome, due largely to a brilliant closing speech by Erskine admitting Gordon's rashness and lack of foresight but asserting his innocence of violent or traitorous intent, was an acquittal. Gordon's mind, always unbalanced, was finally unhinged

---

* Both were to have distinguished careers. Lloyd Kenyon became 1st Baron Kenyon and Lord Chief Justice 1788-1802; Thomas Erskine, later 1st Baron Erskine, was Lord Chancellor 1806-7.

by the strain of the riots and his oppressive feeling of guilt. He abandoned the faith for which he had fought and became an orthodox Jew. He exhibited, as Wraxhall gleefully recorded, 'the strongest attestation of the sincerity of his conversion to Judaism by submitting to one of the most painful ceremonies or acts enjoined by the Mosaic Law . . . and he preserved with great care the proofs of his having undergone the amputation.' [92]

The Gordon riots produced two important effects: the horror of their experiences swung the opinion of the people of London back to the government; and the parliamentary Opposition, and the City, traditionally opposed to the government of the day, understood that public agitation could no longer be considered a safe or acceptable method of expressing their opinions. Lord Shelburne had noted that 'The police of Westminster was an imperfect, inadequate, and wretched system . . . and a fit object for reformation.' [93] In fact there was no police system worth the title and it was to be another thirty-five years before any regular organization was introduced. Until then London was policed by the 'watch and ward', a medieval body recruited from the dutiful citizenry of the parishes, assisted by magistrates, marshals, and beadles. At the end of the century the police of London numbered little more than 3,000 men, all of them unarmed.

The most effective deterrent to increasing crime was the improved lighting of the streets introduced between 1780 and 1790. A foreign visitor reported: 'The lamps are lit while it is still daylight and are placed so close to each other that this ordinary street-lighting glows like a festive illumination.' [94] Such lighting was not to be seen in any other European city, and a German prince visiting London for the first time thought it an illumination specially created for his welcome.

The Gordon riots accomplished what no more constitutional movement could have achieved in the time: the consolidation of public loyalty behind the King and his ministers. They also demonstrated certain entrenched but often forgotten traditions of British behaviour. As a student of history, Pitt must have been already aware that when the people believed the Constitution to be threatened, whether by the sovereign, by parliament, or by a disaffected minority, they united to defend the established order. The Protestant Association, originally a defence of the established

66

Church against an imaginary threat, received public support; but when its aims disintegrated in mob violence, the mass of the people withdrew in alarm behind the security of authority and the rule of law. Pitt was given an early opportunity to see for himself the strength of anti-Catholic feeling in the country; the development of peaceable demonstration into mob violence; the dangers inherent in the use, however necessary, of troops in support of the civil authority; and the instinctive loyalty of the mass of the people to the Crown as representing a Constitution but dimly understood. Though they had helped to maintain a Government which Pitt chose to oppose, the riots held for him lessons which he was later to find valuable.

Towards the middle of June Pitt was called to the Bar. 'Besides', he wrote to his mother, 'the military transactions of the times, I have had to assume within these few days the pacific character of a barrister-at-law, and now want nothing but my wig to qualify me for the Western Circuit.' [95] Before he set out for the West Country he attended a series of dinners organized by the lawyers of Lincoln's Inn to entertain officers of the Northumberland Militia, who had helped to guard their chambers during the recent riots. At one of these the guests included Francis Osborne, Marquess of Carmarthen, and the historian Edward Gibbon. Gibbon, whose reputation had been enhanced by the publication, four years earlier, of the first volume * of his *Decline and Fall of the Roman Empire*, was justly considered one of the best conversationalists of his day. He was also a man of powerful vanity. Wilberforce described him as 'Coxcomb all over; but of great learning as well as very great show of it.' [96] He was accustomed to the centre of the stage, a position from which Pitt, in one of those moods of irreverent humour described by his friends as 'playful', determined to dislodge him. James Bland Burges, who was acting as host, described the occasion:

Mr Gibbon, nothing loath, took the conversation into his own hands, and very brilliant and pleasant he was during the dinner and for some time afterwards. He had just concluded, however, one of his best foreign anecdotes, in which he had introduced some of the fashionable levities of political doctrine then preva-

---

* The second and third volumes were issued in 1781.

lent, and, with his customary tap on the lid of his snuff-box, was looking round to receive our tribute of applause, when a deep-toned but clear voice was heard from the bottom of the table, very calmly and civilly impugning the correctness of the narrative, and the propriety of the doctrine of which it had been made the vehicle. The historian, turning a disdainful glance towards the quarter whence the voice proceeded, saw, for the first time, a tall, thin, and rather ungainly-looking young man, who now sat quietly and silently eating some fruit.[97]

Seeing that Pitt's remarks had made some impression on the company, Gibbon felt obliged to defend his argument. The debate between them 'was conducted with great talent and brilliancy on both sides', but Pitt's argument prevailed. Gibbon 'finding himself driven into a corner from which there was no escape, made some excuse for rising from the table and left the room.' Burges followed him and, finding that he was looking for his hat, begged him to return. The historian refused, saying 'That young gentleman is, I have no doubt, extremely ingenious and agreeable, but I must acknowledge that his style of conversation is not exactly what I am accustomed to, so you must positively excuse me.'

'And away', Burges continues, 'he went in high dudgeon. . . . When we returned to the dining room we found Mr Pitt proceeding very tranquilly with the illustration of the subject from which his opponent had fled, and which he discussed with such ability, strength of argument, and eloquence, that his hearers were filled with profound admiration.'

Pitt's behaviour on this occasion was, perhaps, reprehensible. Gibbon was an honoured guest at a dinner at which Pitt was one of the most junior hosts. The 'playfulness' that William's young friends found so diverting was not invariably beguiling to his seniors. He had wit, some of his mother's charm, and a great intellect; but he lacked tact.

Four months earlier, Pitt's elder sister, Hester Mahon, had given birth to her third daughter. It is clear from Pitt's letters to his mother that Hester never fully recovered. On 18 July she died. Charles, Viscount Mahon—left with three small girls, the eldest of whom, Lady Hester Stanhope, was but four years old—lost no time in taking a second wife. Within the year he had married Louisa Grenville, daughter of Lady Chatham's youngest brother, Henry. Louisa, described by her mother-in-law as 'chilling', and by Lady Hester Stanhope, her stepdaughter, as interested only in pleasure and the details of her toilette, nevertheless provided the Stanhope heir with three sons.

By the beginning of August Pitt had joined the Western Circuit. Among the junior counsel he found one of his friends from Cambridge, St Andrew St John, and soon acquired a circle of friends which included Nathaniel Bond, later Judge Advocate, and Joseph Jekyll. Jekyll later remembered that 'among lively Men of nearly his own time of life he was almost the most lively & convivial in the many Hours of leisure which occur to young unaccompanied Men on a Circuit & joined all the little excursions to Southampton, Weymouth & such parties of Amusement as were habitually formed. . . . His wit, his good Humour & joyous Manners endeared him to the younger Part of the Bar.' [98] Pitt was, Jekyll recalled, excellent in cross-examination, but never addressed a jury. He had, indeed, little opportunity to do so. On 1 September, parliament was dissolved.

Pitt hurried to Cambridge. There were five candidates for the two University seats and his prospects were not favourable. When the results were announced on 16 September he was bottom of the poll, the first two places going to James Mansfield, later appointed Solicitor-General, and John Townshend, who was supported by the Rockingham faction. Pitt, though last of the five, was not disgraced. He had found time for little canvassing, but he polled nearly fourteen per cent of the total votes cast and more than half the number cast for Mansfield. He wrote, disappointed but not surprised, to his mother: 'Mansfield and Townshend have run away with the prize, but my struggle has not been dishonourable. I am going to Cheveley for a day or two, and shall soon return to you for as long as the law will permit, which will now be probably the sole object with me.' [99] Cheveley was the Cambridgeshire home of the Duke of Rutland who, as Marquess of Granby, had been a close friend at the University, and whose succession to the dukedom on the death of his father had created a vacancy in the representation for Cambridge. Rutland had many political contacts, among the most valuable of whom was Sir James Lowther, controller of nine parliamentary seats. It was common at the time for a candidate to offer himself for more than one borough to make sure of his election. In September 1780 Lowther was elected for both Haslemere and Cumberland, and his cousin William for both Appleby and Carlisle. Two seats won at the election were thus at Lowther's disposal. In November he offered the vacant seat for Appleby to William Pitt.

The offer was tempting, but Pitt hesitated to accept it. There was no question of his losing the election: he would be returned, on the instructions of his patron, unopposed; he would not even have to visit his constituents to canvass their support; but he feared that his nomination under such circumstances would restrict his independence of action. Sir James Lowther was 'equally unamiable in public and private' and his reputation as a boroughmonger who exercised a tight control over his members was well known. Pitt went to Cumberland to see him. The result of this interview was, as he told his mother, entirely satisfactory: the offer was confirmed 'in the handsomest Manner. Judging from my Father's Principles he concludes that mine would be agreeable to his own, and on that Ground, to me of all others the most agreeable, desires to bring me in. No Kind of Condition was mentioned, but that if ever Our Lines of Conduct should become opposite, I should give Him an Opportunity of choosing another Person.' [100]

On 23 January 1781 Pitt took his seat in the House of Commons as member of parliament for Appleby. A month later, Samuel Goodenough wrote to Edward Wilson, who had tutored Pitt in his youth: 'I cannot resist the natural impulse of giving pleasure, by telling you that the famous William Pitt, who made so capital a figure in the last reign, is restored to this country.' [101]

VI

Apprenticeship
1781-1782

THE HOUSE OF COMMONS, which William Pitt entered for the first time as a member on 23 January 1781, had occupied the same chamber since the reign of Edward VI. Built as the Chapel of St Stephen, part of the royal palace of Westminster, it had retained, despite subsequent alterations, much of its original character. The Speaker's chair was placed on the altar steps, and the tiered stalls, ranged along the walls on either side for boys of the original collegiate foundation, formed the benches for members. The ceiling had been lowered, and from it hung huge brass chandeliers. Above the benches on both sides ran the Strangers' Gallery, supported on slender columns. Behind the Speaker's chair the windows at the eastern end had been altered and enlarged, and a door, known as Solomon's Porch, cut through the wall. The whole chamber was panelled. Some fifty-eight feet long and thirty-three feet wide, the room had kept some of the college chapel atmosphere, familiar and comfortable to members educated at Oxford or Cambridge, and its very lack of space or grandeur contrived to add an air of informality and intimacy to debates. There was seating only for about 420 of the 558 members, and, when debates were well attended, those who were unable to find seats stood behind the benches.* Few members spoke in debates, and there was constant interruption and disturbance from members entering or leaving the chamber. Carl Philip Moritz, a German visitor in 1782, was scandalized that members wore 'no special clothing' and, worse, 'They enter the House in greatcoats, boots and spurs! It is not unusual to see a Member stretched out on one of the benches while the rest are in debate. One member may be cracking nuts, another eating an orange or whatever fruit may be in season; they are continually going in and out.' He was 'also much shocked by the open abuse which Members of Parliament flung at each other.' [102] In spite of these diversions the standard of oratory was high and the audience critical: speakers who were ill informed or dull were left in no doubt of their shortcomings.

The physical arrangement of the chamber produced a natural division of members between those, on the Speaker's right hand, who formed and supported the government, and those, facing them across the narrow aisle, who opposed it. Stalls at the western end provided 'cross-benches' for some of the independent members. There were those who were identifiable as Whigs or Tories, but the divisions in the House were not governed by party in the modern sense, or by formal organization. Although faction was generally deplored as tending to fragment the essential unity of parliament as an independent limb of the constitution, the majority of members aligned themselves behind heads of families or political patrons, producing a quantity of small parties or groups which coalesced to support or oppose the policies advocated by ministers of the Crown.

Of all the ties that bound members together to form a party, the most important was that of family. A nucleus formed thus by 'connexion' would be strengthened by the accession of friends and political protégé, and by the loose attachment of members of shared interest and opinions. In addition, a chief minister or serious contender for high office could count on the votes of those already under obligation to him or hoping for favours in the future. Lord North's personal following, built on the firm foundation of eight relations, was one of the largest in the House, numbering nearly

* This traditional lack of sufficient seating was deliberately continued when the chamber was rebuilt after the fire of 1834 and again after the House of Commons was destroyed by bombs in 1941.

forty. Lord Sandwich's party, about seventeen strong in 1780, exceptionally owed less to family than to his connections with and influence in the East India Company and the Admiralty. Earl Gower's group, on the other hand, included his son, son-in-law, nephew, brothers-in-law by his two marriages, and several more distant relations. None of these groups was large enough by itself to form a government. It was the business of an aspiring political leader to contrive the coalition of a sufficient number of these groups to establish a majority. In practice this object could not be achieved without the aid of independent members.

The independence of parliament, and most particularly of the House of Commons, was a constitutional principle to which all members subscribed. The independence of the individual member was as highly valued but less easily attainable. After the 1780 election it was estimated that 220 independent members had been returned, about 90 of whom leaned towards one or another group or party. This left a powerful body of 130 truly independent members who, if they could be persuaded either to attend a debate or to vote, might be swayed by argument. They would not vote as a group: to do so would be a contradiction of their belief in individual liberty; but they held among them a power that no minister could afford to ignore. The difficulty was to persuade them to vote at all. They were amateur politicians, prepared to exercise their power in a constitutional crisis, but generally preferring to attend to their duties as landowners, or their pleasures in the hunting field or at race meetings. The independents, often described as the County Members or Knights of the Shires, included a good number of landowning representatives of counties where voting was less easily manipulated by outside influence, but there were others, successful merchants among them, who represented boroughs where the seats were controlled by local independent gentry or won in open contest. They were protected from the pressures of party by their wealth and their lack of ambition.

It is one of the complications of eighteenth-century politics that scarcely any of the familiar terms is applicable in its modern sense. There was no two-party system; there was no systematic opposition based on party, which was considered contrary to the national interest and disrespectful to the Crown, if not actively treasonable;

the term 'Prime Minister', though in use, was considered objectionable as late as 1783 *; the existence and the function of the Cabinet were recognized by 1784, but the theory of collective responsibility was not accepted until some years later; and even a general election was not general by modern standards, for many constituencies were uncontested and no vote was taken. † Nor was a general election an opportunity for the people to choose a ministry. Rather less than one per cent of the population was entitled to vote (and of these about one in twenty-five was able to exercise his right freely), nearly three quarters of the members were returned by influence, and throughout the century no government ever lost a general election. Politics was not considered the business of the people. Daniel Parker Coke, addressing the electors of Nottingham in 1784, 'declined then entering into the discussion of political questions, as they frequently caused confusion'.[103]

Ministries changed when a Chief Minister wished to resign or found he could no longer attract sufficient support in the Commons to enable the government to govern. General elections, always held on the death of the sovereign but otherwise seldom called before the end of the statutory seven years allotted to each parliament by the Act of 1716, were used by the King to adjust the composition of the Commons, to strengthen his government, and to defeat or reduce opposition factions. The responsibility of the First Lord of the Treasury, who was usually also Prime Minister, general elections were managed by the Secretary to the Treasury. It was his task to make detailed assessments of the constituencies and the allegiance of the candidates most likely to be elected, to arrange such support as might be practicable and necessary for those friendly to the government, and to advise the King and his ministers about their best course of action and the probable consequences. From 1770 until 1782 this key appointment was held by John Robinson, a lawyer, who owed his position to the recommendation of Pitt's first political patron, Sir James Lowther. Without Robinson's extraordinary industry and zeal it is doubtful if North's ministry could have survived. It was Robinson's estimate of election results that per-

* George III wrote in 1779 of Lord North's 'wanting to ape the prime minister without any of the requisite qualities'.

† Only two counties (Cambridgeshire and Surrey) polled in 1780; in the elections of 1784 and 1790, seven were contested.

74

suaded the King and Lord North to call a surprise election in September 1780, some twelve months before the end of the parliamentary term.

In theory the King was free to choose his ministers, but in practice this freedom was progressively eroded by the necessity to choose a ministry that could command the support of the House of Commons, and the alliance, however temporary, of powerful groups in parliament to deny such support to anyone unacceptable to the members. In the early years of his reign George III succeeded in asserting his constitutional right to the chief executive authority against the power of the Whig aristocracy. The secure establishment of the Hanoverian monarchy after the failure of the last Jacobite rebellion in 1745, the war with France and Spain which united the people with the Crown against the common enemy, and the absence of an adult heir to the throne to act as a kernel of opposition, had given the first British-born King since James II an opportunity denied to his predecessors; but the Whigs, traditionally the defenders of the Constitution against the Crown, gained strength as the American war continued, and looked for political victory in military defeat.

Parliament was dissolved and a general election called in September 1780 with the clear intention of strengthening the North government's following in the House of Commons, enabling it to last for another parliamentary term. North had begged to be allowed to resign in April, when Dunning's notorious motion against the increasing influence of the Crown was carried, but the King understood the danger of changing his chief minister eighteen months before a general election and, indeed, could find no one of sufficient stature, who was also acceptable to him, to replace North. As the months passed, the rift between the opposition groups led by Rockingham and Shelburne widened until Shelburne withdrew from parliament in disgust. Much encouraged by this development, North had hopes of a coalition with Rockingham, but his attempts to achieve this failed. Rockingham had been prepared to call a truce with the government until the Gordon riots were suppressed and law and order restored, but his terms for making the truce more permanent included the King's permission to recognize American independence if no other course could bring the war to an end, the package of economical reforms already proposed by Burke, the dismissal of Lords Sandwich and George Germain, and the appointment of Fox and the Duke of Richmond to the two vital executive posts as Secretaries of State. The terms were unacceptable to North. To the King they seemed preposterous and impertinent.

On 15 June news had arrived of Sir Henry Clinton's successful siege of Charleston with the capture of 5,000 men and 300 pieces of artillery. Ministers began to think in terms of imminent and final victory. John Robinson's detailed calculations, delivered to the King on 1 August, produced the conclusion that a general election would increase North's majority in the House of Commons from sixty to seventy-two. The decision to dissolve parliament was kept secret. Rockingham and the Duke of Portland did not know of it until 30 August. Rockingham pronounced himself 'exceeding vexed', and denounced the measure as 'wicked'. He was less aggrieved when the results became known. Robinson's calculations had been over-optimistic and misleading. Although his figures had been remarkably accurate, the deductions drawn from them had been proved false. It appeared that North's government was the poorer for the election by some five votes. It was true that a number of the severest critics of the government—including Sir William Howe, Edmund Burke, and Admiral Keppel—had been defeated, but Pitt's brother-in-law, Lord Mahon, John Townshend, and the playwright and actor-manager Richard Brinsley Sheridan had come in for the first time, and Burke and Keppel were soon returned in the by-elections. William Wilberforce, who had celebrated his twenty-first birthday on 24 August, was elected for Hull after a campaign costing him £8,000-9,000 for 1,126 votes. Charles James Fox, who had previously held a seat for Malmesbury in Wiltshire, was returned for Westminster, which he represented for the rest of his life. The Reverend Doctor John Warner saw him campaigning in Westminster, standing 'upon the hustings, bowing and sweltering, and scratching his black ass'.[104]

North had failed to solve his own problems at the polls. The country's difficulties abroad were no less likely to bring down his ministry. In America, Clinton's victory at Charleston had been followed by Cornwallis's defeat of Gates in August; Benedict Arnold deserted to the British; the Carolinas were cleared of resistance, and the army moved into Virginia; but no sooner had the British army left an area of conquest than American rebellion took root there again. For all the hopeful reports of commanders in the field, and the premature expectations of triumph expressed by Germain, it was evident that the war could not be ended by military force alone. The appearance of a formidable French fleet in American waters threatened even the essential British command of the sea. In Europe, British isolation was complete. The combined French and Spanish fleets had taken command of the Channel and the Mediterranean, and in the summer of 1779 they had cruised unmolested on seas traditionally ruled by the British navy. In November, when it seemed that the Dutch would join the League of Armed Neutrality formed by Russia and the Baltic powers, and recognize the independence of the United States of America, Britain had declared war on Holland. Gibraltar was under siege by Spain. In India, British possessions were threatened by the Marathas and by Hyder Ali.* Lastly, although order had been restored in Britain, the urgent danger of insurrection in Ireland had been averted at the last minute by economic concessions lifting restrictions on Irish trade. It could not be said that any major issue had been solved in the previous four years; nor was there any indication that North's government was capable of designing solutions. It is remarkable that in this time of evident ministerial incompetence, when years of neglect had left the navy helpless against the fleets of France, Holland, and Spain; when the army was engaged in a futile war in America; when every overseas possession was threatened; and when Britain had no ally in Europe or, indeed, anywhere else, the opposition was, as Lord Hillsborough told William Eden, 'if not dead at least asleep'.[105]

In his first eighteen months in the House of Commons Pitt made fewer than a dozen major speeches and a similar number of interjections in debates.† He concerned himself with two great subjects, the war and reform, and the impression he made was immediate and striking. The occasion of his maiden speech was

* See pp. 112-113

† Although, by tradition, parliamentary debates were secret, the standing order prohibiting the reporting of proceedings was, also by tradition, ignored. In 1771, the 'printers' case' (when the City of London challenged the House of Commons on this issue) resulted in some relaxation of the rule, but 'newswriters', when they were admitted, were cramped into the back benches of the Strangers' Gallery, where they were often unable to distinguish the speakers, and their long-hand accounts were notoriously inaccurate. The most reliable of all early reporters was William 'Memory' Woodfall, though his political bias is evident in his writings. Newswriters were often helped by carefully edited versions of speeches supplied by the speakers themselves and by the recollections of members. Pitt seldom supplied written texts to the reporters and the records of his speeches are certainly both inaccurate and incomplete.

unique. On 26 February the House was debating the reintroduction of Burke's motion for Economical Reform when members on the Opposition benches began to chant Pitt's name. It is a convention that new members are not expected to speak until they consider themselves ready to do so and then only from a prepared script. Pitt was called upon without warning and in the course of a debate. He rose magnificently to the challenge in an extempore debating speech of remarkable power and lucidity. In it he demonstrated to the House for the first time the mature style of argument—cool, incisive, reasoned, and eloquent—that distinguished the best of his speeches throughout his parliamentary life. His particular strength lay in his ability to isolate any factual weakness in the arguments of his opponents. In his own argument he relied upon the inexorable persuasion of logic. His voice was 'deep, bell-toned', 'rich and striking, full of melody and force', [106] and he used it to illuminate his language, providing the necessary balance of light and shade. He seldom made any appeal to the emotions: his speeches were constructed with an almost mathematical precision, like well-proportioned buildings, more impressive than moving. He was never a great theatrical performer as his father had been. Though tall, he was thin and narrow-shouldered, and his gestures were awkward.* The essence of his oratory, as of his life, was control. In an age when men did not scruple to display the full range of human emotions, Pitt held his own under iron restraint. He confined his gestures, both in his public and his social life, to the frequent use of the admonitory index finger, commanding attention by his logic, by his language, and by the strength of his expression, which the artist John Opie described as 'extraordinary' and 'devilish' in its power.

Pitt's maiden speech established him, at the start of his career, as a speaker of outstanding ability. Fox, with whom he was already on good terms, was the first to congratulate him, and Lord North was heard to say 'that it was the best speech of a young man that he had ever heard'. [108] Burke is said to have exclaimed, 'He is not a chip off the old block: he is the old block itself.' The following evening Pitt wrote with becoming modesty to his mother: 'I know you will have

---

* William Owen, the portrait painter, to whom Pitt sat twenty years later, told Joseph Farington that 'a more awkward, illmade *figure* than that of Mr Pitt could scarcely be, and his cloaths were very ill shaped.' [107]

learnt that I heard my own voice yesterday, and the account you have had would be in all respects better than any I can give if it had not come from too partial a friend. All I can say is that I was able to execute in some measure what I intended, and that I have at least every reason to be happy beyond measure in the reception I met with.' [109]

He spoke twice more before the summer recess: in an economic debate at the end of May; and in June in the debate on the American war, which he described with Chathamite vigour as 'a most accursed, wicked, barbarous, cruel, unnatural, unjust, and diabolical war. It was conceived in injustice; it was nurtured and brought forth in folly; its footsteps are marked in blood, slaughter, persecution, and devastation.' Fox, who had moved for the conclusion of peace, was delighted with the performance. Henry Dundas, Lord Advocate and destined to be one of Pitt's closest friends and political associates, replying for the government, spoke generously of 'so happy an union of first-rate abilities, high integrity, bold and honest independence of conduct, and the most persuasive eloquence', [110] and went on to describe Pitt as a man from whom 'his fellow subjects . . . were destined, on some future day, to derive the most important services.' Less than two months earlier Pitt had celebrated his twenty-second birthday.

The summer recess began on 18 July and Pitt returned to his practice of law on the Western Circuit. The family had suffered another grievous loss. Early in February, news had been received of young James Pitt's death at sea. William wrote to Pretyman on the 7th of 'the loss of a Brother, who had everything that was most amiable and promising, everything that I could love and admire, and I feel the favourite Hope of my mind extinguish'd by this untimely Blow.' [111] Admiral Sir Samuel Hood wrote to his brother, Rear-Admiral Alexander Hood, of the 'noble-minded youth', James Pitt, who 'would have been an honour and a most shining ornament to the Navy'. [112] In the course of three years, death had robbed Hester Chatham of her husband, her eldest brother, her elder daughter, and her youngest son. Harriot still spent much of her time in Somerset when not visiting her brothers or her friends in London, and both Chatham and Pitt visited their mother at Hayes or Burton Pynsent as often as they were able. She had always avoided the social life of London and the Court, and during her husband's long periods

79

of illness and retirement had found little opportunity for it. In her sixties she was content to remain in retirement.

Pitt spent part of October at Kingston Hall, the Dorset house of his Cambridge friend, Henry Bankes, shooting pheasants and partridges, on which, as he told his mother, he had been 'waging war, with increasing success'. More significant to his career was his visit to Lord Shelburne at Bowood, where the company included Lord Camden, Colonel Isaac Barré, and John Dunning. This was a powerful gathering of Chathamites, assembled to discuss opposition tactics in the forthcoming session of parliament. On 25 November news arrived in London that made the meeting even more seasonable: five weeks earlier Lord Cornwallis had surrendered his entire army of 7,000 men to the Americans at Yorktown. When Lord George Germain reported this disaster, Lord North threw up his hands in despair, crying, 'Oh God! It is all over.'

On the 27th, parliament reassembled and the government was immediately assailed by Fox, Burke, and Pitt, among others, but the Opposition was still divided on policy and the ministry survived. One of the most interesting speeches was made by Dundas in reply to Pitt's. Without particularizing, he made it clear that the ministry was itself divided, and that there was a strong faction among North's adherents that favoured bringing the war to an end without delay. It was the first sign of serious internal dissension and a sure indication that North could not long remain in office. The Opposition closed ranks. In January, under threat of a move to impeach Germain and Sandwich, North submitted to the advice of his own ministers and dismissed Germain from his office as Secretary for the American Colonies. By the beginning of March North's majorities in the Commons had sunk to derisory figures, and when the House passed a resolution that it would 'consider as enemies to His Majesty and to this country all who should advise or by any means attempt the further prosecution of offensive war on the continent of America' it was obvious that he could no longer continue. George III sent the Lord Chancellor, Lord Thurlow, to ask the Marquess of Rockingham for his terms for forming a government, but on learning that they included the recognition of American independence, the passage of most of Burke's proposals for economical reform, and permission to exclude from government certain 'obnoxious Ministers', he allowed negotiations to lapse. North did his utmost to persuade his royal master to submit. 'Your Royal Predecessors', he reminded the King,

> . . . were obliged to yield to it [the House of Commons] much against their wish in more instances than one: They consented to changes in their Ministry which they disapproved because they found it necessary to sacrifice their private wishes, and even their opinions to the preservation of public order. . . . The concessions they made were never deemed dishonourable, but were considered as marks of their wisdom, and of their parental affection for their people. Your Majesty has graciously and steadily supported the servants you approve, as long as they could be supported. . . . The Parliament has altered their sentiments and . . . their sentiments whether just or erroneous must ultimately prevail.

The King replied, 'If you resign before I have decided what I will do, you will certainly for ever forfeit my regard.' [113]

After speaking to Shelburne, the King understood that there was to be no escape. Shelburne had already told Rockingham, 'You can stand without me, but I could not without you.' [114] George III was so desperate that he drafted a message to parliament declaring his intention to leave England 'forever'. It was never sent and it is doubtful if it was meant as anything more than a crude piece of blackmail. Whatever the intention, the King prudently thought better of it and resigned himself to accepting Rockingham's terms in principle while ensuring that the most offensive of them should be castrated before maturity by the inclusion in the new ministry of a sufficient number of 'King's men' to provoke divisions in Cabinet.

On 20 March, the House of Commons was to debate a motion for the removal of the King's ministers. North forestalled it by announcing the resignation of the government. Soon after six o'clock the House adjourned for five days to give time for a new administration to be formed. Snow was falling, and members stood shivering at the entrance to the House, waiting for their carriages. As he stepped into his, which had been waiting at the door, North turned and said, with all his usual geniality: 'I *have* my carriage. You see, gentlemen, the advantage of being in the secret.' [115] It was a fine exit. He would have done well to make it final.

From the start the new government was, as the King had shrewdly intended it should be, divided. Rockingham, as First Lord of the Treasury, had with him Charles Fox as Secretary of State for Foreign Affairs, and four others of his most loyal followers in the Cabinet; and further support outside it from Burke as Paymaster and the Duke of Portland as Lord-Lieutenant of Ireland. Two more Cabinet posts went to Thurlow, who survived the change of ministry as Lord Chancellor, and General Conway, wavering, as Commander-in-Chief, between the two main factions. Shelburne, as Secretary of State for Home Affairs and the Colonies, could count on the aid of Lord Camden, Lord President of the Council, and had brought with him John Dunning as Chancellor of the Duchy of Lancaster. Outside the Cabinet, Henry Dundas remained Lord Advocate, and Colonel Barré and Thomas Townshend became Treasurer of the Navy and Secretary-at-War. Honours were also freely bestowed: Admiral Keppel was created Viscount; the Duke of Richmond and Lord Shelburne received the Garter; Dunning was raised to the peerage as Baron Ashburton; and Barré was granted a pension. Dundas, nothing if not a canny Scot, declared on 25 March that the new government was unlikely to last three months.[116] It was hardly to be expected that Pitt would be included; and yet Shelburne had attempted to obtain a Cabinet post for him. When Rockingham was adamant in his refusal, the offer had been made of a Vice-Treasurership of Ireland * at a salary of £5,000 a year which Pitt declined. In a speech, as premature as it was presumptuous, on 8 March, he had told a startled House of Commons, 'For myself, I could not expect to form part of a new administration; but were my doing so more within my reach, I could never accept a subordinate position.'[117] He was sometimes too evidently Chatham's son.

Some three months before North's resignation, Pitt had again stayed with Lord Shelburne at Bowood. With Dunning and Barré they had drafted proposals for parliamentary reform, a subject of which Pitt had made a special study, and on 7 May he moved for 'a Select Committee to take into consideration the present state of the representation of the House of Commons of England.' He spoke for an hour and a half to a full house and crowded gallery.[118] It was a masterly performance, a model of persuasive moderation, intended

* The first official appointment held by Chatham, in 1746.

to conceal divisions by avoiding detailed proposals, and presented the Select Committee as one of inquiry. He asked for a 'moderate and substantial reform', but, in his speech in reply at the end of the debate, he could not resist calling attention to the tone of the petitions that had poured into parliament: 'the people were loud for a *more equal representation.*' He had already defined representation as 'equal, easy, practicable, and complete'. When he turned to attack Crown influence he was on sure ground, expecting the support of the Economical reformers. He spoke out boldly against 'the corrupt influence of the Crown—an influence which has been pointed at in every period as the fertile source of all our miseries—an influence which has been substituted in the room of wisdom, of activity, of exertion, and of success—an influence which has grown up with our growth and strengthened with our strength, but which unhappily has not diminished with our diminution nor decayed with our decay.'

His motion was supported by Fox, who, knowing the bitterness of Burke's opposition to parliamentary reform, had persuaded his friend to absent himself from the debate, and violently attacked by William's cousin, Thomas Pitt of Boconnoc, who was appalled by the mention of equal representation. His fears were shared by other members. When the vote was taken, Pitt's resolution was defeated by 161 votes to 141. Pitt, incurably optimistic, had hoped to win. He might have been less disappointed had he been able to foresee that it would be nearly fifty years before any motion for electoral reform would be run so close in the lobbies. A Bill brought forward ten days later 'to shorten the duration of parliaments', again supported by Pitt and Fox, was rejected by a much larger majority. Burke, who spoke against it, referred back to the earlier debate and, according to Sheridan, 'acquitted himself with the most magnanimous indiscretion, attacked William Pitt in a scream of Passion, and swore Parliament was and always had been precisely what it ought to be, and that all people who thought of reforming it wanted to overthrow the Constitution.' [119] It was a bizarre explosion, and no less so for being detonated at a time when the House of Lords was composed of hereditary peers and more than half the members of the House of Commons were returned by 11,000 electors from a population of eight million.

The reform of parliament was a cause to which Pitt was to devote much of his career, but the movement for reform was never egalitarian, nor truly the people's cause. It was an attempt by the middle class to consolidate their power and reduce the influence of the Crown. It was not at any stage of Pitt's involvement the intention to extend the franchise to a wider electorate, but rather to distribute the membership of the House of Commons more equitably among the electorate already enfranchised. Nor were the reformers agreed about the details or the extent of the reforms required. When Pitt's brother-in-law, Lord Mahon, introduced a Bill to stamp out bribery at elections and facilitate voting by increasing the number of polling stations, it was mutilated by Fox and withdrawn; and Rockingham, though a reformer in principle, was more interested in economical reform as a practical curb on Crown influence than in any electoral changes. Outside parliament the Yorkshire Association, led by the Reverend Christopher Wyvill, was the most powerful reforming organization and the one to which Pitt was most closely allied. Support from elsewhere in the country varied: the London Association resented Wyvill's influence in parliament; some of the counties were lukewarm; and Wales and Scotland showed little interest.

Pitt's first attempt had enhanced his reputation and he had gained powerful friends; but the cause of parliamentary reform, however worthy, was trivial in comparison with the urgent need to end the war.

Rockingham's Cabinet were agreed, and even the King had been persuaded, that Britain must make peace, but they were divided on the method of obtaining it. As Secretary for the Colonies, Shelburne was charged with negotiations with America; as Foreign Secretary, Fox was responsible for talks with France, Spain, and Holland; and they were unable to agree on a national policy. Fox assumed the recognition of the United States and, in consequence, an immediate end to the war in America. With this much achieved, he hoped to be able to make peace in Europe on the basis of restoring the status quo. Shelburne, on the other hand, considered that the formal acknowledgement of American independence must be withheld until terms of peace had been agreed. The settlement of frontiers and the regulation of trade were essential ingredients of the treaty which might be adversely affected by premature recognition of the United States. Shelburne hoped that a generous settlement might secure some measure of American co-operation in the future.

In Paris, where all the treaties were to be negotiated, Fox was represented by Pitt's cousin, Thomas Grenville *, and Shelburne by Richard Oswald. Neither was an experienced diplomat. They were commissioned, respectively, to negotiate with Charles Gravier, comte de Vergennes, Louis XVI's Foreign Minister, and with Benjamin Franklin. Grenville and Oswald were no match for them and their tasks were made no easier by conflicting instructions from their principals. Vergennes and Franklin had little difficulty in playing one off against the other so that neither made progress and each reported to his minister that the other was undermining his authority. Fox, already suspicious of Shelburne, who had access to the King, believed that he was deferring to George III's reluctance to grant independence to the American colonies, with the intention of supplanting Rockingham at the head of the government.

In the midst of the confusion Rockingham died. He was succeeded by Shelburne. On 5 July Fox resigned, and his example was followed by the Chancellor of the Exchequer, Lord John Cavendish. The rest of the Rockingham faction remained in office. Shelburne was left with three vacancies in his Cabinet. Five weeks after his twenty-third birthday William Pitt became Chancellor of the Exchequer.

* Younger son of George Grenville, First Lord of the Treasury 1763-5.

First Office
1782-1783

CHARLES FOX recognized almost at once that his resignation was an error that threatened to blight his political career. However he might try to disguise his motives in obscure talk of threats to the Constitution, or malicious, and all too evidently unfounded, hints that Shelburne intended to invite Lord North to return to office, it was clear, even to his friends in the Cabinet, that his action had been motivated by personal animosity and frustrated ambition. In time of peace his resignation would have been considered imprudent and soon forgiven; in war, when essential and delicate negotiations for which he was responsible were being conducted in Paris, his going was looked upon as dereliction of his patriotic duty. If he had been prepared to serve with Shelburne, he must, in time of national crisis, be prepared to serve under him. There were not many who believed, as Fox professed to believe, that the Duke of Portland would be a better choice than Shelburne to lead the government. Even Burke, who resigned with him, had suggested that Fox should consider remaining in office until the House of Commons had demonstrated some reaction to Shelburne's succession. Nor was it useful for Fox to declare, truthfully, that he had contemplated resignation before Rockingham's death. By waiting he had forfeited the opportunity to stand on principle. The King had tried to persuade Fox to reconsider his decision; but he would not surrender the right to choose his first minister, and he had ample reason to prefer Shelburne to Portland. Fox was capable of extraordinary errors of judgement and, even more damaging, a loss of any sense of timing. He was already acquiring an unenviable reputation for instability: of all the attributes of genius the one least tolerable to the British.

The resignations of Fox, Cavendish, and Burke precipitated a government crisis. The *Annual Register* declared that 'The secession of such a weight of talents and integrity from the government could not be regarded with indifference.' Fox told Pitt, 'They look to *you*; *without* you they cannot succeed; *with* you I know not whether they will or no.' [120] Pitt replied, 'If they reckon upon *me*, they may find themselves mistaken;' but, in his account of this conversation, Fox added, 'I believe *they do* reckon on Pitt, and I believe they will *not* be mistaken.' It was no consolation to him to be proved right: he considered Pitt's acceptance of office a proof of self-interest and greedy ambition. He ignored the shared convictions which drew Pitt and Shelburne together: the doctrine which both had inherited from Chatham. Pitt questioned Fox in the Commons about the reasons for his resignation, and justly accused him of violating one of the great Chathamite principles, of objecting to men not measures. The breach between the two men was widening.

About the middle of August Pitt moved into 'the best Summer Town house possible', a 'vast, awkward House'—Number 10 Downing Street.* After alterations costing more than £700 he was, as he told his mother, as comfortable as a bachelor could be, in part of it. To judge by his letters to Hester Chatham, he took his new responsibilities lightly, but, although they were not arduous during the summer recess, he knew little about his duties and even less about the practical business of government. He had no time in which to fit himself to be, in all but name, leader of the government in the House of Commons †. His secretary was an army acquaintance of his

---

* By tradition the residence of British Prime Ministers, Number 10 was still occupied by Lord North since neither Rockingham nor Cavendish had wished to live there. Shelburne had no desire to move from his house in Berkeley Square.

† The nominal leader was Thomas Townshend, Secretary of State for Home Affairs. Townshend, Pitt, and the Commander-in-Chief, General Conway, were the only commoners in Shelburne's Cabinet.

brother's, but lack of qualifications was no bar to a position that was 'a perfect Sinecure and has no Duty but that of receiving about four Hundred a yr.' He had no private secretary and could not see 'as Yet, any Occasion' for one. As a Cabinet minister he was, to some extent, concerned in the negotiations for peace, but Shelburne never took his ministers into his confidence, preferring to exclude even his Foreign Minister, Lord Grantham, from his deliberations.

The new ministry was insecure. It was estimated that Shelburne could muster no more than 140 votes against North's 120 and Fox's 90. There remained some two hundred members who were not committed in advance to any group but could not be relied upon either to attend debates or to vote. Shelburne had the confidence and support of the King, and hoped to augment his strength by attracting to his side some of the followers of North and Fox as it became clear that his ministry could survive. On the whole his policies were unlikely to prove attractive to the followers of either. He was committed to the negotiation of peace, if necessary by making unpopular concessions to France and America; to reform within the Constitution, preserving the prerogative of the Crown; to the restoration of financial stability, by the simplification of taxation and the establishment of a sinking fund to redeem the national debt; and to the revival of trade by the revision of commercial restrictions along the lines prescribed by Adam Smith *, who advocated the abandonment of the old mercantile system.

The proposals for parliamentary reform were centred on the increase of representatives for the counties, where the electorates were disproportionately large. Apart from distributing the representation more evenly among the electorate, the purpose of this proposal was to shift the emphasis of parliament away from party or faction. Such a shift would have had the effect of reducing the direct influence of the Crown, but an increase in the independent vote would also strengthen the potential power of the 'patriot' element which both Shelburne and Pitt believed to have the support of the people whom they sought to represent.

* Adam Smith's *Wealth of Nations* had been published in 1776. Smith advocated the ending of government interference in industry and commerce on the assumption that private profit would produce public wealth. He considered it 'the biggest impertinence to pretend to watch over the economy of private people'. His theories opened the way for the serious study of political economy.

As the summer passed and the opposition groups held firm it became increasingly urgent for Shelburne to come to some agreement with either North or Fox. He inclined towards North, but Pitt would not stomach coalition with the discredited leader who opposed all reform and whose ineptitude had led Britain into an 'accursed, wicked, barbarous, cruel, unnatural' war. Even towards Dundas, who had been won from North's group and was to become one of his most trusted colleagues, Pitt at first showed some reserve. Fox, on the other hand, was an extremist economical reformer, though his attitude to electoral reform was traditionalist, and he had been one of the most consistent opponents of the American war. He had also attacked North with a savagery unmatched by any contemporary speaker. There was, it seemed, no possibility of his joining with North to bring down the government: on 5 March, in one of his most violent outbursts, he had denounced him as 'void of honour and honesty' and declared himself content to be branded as 'the most infamous of mankind' if ever he should consider making terms with him.

The greatest obstacle to any plan for coalition was Shelburne's reputation for duplicity. Among British Prime Ministers he must be recognized as one of the most gifted but, although he was the architect of many of Pitt's later reforms, his personal achievement was negligible. Distrusting his fellow men, he was distrusted by them. Sensitive to criticism, he surrounded himself with intrigue, and hid his actions in a fog of suspicious secrecy. His manner, often oily and ingratiating, was no more repulsive than Chatham's; his political treacheries, which so disgusted his contemporaries, were no more reprehensible than North's or Fox's; he was no more ambitious—and less self-confident—than Pitt; and yet he inspired dislike, doubt, and mistrust which earned him the pejorative sobriquet 'The Jesuit of Berkeley Square'.

Parliament did not assemble after the summer recess until 5 December. During the interval Shelburne concentrated on the negotiation of peace terms with France and America. The British position was not as weak as at first it appeared. The French were as exhausted by the war as the British. Their gains in the West Indies had been offset by losses in India, and the defeat of their fleet under de Grasse at the Battle of the Saints in February 1782 had restored command of the Atlantic to Britain. If generous concessions were

89

made, the Americans would have nothing to gain from continuing the war. If France and America withdrew from the war, the Spanish and Dutch would be obliged to make peace. Shelburne's proposals were shrewd and far-sighted. By his insistence that a treaty with America must depend upon a treaty with France, he integrated the negotiations in a way that suited neither party. By offering independence and valuable concessions to the Americans, he detached them from the alliance, encouraged them to make peace, and invited them to put pressure on the French to do so. He looked beyond these negotiations to the conclusion of commercial treaties, proposing nothing less than 'a revision of our whole trading system', abandoning the old mercantile policy of restrictions to open up a free trade between the United States of America and all British possessions. Restriction on the westward expansion of the colonies would also be removed, providing a steadily growing market for British goods and the wealth to pay for them. The benefit to British manufacture, and to British shipping, would be inestimable. Had he been permitted to carry his plans into operation the subsequent relationship with the United States would have been transformed.

Shelburne's proposals were explained in a pamphlet published early in the year which served only to strengthen opposition to the whole package of peace terms.[121] The views expressed were rooted in the Chathamite tradition, and there can be little doubt that they reflected Pitt's opinions:

Since the Independence of America hath been reasonably and unavoidably acknowledged, it is our business to make the best use of an event which can never be recalled. By a wise conduct, it may not prove so unfortunate for this Kingdom as might at first be apprehended; and at any rate it was better to submit to it than pursue a destructive and hopeless contest. Whilst we are delivered from the vast expense of maintaining and protecting the Colonies, our commercial intercourse with them will still be productive of many advantages . . . and possibly, if America, as may rationally be expected, should rapidly increase in populousness and cultivation, the benefits of our trade with her may be greater than ever. . . . The system of monopolies and little restrictions in trade, begins to be exploded in the world, and will justly every day grow more and more out of fashion. It is for the real honour and

90

interest of Great Britain to prosecute an enlarged plan of commerce: and to have contended about a few furs, would have been incompatible with a design of such magnitude and importance. . . . If we are so wise as to profit by experience, and to send liberal laws to our remaining Colonies, instead of troops, bad Governors, and machiavelian [sic] systems, we shall be freed from the burthen of transmitting large sums thither, which we can no longer afford, and shall receive considerably more from thence in return, by the necessary balance of our commerce.

Shelburne proposed to follow the trade agreements with America by commercial treaties with France and Spain. His great plan was considered dangerous, and damaging to British interests. Its repudiation sowed the seeds for another, even more pointless and indecisive, war in 1812.

Both Shelburne and Pitt were uneasily aware that, far from gaining strength in its first six months of office, the government was in danger of collapse. Lord Keppel had resigned from the Admiralty, and the Duke of Richmond (Master General of the Ordnance) no longer attended meetings of the Cabinet. Both disapproved of the proposed peace terms, and there were others in the Cabinet who were lukewarm. The protection of the Crown was not enough to sustain the ministry. With George III's reluctant consent Shelburne authorized Pitt to approach Fox. They met during the second week of February. Pitt told his cousin, William Wyndham Grenville, that he had asked Fox whether there were any terms on which he would join the government: 'the answer was, None, while Lord Shelburne remained; and so it ended.' [122] They never again spoke together in private, and it seems certain that Pitt's description of the interview omits much of what passed between them. Dr Pretyman, Pitt's adulatory friend and biographer, and William Adam *, one of North's most loyal followers, give different accounts of the meeting which show Pitt reacting with more vigour. [123] According to Pretyman, who does not name his source, Pitt replied to Fox's rejection 'that if that was his determination, it would be useless to enter into any further discussion "as he did not come to betray Lord Shelburne".' There is no evidence that Shelburne suspected any collusion between North

* Adam had wounded Fox in a duel in 1779, but subsequently became his friend and ally.

and Fox, but intermediaries of both—North's son George, Lord John Townshend, William Adam and William Eden among them—had been busy for some time. Dundas made a last desperate attempt to persuade Lord North at least to support the peace settlement but it was already too late. On 14 February North and Fox met and came to an agreement: they would sink their differences to overturn the Shelburne government; and they would impose upon the King a coalition government under the titular leadership of the Duke of Portland but controlled by themselves as Secretaries of State.

On 17 February both Houses debated the Address on the Preliminaries of Peace. In the Lords, despite the opposition of Richmond and Keppel, both of whom had served in Shelburne's Cabinet, the government scraped a majority of six. In the Commons the government motion was proposed by Thomas Pitt and seconded, at Pitt's special request after William Wyndham Grenville had refused, by William Wilberforce. An amendment moved by Lord John Cavendish was carried against the government by sixteen votes. North spoke with the moderation becoming to one who feels his responsibility for his country's plight, but Fox and Sheridan suffered from no such inhibition, Sheridan declaring that the peace terms 'relinquished completely everything that was glorious and great in the country', and Fox describing it as the 'most disastrous and disgraceful peace that ever this country had made'. The fatuity and insincerity of both criticisms was to be proved within the year, but Fox was as much concerned to defend his own ambivalent position as to condemn the actions of others. He was already aware of the growing revulsion provoked by his alliance with North and he was at some pains to vindicate his behaviour. He was at his most persuasive: '. . . if men of honour can meet on points of general national concern, I see no reason for calling such a meeting an unnatural junction. It is neither wise nor noble to keep up animosities forever. It is neither just nor candid to keep up animosity when the cause of it is no more. It is not in my nature to bear malice, or to live in ill will. My friendships are perpetual, my enmities are not so. . . . When a man ceases to be what he was, when the opinions which made him obnoxious are changed, he then is no more my enemy, but my friend.' [124] His argument would have been more moving if any of the mitigating circumstances he described had been justified by the facts; but Lord North had not, as all knew, ceased to be what he was, nor were the opinions that had made him obnoxious changed.

Fox knew, as his friends were obliged to admit, that he had made a shabby bargain with a man whose political convictions were directly opposed to his own, and that his motive, like North's, was the pursuit of power. It has been suggested that the coalition was no more disgraceful than the elder Pitt's with Newcastle, or 'the alliance of the pure virgin Pitt with Dundas, Thurlow, and Gower'.[125] The comparisons are not valid: the elder Pitt joined with Newcastle at a time when the survival of his country was threatened and patriotism demanded a coalition of the best available talents. Neither he, nor his son in his later coalition, was obliged to jettison cherished principles in order to gain office. Fox, in his junction with North, agreed to give up his struggle for economical reform as the most effective instrument in reducing the influence of the Crown, and to leave the matter of parliamentary reform outside government policy. Both he and North defended their alliance as the only means of forming a stable government, but they were opposing men not measures, the mark to Pitt of the anti-patriot, and the decision to use the peace terms which they were to accept unchanged nine months later as the case for bringing down the government was contemptible. Fox's political creed was expressed in his letter of 24 January 1779 to Rockingham: 'You think you can best serve the country by continuing in a fruitless opposition; I think it impossible to serve it at all but by coming to power.' Confident of his own remarkable abilities he judged his own naked ambition to be both appropriate and patriotic. In others he found it less admirable.

Dundas and Tommy Townshend spoke well for the government, but Pitt's speech in reply to Fox was one of the worst of his life. He did not rise until four o'clock in the morning to speak, from his own exhaustion, to an exhausted House. To a speech lacking fire he added a tasteless error, taunting Sheridan with his theatrical connections. Sheridan's ready wit was more than equal to the occasion and he replied, 'If ever I again engage in those compositions to which the Rt. Hon. gentleman has in such flattering terms referred . . . I may be encouraged by his promises to try an improvement on one of Ben Jonson's best characters in the play of the Alchemist—the Angry Boy.' [126] Soon after the division Pitt wrote to his mother to inform her of the government's defeat: 'This I think decisive. It comes rather sooner than I imagined, though certainly not quite unexpected. We shall at least leave the field with honour.' [127]

Three days later he took the opportunity to restore his reputation in debate. The Opposition amendment, carried in the early hours of the morning on the 18th, had substituted an intention to consider the treaties for a declaration that they had been considered. To bring about the fall of the government it was necessary that the House should go further and disown the terms. Fox and Cavendish concocted the formula: the necessity for making peace was agreed, and the independence of the United States of America accepted, but the concessions to Britain's enemies were condemned. On 21 February the Opposition carried a vote of censure by a majority of seventeen. Fox was rebuked by two independent members for his participation in an 'unnatural alliance' and again defended the coalition at length. During the debate Pitt was taken ill, 'actually holding Solomon's Porch door open with one hand, while vomiting during Fox's speech to which he was to reply.' [128] At one o'clock in the morning he rose to respond. He spoke for three hours, analysing the terms of the treaties and examining in lucid detail the alternative courses and their consequences. [129] He accused Fox of using his 'great abilities . . . to inflame the imagination and mislead the judgement', and coldly indicted the debate as having 'arisen rather in a desire to force the Earl of Shelburne from the Treasury, than in any real conviction that Ministers deserve censure for the concessions they have made. . . . This is the object which has raised this storm of passion—this is the aim of the unnatural Coalition. . . . If, however, the baneful alliance is not already formed, if this ill-omened marriage is not already solemnized, I know a just and lawful impediment, and in the name of public safety I here forbid the Banns!' Turning to North's conduct he declared 'whatever appears dishonourable or inadequate in this peace is strictly chargeable to the Noble Lord in the blue riband *, whose profusion of the public money, whose notorious temerity and obstinacy in prosecuting the war which originated in his pernicious and oppressive policy, and whose utter

* The sash of the order of the Garter, to which Lord North had been appointed in 1772. Informality of dress did not extend to the Court. Those members of both Houses attending the royal levee wore the sashes and badges of their orders on their Court dress or uniform.

incapacity to fill the station he occupied, render a peace of any description indispensable to the preservation of the State.'

The speech was a nicely calculated combination of objective analysis and frigid invective. Wilberforce described it as 'famous', and Lord North, with customary urbanity, began his lengthy reply with a tribute to Pitt's 'amazing eloquence'. This second defeat, and on a vote of censure, convinced Shelburne that he could no longer continue in office. On 24 February he resigned. It has been argued that his withdrawal was premature and unnecessary; that he should have waited for the full horror of the unnatural coalition to drive members to support the government; that his precipitate resignation displayed, as Wraxhall suggested, a lack of fortitude in adversity; but Shelburne had examined the division lists. These revealed that he had received the votes of more than sixty per cent of the independents, an unexpectedly high proportion that was unlikely to be bettered by delay. Shelburne left George III with two recommendations: that his faithful lieutenant, Thomas Townshend, be raised to the peerage as Baron Sydney; and that William Pitt be invited to take office as First Lord of the Treasury and leader of the new government.

Shelburne's recommendation that the King should send for Pitt was seconded by the Lord Chancellor, Lord Thurlow, whose office was traditionally accepted as being above faction and gave him direct access to the sovereign. George III summoned Pitt the same afternoon and invited him to form a government. Henry Dundas urged him to accept and believed that he would do so. He busied himself among North's followers, his former colleagues, in an attempt to persuade them to abstain from opposition to the proposed administration.

Pitt's situation was one of great delicacy. On the one hand there was the temptation to become his country's Prime Minister at the age of twenty-three; on the other the realization that he would be unlikely to succeed where Shelburne had failed. He had friends—the companions of his own generation from Cambridge and Lincoln's Inn and in the House of Commons—but none qualified to advise him. More senior politicians were committed, by interest or ambition, to bringing him in or keeping him out. None could offer the experience, personal knowledge, devotion, or objectivity that he knew his

95

mother could provide. He wrote to her early on Tuesday morning 25 February, 'I wished more than I can express to see you yesterday. I will, if possible, find a moment today to tell you the state of things and learn your opinion. . . . The King, when I went in yesterday, pressed me in the strongest manner to take Lord Shelburne's place, and insisted on my not declining it till I had taken time to consider. You see the importance of the decision I must speedily make . . . I should wish anxiously to know what is the inclination of your mind.' [130] There is no evidence that he was able to see Hester Chatham, and although she would certainly have replied at once, her advice has not been preserved. On Wednesday night, when he wrote to her again, he had still not made up his mind, but at two o'clock on the Thursday afternoon he wrote to inform Dundas of his decision to decline. His reason for doing so was both prudent and honourable:

> I see that the main and almost only ground of reliance would be this,—that Lord North and his friends would not continue in a combination to oppose. In point of prudence, after all that has passed, and considering all that is to come, such a reliance is too precarious to act on. But above all, in point of honour to my own feelings, I cannot form an administration trusting to hope that it will be supported, or even will not be opposed, by Lord North, whatever the influence may be that determines his conduct. The first moment I saw the subject in the point of view, from which I am sure I cannot vary, *unalterably* determined me to decline. [131]

'Nothing', as the King wrote to Lord Shelburne later that day, 'could get him to depart from the ground he took, that nothing less than a moral certainty of a majority in the House of Commons could make him undertake the task.' [132]

From 25 February until 2 April the country was without a government. The King was inflexibly resolved that whatever administration he might be obliged to endure it should not be one formed by 'the most profligate and ungrateful coalition that ever was made in this Kingdom.' [133] For five weeks he twisted and turned, approaching that frequent and unreliable contender Lord Gower, and Pitt's cousins, Earl Temple and Thomas Pitt. He was, indeed, prepared to consider 'Mr Thomas Pitt or Mr Thomas anybody', [134] but none would accept. He even attempted, without success, to prevail upon Lord

North to return without Fox. On 18 March George III capitulated, agreeing to offer Portland the Treasury and tolerate the appointment of North and Fox to be Secretaries of State; but, on learning that Portland required the dismissal of the Lord Chancellor and unconditional approval of his list of ministers, the King sent a curt and hasty note to Downing Street: 'Mr Pitt, I desire you will come here immediately. G.R.'

For five days George III strove to persuade Pitt to change his mind. On 25 March Pitt sent his final answer: 'Mr Pitt received, this morning, the honour of your Majesty's gracious commands. With infinite pain he feels himself under the necessity of humbly expressing to your Majesty, that with every sentiment of dutiful attachment to your Majesty and zealous desire to contribute to the public service, it is utterly impossible for him, after the fullest consideration of the situation in which things stand . . . to think of undertaking . . . the situation which your Majesty has had the condescension and goodness to propose to him.' [135] The King's reply, sent the same day, was an uncompromising rebuke: 'Mr Pitt, I am much hurt to find you are determined to decline at an hour when those who have any regard for the Constitution as established by law ought to stand forth against the most daring and unprincipled faction that the annals of the Kingdom ever produced.' [136] On 31 March Pitt announced in the House of Commons his resignation from the office of Chancellor of the Exchequer.

George III was defeated. He drafted another message of abdication, but again did not send it; he contemplated retiring to Hanover, until Lord Thurlow reminded him that English Kings had found it simple to leave the country but less easy to return; at last he yielded; but he had not left the field. The first British-born Hanoverian King had learnt an important British principle of survival: he had lost a political battle, but he intended to win the constitutional war. It was his constitutional right to choose his ministers that was at stake.

If he were content to be patient, the King was certain to win. Apart from his own growing popularity in the country as a sober and patriotic family man and as the sovereign by constitutional right, and Fox's unenviable reputation as a licentious gambler, the King controlled a large election fund and an effective election organization, and had the power to dismiss his ministers, dissolve parliament, and call an election. He had also control of the creation of peerages.

His first salvo against the incoming ministry was fired the day before it took office when George III told Lord Temple, 'A ministry which I have avowedly attempted to avoid by calling on every other description of men, cannot be supposed to have either my favour or my confidence and as such I shall most certainly refuse any honours that may be asked by them.' [137] For the new coalition this was exasperating, for all ministries relied upon the honours system to reward the faithful and encourage the apathetic among their followers.

On 2 April the Duke of Portland, Lord North, and Charles Fox took office as First Lord of the Treasury and Secretaries of State. Lord Thurlow was dismissed and the great seal of the Lord Chancellor was put in commission with Lord Loughborough presiding. Thurlow continued to see the King in private and became a powerful weapon in his armoury.

The outcry against the 'unnatural alliance' was widespread. One old friend of Fox's described it as 'a most revolting compact', and another wrote 'Unless a *real good government* is the consequence of this juncture, nothing can justify it to the public.' His enemies were more outspoken. An anonymous writer for the *Public Advertiser* put his revulsion into a verse entitled *The Broad Bottom Administration*, a description referring less to the composition of the ministry than to the proportions of its Secretaries:

> Quoth N—— to F——, 'You've got your Ends,
> In spite of all your foes!'
> 'I'd have,' says F——, 'See how my friends
> I do lead by the Nose!'
> 'I see't,' says N—— again; 'such Blocks
> Prove Country's Good a Farce is;
> So we're broad-bottomed'—Right,' says F——,
> 'We bid them kiss our ——.'

The eccentric Earl-Bishop, Frederick Augustus Hervey *, commissioned an appalling Italian sculptor to produce a version in marble of the *Infant Hercules* showing Pitt's head, life-size, on an infant's body strangling the serpents, Fox and North. Fox's sister-in-

* 4th Earl of Bristol and Bishop of Derry.

98

law, Lady Holland, described it accurately as 'a lasting monument to Lord Bristol's bad taste'. North, himself, was 'perfectly miserable' and trembled at 'the vexations and troubles' that hung over him. [138]

Fox's most urgent task was, as Shelburne's had been, the conclusion of peace treaties with America, France, Spain, and Holland. During the next six months he struggled in vain to improve the terms. He succeeded only in alienating the Americans still further by his abandonment of Shelburne's sagacious plan for free trade in favour of mercantilist controls. This was his single, lamentable, contribution to the negotiations. It was not to be expected that he would succeed in obtaining significant concessions. It might have been hoped that he would not have destroyed the one long-term benefit that might have accrued to all parties from the unnecessary war.

In his speech of resignation, Pitt had declared that he would consider himself bound to no party. It was therefore as a truly independent member that he introduced, on 7 May, a resolution for the reform of parliament. Rejecting the idea of universal suffrage as 'a mere speculative proposition that may be good in theory but which it would be absurd and chimerical to endeavour to reduce to practice', he advocated the strengthening of the representation for the counties and larger cities. This proposal should be associated with Bills to prevent bribery and unlimited expenditure at elections, and the disfranchisement of boroughs where electoral practice was proved to be corrupt. The motion, supported by Fox, and from outside the Commons by numerous petitions, was overwhelmingly rejected by a House shocked by such dangerous innovation. Pitt's efforts, later in the session, to effect economies in public expenditure by the reduction of extravagance and the reform of abuses were mercilessly attacked by Burke who accused him of 'prying into the little perquisites of little men in little offices' while ignoring malpractices in high places, of possessing 'that nice olfactory nerve which could smell a ball of horsedung a thousand miles off, but which was not affected by the stench of the dunghill under his very window'. [139] In spite of Burke, Pitt's proposals were passed by the Commons, but they perished in the House of Lords.

The parliamentary session ground towards its close. Members looked forward to a four-month recess and much of the business was routine. Into this relatively calm political scene blundered the disruptive figure of George, Prince of Wales, who chose the approach of his twenty-first birthday as an appropriate occasion to demand an establishment suitable to his majority and sufficient to enable him to pay some proportion of his debts. Without consulting the King, Portland allowed himself to be persuaded by Fox to propose a settlement of £100,000 a year to be voted by parliament. George III was beside himself with fury. His eldest son's debts were already a public scandal and, worse, a personal affront to the King whose parsimonious attitudes were outraged by the Prince's reckless extravagance and ostentation. His passion was fuelled by his hatred of Fox, whose intimate friendship with his son he blamed for the Prince's love of gambling and loose living. He considered the sum disgracefully large and an unjustifiable burden on the public funds. He offered to provide £50,000 a year from the Civil List. Fox, the Prince's 'Dear Charles', found himself in some difficulty. The Prince was his friend. He was also heir to the throne. Eleven years the King's junior, Fox could expect far grander rewards in the future than he could hope to extract from the present. The King contemplated dismissing his government, and Fox believed on 16 June that the administration could not last more than a few days.[140] A compromise was hastily manufactured: the Prince received £30,000 towards his debts, the valuable Duchy of Cornwall, and £50,000 a year from the Civil List. On 16 July parliament rose for the summer recess.

In Pitt's first thirty months in parliament he had witnessed the fall of three ministries and the formation of an unstable fourth. He had held Cabinet office and been pressed by the King to form a government. In one of the most serious constitutional crises of the century he had aquitted himself with precocious coolness, discretion, and resolution. Almost alone among the leading parliamentarians of the period he had preserved unscathed his reputation for independence and patriotism. He would head the government, but he would not lead a party. He was prepared to wait for the opportunity, and he was not to have to wait for long. Before the House rose for the recess, Charles Fox announced his intention to introduce, in the next session, his Bill for the regulation of the East India Company.

VIII

In Opposition
1783

IN PITT'S FIRST TWO AND A HALF YEARS in parliament he had shown himself to be a young man of extraordinary authority, and mature judgement and discretion. His resolve to remain aloof from the politics of faction had gained him a small personal following, particularly among those uncommitted members who were not frightened by his dedication to reform or repelled by the coldness of his manner. In conservative institutions precocity is seldom welcomed, and Pitt's independence, a rarity among professional politicians who looked for preferment, kept him apart from the associations formed by shared interest or the companionship of intrigue. To his friends in private he showed a different aspect of his personality. There is ample evidence that he was not enthusiastic about formal society gatherings, but he accepted the social duties expected of him, accompanying Harriot and her friends to Vauxhall and Ranelagh and to private balls and dinners. He preferred, however, the exclusively male company of Goosetree's Club and his visits to friends who owned houses in the London area.

The London clubs played an important part in the political and social scene of the eighteenth century. They were also the great centres of gaming. At a period when less than four in every hundred of the population had incomes of £200 a year or more, Charles Fox and his brother, Lord Holland, lost £32,000 in two nights' play. Horace Walpole recalled that at Almack's in Pall Mall

> . . . the gaming and extravagance of the young men of quality was arrived now at a pitch never heard of . . . generally there was £10,000 in specie on the table. . . . Nor were the manners of the gamesters, or even their dresses for play undeserving notice. They began by pulling off their embroidered clothes, and put on frieze great-coats, or turned their coats inside outwards for luck. They put on pieces of leather (much as worn by footmen when they clean the knives) to save their lace ruffles; and to guard their eyes from the light, and to prevent tumbling their hair, wore high-crowned straw hats with wide brims, and adorned with flowers and ribbons; masks to conceal their emotions when they played at Quinze. Each gamester had a small neat stand by him with a large rim, to hold their tea, or a wooden bowl with an edge of ormolu, to hold their rouleaus. They borrowed great sums off Jews at exorbitant premiums. Charles Fox called his outward room, where those Jews waited till he rose, the *Jerusalem Chamber*.*[141]

Brooks's, to which Fox had introduced Pitt in 1781, was the heart of high Whiggery and, after the Fox-North coalition of 1783, Pitt never entered it again. White's Club in St James's, to which he also belonged, was Tory and fashionable. After the entry of the Prince of Wales into active politics, Brooks's became the meeting place for his friends in opposition, and White's the club for supporters of the King and the government.

During his early years in London Pitt's favourite was Goosetree's. Founded upon the remains of an almost defunct social club at 5 Pall Mall, this had a small membership of about twenty-five young men of shared political interest who were 'very nice in their admissions'. Pitt was one of the leading lights and, during the winter of 1780-81, supped there every night. Edward Eliot, Lord Euston, Lord Althorp, the Duke of Rutland, Henry Bankes, St Andrew St John,

---

* The Jerusalem Chamber is part of the deanery of Westminster Abbey. Dating from the fourteenth century, it was originally the Abbot's parlour and its walls were hung with tapestries depicting the history of Jerusalem.

and John Pratt were among the members who had been at Cambridge with him, and others included his brother Chatham, his cousin William Wyndham Grenville, Wilberforce, Robert Smith, Thomas Steele, John Jekyll, and later Charles Long and Richard Pepper Arden. In this company Pitt allowed himself to relax.

There was some gambling in all clubs and Goosetree's was no exception. Wilberforce later recollected the 'intense earnestness' displayed by Pitt when he took part in the games of chance, but also that 'He perceived their increasing fascination, and soon after suddenly abandoned them for ever.' Both Wilberforce and Jekyll were among the company that met one evening at the Boar's Head in Eastcheap to celebrate Shakespeare's memory: 'Many professed wits were present, but Pitt was the most amusing of the party, and the readiest and most apt in the required allusions.' Wilberforce remembered him as 'the wittiest man I ever knew'.[142]

Pitt was also high-spirited and not averse to horseplay and practical jokes. Wilberforce had inherited a villa, Lauriston House, on the south side of Wimbledon Common, and his friends often gathered there, or at Bob Smith's at Hampstead, in the evenings or at weekends. Pitt in particular appears to have disliked staying in London at night and made a habit of riding out, sometimes as late as midnight, to sleep at Wimbledon. Wilberforce had become one of his most intimate friends. He was diminutively small, about seven inches shorter than Pitt, and skeletally thin. His face was not handsome, but the expression was lively and mischievous, and he moved neatly, 'with the look of an angel and the agility of a monkey'.[143] He had an excellent singing voice, and a talent for mimicry that he used with merciless effect until old Lord Camden told him that it was 'but a vulgar accomplishment'. Quick-witted, articulate, and charming, he had a gift of warmth in friendship. His spontaneity and lack of inhibition evoked a response in Pitt's nature. With Wilberforce Pitt slipped the chain of his natural reserve and self-imposed restraint, and renewed his youth. At Wimbledon that summer there was a 'fine hot day' when the friends, joined by Edward Eliot, went fishing on the river; a 'delicious day' when they lounged about the grounds of Lauriston House 'foining * at night, and run about the garden for an hour or two'; an evening when Eliot,

* 'Foining' was fencing or lunging with a pointed weapon. The word was also used in low slang for sexual connection.

Pepper Arden, and Pitt rode down from London for 'an early meal of peas and strawberries'; and a morning when Wilberforce's guests rose to find the remains of Dudley Ryder's expensive hat, which he had worn to the opera the previous night, scattered by Pitt ornamentally over the flower-beds.[144] Thomas Orde, reporting the latest political news to Lord Shelburne at Bowood,[145] had to admit that he had found 'no opportunity of particular conversation with Mr. P since yr. Ldship left London. . . . He passes, as usual, most of his time with his young Friends in a Society sometimes very lively— Some little excess happen'd lately at Wimbledon. . . . In the Evening some of the Neighbours were alarmed with noises at their doors, but Nobody, I believe, has made any reflection upon a mere frolic—It has only been pleasantly remarked, that the Rioters were headed by Master P.—late Chancellor of the Ex——, and Master Arden, late Sollicitor Genl.'

A week earlier, Pitt's brother Chatham finally concluded a year of languid courtship and married Mary Elizabeth Townshend, daughter of Tommy Townshend, Lord Sydney. The family association was happy and the political connection valuable. Chatham and his bride spent their honeymoon at Hayes, where they were joined for a few days by William on his way to stay with Earl Temple at Stowe. Pitt had good reason for wishing to consult with his cousin. On 19 July he had received another, though guarded, approach from Lord Thurlow. No longer Lord Chancellor but still the trusted servant of the King, 'old Hurlo Thrumbo' was a constitutional lawyer of considerable learning and ability, unalterably pledged to preserve the prerogatives of the Crown and to oppose reform of any nature. He affected the dress of some forty years earlier, 'great cuffs and massy buttons, great wig, long ruffles'; his large, fleshy face was dominated by enormous black eyebrows; and his voice was deep and portentous, 'a kind of rolling, murmuring thunder'.[146] Some, like John Robinson, admired him: 'He has humours, he is overbearing perhaps in his opinions, sentiments and dictates, his superior abilities may lead to this, but he has a manly firmness and decisiveness about him that gives him great consequence . . . and his judgement is sound.' [147] Others, and they were in the majority, agreed with Gilbert Elliot that he was 'the falsest and most treacherous character in the world . . . an able man, but from temper and character never a useful friend to the government he

104

served with.' [148] Pitt both disliked and distrusted him, but he was obliged to recognize his imposing presence and his great influence with George III.

Thurlow was sent to test the sincerity of Pitt's commitment to parliamentary reform, and to find out whether Pitt, assured of the King's approval and support, would risk an attempt to overthrow the government. The answer was nicely judged: if the King wished for a change and, provided that Pitt and his friends could 'form a permanent system consistent with their principles', he would not refuse office; but his commitment to parliamentary reform was total and immutable. Once more Pitt had asserted his independence. He would oblige the King, and he would serve him, but he would not relinquish his principles in order to do so. He would belong to no party, and he would be no man's lackey. He believed, as he told Lord Temple, that 'what has passed will not tend to delay our having the offer whenever things are ripe for it.' [149] He had good reason for such confidence: the King had no one else to whom he could turn for effective help. To free himself of the Fox-North coalition George III must be satisfied of three conditions, of which only one was under his control: the completion of preparations for a general election, and the prospect of a favourable outcome; an issue on which a challenge to the government would attract a large measure of public support and the defection of government followers; and the emergence of a politician of sufficient stature and courage to stand against the coalition and achieve the majority necessary to stable government. For the first and third he must rely on John Robinson and William Pitt. Ironically, it was to be Charles Fox who provided the second.

Pitt, meanwhile, went to Stowe, 'the most magnificent [house] by far' he had ever seen. There were other guests, among them William Wyndham Grenville, and although the visit was short there was time for 'an abundance of speculation and discourse, all of which was in the greatest degree satisfactory'. [150] His Grenville cousins, it was clear, would stand with him. At the end of July Pitt was in Brighton, where he spent two weeks staying at the Castle hotel and bathing in the sea with Tom Steele and Pretyman. He wrote from 'Brighth elmstone' to Eliot on 4 August: 'By having had the Presence of Mind to jump into the Sea this Morning without a Cap, and being in consequence under the hot Irons for half an Hour, I find at last the opportunity for writing, which I suppose I should never have found otherwise. I came here Friday sennight, and with the Exception of about four and twenty Hours in London, which included a Levee and a drawing Room, and of the Time on the Road, which included the Breaking of my Horse's Knees, and pretty nearly of my own Leg, I have been doing nothing but bathing and reading French ever since.' [151] The holiday gave him relaxation and a much-needed rest from politics, but it also gave rise to rumour and suspicion about his private life that later found expression in lampoons and caricatures and, most notably, in *The Rolliad*.*

Pitt had been reading French to prepare himself for another holiday which he planned to take with Eliot in September. They proposed to spend two or three weeks in Rheims to improve their knowledge of the language before moving on to visit Paris and Versailles. On 22 August Pitt wrote again to Eliot that he expected to arrive at Henry Bankes's house in Dorset on 1 or 2 September, and added, 'I forget whether I told you that I had received a letter from Wilberforce, who wished to know when we set out, and seem'd to intend joining us. . . . I wrote to Him that if he is not at Bankes's the 1st of Septr or in London the 2nd or 3rd, He will have no Chance of going with us.' [152] After a visit to his mother at Burton Pynsent, he rode into Dorset to stay with Bankes. Wilberforce arrived and joined the rest of the party in a day's shooting. Short-sighted and inexperienced, he proved less alarming to the partridges than to his friends.

After a brief return to London, where he attended the King's levee at St James's, Pitt set out for Dover. With Wilberforce and Eliot he landed at Calais on 12 September. None of them had been abroad before, and each had trusted to the other to provide the most necessary of all travel documents in the eighteenth century, letters of introduction. At the last minute Peter Thelluson, the Huguenot merchant and banker, had provided an introduction to a certain M. Coustier, whom they imagined to be someone of consequence in Rheims. It was with some dismay, therefore, that after settling themselves comfortably at an inn they found him, a 'véritable épicier', serving customers with figs and raisins from behind the counter of his shop. Courteous and welcoming as M. Coustier was, he could not arrange introductions to the local nobility, and the three

---

* A series of more or less scurrilous verses about members of parliament, first published in 1784. It was produced by members of the Whig opposition and was directed particularly against Pitt, his friends, and his political associates. See pp 328–329.

Englishmen spent dull days at their lodgings practising their French on one another. At length, after some embarrassed hesitation, they persuaded the worthy grocer to dress himself in his best, with a respectable wig and sword, and to accompany them to the local Intendant of Police, where they introduced themselves. The police officer was charming and sympathetic, promising to explain their predicament to the abbé de Lageard, next to the Archbishop the senior authority in the town.* Privately he was convinced that they were spies, and next day reported to the abbé the presence of 'three Englishmen here of very suspicious character. They are,' he said, 'in wretched lodgings, they have no attendants, yet their courier says, that they are *"grands seigneurs"*, and that one of them is the son of the great Chatham; but it is impossible, they must be *des intrigants.*' He recommended an official investigation. The abbé, 'a fellow of infinite humour and extraordinary humanity', fortunately decided to see these suspect visitors for himself.[153]

Lageard was convivial, generous, and hospitable. He entertained the three Englishmen at home, arranged for them to hunt over the Archbishop's land, and introduced them to his friends. Over dinners, sometimes lasting five or six hours, they discussed politics and compared their countries' institutions. Pitt, whose ear was 'quick for every sound but music', spoke French with fair accuracy and a passable accent and held his own with Lageard, who 'as a French Abbé is not proverbial for silence'.[154] Lageard asked him which part of the British Constitution he expected to be the first to decay. Pitt replied, 'the prerogative of the King and the authority of the House of Peers', and he told the abbé, *'Monsieur, vous n'avez point de liberté politique, mais pour la liberté civile, vous en avez plus que vous croyez.'* When Lageard expressed his bewilderment that a country so moral as England should submit to being governed by a man so wanting in private morals as Fox, Pitt acknowledged the justice of the remark but added, *'C'est que vous n'avez pas été sous la baguette du Magicien.'*

At the end of the month, Alexandre Angélique de Talleyrand-Périgord, Archbishop of Rheims †, returned, and on 6 October Pitt and his friends dined at the palace. Wilberforce noted in his diary,

* Rheims retained the system of episcopal government instituted in the sixth century.

† Uncle of Charles Maurice de Talleyrand-Périgord, the French statesman. It is said that Talleyrand met Pitt at the Archbishop's palace at Rheims, but neither recorded such an encounter, nor does Wilberforce mention it in his journal.

'N.B. Archbishops in England are not like Archevêques in France; these last are jolly fellows of about fifty years of age, who play at billiards, etc., like other people.'

Six days later, armed with introductions from the Archbishop, the visitors left for Paris. They spent a week there, but there was 'little to do but see the sights' as the King had taken his Court to Fontainebleau and 'carried all the world from Paris except the English, who seem quite in possession of the town.' [155] Pitt had timed his arrival to coincide with that of George Rose, previously a Secretary to the Treasury in Shelburne's government, who had been staying at Spa * with 'the Black Mastiff', as Pitt called Lord Thurlow. Though Rose had little news to give him, it was a meeting of some importance. It laid the foundation for Rose's lifelong attachment to Pitt, a blind and jealous devotion that was neither reciprocated nor adequately rewarded.

On 15 October Pitt and his friends followed the Court to Fontainebleau, where they were presented to Louis XVI, 'a clumsy, strange figure in immense boots', and to Queen Marie Antoinette, 'a monarch of most engaging manners and appearance', who chaffed them about their friend the *véritable épicier* in Rheims. They were entertained to suppers, played cards and billiards, and enjoyed the opera and the theatre. Pitt went stag-hunting one day while Wilberforce and Eliot attended the Court. Wherever he went Pitt was surrounded by interested courtiers and 'behaved with great spirit, though he was sometimes a little bored when they talked to him about the Parliamentary Reform'. The Englishmen met Benjamin Franklin at the house of marquis de la Fayette; Vergennes; the author and playwright Jean François Marmontel; and the great statesman and financier Jacques Necker. The latter had married Suzanne Curchod, once unsuccessfully wooed by Edward Gibbon, and they had a seventeen-year-old daughter, Anne Louise Germaine. The ambitious mother saw in Pitt an admirable match for Germaine. It is said that the proposal was made through Horace Walpole and John Pratt, and that Pitt rejected it with the words, 'I am already married to my country', but the evidence for this is thin. Certain it is that Madame Necker favoured the alliance. Years later she wrote to her daughter, 'I did desire that you should marry Mr

* In the Ardennes, about seventeen miles south-east of Liège. In the eighteenth century it was the most fashionable watering-place in Europe and famous for its mineral springs.

Pitt. I wished to confide you to the care of a husband who had made for himself a great name; . . . You were not disposed to give me this satisfaction—Well! All is now forgiven.' [156] Germaine was a girl with a will of her own. If Sir Gilbert Elliot is to be believed, she and Pitt would have been ill-suited: 'She is', he wrote, 'one of those women who are greedy of admiration, and lay themselves out for it in all ways, purchasing any quantity of anybody at any price, and among other forces by a traffic of mutual flattery. She is also to have the whole conversation to herself, and to be the centre of every company she is in.' [157] Lord Palmerston was 'glad to have seen her', but added, 'as far as I could judge I do not like either her appearance, style of conversation or her manners.' [158] By the time Elliot and Palmerston met her, Germaine had achieved fame for herself under her married name, Madame de Staël.

Pitt, it seems, had a fortunate escape. A special messenger arrived for him and he cut short his holiday. On the evening of the 22nd he was back in London. He never left England again.

The reason for Pitt's hurried return is not clear. Parliament was not due to reassemble until 11 November. The peace treaties with America, France, and Spain had been signed at Versailles during the first week in September * without any material changes being made to the preliminaries so bitterly condemned in the Commons nine months earlier; and there had been no significant alteration in the political situation since the start of the summer recess. The war was over, and the coalition, so repulsive in April, was gaining acceptance and strength. The government was loathed by the King, but to the greater number of his subjects it appeared to offer a welcome prospect of stability. The source and content of the message delivered to Pitt in France are not known, but it is evident from his immediate return that it was an urgent recall to political life, and his letter to his brother-in-law Lord Mahon, without hinting at the reason for his sudden change of plan, reveals that the three weeks before parliament met were spent in critical discussions with his supporters. It is possible that his return was connected with an offer from Fox. In spite of their differences, each respected the other's abilities and Fox was anxious to bring Pitt into the government. As

* The treaty with Holland, though also unchanged, was not signed until the following May.

he wrote to his brother-in-law, Lord Ossory, on 9 September, 'If Pitt could be persuaded (but I despair of it), I am convinced if he could, he would do more real service to the country than any man ever did.' [159]

On 11 October Pitt spoke in the debate on the Address, following the King's speech, berating the government for delaying nine months before accepting the peace terms and for the hypocrisy of ministers' attacks on the previous administration, and advocating 'without delay, a complete commercial system, suited for the novelty of our situation'. The Address was, nevertheless, accepted without division. All members, and particularly those opposed to the coalition government, were waiting impatiently for Fox to introduce his India Bill. This he did a week later.

The administration and defence of British possessions in India posed unique problems. In the days of 'Diamond Pitt' less than fifteen hundred British, confined to small coastal enclaves at Surat, Bombay, Madras, and Calcutta, had been content to make their fortunes by trade without thought of conquest. The collapse of the Mogul empire after the death of the last great Emperor Aurangzebe in 1707; the rise of the Marathas to ruthless dominance in northern and central India; the assumption of independence by the Imperial Governors in the south and in Bengal, the loss of authority by the titular Emperor at Delhi; and the establishment of rival French trading posts in the Carnatic and at Chandanagar in Bengal, produced a series of threats to British security and trade which ripened in 1746 with the loss of Madras to the French. Two years later, by the treaty of Aix-la-Chapelle, Madras was restored to the East India Company, but the struggle with France in India continued unaffected by the peace treaty in Europe. Joseph François Dupleix, the French Governor, determined to seize control of southern India by setting puppet candidates on the thrones of the Deccan and the Carnatic. By the genius of Robert Clive and the resolution of Thomas Saunders, President at Fort St David, the French plan was irretrievably wrecked at Arcot in 1751, and three years later Dupleix was recalled in disgrace. Clive's triumph was two-fold; he had destroyed the French plan for dominion; and, by his capture and long and successful defence of Arcot against an enemy force which outnumbered his garrison by nearly forty to one, he had demonstrated the fighting spirit most likely to attract Maratha support. Nor did it pass unnoticed that more than half of his small force was Indian. The consequences of Arcot were far-reaching, and particularly in the change of attitude to the British in India, who ceased to be suppliant traders at the courts of the Emperors and their Viceroys and assumed the power to depose and replace those rulers who obstructed them. Where Dupleix had failed, Clive and his successors, who had learnt from him, succeeded. Until 1754 the troops in India had been employed by the East India Company, but in that year the first regular soldiers of the British army were landed.

The threat from the French was not ended at Arcot. Though cleared from the Carnatic, they still held Hyderabad and retained their influence over the greater part of the Deccan, and continued to intrigue with any native power that showed any inclination to fight the British. Suraj-ud-Daula, the young and greedy Nawab of Bengal, Behar and Orissa, decided to rid himself of the British and seize the rich settlement at Calcutta. He succeeded in taking the city, which was poorly garrisoned, but was as quickly relieved of it by Clive and obliged to sign a treaty of friendship and to make reparation for East India Company property looted or destroyed. Suraj-ud-Daula could not, however, be trusted. When war broke out again in Europe, it became necessary to secure Bengal by taking Chandanagar from the French. This was achieved with Suraj-ud-Daula's consent, but he was becoming increasingly disturbed by the rapid growth of British power. Without the counterpoise of the French he could foresee the extinction of his authority. He therefore opened negotiations with the commander of the French forces in the Deccan, offering him a military alliance. At the battle of Plassey in 1757, Clive with 800 Europeans and about 2,000 sepoys trounced a mixed French and Indian army estimated at 50,000. Suraj-ud-Daula was deposed, and his successor, nominated by the British, needed little prompting to show his gratitude to the East India Company. Seven years later, an army raised by a coalition of Indian princes was destroyed at Buxar. By 1765 the Company had been awarded the revenues of three provinces and the rights of collection for the whole of Bengal, Behar and Orissa. The role of the British in India was changing from trade to dominion. As this development became apparent in England, the need for a change in the administration of the East India Company and its territorial possessions came to be regarded as urgent.

As the East India Company, aiming for security of trade, found itself involved, almost involuntarily, in territorial expansion, it became increasingly rich. As it became rich, so its political influence increased. As its frontiers expanded, so their defence required more troops. More and more the profits of the Company were consumed in the costs of defence and war, in payments to the government at home, and in seepage into private pockets. Few of the Company servants who went to India lived to enjoy the fruits of their speculation, but those who returned to England—the nabobs *—did so in spectacular style. They bought fine houses and large estates, and often seats in parliament. Their enormous fortunes were not always made dishonestly: Company servants were permitted to engage in private trade, and some, like Clive, had also received legitimate rewards for their services; but others had used their position to rob both the Company and the country. In an age when moral standards in English political life were so low, the existence of those who made vast fortunes in India by corruption was less remarkable than the restraint and moderation of those servants of India who did not.

In 1772 the East India Company faced bankruptcy. This situation, variously blamed on corruption and the slump in trade, was in reality caused at least as much by the necessity to pay maximum dividends to shareholders in a period when administrative and defence costs were being multiplied by the extension of the Company's frontiers and responsibilities. In 1773 Lord North introduced his Regulating Act. This provided for an immediate loan to the Company of £1,400,000 and the relaxation of customs duties on the re-export of tea; but the most important provision of the Act was the creation of a supreme power in the person of the Governor-General and a council of four, resident in Calcutta, with authority over the presidencies of Bengal, Madras, and Bombay. The first Governor-General to be appointed was Warren Hastings.

This system of regulation was designed to remain in being until the expiry of the Company's charter in 1780. Meanwhile, government ministers would have access to all dispatches from India. In theory, North's plan combined the minimum of interference in the Company's affairs with the assumption of the authority necessary to

---

* A corruption of the Urdu *nawwab* (or *nawab*), governor or viceroy of a province under the Mogul Empire.

suppress the most vicious abuses. In practice, the sensible compromise was wrecked by the appointment to the supreme council of a majority who, largely from personal motives, opposed and obstructed the Governor-General. It is a sad defect of safeguards in government that they too often rob leaders of the authority they require to exercise their function. To the Indians, accustomed to despotic rule, these safeguards appeared as a sign of weakness. Assailed and traduced by his council, Hastings was also failed and disobeyed by the subordinate governors of Madras and Bombay. The army of the Bombay presidency, forced to surrender to the Marathas in 1779, was rescued by a force dispatched by Hastings across India from Bengal; in the following year the Madras presidency succeeded in provoking both the Nizam of Hyderabad and Hyder Ali, who stormed across the Carnatic to the walls of Fort St George. A confederation of the Nizam, Hyder Ali of Mysore, and the Marathas, assisted by the French who had a powerful naval squadron cruising off the east coast, would have been invincible. By a brilliant combination of diplomacy, bribery, threats, force, audacity, and resolution, Hastings fragmented the alliance of his enemies and reduced them piecemeal. Sir Eyre Coote, a worthy disciple of Clive's, given supreme civil and military authority in the Carnatic, retrieved the territory from Hyder Ali and the French. By the end of 1782 the crisis was over, though peace with Mysore was not concluded until two years later.

While troops and money were poured into America, where British armies surrendered and an empire was lost, Hastings, with puny resources and without aid from Britain, dismembered the alliances of powerful enemies and repulsed every assault upon the territories for which he was responsible. In so doing he secured British possessions, enhanced British prestige, and laid the foundations for the conquest, by a system of alliances and war, of a new empire. The task was Herculean and its achievement heroic. It would have been astonishing if, in such desperate circumstances requiring urgent and imaginative action, and wielding such power, Hastings had not made errors of judgement. It would have been extraordinary had his actions to sustain British trade and possessions against such odds not produced consequences in suffering, loss, and injustice. It would have been even more remarkable if his efforts had not implicated him in financial transactions involving enormous sums of money, and stretched the already overstrained resources of the East India Company to breaking-point.

There was general agreement on all sides of the House of Commons that the administration of British territory in India required to be reorganized. The East India Company, though deeply in debt and unable to offer either the Treasury or its shareholders a satisfactory return on their investments, remained a source of patronage and influence second only to the Crown. Its changing function made reform more urgent. Lord North's plan, produced for him by John Robinson in 1778, had been revised by Charles Jenkinson three years later. Shelburne had admitted the problem, and Dundas had drawn up a Bill, rejected by parliament, that outlined a system of government similar to that later proposed by Pitt. The inherent weakness of all these plans was the presumption that the greatest obstacle to good administration was corruption, and that this could be rooted out as easily as it might be in England. They took little account of the size of the territories, the diversity of their inhabitants, or their differences in tradition and attitudes. Politicians at home made detailed theoretical studies of India: Burke, Fox, and Dundas vied with one another in their knowledge of the East India Company's trade and organization; they were united in their horror of the widespread corruption and oppression reported to them; and they began to evolve philosophical principles of empire associated with a code of morality that did not exist even in Europe. Their intentions were, on the whole, admirable. Their practical ignorance of India and its people remained profound.

Hastings had favoured the division of government function between the Company and the most powerful of the Indian princes and rulers, a system of indirect rule through British influence and local alliances. Politicians in Westminster decided upon the division of power between London and India. Hastings soon discovered that, among the princes, security bred irresponsibility. His system depended upon the maintenance of prestige and was workable only in combination with the frequent display and uninhibited use of strength. The Westminster solution ignored many practical difficulties. Most important, it overlooked the distance between the two governing bodies. Dispatches generally travelled faster than people, but the voyage was a long one, seldom taking much less than four months. Nothing more immediate than long-term policy could be discussed. In effect, whatever the directions from Westminster, the responsibility for decisive action in any emergency remained with the Governor-General.

Reform of the East India Company was a problem of great complexity and dangerous political sensitivity. Burke, who fathered the Bill presented by Fox, failed to understand its implications. Passionate and doctrinaire, he conducted his researches among those who shared his prejudices: the dissatisfied, the disappointed, the jealous; those, in short, who had returned without the rewards for which they had hoped and to which they felt themselves entitled, and those whose investments in the Company had produced unsatisfactory returns. Warren Hastings knew more about India and its peoples than any Englishman of his time. He had, furthermore, a remarkable record of success, Burke consulted only the Governor-General's enemies. His special study of the problem set him on a course of persecution—dedicated, malignant, and occasionally hysterical—that threatened to destroy his own reputation.

On 18 November Fox introduced his India Bill. Inspired and drafted by Burke, it was a genuine attempt to separate the political and commercial functions of the East India Company. A board of seven commissioners, with powers of appointment and dismissal of the Company's officers in India, would be charged with government. Eight assistants would manage the Company's commercial affairs. All would remain in England, answerable for their actions to parliament. The design was unwieldy and impracticable, an example, now all too familiar, of government intervention in a situation imperfectly understood, taking no account of the crucial factors of time and distance. The powers of the Governor-General were to be reduced. By denying him the authority to declare war or negotiate alliances, one of the greatest sources of corruption would, it was thought, be eliminated. It is a tribute to Fox's eloquence, and a measure of the ignorance of his audience, that he was able to present this plan as a magical remedy for the ills of the East India Company. It was not until he explained the details concerning the appointment and tenure of the commissioners that the full extent of his proposals became clear. The seven senior commissioners were to be nominated by parliament for an initial tenure of four years. During this period they could not be removed unless by the King following an address from parliament. The assistants were to be nominated from among shareholders owning £2,000 or more of Company stock. There is no reason to suppose that this method of appointment was chosen deliberately for its political advantage, but it is inconceivable that Fox had not calculated the favourable consequences to his party. The vast patronage of the East India Company was to be put into the hands of Fox and his nominees, impervious to the changing fortunes of governments. Though it was exaggerated at the time, there was at least a theoretical possibility that the Whig government and the board of commissioners might, by the exertion of their powers to the advantage of each other, become mutually self-perpetuating.

The first reading of the Bill, taking the Opposition by surprise, passed without division. The debates on 25 November and 1 December were dominated by Fox, Burke, and Pitt. Fox, with Burke's passionate support, presented himself as the champion of morality, the statesman prepared to risk all to liberate an oppressed people from tyranny. The risk was in fact small: the government's majority never fell below a hundred. Burke, as so often allowing his emotions to subvert history, spoke of 'the rescue of the greatest number of the human race that ever were so grievously oppressed, from the greatest tyranny that ever was exercised',[160] a distortion that Indians in the territories controlled by the Company would have found incomprehensible. To a people accustomed to despotism, robbery was the accepted prerogative of the victor, as bribery was the weapon of the diplomat and subjection the just fate of the weak. Other principles were foreign and engendered distrust or contempt. By 8 December, when the Bill was ready to be passed to the House of Lords, opposition was becoming better organized and East India House began to exercise its considerable influence at Westminster. Lord North, meanwhile, had lost one of his most valuable followers: John Robinson had taken his unique experience of election management into opposition.

On 1 December Lord Thurlow delivered to the King a memorandum from Lord Temple.[161] It contained an exaggerated warning against the India Bill as 'a plan to take more than half the Royal power, and by that means to disable His Majesty for the rest of the reign'. Temple went on to examine the means of circumventing it: 'The refusing the Bill, if it passes the Houses, is a violent means. . . . An easier way of changing his Government would be by taking some opportunity of doing it, when, in the progress of it, it shall have received more discountenance than hitherto. This must be expected to happen in the Lords in a greater degree than can be hoped for in the Commons. But a sufficient degree of it may not occur in the Lords if those whose duty to His Majesty would excite them to appear are not acquainted with his wishes, and that in a manner which would make it impossible to pretend a doubt of it, in case they were so disposed.' Even the convolutions of his style do not disguise the shrewdness of Temple's advice: by exerting his influence in the House of Lords, the King could not only have the Bill defeated but also provide for himself an issue of sufficient importance to justify him in dismissing the government. George III hesitated. There could be no doubt that he had been asked to approve the Bill in outline, for his assent was required to all government measures before they were debated in parliament, but it is unlikely that he was forewarned of its details. His personal intervention to have the Bill rejected might expose him to a charge of double-dealing. The opportunity was tempting, but to make it a practicable proposition the King needed a realistic estimate of the strength of the parties in the House of Commons and a positive reply from the Opposition. For the first he was able to turn to John Robinson. For the second he must consult William Pitt.

Robinson lost no time in making his calculations. By the time the India Bill was ready for the Lords, he had prepared estimates of current voting strengths in both Houses compared with strengths to be anticipated following a general election. From these it appeared that a ministry formed by Pitt and his friends would be in a minority until an election; but thereafter they could hope for a majority of about 180 votes. This landslide change would be attributable to the direct influence of the Crown on the election results, and the general principle that many members, who were opposed to faction, voted with the government unless there was exceptionally good reason for not doing so. Consultation with Pitt was less easy to arrange, and had to be undertaken through intermediaries. The plot, hatched by Temple and Thurlow, enmeshed a proprietor of the East India Company, Richard Atkinson, Charles Jenkinson, Dundas, Robinson, and Lord Clarendon. On 11 December Temple saw the King and brought away with him a written statement 'That His Majesty allowed Earl Temple to say, that whoever voted for the India Bill was not only not his friend, but would be considered by him as an enemy; and if these words were not strong enough, Earl Temple might use whatever words he might deem stronger and more to the purpose.'[162] The following day the King sent for the Archbishop of Canterbury, who, with the proxy held by the Bishop of London, controlled four votes and might be expected to influence more, and made his wishes known. On the 15th the Lords passed by eight votes an Opposition motion to adjourn the debate on the India Bill. Two days later, by 95 votes to 76, they killed it. The King, after what he no doubt considered an adequate and decent interval of twenty-four hours while he waited in vain for the government to resign, sent a note to Lord North requiring him to give up the seals of his department 'and to acquaint Mr Fox to send those of the Foreign Department'.[163] 'I choose this method', he wrote, 'as Audiences on such occasions must be unpleasant.'

The King's actions could be interpreted as unconstitutional in spirit if not in fact. By intervening, albeit indirectly, to obtain a vote in the House of Lords, he had violated parliamentary freedom of debate. On the other hand it could be argued that while the King retained his right of veto, a right which he correctly believed Fox intended to deny him, he was entitled to avoid an open dispute with his ministers by using his influence to defeat measures of which he could not approve. The constitutional debate remains unresolved. The shabbiness of the manoeuvre, at least as dishonourable as the coalition it destroyed, could not be concealed. Nor could it be maintained, as his most distinguished biographer has claimed, that Pitt 'had taken no part in these transactions'.[164] Pitt never denied his ambition. He had declared that he would take office whenever he could do so on his own terms and with some prospect of attracting the necessary support to enable him to govern. For him the best interests of the nation were paramount; and he had inherited his father's ability to identify those interests with his own.

In the House of Commons, on the afternoon of 19 December 1783, Richard Pepper Arden rose to move a new writ for the borough of Appleby 'in the room of the Right Honourable William Pitt, who, since his election, has accepted the office of First Lord of the Treasury and Chancellor of the Exchequer'. His announcement was received with a great shout of laughter.

IX

The Mince-Pie Administration
- 1783-1784

THE RAUCOUS LAUGHTER that greeted the announcement of Pitt's appointment was, in the circumstances, amply justified. Apart from Pitt's extreme youth and inexperience, the calculations on which the King and his allies had based their gamble showed the new Prime Minister and his followers mustering only 149 certain votes against the Opposition's 231. The remainder, divided among 'hopefuls' and 'doubtfuls' would, at best, leave him about sixty votes short of a majority. The inference was plain: Pitt's ministry could not survive without a general election. Fox and North, two of the most astute tacticians in parliament, were determined to prevent the dissolution which they assumed must be announced. On the day Pitt took office, Fox fulminated against the use of the King's prerogative to call an election 'to suit the convenience of an ambitious young man', and hinted at an intention to call for the impeachment of those who advised the King to exercise it. His supposition that a general election would be called immediately was logical but mistaken. He underrated Pitt's resilience. In the personal struggle that developed between them, Fox was outwitted.

Pitt had no intention of asking the King for a precipitate dissolution of parliament. John Robinson's forecast of results was encouraging, but Pitt believed that time would strengthen his following in the House of Commons, not weaken it. In this he displayed both audacity and mature judgement, but it is doubtful if he anticipated the full extent of his difficulties. His first and most dispiriting task was the formation of a government. Lord Temple accepted the seals of Secretary of State on the morning of 19 December, Thurlow returned as Lord Chancellor, and the elderly and influential Earl Gower gallantly volunteered to serve in any office in which he might be useful, an offer which Pitt accepted with gratitude; but the Duke of Grafton, Lord Cornwallis, Lord Grantham, and Chatham's old and trusted friend Lord Camden, all refused. On the evening of Sunday 21 December, Temple resigned.[165] Dr Pretyman later recalled this as 'the only event of a public nature which I ever knew to disturb Mr Pitt's rest while he continued in good health . . . when I went into Mr Pitt's bedroom the next morning he told me that he had not had a moment's sleep. He expressed great uneasiness at the state of public affairs, at the same time declaring his fixed resolution not to abandon the situation he had undertaken.' [166] Wilberforce reported Pitt as 'nobly firm' on the morning of the 23rd, and that evening the Cabinet was formed. Gower was Lord President of the Council, the Duke of Rutland Lord Privy Seal, and Earl Howe First Lord of the Admiralty. Lord Sydney and the Marquis of Carmarthen, as Secretaries of State, once more divided the office relinquished by Temple. Pitt was the first Commoner to be Prime Minister since his father twenty-six years earlier, and the single member of his Cabinet in the House of Commons.

Lord Temple's resignation remains unexplained. It has been variously attributed to his disappointment at not being elevated to a dukedom, a quarrel with Pitt about the latter's resolution not to ask for an immediate dissolution, and a desire, stated by his brother in parliament, to meet as a private citizen any charge that might be made against him for his part in bringing down the Fox-North coalition. This last referred to a motion, passed by the Commons on 17 December, and clearly aimed at Temple, to declare any attempt to influence a vote by reporting the King's opinion 'a high crime and misdemeanour' and a breach of privilege. It seems most likely that Temple resigned to save both himself and Pitt's ministry. He never again held Cabinet office.

To offices outside the Cabinet, Pitt appointed Lloyd Kenyon (Attorney-General), Pepper Arden (Solicitor-General), George Rose and Tom Steele (Secretaries of the Treasury), Sir George Yonge (Secretary-at-War), Henry Dundas (Treasurer of the Navy), and William Wyndham Grenville (Paymaster of the Forces). The ministry lacked debating talent. In the Lords, Thurlow alone spoke with authority. Ill-tempered, domineering, and untrustworthy, he was loathed but respected. In the Commons, Pitt had the support of Grenville and Dundas, but neither had then acquired the influence he was to wield in the future. They were not yet a match for North, Fox, Burke, and Sheridan. The most obvious omission from Pitt's government was Lord Shelburne, but no feeling of gratitude could subdue Pitt's certainty that Shelburne's return would be irreparably damaging to the government's respectability. Nor would he have been an easy colleague. Pitt intended to be supreme in Cabinet.

Those who had supported the coalition did not take the new government seriously. Sir Gilbert Elliot told his brother it must be 'considered as a set of children playing at ministers, and must be sent back to school, and in a few days all will have returned to its former course'; Mrs Crewe *, the great Whig hostess, described the government as 'a mince-pie administration', indicating that it would not last long after Christmas; and Gibbon, remembering perhaps his discomfiture at the Lincoln's Inn dinner in 1780, gave it as his opinion that 'Billy's painted wagon' would 'soon sink under Charlie's black collier'. Fox himself declared, 'We are so strong that nobody can undertake without madness; and if they do, I think we shall destroy them almost as soon as they are formed.' [167] Members did not disperse for Christmas until the evening of 26 December, and on the insistence of Fox it was agreed that parliament should reassemble on 12 January. Writing to his mother, Pitt managed to assume a guarded confidence that few of his followers found reason to share: 'Things are in general more promising than they have been, but in the uncertainty of effect the persuasion of not being wrong is, as you say, the best circumstance and enough; though there is satisfaction in the hopes of at least something more.' [168]

Pitt appears to have understood, as George III did not, that the outcome of the struggle depended on his remaining in office,

* Frances Anne, wife of John (later Baron) Crewe.

regardless of the strength of the opposition, until his own performance in parliament, and the powerful forces exerting their influence for him outside, could effect the necessary swing of opinion in his favour. The proprietors and directors of the East India Company were hard at work on his behalf. Two celebrated caricatures attacking Fox's India Bill had already appeared: the first showing him carrying away the wreck of East India House on his shoulders; and the second, and more famous, by James Sayers, depicting him as Carlo Khan, mounted on an elephant Lord North, led by Edmund Burke in triumph through the City. Fox stated it as his belief that these two caricatures had done him more harm than all the debates in the Commons.[169] In addition to the funds of the East India Company, part of the King's secret service fund of £100,000 could be made available for the financing of propaganda. Sayers was later rewarded by Pitt with the appointment of Marshal of the Exchequer for his anti-Fox caricatures published in 1783 and 1784.

During the first three months of 1784 the struggle between the Crown and the Opposition majority in the House of Commons was fought personally by Pitt and Fox. George III was defending not only his prerogative to choose his ministers but also his right to refer to the electorate by the dissolution of parliament. Both were accepted constitutional rights without which no sovereign could continue to govern. It was the essential weakness of Fox's chosen position that he was obliged to resist the calling of a general election. By doing so, he set parliament above both the Crown and the people. It was also implicit in his argument that the voters were either gullible or venal. As this became clear to the House of Commons, his majority melted away.

The political events of the two years after North's resignation in March 1782 served to aggravate differences between Pitt and Fox until the breach became both inevitable and irreparable. They had much in common, but it is doubtful if they could ever have worked together. Neither would have been content to serve under the leadership of the other, and it is difficult to imagine any division of responsibility that would have satisfied them. Any such possibility was, between 1782 and 1784, annihilated by Fox's coalition with North and his passionate hatred of the King. The antipathy was mutual and it excluded Fox from office for twenty-three years. Pitt's refusal to join the coalition or take part in factional politics, and his acceptance of office after the intrigues of December 1783, were never forgiven by Fox. As the years passed, the memory of these injuries was renewed with every day of his exile on the Opposition benches.

Fox was, as Carl Philip Moritz observed, 'dark, small, thickset, generally ill-groomed' and looked 'rather like a Jew'. His features were coarse, 'harsh and saturnine', distinguished by shaggy black eyebrows 'which sometimes concealed, but more often developed, the workings of his mind'. Walpole described him in 1783: 'Fox lodged in St James's Street, and as soon as he rose, which was very late, had a levée of his followers, and of the members of the Gaming Club at Brooks's, all his disciples. His bristly black person, and shagged breast quite open, and rarely purefied by any ablutions, was wrapped in a foul linen nightgown, and his bushy hair dishevelled. In these cynic weeds, and with epicurean good humour, did he dictate his politics—and in this school did the heir of the Crown attend his lessons and imbibe them.' All contemporary accounts are agreed that his appearance was not engaging; and yet the charm of his personality was such that few could withstand it. He had a warmth, good-nature, and impulsive generosity described by William Wordsworth as 'constant predominance of sensibility of heart', and his smile was 'irresistible'.[170]

Born in January 1749, he was the younger son of Henry Fox, Lord Holland, who had made a vast fortune from his dealings as Paymaster of the Forces between 1757 and 1765. As a child, Charles was grossly spoilt, and when he was fourteen he was taken to Paris where his father is said to have acted as 'pimp and bookmaker' to him. A year later he went up to Hertford College, Oxford, where he managed to combine serious study with heavy gambling and the satisfaction of his voracious appetites. In September 1767 he complained to his cousin, Richard Fitzpatrick, 'I have had one pox and one clap this summer. I believe I am the most unlucky rascal in the universe.' The following July he was in Nice, bemoaning his boredom in 'perhaps the dullest town in the world, and what is a terrible thing there are no whores . . . my poxes and claps have weakened me a good deal, but by means of the cold bath I recover apace.'[171] Two months earlier he had been elected, in his absence, member of parliament for Midhurst in Sussex, and he took his seat in November 1768 while still nineteen. On his return from his travels in France and Italy, he made his appearance as a man of fashion, in red-heeled shoes and with his hair powdered blue. Later he affected, as did many of his followers, the blue coat and buff waistcoat worn by American troops in the revolutionary war.

It is not easy to understand the mastery Fox exercised over the House of Commons. Even allowing for their incompleteness and inaccuracy, the printed records of his speeches make wearisome reading; but as Fox himself said, 'The very identical things which make a speech good to hear make it bad to read and vice versa.' [172] His most admired speeches are too long and too repetitious for modern taste, and even his contemporaries were agreed that he was 'deficient in the great point of knowing when to have done and how to avoid fatiguing his auditors'. [173] In the lower register his voice was pleasant and musical, but when raised it became shrill and discordant. He spoke rapidly, and his diction was often indistinct. In his speeches, as in his life, he was an opportunist, and his lack of preparation or orderly train of thought led him into the repetitions that are acceptable and even effective in oratory but irritating in print. He 'went forward and backward, not satisfied with his first expression. He would put it another way'. [174]

Fox's private life was a public scandal. He was 'dissolute, dissipated, idle beyond measure', drinking, gambling, and whoring all night and then stumbling, frowzy and unshaven, into the House of Commons to make a spellbinding speech lasting two hours or more. Sir Gilbert Elliot thought him the best speaker in the House, and even Walpole admitted that he had genius. Burke described him as 'one of the pleasantest men in the world, as well as the greatest Genius that perhaps this country has ever produced'. [175] George III loathed him, not only for his violent attacks on the royal prerogative but also because he held him responsible for the dissolute behaviour of the Prince of Wales. It was Fox who introduced him to his mistresses and companionably shared their favours. The King might forgive him his political views, though it cannot have been captivating to know that Fox compared him with Satan and looked forward to his early demise, but for debauching the heir to the throne there could be no absolution. Fox's hatred of Pitt sprang from the false assumption that it was Pitt who had robbed him of the highest office; but at no time after 1783 would George III have accepted Fox as his Chief Minister.

Fox possessed all the qualities of a great politician, and he was one of the greatest parliamentarians of his century. He lacked one essential quality of the statesman: self-control. His natural spontaneity and lack of moderation led him to take up battle standards that he later found himself obliged in some embarrassment to throw away, and to entrench himself in positions that he soon found to be indefensible. His early speeches declaring the inviolability of the constitution later contrasted oddly with his arguments for the sacrosanctity of parliament, his assumption of the right to speak for the people, and his disastrous defence of the hereditary rights of the Prince of Wales. In 1771, speaking of the 'imaginary infallibility of the people',[176] he said 'We have sworn to maintain the constitution in its present form; to maintain the privileges of parliament . . . and neither to encroach upon the legal jurisdiction of the peers, nor the just prerogatives of the sovereign. . . . What acquaintance have the people at large with the arcana of political rectitude, with the connexions of Kingdoms, the resources of national strength, the abilities of ministers, or even with their own dispositions? . . . I pay no regard whatever to the voice of the people.' Ten years later, as the self-appointed voice of the people, Fox must often have wished that speech expunged from the record. Early in 1784 a pamphlet appeared entitled *Beauties of Fox, North & Burke*, listing the various attacks made by each upon the others. Accurately documented, and well indexed, by far the greater part of the pamphlet was taken up by Fox's vitriolic invective against North. It was an effective broadside against the Opposition.

Fox's disorderly genius was the antithesis of Pitt's glacial control. In appearance and behaviour the two men were opposites: Fox, short and corpulent, coarse-featured, impulsive, genial, and libidinous; Pitt, a little over six feet tall, auburn-haired, thin, awkward in his movements, shy, cool, and in his public life austere. Wraxhall, unforgiving in the disappointment of his hopes of office, remembered Pitt's manner as 'cold, stiff, and without suavity or amenity. He seemed never to invite approach, or to encourage acquaintance, though when addressed he could be polite, communicative, and occasionably gracious. Smiles were not natural to him. . . . From the instant that Pitt entered the doorway of the House of Commons, he advanced up the floor with a quick and firm step, his head erect and thrown back, looking neither to the right nor to the left, nor favouring with a nod or a glance any of the individuals seated on either side. . . . It was not thus that Lord North or Fox treated Parliament.' But it was also Wraxhall who wrote of Pitt's 'perspicuity, eloquence, rapidity, recollection, and talent altogether wonderful, which carried the audience along with him in every arithmetical statement, [and] left no calculation obscure or ambiguous.' [177] In their style of oratory, the essential difference between Pitt and Fox was neatly summarized by the great Greek scholar, Richard Porson: 'Mr Pitt conceives his sentences before he utters them. Mr Fox throws himself into the middle of his, and leaves it to God Almighty to get him out again.' [178]

During the brief Christmas recess, Pitt drafted his India Act. Although firmly based upon work done by Dundas in 1783, the Act was produced in an astonishingly short time. The greater part of it appears to have been completed between 5 January, when Pitt met representatives of the East India Company to discuss his proposals, and 10 January when they were approved in detail by an overwhelming majority of those present at a meeting of the Company's General Court. He also found time for two other important tactical moves: he recommended to the King the creation of four new peerages; and he disposed of the vacant Clerkship of the Pells. Two of the peerages were bestowed on Edward Eliot, father of one of his most intimate friends and controller of seven parliamentary seats in the West Country; and on his cousin, Thomas Pitt, who was raised to the Barony of Camelford. These creations were more than a deliberate affront to Fox and North, who had been denied the opportunity to reward their followers, they were an explicit declaration of the King's faith in his new ministry and of the prizes once more available to those loyal to the Crown. The Clerkship of the Pells, a sinecure worth £3000 a year, and in the gift of the Prime Minister, fell vacant following the death of Sir Edward Walpole. It was assumed that Pitt, who unlike his rivals had almost no private income, would take the post for himself. There were ample precedents for such action, and the Lord Chancellor was among those who urged him to ease his financial burdens by this means. Pitt chose, instead, to give the post to Colonel Isaac Barré in return for his resigning a pension awarded to him by Rockingham. This transaction saved the Exchequer the whole of Barré's pension for the remainder of his life, a sum totalling more than £57,000, and enabled Pitt, by a sacrifice that he evidently could not afford, to put on public display the same disinterestedness

126

and integrity that had distinguished his father and won him the respect and trust of the people. No two moves could have been more nicely judged simultaneously to strengthen Pitt's position in the country and to enrage the Opposition.

When parliament reassembled on 12 January, it was immediately clear that Fox intended to control the proceedings. He launched a vicious and effective onslaught against the government, and against the Prime Minister in particular. Pitt defended himself ably, but the government was defeated twice, by majorities of thirty-nine and fifty-four, and five Opposition motions were carried without a vote. Such a daunting display of Opposition strength might have shaken more experienced ministers than Pitt, and he was grateful when the Duke of Richmond, who had already agreed to become Master General of the Ordnance, pledged his loyalty by accepting the Cabinet post he had previously declined. Four days later, a motion requiring the dismissal of the King's ministers was carried by a majority of twenty-one. On the 23rd, Pitt's India Bill was thrown out by 222 votes to 214.

The government's situation was desperate, but Pitt stolidly ignored the demands for his resignation. He also resisted the King's increasingly urgent advice to ask for the dissolution of parliament. His stubborn refusal required all his courage and natural optimism, but there were encouraging signs that the tide was beginning to turn in his favour. The Fox-North majority had fallen from 106 on 3 December to eight on 23 January, showing the gradual return of the independent members to their traditional support of the government, and the reassertion of a general intention to renounce faction and vote according to the merits of measures. Pitt believed that his greatest danger lay in the last sanction of a majority Opposition, the refusal to vote supplies, the essential financial grants without which no government could continue. He had voiced this fear to his brother-in-law, Lord Mahon, in December, but Mahon had answered with conviction, 'They will not stop them, it is the very last thing they will do.'[179] Nevertheless Fox was tempted, and on 18 February succeeded in postponing consideration of supplies for the ordnance.

In this intolerable situation, Pitt's defiance was beginning to arouse public sympathy and support. The almost single-handed defence of the King's constitutional prerogative by a twenty-four-year-old Prime Minister, who had already given proof of his integrity of purpose, appeared virtuous and heroic in comparison with the disreputable coalition of Fox and North, and the general abhorrence of faction was strengthened by the propaganda instigated and financed by the East India Company. Addresses to the King, expressing gratitude for his dismissal of the previous ministry, began to arrive from all parts of the country. Two were from Westminster and Banbury, the constituencies that had elected Fox and North. Pitt was voted the Freedom of the City of London and a gold box in recognition of his services.

On 26 January fifty-three independent members of parliament met at the St Alban's tavern and agreed upon an address to Pitt and the Duke of Portland, First Lord of Treasury in the previous ministry, urging them jointly to explore the possibility of forming a new government to include the best abilities of both groups. A week later, a motion declaring that the state of the nation called for 'a firm, efficient, extended, united Administration' was passed by the House of Commons without dissent. Portland and Fox, while accepting the principle of another coalition, made the resignation of the ministry a prior condition of any negotiation. Pitt refused to resign. On 11 February Fox declared himself willing to serve with Pitt in a new administration. In response to Pitt's refusal to serve with North, the latter at once announced his readiness to stand aside if this would facilitate the desired reconciliation. Much against his will, the King gave Pitt permission to negotiate with Portland on the clear understanding that no more than equal terms should be offered to the Opposition; but Portland refused to meet Pitt until the offer of equality in the proposed administration should be set out in detail.

The plain fact, which all were at pains to disguise, was that none of the parties concerned genuinely wished to reach an agreement. The King regarded the Opposition as 'a most desperate and unprincipled faction' and would allow Portland or Fox to take office only as a last resort; Pitt, believing that delay and a well-timed general election would confirm him in office, had nothing to gain by compromise; Portland and Fox would not serve under Pitt and would consider no arrangement that did not exact his resignation. All, on the other hand, were obliged to make a convincing show of moderation and a desire to negotiate in deference to public opinion and the independent members of the House.

128

On 28 February Pitt drove in procession to the Hall of the Grocers' Company * to receive the Freedom of the City of London, presented to him in a hundred-guinea gold box. He was accompanied by the City Marshal and Sheriffs, and a cheering crowd which had assembled outside his brother's house in Berkeley Square where he was staying. His return, after dinner at the Hall at which one of the most laudatory speeches was made by the City Chamberlain, John Wilkes, was described thirty-eight years later by Chatham, who was with Lord Mahon in Pitt's carriage:

. . . he was attended by a great concourse of people, many of the better sort, all the way down the Strand, as well as by a considerable Mob. The Populace insisted on taking off the Horses and drawing the Coach. A Mob is never very discreet, and unfortunately they stopped outside Carlton House and began hissing, and it was with some difficulty we forced them to go on. As we proceeded up St James's Street, there was a great Cry, and an attempt made to turn the Carriage up St James's Place to Mr Fox's house . . . in order to break his windows and force him to light, but which we at last succeeded in preventing their doing. I have often thought this was a trap laid for us, for had we got up, there, into a Cul de Sac, Mr Pitt's situation would have been critical indeed. This attempt brought us rather nearer in contact with Brooks, and the moment we got opposite (the Mob calling for lights) a sudden and desperate attack was made upon the Carriage in which were Mr Pitt, Lord M[ahon], and myself—by a body of Chairmen armed with bludgeons, broken Chair Poles—(many of the waiters, and several of the Gentlemen among them). They succeeded in making their way to the Carriage and forced open the door. Several desperate blows were aimed at Mr Pitt.[180]

Seeing his danger, a mixed party of chairmen and members of White's rushed to Pitt's assistance, and, covered by them, he succeeded in escaping into the Club. Chatham recalled that 'The Coachmen, and the Servants were much bruised, and the Carriage nearly demolished.' Among the crowd of attackers Chatham recog-

* One of the twelve great livery companies of the City of London; founded in the fourteenth century.

nized Fox's friends James Hare and John Crewe. He added, reasonably, 'I never went to Brooks any more.'

To the relief of all his supporters, and most particularly of the King, to whom even a temporary absence might have proved disastrous, Pitt was uninjured. The widespread suspicion that Fox was personally implicated in this outrage was unfounded, and he defended himself by declaring that he was at the time in bed with his mistress, Elizabeth Armistead, who was prepared to substantiate his story on oath; but there could be no doubt that this attack was the work of his followers, and his reputation was not enhanced. On 1 March his resolution in parliament demanding Pitt's dismissal was carried by twelve votes, but a week later a similar motion was given a majority of only one. Next day, the Mutiny Bill, which renewed each year the legality of a standing army, and which Fox had threatened to oppose, was allowed to pass without division. Pitt wrote to the Duke of Rutland that he was 'tired to death, even with victory, for I think our present state is entitled to that name'.[181] He was right. The supplies were voted. Everything was now ready, and Pitt arranged for the King to dissolve parliament on 24 March.

The Opposition made one last attempt to delay Pitt's public victory. Early in the morning of 24 March, thieves broke into the Lord Chancellor's house in Great Ormond Street and stole the Great Seal of England. After a hurried Council at St James's Palace, orders were given for craftsmen to work through the night to make a new Seal. It was finished at noon on the 25th and parliament was dissolved by royal proclamation. The stolen Great Seal was never recovered. The theft was, as Pitt told Wilberforce, 'a curious manoeuvre'. In 1688 King James II had dropped the Great Seal into the Thames in order temporarily to prevent the functioning of government under his successor. It was impossible to avoid the conclusion that misguided followers of Fox had tried to prevent the dissolution of parliament by similar methods. Their enemies spread the colourful story that Fox and Mrs Armistead had been seen on the night of the robbery, creeping through the streets armed with a lantern and crowbars.

The general election of 1784 exceeded both Pitt's most optimistic expectations and Fox's worst fears. No less than 160 Opposition members were unseated. At Cambridge, where Pitt, despite the doubts of his friends, stood again for the University where he had been defeated in 1780, he was returned at the head of the poll with his friend Lord Euston second over Lord John Townshend and James Mansfield. Pitt continued to represent Cambridge for the rest of his life. All over the country the victory of the government was most apparent in the counties and the large boroughs, those constituencies where the results were least subject to the influence of patrons or parties. The successes in Yorkshire, where Wilberforce scored a personal triumph, and in Middlesex, were specially significant, for, as Fox said, 'Yorkshire and Middlesex between them make all England.' [182]

As one of the candidates for two places at Westminster, Fox found himself fighting for survival. The government had brought in the popular naval hero, Lord Hood, and Fox's former colleague, Sir Cecil Wray, had switched from Opposition to support of the government. From the start it was clear that Hood would head the poll, and the vital contest would be fought by Fox and Wray for the second seat. While Fox wielded his 'magician's wand' on the hustings, a number of England's most beautiful women—among them Georgiana, Duchess of Devonshire, Elizabeth, Countess of Derby, and Frances Crewe—canvassed for him in the streets. The Prince of Wales himself rode through Westminster, wearing the blue coat and buff waistcoat of the Whigs and sporting the cockade of a fox's brush entwined with sprigs of laurel in his hat. Pitt wrote to Wilberforce on 8 April, 'I can never enough congratulate you on such glorious success . . . Westminster goes on well, in spite of the Duchess of Devonshire and the *other women of the people*.' [183] But as the polling continued it was clear that Fox was gaining ground. On 17 May the final vote was announced: Hood, as expected, led the poll; Fox was second, with 235 votes more than Sir Cecil Wray. His was one of only two Opposition successes in the London area.

Even allowing for the strength of Crown influence, the organized support of the East India Company, and the proved predisposition of the electorate to vote for the government, the completeness of Pitt's victory was, as the *Annual Register* noted, 'scarcely to be credited'. There was good reason to believe that, in spite of the deficiencies and eccentricities of the electoral system, the victory truly represented the will of the people. The King rejoiced at his delivery from Fox and faction. He had found a Prime Minister whose stature, ability, and loyalty were beyond question. If George III also expected subservience he was to find himself sadly mistaken.

X

Retrenchment and Revival
1784-1792

THE WESTMINSTER ELECTION, described by Pitt as 'forty days' poll, forty days' riot, and forty days' confusion',[184] had been the most sensational and the most furiously fought of all contests in the spring of 1784. Apart from its significance as Fox's constituency, it was also numerically the largest in Britain and the only one in the country in which every householder was enfranchised. Both parties had put out their maximum strength in the struggle between 'the Fox, the Lion, and the Ass' and there had been violent scuffles between Irish chairmen employed by Fox, and bruisers dressed as sailors hired by the government. As the King rode down the Mall to open the new parliament, he passed Carlton House, where the Prince of Wales was holding a large garden party to celebrate the success of Fox and 'buff and blue'.

The election was not, however, over. More than 18,500 votes had been counted, and there was good reason to suppose that this total exceeded the number of registered voters. Sir Cecil Wray's application for a scrutiny on the grounds of corruption was granted by the High Bailiff, who declined to make any return for Westminster until it had been completed. Had Fox not taken the precaution to have himself elected also for Orkney and Shetland, he would have been temporarily deprived of his seat in parliament.

Fox immediately challenged the legality of the High Bailiff's decision, but the House voted by a comfortable majority for a scrutiny and continued to defeat Opposition motions to prevent it. On 8 June the High Bailiff was ordered to undertake the scrutiny 'with all practicable dispatch'. Eight months later, when it was evident that while Westminster remained unrepresented nothing constructive was being achieved, the Opposition renewed its complaints. Pitt's majorities wilted and finally withered. On 3 March the government was defeated, the scrutiny abandoned, and Hood and Fox were officially returned for Westminster. The still uncompleted scrutiny had, by this time, detected 316 false votes: 107 for Fox, 106 for Hood, and 103 for Wray.

For Pitt the exercise was a damaging fiasco. It is understandable that he should have been tempted by his overwhelming majority in the House of Commons to exact the maximum penalty from Fox, but the stubborn pursuit over a period of eight months in the face of the growing concern and finally the opposition of his friends seemed to show a distressing lack of magnanimity and imagination. It was certainly an early indication of his lack of understanding of his fellow men and his dangerous capacity to lose touch with the feeling of the House. Pitt had come to power with the aid of the King and the East India Company, but the election results showed that the greater influence had been the wave of favourable public opinion in the counties and the largest boroughs where the contest could be considered, by standards of the period, open. Pitt's decision to fight an open election at Cambridge instead of retaining his safe seat for Appleby was a public assertion of his independence of patronage or favour and his rejection of faction. He could not afford to alienate the independent members. They would, as always, vote irregularly and as they wished, but if they were neither neglected nor offended they would sustain the government when they were most needed. In Pitt, the Crown and the people, as represented by the independent interest in parliament, had discovered a unifying champion.

This form of political partnership did not, however, allow Pitt the power or freedom that his great victory in the general election might be thought to have given him. His repudiation of party obliged him to invite ordinary members of parliament to accept or reject his legislation on its merits. The King, too, remained uncommitted to Pitt's proposals for reform. He was prepared to allow him to bring them forward, but he would not exert his influence to have them passed into law. This lack of guaranteed interest or favour involved Pitt in a series of defeats and the postponement or renunciation of some of his most cherished plans.

Some measure of executive solidarity was urgently needed. Pitt's was the fourth ministry in two years. Frequent changes of government and the failure, through incapacity or lack of parliamentary consent, of successive administrations to come to grips with the country's formidable problems had created a shocking legacy of accumulated debt and overdue legislation. The most crucial issues, demanding immediate attention, were the regulation of the East India Company and the threat of national bankruptcy. The first was accomplished by a new India Bill introduced in July. The second required the radical revision of taxes and trade. The revival of the national credit could not be achieved by legislation alone, but remedial measures were urgently needed to halt the rapid decline to insolvency.

Pitt's second India Bill was introduced on 6 July. Compared with the Bill prepared by Burke and Fox it had the inestimable advantage of having the approval, though it was not enthusiastic, of the Directors of the East India Company, with whom its main provisions had been discussed in January. The Company was to be ordered by a board of control consisting of six privy councillors, nominated by the King and, in contrast to Fox's proposals, subject to change with any change of ministry. The Board would have access to all the Company's papers and dispatches, and no orders would be sent to India without the Board's approval. In emergencies, the Board might transmit orders direct to India. The Governor-General and his council in Calcutta were given absolute authority over the three provinces in matters of foreign policy, and none of the Governors was permitted to declare war or engage in a treaty liable to lead to war. British subjects were to be answerable for their behaviour in India to the courts in Britain. The Company retained all patronage—the appointment to offices in India including that of Governor-General—subject to powers of removal by the King, the Board, or the Directors. Some attempt was also made to curb the speculation and

134

corruption that had made it possible for officers to enrich themselves while their company faced financial collapse. Pitt had made concessions to the East India Company in order to obtain acceptance for his Bill from the Proprietors and the Court of Directors, but the new Board of Control nevertheless took over the government of all British territories in India. By vesting the power of appointment to the Board of Control in the King, Pitt had removed the government of India from any taint of faction. In debate Fox complained bitterly that the Board would be a party of ministers responsible to the Crown and not to parliament, but it was a poor argument that failed to convince anyone who remembered his own proposals. The Bill was passed, with amendments, and became law on 13 August. The single serious weakness of the design, the failure to give the Governor-General powers to overrule his Council, was amended two years later. With minor changes this sytem continued in operation for more than seventy years.

The first members of the Board of Control were Pitt, Dundas, William Grenville, Lord Sydney, Lord Mulgrave, and Lord Walsingham. Dundas, who presided at most of the meetings, rapidly made himself the government authority on Indian affairs, and Pitt was content to entrust them to him. He needed to free himself for matters better suited to his particular talents: the reform of the economy and the reorganization of civil administration.

The country's economic condition at first appeared to be bordering on catastrophe. The National Debt had reached an unprecedented figure, approaching £250 millions, almost double what it had been at the end of the Seven Years' War and nearly twenty times the annual revenue from taxes.[185] The annual interest on government borrowing, some two-thirds of the total revenue, automatically produced an annual deficit which, in turn, was funded by further borrowing resulting in increased interest and an even greater deficit. If national bankruptcy were to be averted, this inexorable progress must be halted and then reversed. There were three methods by which Pitt could hope to master the situation: by increasing taxes; by cutting government expenditure; and by stimulating trade. It was clear from the outset that he would be obliged to employ them not as alternatives but as complementary parts of a single policy. The printing by governments of devalued currency had not then become an acceptable alternative to an economic policy. Nor was the delay inseparable from administrative change considered adequate excuse for inactivity.

The gravity of the situation demanded nothing less than a reconstruction of the country's economy, and in his design Pitt deployed all the powers at his command to provide both short-term relief and a solid foundation for permanent solvency. He was, above all, determined to avoid the error that had destroyed all his predecessors' attempts to stabilize the economy: commitment to a long war. It is ironical that a minister of such peaceable intentions should have been responsible for engaging his country in the longest war in its history.

Proposals for raising revenue by the conventional means of introducing additional taxes, or raising those already levied, were customarily announced in the Chancellor of the Exchequer's annual budget, and valuable time must be lost before they produced any effect. Moreover, the massive weight of tax needed could not be presented to the House of Commons in one package without the risk of stimulating opposition strong enough to repudiate the entire policy. Pitt therefore gave priority to those measures that would raise the least controversy and produce the quickest effect, concentrating his effort on the more efficient collection of tax and the prevention of evasion. His first target was the smugglers, and the weapons, already forged by previous administrations, were conveniently at hand. Trade in contraband goods had grown during the years of war with America until it was estimated to exceed twenty per cent of imports, and the East India Company believed that the illegal trade in tea approximated to the quantity passing through customs at authorized ports of entry. Reports of a Commons committee set up by the coalition government recommended the strengthening of laws against smuggling but concluded that the most effective deterrent would be a reduction of duties 'to make the temptation no longer adequate to the risk'.[186] In the short term, the resulting loss in revenue must be made up by the increase or imposition of other taxes, but it was reasonable to suppose that a general expansion of trade and increased home consumption following the reduction in price would, in time, compensate for much of the loss.

Pitt's previous discussions with the East India Company had brought him into contact with the tea merchants and he listened with care to their objections and suggestions. His Bill, introduced in June 1784, became law in amended form on 20 August. The varied duties on tea, averaging 119 per cent, were reduced to a uniform twenty-five per cent on value. There were, of course, complications: stocks proved to be inadequate, and the wealthiest smugglers banded together to force up prices in the auction rooms; but Pitt, with the active co-operation of the East India Company and the merchants, crushed or circumvented all attempts to break his policy. Within five years the quantity of tea passing through customs at the lower rates of duty had doubled, the smugglers' trade in tea had been stunted, and the finances of the East India Company improved. A graduated rise in the window tax * had more than compensated for the loss in revenue. At the end of the first year the Exchequer had benefited by an additional £200,000.

The success of this measure persuaded Pitt to extend the principle to duties on wines, spirits, and tobacco. The trade in contraband was not, of course, eliminated, but supported by more stringent penalties and a strengthened revenue service. Pitt's policies had by 1792 augmented the annual revenue by some £3 millions, of which the greater part was attributable to duties on increased consumption.

Pitt's proposals for direct taxation were more controversial, though few of them were new. He did not attempt a concentrated assault on wealth, preferring to spread a number of taxes thinly over a wide range of goods, possessions, and services. This policy, much criticized by historians and modern economists, provides evidence of his qualities as a politician. A single tax, although more efficient and simpler to collect, would have created a focus for opposition in parliament; but the series of smaller taxes allowed him room to concede any that raised too great a storm of protest without endangering his budgeted revenue. He has been accused of 'tinkering with the economy', but by this means he was able, during the years of peace, to make minor alterations without serious opposition.

---

* Contrary to popular belief, the tax levied on the number of windows in each house was neither invented nor introduced by Pitt. It was first imposed in 1697 and finally repealed in 1851. Though ridiculed by historians (and made to seem ridiculous by the number of bricked-up windows still visible in England) it was easily administered, difficult to evade, and, after Pitt's withdrawal of the tax in 1792 from houses with less than seven windows, a direct form of taxation which bore equitably upon those best able to pay it. It was, in time, both fairer and easier to assess than the modern rating system, though this cannot be considered a recommendation.

137

It is undeniable that some of his tax proposals were misconceived: he was obliged to abandon his intention to tax coal in 1784, and the taxes on linens and calicoes, and on female servants, in 1785. This last made him the butt of many ribald verses and cartoons illustrating his apparent lack of enthusiasm for the company of women. Most unpopular of all, the shop tax, which Pitt agreed to amend, and four years later to repeal, caused minor riots in London where his effigy was burnt in the streets. Such a reaction to his taxation policy was rare. On the whole, although resisted in form by the Opposition in the House of Commons, his new taxes, and the increases on those already exacted, were accepted, with reluctance, as necessary medicine. The objects taxed, mainly but not exclusively the possessions or pleasures of the rich, included bricks and tiles, gold and silver plate, imported silk, men's hats and ladies' ribbons, perfumes and hair powder, horses and carriages, sporting licences, and bachelors (according to the number of their servants).

This increase in revenue by changes in taxation was accompanied by a detailed but gradual reduction of government expenditure. Pitt excelled in the field of administration, and he possessed the patience to carry out radical reforms over a period of years so that their effects did not fall precipitately upon government servants. The principle upon which his reforms were founded was his belief that government administration, the functions of the civil service, should not be left in the hands of amateurs rewarded by fees, but should be directed and carried out by trained and salaried professionals. He aimed for a massive, long-term, reduction of expenditure which could be achieved only by fundamental reorganization. He employed two methods: the amalgamation of offices, with a consequent reduction in staff; and the gradual abolition of those profitable sinecures which had been used to purchase political allegiance. It was characteristic of Pitt's shrewd judgement that he did not attempt to accomplish his aims by aggressive legislation, the bludgeon so eloquently advocated by Burke and guaranteed to provoke opposition in sufficient strength to threaten the principle. The abolition of sinecures would be costly: compensation of £700 a year for life was paid to each of the auditors of the imprests who were dismissed in 1785; but the savings, once made and paid for, were permanent. Whenever he could afford to wait, Pitt's economies were accomplished for him by the death of the sinecurist, whose position was not again filled. Pitt was content to wait thirteen years until the death of Horace Walpole enabled him to abolish the grandiose but unproductive office of Usher of the Receipt of the Exchequer and to replace it by an efficient Stationery Office under proper control.

Pitt's administrative reforms were detailed and complex, and not all were successful. In spite of his patience and moderation, there were occasions when, obstructed by power and influence, he was obliged to compromise or withdraw. An example was his support of John Palmer, whose proposal to revolutionize the inefficient and vulnerable postal service by the introduction of fast mail coaches in the charge of armed guards offered obvious improvements in the service for which substantially increased charges might be made. Pitt, impressed as much by the benefit to the revenue—urgently needed to replace the coal tax which he had been obliged to withdraw—as by the increased efficiency and security promised by Palmer's scheme, introduced it, without adequate consultation, in June. He reckoned without the opposition of Anthony Todd, whose family had controlled the operations of the Post Office for more than thirty years, and of one of the joint Postmasters-General. In the ensuing struggle, Pitt, who had given the new service the full support of the Treasury, was not helped by Palmer's intractability and evident ambition or by the administrative irregularities revealed by an official examination conducted between 1787 and 1790. The mail coach system survived, but its author did not. After five years of bitter argument, involving the dismissal of the Postmaster-General, a Commission of Enquiry, and Pitt's being challenged to a duel by young Charles Grey, Palmer was pensioned off for £3,000 a year. Todd, who had lost his battle against the mail coaches, had already accumulated a fortune of £100,000 from his office as Secretary.

Pitt's decision to withdraw his support from Palmer has been condemned as desertion. This is a convenient adornment to similar accusations concerning Warren Hastings and Dundas, but there is no evidence that anyone thought of it in that light at the time. In fact Pitt did not agree to the dismissal of Palmer until 1792, eight years after his first employment, and after the Commission of Enquiry had produced convincing evidence of the financial mismanagement of Palmer's organization. The pension granted to him, though not princely, was equal to that attached to the Clerkship of the Pells, awarded to Barré in 1784 *, and more than double the salary of a

* See p. 126.

Treasury Commissioner. This incident, though minor in the long history of Pitt's administration, was an important early test of his powers. He learned from it that the reform of established institutions could best be achieved through discussion and persuasion, not by the issue of directives.

Cuts in government expenditure, and the increased revenue from customs duties and taxes, converted the annual deficit into a surplus. In the first eight years of his administration Pitt raised the revenue by £6 millions, nearly fifty per cent of the annual receipts in 1783, the greater part of which had come from the increased yield on expanded trade encouraged by his reductions in indirect taxation. Having laid the foundations of his system to produce a surplus of income, Pitt turned his attention to the more formidable problem of the nation's capital debt. Funded long-term liabilities amounted to the unprecedented sum of £243 millions; and in addition to these funded loans, commonly known as the National Debt, there were short-term, unfunded debts, mainly incurred by the ordnance and the navy in anticipation of revenue, amounting to some £14 millions. The interest on these temporary debts was paid from sources of revenue not already allocated to the National Debt and was not guaranteed.* Pitt determined to fund the floating, short-term debts, and to maintain a steady flow of surplus revenue into a separate sinking fund to liquidate part of the National Debt. The funding of the floating debts, undertaken over a period of two years in order to avoid flooding the market with new government stock issues, gave Pitt the opportunity to proclaim the apparently paradoxical theory that the government would benefit from offering higher rates of interest.[187] Lord North, in a desperate attempt to reduce the burden on the revenue, had borrowed at three or four per cent interest; but in order to do so in an open market where six per cent could be obtained he had been obliged to offer £150 of stock at three per cent and £25 of stock at four per cent for every £100 borrowed. The capital debt was thus hugely increased and the government paid interest at artificially low rates on sums that were never received by the exchequer. By funding the floating debts at five per cent Pitt avoided overloading the capital debt. He calculated that improved revenues could support the payment of the higher rates of interest.

* Payment of interest (and in some instances, repayment of the principal) on the National Debt was 'guaranteed' as a first charge on specific revenue funds.

The establishment of a sinking fund to reduce the National Debt appeared at first less practicable and even more incongruous, but by the beginning of 1786 Pitt was able to forecast a revenue surplus of £1 million which he proposed to use to redeem capital loans. The method he chose owed much to the advice of Dr Richard Price, a friend and protégé of Shelburne's, whose *Appeal to the Public, on the Subject of the National Debt* had been published in 1772. The kernel of Price's theories was the use of compound interest to develop capital. He chose an arresting example as illustration: 'ONE PENNY, put out at our Saviour's birth to 5 *per cent* compound interest, would, before this time, have increased to a greater sum, than would be contained in A HUNDRED AND FIFTY MILLIONS OF EARTHS, all solid gold.—But if put out to *simple* interest, it would, in the same time, have amounted to no more than *seven shillings and four pence halfpenny.*' [188]

In December 1783, shortly before Pitt took office, a parliamentary commission had reported to Lord North that the National Debt must be reduced by the creation of a fund 'appropriated and invariably applied' from the surplus of income produced by increased revenue. On 30 September 1785 Pitt wrote to Wilberforce that he was 'half mad with a project which will give our supplies the effect almost of magic in the reduction of debt'. [189] That project was the application of £1 million annually, at compound interest, to a sinking fund.

Pitt's plan, evolved after correspondence with Dr Price [190] and lengthy discussion with his own advisers, was a masterpiece of simplicity requiring no more than a consistent annual surplus of £1 million to guarantee the liquidation of the National Debt. This sum, administered by a commission created for the purpose, was to be applied to the purchase of government stock, giving preference to any that stood below par. The stock required was not to be redeemed or cancelled but would continue to earn interest which, in turn, would be used for the purchase of further stock. To the principle of consistent annual saving was thus added the multiplying factor of compound interest. Pitt's Bill to give effect to this magic remedy was passed in May 1786. In the following eight years the commissioners received £8 millions with which they bought more than £10 millions of stock. It was calculated that within thirty years the fund would be earning interest at the rate of £4 millions a year.

There was, of course, a major obstacle: the full benefit of the scheme could not be achieved without a consistent surplus of revenue. This was attainable in time of peace, though there were deficits in 1785 and 1787, and by 1792 it appeared that the system was securely established. It was, however, vulnerable, unless the burden of taxation were to be greatly increased, to pressure when unexpected expenditure produced a deficit. Pitt secured the sinking fund, by Act of parliament, as inviolable. It therefore happened that in years of deficit the government borrowed money at a high rate of interest in order to enable the commissioners to purchase stock bearing a lower rate. This was acceptable only if it was occasional. The longest war in British history, imposing strains on the British economy unparalleled even at the height of the war with America, made nonsense of the system.

Pitt, at the age of twenty-four, took charge of a national economy that was staggering under a weight of debt, automatically made heavier each year by increasing loan interest, towards bankruptcy. In eight years he succeeded in halting the process and reversing it. His achievement was, by any standards, remarkable. The instruments he chose were not original: they were designed by Adam Smith, and Richard Price, or they were hammered out in conversation with advisers from methods used or advocated by previous administrations; but he made use of them, in combination, to create a practicable pattern of retrenchment and recovery that was his own, and he did not feel obliged to make public acknowledgement of his debt to the theories of others.

The national recovery could not have been accomplished without a substantial increase in trade. Pitt had far-sighted plans for the expansion of trade with America and Ireland by the reduction or rationalization of duties and restrictions, and negotiations were opened for commercial treaties with Spain, Portugal, France and Russia. The gesture towards Ireland raised a storm of protest from British manufacturers, and the Navigation Laws which protected the merchant service and indirectly secured the manpower of the navy proved to be an insurmountable obstacle to any agreement with America. It was, perhaps surprisingly, the French who were most anxious to make terms. Pitt, who believed in employing the best man available without regard to his political allegiance, chose William Eden as his negotiator. It was the beginning of a long association, valuable to both men, that was also to have an important part in Pitt's private life.

William Eden was fifteen years Pitt's senior. An experienced and shrewd politician, he had also proved himself, as a Commissioner of Trade, Commissioner to America, and Vice-Treasurer of Ireland in the previous Whig administrations, an able administrator. He had been a determined opponent of the new government, particularly during the period of Pitt's struggle to negotiate a settlement with Ireland,* but his personal ambition and hunger for recognition were greater than any ties of friendship or party. His political patron, the Duke of Marlborough,† had given him a clear indication of his own attitude: 'the more the late Members of Opposition keep together, the more the present Government will be embarrassed—But that does not seem to me to be a good reason for keeping together. I should hope that they would not keep together, but that some of the late Opposition who are Men of Business, would think it for the good of the Country to offer their assistance and come over, or be Rats if you please.' [191] This point of view was respectable among those who believed that they owed their first loyalty to the Crown and the elected government. Eden's desire for advancement acted as a sharp spur to him in the recognition of his public duty. In September 1785 he began to correspond with Pitt to obtain a government appointment.

Pitt's reaction was favourable. His administration was not overloaded with men of great ability and there could be no doubt that Eden, a professional and tried 'man of business', would be a useful acquisition. It would also be worthwhile to remove him from the ranks of the Opposition. Senior members of his government were, however, less than enthusiastic. The right of independent members to support measures on their merits, and the convention that administrators, men of business, should make their abilities available to the King and his government without regard to party, were not questioned; but Eden had been a politician of faction, a close associate of Fox, and the friend of North. He was turning his coat, and Pitt's colleagues regarded him with mingled suspicion and

* See pp. 149–161.

† George, 4th Duke of Marlborough (1739-1817), held the nominations for the constituencies of Heytesbury and Woodstock, which Eden represented in 1774 and from 1778 to 1784.

143

contempt. Eden's appointment to a senior political post would undoubtedly have created serious dissension in the Cabinet. After careful consideration, Pitt entrusted to him the negotiation of a trade treaty with France. It was an assignment, carrying the rank and salary of a minister, for which Eden was admirably fitted.

Eden left for Paris at the end of March 1786 and in spite of the complexity of the negotiations, exacerbated by the opposition of leading statesmen of both countries to any form of commercial agreement, concluded a treaty signed at Versailles on 26 September. It was, moreover, a treaty so triumphantly favourable to Britain as to astonish even the most aggressive opponents.

The purpose of the treaty was the settlement of duties to allow the principal products of each country to be exported, with the minimum of restriction, to the other. In return for low rates of duty on oil and vinegar, the reduction of the duty on wines to the lowest rate then charged on the wines of any other country, reciprocal levies on such common products as textiles, pottery, and saddlery, and an agreement that either country, while it remained neutral, might carry goods freely during a war in which the other was engaged, the French accepted special concessions for Ireland and the exclusion of silk from the treaty and thus from Britain. The apparent concessions obtained by France were illusory. There was nothing to prevent Britain from further reducing the duties on Portuguese wines, without any similar reduction for the French, and it was later accepted that Spanish wines might be dutiable at the same rate. The agreement on the carrying trade was unlikely to benefit the French since the possibility of Britain's being engaged in a war that did not also involve France was remote; but it was possible, even probable, that Britain might remain aloof from a war in Europe that engaged France. Where reciprocal duties applied, it seemed certain that British manufacturers would gain the greater profits. The exclusion of French silk, on the other hand, protected the hand-weavers of Spitalfields who would have been ruined by direct competition with Lyon. Most important of all, the treaty opened to British manufacturers a market which, as Adam Smith had pointed out ten years earlier [192], was eight times as populous as the American Colonies and, because of its proximity, able to trade three times as fast.

Pitt congratulated Eden on an outcome 'far beyond our most sanguine wishes', and Dundas described the treaty as 'the greatest boon the Manufacturers ever received'. Even Lord Sheffield, whose friendship with Gibbon was partly responsible for his profound distrust of Pitt, could not discover 'a single advantage the French have gained.' [193] The combined opposition of Fox and Burke attracted little honest support in the House of Commons. Fox seemed unable to distinguish between commerce and foreign policy, or trade from alliance. Burke's hatred of the French was already developing into mania. In the debates on the treaty Pitt turned on them the full power of his disdainful logic.

Fox was bitterly aware of his loss of power, his failing influence, and his agonizing difficulties in keeping his followers together. As usual, his desperation led him into increasingly immoderate arguments and the obstinate defence of indefensible postures. He insisted that trade with France implied the subjection of Britain in foreign affairs; that the commercial advantages lay with the French; and that France was 'the natural political enemy of Great Britain'.[194] He was wrong, and his theories, though asserted with his customary vehemence and skill, impressed his audience more with his determination to oppose for opposition's sake than by any merit of his argument. Realizing that he would be accused of being 'possessed by illiberal and vulgar prejudices against France,' [195] he sought to turn this to his advantage by an appeal to patriotism. It was ill-chosen ground on which to challenge Chatham's son. In the negotiations with France Pitt believed, correctly, that he bargained from strength. His continuing and realistic distrust of France was expressed privately to Eden: 'Though in the Commercial business I think there are reasons for believing the French may be sincere, I cannot listen without suspicion to their professions of political friendship.' [196] Pitt's economic policy was founded upon the preservation of peace, and good trading regulations were doubly effective instruments; but they were never allowed to dictate his foreign policy or to diminish his vigilance. He rejected with scorn Fox's repeated assertion that France was unalterably Britain's enemy, but he did not, at any time, assume that trade was testimony of friendship.

XI

Failure in Ireland
1784-1785

THE RESUSCITATION of the national economy, requiring a comprehensive expansion of trade, was associated with a problem that did not yield to logic: the settlement of Irish grievances. It was one with which Pitt was already familiar through his connection with the Grenvilles * and his own brief experience as Chancellor of the Exchequer. Nothing in this experience should have given him reason to suppose that the Irish problem was open to a quick solution, but Pitt's natural optimism was even stronger than his growing self-confidence. He was determined to right old wrongs, and believed that in doing so he would heal old wounds. He sadly underrated the ability of the Irish to reopen scars and nourish new abrasions.

There could be no doubt that the Irish had ample cause for complaint. For ninety years after the Revolution of 1688, Ireland had been kept in a political and economic straitjacket, dependent upon England and under harsh regulations imposed by the Westminster parliament. More than three-quarters of all Irish land was owned by English or Anglo-Irish Protestant families, many of them absentee landlords whose rents were remitted to England. Intermittent

* Pitt's first cousins, the 2nd Earl Temple and William Wyndham Grenville, had been, respectively, Lord-Lieutenant of Ireland and Chief Secretary in the Shelburne administration.

146

rebellion had resulted in ever more oppressive and intolerable laws designed to deprive the Catholic population of their already scant rights of citizenship. Catholics, who outnumbered the Protestants by little less than two to one,[197] had been excluded from ownership of freehold property, from parliament, from the professions, and from juries. Ireland's most important product, wool, was permitted to be exported only to England, and the manufacture of woollen goods was forbidden. Irish ships might not be used for trade with British colonies. Ireland's subsistence depended upon the cultivation of the potato, and the export of linens which the English were unable to make. In these unfavourable conditions, and despite mass emigration to America and recurrent famine, the population doubled. Nowhere else in Europe were the people reduced to poverty so abject as that of the Irish.

The Dublin parliament, subservient in all but its right of taxation to the parliament at Westminster, was no more than a debating chamber, and the majority of its three hundred members was nominated by Protestant landowners whose allegiance to Britain was purchased by rewards of titles or land. The management of the government was in the hands of 'undertakers', a self-seeking and generally corrupt group of men of business who held the real political control and owed loyalty to no one but themselves. They had achieved a satisfying position of power without responsibility, and successive Lord-Lieutenants, English representatives of the King and his government, found any plan to reform the system obstructed and destroyed. The English Viceroys, and thus the parliament in Westminster, were regularly outmanoeuvred. Ireland had come to be governed, in practice, for the benefit of neither the English nor the Irish people, but for the personal profit of a select group of Protestant Irishmen who manipulated disparate factions into occasional and uneasy alliance in order to maintain their own positions of power.

Ireland, bound to England by political and economic regulations designed to deny to the population any hope of prosperity or those few rights enjoyed by the peoples of other western European countries, was itself split into separately dissident factions, differing in their grievances and seldom united in their aims. The country nevertheless presented an impression of general and dangerous unrest which troubled successive British ministries. During the

American war, when all available troops were needed for service elsewhere, Ireland's vulnerability to invasion from France led to the formation of the United Volunteers. Organized by Henry Grattan and his patron, James, Earl of Charlemont, the Volunteers declared their undivided loyalty to the King; but they also proclaimed their resolution to obtain freedom of trade and the independence of the Irish parliament. The British government, at war in Europe and floundering in a quagmire of disaster in America, was in no position to resist the demands of eighty thousand trained and armed volunteers drawn from the Protestant governing class but claiming to represent all Ireland. The lesson, from America, that armed rebellion extracted concessions not obtainable by loyalty and reasoned discussion, was well understood in Ireland.

Lord North regarded the problem with sincere anxiety. The shrewdest of politicians, he was also one of the most incurably supine, believing from long experience that the most intricate questions, when ignored, tended either to disappear or to answer themselves. The solution to the Irish problem, as it was presented to him during his last ministry, seemed unlikely to be found either in inaction or in any practicable action he could devise. Any attempt to reform the Dublin parliament was attacked by the undertakers as yet another authoritarian regulation of Irish government; North's efforts in 1778 to remove some of the restrictions on Irish commerce raised a storm of protest from manufacturers and traders in England, who feared competition; and the influential Protestant landowners were united in their alarm at the threat of any concession that might result in the taxation of their Irish rents.

The Opposition made the most of North's discomfiture. Fox was in correspondence with Grattan, though he was careful not to commit himself to the support of precise claims. Irish legislative independence required the repeal of the Declaratory Act of 1719, the formal instrument asserting the supremacy of the Westminster parliament. Grattan insisted upon the parallel with the situation in America: 'Can England cede with dignity? I submit she can; for if she has consented to enable his majesty to repeal all the laws respecting America, among which the declaratory act is one, she can with more majesty repeal the declaratory act against Ireland, who has declared her resolution to stand and fall with the British nation, and has stated her own rights by appealing not to your fears but to your magnanimity.' [198] It was a persuasive argument, but it offered no corrective for the venality of the legislature; nor did Grattan suggest any change in the method of nomination of the executive appointed in London. Again following the American example, Irish demands for commercial freedom were reinforced, in 1779, by non-importation agreements.

The reaction of George III to such threatening behaviour was characteristically resolute and unimaginative. He was convinced, as it proved rightly, that 'opening the door encourages a demand for more',[199] and reprimanded his liberal-minded Lord-Lieutenant, John Hobart, Earl of Buckinghamshire, for his preoccupation with Irish affairs and neglect of proper duty to his own country. To the suggestion that the anti-Catholic laws should be repealed, he replied that no man in his senses could consider such a dangerous course of action.[200] This was his sincere conviction, rooted in his interpretation of his duty to the British Constitution, from which he never departed. It was the rock against which all possibility of a lasting Irish settlement foundered, and Pitt's failure to appreciate its strength was later to put an end to his effective career.

The British government was nevertheless obliged to make concessions. In 1779, Irish ships were permitted to sail as British, and in the following year Ireland was granted freedom of trade with the colonies and the right to export wool and glass. A modest gesture was made to the Catholics by allowing them to inherit property and to own long leaseholds. In 1782, the Rockingham government finally repealed the Act of 1719 and freed the Irish parliament and courts from the jurisdiction of Westminster. This renunciation of power, greeted in Ireland as a victory and accepted in England as a necessary evil from which peaceful co-operation might blossom into a genuine unity of purpose, served further to confound consitutional issues already sufficiently confused. The legislature was freed, but the executive remained fettered to England. The Lord-Lieutenant continued to act for the King, who was the head of the executive for both countries. In theory the Dublin parliament assumed a constitutional position similar to that of the parliament in Westminster, the legislature acting as a proper check against the power of the executive. In practice the situation was very different. In England the King's choice of ministers was restricted to those acceptable to the House of Commons, but there was no requirement that those same ministers must be acceptable, also, to the Irish parliament. Nor was it likely that the two parliaments could ever have been brought to agree upon any choice made by the King, even had it occurred to anyone that the Irish should be consulted. The King and his ministers continued to be represented in Ireland by the Lord-Lieutenant and his Chief Secretary, both appointed in London and both responsible to an English government dependent upon the English parliament. The Irish believed that their legislative freedom was largely an illusion, and they were right. To redress the balance and impose the desired check against executive power, Irish politicians adopted the attitude most natural to the national temperament: permanent opposition.

Pitt, understanding that the commercial expansion essential to Britain's recovery depended upon freedom of trade, determined to remove the artificial restrictions that impoverished the Irish population. His policy was unsentimental: a prosperous Ireland would provide an increasingly valuable outlet for British manufactures; and a settled Ireland would cease to be a magnet to Britain's enemies in any future European war. He was aware that settlement involved more than trade: there could be no peace in Ireland until the Dublin parliament was reformed and the Catholic population relieved of the disabilities which deprived the majority of representation or executive responsibility; but Pitt was not yet ready to advocate such radical measures and neither of the two parliaments was ready to receive them. The freeing of trade was the logical first step, and the unrest reported from Dublin made some conciliatory gesture a matter of urgency.

In February 1784 Pitt sent his friend Charles, 4th Duke of Rutland, to Ireland as Lord-Lieutenant. With him, in the crucial post of Chief Secretary, went one of Shelburne's ablest disciples, Thomas Orde. Five years Pitt's senior, Rutland had been his loyal supporter since he first entered parliament, and had been among those who had accepted office in Pitt's first derided ministry. He was better known for his love of lavish entertainment than for any ministerial capacity, but he applied himself with earnest thoroughness to his complex task and displayed greater intelligence and competence than might have been expected of him. Orde, a barrister, and member of parliament for Aylesbury since 1780, had been Secretary to the Treasury in Shelburne's government. At thirty-six, he had acquired a just reputation for exceptional ability, diligence, and discretion. He could be relied upon to judge from evidence, to report with accuracy, and to negotiate with patience. Shortly after his arrival he was returned, by government influence, as member for Rathcormack, becoming the British government spokesman in the Irish parliament.

Rutland found Ireland in turmoil. The disastrous harvest of 1783, and the self-inflicted wounds caused by non-importation agreements, had aggravated the already intolerable poverty of the mass of the population, embittering relations between Irishmen of different classes, persuasions and faiths, and providing an excuse for explosions of violence. This climate of general unrest was particularly favourable to the Volunteers, who had come to be regarded as representative of the nation. The King was petitioned to dissolve the Irish House of Commons, which, Rutland admitted, did not 'bear the smallest *resemblance to representation*'.[201] By August he was also forced to confess that Dublin was in a state of riot. 'This city', he wrote, 'is in a great measure under the dominion and tyranny of the mob. Persons are daily marked out for the operation of tarring and feathering; the magistrates neglect their duty; and none of the rioters—till today, when one man was seized in the fact—have been taken, while the corps of volunteers in the neighbourhood seem as it were to countenance these outrages. In short, the state of Dublin calls loudly for an immediate and vigorous interposition of the Government.'[202] Sir Joshua Reynolds declined the invitation of the Duke, his friend and patron, to visit Dublin, and the great actress, Sarah Siddons, 'came away in a terrible fright'. Already, in June, Rutland had given Pitt a judicious warning: 'Whatever advantages Great Britain may be enabled and disposed to grant, let them be declared to be *conclusive*. I must press this idea on your mind as . . . indispensable, for as long as anything indefinite remains for expectation to feed upon this country will never be at peace.'[203] Fox had expressed a similar view two years earlier in a letter to his lifelong friend, Richard Fitzpatrick, then Chief Secretary for Ireland*: 'My opinion is clear for giving them [the Irish] all that they ask, but for giving it to them so as to secure us from further demands.'[204] It was the continuing and realistic misgiving haunting all British ministers that

* Fitzpatrick was appointed Secretary-at-War in the Fox-North coalition formed in April 1783.

whatever might be granted, the Irish would demand more. Another century passed before the British fully understood the Irish capacity for altering a demand while it was being conceded. Rutland, after less than four months in office, predicted that 'Without a *union* Ireland will not be connected with Great Britain in twenty years longer.' [205]

Pitt corresponded regularly with Rutland, but it is plain that he attached greater importance to the information, opinions and advice he received from Orde. The Chief Secretary was experienced and outspoken, and his sources of intelligence were reliable and well organized. It was Orde who first reported to Pitt that the French were intriguing in Ireland to provoke insurrection, and it was also he who stated, without prevarication, the opinion that widespread disorder was being stimulated to divert attention from a design that embraced not merely the removal of all commercial restrictions and the reform of parliament, but also the 'entire dissolution of the subsisting connection with Great Britain', supported by foreign arms. He expressed his views freely to Pitt, often using language that made his advice read more like instruction. 'I shall repeat', he wrote on 25 August 1784, 'what I have always said—everything tends to strengthen the sentiment: act towards Ireland with the utmost liberality consistent with your own safety; it must in the long run be the wisest policy. But you are nevertheless not to forget that you must not hope to please everybody, and specially in this country. You will have regard only to what in reason *ought to satisfy* Ireland, and not to what will satisfy her.' [206]

Pitt accepted such lectures with admirable humility. 'No man', as Wilberforce was to bear witness, 'ever listened more attentively to what was stated against his own opinions.' [207] In fact, Pitt was always inclined towards more generous concessions, and more hopeful of finding an ultimate solution, than either Orde or Rutland, but he was, as he told Orde, 'completely open to information and to reasoning'. He understood, as did few of his contemporaries, the additional complications arising from the legislative independence of the Irish parliament. 'We must,' he wrote to Orde in September, 'in order to make a permanent and tranquil system, find some line according to which the Parliaments of the two countries may exercise the right of legislation, without clashing with each other on the one hand, or, on the other, being encumbered by the necessity of actual and positive concert on every point of common concern.' The Dublin parliament must, he was convinced, be reformed, but he was equally certain that reform could not be so extensive as to include the opening of the doors of the Irish House of Commons to Catholics. This, he believed, would forfeit the goodwill of the Protestants to such an extent as to threaten his own government. Indeed, he proposed to employ reform as a means of destroying the growing threat of Protestant and Catholic uniting against Britain as the common foe. He was quick to learn the lesson that, deprived of a unifying enemy, the Irish would inevitably discover an excuse to fight among themselves. He was aware that a more representative parliament might be less acquiescent to the rule of a British executive, but declared that 'Government can never be carried on to any good purpose by a majority in *Parliament alone,* if that Parliament becomes generally and lastingly unpopular. We may keep the Parliament but lose the people.'

With 'some reservations arising from actual circumstances', he believed that 'the system of commerce should be so arranged as to extend the aggregate wealth of Great Britain and Ireland to its utmost limit, without partiality or preference to one part of the Empire or the other.' He proposed as 'fundamentally requisite' that part of the increased wealth of Ireland should be used, in the future, to relieve England of the heavy burden of Irish defence. It was not his intention to put the Irish 'in possession of any actual force capable of being at any time independently exerted under their separate direction', but rather to obtain a contribution from increased revenue towards the cost of maintaining the army in Ireland and, more particularly, employing the navy to safeguard Irish shores.

He was, as always, hopeful, but his summary of the situation shows that he had not allowed himself to be blinded to the realities. 'After all,' he wrote,

the great question remains: *What is it* that in truth will give satisfaction and restore permanent tranquility to Ireland? Much has been given already, and the effect has been very little in proportion. It will be idle to make concessions without having good ground to think that they will attain their object. I believe what you have stated to be perfectly just—that the internal poverty and distress of the country is the radical cause of all the discontent that prevails. Of that the cure must be gradual and probably slow. The present effect, then, of any measures we can take will be to remove or diminish the pretexts of discontent, and to eradicate the cause of it must be the work of time; or at most, if we remove some things that are perhaps not barely pretexts but real additional causes of discontent, *that one great cause* will still remain. In such a situation we can only hope to prevent in some degree the most mischievous effects of what we cannot at once remove, and must trust to the progressive operation of a prudent system to extinguish at length the seeds of the disorder.[209]

Pitt's understanding of the problem was sensitive and astonishingly quick. He was not, however, beguiled by self-confidence or optimism, or persuaded by the evident urgency of the situation, into imposing an over-hasty and ill-considered solution. He examined the evidence with exemplary patience, and approached the delicate negotiations with caution. At the end of October, Orde, who had visited London in June, returned, accompanied by John Foster, Irish Chancellor of the Exchequer, and John Beresford, Chief Commissioner of the Revenue. They found Pitt and Dundas 'very liberal in their ideas', but both Foster and Beresford, whose influence in the Irish parliament might be decisive, protested against the intention to levy any specific sum as a contribution to defence costs. They proposed, instead, that the amount should be left to the goodwill of the Irish government. Even if Pitt could have been persuaded to agree to this, he knew that there was no possibility of its being accepted by the Westminster parliament. Nothing less than a guarantee would satisfy the House of Commons whose assent to the commercial concessions must be expected to be grudging. Pitt swiftly put forward a compromise: the amount of the contribution should be assessed annually, rising or falling according to the upward or downward movement of Irish revenues. This early form of index-linking could be most easily achieved by using the Irish hereditary revenue, a fund accumulated mainly from customs and excise receipts, as a regulator. Taking the average receipts of the past five years as a base, the annual surplus, a fair reflection of Ireland's increased prosperity resulting from more favourable commercial conditions, would be paid as contribution towards the costs of defence.

The plan was ingenious, and, Pitt believed, acceptable to both parliaments. Writing to Rutland in January 1785, he restated his prescription for a settlement: 'In the relation of Great Britain there can subsist but two possible principles of connection. The one, that which is exploded, of total subordination in Ireland, and of restrictions on her commerce for the benefit of this country, which was by this means enabled to bear the whole burden of the empire; the other is what is now proposed to be confirmed and completed, that of an equal participation of all commercial advantages, and some proportion of the charge of protecting the general interest.' [210] He emphasized, once again, 'the essential point of reciprocity'. There were, of course, details to be determined, but it was settled that the principal proposals should be put before the Irish House of Commons on 7 February. In return for the reduction of duties on all manufactures and produce of both countries to the lower rate levied by either, and the freedom to import from Britain and export into Britain the merchandise of other countries without increased duties, the Irish should remit the receipts of the hereditary revenue, exceeding a sum to be agreed, to the British exchequer as a contribution towards defence costs. If these propositions were accepted by the Irish parliament, Pitt was confident that they would be approved by the House of Commons at Westminster.

In spite of Orde's best endeavours, Pitt's proposals, contained in ten resolutions presented to the Irish parliament on 7 February, were received with such general disfavour that nothing but a last-minute concession, hastily cobbled together without reference to London, could save them. A new resolution was added, providing for the peacetime annual surplus of the hereditary revenue over the sum of £656,000 to be paid for defence, but only after the Irish budget had been balanced. In time of war the surplus would be handed over without regard to the balancing of the budget. Pitt, while acknowledging Orde's difficulties, confessed that he wished 'any consequence had been risked rather than such a concession'. He added, with commendable restraint, 'It is and will be considered here as rendering the whole effect of the surplus *precarious*. Everything, therefore, depends upon having the difficulty removed.' [211] In fact, as he was well aware, the new resolution passed by the Irish parliament annihilated the certainty of any Irish contribution for the foreseeable future. Whatever the benefit to Irish prosperity and the growth of the hereditary revenue, increased expenditure would be allowed to absorb the surplus. One might, as Fox suggested, trust everything to the generosity of the Irish, but not much to their prudence.

Pitt realized that there was no possibility that the resolutions, with the Irish amendment, would pass the House of Commons, and he contemplated the postponement of debate in the English parliament until some mutually acceptable form of guarantee could be devised. Failure to inform the House officially of the passing of the resolutions in Ireland would, however, have cast suspicion on the entire project. On 22 February, therefore, he presented his proposals to parliament, asking for approval in principle but suspending discussion of the details until some satisfactory alternative to the disputed resolution should have been found by the Irish government. Once more, he proposed a solution. If the Irish would remove the resolution making their contribution dependent upon a balanced budget, and acknowledge in the form of an Address the need for an economical administration, he would accept an altered form of commitment that, falling short of an absolute guarantee, nevertheless confirmed, in mutual trust, the principle of contribution from increased prosperity. With some reluctance the Irish government accepted this application of thin veneer to a rejected piece of political craftsmanship the construction of which remained unchanged, and Orde returned to London to polish the details. He anticipated that the work would be completed in 'a matter of a few hours'.

On his arrival, Orde found the situation sadly changed. Throughout the negotiations Pitt had assumed, and with some justification, that if the Irish parliament could be brought to agree to terms he had himself framed, his majority at Westminster would ensure the assent of the British House of Commons. He had taken the wise precaution of consulting manufacturers. Their evidence, given to the Committee of Trade in February, showed a general approval of his commercial proposals and confidence that, in conditions of equal competition, the British manufacturer would show himself 'equal, if not superior, to any other manufacturer of the world'.[212] As late as 3 March, when the debate was reopened by Pitt in the House of Commons, he gave no sign that he anticipated any organized opposition from commercial interests. He knew enough about the Irish character to understand that delay might prove fatal: while others might have welcomed a period of discussion to consolidate agreement, the Irish were more likely to use the time to discover fresh grievances, the adjustment of which would be made a condition of a bargain already settled.

Pitt announced that in the continuing absence of evidence of powerful and concerted opposition from manufacturers, he would ask the House to adopt the resolutions in one week's time. That day he wrote to the Duke of Rutland, full of confidence that 'there is nothing now remains that ought to be an obstacle between the two countries', and expressing the opinion that the opposition at Westminster would be 'less than was threatened'.[213] He appears either to have failed to notice, or to have chosen to ignore, ominous signs of growing resistance to his intentions, roundly declaring to Rutland, 'All the objects of commercial equality will be attained, and the whole arrangement will be established on the best of all securities, the mutual satisfaction of both countries.'

Pitt's plan for Ireland sprang from a sincere desire to redress injustice and to provide for the commercial prosperity of both countries. His determination to obtain a contribution towards the costs of defence was less an indication of an obstinate sense of propriety than a realistic assessment of parliamentary opposition. Having arrived, as he believed, at a satisfactory compromise, he was confident that he could carry the Westminster and Dublin parliaments with him. An abridged draft of the report of the Committee of Trade, published at the beginning of March, contained evidence taken from manufacturers that effectually disposed of the Opposition's most telling arguments. Behind the scenes, however, two astute men of business, Lord Sheffield and William Eden, were organizing a concerted assault on the Irish resolutions. They chose their ground, the threat to the Navigation Act,* shrewdly. Apart from its automatic involvement of the powerful West Indian interest in parliament, no aspect of the Irish proposals was more likely to rouse the opposition of the independent members. The co-operation of manufacturers was essential, and Eden and Sheffield set about

---

* The principal Navigation Act, passed in 1651, directed that English imports must be carried in English ships or in ships of the country from which the goods originated. All English exports must be carried in English ships. These regulations were also applied to British territories overseas. Although modified in detail by a succession of subsidiary Acts, the principle of protection remained unchanged, securing for Britain the greater part of the carrying trade of the world, and also an unrivalled merchant marine from whose ranks trained seamen were drawn for the navy in time of war.

canvassing their support. They found an able champion in Josiah Wedgwood, the great potter. In evidence to the Committee of Trade on 19 February, Wedgwood had said, 'I certainly apprehend that there might be danger of a competition in time, in their own [the Irish] and every foreign market. I should think we were safer if earthenware was allowed to be imported free of all duties into both countries, because the Irish would not have then so much encouragement to begin to set up Potteries, or to establish them to any extent.' [214] Less than three weeks later he was elected first chairman of the executive committee of the newly formed Great Chamber of the Manufacturers of Great Britain, pledged to oppose the Irish resolutions.

From 12 March, when Wedgwood published an official notice of the manufacturers' opposition, he campaigned tirelessly to have the resolutions amended. His connection with Eden and Sheffield was well known, and the deputations from the Chamber of Manufacturers were received by Pitt with frigid reserve. Wedgwood's earlier pronouncements in favour of freer trade now laid him open to a charge of playing factional politics. For his part, Wedgwood believed that manufacturers who failed to oppose the resolutions, did so from motives unconnected with either political conviction or patriotism. As he wrote to Matthew Boulton *, 'The button maker makes buttons for his majesty, and so he is tied to his Majestie's minister's button hole. In short the Minister has found so many buttons and loop holes to fasten them to himself, that few of the principal manufacturers are left at liberty to serve their country.' [215]

There can be little doubt that Wedgwood and the manufacturers who joined him in opposition to the resolutions had been misinformed, perhaps deliberately, by Eden and Sheffield. Pitt's declared intention was the equalization of duties at the lower rate, and not, as the manufacturers were encouraged by the opposition press to believe, equalization by an increase in duties on British goods. Eden put forward another, more scrupulous argument: '. . . it is idle and visionary to place on the same commercial ground two neighbouring

---

* Matthew Boulton (1728-1809) FRS, engineer, silversmith, and merchant in cut steel and ornamental brassware; formed a partnership with James Watt (who had perfected his steam engine seven years earlier) in 1775; associated with Wedgwood in the Great Chamber of Manufacturers, and the Cornish Mining Company, and provided cut steel and silver mounts for Wedgwood's jasperware.

nations, when the one is highly taxed, and the other comparatively without taxes.' [216] He might justly have added that Irish labour was cheap. What Wedgwood failed to understand, or ignored, was Ireland's lack of the natural resources required to support a pottery industry. The theoretical establishment of competitive potteries in Ireland at some unspecified date in the future played no great part in the opposition to the Irish resolutions, but Wedgwood's intervention was material. The Chamber of Manufacturers, founded at Wedgwood's instigation and maintained by his energy, commanded attention and respect, though it was unable to attract the active support of many of its most important members, and its sudden appearance in opposition, when Pitt was anxious to avoid any obstacle or delay, was sufficient to raise serious doubts in the minds of members of parliament who were uncommitted.

During the next five months, confronted by the opposition of disparate but powerful interests, Pitt was obliged to accept the gradual erosion, by compromise, of his design. Under increasing pressure from the East India Company, the West Indian interest and the Chamber of Manufacturers, the resolutions were increased in number and complexity until their chances of acceptance in Ireland were seriously jeopardized. Wedgwood wrote jubilantly to Joseph Priestley, 'We have already convinced the Minister of 16 capital errors in the arrangement, and he has now brought into the house a system so much altered, and with so many additions, that it may be called a new one, and in every one of these, new alterations and amendments are made before it passes. . . . If they do at length get through the house, Ireland cannot acknowledge or know them; and as she declared she would not admit an alteration of a single iota, she must certainly herself reject what one party is labouring so hard to provide for her and the other to keep from her.' [217]

By the end of May, when the propositions were passed in the House of Commons, they had been increased to twenty. Pitt described the amendments and alterations as 'perfectly consistent with the general tenor of the resolutions', but he was aware that his plan had been mutilated. The existing monopoly of the East India Company was reaffirmed; the West Indies were protected against the competition of French or Spanish colonial products carried in Irish ships; the Navigation Acts were to be binding on Ireland; no duty on commerce between the Kingdoms was to be less than ten and a half per cent; and the defence contribution was to be paid regardless of the Irish national budget surplus or deficit. Even with these fundamental alterations it is possible that the resolutions might have been rejected by parliament, but their passage was eased by the behaviour of leading Opposition speakers. Knowing that the final decision must be taken in the Irish parliament, Fox and Sheridan concentrated their attack on one of the most important amendments insisted upon by their own party: the application of the Navigation Acts to Ireland. This, they claimed, violated the independence of the Irish legislature and reduced Ireland to a subordinate state. Fox chose, also, to condemn the compulsory contribution to defence costs. 'I will not', he declared, barter English commerce for Irish slavery: that is not the price I would pay, nor is this a thing I would purchase.' [218] His refusal to believe that any system of unfettered trade between the two countries could be to their mutual benefit might have been forgiven: he scoffed openly at the work of Adam Smith, which he admitted he had never read, and he had no knowledge or understanding of commercial affairs. What sickened many among his audience in the House of Commons was his transparent hypocrisy and his irresponsible determination to inflame prejudice for his own political advantage.

The disfigured resolutions were passed by the House of Commons on 31 May and approved by the Lords in July. On 13 August, Orde's motion to present them was passed by the Irish House of Commons by nineteen votes, a majority so meagre as to make their defeat in full debate certain. Two days later the measure was withdrawn. For Pitt, the rejection of the Irish proposals was a personal failure. He had justified the plan to Rutland on the principle 'that for the future the two countries will be to the most essential purposes united', [219] and it is clear that he hoped that unity of interest and purpose might lead to a permanent and voluntary fusion. Rutland had already forecast * that without union the connection with Ireland would not last twenty years. Wedgwood, who had so earnestly opposed the resolutions, nevertheless favoured union. On 3 October 1785 he wrote to his friend, Richard Lovell Edgeworth †, 'An Union of Ireland with Great Britain will doubtless meet with strong opposition on your side of the

* See p. 152.
† Irish author, and father of the novelist, Maria Edgeworth (1767-1849).

water. . . . And yet however forbidding the plan may at first sight appear, I do not utterly despair that . . . mature reflection may in the end convince your nation of its *equity*, and even of its *expediency;* for the fundamental principles of political and commercial connection seem to me to require an equal participation of burthens as of benefits, of expenses as of profits.' [220]

The opposing sides in the argument, fought with such bitterness in Britain, were not, in principle, so far apart. Their divisions were ruthlessly exploited for political advantage. A far-sighted and liberal design, thwarted by malice, prejudice, and ignorance, ended in acrimony and deepened distrust. Pitt was disappointed but not despondent. As he wrote to Rutland, 'We have the satisfaction of having proposed a system which I believe will not be derided even by its failure, and we must wait times and seasons for carrying it into effect. . . . I believe the time will yet come when we shall see all our views realized in both countries, and for the advantage of both.'

A great opportunity had been lost, but, in spite of Fox's triumph and Pitt's disappointment, the immediate effects were negligible. As the benefits from freedom to trade with the colonies, granted in 1780, worked through the economy, Irish national finances were strengthened. This improvement coincided with a considerable advance in agricultural prosperity and provided a stimulus to manufactures. For a few years the Irish problem was muffled. It remained in ambush for the future.

In British manufacturing towns Fox was fêted as a hero, but in parliament he gained nothing. Pitt's failure had not been the consequence of defeat in the House of Commons, nor would such a defeat have led to the fall of his government. His general policies of economic and administrative reconstruction and reform commanded substantial majorities; his exceptional ability and sincerity were scarcely questioned. Above all, Pitt was trusted, as Fox was not. The manufacturers, glad to employ Fox as their spokesman, showed no desire to champion his claims to be Prime Minister, and even Eden was convinced that Pitt's position was secure. 'The Ministry', he wrote loftily to his brother on 8 September, 'wants Strength & Consistency & effect.' [222] Before the end of the month he was negotiating to join it.

161

XII

Burdens of Affection
1785-1786

THE FAILURE of Pitt's proposals for the settlement of Ireland was not
the only defeat he suffered in 1785. His hounding of Fox through the
Westminster scrutiny had been halted by the Commons in June,*
and two months earlier his motion to introduce some measure of
parliamentary reform had been lost by seventy-four votes. On this,
as on the Irish proposals, Pitt had made his personal conviction and
purpose clear. Both were defeats of ministerial policy, and frustrated
cherished hopes. Both demonstrated the ability of the House of
Commons to curb ministerial power. Three times in 1785 Pitt's great
majority in the House was enfeebled or wiped out in votes on
measures to which he was personally pledged: and yet he continued
to command massive majorities for his general policies, and much
government business was accepted without debate. This implied
contradiction is explained partly by the exceptional independence of
the House of Commons elected in 1784, and partly by Pitt's failure,
which appears to have been deliberate, to gather round him a
personal party or following comparable in strength with those of Fox
or other contemporary leaders. Though he was often hurt to find his

* See pp. 132–133.

friends absenting themselves from important debates, or voting against him, he seldom allowed their public defections to interfere with his private friendships. Wilberforce and Bankes, in particular, made a habit of opposition. Pitt encouraged his personal friends to vote according to their own opinions, but in return he would not use his own power in any way he considered improper or illegitimate on their behalf. To obtain the passage of a measure to which he was pledged he was prepared to use 'such means as are fairly in the hands of Ministers',[223] and never hesitated to employ the accepted methods of appointment and promotion or to apply pressure; but he set himself a standard of incorruptibility and remained indifferent to claims on his patronage.

Pitt's Parliamentary Reform Bill was presented to the Commons on 18 April 1785. When, at the King's request, Thurlow had approached Pitt in July 1783 to discover whether he was prepared to take office, Pitt had told him that he was 'personally pledged to Parliamentary Reform' on principles that he had already explained, and that he would support it 'on every seasonable occasion'.[224] The Westminster Scrutiny debates, and two long negotiations to find an Irish settlement, had delayed his preparation of a new Bill, but in December 1784 he called the Reverend Christopher Wyvill, the leader of the influential Yorkshire Association, to Downing Street and told him of his intention to 'put forth his whole power and credit, *as a man* and *as a minister, honestly* and *boldly* to carry a plan of reform'.[225] Wyvill began immediately a campaign to rouse support in the country. Pitt was concerned to secure the active co-operation of his Cabinet colleagues and the approval, or at worst the neutrality, of the King. Government ministers and close supporters were warned that failure would endanger the credit of the Prime Minister and the stability of the administration. The campaign was not a success. The country failed to respond to Wyvill, and the expected flood of petitions did not materialize. George Rose and William Wyndham Grenville were unalterably opposed to reform and, at the end of the debate, voted against it. The King agreed to refrain from applying influence to have the Bill rejected but continued implacable in his private opposition to it. 'Mr. Pitt', he wrote on 20 March, 'must recollect that though I have thought it unfortunate that He had early engaged himself in this measure, yet I have always said that as He was clear of the propriety of the measure He ought to lay his thoughts before the House; and that out of personal regard to Him I would avoid giving any opinion to anyone. . . .' [226]

Pitt's Bill was a model of moderation. The changes he proposed were modest and to be effected gradually. Thirty-six small boroughs were to be purchased, by consent of the electors, and their seventy-two seats distributed among the counties and the city constituencies: the franchise was to be extended to forty-shilling copyholders and long leaseholders. Other minor and less controversial proposals referred to the proper regulation of elections. There was little in the Bill to offend the most conservative susceptibilities, and yet it was known that the majority of independent members opposed any change. Fox contrived to vote for the Bill while, at the same time, condemning it in detail, and most of his supporters voted against it. The motion was lost by 248 votes to 174. Pitt withdrew from the struggle and the reform of parliament was postponed for nearly fifty years.

In spite of these rebuffs and disappointments, Pitt remained confident and hopeful. He described the end of the parliamentary session as 'in all respects triumphant', and declared 'everything essential to the strength of our Government as satisfactory as possible.' [227] He was buoyed up by an indomitable optimism, a vigorous conviction of coming achievement that dispelled doubt. His failures had not damaged his reputation. He had set out to attract 'the approbation of impartial and independent men', and in the greater part of the legislation put before parliament he had succeeded. Lord Mansfield's opinion of him was judicious: 'He is not a great minister: he is a great young minister.' [228] Gibbon, a loyal Whig with no reason to love Pitt, viewing events in Westminster from Lausanne, admitted that 'A youth of five-and-twenty, who raises himself to the government of an empire by the power of his genius and the reputation of virtue, is a circumstance unparalleled in history, and, in a general view, is not less glorious to the country than to himself.' [229]

Pitt's popularity in the country was generally unimpaired, though the Irish proposals had not endeared him to the people of the manufacturing towns, and he commanded the support of all but the Foxites in the Commons for any government business that did not involve radical change. Most important of all, he was gaining the confidence of the King, who had at first recognized his precocious brilliance as the only practicable alternative to the appalling Fox, but was coming to appreciate his young Prime Minister's integrity and fortitude as much as he welcomed his invariable punctuality. There was little warmth in the relationship, but there was a steady growth of mutual respect and trust that sprang from mutual dependence.

In his first eighteen months of office, Pitt had accomplished an astonishing amount of work. In August 1784 he had rented a house on Putney Heath, to which he rode out for occasional nights and working weekends, and he succeeded in spending a few days at Brighton with friends, but he could not find time to visit his mother at Burton Pynsent and most of his time was spent at Downing Street. His sister, Harriot, paid frequent visits to him there, and in 1785 made her home at Number 10 to act as his hostess. She was vivacious, witty, and charming, and William was devoted to her. As Pretyman's wife Elizabeth observed, 'twas a pity she was his *Sister*, for no other woman in the World was suited to be his wife.' [230] Pretyman was a constant companion. He had become Pitt's private secretary, and his wife formed a close friendship with Harriot.

Pitt's letters to his mother during this period contain little of interest about either public affairs or his private life. 'I only wish', he wrote to her, 'you were a nearer spectator, and that I could have an opportunity of telling you all you would like to hear.' [231] He was concerned to learn from Harriot that Lady Chatham was obliged to make severe economies at Burton Pynsent because her pension was constantly in arrears. The difficulty was temporary, and while he was using his position to have the arrears paid and to regularize payments for the future, he assured her that 'The income of the Lord of the Treasury and Chancellor of the Exchequer together will really furnish more than my expences can require; and I hope I need not say the surplus will give me more satisfaction than all the rest, if it can contribute to diminish embarrassment where least of all any ought, I am sure, to subsist.' [232] His combined salaries amounted, at the time, to a net figure of a little less than £7,000, but these, too, were in arrears, and he was spending freely. Lady Chatham's financial problems continued to cause her anxiety, and in 1786 Pitt transferred to his mother the lump sum of £5,800, raised by a loan on Burton Pynsent from his loyal friend Thomas Coutts, on which he paid the interest. [233] This anticipated the unpaid remainder of his inheritance from his father, and represented his entire capital.

Pitt was about to involve himself in a transaction that contributed largely to his effective bankruptcy. In August 1785 he was offered the chance to buy a country property, Holwood House, in Kent. By the standards of the period, and of the mansions of his friends, the house was small. Built of brick already mellowed by some two hundred years of English weather, it contained six main bedrooms, a drawing room, dining room, and study, with adequate servants' quarters. With Downe farm, which was also for sale, the estate of two hundred acres with the house, farm buildings and some stock could be purchased for about £7,000, little more than a year's salary. He raised £4,000 on mortgage and bought both properties. Had he been content to enjoy his estate unaltered, he might have been able to maintain it from his earnings and even to repay the debt; but he had inherited his father's delight in 'improvements' and to the Pitts improvement involved enlargement. During the following eight years he bought parcels of land and indulged what he aptly described as 'my passion for planting'. Walks and vistas were cut through existing woodland and shrubbery, and, with sadly characteristic indifference to antiquity, he had part of Caesar's Camp, a large and unusually fine example of Iron Age earthwork fortifications, levelled and planted. Great numbers of labourers were employed, and Pitt liked to work with them 'for whole days together, undergoing considerable bodily fatigue, and with so much eagerness and assiduity, that you would suppose the culture of his villa to be the principle occupation of his life'.[234] Friends invited to stay at Holwood were encouraged, if not expected, to join him in uprooting shrubbery, clearing brambles, and preparing sites for planting.

The Holwood furniture, much of which had been acquired with the house, was solid, elegant mahogany of the period, and all the curtains and chair covers in the reception rooms were green or green and white striped cotton. The same colour predominated in the furnishings at Downing Street and was evidently Pitt's personal choice. The house commanded extensive and magnificent views of the Kent countryside. It was, as Pitt told Wilberforce, 'a most beautiful spot, wanting nothing but a house fit to live in',[235] but he admitted that its purchase was a foolish extravagance. He moved in on 5 November and it was not long before his financial troubles became so pressing that he was obliged to ask for advice. He turned to Bob Smith, the banker and member of parliament for Nottingham, who had been among his circle at Goosetrees and had become one of his intimate friends.

Pitt displayed a genuine indifference to money worthy of his father; but where Chatham had little, if any, understanding of economies and overspent largely through ignorance, Pitt's extravagance seems to have sprung from a curious mixture of optimism and neglect. Pretyman's efforts to induce him to examine his accounts were unavailing. Nor, as Pitt's secretary and intimate friend, does he appear to have succeeded in protecting him against the depredations of tradesmen. Bob Smith uncovered unpaid bills amounting to nearly £8,000. He also discovered that Pitt was being systematically robbed by servants and suppliers. The bills for provisions, which included one for thirty-four hundredweight of meat delivered in January 1785 when Pitt was regularly dining out, exceeded, as Smith told his cousin Wilberforce, 'anything I could have imagined . . . I can scarcely conceive a private house in the Kingdom where such a quantity of provisions, as charged, could be consumed.'[236] Even more serious was the astonishing record of Pitt's expenditure on his horses and carriages: nearly £17,000 in 1783-4, and £12,500 in 1784-5.[237] These were costs comparable with those of a substantial racing stable; but Pitt kept no racehorses.

Apparently impervious to Bob Smith's remonstrances, Pitt continued to spend on a scale he could not afford, to offer financial support to his mother, and to raise loans to bridge the widening gap between his income and his expenditure. It is remarkable that the man who initiated policies to rescue the national economy from debt originating in overspending and progressively aggravated by mounting interest on spiralling loans, was undisturbed by his own analogous insolvency. There is evidence that Smith's efforts produced some economies, but they were inadequate and temporary. Pitt's expenditure at Downing Street, £2,848 in 1785, was reduced to less than half that figure in 1787 and only once rose above £1,700 during the next five years; at Holwood the expenses were also halved, but rose again in 1790 when Pitt embarked upon more 'improvements'; and his stables account was similarly reduced.[238] He was, nevertheless, still spending almost twice his income in addition to paying the interest on loans totalling nearly £16,000. He negotiated new loans to repay the old, and was obliged to borrow more to pay the interest. He pledged his expectations as security, and mortgaged his property as he bought it. It was characteristic that he should have refused to take the sinecures enjoyed by his predecessors. He refused, also, to accept loans from his friends or the gift of £100,000 offered by a group of London merchants. He would not fund his debts at public expense, nor would he allow himself to be put under financial obligation to anyone whose interests it was in his power to promote. His reputation for personal integrity was preserved and untarnished. He continued to be cheated by tradesmen and servants. He remained unmoved by the problem, which consequently remained unsolved.

In the midst of his negotiations to buy Holwood he was called upon to use his influence, on Harriot's behalf, with Lord Eliot, whose son, Edward, had been one of Pitt's most intimate friends since their days together at Cambridge and had accompanied him and Wilberforce on their holiday in France in 1783. In August, Edward Eliot's proposal of marriage was accepted by Harriot and gladly approved by her mother and brothers. Lord Eliot, however, made it clear that his financial situation precluded the possibility of his making a suitable settlement on his son, and advised delaying the match until Edward should inherit from his kinsman, Lord Nugent,* from whom he had considerable expectations. Pitt, writing from Downing Street on 8 September, was firm: 'A further delay, such as you now desire, could not I am persuaded be reconciled to the happiness of either of them, or under all the circumstances be productive of any possible advantage.' [239] He suggested a provisional settlement repayable upon Nugent's death, or postponed until that event. It appears that his intervention was successful: Lord Eliot yielded, and the marriage took place on 21 September. A week later Pitt was in Brighton, and in the first week of October he met the honeymooning couple at Salisbury on his way to stay with his mother at Burton Pynsent. Later in the month he had a day's shooting with Bankes in Dorset, 'notwithstanding all the perils of thunder and lightning' but 'attended with no more consequences than a complete wetting'. By 20 October, after a few more days in Brighton, he was back at work in Downing Street. [240]

Edward and Harriot rented a house in Putney, but they spent

---

* Robert, Earl Nugent 1702-88, was thrice married, twice to rich widows. From this comfortable ability to acquire wealth by marriage, Horace Walpole coined the verb 'to Nugentize'.

most of their married life at Downing Street, where Harriot continued to act as hostess for her brother. They paid a number of visits to 'Holly Wood', and Harriot, knowing her brother's dislike of large parties, thought him lucky to have found 'a small House that will not allow of many Visitors'.[241] Pitt was not naturally gregarious: as Wilberforce noted sadly in his diary, 'Pitt does not make friends.'[242] His comment was made in reference to the controversial Irish proposals, but it was true in a wider sense. In private, with any of his small, intimate circle, Pitt was good-humoured, witty, kind and addicted to innocent and occasionally tiresome schoolboy pranks; but in his public life, or with strangers, he appeared cold, haughty and aloof. Even Shelburne, who had been his mentor and friend, wrote to a young man about to have an interview with the Prime Minister, 'I know the coldness of the climate you go into and that it requires all your animation to produce a thaw.'[243] This dichotomy in his behaviour is explained partly by Pitt's touching confession to Wilberforce—'I am the shyest man alive'[244]—and partly by the iron control he exercised over his emotions. Wilberforce confirmed that Pitt's 'great natural shyness (for he was one of the shyest men I ever knew) and awkwardness (French *gaucherie*), often produced effects for which pride was falsely charged on him.'[245]

Hester Chatham was aware of her son's lack of enthusiasm for entertaining and wrote to remind him of his social obligations. Harriot Eliot replied on 28 February 1786 that there were to be 'three or four more Assemblies to *take in every Body* . . . and ye Young World are *very* desirous of it. . . . I hope you will like this Plan, and indeed I believe your having said so much about ye *tristesse* of our Administration made my Brother think of it.'[246] Harriot was expecting her child in September and it was decided that the baby should be born at Downing Street. On 20 September Pitt wrote to his mother, 'I have infinite joy in being able to tell you that my sister has just made us a present of a girl and that both she and our new guest are in every way as well as possible.' But two days later, as he told Wilberforce, Harriot was feverish. On 25th he wrote to Mrs Stapleton, his mother's friend and companion, asking her to judge whether to break the news to Lady Chatham that Harriot was not expected to recover. She died a few hours later.

Pitt was stricken. The depth of his grief alarmed his friends, and the King, who had been charmed by 'this aimiable Lady Harriot

Elliot [*sic*]', admitted, 'I owne I dread the effect . . . on Mr Pitt's health.' Pretyman stated that it was some days before Pitt would see anyone or transact any business except through his secretary. In his anguish Pitt did not forget the needs of his mother and his broken-hearted brother-in-law. On the 26th he wrote to Hester Chatham, 'I will not suffer myself at this most sad moment, my dear Mother, to express my own feelings, which I know are but too deeply yours also. . . . I should not lose a moment, you will believe, in coming to Burton, but I am sure you will approve of my not leaving poor Eliot at this time.' Edward Eliot was inconsolable. He made his home with Pitt at Downing Street, seldom mixing in society and unable to regain the gaiety that had enlivened his friendships and found a ready response in the high-spirited Harriot. On 4 October, the day after the funeral, Pitt went to Burton Pynsent. His mother wept 'inconstrain'd' and spoke continually of her 'beloved daughter'. The baby Harriot was christened at the end of the month, and a few days later Eliot took her to live with her grandmother. The child was, as Hester Chatham told Eliot, 'the most enchanting little thing that ever was'.[247]

Pitt's burdens at this time were intensified by physical pain. By the beginning of the year, a cyst on his cheek, which had first appeared when he was at Cambridge, had grown again and was causing him some discomfort. An operation, originally planned in February, was postponed until the parliamentary recess and carried out by John Hunter * at Downing Street just three days before Harriot's death there. Pitt bore the pain with predictable stoicism, refusing to have his hands bound as was the custom, remaining motionless as he had promised for the six and a half minutes required for surgery, and chiding Hunter for exceeding his estimated time by thirty seconds. He wrote to Wilberforce on 22 September, 'Having yesterday parted with the ornament on my check, and two or three handkerchiefs for the present occupying the place of it, my appearance is better suited for correspondence than conversation.' [248]

Pitt's friendship with Wilberforce had cooled. Throughout the summer session of parliament in 1785, Wilberforce had worked with

---

* John Hunter 1728-93 FRS, Surgeon Extraordinary to George III. One of the most celebrated surgeons and anatomists of the century.

Pitt on the provisions of the Reform Bill, and they had dined together, in London or at Wimbledon, two or three times a week. In the autumn, however, it became clear that Wilberforce's attitudes were changing: he seldom went to the theatre or to Almack's club, and he had become strict in his observance of Sunday as a day of rest. Through the influence of John Newton and Isaac Milner *, Wilberforce had been converted to Evangelicism: the belief that nominal Christianity was not enough. This he expressed in a letter to his sister Sarah in December: 'There is no opinion so fatal as that which is commonly received in these Liberal days, that a person is in a safe state with respect to a future world, if he acts tolerably up to his knowledge and convictions, though he may not have taken much pains about acquiring this knowledge or fixing these convictions.' Later he recalled, 'It was not so much the fear of punishment by which I was affected, as a sense of my great sinfulness in having so long neglected the unspeakable mercies of my God and Saviour; and such was the effect which this thought produced, that for months I was in a state of the deepest depression, from strong convictions of my guilt. Indeed nothing I have ever read in the accounts of others, exceeded what I then felt.' The Evangelicals sought to take Christianity into every aspect of life, and to bring all life within its control. Reaction was later well summarized by Lord Melbourne who, after listening to an Evangelical sermon, remarked,[249] 'Things are coming to a pretty pass when religion is allowed to invade public life.'

In this spiritual crisis Wilberforce considered leaving politics. He wrote to Pitt, and to others of his friends, at the beginning of December, explaining his new-found faith and the consequences of his conversion. 'I told him', he wrote later, 'that though I should ever feel a strong affection for him, and had every reason to believe that I should be in general able to support him, yet I could no more be so much a party man as I had been before.' This was a remarkable piece of self-deception. Pitt had never encouraged the formation of a party, and, among his close friends, Wilberforce's record of failure to vote

* The leaders of the Evangelical movement were Thomas Babington, Zachary Macaulay, Isaac Milner, John Newton, Hannah More, Henry Thornton, John Shore (First Baron Teignmouth), James Stephen and William Wilberforce: a landowner, a slave-owner, the Professor of Natural Philosophy at Cambridge, an ex-slave turned clergyman, a poetess and playwright, a banker, a Governor-General of India, a lawyer and a politician.

171

with him was second to none. Pitt's reply, written on 2 December, reveals the patience and warmth in friendship of which he was capable, and the human emotion he was at such pains to conceal:

My dear Wilberforce,

Bob Smith mentioned to me on Wednesday the letters he had received from you, which prepared me for that I received from you yesterday. I am indeed too deeply interested in whatever concerns you not to be very sensibly affected by what has the appearance of a new era in your life, and so important in its consequences for yourself and your friends. As to any public conduct which your opinions may ever lead you to, I will not disguise to you that few things could go nearer my heart than to find myself differing from you essentially on any great principle.

I trust and believe that it is a circumstance which can hardly occur. But if it ever should, and even if I should experience as much pain in such an event, as I have found hitherto encouragement and pleasure in the reverse, believe me it is impossible that it should shake the sentiments of affection and friendship which I bear towards you, and which I must be forgetful and insensible indeed if I ever could part with. They are sentiments engraved in my heart, and will never be effaced or weakened. If I knew how to state all I feel, and could hope that you are open to consider it, I should say a great deal more on the subject of the resolution you seem to have formed. You will not suspect me of thinking lightly of any moral or religious motives which guide you. As little will you believe that I think your understanding or judgement easily misled. But forgive me if I cannot help expressing my fear that you are nevertheless deluding yourself into principles which have but too much tendency to counteract your own object, and to render your virtues and your talents useless both to yourself and mankind. I am not, however, without hopes that my anxiety paints this too strongly. For you confess that the character of religion is not a gloomy one, and that is not that of an enthusiast. But why then this preparation of solitude, which can hardly avoid tincturing the mind either with melancholy or superstition? If a Christian may act in the several relations of life, must he seclude himself from all to become so? Surely the principles as well as the practice

172

of Christianity are simple, and lead not to meditation only but to action.

I will not, however, enlarge upon these subjects now. What I would ask of you, as a mark both of your friendship and of the candour which belongs to your mind, is to open yourself fully and without reserve to one, who, believe me, does not know how to separate your happiness from his own. You do not explain either the degree or the duration of the retirement which you have prescribed to yourself: you do not tell me how the future course of your life is to be directed, when you think the same privacy no longer necessary: nor, in short, what idea you have formed of the duties which you are from this time to practise. I am sure you will not wonder if I am inquisitive on such a subject. The only way in which you can satisfy me is by conversation. There ought to be no awkwardness or embarrassment to either of us, tho' there may be some anxiety: and if you will open to me fairly the whole state of your mind on these subjects, tho' I shall venture to state to you fairly the points where I fear we may differ, and to desire you to re-examine your own ideas where I think you are mistaken, I will not importune you with fruitless discussion on any opinion which you have deliberately formed. You will, I am sure, do justice to the motives and feelings which induce me to urge this so strongly to you. I think you will not refuse it: if you do not, name any hour at which I can call upon you to-morrow. I am going into Kent, and can take Wimbledon in my way. Reflect, I beg of you, that no principles are the worse for being discussed, and believe me that at all events the full knowledge of the nature and extent of your opinions and intentions will be to me a lasting satisfaction.

Believe me, affectionately and unalterably yours,
W. Pitt.

The two friends met for two hours the next day. 'He tried', Wilberforce wrote, 'to reason me out of my convictions but soon found himself unable to combat their correctness, if Christianity was true. The fact is, he was so absorbed in politics, that he had never given himself time for due reflection on religion.' [250] This was not strictly true. The teaching and influence of Dr Pretyman had left their mark on Pitt, and he was well versed in Christian doctrine and religious argument. The truth, distressing to Wilberforce and therefore rejected by him, was that Pitt was unable to accept the faith or the doctrine on trust, and deployed knowledge, intellect, and debating ability in challenging them. They remained friends, but their friendship was changed. They never again enjoyed the intimacy of earlier days, when they had shared their thoughts, their ambitions, and their laughter. For the future, Wilberforce acted—sometimes voluntarily consulted, but more often importunate and inconvenient—self-appointed, as Pitt's conscience.

As Prime Minister, Pitt had, however unintentionally, become the focus of a party. As the King's minister, his party could not be accused of faction, but membership was not reconcilable with the independence adopted by Wilberforce. Nor were his convictions in harmony with the business of political management. He believed that if Pitt 'had then generously adopted the resolution to govern his country by *principle* rather than by *influence,* it was a resolution he could have carried into success.' [251] That Wilberforce believed this at the time, when he knew from his own close involvement how small was Pitt's personal following, must be considered astonishing; but his declaration was written many years later, after sufficient time for mature reflection. It reveals a preposterous ignorance of the workings of parliament. For all his incurable optimism, Pitt was a political realist. He was capable of misjudging the temper of the House of Commons, and the obstinacy of the King, but he became increasingly a professional in his understanding and exercise of the means of government. Wilberforce, a prey to his galling guilt, might have been torn between idealism and loyalty, but the political doctrine he enunciated was abstract and it is hard to escape the conclusion that he was aware that this was so. For twenty years he pursued Pitt with the demands of his awkward conscience, but it was seldom that he voted against him. Pitt listened to the demands and tolerated his opposition with unfailing patience and understanding. Wilberforce's conversion created a barrier. It was inevitable that, as their styles of living diverged, both should choose new friends; but there was no rift between them. Wilberforce's admiration remained undimmed. Pitt's affection endured.

Before the end of the year, Pitt received news of a connection of far greater public interest than Wilberforce's alliance with the Evangelical movement. It was, as his brother Chatham told him, rumoured that the Prince of Wales had married the twice-widowed Maria Anne Fitzherbert. Sir Gilbert Elliot picked up the same gossip from 'a half-hour's sitting at Lady Palmerston's toilet . . . the report is', he told his wife, 'that Mrs Fitzherbert is, or is to be, at Carlton House; that she was married by a Roman Catholic priest, is to have £6000 a year, and is to be created a Duchess.' By February 1786 the rumours were accepted as public knowledge, and in March Gillray issued a celebrated cartoon entitled *Wife & no Wife* 'designed by Carlo Khan'. This shows the marriage conducted by Burke, dressed in Jesuit robes (a reference to his advocacy of Catholic emancipation) while Lord North, as the royal coachman, slumbers in the foreground. The bride is given away by the Prince's 'dear Charles' Fox.*

In essence, the gossip was true. On 11 December the Prince had written to Fox in shocked denial: 'My dear Charles . . . Make yourself easy, my dear friend; believe me the world will now soon be convinced that there not only is not, but never was, any ground for these reports which of late have so malevolently been circulated.' [252] Four days later he was married to Mrs Fitzherbert at her house in Park Lane. The ceremony was conducted by the Reverend John Burt, an Anglican priest who had been confined in the Fleet Prison for debt. He was paid five hundred pounds for his services. The Prince of Wales and his bride set off for a week's honeymoon at Richmond. Their carriage broke down in deep snow at Hammersmith.

George, Prince of Wales, suffered as much as anyone of his period at the hands of the caricaturists. They bequeathed to history a composite portrait of an obese, spendthrift, drunken lecher, whose vulgarity is preserved for posterity in the unrestrained furnishings of the Brighton Pavilion. The image is lively, and truthful enough to be convincing, but it is as extravagant as its subject. As a young man he was handsome, well-proportioned, witty and attractive: 'brighter than sunshine . . . graciousness personified', a 'most captivating Prince'.[253] He was an energetic horseman, on one occasion riding the 108 miles to Brighton and back in one day. He spoke French fluently, and an early predisposition towards the art and culture of France was enhanced by his friendship and political association with leading Whig Francophiles. The architect Henry Holland, who had

* Another, far more explicit, appeared, showing 'His Highness in Fitz'.

built Brooks's Club for the Whigs in 1776-8, was a leading exponent of a style in decoration derived directly from contemporary France *. At Carlton House, where he began in 1783 a task that was continued for nearly thirty years, he created for the Prince, at stupefying cost, a palace that stood comparison with Versailles. The Prince of Wales was widely ridiculed and condemned as a prodigal dilettante, with a regrettable taste for foreign ostentation. In truth he was a prodigal patron who became a dedicated collector and a genuine connoisseur.

Generous, exuberant and charming, the Prince of Wales enchanted his friends, and gave hope to the ambitions of the Whig Opposition: but he was a sore trial to the King and Queen, to the government, and to his country. As profligate in his affections as he was with his money, his private life was a public scandal and his personal debts a national burden. The King's refusal to increase his allowance or to satisfy his creditors provoked petulant outbursts: 'The King hates me. . . . He won't even let Parliament assist me till I marry. . . . He hates me; he always did, from seven years old. . . . The King has used me ill . . . I never will marry! My resolution is taken on that subject.' Sir James Harris had the greatest difficulty in persuading him that, without the King's permission, which had been refused, he could not leave the country.[254] The Prince's passion for Maria Fitzherbert was no passing infatuation, and it was inflamed by her refusal to become his mistress. He threatened suicide if she would not marry him; he attempted to pursue her when she fled abroad; and he promised to renounce the throne. In spite of these protestations, he must have been aware that nothing he could do would legalize their marriage. Maria Fitzherbert was a Roman Catholic and the Prince was not yet twenty-five. Renunciation of the throne would release him from the anti-Catholic restrictions of the Act of Settlement, but the Royal Marriage Act of 1772 forbade, in law, his marriage without the King's consent before August 1787.

In 1783, when he came of age, the Prince had been given Carlton House, an income of £62,000 a year †, and the sum of £29,000 towards the settlement of his debts. During the next three years he spent £370,000, of which more than £250,000 remained unpaid at the end of 1786. His repeated denials of his illegal marriage, his

---

* *Le style Louis XVI*.
† £50,000 from the Civil List, and £12,000 from the Duchy of Cornwall.

deception of Fox, and his desperate financial straits were dangerous weapons in the hands of the government. Pitt had no wish to use them; but the fortunes of the Prince of Wales had become ravelled in the ambitions of the Opposition, and the possibility of hanging both from the same rope was not one to be disregarded. Meanwhile, with the return of Warren Hastings from India, Pitt faced one of the most painful moral decisions of his career.

XIII

The Trials of Warren Hastings
1782-1795

IN APRIL 1782, the House of Commons had passed a vote of censure on the Governor-General of India, Warren Hastings, and, in response to a request from the government, the Court of Directors issued an order recalling him. The Court of Proprietors, however, exercised their superior powers, withdrew the notice of recall and confirmed Hastings in his position, where he enjoyed the support neither of the government, his Court of Directors, nor his own Council. Seeking simultaneously to reassert the supreme authority of parliament, and to reform the administration of the East India Company, Fox introduced his India Bill *, which gave the King an opportunity, long-desired, of dismissing the coalition government. In doing so he solved his own most urgent problem, but the solution for India remained to be found.

Pitt had not had time to give to any detailed study of Indian affairs. He shared with Dundas, and with Fox, the determination to regulate the East India Company, and his India Bill, passed in August 1784, transferred much of the effective power to the Board of Control, of

* See p. 115–116.

which he was the senior member. It was, however, Dundas who presided over most of the meetings, and it was he who made himself master of Indian policies and Indian patronage. Pitt was content to leave the detailed administration and the formulation of policy to Dundas, whose influence in government and friendship with Pitt grew steadily as the extent of his abilities came to be recognized. After Wilberforce's conversion, Pitt relied more and more upon the advice of Dundas and Grenville, and they provided respectable support in the House of Commons against the formidable opposition of Fox, Burke, and Sheridan. Between Dundas and Grenville there sprang up an intense loathing which blossomed in direct proportion to Dundas's strengthening friendship with Pitt.

Henry Dundas was born in 1742 into a family of distinguished Scottish lawyers *. His father, Lord Arniston, was Lord President of Session from 1748 to 1753, and his half-brother Robert, thirty years his senior, was appointed to the same office in 1760. Henry became Solicitor-General for Scotland in 1765. Nine years later, through the influence of Lord North, he was elected member of parliament for Midlothian and appointed Lord-Advocate. He soon made a reputation for himself as 'a fine manly fellow', outspoken, and 'afraid of nobody'. He was tall and broad-shouldered, with rugged features, 'pleasingly expressive, though tinged with convivial purple', heavy brows, and deep-set eyes remarkable for their 'brilliant and piercing gaze'. He was an effective speaker, in 'his strange barbarous but forcible way': his language was unadorned, and his speeches were delivered in a strong voice and thick Scottish accent that often provoked laughter from his opponents.[255]

He had been a sincere and loyal follower of North's and had declared his intention in February 1782 to leave politics if North fell from power; but he had been among the first to pay tribute to Pitt's 'first rate abilities, high integrity, bold and honest independence of conduct, and most persuasive eloquence'.[256] In Shelburne's administration he had become Treasurer of the Navy, but the Fox-North coalition had removed him from the office of Lord Advocate of Scotland. By then it had become clear that he intended to attach his fortunes to Pitt's. He was ambitious, shrewd, and industrious, and

* His great-grandfather and grandfather were lords of session: his father, half-brother and nephew were, as he was himself, Solicitors-General for Scotland and Lords Advocate.

provided a sturdy buttress to Pitt's authority. In *The Rolliad* he was condemned as unscrupulous and insincere:

> Alike the advocate of North and Wit,
> The friend of Shelburne, and the guide of Pitt,
> His ready tongue with sophistries at will,
> Can say, unsay, and be consistent still;
> This day can censure, and the next retract,
> In speech extol, and stigmatize in act. . . .[257]

The resignation of Warren Hastings, and his return to England, gave the Opposition plenty of opportunity to renew this charge, for it was Dundas who had moved the vote of censure on him three years earlier.

Although there is some evidence that his opinion of Hastings was changing, there can be no doubt that Dundas continued to look upon him as a threat to the authority of the Board of Control. In October 1784 he wrote to Grenville, deploring the fact that Hastings remained at the head of the civil administration, and four months later he informed Lord Thurlow, who refused to co-operate with him, of his intention to replace Hastings by Lord Macartney.* [258] He had not then received Hastings's official resignation, written in January. Macartney declined the post of Governor-General and sailed for England. The Governor-Generalship of India had become a job that no one who knew anything of it wished to take.

Hastings, who had fought his way out of a position of siege, beleaguered by enemies in government, in the Company, in his own Council, and in the territories he administered, had hoped for better things from Pitt. The India Bill of 1784 had failed to invest in him the prerogatives he knew to be essential to the effective exercise of responsibility: the authority to overrule his Council, and the powers of Commander-in-Chief. Both were granted in 1786 to Cornwallis, who had less need of them but would not accept the post without them.

On 11 December 1784, Hastings wrote a long letter to Pitt.[259] Part self-justification and part an exposition of the principles on which

---

* George, Baron (later 1st Earl) Macartney, Governor of Madras 1780-86; subsequently ambassador extraordinary and plenipotentiary to Peking.

future policy should be founded, it was his last attempt to influence the government; but he did not wait for an answer before sending in his resignation *. 'My health & Bodily Strength', he wrote, 'are no longer equal to the charge of this Government and unless compelled to retain it by authority which I may not resist, I shall have resigned it before this letter can attain its destination.' He denied the charge of insolvency laid against the East India Company, calling attention to the size of the debt he had inherited in 1772, cleared within two years and shortly afterwards converted into an even larger balance, the expenses borne during the war with France, and the resulting debt which was still less than half the annual income of the Company. He declared that the government of India had been

a scene of continual Warfare between its constituent members; & every infirm Servant has enlisted in one or other party. This may be naturally supposed to extend & enlarge the gifts of Patronage and the multitudes of recommendations from high authority in England augmented the evil. The civil establishments are greatly overloaded with incumbents who all claim the right of subsistence.

He deplored the dependence of his administration upon changing governments and policies: 'this state distant beyond the reach of more than general instruction and liable to daily contingencies which require both instant discussion & a consistency of system cannot be ruled by a Body of men variable in their succession, discordant in opinion, each jealous of his Colleagues and all united in common Interest against their ostensible leader.'

Hastings made a plea for both supreme authority and independence of action for the 'first executive' in India who would need two qualifications only: 'an approved integrity & a Judgement impracticable by [impervious to] the byass of external Opinion'. 'This may be', he admitted, 'an unpopular Doctrine and repugnant to our domestic Constitution . . . I affirm only what ought to be.'

It is probable that both Pitt and Dundas, appreciating his achievements, agreed with him: it was clear that there must be a supreme authority in India who could act, in emergency, without consultation with the Board of Control in England, and that authority

* There appears to be no evidence that Pitt ever replied to it.

was given without undue hesitation to Cornwallis and his successors; but Dundas was not prepared to give it to Hastings. He had been charged, and not without cause, with tyrannical behaviour and megalomania. He was widely regarded, unjustly, as the cornerstone of corruption. His policies, the distillation of a lifetime's experience and dedicated exertion, must be entrusted to others.

Warren Hastings landed at Plymouth on 13 June 1785, after a voyage of four months, much of which he had spent in writing a self-applauding account of the state of Bengal. He met Pitt on the 17th. The encounter was not reassuring: Pitt was courteous but cool, and there was no mention of the honours Hastings was expecting. Three days later Burke gave notice in the House of Commons of his intention to move certain resolutions regarding 'a gentleman just returned from India'. Hastings was unperturbed. He was well received by the King and accepted the formal thanks of the Court of Directors. With his wife Marian, who had preceded him to England and caused something of a social stir in her fine silks and splendid diamonds, he visited old friends, took the waters at Cheltenham, and negotiated for property. His fortune was estimated at £74,000 [260], a sum that does not indicate corruption on a grand scale, and puny beside those of others of the Company's servants whose positions had been junior and opportunities less.

Hastings and his wife were regularly lampooned and libelled by the cartoonists, and he was hurt and angered by the imputations against Marian, but he was accustomed to being reviled and believed his position to be too secure to be overturned either in parliament or out of it. Two signs should have warned him that he was vulnerable: the offer of the Governor-Generalship to his enemy, Macartney; and the government's ominous silence on the matter of honours. Hastings was aware, as were the King and every member of Pitt's ministry, that his achievements merited the award of a barony, and even a marquessate—provided it were in the Irish peerage—would not have been considered overindulgent. It was unfortunate that the most energetic advocate of his elevation should have been Lord Thurlow. More serious was the fact that most of Hastings's friends and protagonists at East India House had either retired from the service or died.

While Hastings waited with ill-concealed impatience for his just reward, Burke was preparing the case against him. In this he was abetted by Sir Gilbert Elliot and William Windham, both recent converts to his views, and by Philip Francis, Hastings's most implacable enemy, who had worked with Burke since the censure motion of 1782. Francis had been appointed, from outside the Company, to the Bengal Council in 1772 and, with Colonel George Monson and General John Clavering, had at once set himself the task of forming a majority against Hastings and thwarting his policies. He was intelligent, able, eloquent, bigoted and vicious, believing that all servants of the Company were corrupt and that Hastings was motivated entirely by personal ambition, avarice, and lust for conquest. He was blind, and succeeded in blinding others, to the realities of Company policy, the frequent and inescapable choice between conflicting evils, and the necessity for urgent decisions based upon local customs and conditions and in the face of extraordinary contingencies. He refused to accept responsibility for Company policy towards the Indian rulers, and denied the need for any such policy. Using trumped-up evidence from the most dis-creditable sources, Francis conspired to have Hastings charged with corruption. The charge failed. The two main witnesses were accused of forgery, found guilty by the Supreme Court, and executed. It is remarkable that Hastings, who in his years as Governor-General published his acceptance of gifts amounting to £300,000, all of which he gave to the Company for its use, was indicted by Francis, who published none of the gifts he accepted and returned to England with a great, but undeclared, fortune. Clavering, having heard that Hastings had offered the government his resignation, declared himself Governor. The Supreme Council ruled this declaration illegal, and Hastings was confirmed in his appointment. Shortly afterwards, both Monson and Clavering died.

The continuing quarrel between Francis and Hastings was brought to a point at a critical moment in the Maratha war, when Francis refused to support the Governor-General's military measures in spite of an earlier undertaking to do so. Hastings, aware of Francis's much-publicized claims to supplant him as Governor-General, wrote him a minute accusing him of a breach of faith, obstruction and subversion. 'I judge', he wrote, 'of his public conduct by my experience of his private, which I have found to be void of truth or honour.' Francis, as Hastings intended, challenged him to a duel. They met on 17 August 1780. Francis was wounded and soon afterwards resigned. He sailed for England in December. His last powerful enemy in Council removed, Hastings was freed to defeat the enemies of the Company in India. 'I have power', he wrote, 'and I will employ it.' He did so, heroically, waging war with pathetic resources against overwhelming odds, and winning victory and peace. These achievements, in such forbidding circumstances little short of miraculous, were not enough for the prejudiced and ignorant among his fellow countrymen in England. They affected to believe that government could be exercised without the use of power, that war could be waged without suffering, and victory achieved without injustice.

The resignation of Francis had relieved Hastings of his most formidable enemy in India, but only to transfer him, his festering vindictiveness convincingly clothed in experience at first hand of the evils he denounced, to England. To protect himself, Hastings sent home, as his personal agent, Major John Scott. No choice could have been less suitable. Scott combined, in immoderate proportions, unquestioning devotion with misplaced activity. Ignorant of politics, he was also totally lacking in judgement. His reports to Hastings, always sent in duplicate and on occasions multiplied to as many as ten copies, radiated unjustifiable confidence and abounded with pronouncements ranging in depth from the superficial to the puerile. The provision of a parliamentary seat supplied him with some social standing, but it gave him also a forum for his ill-digested opinions and an opportunity to display his unrivalled capacity for injudicious statement and ill-timed intervention. On the first day of the new session of parliament, in January 1786, Scott rose and challenged Burke to move the resolutions of which he had given notice in the previous June.

Burke, undeterred by the advice of senior members of the Opposition, who had met a few days earlier at the Duke of Portland's and urged him to drop his motion of censure, responded by demanding the rehearsal of the resolutions of May 1782. He suggested that Dundas, who had moved them, might now prefer to take the lead in the prosecution against Hastings. The familiar charge of inconsistency was scotched by Dundas who reminded the House that the motion of 1782 had been intended to achieve the recall of Warren Hastings, not his prosecution; and, since then, Hastings had been three times reappointed to or confirmed in office as Governor-General, serving in that capacity under the North-Fox coalition government in which Burke had been Paymaster.

184

After some skirmishing, in which Opposition applications for confidential government papers were refused by Pitt, and sixteen motions for other papers were accepted, and the House rejected Burke's demand that prosecution witnesses should be heard, Pitt insisted that Hastings be given the opportunity to make a statement in his defence. There is no reason to doubt the honesty of his intention. Hastings's defence should be general: 'if his conduct in some parts of his administration had been faulty, yet those faults were highly compensated and fully counterbalanced by the general tenor of his conduct.' [261] Pitt could not have anticipated that Hastings would choose to answer every one of the twenty-two charges brought against him, individually and at tedious length. The reading of Hastings's statement, which occupied two full days, required the assistance of the clerks of the House, and emptied the Commons benches on both sides, was disastrous to his cause. Many speakers had bored the House, though seldom at such length; for that, Hastings would have been forgiven; but his statement displayed an unyielding self-righteousness, a remorseless denial of any possibility of error or miscalculation, that members found distasteful and inconsistent with his claims of moderation, humanity and the administration of justice.

The account read by Hastings at the bar of the House in May severely damaged his reputation, but it was generally assumed that when evidence was called against him he would be supported by Pitt and his ministers. Burke and Fox, though hoping for political advantage from the debates to come, did not expect to overturn the majority that Pitt could expect to command if he mustered a full government vote. If their campaign succeeded, Hastings would be accused, and sufficiently discredited to prevent his elevation to the peerage or further employment; the government would be embarrassed; and Burke and Fox would gain public esteem by their exposure of corruption, cruelty and injustice allowed, through political influence, to go unpunished. Such ends would amply justify any means the Opposition might choose to employ. Their forecast was logical and attractive, and in the event totally mistaken.

On 2 June, evidence was presented on the first charge: the conduct of the Rohilla war, fought twelve years earlier and clearly condoned, though not approved, by all governments since 1775. The motion for impeachment was defeated by 119 votes to 67, the majority following the lead given by Pitt, Grenville, Dundas and

Wilberforce. There seemed to be nothing to prevent the rest of the long series of charges being dismissed as decisively as the first. The argument, put forward by Dundas, that whatever might be the rights or wrongs of Hastings's actions they had been condoned by his continuance, thrice confirmed, in office, could be extended to all the charges, and although Dundas was not committed to Hastings's defence it was clear that he was reluctant to assist in his prosecution. Grenville and Thurlow were certain to support Hastings, as were other senior members of the Cabinet. Pitt was assumed to be committed to Hastings, and it followed from this assumption that Burke and his friends would present only a small number of the charges before rising majorities against them provided convincing proof of the futility of their continuing.

This assumption was false. Pitt was committed to no man. He recognized the value of Hastings's work without understanding the conditions under which he had laboured or the extent of the obstacles he had overcome. The Amending Act, passed in April, granted to Lord Cornwallis as the new Governor-General precisely the powers denied to Hastings: the authority to overrule his Council, the right to hold the appointment of Commander-in-Chief in India, and increased freedom of action in an emergency. It seemed essential that these enhanced powers should be accompanied by a public reaffirmation of the impartial administration of justice. Pitt had stated his position in parliament: 'I am neither a determined friend nor foe of Mr. Hastings, but I will support the principles of justice and equity. I recommend a calm dispassionate investigation, leaving everyone to follow the impulse of his own mind.' [262] He preserved his right to independence of judgement, and he exercised it with cold objectivity.

On 13 June Fox introduced the second charge against Hastings, relating to his treatment of Rajah Chait Singh, Zamindar * of Benares. During the Maratha war the resources of the East India Company were even more than usually strained. The Company

* Literally a landowner, but the term held different meanings in different parts of India. In Bengal, the Zamindars collected the King's share of the harvest or revenues, retaining the whole or a part according to their standing. They also acted as local judges, with powers of summary justice over Mogul subjects. The rights of Zamindars, often awarded to officials instead of salaries, became in unscrupulous hands, hereditary. To others the rights were assigned as pensions, or *jagirs*. These rights were incredibly complicated, and their exercise an open invitation to corruption.

186

called upon its dependent rulers for financial and military assistance. Chait Singh, required to pay a war contribution of five lakhs * a year and 1,000 horsemen in addition to his annual taxes of 22½ lakhs, delayed his payments but sent Hastings a personal bribe of two lakhs which the Governor immediately used for Company war expenses. The Company's need of money was desperate: the presidency at Madras was bankrupt, and Bombay was drawing on Bengal. The Council had borrowed all it could, the armies must be paid, and the French fleet was daily expected to return. In such an emergency Hastings felt himself justified in taking extreme measures. He visited Benares in state, resolved to fine Chait Singh half a million pounds and to depose him. To Hastings's demand for an explanation of his 'disaffection and infidelity' the Rajah returned an answer denying responsibility for the delay in payment which Hastings interpreted as a refusal to pay. He gave orders for Chait Singh's arrest. The Rajah's troops promptly attacked the Governor's bodyguard, killing more than two hundred, and Hastings was besieged while Chait Singh escaped. Hastings deposed him, enthroned another Zamindar, and increased the annual contribution to forty lakhs.

Pitt admitted to Eden that he had 'hardly hours enough to read all the papers' [263] on the Benares charge before it was debated, but he showed no sign of being ill-prepared when he rose to speak. He exposed, with complete mastery of the details of his subject, the ignorance of Fox and the malicious misrepresentations of Francis; but, while accepting Hastings's policy as dictated by necessity, he denounced his methods, accusing him of acting in 'an arbitrary and tyrannical manner'. The fine was 'beyond all proportion exorbitant, unjust and tyrannical'. Hastings was guilty of a 'very high crime', an 'act of oppression' which 'ought to be made one of the articles' if there were to be an impeachment. [264] The motion was passed by 119 votes to 79, Pitt and Wilberforce voting with Burke, Fox and Sheridan. From that moment, the outcome of the parliamentary proceedings was settled: Hastings would be impeached.

Thirty years later, Hastings declared that Pitt had been persuaded to vote for the motion by Dundas at breakfast that morning. Wilberforce, a far more likely author of any conversion, recalled that during the Opposition speeches Pitt beckoned him behind the

* The lakh (100,000 rupees) was worth about £10,200.

Speaker's chair and asked, 'Does not this look very ill to you!' 'Very ill indeed,' Wilberforce replied.[265] Fortified by this opinion Pitt condemned Hastings to impeachment. There is no good reason to suppose that Pitt was 'converted' by anyone, but it is nevertheless difficult to account for his choice of argument. The size of the fine, which was not in fact ever levied, was certainly a measure of Hastings's high-handed methods to meet an emergency, but it was just that ruthless grasp of opportunity that had enabled him to deliver the Company from its enemies. It was not a secure foundation for impeachment.

In May 1787 the articles of impeachment were approved. Pitt had spoken and cast his vote against Hastings on more than one occasion, notably after the debate concerned with the spoliation of the Begums of Oudh when Sheridan made one of the most famous speeches in the annals of parliament. On the 21st Hastings knelt at the bar of the House of Lords, a ceremonial he described with bitter accuracy as 'punishment not only before conviction, but before the accusations', [266] to hear a recital of the articles. He knelt there again on 28 November to deliver his reply. The impeachment proceedings were set to begin in February.

Pitt's decision has never been satisfactorily explained. It was his vote on the Benares charge that led the House of Commons to call for impeachment, and his votes against Hastings in subsequent debates dispelled any lingering doubts of his intention. He has been condemned for abandoning Hastings for the most devious motives: a determination to assert his authority over India House; a desire simultaneously to reassure Dundas and dispose of a powerful rival; a cunning diversion to distract the Opposition from paying attention to more important matters of policy; or a timely reminder to the King, who supported Hastings, of his independence. None is convincing. Towards the end of his life Wilberforce denied that Pitt had acted from political motives: '. . . he was always weighing in every particular whether Hastings had exceeded the discretionary power lodged in him. . . . He paid as much impartial attention as if he were a juryman.' [267] This is the simplest explanation and also the most credible. It accords with Pitt's reputation for frigid integrity. He judged Hastings according to his own exacting standards of honour, conceding nothing to circumstances or human fallibility.

There is a suspicion of irony, as well as his customary common sense, in the King's letter to Pitt, written the day after the Benares vote: 'Mr Pitt would have conducted himself yesterday very unlike what my mind ever expects of him if, as he thinks Mr Hastings's conduct towards the Rajah was too severe, he had not taken the part he did, though it made him coincide with [the] adverse party. As to myself, I own I do not think it possible in that country to carry on business with the same moderation that is suitable to an European civilized nation.' [268] Pitt did not abandon Hastings: as he made clear, he was never his friend. Hastings was convinced that Pitt had 'always been my personal and inveterate enemy'. [269]

Pitt judged Hastings with Olympian detachment, without regard to the consequences of his personal verdict. He was troubled by his decision and sincere in his conviction, but he was dangerously wrong. No Prime Minister, and least of all one whose influence was as great as Pitt's, could afford the luxury of acting in isolation as if that influence did not operate. In theory Pitt had called for a free vote, 'leaving every man to follow the impulse of his own mind'; but in practice, as he was well aware, his own vote would determine the votes of the majority. By affecting to renounce responsibility Pitt unintentionally made himself responsible for Hastings's ruin. It is possible that he realized his mistake, for when the Opposition attempted the impeachment of Sir Elijah Impey, Hastings's Chief Justice, Pitt made it a matter of ministerial policy to have the motion rejected. This was, on the face of it, a curious decision. Lord Cornwallis voiced the opinion of many who had first-hand knowledge and experience of administration in India: '. . . it is not fair to judge his [Hastings's] conduct many years ago by the temper of the present times'; but he added, 'If you are in the hanging mood, you may tuck up Sir Elijah Impey, without giving anybody the smallest concern.' [270]

Having condemned Hastings to be tried, Pitt made some effort to ensure that the proceedings were conducted with proper judicial impartiality. The articles of impeachment, though unwieldy and poorly devised, were framed in consultation between both sides of the House. Pitt and his ministers refused to take any part in the management of the trial, and the list of managers was therefore drawn from the Opposition, but he succeeded in having the most vindictive of Hastings's enemies, Philip Francis, excluded.

At noon on 13 February 1788 Warren Hastings knelt before his accusers and a vast and fashionable audience in Westminster Hall to hear the charges against him. He was then allowed to take his seat, separated only by the witness box from the hostile managers. The Hall had been transformed for the occasion into a great auditorium suitable for a theatrical performance. To Hastings's left sat the peers, to the right the Commons; and above them the galleries provided seating for peeresses and ticket-holders. At the far end of the Hall the throne and boxes for the royal family were raised upon a dais. Below them sat the Lord Chancellor and the judges. Hastings, five feet six inches tall and weighing 122 pounds, was a diminutive figure in his plain crimson-coloured suit, and looked pale and ill. The trial lasted seven years *, and although public interest waned, Hastings's suffering must have been all but intolerable. He was put up as a public spectacle, and society made the most of it. On the first day the Queen and the Princesses were in the Duke of Newcastle's party, the Prince of Wales and Mrs Fitzherbert graced one of the royal boxes, the Court, foreign ambassadors, representatives of the arts and the stage, the rich, the great and the fashionable thronged the Hall. Four months later their enthusiasm was unabated. Sir Gilbert Elliot wrote on 2 June to his wife, 'You have no conception of the rage and clamour for tickets.' The following morning he was up before seven to accompany a lady to Westminster Hall. 'She will,' he wrote, 'have to mob it at the doors till nine, when the doors open, and then there will be a rush as there is at the pit of the playhouse when Garrick plays King Lear. . . . Some people, and, I believe, even women—I mean ladies—have slept at the coffee-houses adjoining Westminster Hall, that they may be sure of getting to the door in time.' Later he added,

We stood an hour and a half in the street in the mob, and at last the press was so terrible, that I think it possible I may have saved, if not her life, at least a limb or two. I could not, however, save her cap which perished in the attempt. Shoes were, however, the principal and most general loss. Several ladies went in barefoot: others, after losing their own, got the stray shoes of other people, and went in with one red and one yellow shoe.

* The hearings were intermittent: between 1788 and 1794 they occupied 143 days; the concluding sessions, mostly in the House of Lords, were held between January and April 1795.

Elliot heard Sheridan, who spoke for four and a half hours on the 5th, a further three and a half on the 6th, and concluded his speech on the 14th. '. . . there were few dry eyes in the assembly; and for myself, I never remember to have cried so heartily and so copiously on any public occasion.' Mrs Siddons was among those who fainted, and Thomas Gainsborough caught there the chill that brought on his last illness. Gibbon was there too: 'Sheridan, on the close of his speech, sunk into Burke's arms, but I called this morning, he is perfectly well. A good actor.' * [271]

The trial, which began as a grand theatrical occasion apparently designed to show Sheridan and Burke in their most taxing dramatic roles, rapidly deteriorated into an obscene travesty, and sank finally into a series of amateur recitals of such length and tedium that the galleries were emptied. Important witnesses, and about a third of the peers, died before the verdict. † The judges frustrated all attempts by the managers to conduct the trial outside the rules of law governing procedure in the courts, but they were unable to prevent Burke's manipulation of testimony or the vulgar abuse he poured over Hastings and all who had been associated with him. He bullied and insulted witnesses, defamed all who disagreed with him, and introduced malicious gossip, rumour and slander as evidence of crimes which Hastings had not been called upon by parliament to answer. In November 1788 Sheridan confessed that he was already heartily sick of the proceedings and wished that Hastings would run away and Burke after him. A year later Fox was considering an 'honourable retreat'. He had acted from mixed motives of opportunism and idealism; Sheridan from opportunism and vanity; but Burke, great-hearted and compassionate, the obdurate champion of the oppressed, had been corrupted by his association with Francis, and he acted from paranoid malice.

On 23 April 1795 Hastings was honourably acquitted on all charges, no more than six peers voting against him on any charge. He had spent £71,000 on his defence. In March 1796 the Company awarded him a pension of £4,000 a year, to run for twenty-eight years from 1785, and a loan of £50,000, but he was beset by financial difficulties for the rest of his life. He lived on for twenty-three years,

---

* Tickets for Sheridan's performance changed hands for fifty guineas.

† By agreement, only those peers who had attended the trial continuously were eligible to vote on the verdict. They numbered twenty-nine.

surviving Burke, Sheridan, Fox, Dundas and Pitt. In March 1812, at the age of eighty-one, he was summoned before the House of Commons to give evidence on the renewal of the East India Company's charter. When he left the Chamber, after three and a half hours of examination, the members rose to him, a mark of respect, as he proudly told Marian, shown only to Kings and Princes. Next month the Lords paid him the same tribute. He died in 1818, in the same year as Philip Francis. Twenty-seven years earlier, in Westminster Hall, he had told his persecutors: 'I gave you all; and you have rewarded me with confiscation, disgrace, and a life of impeachment.' Henry Addington, who had examined all the charges with typical industry, produced the verdict of history a week before the first evidence was produced in the House of Commons and twenty-one months before the trial: 'I am convinced Hastings is not blameless; but I think I see enough to satisfy me, that if there is a bald place on his head, we ought to cover it with laurels.' [272]

The impeachment reflected little credit on anyone except Hastings. Fox's plan to lure the government into a defence of the Governor-General that would burden it with the justification of every error made in India since 1772 had been thwarted, but at the cost of condemning Hastings to seven years of purgatory. If he felt any remorse, Pitt could at least view with some satisfaction the general revulsion against Burke and the rest of the Opposition managers. He was to need all the parliamentary support he could find. Long before Hastings's acquittal, Pitt was absorbed in the conflicts of a constitutional crisis, the threat of revolution, and the catastrophe of war.

XIV

The Regency Crisis 1788-1789

IN HIS FIRST FIVE YEARS OF OFFICE Pitt had gained the King's respect and confidence. They had disagreed frequently on major policy matters, and Pitt's unbending reserve precluded intimacy even had the King encouraged it, but there had grown up between them a mutual regard based on integrity and candour. George III was no tyrant demanding unquestioning obedience: on the contrary he admired strength of purpose and tenacity of principle. He was both physically and mentally tough, combining a steely obstinacy with absolute faith in the rightness of his opinions, and he expected the same determination and fibre—or, as he described it, 'bottom'—from his ministers. His once-adored Bute had failed him in crisis, Chatham had turned against him, Grafton had deserted him, and North had collapsed under pressure. Pitt, alone, had 'bottom' without the hectoring, authoritarian manner the King had found intolerable in George Grenville.

George III did not, as he told his son, 'pretend to any superior abilities', but he was extraordinarily industrious. He was also, after a quarter of a century as King, more experienced in government than any of his ministers. In matters affecting the Constitution, his opinions were more often right than wrong; and his convictions, dictated by high moral principles, common sense, and a genuine desire to protect and further the best interests of his country and his people, were worthy of respect. His life was active and regular. He rose at about six o'clock every morning, shaved himself, dressed, and then attended to correspondence that had arrived during the night. He always went for a ride before breakfast. When in London he held a levee or drawing room which usually lasted until dinner * which he took at about four o'clock. He then continued with correspondence and dispatches until tea at seven. He seldom entertained at dinner, and there is no record that Pitt ever dined with him, but he was often joined by guests for supper at ten. His meals were frugal, and he drank wine, or large quantities of tea, but never spirits. He was an excellent horseman and an enthusiastic walker, often wearing out his courtiers and servants with casual strolls of twelve miles or more. When he travelled with the Queen, he rode beside her coach, apparently impervious to foul weather.

In 1762, just two years after his accession, George III suffered from what was then described as 'a feverish cold'. His symptoms included a violent cough and chest pains, and it is plain from the treatment prescribed that his doctors feared consumption. Fox heard that he was 'very very ill', and, like others who knew of the seriousness of the King's illness, lamented the lack of any constitutional provision for a regency in the event of the sovereign's death or minority. [273] After three weeks of the violent treatment favoured at the period, which included frequent purging, bleeding and blistering,† the King's natural reserves of strength restored him to health. Three years later he was taken ill again, with similar symptoms that lasted intermittently for nearly three months, though he was not confined to bed for more than a few days at a time. The illness was, however, serious enough to occasion a bitter quarrel between the King and his ministers about the composition of a Regency Council, and resulted in the passage of the Regency Act of May 1765, appointing the King's mother and 'others descended from the late King now resident in England' to form the Council.

---

* Luncheon was not a meal known in the eighteenth century. The King had nothing to eat between breakfast at nine and dinner at four.

† Poultices of mustard and cantharides were applied to the skin of the patient (generally to the legs or feet) raising painful blisters which were allowed to burst and suppurate. This, it was thought, allowed poisoned fluids to escape.

In August 1786 the King's life was threatened. Margaret Nicholson, a middle-aged and deranged spinster, tried to stab him as he stepped out of his carriage at St James's Palace. According to Wraxhall, she 'only failed from the knife being worn so thin about the middle of the blade that it bent with the resistance of the King's waistcoat instead of entering his body'.[274] She was easily overpowered, and arrested by a yeoman of the guard. The King 'immediately held his levee with the most perfect composure.' At five o'clock that afternoon, Margaret Nicholson was examined by Pitt and the Law Officers, and later by Dr Thomas Monro *. She was confined for life in Bethlem Hospital, where she died in 1823. The Whigs refused to join in the celebrations for the King's escape.

Two years later, Whig hopes were revived. On 11 June the King 'was seized with a bilious fever, attended with violent spasms in his stomach and bowels'.[275] Next day he wrote to Pitt, 'I certainly mend, but have been pretty well disciplined [purged] this day.' [276] He was attended by Sir George Baker, President of the Royal College of Physicians, and Fellow of the Royal Society, whom he was later to describe as an 'old woman'. The disorder seemed not to be serious, though the patient was weakened by the blood-letting and purging prescribed by his doctor. Lord Fauconberg offered him his house, Bays Hill Lodge, for his convalescence, and on 12 July the King and Queen and three Princesses left Windsor informally for Cheltenham. There the King drank the waters, much recommended for the cathartic effects though the 'smart brackish irony taste' and 'slight fetid odour' cannot have been inviting. Fanny Burney, who accompanied the Queen as second Keeper of the Robes, left evidence of the welcome offered to the royal family: 'Every town seemed all face; and all the way upon the road we rarely proceeded five miles without encountering a band of most horrid fiddlers, scraping "God save the King" with all their might, out of tune, and all in the rain.' [277]

In Gloucestershire the King was in his element. He was by preference a countryman, and genuinely interested in farming. He walked, unescorted, about the fields, talking freely with anyone he happened to meet about the quality of the soil and the price of sheep. The royal party visited the playhouse at Cheltenham,

* Later (1792-1816) physician at Bethlem Hospital, London (Bedlam). A connoisseur of art, he was the patron of some of the greatest of English artists of the eighteenth century, including J. M. W. Turner, John Linnell, Peter de Wint, John Varley, and Thomas Girtin.

renamed the Theatre Royal in their honour, the Gloucester infirmary and the County Gaol, and at the King's particular request the date of the Three Choirs Festival at Worcester was advanced so that the Royal Family might attend. Wherever he went he was greeted by great crowds of people and spontaneous evidence of his popularity. After five weeks' holiday he returned to Windsor in excellent spirits and apparently quite recovered. Apart from some pain in his face, which he reported to Pitt as lasting for several days during the third week of September, he seemed to be in good health.

Early in the morning of 17 October, Sir George Baker was summoned to Kew. There he found the King complaining of acute pains in the stomach, a recent rash, and severe cramps in his legs at night. Baker gave him castor oil and senna. These increased the pain, which he was then obliged to relieve by laudanum, which counteracted the purgatives. Within twenty-four hours the King obediently took three doses of each. During the 19th and 20th he was in great pain. On the evening of the 20th he made a gallant attempt to deal with correspondence and dispatches but found his hands shaking and his concentration flagging. He wrote pathetically to his Prime Minister: 'I am afraid Mr Pitt will perceive I am not quite in a situation to write at present, but I thought it better even to write as loosely as I have here than to lett the box return without an answer.'[278] Next day, at his request, Pitt went to see him at Kew. He found him in pain and evidently very tired. On the 22nd Baker noted the first signs of delirium, but the King insisted on returning to Windsor where, two days later, he appeared with his legs wrapped in flannel at the levee. This was a deliberate act of courage to scotch exaggerated rumours and to stop 'any fall in the stocks'. Pitt, as the King noticed, was unable to disguise his distress. When they met again, on the 29th, the King's health had deteriorated and, most ominous, it was clear that his mind was affected. On occasions he babbled incessantly, and his eccentric behaviour towards his family and the royal servants was giving further cause for concern. His eyesight and hearing were also impaired.

The King was painfully aware of his situation. On 3 November he wrote a letter of moving and determined optimism:

The King thinks it must give Mr Pitt pleasure to receive a line from him. This will convince him the King can sign warrants without inconvenience: therefore he desires any that are ready may be sent, and he has no objection to receive any large number, for he shall order the messenger to return to town and shall sign them at leisure. He attempts reading the despatches daily, but as yet without success; but he eats well, sleeps well, and is not in the least fatigued with riding, though he cannot yet stand long, and is fatigued if he walks. Having gained so much, the rest will soon follow.[279]

It was his last letter to Pitt for sixteen weeks.

That day Sir George Baker called for a second opinion from Dr William Heberden, an eminent, if somewhat ancient, physician who lived in retirement at Windsor. Two days later the King became delirious and foamed at the mouth. Baker and Heberden agreed to call in the Prince of Wales's physician, Dr Richard Warren. The King refused to see him. In no way deterred, Warren made his diagnosis by listening at the door while Baker examined the patient, informing the Prince that the King's life was in danger and that 'if he did live, there was little reason to hope that his intellects would be restored.'[280] Baker reported to Pitt that there was no change either for the better or worse, but it appeared to the doctors that the King was dying. A fourth physician, Dr Henry Revell Reynolds, was summoned. All were baffled. As Grenville wrote of them: 'The cause to which they all agree to ascribe it, is the force of a humour * which was beginning to show itself in the legs, when the King's imprudence drove it from thence into the bowels; and the medicines they were obliged to use for the preservation of his life have repelled it upon the brain. . . . The physicians are now endeavouring, by warm baths and by great warmth of covering, to bring it down again into the legs, which nature had originally pointed out as the best mode of discharge.'[281]

The doctors had, in fact, tried all the most respected remedies: purging, cupping, bleeding, blistering, doses of laudanum and St James's powder, and a course of 'the bark' †, to no avail. The King

---

* Four body fluids—blood, phlegm, choler, and melancholy (black choler)—were believed to determine a person's physical and mental constitution.

† St James's powder, a febrifuge, was roughly the equivalent of the modern aspirin; 'bark' was another name for quinine.

was, by turns, delirious, violent, and deranged. Dr Warren, still considering examination superfluous to diagnosis, pronounced that the King was suffering from 'an ossification'. On 11 November the *Morning Chronicle* found it necessary to contradict rumours of the King's death, and Lord Bulkeley reported to Lord Buckingham that 'poor Rex's state seems worse than a thousand deaths. . . . The Prince has taken the command at Windsor, in consequence of which there is no command whatsoever. . . . The Stocks are already fallen 2 per cent, and the alarms of the people of London are very little flattering to the Prince.' [282]

Pitt's acute anxiety was not for the King alone. To his friend, Dr Pretyman, recently promoted at his request to the Bishopric of Lincoln and Deanery of St Paul's, he wrote, in a letter superscribed 'secret', that the King's illness

> . . . has hitherto found little Relief from Medicine, and what is worst of all that it is attended with a delirium the Cause of which the Physicians cannot clearly ascertain . . . there is some Room to apprehend the disorder may produce danger to his Life, but there is no immediate Symptom of danger at present. The Effect more to be dreaded is on the understanding. If this lasts beyond a certain Time, it will produce the most difficult and delicate crisis imaginable in making Provision for the Government to go on. It must however be yet some Weeks before that can require a Decision. [283]

The situation was, as he well knew, already both difficult and delicate. If the King were to be adjudged insane by his physicians, there could be little doubt that the Prince of Wales would become Regent. If the King were to die, the Prince would succeed him. In either circumstance Pitt's government would be dismissed. Nor could he expect to retain the votes of more than a handful of his most devoted supporters. Already Captain Jack Payne, one of the Prince's most disreputable associates, was putting in hand backstairs negotiations with the Lord Chancellor, Lord Thurlow, while simultaneously assuring his rival, Lord Loughborough, of the certainty of his succession to the Woolsack. It would not be long before rats began to show themselves on the government benches.

Pitt understood the need to play for time, and he was prepared to use any constitutional means at his command to defend the King and thus his own ministry. It was fortunate for him that the physicians attending George III were unable to agree upon a prognosis. The introduction of a fifth, Sir Lucas Pepys, did nothing to promote unity among them, and on 24 November Pitt proposed that the doctor of his childhood, Dr Anthony Addington *, should be consulted. After one examination, Addington diagnosed 'a morbid humour, flying about and irritating the nerves'.[285] A seventh authority, Dr Thomas Gisborne, did no better. The *London Chronicle* announced that it was 'now authenticated from the best authority that the King's late disorder was owing solely to his drinking the waters at Cheltenham', an opinion that produced a disastrous and long-lasting effect on the spa.

The physicians' inability either to recognize the malady or to come to any agreement on a prognosis is not surprising. Not only were they confronted by a disease of which they had no knowledge or experience, but they were also working under pressure to suit their opinions to the political ambitions of their patrons. As Grenville told his brother, 'All the private accounts are so strongly tinctured by the wishes of those who send them, that no reliance can be placed upon them; and the private letters of the physicians are frequently inconsistent with each other, and even with the public account which they send to St James's. In general, that account has been uniformly found to be the least favourable.' [286]

The King's mental condition fluctuated, without warning, between extreme excitement and irritation, and comparative calm; between periods of understanding that his mind was disturbed, and positive conviction that his delusions were reality. When capable of action, his actions were apparently purposeful, but the purpose was irrational. An equerry recorded that he babbled incoherently for nineteen hours 'without scarce any intermission'. He frequently refused to eat or to be shaved, and the Queen, to whom he was devoted, was terrified of him. The Prince of Wales later insisted that his father had attacked him, seizing him by the collar and thrusting him against the wall. In the circumstances of their relationship at the time, the action might have been considered long overdue and a

* Unkindly, and inaccurately, described by Grenville as 'eighty-six and reckoned an old woman twenty years ago',[284] Addington was a mere seventy-five.

welcome sign of lucidity. Fanny Burney recalled the scene, the Prince in tears and the Queen in hysterics. The King was certainly sane enough to object to being examined or treated by Warren, whom he had always regarded, not without reason, as a fashionable quack.

At the end of the month it was decided, on Addington's advice, to move the King to Kew, where he might benefit from fresh air and exercise in greater privacy. It is not altogether surprising that Addington's proposal should have been accepted. Sometime keeper of a madhouse, he was the only one of the seven doctors attending the King to have had any specialist experience of the mentally deranged; and Kew was more convenient than Windsor for those with London practices, as it was also for the Prime Minister and Lord Chancellor. The Queen, who knew her husband's preference for Windsor, objected. The King refused to go. The Cabinet was called to Windsor to persuade him. Pitt and Thurlow saw him separately on the 28th. Both were much moved by the King's pathetic condition, and the royal attendants were treated to the unusual spectacle of the rugged Lord Chancellor in tears. Pitt tried again, by himself, the next day, but without success, and finally retired to the ante-room to write the King a letter: 'Mr Pitt humbly begs leave to acquaint your Majesty that he finds the physicians think it of the greatest consequence to your Majesty's recovery to change the air; and they have informed Mr Pitt that they think themselves obliged not to permit Mr Pitt to pay his duty personally to your Majesty again until your Majesty's arrival at Kew.' [287] This was signed also by Baker, Pepys, Addington and Reynolds. The King attempted to pen a reply but, finding himself unable to do so, hid himself behind his bed curtains. At last, told that he would be removed by force, he allowed himself to be dressed and driven away, escorted by a troop of cavalry.

At the palace at Kew, designed as a summer house and atrociously cold and uncomfortable in winter, the King was treated as a prisoner. He made several attempts to escape, and was punished by being locked in his room and tied to his bed at night. Obliged to pass the winter with her deranged husband in a freezing house without carpets, where draughts were imperfectly excluded by sandbags at the doors and windows, the Queen, who had borne up wonderfully under terrible strain, drifted into melancholy.

While the Prince of Wales was required to be with his father at Windsor, he succeeded in assuming a respectable air of filial anxiety and gloom. The King's imprisonment at Kew allowed him a freer rein of which he was quick to take rash advantage. His closest intimate was his younger brother the Duke of York, and together in London they made no secret of their expectation of a speedy, merciful, and conclusive release from the King's puritanical influence. The Prince boasted openly of his choice of ministers, and lists, claimed to be authentic, were published in the newspapers. In the absence of Fox, holidaying, no one knew where on the Continent, with his mistress Elizabeth Armistead, Sheridan tried in vain to restrain the Prince.

Fox landed in England on 24 November. Informed, on his arrival in Lausanne, that there was an express from England awaiting him, he jumped to the conclusion that this must contain news of the death of his nephew, Lord Holland. As heir to the family barony, Fox would be translated by Holland's death to an unwanted seat in the House of Lords. When he learnt that the news was of the King's illness, and that he was not expected to live, Fox 'was so much affected as to fall down on a couch and cry violently for some time' with relief. Sir Gilbert Elliot noted indignantly, 'It seems extraordinary that such a man as Fox could be from September to November without receiving one line from England . . . and that no man in England should know with the least certainty where he was. . . . He never asked for a newspaper, either foreign or English, the whole of his absence, except once, and that was to look at the Newmarket article; and when he had seen that he did not read another word.' Fox was ill. He was suffering from dysentery, which malicious rumour attributed to his having to eat his own words without being able to digest them, but he was ready to grasp the unexpected opportunity. Pitt had gained time by moving the adjournment of the House for two weeks, but parliament was due to reassemble on 4 December and a debate on the creation and nature of a Regency could not be long delayed. The government's position was precarious, its survival depending upon the King's recovery. Addington, alone among the seven doctors attending the King, believed this possible. It was generally thought certain that, even if the King lived, he would be insane for the rest of his life. Elliot told his wife: 'People begin to talk as if the ministers considered the game was up; there are even reports of Pitt's talking of returning to the bar.' The

Prince was, he added, determined never to have anything to do with Pitt 'who was very absurdly arrogant in his good fortune, and insulted the Prince.' Pitt, he considered, would 'continue to couple the violent affection and compassion of the people for the King in his present affecting situation, with his own fortunes', and would 'certainly make a very popular if not at first a very powerful Opposition'.[288]

With another parliamentary session about to begin, the Privy Council met on 3 December to examine the King's physicians * on oath to ascertain whether the King was capable of attending parliament, or dealing with business, the likelihood of his recovery, when this might be anticipated, and whether the doctors could substantiate their opinions by citing experience of similar cases. All were agreed that the King was unfit to attend to any business. All, astonishingly, except Warren, followed Addington's lead and agreed that recovery was possible, though none would hazard a guess at the time required. Warren was pompous and wordily evasive. That day the Prince of Wales wrote to his brother, Augustus, that their father was 'a compleat lunatick'.

In parliament on 4 December it was agreed that a Commons committee should be appointed to question the doctors. By the time it met, five days later, a further conflicting factor had been added. On 5 December the Reverend Dr Francis Willis, 'keeper of a mad-house in Lincolnshire', arrived at Kew. The King knew of Willis's work and made a special effort to appear rational before him. He

> received Dr Willis with composure & began immediately to talk to Him & seemed very anxious to state to Him that He had been very ill, but that He was now quite well again. . . . He told Dr Willis that he knew where he lived, & He asked Him how many patients He had with Him under his Care—He then thus addressed Dr Willis. 'Sir, your dress & appearance bespeaks You of the Church, do You belong to it.' Dr Willis replied, 'I did formerly, but lately I have attended chiefly to physick.' 'I am sorry for it,' answered the King with Emotion and Agitation, 'You have quitted a profession I have always loved, & you have Embraced one I most heartily detest.'

* All were present except Heberden.

Willis is said to have replied, 'Sir, our Saviour himself went about healing the sick;' 'Yes, Yes,' retorted the King, 'but he had not £700 a year for it.' The King went on to rail against his doctors, especially Warren and Pepys, and 'most earnestly begged that Dr Willis would take the former under his care as one of his Patients & remove him to Lincolnshire.' [289] Such a deal of sense gave hope for the King's return to perfect sanity.

Willis brought with him his son, Dr John Willis, three muscular assistants, and a straitjacket. He told the King firmly that his mind was deranged and that he required 'attention and management'. The King, enraged, became violent. He was promptly put into the straitjacket and kept there until he was calm again. During the next three months Willis conducted two separate but closely linked struggles for ascendancy: against his patient; and against the seven attending physicians. The King could be forcibly restrained. The other doctors must be so humiliated or irritated as to oblige them to withdraw. From the first, he ensured to himself the support of the government by his adamant assertion that the King could be cured and that he could effect the cure.

When the Commons committee met on 9 December, Warren and Baker, by refusing to attribute the King's disorder to any specific cause, implied that he was insane. These two became the 'opposition physicians'. Willis's evidence was bold and clear: he had 'great Hopes of His Majesty's Recovery'; and he had experience of such cases over a period of twenty-eight years, treating more than eight hundred patients, nine out of ten of whom had recovered. [290]

Next day in the House of Commons Pitt introduced another tactical manoeuvre to delay the establishment of a Regency. Although, he declared, the physicians' evidence gave him room to hope that the King would recover from his illness, it was the duty of parliament to consider the proper constitutional procedure to ensure the continuing functions of government. He therefore moved the appointment of a committee 'to examine into, search for, and report precedents'. This was excellent lawyers' language, impeccable in its appeal to the deeply rooted English love of well-worn custom and the bleak mistrust of precipitate change, or indeed of any change unsupported by usage and tradition. It was also, though less deliberately, the move best designed to inflame the Opposition. Fox was too experienced a politician to be deceived by Pitt's bland assumption of the necessity to examine precedents. He was also ill, irritable, and, after five years of unprofitable opposition, frustrated. He thought he saw power within his grasp and he would suffer no delay. Replying to Pitt, he argued that any search for precedents would be a waste of time, for no relevant precedents existed. 'The Prince of Wales had as clear, as express a right to assume the reins of government, and exercise the power of sovereignty during the continuance of the illness and incapacity with which it had pleased God to affect his majesty, as in the case of his majesty's having undergone a perfect and natural demise.' [291] At this, Pitt is said to have slapped his thigh and whispered to his neighbour on the government front bench, 'I'll un-Whig the gentleman for the rest of his life!' [292]

Fox's customary lack of restraint had led him into a disastrous blunder. That anyone should attempt to reduce the function and duty of parliament to a passive ratification of the Prince's wishes was shocking enough; but that he, who had throughout his career attacked and condemned the royal prerogative of the King, should, from the obvious motive of personal ambition, assert the royal prerogative of the Prince of Wales appeared particularly disgraceful. Nor was he correct in declaring that no relevant precedents could be found. There was, it was true, no precedent for the creation of a Regency in identical circumstances; but Regents, Protectors, and Councils of Regency had been named on numerous occasions in the past, during a monarch's temporary absence or his minority, and during the period of Henry VI's madness in 1454-5. On every occasion parliament had imposed restrictions on the Regent's exercise of sovereignty. It was beyond doubt that the constitutional appointment of a Regent required the sanction of both Houses of Parliament and that they had the right and duty to restrict the powers of the Regent. Pitt, who had already studied the intricate constitutional issues involved, defined the position with crystal clarity: 'However strong the arguments might be . . . in favour of the Prince of Wales . . . it did not affect the question of right; because neither the whole, nor any part, of the royal authority could belong to him in the present circumstances, unless conferred by the two houses of parliament.' [293]

Fox was aware, almost at once, of the extent of his imprudence. In a second speech, and another on 12 December, he attempted to retrieve the situation, but he succeeded only in confusing the issues. The impression remained that he was prepared to abandon all principle in order to gain power. His own followers were dismayed and angry. Sheridan, who had so assiduously nursed the Prince of Wales in Fox's absence, counselling patience and discretion, understood the need to subordinate every consideration to the first priority: that of unseating the government by the creation of a Regency. Given due time for consideration, parliament was certain to recognize the Prince's claim. The new Whig government could surely remove whatever restrictions might be imposed on his powers. Pitt had handled a delicate situation with great skill, but the government could not act, nor could parliament function, without royal authority, and the Commons would not accept delays that members construed as unconstitutional. The Prince's claim to the Regency was paramount. With the exercise of a little patience, the Opposition must inevitably come to office.

Debates in the Lords were distinguished by a lachrymose display of hypocrisy by Thurlow, who, deep in negotiations to retain his office under the coming Regency, sobbed out his gratitude for the King's many favours 'which, when he forget, may God forget him'.[294] Pitt was among the members of the Commons present to hear him, and walked out of the Chamber in amused astonishment, muttering, 'Oh what a rascal!'[295] The comments of Wilkes and Burke were predictably less restrained.

Although the government's motion was passed by both Houses, there were uncomfortable signs of defection among its supporters. A group known as the 'Armed Neutrality', led by the Duke of Northumberland and Lord Rawdon, was thought to number about twenty peers and thirty members of the Commons, and the loyalty of others was uncertain. When Lord Carmarthen, who had become Foreign Secretary after Temple's resignation in 1783, heard it said that Fox's insistence on the Prince's right to the Regency had let the cat out of the bag, he replied, 'So much the better—the rats are grown very troublesome.'[296]

The Prince complained to Thurlow that he had no knowledge of the government's plans for the Regency. Pitt replied to him on 15 December: 'The Lord Chancellor delivered to me last night a letter which he had received from your Royal Highness, from the contents of which, I have the unhappiness to perceive, that both my general conduct, & what I have said in the House of Commons, has been represented to your Royal Highness in a light which I flatter myself I do not deserve.' [297] He went on to deny that any detailed arrangement had been agreed by the Cabinet, and required permission not to enter into any discussion of such details. He added his opinion that 'whatever portion of Royal Authority might appear necessary to be exercised during the present unhappy interval should be vested in your Royal Highness unrestrained by any permanent Council & with the free choice of the Political Servants to act under your Royal Highness. Precisely what portion of the Royal Authority ought to be given, & what ought to be withheld I conceived it would be improper then to discuss.' If the Prince found any comfort in the assurance that he would be permitted to choose his own ministers, it must have been nugatory beside his irritation at the reference to 'the present unhappy interval' and the repetition of the word 'portion' applied to the royal authority. Though respectfully phrased, Pitt's letter was a deliberate and unwelcome reminder of the sovereignty of parliament.

The next day's debate did nothing to encourage the Opposition. Pitt moved that the personal exercise of royal authority by the King was 'interrupted', and it was the right and duty of parliament 'to provide means for supplying the defect'. In spite of well-reasoned resistance, especially from Fox and North, the resolutions were approved by 268 votes to 204, a far larger majority than either side had anticipated. On Christmas Day Thurlow told Fox that he no longer wished to continue with his negotiations. He had come to the end of what Elliot described as his 'shabby trimming game'.

Public opinion was concentrating behind the government. Both sides made full use of the newspapers, the Prince's Dutch *maître d'hôtel*, Louis Weltje, being employed to buy the *Morning Post* for the Opposition; and cartoons, pamphlets and handbills were commissioned for distribution throughout the country. A typical Opposition publication accused the Prime Minister of attempting to seize supreme power:

PRINCE PITT! or the Minister of the Crown. Greater than the HEIR APPARENT! who, having already destroyed the People's Rights by an undue Exertion of the Prerogative of the Crown, is

206

now willing to raise himself above the Prerogative by *seizing on the Sovereignty of these Kingdoms*.

This echoed Sir Gilbert Elliot's fear that the people 'would be content and pleased to set aside the whole of the Royal Family, with the Crown and both Houses of Parliament, if they could keep him [Pitt] by it.' [298] William Eden's brother wrote to him on 11 December: 'Many people seem to think the minister means to have a committee of Regency, himself the chief *(King William the Fourth)*, but I am not of this opinion; however he seems to have spoken so freely of the Prince of Wales as to indicate a design of retiring if the Prince becomes Regent.' [299]

Pitt's weakness lay in the doubts of the King's recovery. Since the arrival of Dr Willis at Kew, the King had been straitjacketed and strapped to his bed at the slightest sign of intractability. Pepys, Reynolds and Gisborne stayed, alternately, from four o'clock each afternoon until eleven, and Warren and Baker visited the King every morning for a consultation. Willis and his son were always in attendance, with their own staff. Willis and Warren were[301] at loggerheads: Warren, fashionable, patronizing and authoritarian, was the Prince's man; Willis, experienced, dogmatic and determined, was staking his reputation on the King's recovery. When the King's condition was seen to be worse, he was repeatedly blistered. The festering sores on his legs were later reported as having 'discharged well and for weeks', doubtless removing all sorts of debilitating 'humours'. Meanwhile his stomach was subjected to regular assault by doses of digitalis, calomel and saline draughts. Anxious, confused, often terrified and always in appalling and unnecessary pain, the King was held prisoner at Kew while his government fought his eldest son and His Majesty's Opposition for the support of parliament and the people. On 18 December, Willis reported that the King had had a good night and that his 'compleat recovery' was assured.

His reasons for such an assertion are obscure. He had no more idea of the nature of the King's illness than any other of the attending physicians, and his confidence appears to have been founded upon conceit and hope. It now seems certain that the King was suffering from acute intermittent porphyria, a rare hereditary disease first classified a hundred and fifty years later.[300] Porphyria, a metabolic disorder leading to an accumulation of toxic chemical substances which damage the nervous system [301], is thought to have been passed down to the Hanoverians through George III's great-grandmother, the Electress Sophia, who inherited it, in the Stuart line, from Mary Queen of Scots. The symptoms, which include weakness of the limbs, hoarseness, constipation, discolouration of the urine and vomiting, followed in more acute stages by insomnia, irritability, excitement, hallucinations and delirium, are recognizable in four of the King's children, including the Prince of Wales, and the Prince's only child. Though prescribed in good faith, the treatment received by George III would have killed many a healthy patient, and it is a measure of the extraordinary strength of his general constitution that he was able to survive not only a serious attack of the disease but also the ministrations of his well-intentioned but uninformed physicians.

The King showed no obvious sign of recovery. On Christmas Day, just a week after Willis's confident assertion, one of the King's equerries reported that 'He was as deranged as possible. . . . Among his extravagancies of the Moment He had at this time hid part of the Bed Clothes under his bed, had taken off his Night Cap, & got a Pillow Case round his head, & the Pillow in the bed with Him, which he called Prince Octavius *, who He said was to be new born this day.' [302] Two days later, the Reverend Thomas Willis joined his father and brother in attendance on the King.

On 30 December Pitt's proposals for the Regency were sent to the Prince of Wales. The planned limitations were severe, as Sir Gilbert Elliot explained to his wife: 'No Power to make Peers / No power to grant places for life / No share in managing the King's real or personal estate / The Household to be at the Queen's disposal / No time fixed for the duration of these proposals.' [303] The Prince, aided by Burke, wrote a strong but dignified letter of protest. The restrictions on the granting of pensions and the creation of peerages (except for the King's issue after they had attained the age of twenty-one) would cripple any new ministry by denying it the most powerful rights of patronage.

The resolutions were not debated until 16 January 1789, owing to the sudden death of the Speaker of the House of Commons, Charles

* The King's youngest son, who had died, aged four, in 1783.

208

Cornwall *, who succumbed on 2 January to a pleurisy and the treatment prescribed by Dr Richard Warren. On the 5th, to the mortification of the Opposition, William Wyndham Grenville was elected Speaker by a majority of 215 votes to 144. In a last attempt to prove that the King's illness was not temporary, the Opposition insisted upon yet another examination of the attending physicians before the debate on the Regency. This wasted a further five days and the evidence filled four hundred pages. It supplied Pitt with the knowledge, dispiriting to the Opposition, that Gisborne, Reynolds and Sir Lucas Pepys were veering in their opinions towards Willis's in believing that there was reason to hope that the King might recover.

By 23 January, after a week of debates, Pitt's resolutions had been passed by both Houses. A formal Bill, giving effect to the resolutions, passed through the Commons during the first week in February.† The abject failure of the Opposition owed much to Fox's first shocking blunder, his continuing illness, and finally his absence; but it was also the result of the Prince's conduct and the disunity of his supporters. Since his return from Windsor at the time of the King's removal to Kew, the Prince had behaved with increasing indiscretion, publicly insulting his father, quarrelling with his distracted mother, allocating posts in his government, and celebrating with his cronies his imminent succession. News, and also exaggerated rumours, of this unfilial exhibition were not slow to circulate, and they disgusted all but his most dedicated parasites and admirers. The devoted Whig hostess Georgiana, Duchess of Devonshire, wrote that there was 'Great private treachery . . . Sheridan courting the Prince and encouraging the praise of him where Fox is abused.' [304] Charles Grey, a rising young hope of the Opposition, was also at the centre of party quarrels. By the middle of January, Pitt's championship of his ailing King and the sovereignty of parliament against the assumed prerogatives of the Prince was attracting addresses of support from all parts of the country, and the City of London voted Pitt an annuity of £3,000 if he should be removed from office. Antony Storer wrote

* Cornwall was chiefly distinguished for his habit of refreshing himself at frequent intervals during debates with draughts of porter from a supply kept beneath the Speaker's chair.

† Parliamentary Bills require the royal assent. This was by-passed by invoking the authority held to reside in the great Seal, an instrument of authority sanctified by precedent.

to William Eden, 'Mr Pitt is so powerful that he may do as he pleases.' [305]

The Opposition case may be considered to have been finally ruined by Burke. In a desperate attempt to fill the void left by Fox's absence at Bath, where he was racked by dysentery, Burke made a speech of such violence that even those who had heard his diatribes against Warren Hastings must have feared for his sanity. He declared that he had 'taken pains to make himself master of the subject, he had turned over every book upon it, and had visited the dreadful mansions' where the insane were confined. [306] He stressed the dangers of 'an uncertain cure' and 'sudden relapse', and excelling himself in tactlessness, quoted the cases of patients who, presumed cured, 'had butchered their sons'. Others, he claimed, had 'done violence to themselves by hanging, shooting, drowning, throwing themselves out of windows'. It was, perhaps, the least felicitous performance of his parliamentary career.

By mid-February the Regency Act was ready to go to the Lords. On 19 February Thurlow announced to a crowded House that the King was convalescent, and moved the adjournment. The crisis was over. Four days later, the King wrote his first letter to Pitt since November, and on the 24th Pitt and Thurlow visited him at Kew. The *London Gazette* announced that the daily bulletins on the King's health would be discontinued, and by 1 March all the doctors had reached agreement for the first time in four months: the King was cured. He was thin, his voice was still hoarse, and he was bewildered by the hallucinations he had experienced, but he was calm and rational, and able to preside at a Privy Council at Kew on 9 March. Two days earlier, to his relief and joy, Willis and all his assistants had left.

The King's recovery was celebrated by public rejoicing. On 10 March 'London displayed a blaze of light from one extremity to the other; the illuminations extending . . . from Hampstead and Highgate to Clapham, and even as far as Tooting: while the vast distance between Greenwich and Kensington presented the same dazzling experience.' It was, according to Wraxhall, 'the most universal exhibition of national loyalty and joy, ever witnessed in England.' The Whig Elliot, though less enthusiastic, was obliged to admit the magnificence of the illuminations and the ingenuity of the 'devices of different sorts in coloured lamps and transparent paintings'. The

Prince of Wales and Duke of York were mobbed in their coach on the way to the opera and narrowly escaped injury. Lord Palmerston noted a popular Opposition verse in his journal:

> Still London exhibits a prospect that's sad
> Though the King is recovered the Town is run mad.
> This scene of delusion will quickly be over
> When the monarch relapses the town will recover.[307]

Such was not, however, popular sentiment. The Opposition had suffered its worst defeat in the history of Pitt's ministry, and his stand against Fox had confirmed him in the role of public hero.

On 26 March the King was in London for the first time since his illness, and on 1 April an 'excessively fine' ball was given by White's Club at the Pantheon in Oxford Street. It was attended by some two thousand people, Pitt joining a supper party which included the Duchess of Gordon, Dundas, Lord and Lady Chatham and the celebrated Dr Willis. The Prince of Wales and Duke of York did not join in this festivity; they allowed their complimentary tickets to be offered for sale in Bond Street. The Opposition ball was given, with deliberate effrontery, on 22 April, the eve of the St George's Day thanksgiving service at St Paul's.[308]

The King survived the five-hour ceremonies in the Cathedral with perfect composure, but the two Princes behaved with offensive vulgarity, pointing, talking loudly, guffawing and, according to one account, munching biscuits during the sermon. Fox, who 'sat quite back in his coach, not to be seen', was greeted by 'an universal hiss which continued with very little intermission until he alighted at St Pauls'.[309] Elliot, who three weeks earlier had declared sourly, 'I certainly do not feel any new affection or respect for the King, whom I do not think either better or worse for being mad', found his 'eyes running over' at the sight of the King greeted in the Cathedral by '6,000 children from the different charity-schools in the city, in their different habits and colours' singing the Hundredth Psalm.[310]

On 9 June, George III drove through enthusiastic crowds to the House of Lords to receive the newly elected Speaker of the House of Commons. After less than five months, Grenville had resigned, causing Burke to refer to the Speaker's Chair as 'a hot bed for statesmen'. Pitt nominated his childhood friend, Henry Addington, and he was elected by a large majority. Elliot, disappointed for the second time, wrote bitterly: 'Pitt could not have made a more obnoxious choice. . . . He [Addington] is the son of Lord Chatham's physician and is in fact a sort of dependent of the family. The Chair has hitherto been filled by persons of quite a different description.' [311] This was true, but not in the sense he intended: of previous Speakers since the great Arthur Onslow, Sir John Cust had been feeble, Fletcher Norton partial, Charles Cornwall an indolent nonentity, and Grenville reluctant. Addington had not greatly distinguished himself as a member of parliament, but he was understood to be without personal ambition, and known to be tactful, conciliatory and well-versed in parliamentary procedure. He turned out to be an excellent choice. Pitt was glad of the change: apart from the opportunity to reward a loyal friend, he welcomed the chance to strengthen his Cabinet by the inclusion of Grenville, as Home Secretary, in succession to Lord Sydney who had resigned.

At the end of the month the King set out for Weymouth, where he was to continue his convalescence. All the way through Hampshire and Dorset the people came out to greet him with flowers and music. 'Think', wrote Fanny Burney in Weymouth, '. . . of the surprise of His Majesty when, the first time of his bathing, he had no sooner popped his royal head under water than a band of music, concealed in a neighbouring [bathing] machine, struck up "God Save great George our King".' [312]

George III was restored to health, Pitt had triumphed, and the people rejoiced in the summer sunshine. Across the Channel, clouds had been gathering for two years. On 14 July, the workers of the Faubourg St Antoine stormed the Bastille.

XV

The Return to Europe
1784-1791

PITT CAME TO POWER at a time when British prestige in Europe had
been severely damaged by the loss of the war in America. The
Emperor Joseph II of Austria considered that Britain had declined
for ever to the rank of a second-rate power comparable with
Denmark or Sweden, and Frederick the Great looked forward, more
in hope than genuine expectation, to the day when Pitt might
'restore his country to the importance which she formerly held in the
scale of Europe'.[313]

Pitt was not immediately interested in Britain's place in Europe.
He was preoccupied with the restoration of the economy, with the
intractable problem of Ireland, and with India. He required a period
of peace and stability, of retrenchment accompanied by a massive
increase in manufacture and trade, of commercial alliances without
military commitment. Carmarthen, the Secretary of State for Foreign Affairs, was anxious to lay the foundations of a practicable
foreign policy, but he was working under severe handicaps, not the
least of which were his own limited abilities and lack of experience.
Sir James Harris, who had followed his early success in Madrid * by

* See p. 36.

213

successive appointments as minister in Berlin and ambassador at St Petersburg before Pitt had him appointed in 1784 to The Hague, was not alone in thinking that 'if any good is ever done . . . it must be effected through the King's Ministers abroad, and not by those about his person.' He added, 'Long experience has taught me this; and I never yet received an instruction that was worth reading.' [314]

Even in more capable hands than Carmarthen's, and with more enthusiastic support from Pitt, the outlook would not have been promising. France already had alliances with Austria and Spain *, and traditional ties with Sweden, while Austria had a treaty with Russia; peace had not been concluded with the Dutch until 1784; and Frederick the Great was not eager to yoke Prussia to an enfeebled Britain unless as part of a quadruple alliance to include Denmark and Russia. Indeed, it seemed that Denmark alone was interested in any proposal, but such a connection might involve Britain in a quarrel with Sweden that might, in turn, involve France. Carmarthen juggled with a series of imaginative permutations, but none could be found that did not conflict with Pitt's instruction not to seek an association that might lead to military action in any European dispute.

Britain appeared to be isolated; but there were cracks in the structure of existing European alliances, and it soon became clear that these might be widened to restore a more secure balance of power. Sweden was Russia's rival in the Baltic; the Austrian Netherlands provided fertile ground for seeds of dissension between Austria, France and the United Provinces †; and the relationship of France with Spain, always an uncomfortable bed-fellow, was showing signs of strain. Russian ambitions included the conquest of Turkey, a

---

* These alliances were cemented by the marriages of Joseph II's sister, Marie Antoinette, to Louis XVI of France, and of his brother, Leopold (later the Emperor Leopold II), to Maria Luisa of Spain.

† The Protestant union of the seven northern provinces of the Netherlands, which, under the leadership of William I ('The Silent') and, after his death, of his sons, overthrew Spanish rule and gained, by the treaty of Münster (Westphalia) in 1648, recognition of their independence. Holland, by far the largest of the provinces, containing more than half of the total population and wealth, contributed more to the federal revenue than the aggregate of the other six. The provinces were governed by their own Estates, formed from delegations sent by the larger towns and the nobility. In practice, the delegations were controlled by the corporation, known as the 'regents', of each town. The federal parliament, the States-General, sat in permanent session at The Hague.

William Pitt, by John Hoppner

Hester, Countess of Chatham, by Thomas Hudson

William Pitt, First Earl of Chatham, by William Hoare

John, Second Earl of Chatham, Studio of Hoppner

William Wyndham Grenville, First Baron Grenville, by John Hoppner

William Wilberforce, by Karl Anton Hickel, 1792

Bishop George Pretyman Tomline. Engraving by R. Cooper after Henry Edridge, 1814

Henry Dundas, First Viscount Melville, by Sir Thomas Lawrence, 1810

Henry Addington, First Viscount Sidmouth. Artist unknown

Charles James Fox, by Karl Anton Hickel

William Cavendish Bentinck,
Third Duke of Portland, by Matthew Pratt

Edmund Burke, Studio of Reynolds

Richard Brinsley Sheridan, by John
Russell, 1788

William Windham, by Sir Joshua
Reynolds, 1788

William Pitt, by James Gillray, c. 1789

GOD SAVE THE KING,—in a Bumper, or—an Evening Scene, three times a Week at Wimbleton. *Caricature by Gillray, 1795. Dundas to Pitt: "Send us Victorious, Happy and glorious, Long to Reign,—go it my Boy—Billy my Boy, all my Joy,—God Save the King!"*

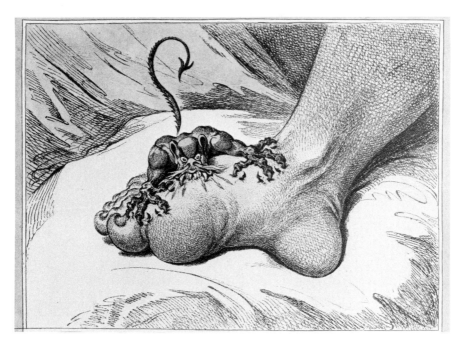

The GOUT. *Caricature by Gillray, 1799.*

King George III, by Johann Zoffany.

A Voluptuary under the Horrors of Digestion. *Caricature by Gillray, 1799.*

Edward, First Baron Thurlow, by Thomas Phillips, 1806.

Alexander Wedderburn, First Baron Loughborough and Earl of Rosslyn, by William Owen.

project that required the co-operation of Austria and consequently the friendship of France; and this conflicted with French support of Swedish aims in the Baltic. There was room for manoeuvre.

The most immediate area of concern was the Low Countries. Joseph II had long wanted to rid himself of the Austrian Netherlands in exchange for Bavaria. This scheme, strongly opposed by Frederick the Great at the head of a league of the German principalities, was abandoned in favour of redeveloping the Belgic provinces as a centre of trade. This second plan, however, required the Dutch to open the estuary of the Scheldt below Antwerp, control of which had been granted to them by the treaty of Münster. In spite of severe pressure, the Dutch rejected all Austrian demands, and it seemed that the dispute could not be resolved without war. Carmarthen hoped that Britain might gain prestige by mediating between Austria and the United Provinces, but Pitt accurately predicted that negotiations, and the credit for them, would be the prerogative of the French. Though obliged to concede a small area of territory below Antwerp, the Dutch retained control of the Scheldt estuary. War had been averted, but the cause of the crisis remained.

The Emperor reverted to his earlier scheme, the Bavarian exchange. This was potentially more troublesome to Britain. It was a fundamental doctrine of British foreign policy that no hostile power should be allowed to dominate the coastline from the Rhine to the Scheldt. The suggested Bavarian exchange would plant in the Belgic provinces a German prince who owed his position, in some degree, to French influence. An additional complication was George III's role as Elector of Hanover. His policies and actions in this capacity were strictly nothing to do with the British government or parliament. The King's ministers were not expected to give advice or state opinions on the subject unless they were sought by the King. The maintenance of this polite fiction had been one of the most frustrating tasks of successive first ministers since the accession of George I. In fact, the policies of the Hanoverian Kings as Electors could not be divorced from the policies they approved as British monarchs. George III was mercifully far less interested or involved in German politics than either of his predecessors but he could not ignore his responsibilities. In July 1785 the Fürstenbund, a league of Princes that included Prussia, Saxony and Hanover, was founded to resist, if necessary by war, the Bavarian exchange. Joseph II again relinquished his plan, but Carmarthen's bright hopes for an alliance with either Austria or Russia, which supported the exchange, were crushed.

There remained the problem of growing unrest in the United Provinces. The Dutch had not been united in their enthusiasm for war with Britain, which had cost them the cession of Negapatam in the Carnatic. It had become the custom for the federal provinces to call upon the hereditary Stadtholders, the Princes of Orange, for leadership in times of crisis, and resentment for failure was therefore directed at William V, the Anglophile son of an English princess *. This was aggravated by the Prince's attempts to introduce further centralization of government and control of the armed services to provide for emergencies. Weak and vacillating, he had married Frederica Sophia Wilhelmina, niece of Frederick the Great and sister to his heir. She was both capable and domineering.

Pitt's appointment of Harris to be minister at The Hague was astute. He was no stranger to the Netherlands, having spent eighteen months at the University of Leyden after coming down from Oxford, and his four years in Berlin had made him familiar with the Court of Frederick the Great. If there were to be trouble in the United Provinces, 'ce rusé et audacieux Harris', as Mirabeau described him,[315] was more likely to extract from it the maximum benefit to Britain than any envoy in government service. A staunch Whig, Harris was first a professional diplomat: 'In all matters of publick concern,' he wrote, 'my education, habits and I may add . . . principles, lead me more to measures than men.'[316] He became one of the great Whig triumvirate—James Harris, Gilbert Elliot, William Eden †—whose abilities as 'men of business', and readiness to put measures before men, were to prove so valuable to Pitt. The fact that by serving Pitt they also served themselves does not detract from their achievements.

In December 1784 Carmarthen sent Harris a firm instruction based on his understanding of Pitt's intentions and also his knowledge of Harris's loathing of the French: 'The general line of your conduct must ever be to crush, as far as possible, the assumed and

---

* William IV, 6th Stadtholder, had married Anne, daughter of George II.

† They were related by marriage: Harris and Elliot married sisters. Harriet and Maria Amyand; and Eden's wife, Eleanor, was Elliot's sister. They were not, however, always on good terms.

despotic influence of France . . . yet even the attainment of this object must not be purchased at the expense of having to support at all events, the enfeebled and impoverished remains of a distressed and divided country.' [317] Harris responded early in February, enclosing with his letter a penetrating analysis of the European political situation. 'I know, my dear Lord,' he wrote, 'from frequent conversations with yourself and Mr Pitt, how inconvenient, even to distress, it would be to risk a war. . . . But it is not the evil of the day we are to attend to, it is to those many great and inevitable ones which if we allow them to go their time, will in the end crush us entirely.' [318] Of Joseph II he wrote, 'his ambition is greater than his wisdom; his means, I trust, are less'. He considered the general situation 'never to have been so critical at any epoch since the breaking out of the Thirty-years' war.' The emergence of Russia as a power in Europe had upset all previous concepts of balance in Europe and, he believed, 'the moment is not very distant when England will be called upon to take, once more, a share in the concerns of the Continent; and one may venture to pronounce that the line of conduct she holds at this important conjuncture will decide whether she is again to become a leading power, and regain her former influence, or whether she is to remain exposed to all the dangers of an isolated system.' He warned against allowing the barrier of the Low Countries, created by the Treaty of Utrecht, to be broken down by conquest by France or any subject ally of the French, giving them command over 'that whole extent of coast which reaches from Ostend to the Texel'.

Neither the warning nor the implied reproof were lost on Pitt, but he knew, better than any other, the extent of Britain's weakness, and he was determined to keep Europe at a distance while the nation's economy and defences were repaired. The King, too, though he was thought to have got himself into a 'd——d scrape' by the commitment of Hanover to the Fürstenbund, hoped that Britain might again become 'respectable, if she has the sense to remain quiet some years, and not by wanting to take a showy part in the transactions of Europe again become the dupe of other Powers, and from ideal greatness draw herself into lasting distress. The old English saying is applicable to our situation: "England must cut her coat according to her cloth".' [319]

George III's involvement with the Fürstenbund, although no part of British policy, caused deep offence to Russia and Austria. The Empress Catherine sent a sharply worded protest, demanding the withdrawal of Hanover from the treaty, but the King remained firm. The Bavarian exchange was unacceptable to the German Princes and an uncomfortable prospect for Britain. The alliance of Hanover with Prussia provided a link that, with patient diplomacy, might be forged into an alliance between Prussia and Britain. That such a prospect became a practicable possibility owed much to the tireless efforts of Joseph Ewart in Berlin and Sir James Harris at The Hague.

In November 1785 the French followed up their success in mediating between the United Provinces and Austria, and concluded a treaty of alliance with the Dutch. Through Carmarthen, Pitt urged Harris to do everything in his power to prevent ratification of the treaty, but Britain had nothing to offer to the United Provinces and there was no possibility that Harris could succeed. The French Minister for Foreign Affairs, Charles Gravier, comte de Vergennes, was a statesman of outstanding ability, implacably hostile to England. The treaty with the Dutch completed his design. The alliance with Austria, the cornerstone of his policy, was secured through Marie Antoinette; the Empress Catherine would remain on terms of friendship while she required the compliance or co-operation of Austria in her plans to conquer Turkey; and the new treaty with the United Provinces paved the way for co-operation between the French and Dutch East India Companies. The Duke of Richmond, Master-General of the Ordnance, issued a dire warning: 'Holland seems lost to us both in Europe and the East Indies; and should the Emperor and Russia unite with France, Sweden must follow, and Denmark dare not be our friend. Under such circumstances what are we to look for but utter ruin?' [320]

Pitt refused to be stampeded into precipitate action. It was already too late to frustrate the French design and he had chosen to ignore the slender opportunity to do so. While the great powers of Europe concentrated their attention upon foreign affairs, their national economies were allowed to wither. Inaction involved enormous risks, but if war could be avoided for as long as five years, Britain need not be drawn into it unarmed. In the meantime, Pitt was content to effect diplomacy through trade.

During the next seven years, talks for commercial treaties were held with eight European countries—Spain, Portugal, France,

Prussia, Russia, the United Provinces, Poland, and the Kingdom of the Two Sicilies—and Morocco. Transactions were also considered with Sweden, Turkey, and the Austrian Netherlands. As the *Public Advertiser* announced with pride, 'There never was in the country, or perhaps in the world, a Minister who engaged in so vast, so intricate, so complete, and consequently so difficult an undertaking, as that which at present occupies the attention of Mr Pitt. It is no less than a general arrangement of the commerce of the greatest commercial power that ever existed, with almost all the great commercial powers of the world.' [321] All the negotiations, except those with France and Morocco, failed, and they may fairly be said to have done so as a direct result of Pitt's personal direction and not in spite of it. If he had been prepared to make greater concessions, the negotiations with Russia, Spain and the United Provinces might have succeeded, but he never lost sight of the need to protect the British carrying trade and thus the manpower reserves of the Royal Navy. Any relaxation of the Navigation Acts was unthinkable, and, even had he been prepared to consider such a concession, it would not have been approved by parliament.

There were, of course, other contributory causes of failure. Apart from the French, none of the governments of the countries concerned was in urgent need of a commercial treaty with Britain: on the contrary, there was considerable apprehension that the mutual relaxation or removal of tariffs would enable British manufacturers, whose products were recognized as superior in quality and available in great volume, to flood the Continent, creating large trade deficits in Europe and a corresponding surplus for Britain. Nor was it considered practicable, or even possible, to separate commerce from foreign policy. Pitt insisted that a commercial contract was not to be regarded as a treaty of alliance, and he could cite the French treaty negotiated by William Eden in 1786 * as evidence of this truth. Fox was not alone in believing it to be an ill-conceived exception. Events did not prove Pitt's theory wrong, but they did show it to be impracticable unless the move towards the elimination of protective tariffs was accompanied by an equivalent move towards free navigation. During the period of the negotiations, the British adverse trade balance with Europe was transformed into a substantial surplus. It

* See p. 144.

219

was not long before the French were denouncing the commercial treaty as the cause of their economic plight, and viewing with increased rancour the trade partners whom they held responsible for it. Intended as a step towards the improvement of traditionally hostile relations, the treaty came to be regarded in France as an added reason for irreconcilable antagonism.

Five weeks before the French commercial treaty was signed at Versailles, Frederick the Great died. He left the care of Prussia to his nephew, the handsome, extravagant and temperamentally unstable Frederick William II *. The new King seemed indifferent to his sister's rapidly deteriorating situation in the United Provinces. The 'Patriots', representing primarily the middle class and looking to France for help in their struggle against the Stadtholder, were supported by the overwhelming majority of the urban population. The Stadtholder retained the allegiance of the rural population, even in Holland, and also of three of the smaller provinces, but his position was becoming increasingly precarious. The Estates of Holland had deprived him of his command of the Province's regular troops, and the appearance of the Free Corps, formed from groups of armed burghers, was particularly alarming. It was clear that the Patriots were receiving substantial financial aid from France. French troops were also being fed secretly into the Free Corps. Unless some urgent and positive action were taken, the United Provinces must inevitably fall under the domination of France. Harris, called to London for consultation with the Cabinet, pleaded for a commitment to military intervention. The French had let it be known that any outside interference would be opposed by force, but Harris expressed his conviction that 'till France is ready, *nothing will provoke* her to quarrel with us, and when she is ready, nothing will prevent it.' [322]

Pitt, fully aware of the extreme dangers, not only to the stability of the Low Countries but also to British possessions in India, insisted upon further delay. Funds were made available to Harris for the support of the loyal provinces, enabling them to employ troops who had deserted or had been dismissed from the army of the Province of Holland, but he was not permitted to offer the Stadtholder's party any assurance of military aid. Three events gave Pitt the opportunity

* Aptly described by Frederick the Great as 'my booby of a nephew'.

for which he had been waiting. The first was the curt rejection by France of Prussia's proposal of joint mediation. This rebuff was accompanied by a harsh warning that Prussian interference would provoke serious consequences. Frederick William's anger was further inflamed by the news, late in June 1787, that his sister, while attempting to travel to The Hague, had been arrested by troops of the Free Corps and forced to return to Nijmegen. The Princess of Orange, who had deliberately engineered this incident, appealed to Prussia and Britain for protection. The King of Prussia sent a note to the States-General, the majority of whose members remained loyal to the Stadtholder, demanding an immediate apology from the Province of Holland. This was not forthcoming. Meanwhile, there were rumours of French troops mustering on the frontier of the Austrian Netherlands, and of French naval preparations.

Grenville, dispatched to The Hague, confirmed Harris's reports and underwrote his opinion that the Stadtholder must be supported. For the first time, a firm assurance was given to the Orange leaders that Britain would not desert them. Preparations were made to hire 5,000 Hessian troops for British service on the Continent, and the Prussian King was secretly informed that the British fleet would guard the Dutch coast against any French attempt to land in the United Provinces. Harris, whose tireless intrigues had helped to keep the Orange party together, redoubled his efforts with greater confidence in his ability to honour his promises.

On 7 September the Turks declared war on Russia. This removed any threat that Austria, already pledged to a Russian alliance, would become involved in affairs in the Netherlands unless Austrian territory was violated. Two days later, Frederick William sent an ultimatum to Holland, giving the province four days to reply. On 14 September, no apology having been received, the elderly Duke of Brunswick led 20,000 troops across the Dutch frontier.

Almost everywhere in the United Provinces the Prussian army was accorded a rapturous welcome. Resistance by the Free Corps was negligible, and the claim that the Patriots represented the people was discredited. On 20 September, the Prince of Orange made a triumphant entry into The Hague, greeted by cheering crowds. Harris, who received a personal ovation, lost no time in persuading the Estates of Holland to rescind their Acts depriving the Stadtholder of his constitutional authority. He crowned this achievement by obtaining their agreement to withdraw an appeal to France made on 9 September.

There was still some reason to fear that the French might act, but they had been outmanoeuvred and were bitterly aware that secret British negotiations were largely responsible for their discomfiture. They were further aware that Britain was rearming. A formal declaration that France was committed in honour to the treaty of alliance with the United Provinces and thus to the support of the Estates of Holland was answered by a frigid assurance that any such intervention would be opposed. The Franco-Dutch treaty had been concluded with the States-General, which, with encouragement from Harris, had maintained a constant majority for the Stadtholder. The Estates of Holland were not even truly representative of the Province. 'His Majesty', wrote Pitt, 'has repeatedly declared the impossibility of his being indifferent to any armed interference of France in the affairs of the Republic, which, if unopposed, must necessarily lead to consequences dangerous to the constitutional independence of those Provinces, and affecting in many respects the interests and security of his dominions. His Majesty has therefore found himself under the necessity of taking measures for equipping a considerable naval armament and for augmenting his land forces.' [323] Grenville was sent to Paris to reinforce Eden, but his presence, resented by Armand, comte de Montmorin, who had succeeded Vergennes as Foreign Minister, made no difference to the outcome. The final blow to French hopes was delivered by the Emperor Joseph II, who made it clear that he approved of the reinstatement of the Stadtholder. On 27 October Montmorin signed an extraordinary document declaring that it had never been the French intention to interfere in Dutch affairs and affirming a decision to disarm. This amounted to a public humiliation and it created a sensation in Europe. After a long absence, Britain was understood to have returned in strength to the European political scene.

Pitt's handling of his first major venture into foreign policy had been a triumph. The House of Orange had been restored, and French plans frustrated, and all without British military involvement. There was also a marked distinction, that did not pass unnoticed, between the open support of constitutional authority, however motivated, and a devious attempt at subversion for the purpose of creating a dependent or subject state. Pitt had displayed steadiness and tenacity, and a remarkable sense of timing. Towards the end of 1786 he had written to Harris cautioning him to avoid any firm commitment and to refrain from encouraging the Orange party to take risks that could not be justified without support, but he added, 'The great objective now . . . [is] *to endeavour to keep together a party which may act with advantage, both for their own country and for us, on some future day, if it should arrive.'* [324] For the next ten months he had taken personal control of the direction of foreign affairs, relying upon Harris and Grenville, but without undermining the authority of Carmarthen. In Harris he had discovered a diplomat of exceptional ability, a man of experience, tact, tenacity and daring, who was nevertheless prepared to obey his instructions. In 1788 Harris was rewarded by promotion to the rank of ambassador and elevation to the peerage as Lord Malmesbury.

The most important long-term advantage to be gained from Britain's diplomatic victory was the prospect of renewing alliances with the United Provinces and Prussia. The Anglo-Dutch treaty, a defensive alliance guaranteeing the Dutch Constitution, was signed in April 1788, coinciding with a similar treaty between the United Provinces and Prussia. The Dutch had hoped to obtain the restoration of Negapatam, but Pitt rejected the suggestion. The defensive Anglo-Prussian treaty was signed in August. * Both parties to it were anxious not to provoke the formation of hostile alliances in response, and each was wary of the other's ambitions and commitments. Prussia hoped for territorial gains, by a manoeuvre of extraordinary complexity involving a series of interdependent exchanges, from the war between Russia and Turkey. Britain had no desire to be drawn into campaigns in eastern Europe. Prussia, on the other hand, wanted no part in British maritime adventures.

The Triple Alliance † owed its existence to the outbreak of war between Turkey and Russia, which, by involving Austria, had isolated France. It was this consequential shifting of balance, with all the attendant dangers of commitment to policies beyond his control, that had made Pitt reluctant to entangle Britain, by alliances, in the convoluted affairs of Europe. Isolation, on the other hand, was

---

* A provisional treaty had been signed in great secrecy by Malmesbury in June.

† A popular misnomer as no single treaty was signed by all three parties. As John Ehrman has pointed out (*The Younger Pitt: the Years of Acclaim*, p. 542) the alliance was triangular.

dangerous to Britain and her colonial possessions, and strong defensive alliances might be valuable in their exercise of mutual restraint, in their restraining influence upon others and in their power of mediation. Pitt would have preferred an alliance with Russia or Austria, but all overtures to Joseph II and the Empress Catherine had been rejected. The recovery of the Dutch alliance was a brilliant achievement, but Pitt viewed the Prussian connection with acute and justifiable suspicion.

It was not long before his worst suspicions were confirmed. In the summer of 1788 Gustavus III of Sweden declared war on Russia. He demanded the cession of Carelia and Livonia, and the return to Turkey of the Crimea, seized by Catherine five years earlier. In support of these remarkable claims, he marched his army across the frontiers of his Finnish province and advanced towards St Petersburg. Catherine, caught unprepared, was obliged to withdraw troops from her Turkish campaigns, exposing the Austrians to a series of humiliating defeats. The Swedish navy was defeated by the Russian fleet * in the Gulf of Finland, and the army, almost within striking distance of the Russian capital, halted, mutinied and retreated. The Danes chose this favourable moment, in spite of warnings from Prussia, to honour a secret treaty with the Russians, and invade Sweden. Urgent action was needed to prevent the dismemberment of Sweden by Denmark and Russia. Britain and Prussia, acting in concert, offered to mediate, and Prussia threatened to invade the Danish Duchy of Holstein. Neither the offer nor the threat would have saved Gustavus without the extraordinary and unauthorized behaviour of Gilbert Elliot's brother Hugh, the flamboyant and reckless minister at Copenhagen. Elliot obtained from the dejected Gustavus his authority to negotiate, and succeeded, by a curious mixture of diplomacy and coercion, in arranging an eight-day armistice. This was later prolonged to six months and ended in the Danish withdrawal from the war. This brilliant achievement was greeted in London with mixed feelings. Pitt had particularly wanted to avoid any commitment offensive either to Denmark or Russia, or too close an identification with Prussian policy. Elliot's actions had

* The Russian fleet was commanded by Admiral Sir Samuel Greig (1735-88), who had served in the Royal Navy until 1763, and officered largely by Scots. Greig is generally credited with having founded the modern Russian navy.

saved Sweden, but at the heavy cost of a further deterioration in relations with Russia.

The Prussians, meanwhile, were pursuing their ambitions in eastern Europe, and, even more dangerously, in the Austrian Netherlands. The Poles had, in the spring of 1789, shaken off the control of Russia. Frederick William seized the opportunity to negotiate an alliance with Poland, at the same time encouraging Gustavus III to continue the war against Russia. The British, noting with apprehension the Prussian view that Sweden's continued involvement was advantageous as a *diversion in case the Allies should take part in a Turkish War,'* [325] sent urgent warnings of disapproval which temporarily cooled Prussian ardour, but in March 1791 the Prussians and Poles signed a treaty of mutual support that brought the eastern conflict threateningly close to Britain.

In the Netherlands, as in others of the Austrian possessions, there were signs of revolt against Joseph II's attempts to centralize government and raise funds for the Turkish war. In June 1789, the Emperor dispossessed the Estates of Brabant of their ancient rights and privileges, provoking revolution and a declaration for a Belgian Republic under the guarantee and protection of the Triple Alliance. Envoys were dispatched to Berlin and The Hague, where they received a cordial welcome, and to London, where their reception was more guarded. Unlike the Prussians, the British had no reason to hope for the weakening of Austria, and good cause for maintaining friendly relations at a time when the Emperor was believed to be dying. His brother Leopold, who would succeed him, was understood to favour policies very different from Joseph's. An independent Belgian republic would be far more vulnerable to French influence or conquest than the semi-independent provinces under Austrian rule. While the removal of the Estates was not a welcome development, the overriding concern of Britain was the security of the Austrian Netherlands against the French.

Once more, as the Prussians tried to force the pace for recognition of the Belgian Republic, the conflict of interest within the Triple Alliance became apparent. In January 1790, the British and Dutch succeeded in restraining Prussia by a tripartite agreement that there should be no intervention without Austrian consent. Soon afterwards, the deputies of the Belgic provinces issued from Brussels a declaration deposing the Emperor Joseph II and setting up a Federal

Congress. An appeal to France for aid was, fortunately for Britain, rejected.

This dangerous situation was transformed, though not immediately, by the death of Joseph II in February. Leopold II lost no time in asking Britain to act as mediator in negotiations for a general peace. Pitt agreed, with the proviso that the terms proposed should be on the basis of the *status quo ante bellum*. A settlement on these lines was reached by Austria and Prussia at Reichenbach on 27 July. The Austrians agreed to withdraw from the war with Turkey and to restore the rights and privileges of the Netherlands. In return, the Triple Alliance would use its influence to end the Russo-Turkish war and to persuade the Belgian provinces to accept Austrian rule. This happy outcome appeared to be another triumph for Pitt. Prussia had been restrained from entering the war, and Austria had withdrawn from it; the Austrian Netherlands had neither gained their independence nor been swallowed by France; the alliance of the great Imperial powers had been shaken; and British prestige as the mediator, if not the arbiter, of Europe had been enhanced. The achievement was substantial, but there were dangerous legacies, not the least of which was the continuing war between Russia and Turkey. It was one of the ironies that his success in making peace had led Pitt to commit Britain irrevocably to participation in Europe.

The events in eastern Europe had distracted attention from the internal struggles of France. The Revolution was not ignored: in England it was at first viewed with sympathy; but by the end of 1789 the fears of French intervention had been dispelled. It was recognized that for the time being the influence of France could be discounted. This was particularly fortunate for Britain at a time when a serious dispute, threatening war, had arisen with Spain. On 21 January 1790, eight months after the event, news reached London that a British vessel trading on the north-west coast of America had been seized by the Spanish, and the captain and crew treated with brutality. Later it became known that a number of ships had been involved, in separate incidents, at Nootka Sound, a natural harbour on the west coast of Vancouver Island *. The first news was soon followed by an official protest from the Spanish government asserting the sovereignty of Spain over the waters of the Pacific Ocean and the

* Then part of California.

226

west coast of America as far north as the Gulf of Alaska. The Spanish note required the prevention of any further trespass and the punishment of offenders. As Foreign Secretary, the Duke of Leeds * had already dispatched a curt demand for the immediate release of the captured vessel. In reply to the Spanish note he repeated the demand for the return of all confiscated property, and declined to discuss Spanish claims to sovereignty in the area until compensation had been received.

On the face of it, the incident was trivial, involving a few ships and their crews, and some trading rights on a coastline so obscure that few people had ever heard of it. The Spanish claim, founded upon a Papal Bull of 1493 granting to Spain all territories outside Europe not at that date occupied by another European power, had never been accepted by England. Vancouver Island had been named by Captain Cook in 1778, and during the next ten years a small, thriving settlement had been founded there, trading in furs and ginseng with China. The principle of Spanish sovereignty over the Pacific coastline was unacceptable, particularly in view of the developing whaling industry. The Spanish reply to Britain's demand was uncompromising: the crews had been released, but no compensation was offered for the insult or loss of property; and Spanish sovereignty over the Pacific coast was reaffirmed.

The Cabinet authorized the dispatch of a further demand for 'immediate and adequate satisfaction for the outrages committed', and the mobilization of the fleet. On 24 July Spain agreed to return the captured ships and compensate their owners, but the principle of rights and the ownership of the settlement at Nootka Sound remained unresolved. Preparations for war continued while ambassadors of both countries scurried round the Courts of Europe soliciting support. Britain quickly obtained promises of help from her partners in the Triple Alliance: Prussia offered military aid in Europe; and the Dutch agreed to provide ten ships of the line. Spain, on the other hand, received little sympathy from Austria, Russia or Denmark, and was thus thrown back on the hope that France would honour the Family Compact.† It seemed, at first, that

---

* The Marquess of Carmarthen had succeeded, in 1789, to the title of 5th Duke of Leeds.

† The secret *Pacte de Famille*, signed in 1761 by all the Bourbon monarchs—Louis XV of France, Carlos III of Spain, Ferdinand IV of Naples, and Filippo of Parma—for mutual defence, and with the specific and declared aim of ending British maritime supremacy.

the French would support Spain. In August, the National Assembly approved the fitting-out of forty-five ships of the line, but by the beginning of October sentiment in France had changed.

Pitt had, as usual in an emergency, taken charge of the negotiations. While talks were being held to persuade the Prussians and Dutch to promise aid, and it seemed possible that the French would support Spain, his attitude had been firm but not unyielding. Early in October he saw that Spain was, perhaps temporarily, isolated. He seized the opportunity to present Spain with an ultimatum. On 28 October the Spanish Foreign Minister signed a convention, agreeing, without significant alteration, to the British terms. The settlement at Nootka was restored and Spanish claims to sovereignty over the Pacific coast were renounced. The British were granted the freedom to trade and fish in the Pacific, but all commerce with Spanish settlements was prohibited, and British ships were forbidden to approach within ten leagues of their shores. North of the established Spanish territories, both countries were free to trade and settle at will. There were details to be worked out, and it was more than three years before they were finally agreed; but the crisis was over.

Once more, the threat of war had been averted, and again it was Pitt's immaculate sense of timing that had been responsible for his success. The Nootka Sound crisis, however, cast new light on Pitt's strategic aims and on his abilities. In the negotiations concerned with the Dutch and Austrian Netherlands, and the Turkish War, his aims had been clear: to re-establish British strength and prestige in Europe by a combination of alliances and mediation, without entering into any commitment that might lead to war; to prevent French domination over the Netherlands; and to use the period of peace to restore the British economy, providing a solid foundation for defence and future expansion overseas. His direction of negotiations had been notable for patience, moderation, candour, and imperturbability. These qualities had been replaced, in the Nootka Sound dispute, by a steely determination bordering on ruthlessness. He had shown none of the caution and painstaking perseverance that had distinguished his earlier efforts.

The reason for this change of tactics was two-fold. The Spanish claim was, as he told the House of Commons, '. . . the most absurd and exorbitant that could well be imagined . . . indefinite in extent,

228

and which originated in no treaty.' [326] He added, significantly, that if the claim were accepted, it would exclude the British from 'an infant trade, the future expansion of which could not but prove essentially beneficial to the commercial interest of Great Britain.' This was the authentic echo of his father's voice from fifty years earlier: 'When trade is at stake it is your last retrenchment, you must defend it or perish.' [327] It was the fundamental principle upon which Pitt's policies were founded. The preservation and future expansion of British trade was of paramount importance: national security must be risked for it, for national security would be endangered if it were lost. His second reason for using coercion against Spain was his apprehension that the Russo-Turkish war might yet fragment the Reichenbach agreement. The pressure and influence exerted by Britain had succeeded with Prussia, Austria, the Netherlands, Sweden and Denmark, but all attempts at negotiation with Russia had failed. The ambitions of the Empress Catherine were unsatisfied and continued to threaten the delicate balance. To be ready to meet this threat, Pitt must obtain, by any means at hand, a speedy solution to the dispute with Spain.

Though he viewed the upheaval in France with concern, he had no cause to suppose that the effective absence of the French from the councils of Europe could be anything but beneficial.

By the end of 1790, the unbroken success of Pitt's negotiations had helped to restore some semblance of a balance of power. Britain's position, fortified by the Triple Alliance, had been transformed from that of an isolated and bankrupt petitioner to one of stability and authority. Pitt's personal credit was at its peak, and the Opposition in disorder. Within eight months his policies appeared to be in ruins, the Triple Alliance was breaking up, his ministry shaken to its foundations, and the Opposition reunited.

This remarkable reverse was the result of a disastrous error of judgement arising from that curious mixture of optimism, obstinacy and arrogance that occasionally robbed Pitt of his natural caution. Pitt's determination to bring the Russo-Turkish war to an end was not motivated solely, or even primarily, by his desire for peace in Europe. The failure of trade talks with Russia, and friendly overtures received from the Poles, who were interested in the possibility of joining the Triple Alliance, convinced him of the necessity of a peace treaty based on a return to the *status quo*. Such a treaty would have the multiple advantages of securing new markets, preventing the Russians from gaining access to the Mediterranean, and encouraging the accession of both Poland and Turkey to the Triple Alliance. Under these conditions, Sweden and Denmark might also be persuaded to join the Alliance, forging a defensive chain from the Baltic to the Black Sea.

This grand design was made unattainable by the successes of the Russian armies and the delay in confirming by treaty the agreement made between Austria and Turkey at Reichenbach. The Prussian Foreign Minister intrigued secretly with Russia. Leopold II re-opened negotiations with Catherine, and Gustavus III put the use of his army up to auction. It soon became clear that the success of any negotiation for peace hinged upon Catherine's determination to retain the district of Ochakov, captured in 1788. The town itself, close to the entrance of the estuary formed by the Dnieper and Bug rivers, was believed to be of essential tactical importance to the Turks in the defence of Constantinople against naval assault from Sebastopol and Kherson, and to command the Polish commercial route down the Dniester to the Black Sea. Both Joseph Ewart in Berlin and Charles Whitworth in St Petersburg believed that determined and united action by the Triple Alliance would oblige Russia to make peace. William Eden, who had been rewarded for his services in France by elevation to the barony of Auckland, and had succeeded Malmesbury at The Hague, warned against relying upon the support of Prussia. He also provided convincing evidence, obtained from a Dutch admiral who had served with the Russian fleet, that the military importance of Ochakov had been greatly overstated.[328]

Pitt remained unconvinced, but in March 1791 the Duke of Leeds received, through the Prussian minister in London, a letter from Frederick William II requiring a definite statement of British support for the return of Ochakov to Turkey as a condition of peace. It was plain that the Prussian King expected Britain's help in return for the support given by the Triple Alliance in the Nootka Sound dispute. If Catherine II refused the terms, she was to be threatened with war. On 25 March an ultimatum was drawn up, and two days later the Dutch were requested to prepare a naval squadron to join the British fleet in the Baltic.

The Cabinet was divided, the Duke of Leeds advocating firm

resistance to Russian encroachment into the eastern Mediterranean with all the consequential effects on British commercial interests in the area and the shorter route to India, while the Duke of Richmond, mistrustful of Prussia, resolutely opposed any commitment to war with Russia. The feeling of parliament was tested in both Houses at the end of March and during the first two weeks of April. The Opposition, relishing Pitt's difficulties, united to attack his policy, but Sheridan's true opinion may be assessed from the light-hearted summary he wrote to Lady Bessborough:

> If the Empress can gain an ascendancy in Poland and by commanding the navigation of the Dnieper and the Dniester get complete possession of the Black Sea, then, Ma'am, with the future contrivance or assistance of the Emperor, she may certainly get actual possession of Constantinople and the European Provinces of Turkey which is all that's necessary, and then, Ma'am, turn the Black Sea into a Wet Dock, and floating down her stores from the North, fit out such a fleet, when no one can peep at her, that out they will come into the Mediterranean [and] swallow up all the States of Italy like larks; and at last a Russian Brigadier may be quartered at Roehampton *, for aught I know, within these hundred years, so on your account, Ma'am, I am rather for the Balance of Europe.[329]

In the Commons debates he derided Pitt's policy of resistance to Russia.

Fox, who had approved of intervention in the Low Countries, chose to base his argument on the futility of intervention except in circumstances that endangered British interests: 'If our allies were attacked or threatened, then, indeed, the honour of the nation would be concerned to interfere. We had no alliance with Turkey, and were only called upon to gratify the pride of our ministers, and to second the ill-judged policy of Prussia.' He advocated alliance with Russia, though he did not suggest how this might be achieved: 'Her extent of territory, scanty revenue, and thin population, made her power by no means formidable to us; a power whom we could neither attack, nor be attacked by; and this was the power against whom we were

---

* Where the Bessboroughs had a house.

going to war!' [330] He weakened his case by using the Ochakov debate for an ill-timed panegyric on the French Revolution, which affronted many of his own supporters, but there was little doubt that his attacks on the government had been effective.

Pitt's replies, as coolly logical as ever, lacked conviction. Even his assertion that a strengthened and united Poland, under the protection of the Triple Alliance, would be able to supply essential naval stores for which Britain was then obliged to rely on Russia, failed to make any great impression. The government's majority sank to eighty, and Fox forecast that if war were declared the House would refuse to vote supplies. However unlikely it might be that such a move would succeed, Fox was gaining support, and Pitt knew that the credibility of his ministry was at stake. His position was further shaken by continuing Russian victories and the news, received from Auckland, who had 'happened to see' a cipher letter from Frederick William II to his minister in London, that Austria was arming in preparation for a denial of the Reichenbach agreement. [331] On 10 April, Pitt informed Ewart that he was prepared to seek a compromise solution. According to Ewart, he announced this with 'tears in his eyes', admitting that he had contemplated resigning. [322] On the 21st, Leeds, who refused to accept the change of policy, resigned. He was succeeded at the Foreign Office by Grenville, who had been awarded a barony in November.

Following lengthy negotiations, Catherine II agreed to make peace with Turkey on her own terms. She graciously accepted, as her reward, all Turkish territory east of the Dniester, but agreed to permit free navigation of the river. All the demands of the Allies were rejected, and Poland, so recently reborn under an hereditary monarchy and 'a constitution better than that of England' [333], was abandoned. It was a disgraceful and humiliating outcome of Pitt's policies, and one for which he was personally responsible. It was also a classic example of his over-optimism, amounting at times to arrogance, and his failure to respond to altered circumstances. He had been, it is true, hampered by the duplicity and indecision of Prussia, the threat of Austrian betrayal, the ambivalent attitude of Sweden, lack of unanimity in the Cabinet, and the undoubted opposition of the British people; but by delaying too long he allowed Russia time to consolidate early success and build victory upon it, and he did not recognize the implications of the revolution in France.

Catherine II made peace, on terms that were far more reasonable than her victories gave her strength to exact, because she saw the revolution as a menace to the principle of absolute monarchy. In recognition of his part in the British humiliation, she ordered a bust of Fox. As she told her ambassador in London, *'Je veut le mettre sur ma Colonade [sic] entre ceux de Démosthène et Ciceron. . . . Il a délivré par son eloquence sa Patrie et la Russie d'une guerre à la quelle il n'y avoit ni justice ni raisons.'* [334] Fox's promotion to such elevated company, where he supplanted the suddenly discredited Voltaire, was temporary. His impassioned championship of the revolutionaries soon caused his likeness to be consigned, with those of others suspected of democratic principles, to the darkness of the palace cellars. His political reputation in England was soon to suffer similar eclipse.

XVI

The Impact of Revolution
1789-1792

ON 21 JULY 1789 the *Morning Post* announced the fall of the Bastille in terms of glowing approval: 'An Englishman not filled with esteem and admiration at the sublime manner in which one of the most IMPORTANT REVOLUTIONS the world has ever seen is now effecting, must be dead to every sense of virtue and of freedom.' Nine days later, Fox, the dedicated Francophile, was hailing it as 'How much the greatest event . . . that ever happened in the world! And how much the best!' [335] The Revolution aroused widespread sympathy and support, motivated partly by self-interest and a sense, later proved to be false, of secure immunity to its consequences. The financial collapse of France dispelled any fears of renewed rivalry in India or anywhere else, and there was thought to be no possibility that dangerous 'democratical' opinions would cross the Channel and take root in Britain. Pitt, with some satisfaction, declared France to be 'an object of compassion'. [336]

Fox, as intemperate as ever in his emotional reactions, persuaded himself that he saw a close parallel between the Revolution in France and the Revolution of 1688: representative government, freedom of speech and thought, and the rule of law, would supersede the despotism, repression and prohibitions of the *ancien régime*. The use

234

of violence was to be regretted, but such a glorious purpose could not be achieved without sacrifice. He was not alone in his enthusiasm. In 1789, the majority of people of education and enlightenment sympathized with the revolutionaries, and diminishing but still significant patronage was evident at least until the establishment of the Jacobin dictatorship under Robespierre in 1794. In Britain they attracted support from all classes, but particularly from the 'middling' class scientists and industrialists, and from the poets. Josiah Wedgwood the potter, John Wilkinson the ironmaster, and Thomas Telford the engineer, were partisans, as were the poets William Wordsworth, Samuel Taylor Coleridge, William Blake and Robert Burns. Joseph Priestley the chemist and dissenting minister was another disciple of the Revolution and suffered for his beliefs in 1791, when the Birmingham mob burnt down his house, destroying his books, papers and scientific apparatus. Wedgwood considered the Revolution 'a very sudden and momentous event' and forecast that its consequences would be 'extensive beyond anything perhaps that we can at present imagine'.[337] He did not, however, imagine that these consequences would be confined within the frontiers of France: 'When', he wrote, 'the rights of men are ascertained with such precision, and laid down from such authority as the National assembly of France, other nations will begin to consider whether they are not men, and if men whether these rights do not belong to them.' It was a prospect that many then applauded. The comparison with the Glorious Revolution of 1688 was, as Burke was to show, false. The revolution in England had been the work of the aristocracy in defence of the Constitution. It had achieved its aims, and created no pattern for revolution elsewhere nor left any mark on other countries. The French Revolution began as an attempt by the aristocracy to regain control of the State, and developed, through a series of terrifying convulsions, into a rebellion, led by the middle class, that overthrew the State and formulated a constitution. The dream of 'the Enlightenment', the freedom of the individual declared in the revolutionary slogan 'Liberty, Equality and Fraternity', would have shocked Englishmen in 1688. It was dispelled by Napoleon, but the vision remained as the inspiration of all revolution. It was France, not England, that invented the vocabulary of revolution; and it was France that discovered the concept of mobilization. Had he known of its existence, Fox might have found a closer parallel in the

Industrial Revolution already gathering momentum in England.

Sympathy in Britain for the French Revolution sprang as much from the hope that it would transform French attitudes and policies as from any accord with its aims. Hostility towards France had been the dominant influence in English foreign policy since the middle Ages, and in the eighteenth century it was the most consistent thread running through English thought. As the abbé le Blanc wrote in 1747, 'the bulk of the English nation bear an inveterate hatred of the French, which they do not always take the pains to conceal from us.' [338] Mistrust and fear persisted in spite of adventures in Anglo-French co-operation or alliance during the reign of George I, and the commercial treaty of 1786. France was Britain's most dangerous rival in commerce, colonial expansion, and the struggle for command of the sea; and she was also, as the greatest Catholic power, the repository of the hopes of the Pretenders and the centre of the Bourbon family alliance. The history of Anglo-French relations since 1688 had been one of a century of war, briefly interrupted by ill-founded alliances and a series of treaties, of which only that of Utrecht, in 1713, lasted more than ten years. French intervention in the American Revolution had further embittered British sentiment. By bankrupting France it had also led more directly to revolution than the comparatively paltry extravagances of Louis XVI's court.*

The British tended naturally to align themselves with the Protestant powers—the United Provinces, Prussia and the German States, and the Scandinavian countries—against France, Spain, Austria and Italy, and this association had helped to maintain a balance of power. The Dutch alliance had been, and remained, particularly important to the preservation of British superiority at sea and thus to colonial expansion and trade. Chatham had been content to contain France in Europe, by much-criticized diversionary or 'eccentric' attacks on the coast and a liberal use of subsidies to allies, while he mopped up the French colonial empire. This called forth the accusation from the duc de Choiseul, French Foreign Minister during the Seven Year's War, that Britain was 'pretending to protect the balance on land which no one threatens, [while] destroying the balance at sea which no one defends.' [339] Pitt, by the commercial treaty of 1786, had attempted to lessen the effects of economic rivalry, which had made a lasting

---

* These amounted to little more than six per cent of government expenditure.

peace impossible. Though he denied that commercial agreement implied alliance, this was a clear indication of his understanding that trade was replacing religion as the most important influence on foreign policy.

The French Revolution appeared to offer Britain further time for economic revival. Pitt resolutely refused to make any judgement, in either moral or constitutional terms, and would have nothing to do with demands for intervention. He was content to watch the French struggle from a safe distance while at home the Opposition tore itself apart in a fury of internecine contention.

This it did with a dramatic effect worthy of a party that included the greatest actor-manager of the period. The old friendship between Fox and Burke had been showing signs of strain since the impeachment of Hastings, and it had not been improved by Fox's behaviour during the Regency crisis. It was shattered by the French Revolution. The first signs of a serious rift appeared during the debates on the Army Estimates in February 1790. Pitt, under attack from the Opposition for proposing a modest increase in the army, was careful, without mentioning either the necessity of presenting a firm front to Russia or the rumours of a dispute with Spain, to make it clear that the increase was not prompted by events in France. Indeed, he said, 'The present conditions of France must, sooner or later, terminate in general harmony and regular order; and though the fortunate arrangements of such a situation may make her more formidable, it may also render her less obnoxious as a neighbour. . . . Whenever the situation of France shall become restored, it will prove freedom rightly understood; freedom resulting from good order and good government; and thus circumstanced France will stand forward as one of the most brilliant powers in Europe; she will enjoy just that kind of liberty which I venerate.' Fox had already expressed his exultant approval of the Revolution, and unguardedly stated that '*a man, by becoming a soldier, did not cease to be a citizen*'.[340] Coming on top of reports of disobedience, indiscipline and riot among French regiments, this was considered tantamount to condoning mutiny. For members who remembered the necessary use of troops to quell the Gordon Riots, Fox's words were an ominous reminder that law and order depended upon the loyalty of the army.

In a long and reasoned speech, demolishing the argument that the French Revolution could be considered analogous to the Glorious

Revolution of 1688, Burke warned against the contagion of democratic principles and the peril of underrating the strength of France. He softened the implied rebuke, attributing Fox's enthusiasm to his love of liberty, but added that he would 'abandon his best friends, and join with his worst enemies . . . to resist all violent exertions to the spirit of innovation'. Fox in reply paid a generous tribute to Burke's high principles, judgement, and friendship, dissociated himself from any desire to introduce democracy into England, professed his faith in the Constitution, and distinguished between dangerous innovation and desirable development; but he reiterated his admiration for the Revolution and reaffirmed his faith in an outcome as favourable to Britain as to France. Burke was mollified by Fox's warm response and 'The day ended with sentiments not very widely divided and with unbroken friendship.' He could not, however, forgive Sheridan, who 'broke out into the most violent invective against him and asked "Whether the honourable gentleman had found his doctrine among the stones of the Bastile [sic]".' Burke, declaring in disgust that he and Sheridan were, from that time, 'separated in politics', also deplored the discovery that 'there were persons in this country who entertained theories of government incompatible with the safety of the state.' [341]

It was more than a year before the quarrel between Burke and Fox finally exploded. During the interval Burke published his *Reflections on The Revolution in France*.* It was a brilliant, though prejudiced, analysis of the harsh realities that lay half-hidden beneath the thin disguise of democratic principles and libertarian slogans. In contrast, he explored in detail the principles of the British Constitution, making full use of his painstaking studies of the Glorious Revolution and drawing from the comparison conclusions that were as clear and logical as they were persuasive. It was an astonishing performance from a man whose career had seemed to be dragging to a discredited and embittered end, and its immediate public impact was electrifying. In a flurry of superlatives, the impressionable Fanny Burney described it as 'the noblest, deepest, most animated and exalted' work she had ever read, and her excitement was not untypical of conservative reaction. The book was predictably well received in Court circles and by the government, but it also stimulated a

---

* Published November 1790. Extracts appeared in the *Public Advertiser* from 2 November.

favourable response from among the Whigs. Burke's passionate belief in the fundamental principles of the British Constitution was expressed in a clarion call for its defence, and this could not fail to appeal to all but the most extreme reformers. Though it was widely read in France, his work was, as he admitted, directed to his own country, where the growth of 'reforming societies', whose intentions were regarded as subversive, was already causing alarm. As always, Burke overstated his case: religious dissenters were identified with reformers, and all were assumed to be revolutionaries. The cause of moderate reform, espoused by Pitt, received a blow from which it was not to recover during his lifetime.

The Whig Opposition, which had closed ranks for a general election in the summer of 1790, was once more in abject disarray. The election made little difference to the strengths of the parties, and the satisfactory settlement of the Nootka Sound dispute had justified the government's belligerent attitude towards Spain. The publication of Burke's *Reflections* was deliberately timed to achieve the greatest possible effect on the new parliament. The gap between Burke and Fox was widening. As Burke was increasingly disturbed by Fox's jubilant praise for the Revolution, so he was also disgusted and saddened by Fox's indifference to the prosecution of Hastings. Addington's first important decision as Speaker was to rule, in December, that the dissolution of parliament had not abated the Hastings impeachment. The decision was controversial, but it was supported by both Pitt and Dundas. Pitt was sickened by the prolonged torture of Hastings and by Burke's obdurate malevolence, but the question was one of sufficient constitutional significance to override personal inclination. If dissolution automatically put an end to impeachment proceedings, it would be in the power of the King to protect a favourite servant by calling an election. It would also be possible for the House of Lords to achieve a similar result by deliberately prolonging proceedings beyond the life of the elected parliament. Burke, who was determined to continue the persecution at any price, found himself in closer accord with ministers than with his own party.

In March Pitt brought forward his Bill to reform the government of Canada. The Quebec Act of 1774, by providing for the preservation of French laws and customs as protection for the overwhelming majority of the population, had offended British settlers and imposed unnecessary and unacceptable restrictions upon merchants. The Act of 1791, drafted and amended by Sydney, Grenville and Dundas, sought, in Pitt's words, 'to promote the happiness and internal policy of the province and to put an end to the differences of opinion and growing competition that had for some years existed in Canada between the ancient inhabitants and the new settlers from England and America * . . . and to bring the government of the province, as near as the nature and situation of it would admit, to the British Constitution.' [342] His solution to this problem was the division of Canada into an Upper and a Lower Province, conforming approximately to the distribution of the two estranged populations. The Bill became law in May, and its provisions remained in force until the Act of Union in 1841.

During the Ochakov debate on 15 April, Fox had infuriated Burke by using the occasion to deliver his famous panegyric upon the French Revolution, 'the most stupendous and glorious edifice of liberty, which had been erected on the foundations of human integrity in any time or country.' [343] Burke, denied an opportunity to reply at the time, determined to do so during the debate on the Canada Bill. On the morning of 21 April Fox called on Burke and they walked together, arm in arm, to the House of Commons. Two weeks later, the last embers of their friendship were extinguished. During that brief interval, leading Whigs, aware of Burke's intention, endeavoured to dissuade him. The Duke of Portland, leader of the party, was satisfied that the crisis would pass, leaving the Opposition more united than before. The *Morning Chronicle* of 4 May expressed the pious hope that 'no altercation will occur on the subject of French politics that might in its effects weaken the present virtuous and formidable minority'. All were destined to be disappointed.

In the debate on the Canada Bill on 6 May, Burke made no attempt to speak to the motion, being called to order six times in the course of a long speech for defying the rules of the House. In reply, Fox remarked that 'it seemed that this was a day of privilege when any gentleman might stand up, select his mark, and abuse any government he pleased whether it had any reference or not to the

* The American war had driven thousands of 'United Empire Loyalists' from the United States into Canada where they had settled in the Maritime Provinces (principally in New Brunswick) or close to the Great Lakes.

point in question.' He recognized Burke's strictures as being aimed at him and reproved Burke for his 'manifest eagerness to seek a difference of opinion, and anxiety to discover a cause of dispute'. He went on to repeat his description of the French Revolution as 'one of the most glorious events in the history of mankind'. Burke responded with a measured defence of constitutional monarchy, and added that he would risk the loss of everything in his adherence to it. Fox interrupted him to whisper that 'there was no loss of friends'. Burke retorted 'Yes, there was a loss of friends—he knew the price of his conduct—he had done his duty at the price of his friend—their friendship was at an end.' On hearing this, Fox burst into tears, and it was some minutes before he could compose himself to reply. He began by trying to effect a reconciliation, but, as he spoke, his feelings of wounded pride took command and he ended by declaring that he would avoid Burke's company until he should have moderated his opinions.

Pitt, with cool deliberation, both fostered and aggravated the quarrel. He had known of Burke's intention to use the Canada Bill debate for a reply to Fox's speech of 15 April; he had spoken in Burke's favour when he was called to order; and he congratulated Burke warmly on his speech, thanked him for his timely warnings, and promised his co-operation in 'taking every possible means' to preserve the Constitution.[344]

The wanton destruction of his friendship with Fox condemned Burke to isolation. Later it came to be looked upon as a symbol of the disintegration of the old Whig party but its effect at the time was small. Burke's personal following had never been large. He was admired for his intellect, his loyalty and his integrity, but his increasing irritability and the violence of his crusading spirit made his colleagues as uneasy as Fox's wild inconsistencies and ungoverned emotions. Fox was easily forgiven because he offered a genuine and comforting warmth in friendship; Burke was isolated because he cauterized his own wounds with a fire that blistered all around him.

It should not be supposed that Pitt nourished the destructive wrangle between Fox and Burke merely from personal malice. Though he was seldom slow to take advantage of Fox's impetuosity or distress, he could not afford to be seen to be taking either side in the quarrel. It would, however, have been the nadir of political incompetence to neglect an opportunity to widen the rift in the Opposition by emphasizing the differences between the factions. Fox had asserted that the rights of man were 'the basis and foundation of every national constitution, and even of the British constitution itself'. Burke insisted that the Constitution was 'founded upon the wisdom of antiquity, and sanctioned by the experience of time'.[345] This was the essential difference of principle that divided the Opposition. By appearing to offer renewed friendship in return for grievous injury, Fox had attracted sympathy and respect, but it was Burke's principles, those of the old Rockingham Whigs, that finally prevailed.

The Duke of Portland approved of Burke's *Reflections*, and there were many others among the Whigs, probably a majority, who sympathized with the principles affirmed in the book and in Burke's speeches in the House of Commons; but the extravagance of his language intimidated those who at heart endorsed his opinions. His enthusiastic championship of the cause of the French *émigrés*, and his persistent efforts to bludgeon ministers into abandoning their policy of neutrality, not only frightened his own party but also irritated Pitt and Grenville.

The ill-judged flight of Louis XVI and his family, and their recapture at Varennes in June, provoked a temporary reaction against the Revolution and the political societies in England, but the French King's acceptance of the new Constitution in September 1791 renewed hopes that the aims of the revolutionaries might yet be accomplished without further violence or excessive bloodshed. Fox, meanwhile, was playing the trimming game of which he was master. He announced his disapproval of Thomas Paine's revolutionary *Rights of Man*, published in two parts between 1791 and 1792, and, by insisting that the division in the party was one of emphasis rather than principle, sought to conceal the real issues behind a cloud of ambiguous language. He did not succeed because he was temperamentally incapable of restraining himself in debate. The most unscrupulous of politicians, he possessed an innate probity that burst unbidden from the shackles of his ambition.

In January 1790 Tom Paine had written to Burke, 'The Revolution in France is certainly a Forerunner to other Revolutions in Europe.'[346] It was this, above all, that Burke feared. In common with Fox, he had known little about France until the Revolution; but, unlike Fox, he had applied himself with all his customary zeal and industry, to a study of events, accumulating evidence to support the opinions he had already formed. He was shocked by Fox's equally prejudiced but less informed convictions, and dismayed by the failure of ministers to understand that Britain was threatened.

The winter and spring of 1791-2 brought disturbing signs of unrest. The London Society for promoting Constitutional Information was revived * in December, and at the end of January the London Corresponding Society for the Reform of Parliamentary Representation was founded by a Westminster shoemaker. At the same time an association was formed in Sheffield which reprinted and distributed 1,600 copies of the first part of Paine's *Rights of Man*. These groups were not so innocuous as their names implied. Their formation was the first significant expression of independent political action among the working class. On 17 February Paine published the second part of his *Rights of Man,* advocating republican and egalitarian doctrines that went far beyond his first thesis and created an even greater sensation. It was ironical that Pitt should have chosen the same day to declare in the House of Commons that 'unquestionably there never was a time in the history of the country when from the situation of Europe we might more reasonably expect fifteen years of peace than we may at the present moment.' [347] Within two months of this pronouncement, France had declared war on Austria.

During the previous year, Louis XVI's brothers, the comte de Provence and the comte d'Artois †, had led at Coblenz the rapidly increasing assembly of *émigrés* in their efforts to persuade the Austrian Emperor to intervene in French affairs. The arrest of Louis XVI and Marie Antoinette played into their hands. It became the duty of Leopold II to avenge the insult to his sister and to rescue her from the revolutionary government, but he had no intention of attempting this without the active support of Prussia and Britain. His urgent request to George III to join with the European monarchs in demanding the release of the French King and Queen and in a formal declaration of intent to assist them in putting down insurrection in their country, received a cool reply that shows every sign of having

---

* It had expired of disgust, in 1784, as a result of Fox's coalition with North.
† Later Kings Louis XVIII and Charles X.

been drafted by Pitt and Grenville. George III was not, it seemed, indifferent to the plight of the French royal family, but considered that a treaty between Austria and Turkey, in fulfilment of the Reichenbach agreement, must be concluded before he could contemplate any association between Austria and the Triple Alliance. The French *émigrés* dispatched Charles Alexandre de Calonne, formerly French Minister of Finance, to obtain at least an assurance of British neutrality in the event of 'an attempt being made by the Emperor and other Powers in support of the royal party in France,' [348] but Pitt and Grenville refused to see him and sent a letter to the comte d'Artois rejecting the suggestion. Gustavus III of Sweden was prepared to act, but feared to do so without the guaranteed neutrality of the British navy. Leopold's hopes, therefore, rested on Frederick William II of Prussia.

On 25 July the Foreign Ministers of Prussia and Austria signed an agreement of mutual defence, and a month later the two rulers published the Declaration of Pilnitz expressing the hope that the sovereigns of Europe would unite to restore the rule of monarchy to France, and 'in that case' the Emperor and the King of Prussia would act together, and in such force as they deemed necessary to achieve that end. The careful insertion of the words *'alors, et dans ce cas'* negated the fine flourishes of boldness, and Louis XVI's acceptance, in September, of a new Constitution limiting his powers, gave the signatories an even more satisfactory excuse for inaction. Any prospect of a united invasion of France was obliterated by the sudden death of the Emperor Leopold on 9 March. A week later, Gustavus III was assassinated.

In England the growth of associations declaring their sympathy with democratic principles continued. The decay of the Whig party was accelerated in April by the founding of the society known as The Friends of the People. Among its members were Sheridan, Philip Francis, Charles Grey, and Fox's closest friend in the party, Lord Edward Fitzgerald. Fox prudently refused to join, and urged Grey to avoid any connection with the organization. Although the first aim of the society was professed to be the purification of the Constitution by correcting the abuses of the past hundred years, it became identified with the republican views of the Corresponding Societies, which were in turn, considered to be the British equivalent of the Jacobin

Clubs of France *. Particularly disturbing was the meeting of delegates from the United Constitutional Societies at Norwich in March, celebrating the foundation of 'some hundreds' of groups of reformers and recording their gratitude to the inspiration of Paine's *Rights of Man*. Sir Gilbert Elliot thought he discerned, in March, 'an appearance of greater moderation about the French affairs, and our own constitution etc., than there seemed to be last year,' but he added, 'There are certainly a number of people in the Kingdom who are desirous of confusion.' [349]

To Pitt, coolly indifferent to the effects of the Revolution upon the people of France, the threat of serious unrest or revolution at home was real, and it induced him to abandon one of his most cherished ambitions: the reform of parliamentary representation. On 30 April, Grey gave notice of a motion for reform to be introduced in the next session. In the debate that followed, Pitt attacked the proposal as an invitation to anarchy. He knew that Grey's motion would include a demand for universal suffrage, the acknowledged aim of the Societies following the principles laid down by Paine. This had never been any part of his own plans for reform and he was resolutely opposed to it. He knew, too, that the feeling of the House was against reform of any kind. Even Fox, although he joined Sheridan in supporting Grey, was doubtful of the wisdom of introducing the proposals at such a time. It is possible that Pitt's great influence might have persuaded the House to accept a reform more moderate than Grey intended, but the chances of success were small and the risk of failure great. It does not, however, seem to have occurred to Pitt that he should continue to support reform of any kind. He had joined the ranks of those who looked upon all change with suspicion, and all reformers as party to a subversive conspiracy of the Societies to overthrow the Constitution. 'My object', he declared, 'always had been, and is now more particularly so, to give permanence to that which we actually enjoy rather than remove subsisting grievances.' Philip Francis retorted bitterly, 'You look for our principles not in our declarations, but in the supposed views and projects of other men.' [350] This was

* The Jacobin Club (taking its name from the Dominican monks whose first monastery in Paris was dedicated to St Jacques) was housed in the former monastery in rue St Honoré. Its members formed the most radical group of revolutionaries under the leadership of Robespierre. Jacobin Clubs were started in all the cities of France.

true, but Pitt's reaction was a fair reflection of the feelings of the House. The Friends of the People were regarded with deepening mistrust. Fox, who was the undisputed party leader in all but title, found himself acting as mediator between the followers of Portland and the new reformers led by Sheridan and Grey. He succeeded, for a brief period, in maintaining a façade of party unity, but his efforts found favour with neither faction. The Friends of the People were the enemies of the party.

In April, Talleyrand returned to London. He had seen Pitt and Grenville in March to ask for an assurance that Britain would not intervene in France on behalf of the *émigrés*. The purpose of his second visit was to extract a promise of neutrality in the French defensive war against Austria. French plans included the annexation of the Austrian Netherlands and aid to any consequent 'patriot' rebellion in the United Provinces. In return for neutrality and the guarantee of a massive loan to be raised from the London banks, Britain would be offered the island of Tobago, ceded to France in 1783. Talleyrand, acting with the French ambassador, the marquis de Chauvelin, was authorized to negotiate an alliance with Britain with the intention of dissolving the Triple Alliance and preventing the further spread of war in Europe. Although based on an understanding of Pitt's desire for peace, the proposals were unrealistic. Even if Britain had been prepared to renounce the Treaty of Utrecht and the Reichenbach agreement, which guaranteed Austrian possession of the Belgic Netherlands, it was inconceivable that the Stadtholder should be abandoned and the alliance with the United Provinces lost.

Chauvelin and Talleyrand claimed to represent the King and the Girondin ministry, and came armed with a letter from Louis XVI, but it was evident that the King was acting under instructions as the prisoner of his government. This approach from France, however remote its chances of success, was nicely judged. If Pitt accepted the demand for British neutrality, the Triple Alliance, already damaged, would be destroyed and Britain would again be isolated; but the outright rejection of the French advance would imply active support for Prussia, and thus also for Austria, in a concerted war against France. Both alternatives threatened disastrous consequences. An alliance with France, an unthinkable reversal of traditional policies, would lead to war with the rest of Europe.

Pitt determined to preserve British neutrality without severing the last threads of alliance with the Prussian and the Dutch. While Grenville made it known to the French that occupation of the Austrian Netherlands and interference in the United Provinces could not be condoned, Pitt turned his attention to the internal security of Britain. From the summer of 1792 he concentrated on imposing peace at home as a precaution against war in Europe.

Slavery and Suppression
1788-1792

FOR FOUR YEARS Pitt succeeded in preserving Britain from direct involvement in French affairs, but he was unable to shelter the country from the concussion of the Revolution or his own principles from the assault of alien ideology. As Prime Minister he had led the movement for reform—of parliament, of the national economy, of the civil administration—and he had presided over attempts to settle, by radical change, the government of Ireland and of the British territories in India. There can be no doubt of the sincerity of his zeal for reform, but he never allowed emotion to interfere with his understanding of politics as the art of the practicable. He owed his position to the King and the independent members of parliament at least as much as to his own transcendent abilities, and there was no cause, that did not affect the safety or well-being of the country, for which he was prepared to sacrifice it. He secured and maintained his strength in the House of Commons by the ability, which seldom deserted him, to measure the temper of the House, and his willingness to suit his measures to its moods in a spirit of moderation and compromise. He would lead where parliament might not follow, but he would not, unlike Fox, persevere in a lost or overwhelmingly unpopular crusade. The French Revolution imposed on him severer restraints than upon any man in England. For the sake of his country he was obliged to refrain from making any public declaration of opinion that might be regarded as partisan. For the sake of his position, which he was determined to retain because he believed that he alone could hold back the tide of republicanism and anarchy, he was obliged to draw back from some of his most libertarian intentions.

His expedient disavowal of parliamentary reform was a bitter disappointment. As important to him, and politically less damaging, was Wilberforce's campaign for the abolition of the slave trade. For personal as well as moral reasons, Pitt resolved to give it his unstinting support, and he continued to do so long after it had become clear that the shock of the French Revolution had destroyed all possibility of its success.

Negro slaves from the west coast of Africa were sold for the first time in Lisbon in 1444. Sixty years later, to supply labour for the new settlements in America, the Portuguese started what soon became regular shipments across the Atlantic. For two hundred years the English took little part in the trade *, but by the Treaty of Utrecht Britain acquired from Spain sole rights to the slave trade with the Spanish colonies. Conquests in Africa during the Seven Years' War gave her, so Chatham boasted, something approaching a monopoly.† Although an Act of parliament passed in 1750 expressly forbade the abduction of blacks, none but the Society of Friends, who agreed to expel any member discovered to be guilty of kidnapping slaves, paid any regard to the law, and Liverpool overtook Bristol and London to become the most prosperous slaving port in the world. In 1772, Lord Mansfield overturned previous legal opinions by his reluctant judgement in the case of a runaway Negro slave, James Somerset, whose owner claimed title under Virginian law. Mansfield declared that such a claim to property had never been in use or acknowledged by the law of England, and that 'the claim of slavery never can be supported'. This, *de jure*, freed some 14,000 slaves in Britain. This

---

* Queen Elizabeth I severely reprimanded Sir John Hawkins for his two slaving adventures, and warned him that the forcible abduction of black Africans would 'call down the vengeance of Heaven'.

† Chatham's claim was inaccurate. Estimates vary widely, but it appears that Britain shipped little over half the total number of slaves, France less than a third, and the remaining trade was shared between the Dutch and the Danes.

important decision, however, had no effect upon the slave trade, and jurisdiction was not extended to foreign ships carrying slaves in British ports or waters.

In May 1787 the Committee for the Abolition of the Slave Trade was founded, with Granville Sharp as Chairman. Sharp and Thomas Clarkson, who was a member of the Committee, were the heart and brain of the movement. In William Wilberforce they found the voice. Intensely religious, compassionate, idealistic, and politically experienced, Wilberforce was also the friend of the Prime Minister and one of the best speakers in the House of Commons. Pitt was reported as saying, 'Of all the men I ever knew, Wilberforce has the greatest natural eloquence.' [351] Urged by Sir Charles and Lady Middleton, and later by Clarkson, to lead the campaign in parliament, Wilberforce made his own inquiries and, having assembled his facts, went down to Holwood to consult Pitt. Later he recalled that 'after a conversation in the open air at the root of an old tree at Holwood, just above the steep descent into the vale of Keston, I resolved to give notice on a fit occasion in the House of Commons of my intention to bring the subject forward.' [352] Pitt had recommended him to lose no time 'or the ground may be occupied by another'.

The abolitionists were faced by a delicate decision. There was a clear distinction between slavery and the slave trade. An attack on the first, which would be understood to be an attack on property, would provoke angry and powerful opposition even from among those who were not personally interested, but it would automatically destroy the trade. The abolition of the trade, on the other hand, could be expected to excite the animosity of the West Indian interest without inviting the hostility of any other group, and it would bring slavery to a gradual end, the inevitability of which might encourage planters to treat their slaves with greater humanity. Clarkson and Wilberforce agreed to aim their campaign at the trade. They were aware of the dangers inherent in suddenly granting to thousands of slaves the freedom to turn on their masters, and in the light of later events in the French island of St Domingue *, there is good reason

* The western half of the island discovered by Columbus in 1492 and named Española (Hispaniola); now Haiti. Wilberforce, and most of his English contemporaries, used 'St Domingo' to describe both the Spanish colony of that name occupying the eastern half of the island, and the French colony of St Domingue.

to applaud their decision. Clarkson began to assemble a mass of evidence and to compile a list of witnesses.

During the spring of 1788 Wilberforce was seriously ill and Dr Warren decided that he would be dead within twelve months. In common with others of Warren's patients, Wilberforce did not oblige him by confirming his prognosis, but it was obvious that he would not be fit in May to give notice of a motion for abolition as he had intended. Pitt went to visit him at Wimbledon and, as Wilberforce wrote later, promised 'with a warmth of principle and friendship that have made me love him better than I ever did before,' to take over the leadership of the parliamentary campaign until Wilberforce's return. Accordingly, on 8 May, Pitt formally proposed a debate on the subject of abolition for the next session of parliament. The motion was carried without division. Sir William Dolben then introduced a Bill to limit the number of slaves to be carried in proportion to the ships' tonnage. He proposed that the limitations should remain in force for a trial period of twelve months, when they would be reviewed. This, too, was passed, by fifty-six votes to five. The Lords took a different view. Lord Chancellor Thurlow, whose behaviour was daily becoming more irksome to Pitt, spoke powerfully against the Bill, as did the naval hero, Lord Rodney, and other senior navy officers. Pitt, in fury, let it be known that opponents would not be allowed to continue in the government, but the Bill, much amended, was returned to the Commons. A new Bill, incorporating many of the amendments, was passed by both Houses before the end of the session. According to Wraxhall, Pitt persuaded the King not to prorogue parliament until the Bill had received royal assent.[353] Wilberforce was much cheered to receive Pitt's assurance: '. . . there seems not a shadow of doubt as to the House of Commons next year',[354] but he may have noticed the omission of any mention of the Lords.

Opposition to abolition of the slave trade centred upon three objections: the ruin of the West Indian Islands' commerce which depended on slave labour; the injury to the navy, which benefited from the slave trade as 'a considerable nursery for seamen'[355]; and the futility of renouncing a profitable trade that the French would immediately appropriate. It was also contended that the accounts of slaves' sufferings were grossly exaggerated.

When Wilberforce was able to introduce the motion in May 1789,

251

he replied to these objections in detail, and with refuting evidence. The debate was delayed by the King's illness and the Regency Crisis, and by the time it took place the Privy Council had completed an inquiry into the slave trade, begun more than a year earlier. The evidence presented to the inquiry was published without comment, but the bulk of it, in spite of misrepresentations and contradictions, supported Wilberforce's case. His speech on 12 May was sober, factual and persuasive. He spoke for three and a half hours, presenting his arguments with clarity and moderation: a pleasant change for a House accustomed to the dithyrambics of Burke and the acrimony of Fox. Burke was generous in his praise: 'The House, the nation and all Europe, were under very great and serious obligations to the hon. gentleman, for having brought the subject forward in a manner the most masterly, impressive and eloquent. Principles so admirable, laid down with so much order and force, were equal to anything he had ever heard of in modern oratory.' Pitt and Fox joined in support of the motion. Fox, referring to a proposal that the trade might be regulated rather than abolished, declared that 'He felt no difficulty in saying, that without having seen one tittle of evidence he should have voted for abolition. With respect to a regulation of the trade, a detestation of its existence must naturally lead him to remark, that he knew of no such thing as regulation of robbery or a restriction of murder. There was no medium; the legislature must either abolish the trade or avow their own criminality.' [356] On 21 May the Commons decided to postpone a vote until evidence had been heard before the bar of the House. When parliament rose at the end of the session, the hearing was still incomplete. It was not finished until April 1790.

Meanwhile, the campaign for abolition was attracting public sympathy. A print, drawn by Clarkson, showing the appalling conditions aboard the *Brookes* slaving vessel, was being freely circulated, as was William Cowper's poem, *The Negro's Complaint;* Wedgwood produced a black and white medallion, showing a kneeling slave in chains and inscribed 'Am I not a Man and a Brother?' which, set in brooches, bracelets and patch-boxes, found favour with society ladies; and abolitionist societies were founded all over the country. The prospect should have been fair. In the country at large, outside the traditional slave-trading ports, there was general support for abolition. In the House of Commons, the proposals would be forwarded by Wilberforce, Pitt, Fox, Burke and Sheridan, a combination of such power as the House had seldom seen. Grenville, translated to the Lords, would be a match for the intractable Thurlow and help to mobilize the peers in support of the Bill.

Wilberforce moved the abolition of the trade on 18 April 1791. He made another fine speech, and Fox one of the great speeches of his life. Pitt concentrated on a convincing statistical refutation of contrary arguments. The debate continued until half past three in the morning, when the vote was taken. Wilberforce's motion was lost by 88 votes to 163.

The explanation for this reverse, which came as no surprise to Wilberforce, lay in the progress of the French Revolution and the growth of radical societies in Britain. The connection between these circumstances and the slave trade appears, in retrospect, to be obscure, but it was not so to those who voted against the Bill. Their conviction that 'democratical' ideas and revolution were the natural consequence of increased freedom was, in their view, justified and confirmed by later events in the French colony of St Domingue. A rising by the mulatto community against the white colonists had been ruthlessly suppressed at the beginning of 1790. On 15 May 1791, by decree of the National Assembly, all slaves in the French colonies were freed and granted rights of citizenship. Three months later the slaves rose in rebellion and butchered their masters. St Domingue, the most prosperous of the French sugar islands, was ruined by a triangular war between whites, mulattos and blacks, which lasted, with unsolicited British and Spanish interference, for twelve years.

Accounts of the worst atrocities committed on the island were not received in England until the new year. The cause of abolition was gravely injured. Wilberforce, who was preparing to move for abolition again in April, told Babington: '. . . people here are all panic-struck with the transactions of St Domingo, and the apprehension or pretended apprehension of the like in Jamaica, and other of our islands. I am pressed . . . to defer my motion till next year.' Foremost among those who advised postponement was Pitt, who 'threw out against Slave motion on St Domingo account.' Wilberforce feared that he must choose between his crusade and his friendship, for, as one of his associates wrote, 'From London to Inverness Mr

253

Pitt's sincerity is questioned.' He resolved to go on with his Bill, reassuring Babington that 'This is a matter wherein all personal, much more all ministerial, attachments must be as dust in the balance.' [357] He was not helped by Clarkson's all too public enthusiasm for the French Revolution, which served to identify abolitionists with Jacobins.

Pitt, having cautioned Wilberforce against reintroducing his motion in such an unfavourable climate of political opinion, remained steadfast in his loyalty. There was, indeed, nothing to be gained by defection: there was no party division on the issue; all the greatest orators in the House would speak in favour of the motion; and the internal security of the country, which was his most urgent concern, would be unaffected by the outcome. On 2 April 1792 the House of Commons again debated the abolition of the slave trade. Wilberforce repeated many of his previous arguments, illustrating hem with examples of recent barbarity and revealing the names of brutal captains. The House had heard him twice before, and at length, on the subject and he had little new to add. It was not one of his better speeches; nor was it enriched by an ill-considered display of pious self-congratulation quite out of character with the agonies of self-doubt confided to his diary. It was Dundas, declaring himself a sincere advocate of abolition, who, more than any speaker, influenced the final vote by proposing gradual abolition of the trade, which he hoped would lead to the end of hereditary slavery. Fox condemned this 'moderate' suggestion as tantamount to a declaration that there might be moderation in murder.

The last contribution to the debate was made by Pitt in a speech that came to be regarded as one of the greatest ever made in the House of Commons. He began by speaking of his satisfaction that members were generally in favour of abolition. Though there might be some lack of accord as to the period required for achieving this end, it must be only a matter of time before mankind would be delivered from 'the severest and most extensive calamity recorded in the history of the world'. He analysed and rejected Dundas's proposal for gradual abolition and asserted that, given better conditions, the black population in the colonies would increase without the assistance of trade that involved shocking cruelty and loss of life. If the population decreased, it could only be from continuing ill-treatment. He demolished the argument that the trade renounced by Britain would be taken up by others: France and Denmark had already abolished slavery; it was more likely that others would follow the example already set than that they would attempt to expand their trade. 'This miserable argument, if persevered in, would be an eternal bar to the annihilation of the evil. How was it ever to be eradicated, if every nation was thus prudentially to wait until the concurrence of all the world should be obtained?' On the contrary, if the House voted against abolition, other nations might say, 'Great Britain has not only not abolished, but has refused to abolish, the Slave Trade. She has investigated it well. Her senate had deliberated on it. It is plain, then, she finds no guilt in it.' Britain would be responsible for the crimes of Europe.

Pitt went on to compare the state of Africa with that of Britain under Roman rule. The Romans might have talked then of the 'natural incapacity' of their British slaves, and spoken of Britons as 'a people destined never to be free' as members that night had spoken of blacks. He drew a vivid, imaginative picture of Africa delivered from the chains of slavery, developing in peace to enjoy the benefits of science, culture and prosperity. Dawn was breaking as he came to the end of his speech, and he chose two lines from Virgil to illustrate the long-delayed coming of dawn to Africa:

> Nos primus equis Oriens afflavit anhelis;
> Illic sera rubens accendit lumina vesper.

As he spoke these words, a shaft of light from the rising sun poured through the east windows of the Chamber and illumined his face.[358] It was a dramatic demonstration of Pitt's ability to harness his memory to the occasion. Fox, Grey and William Windham, leaving the House together in the early sunshine, agreed that Pitt's speech was 'one of the most extraordinary displays of eloquence they had ever heard. For the last twenty minutes he really seemed to be inspired.' Sir Gilbert Elliot admitted, 'Pitt delivered one of the greatest and most eloquent speeches I ever heard in my life, and *being right*, it went so far that one could hardly help almost liking him.'[359]

It was all in vain. But for Dundas's intervention the motion might have passed through the House of Commons, though its fate in the Lords was less promising. By introducing the possibility of compromise, Dundas drew from the abolitionists' side those who, for reasons of conscience, had honourably suppressed their greed or overcome their prejudices. Dundas offered them an escape from decision and they accepted it with relief. Wilberforce's motion was defeated by 230 votes to 85. Dundas's amendment was passed by a majority of 68.

Four days later Dundas moved the gradual abolition of the slave trade, to put an end to it in 1800. This date was amended to 1796 and his resolution accepted. In spite of vigorous lobbying by Pitt, and a determined effort by Grenville, the Lords voted to hear all the evidence again. Thurlow swayed a number of votes, including that of the Archbishop of Canterbury who bitterly regretted his decision, by assuring the peers that the hearings would not impose undue delay. After hearing five witnesses on 5 June, the Lords postponed all further examination of the evidence until the following year. In exasperation at Thurlow's obstruction and malice, Pitt persuaded George III to dismiss his Lord Chancellor. In ridding himself of the most intractable, and at the same time the most unpopular, member of his Cabinet, Pitt opened the way to a strengthening of his government that might make it impregnable.

In 1788, Pitt had brought his brother, Chatham, into the Cabinet as First Lord of the Admiralty in succession to Lord Howe. It was a remarkable choice, and it is hard to believe that it was prompted by any faith in Chatham's energy or competence. He was as indolent as ever, and soon acquired, by his congenital impromptitude, the sobriquet of 'the late Lord Chatham'. Pitt admitted to his mother his doubts 'whether the public may not think this too much like a monopoly',[360] but added 'that doubt is not sufficient to counterbalance the personal comfort which will result from it and the general advantage to the whole of our system.' 'To those who know him,' wrote Grenville, spitting into the wind, 'there can be no doubt that his abilities are equal to the undertaking.' [361] In fact, apart from providing the necessary direct communication between the Prime Minister and the Admiralty, there was no requirement for Chatham to exercise any ability he may have possessed. The work of his department was in the skilled and experienced hands of Rear-Admiral Sir Charles Middleton, and the Board was reinforced by the addition to it of Vice-Admiral Lord Hood.

The appointment of Grenville to succeed the Duke of Leeds at the Foreign Office was generally welcomed, but his elevation to the peerage was received with less enthusiasm. Though he believed that the House of Lords was 'certainly becoming too numerous', which he feared would 'be found rather inconvenient', the King agreed that Grenville's abilities were needed in the Upper House, where the ministry was inadequately represented by Lords Thurlow and Hawkesbury *. He also hoped that Grenville's 'conciliating temper' would 'aid in keeping matters smooth with the Chancellor'. Evidence of Thurlow's treachery during the King's illness had been kept from him as far as possible, and he continued to believe that 'with all his appearance of roughness, he has a feeling heart'.[363] Pitt, on the other hand, was preparing the ground for Thurlow's dismissal and needed Grenville to lead for the government in the House of Lords.

The Duke of Richmond wrote Pitt a long letter of indignant complaint.

> I believe this country will not be satisfied to see you two younger brothers take the lead of the two Houses of Parliament, and by yourselves govern the country. With your abilities—which, without a compliment, are very transcending—you may take that lead in the House of Commons; but Mr Grenville, whose parts, however solid and useful, are certainly not upon a level with yours, cannot, as I conceive, succeed in taking the lead in the House of Lords, where something of higher rank and more fortune and dignity is required; and I do apprehend that both of you being in such situations, so nearly related with Lord Chatham at the Admiralty, will be thought engrossing too much in one family.[364]

He was mortified that Pitt had not thought to consult him in advance, and announced his intention to retire from public business. He added, 'In so doing I shall endeavour not to give it the appearance of any dissatisfaction with you, for in truth I feel none, believing, as I do, that your conduct does not proceed from any intentional want of kindness towards me, but from (you must forgive me for saying so) an idleness in your disposition that too often makes you neglect to cultivate the friendship of those who are most attached

---

* Charles Jenkinson, 1st Baron Hawkesbury (1786), and 1st Earl of Liverpool (1796). The rest of the Cabinet peers were all too reticent: 'The Duke of Leeds . . . never took a very active part in debates . . . Lord Chatham has never yet spoken. Lord Camden is idle and grows old. Lord Stafford will seldom speak, and but a few words.'[362]

to you, and which makes you expose your judgement to be biassed by the opinion of the narrow circle to which you confine your intimacy.'

This last criticism was both accurate and just. Pitt's treatment of many of his most loyal adherents—particularly those whose personalities he found dull or uncongenial—was cavalier; and he was already showing a preference for government by an 'inner Cabinet' of two or three intimate friends. This was politically damaging, and accounted for the paucity of his personal following.

He was criticized, too, for his use of patronage, and in particular for his creation of titles and promotions in the peerage. The majority of members of the House of Lords owed their position and allegiance, and not infrequently their pensions or offices of profit, to the Crown. For ministerial business, approved by the King, Pitt could rely on a substantial majority in the Upper House; but there, as in the Commons, his own party was too small to wield a decisive influence. The creation of peerages, and promotion within the peerage, were the prerogative of the King, but he was prepared to consider favourably any recommendations made by Pitt and seldom rejected them.* He had firm ideas about the sorts of people who were suitable for ennoblement: respectable landed families, particularly if they had rendered good service to the Crown; naval and military heroes; colonial governors; distinguished diplomats; loyal politicians; and members of the royal household; all were eligible. People engaged in, or directly connected with, trade were not. During the periods of Pitt's ministries, he created eighty-nine English peers †, all but two of whom were ennobled in the first ten years. Wilberforce thought that 'no little injury had been done to the credit and character of the House of Commons by the numerous peerages that were granted to men who had no public claims to such a distinction, and whose circumstances clearly manifested that borough or parliamentary interest was the basis of their elevation.' Even Pitt acknowledged that 'a variety of circumstances' had prompted 'a larger addition to the British Peerage than I like, or than I think quite creditable.' He was responsible for enlarging the membership of the House of Lords by some forty per cent. Leaving

---

* He nevertheless refused to promote either Shelburne or Temple to dukedoms, saying that, for the time being, new dukedoms must be reserved to his own sons.

† These in addition to creations in the Scottish and Irish peerages.

aside those peerages awarded for military services, by far the greater number were created from political motives. The rest were due, according to George Rose, to his 'uncommon share of good nature'.[365]

Pitt wanted nothing for himself. In 1790 the King had offered him the Garter. It was politely but firmly declined, but Pitt wrote a separate letter requesting the honour for his brother. On 14 December George III replied: 'Mr Pitt's note is just arrived, intimating a wish that I would confer the third vacant Garter on his brother Lord Chatham. I trust he is too well convinced of my sentiments to doubt that I with pleasure shall tomorrow give this public testimony of approbation, which will be understood as meant to the whole family.' His words were carefully chosen. He was determined to reward Pitt for his services, and in August 1792 he seized the opportunity afforded by the death of the Earl of Guilford * to offer Pitt the office of Warden of the Cinque Ports, a sinecure carrying a pension of £3,000 a year. This time he was not to be denied: '. . . the Wardenship of the Cinque Ports is an office', he wrote, 'for which I will not receive any recommendations, having positively resolved to confer it on Mr Pitt as a mark of that regard which his eminent services have deserved from me. I am so bent on this, that I shall be seriously offended at any attempt to decline.' [366]

The vacancy left by Grenville at the Home Office was filled by Dundas. In 1789 he had refused the Lord Presidency of the Scottish Court of Session, explaining to Grenville 'My secession from all political life at this time would be a very fatal step to the Strength and hold Government has in Scotland. A variety of circumstances happen to concur in my person to render me a cement of political strength to the present Administration, which, if it were dissolved, would produce very ruinous effects.' This was true. His influence in Scotland was essential to Pitt. Malmesbury wrote of him, 'Dundas is more active and more diligent than any other, but also selfish and Scotch. Pillage and Patronage—pillage by conquest, patronage at home.' His influence was also apparent, as Malmesbury knew, in what Lord Rosebery was later to describe as 'the Scotticization of India', but Lord Cornwallis, who was in a better position than most to judge Dundas, said that he had 'never met with a more fair or

* Frederick, Lord North, had succeeded his father as 2nd Earl of Guilford in 1790, but survived him by only two years.

259

honourable man'.[367] His promotion to senior cabinet rank was merited. With Grenville, he was a member of the 'inner circle'.

The ministry still lacked strength. Pitt's friend, the Duke of Rutland, had died suddenly in 1787 in Dublin. The Marquess of Stafford, who had succeeded him as Lord Privy Seal in 1784, and Earl Camden *, Lord President of the Council, were elderly and ineffective, and Pitt wanted to dismiss the malignant Lord Chancellor. Threatened, as he believed, by unrest at home and the growing peril of involvement in war in Europe, Pitt acted with characteristic boldness. Thurlow gave him the opportunity he desired by ridiculing a ministerial finance Bill at the committee stage in the Lords, describing Pitt's proposal as 'nugatory and impracticable' and adding, 'the inaptness of the project is equal to the futility of the attempt.' This was intolerable, and Pitt immediately dispatched letters to the King and the Lord Chancellor. 'My Lord,' he wrote to Thurlow on 16 May 1792, 'I think it right to take the earliest opportunity of acquainting your Lordship that being convinced of the impossibility of His Majesty's service being any longer carried on to advantage while your Lordship and myself both remain in our present situations, I have felt it my duty to submit that opinion to His Majesty, humbly requesting His Majesty's determination thereupon.' The King's 'determination' was made that same evening. He wrote to Dundas, instructing him to call upon Thurlow and require the return of the Great Seal 'at the time most agreeable to the Lord Chancellor, and least inconvenient to either the business of the House of Lords or Court of Chancery'.[368] The Great Seal was placed in commission, awaiting the appointment of Thurlow's successor.

Five days later a Royal Proclamation solemnly warned the King's loving subjects against 'divers wicked and seditious writings'. It instructed magistrates to discover and prosecute authors, printers and distributors of all such material and to take all necessary steps for the preservation of order and 'a due submission to the laws'. This proclamation has been condemned by almost every historian of the period as an overreaction against largely imaginary dangers, an incitement to violence, and the first in a series of reactionary and repressive measures dictated by ministerial panic. In retrospect the

* Lord Gower had been created Marquess of Stafford and Lord Camden promoted to an earldom in 1786.

proclamation and the moves that followed it were unnecessarily harsh, but it is well to remember that the avowed object of the Constitutional Societies was to unite in 'a radical Reform of the country . . . established on that system which is consistent with the Rights of Man'.[369] This extension towards a national movement, already spread through several hundred provincial clubs and societies, was menacingly like the development of the Jacobin Clubs in France and it is ingenuous to suppose that the reforming ambitions of the British Societies were confined to the ballot box. They had absorbed and publicly approved both parts of Paine's *Rights of Man,* the second of which advocated action that could only be regarded as revolutionary. If Pitt overreacted, it was because he chose not to distinguish between the aspirations of moderate reformers and the demands of extremists. He was influenced, too, by the French declaration of war against Austria. The closer the threat of European war, the more necessary it became that peace at home should be assured.

Outbreaks of violence in Scotland served only to confirm Pitt in his view that repressive measures were necessary. William Honeyman reported to Dundas 'an almost universal spirit of reform and opposition to the established government and legal administration'; there were riots in Edinburgh on the King's birthday in June; and Dundas was burnt in effigy in Aberdeen, Perth and Dundee. An anonymous correspondent signing himself 'Patriotticus' wrote to him: 'I am exceedingly happy to inform you that your effeigee's mett with the Just fate you yourself deserves and woud have gott, had you dared to have ventured here. . . . You may inform Mr Pitt and the d——d idiot of a King that I wrote this by the order of the Committee of Revolutioners in Scotland.' [370] This type of letter, more a cause for entertainment than apprehension, could not be taken seriously; but it was one of many, and the gravity of the situation in Scotland, where troops had to be called out to restore order, was not in doubt. If national security was to be preserved, stern measures would be required. Pitt had strengthened his ministry from within, but it was still too vulnerable to be entirely effective in the face of the dual threats of insurrection and war. In June 1792, therefore, taking advantage of the renewed quarrels among the Opposition, he began to make overtures to the Whig leaders.

Dissection of the Whigs
1792-1793

THE DISMISSAL OF THURLOW in June 1792 left vacant the office of Lord Chancellor and it was important for the functioning of government that there should be no undue delay in appointing his successor. There was only one serious candidate: Lord Loughborough, a pillar of the Whig Opposition. His ability was not in doubt, but he was as disloyal as Thurlow, and without the latter's blunt and aggressive candour. He was an ambitious, professional schemer, complex and sophisticated, distrusted by both sides but valued for his intellect and experience.* He bore Fox a long-standing grudge, believing that he had been responsible for depriving him of the Lord Chancellorship in the Rockingham administration, and he was bitterly jealous of Thurlow and prepared to go to any lengths in political intrigue to succeed him. Pitt was not anxious to replace open perfidy by secret treachery and made a cautious approach to the Solicitor-General, Sir John Scott; but even if Scott's loyalty to Thurlow had permitted him to accept the appointment it is doubtful if Pitt could have offered it to him without forfeiting any chance of an alliance with the conservative Whigs.

---

* He had been Solicitor-General in 1771, Attorney-General in 1778, and Chief Justice of Common Pleas since 1780.

In May 1792 Pitt embarked upon a series of intricate negotiations that illustrate his mastery of political manoeuvre. His aim was nothing less than the destruction of the Opposition. His pretext for talks was the threat to national security, and Loughborough was well placed to act as a willing go-between. By holding out to the Whigs the invitation to discuss national policies, Pitt was also admitting the possibility of coalition. If his offer was accepted, a wedge would be driven between the conservative Whigs and the reformers that might divide the party into irreconcilable halves; if it was rejected, he would have demonstrated, once again, the intransigence and factional interest of the Opposition. The Whig leader, the Duke of Portland, was suspicious of Pitt's overtures, but he was also tempted. If Pitt really intended to propose coalition, the Whigs could expect to take half the Cabinet seats; and as it was clear that neither Pitt nor Fox would serve in an administration led by the other, the natural choice for First Lord of the Treasury and the premiership would be Portland.

Pitt did not inform the King of his negotiation; nor did he mention to him any possibility of coalition. This omission has been interpreted as evidence that he did not consider coalition a serious proposition and thus that the entire exercise was no more than a devious charade.[371] Though he could hardly expect that his first approach would result in a formal alliance in government, there was good reason to make a convincing offer of coalition and much to be gained if it were accepted on Pitt's terms. His scheme combined all the virtues of simplicity and lack of risk with the certainty of political advantage.

Pitt made his first move a month before Thurlow's dismissal. He proposed that Opposition leaders should attend a meeting of the Privy Council to consider government proposals to deal with the threat of insurrection. Portland responded cautiously, refusing the invitation but agreeing that some measure of co-operation was possible. 'We may', he wrote on 13 May, 'act in concert though not in conjunction.' [372] By the 24th, however, startled by Loughborough's reports that he had been offered the Lord Chancellorship and that Dundas had spoken of coalition, Portland had lost his nerve. Hastily consulting Fox and the Earl Fitzwilliam, he wrote to tell Pitt that Opposition support for the proclamation against seditious publications might not be unanimous. He informed Lord Loughborough that any proposal of coalition was 'utterly inadmissable [sic]'.

This was not discouraging. The seeds for further dissension had been sown, and Loughborough, scenting power, could be relied upon to use all his considerable influence to bring about some form of coalition. In this he was joined by Burke, who was determined, at all cost, to isolate and disable the reformers. Malmesbury was in the thick of the discussions. On Saturday 10 June, he had a 'Long tete-a-tete conversation with Duke of Portland. He agreed that the circumstances of the times made a Coalition with Pitt a very necessary measure; that the security of the country required it. . . . That Pitt was of such consequence in the country, and the Prince of Wales so little respected, that we considered it impossible . . . to form an Administration of which Pitt was not to be a part.' Three days later Malmesbury noted Portland's report of a three-hour conversation with Fox who had declared himself 'a friend to Coalition' but 'only wished it to be brought about in such a way as it should appear they had not *acceded* to Pitt's Ministry, but went to it on fair and even conditions to share equally with him all the power, patronage, etc.' Malmesbury added that it was the 'Duke' idea that Pitt should not keep the Treasury.' According to Loughborough, Pitt had said that a coalition would please the King and that 'the only difficulty at all likely to arise was about Fox.' [373]

Portland and Malmesbury were agreed that any form of alliance with the government must depend on mutual agreement on such major matters of policy as reform, and the government's attitude towards the French revolutionary government and internal security. Such agreement between the conservative Whigs and the ministry presented little difficulty; but there was no sign that the two wings of the Opposition could be brought to agree. Loughborough, unwilling to accept the Seals without the support of party colleagues in the Cabinet, wrecked the negotiations by his congenital passion for manipulation. To satisfy Portland, he reported to him that Pitt would be prepared to give up the Treasury; but, believing that any such suggestion would shock the ministry into withdrawing from the discussions, he did not inform Pitt that this change would be a condition of coalition. On 16 June, Malmesbury dined with Fox and Loughborough. Fox 'doubted Pitt's sincerity and suspected he had no other view than to weaken their party and . . . that to divide the opposition was his great object.' He added that 'it was impossible ever to suppose Pitt would admit him to an equal share of power . . .

Pitt *must* have the Treasury.' Malmesbury noted Fox's 'peevishness and obstinacy' and that he 'spoke *with acrimony* of Pitt, and repeatedly said "the pride of the Party must be saved".' Burke told Malmesbury, 'Mr Fox's coach stops the way,' and complained 'how very hard it was that on *his account* an arrangement calculated to preserve the country should be broken off . . . there was no doing without Fox, or with him.' [374]

Pitt's stratagem was working admirably. Although there was no immediate prospect of coalition, which would destroy the power of the Whig party, the discussions, hideously mismanaged by Loughborough, had opened a rift in the Opposition that Portland seemed unable to bridge. In July, Fox, who had watched with growing anxiety the fumblings of Whig leaders, outwitted by Pitt and deceived by Loughborough, found himself obliged to use all his influence and ingenuity to prevent his party destroying itself. He had already declared himself 'a friend to Coalition', provided that it should be constructed from both sides on equal terms, but he had later insisted upon the exclusion of Pitt from office. His retreat from this impossible stipulation to a prepared position, which he intended to hold, of insisting that Pitt should give up the Treasury, was intended to demonstrate the sincerity of his desire to accept whatever might be best for the country. Malmesbury was too shrewd to be hoodwinked by this manoeuvre, but Portland trusted Fox and respected his political acumen. On Fox's advice, Portland succeeded in persuading the Duke of Leeds that Pitt was prepared to hand over the Treasury to a third party so that he and Fox might serve together in a coalition ministry. Leeds, under the mistaken impression that he was being approached with an unofficial offer of the Treasury, requested an audience of the King, with whom he discussed the formation of a coalition government. Since the King knew nothing of any such proposal, the interview was an embarrassing farce, from which Leeds withdrew nursing a renewed feeling of grievance. The King appears to have assumed that the whole affair was a Whig plot designed to humiliate him and discredit his Prime Minister. His insistence, next month, that Pitt accept the profitable sinecure of Warden of the Cinque Ports is proof that he did not blame him for the situation. Fox's ingenious counterthrust had failed, but there was still a chance that he could save his party from disintegration. There was, indeed, no one else who could hope to do so.

Fox was rightly suspicious of Pitt's intentions. He was convinced that Pitt's approaches were insincere but he failed to understand that the weapon of negotiation was double-edged. He succeeded in persuading himself that although Pitt did not genuinely desire it he had proposed coalition in order to save his tottering administration from defeat. By asserting his influence over Portland, Fox had again taken over the effective leadership of the party and held it together, but he had done nothing to close the gap between the conservatives and the reformers. The Whigs had, in fact, been further subdivided by the prospect of coalition. Portland's group trusted Fox and had drawn together in their rejection of coalition without him; Loughborough and his circle disapproved of Fox's renewed diatribes against Pitt and his determination to bring down the government, a conclusion that Loughborough considered it his public duty to prevent; [375] and the reformers—the Friends of the People—mistrusting and mistrusted, looked to Fox for leadership which, while he strove to hold the party together, he could not give them. For a little while Fox was able to restrain himself and to avoid taking sides. Those who knew him waited apprehensively for his undisciplined honesty to break out of the prison of political expediency.

Pitt, too, waited for the move that would complete for him the rout of his opponents. Given time, Fox could be relied upon to make the error that would exclude him from the councils of the conservative Whigs and ally him with the reformers. The way would then be open for a coalition, with Pitt at the Treasury, that would be impregnable. Meanwhile, Pitt acquired from the Whigs one of their most promising young recruits. On 26 July, George Canning wrote to the Prime Minister asking permission to call on him. He explained that although he knew most of the senior members of the Opposition he was not committed to them. The two men met at Downing Street on 15 August, when Canning made plain his intention to enter parliament without obligation to any party but to give his allegiance to Pitt personally. Both were shy at this first meeting, but Pitt was charmed by the open admiration of the brilliant twenty-two-year-old and promised to help him. For Canning it was the beginning of a great career in which, for the first fourteen years, his guiding principle was an unquestioning devotion to Pitt.

The French declaration of war against Austria on 20 April 1792 was made in response to intense provocation and in the sure knowledge that Austria and Prussia would combine for an invasion of France before the summer was far advanced. If the Girondins believed that enthusiasm was an adequate substitute for military training, they were to be sadly disillusioned. A French rabble poured into the Austrian Netherlands, came up against Austrian troops, murdered their general, and fled back into France. For the rest of Europe this was distinctly encouraging. The Austrians did not immediately pursue the beaten French. In May, Catherine II, taking advantage of the preoccupation of Austria, invaded Poland. The Prussians, to whom as allies the Poles might have looked for help, had already been bribed by Catherine with promises of territory. When, in desperation, the Poles applied to France for aid, the Prussians invaded Poland from the west. Pitt had suffered one humiliation at the hands of Catherine II and he was not prepared to risk another. Grenville wrote to the British envoy in Warsaw: 'No intervention of the Maritime Powers * could be serviceable to Poland, at least not without much greater exertion and expense than the importance to their separate interests could possibly justify.' [376] Poland was abandoned to the mercies of Russia, Prussia, and Austria. Settlement of the partition became the cause of damaging dissension among them, distracting them from the struggle against France and helping to fragment the alliance against revolution.

The rout of the French army in the Netherlands was seen as proof of weakness and disorganization that would make the overthrow of the revolutionary government and the restoration of the monarchy a simple task to be accomplished at leisure. Not until 16 July did the Emperor Francis and the King of Prussia meet at Mainz among a blaze of lesser princes to co-ordinate a policy, and it was a further eight days before Frederick William II declared war on France. Two weeks later, the Prussian Commander-in-Chief, the Duke of Brunswick †, issued a manifesto to the French people: all 'rebels' were to surrender unconditionally; and if the King were to be harmed in any way Paris would be razed to the ground. By then the circumstances were radically altered. Far from being cowed by

* Britain and the United Provinces.
† Charles, Duke of Brunswick (1735-1806), nephew of Frederick the Great, was married to George III's elder sister, Augusta. Their daughter Caroline later married George, Prince of Wales.

defeat, the French had been galvanized into national mobilization. The Assembly called upon the people of France to defend their frontiers. The arrival of Brunswick's clumsy manifesto coincided with intensified anger against the King. On 10 August the Tuileries Palace was attacked and the Swiss Guard massacred. Three days later the royal family was imprisoned. The Prussian army had crossed the frontier, and on 1 September Verdun fell. Two ragged French armies, under General Charles François Dumouriez at Sedan and François Christophe Kellerman at Metz, stood between the Prussians and Paris. There, on 2 September, the suspected 'traitors' held in the prisons were slaughtered. Of the sixteen hundred who were butchered in panic, the majority were the more liberal-minded aristocrats who had preferred loyalty to the King above their own safety. Among them was Marie, princesse de Lamballe, 'a silly, good-natured, inoffensive woman' [377] who refused to take the oath against the monarchy and was torn to pieces by the mob as she left the court. Her heart was cut from her body while she was still alive, and her severed head was carried on a pike to the Palais Royal where Louis Philippe, duc d'Orléans,* was about to dine. Glancing at it, he said, *'Je sais ce que c'est'* and went in to dinner with undiminished appetite.

While volunteers flocked to the army from every town and village in France, the Prussian army was halted at Valmy. Torrential rain had reduced the plains of Champagne to a sea of mud and Brunswick's army was enfeebled by dysentery. On 21 September the Revolutionary Convention met to abolish the monarchy and declare a republic. At the end of the month the Prussians began their retreat. The French pursued them. Within five weeks Adam, comte de Custine, 'General Moustache', had captured Mainz and was striking towards Frankfurt; on 28 October Dumouriez brushed aside the Austrian garrisons of the frontier fortresses and crossed into the Belgian Provinces; and by the middle of November Brussels had fallen to the French army. The Convention declared the Scheldt estuary open to international traffic and prepared to invade the United Provinces. On 28 November Antwerp was taken and the

---

* Known, for his democratic opinions, as Philippe Egalité. He had visited England and was described by Hannah More as 'a low, vulgar, vicious fellow'. Harriot Eliot told Lady Chatham '. . . he wears upon his Buttons an Intaglio of a Horse and Mare in a *gay disposition* which he presents to ye Ladies for their inspection.'[378]

Dutch made a formal request to Britain for naval assistance. The war that Pitt had laboured to avoid appeared to be inevitable.

The crisis on the Continent aggravated discussion among the Opposition, and the September massacres, confirming Burke's most lurid predictions, shocked even the reformers into temporary silence. Though he admitted his disgust at the brutality of the Paris mob, Fox could not conceal his delight at the news of the Allies' retreat.[379] He continued to exercise a powerful influence over the Duke of Portland but he was losing the support of the party. Confined within the frontiers of French territory the rising of the people against despotism had appeared at best admirable and at worst no concern of the British; but the spread of democratic principles in Britain, invigorated by Paine's *Rights of Man* and evidenced by the growth of the Societies, and the astonishing defeat of the Prussian army and French conquest of the Austrian Netherlands, alarmed the majority of those liberal-minded Englishmen who had seen the Revolution as a justifiable and laudable fight for freedom against oppression. The menacing aspect of the Revolution was intensified by the declaration by the French on 19 December of a resolve to 'grant fraternity and assistance to all people who wish to recover their liberty', and the election of Thomas Paine to represent Calais in the French National Convention.

Sympathy for the royalists was strengthened by the arrival in England of large numbers of *émigrés*, whom Elliot described as 'extremely well-bred gentlemanlike people'.[380] 'I assure you', he told his wife, 'you must take to studying French, as the whole island will be full of them soon. The emigration is growing greater and greater every day.' As support for the cause of democracy waned among the country's ruling and professional classes, so the voice of the reforming societies became louder and shriller in praise of revolution. Addresses expressing sympathy and admiration were sent to the National Convention and reprinted for public distribution in France, and manifestos demanding reform were issued by the Corresponding Societies. Seven of the most influential newspapers * were against the government, and it became necessary to start two new publications, the *Sun* and the *True Briton,* to spread ministerial propaganda among those who did not read *The Times*. Among the

---

* *Morning Post, Morning Chronicle, English Chronicle, Star, World, Argus,* and *Courier.*

poor in the cities, ignorant of the September massacres and indifferent to the threat to the United Provinces, the overthrow of the French monarchy and the victories of the revolutionary armies were seen as blazing beacons heralding the downfall of tyranny and the coming of a new era of freedom and equality. The failure of the harvest in 1791 was followed by torrential rains in September and October 1792 which ruined the crops and led to a disturbing rise in bread prices. There were strikes of the dockers in Liverpool and of the colliers in Wigan; there were bread riots in the north and Midlands; and in Sheffield and Manchester troops had to be called out to deal with the mob. These were understood by Chauvelin, and thus by the National Convention to whom he reported, as the stirrings of revolution which would so weaken Britain as to prevent her intervention in Europe.

This exaggerated view was based on the false premise that newly sown seeds of democracy would prove stronger than deeply rooted national pride and long-established hatred of France, and ignored the evidence that the professional class, who must lead the revolution, stood for reform without violence and within the Constitution. The majority of those moderates who had been prepared to advocate liberal reform had anticipated that the changes they sought would be achieved under conditions of strict control. They displayed little enthusiasm for unregulated democracy manifested in mob rule. As Portland and the conservative Whigs drew nearer to the government, moved by the inescapable urge of the British ruling class to close ranks in the face of any threat to national security and their own privileges, Fox found himself thrust into the welcoming arms of the extremists whose irresponsible manoeuvres were nourishing the seeds of revolution among the poor.

On 1 December the ministry published a royal proclamation calling out some two-thirds of the Militia and summoning parliament to reassemble *. Fox, enraged, wrote that day to Portland: 'If they mention danger of *Insurrection*, or rather as they must do to legalize their proceedings, of *Rebellion*, surely the first measure all honest men ought to take is to impeach them for so wicked and detestable a falsehood.'[381] Soon afterwards he met Portland at Burlington House where they were joined by Fitzwilliam. Fox's unrelenting opposition

---

* It was a statutory condition of the embodiment of the Militia that parliamentary approval must be obtained within fourteen days.

to government measures which both Portland and Fitzwilliam regarded as essential to the preservation of internal order dismayed them. Three days later, at a meeting of the Whig Club, Fox made a violent attack on the Loyal Associations which had been forming throughout the country pledging support to the government for any measures taken to safeguard the nation. When the party leaders met again on the eve of the debate in the Commons and agreed not to divide the House in opposition to Pitt's policy, Fox 'with an oath declared that there was no address at this moment Pitt could frame, he would not propose an amendment to, and divide the House upon.' Malmesbury, who was present with Portland, Fitzwilliam, the Duke of Devonshire and Tom Grenville, reported that 'Fox treated the alarms as totally groundless . . . there was not only no insurrection, or imminent danger of invasion—but no *unusual* symptoms of discontent, or proneness to complain in the people; that the whole was a trick . . . *None* of the company agreed with him.' [382]

In the debates of 13-15 December Fox went further, not only denouncing the government's measures, which included an Aliens Bill to regulate the movement and settlement of the thousands of *émigrés* entering the country, but demanding official recognition of the French Republic. In language and construction the speech was one of the finest of his life, but it exposed to public view his pernicious lack of political judgement.

The declaration by the National Convention on 3 December that Louis XVI was to be tried for his life had shocked the old Whig aristocracy, who agreed with Burke that in a trial in which the prosecution were also the judges the verdict was a foregone conclusion. None but members who were Friends of the People spoke in support of Fox, and more than a hundred of his party voted with the government against him. Sheridan was wavering, still unable to believe that Fox would deliberately precipitate a final rupture of the party, and Grey and Thomas Erskine were among those who remained loyal to him; but many, including William Windham, were inclined or ready to go over to the government. Nothing but the timidity or inertia of Portland prevented the formation of a national party that might, by showing a united and determined front to the French, have convinced them of the British will to resist revolutionary expansion. In the absence of any such certain sign of unity the French convinced themselves that Pitt's ministry was about to be overthrown. On 15 December the Convention issued a decree announcing that any country occupied by French troops should be revolutionized according to democratic republican principles, that the cost of maintaining the 'liberating' army should be defrayed by the people on whom the benefits of liberty had been conferred, that the navigation of all rivers should be freed to all nations, and that any nation refusing to accept French principles of republican government should be regarded as an enemy.

Sir Gilbert Elliot told his wife that Fox was 'losing the good opinion and confidence, almost irrecoverably, not only of the country, but of many who were most attached to him', and added, 'The Duke of Portland's indecision and feebleness of character is doing much mischief.' Lady Malmesbury wrote to her sister, 'As for Fox and Grey, I wish they would utter treason at once, and be beheaded or hanged.' She compared Portland to the Duke of Brunswick: 'no party will be led to victory by either.' Such sentiments might be interpreted as evidence of an immediate desire for coalition, but Elliot expressed the majority Whig view when he wrote, 'Our wish is not to join *Ministry*, but to support *Government* in a separate body. The Duke of Portland is, however, making this difficult, and if he continues many days more, most of his party will go over individually to Ministry.' [383]

Portland's dilemma was acute. Fox, who had for so many years kept the party together, had put his personal convictions above party unity and might be thought to have put himself outside the party; but Portland could not contemplate the future of the party without Fox, and feared his emergence as the powerful and politically damaging leader of a group of republican Whigs formed from the Friends of the People. With Fox the party would be discredited; but without him it would be irretrievably split. The vision of a coalition government with Portland at its head had proved to be a seductive illusion. The reality was a party divided in principle and emasculated by its division. The situation engineered by Pitt had been aggravated by events in France, but it was Fox's failure to lead the party in the direction demanded by the national interest, a failure of political common sense dictated at least as much by personal animosity as by devotion to principle, that fragmented his party.

On Christmas Eve Malmesbury, Elliot and Windham met Port-

272

land again at Burlington House and jointly declared that 'Mr Fox and some gentlemen formerly acting with our party, having taken a line and expressed sentiments in Parliament contrary to those of the majority of our party, and on subjects which we think too important to the interests and safety of the country to make it possible that we acquiesce in, a division has thereby taken place in the party.' They urged the Duke to announce this division publicly, and, by gathering together all who agreed, prevent 'the dispersion of the party'. Portland seemed convinced by their argument and told them that he had hesitated so long only on account of his personal affection for Fox; but on the 26th, when everyone was expecting him to speak in the Lords, he sat 'as fixed as the lady in Comus . . . without uttering a syllable.' Elliot said of him that he was 'as unhappy and miserable afterwards as we were angry.' Two days later Elliot took the initiative himself and spoke out in the House of Commons. He wrote to his wife, 'I . . . stated my opinion that it was my duty to give a fair and honourable support to the Government in defending the constitution and saving the country . . . I was fortunate enough to believe that I agreed with the majority of those with whom I had been elected.' [384]

The immediate break-up of the Opposition was averted by the delayed three-week Christmas recess, which began on 4 January, but Pitt made sure that the breach was kept open by choosing that moment to offer Loughborough the Seals. Determined as ever to be Lord Chancellor, and despairing of driving Portland to a decision to break with Fox and bring his own followers into the government, Loughborough accepted. Three days later the news was received in London that Louis XVI had been condemned to death, and on 24 January it was known that the sentence had been carried out. Even the September massacres had not so outraged public opinion, and the Loyal Associations began to agitate for more stringent measures to be taken against the threats of subversion at home and assault from abroad. Loughborough's decision, which might earlier have been looked upon as defection motivated by personal ambition, as indeed it was, became transformed by events into an act of selfless patriotism.

When parliament met again at the beginning of February, Fox and his supporters discarded the last remnants of political caution. With sadly characteristic mistiming Fox chose the day on which the National Convention voted for war against Britain and Holland to launch a spirited defence of French actions since the publication of the Prussian manifesto in August. His realization that war was unavoidable drove him to shrill denunciation of the government. His recognition of failure in his personal struggle against Pitt provoked him into striking attitudes that none but he could have attempted to sustain. His angry affirmation of faith in the sovereignty of the people contrasted oddly with his earlier declaration, 'I pay no regard whatever to the voice of the people . . . I stand up for the constitution, not for the people.' When he claimed that the British Crown was elective, there were many who were reminded of his words to the House, 'I am for maintaining the independence of parliament, and will not be a rebel to my King . . . for the loudest huzza of an inconsiderate multitude.'[385] Portland was shocked, but unshaken in his belief that a clear break with Fox would destroy the party.. The voting figures for the House of Commons confirmed this view. Fox still commanded the support of more than sixty Whig members including Sheridan, Philip Francis, Charles Grey and Erskine. Portland's personal following was little more than fifty. The remaining Whig members, led by William Windham, Sir Gilbert Elliot and Lord Sheffield, formed a 'Third Party' which numbered thirty-eight including twelve independents.[386] Fox and his adherents therefore made up the strongest of the groups, both in numbers and in debating talent. As Elliot wrote to Malmesbury: 'The existence of our party depends on his [Portland's] *firmness, decision, vigour, activity, consistency,* uniformity of conduct, and *honourable support* of his friends, as head of the party . . . I fear the Duke has proved himself *entirely* unfit for his station, both in character and talents.' [387] The power of the Whigs, as a united party or as a credible alternative government, was broken.

When the French declaration of war was received in London on 8 February, Pitt's political victory was complete. Never again during Pitt's lifetime was Fox able to command sufficient support in parliament, or in the country, to make him a serious contender for the highest office. It was clear that if Pitt were to be defeated it must be because he chose to reject victory. No one but the King could bring him down. No one but Pitt, himself, could provide the occasion.

XIX

Lost Opportunity
1793

IF PITT had just cause to celebrate the disintegration of the Opposition and the defeat of Fox, he had also every reason to lament the circumstances that had made his victory certain. During lengthy negotiations with the French,[388] and in spite of deliberate and repeated provocation, he had clung obstinately to his determination to prevent French conquest of the United Provinces. He believed, and even Fox admitted privately that he agreed with him, that the Dutch coastline must not be allowed to fall into French hands. Unless Britain abrogated the Dutch treaty and abandoned the United Provinces to the French, war was inevitable, and hasty preparations were made to increase the strength of the armed forces. Seven years later Pitt admitted that the army and navy had been foolishly neglected: '. . . the reduction of our Peace Establishment in the year 1791, and continued to the subsequent year, is a fact from which the inference is indisputable; a fact, which, I am afraid, shows not only that we were not waiting for the occasion of war, but that, in our partiality for a peaceful system, we had indulged ourselves in a fond and credulous security, which wisdom and discretion would not have dictated.'[389]

Pitt was not uninterested in the navy. He appreciated that it was the bulwark of British defence and the pre-requisite of trade and empire. His younger brother had served in the navy, and he had appointed John Chatham to the Admiralty. In July 1791 he had visited the fleet with Dundas, dining as the guest of Lord Hood aboard the *Victory*. Hood told his brother *, 'Mr Pitt I never saw in better Health and Spirits. . . . I gave them the best Turtle they ever eat [sic], and as good wine as they ever drank, and at seven they left me very highly delighted with the events of the day.' [390] By this time Pitt and Dundas had become energetic drinking companions and their delight in their day with the navy was no doubt enhanced by the excellence of the Admiral's wine.

As early as 1784 Pitt had instituted an inquiry into the state of the navy and the naval dockyards, and, although he had been prevented by parliament from putting into effect the Duke of Richmond's plans for the extensive rebuilding of the defences of Portsmouth and Plymouth in 1786, he had raised the strength of the navy to 18,000, the highest total known for a peacetime establishment, and allotted £2,400,000 for the building of warships. By 1790, at the time of the crisis with Spain, thirty-three ships of the line † had been built and sixty more were ready for commission. Pitt paid frequent visits to the Navy Office to discuss affairs with Sir Charles Middleton, one of the greatest of all naval administrators. Middleton had been Comptroller since 1778 and was committed to a series of reforms in organization which had not met with the wholehearted approval of successive First Lords of the Admiralty. When Lord Howe resigned in July 1788, Pitt chose Chatham to succeed him because he would provide a direct channel through which the Prime Minister could exercise control of national defence, and because he would offer no opposition to Middleton's proposals. In the event the King's illness and the Regency Crisis intervened, and Middleton's reforms were postponed. In March 1790 he resigned; but he remained on good terms with Pitt and Chatham, and continued to advise them unofficially on naval affairs. In his budget speech on 5 May 1788, Pitt

---

* Admiral Sir Alexander Hood, later 1st Viscount Bridport.

† Ships of the line were those considered fit to lie in the line of battle, a formation introduced in the seventeenth century. In the second half of the eighteenth century no ships smaller than third rates—warships that, for the most part, carried seventy-four guns—were rated as ships of the line. First and second rates, three-deckers carrying upwards of ninety guns, were few in the British fleet, which depended for its superiority on a large number of seventy-fours.

was able to point with pride to an expenditure of seven million pounds on improvements to the naval service. When Middleton resigned he was able to declare with truth that the fleet and dockyards had never been in a better state of preparation for war. Nothing, indeed, was needed but the crews to man the ships.

The state of the army was less happy. A standing army, quartered upon the people, and available to enforce the law and impose order, was looked upon with general suspicion and distaste. It was therefore kept contemptibly small, and two-thirds of its strength was dispersed in India and the West Indies, leaving less than 14,000 men in the British Isles. The Militia, ill-trained and inexpertly officered by country gentlemen under the command of the county Lord-Lieutenants, could not be called upon to serve outside Britain. There was, therefore, no army available for war on the Continent and it was understood that the British part in an alliance against France must be primarily naval. It was nevertheless necessary that Britain should be represented in the land war, and, until such time as the army might be increased by recruitment, the meagre British regiments must be augmented by mercenaries. Fourteen thousand were employed from the King's hereditary Electorate of Hanover and a further eight thousand hired from Hesse-Darmstadt.

Not only was the army negligible in numbers, but it was also shockingly administered. The King was by tradition the active head of his army,* liable to take command of it in the field as his grandfather had at Dettingen fifty years earlier, and the fount of all policy, promotions and patronage. His routine administrative duties were carried out, under his supervision, by the Secretaries of State and the Commander-in-Chief. The Secretary at War, at the War Office, was a subordinate minister who was not a member of the Cabinet but acted in the Commons as government spokesman on army administration. The payment of the forces was the responsibility of the Paymaster; and the control of the Militia, the greater part of the army in India, and the artillery and engineers was variously exercised by the Home Secretary, the East India Company and the Master of the Ordnance. There was for the army no central, professional board of control comparable with the Admiralty. Nor

* George II was the last British monarch to command his army in battle. George III assumed command of his troops during the Gordon Riots.

was there a reserve of lively, highly trained and enthusiastic young officers waiting to lead a British army, if such existed or could be raised, to brilliant victories. Since the death of James Wolfe at Quebec in 1759, no one had come forward capable of doing for the army what Lord Anson had done for the navy: to educate a nucleus of leaders who would train commanders to succeed them. Disillusioned by failure in America and despised by the people, the army had forgotten the proud fighting traditions established under Marlborough, Clive and Wolfe. Its officers were gentlemen amateurs; its men were for the most part the otherwise unemployable debris from the gutters and the prisons; and its reputation was deservedly at its lowest ebb. On 30 April the man who was to restore Britain's military reputation, and to raise it above that of any country in the world, was promoted to the rank of major. His name was Arthur Wellesley.[391]

The French declaration of war at the beginning of February found both Britain and the United Provinces weak and unprepared; but their allies, Prussia and Austria, had already put into the field armies which, competently employed under a united command, must have annihilated the republican armies in a matter of weeks.* The French were saved, improbably, by Poland. Unable to resist the opportunity to share in the rape of that unfortunate country by Russia, Frederick William diverted an army for that purpose from the more urgent task of fighting the Revolution. In return for his acquiescence in this disgraceful act of treachery, the young Emperor Francis II was promised the support of Russia and Prussia in his renewed attempt to exchange the Austrian Netherlands for Bavaria. The priorities of the Allies were therefore widely divergent: for Prussia the first requirement was the partition of Poland; for Austria it was the reoccupation of the Netherlands in order to exchange them for Bavaria; for the British and the Dutch the protection of the United Netherlands was of prime importance. To the east, the armies of Russia, temporarily engaged in Poland, might be employed wherever there was the promise of territorial gain. Although all proclaimed their hostility to the Revolutionary government, none of the nations involved was primarily concerned to topple the French Republic or to defeat the armies of France within her own frontiers. For Britain the war was

* The Austrians claimed to have nearly 140,000 troops under arms; the Prussian armies already in the field numbered 80,000; other German States had raised 27,000; and the Holy Roman Empire had promised a further 120,000.

defensive; for Prussia and Austria it was an opportunity for territorial aggrandizement.

In spite of the incompatibility of their aims, Grenville nevertheless succeeded in concluding treaties before the end of the summer with Russia, Prussia, Austria, Spain, Sardinia and Naples. All promised military aid against France, though the Prussians and Austrians demanded substantial subsidies to keep their armies in the field. Pitt was prepared to endorse this arrangement as more practicable and no more expensive than raising an adequate army in Britain, and one that would enable him to use the paltry force available against French possessions in the West Indies. He saw Britain's role as naval and financial. The British army, too small to make any useful contribution to the land war in Europe, might be profitably employed with the invincible navy in capturing the colonial wealth of France.

This attractive design, the 'blue water' policy of the elder Pitt, was frustrated by the unforeseen boldness of the French. On 16 February Dumouriez broke camp at Antwerp and struck across the Dutch frontier towards 'Breda, which he captured ten days later. Auckland, at The Hague, had already sent an urgent entreaty for British troops and it was clear that some gesture of aid must be made towards the Dutch. On Tuesday 26 February, as Dumouriez's troops entered Breda, Sir Gilbert Elliot rose at five-thirty to watch three battalions of Foot Guards march off to Greenwich to embark for Helvoetsluys. The force numbered about two thousand, 'all young, and almost all fine men; some uncommonly so. They were all animated by a spirit natural on the occasion, not to mention spirits of a different sort. . . . Many were too drunk to walk straight.' The King, the Duke of York, who was to command the brigade, the Dukes of Clarence and Gloucester, and the Prince of Wales were on parade: the Prince sulky at his father's refusal to promote him to the rank of general; * and the King 'in the character of an equestrian statue on a fierce white charger'.[392]

The arrival of this British contingent, pathetically small as it was, seems to have encouraged the Dutch. More important, the Austrians, who had been preparing without undue enthusiasm for a

* Although appointed in 1793 to the colonelcy of the 10th Regiment of Light Dragoons, the Prince of Wales was never promoted, as were four of his younger brothers, to the rank of general.

leisurely campaign, broke through the eastern flank, forcing Dumouriez to withdraw to Neerwinden where he was decisively defeated. The French levies crumbled and began to desert. By the end of the month the Austrian army had taken Brussels, and on 5 April Dumouriez, disgusted by the intrigues of the Jacobin rulers of France, rode into the Austrian lines. He had planned to take his army with him, but, finding that it would not follow him, defected with one regiment.

The way was open for a concerted assault against the northern frontiers of France, but the Allies were not ready to take it. The Austrians had rejected the Prussian design for the partition of Poland and Frederick William had retaliated by withdrawing his army. Josias, Prince of Saxe-Coburg, commanding the Austrian army, called upon the British and Dutch to supply the strength he lacked. The Duke of York's instructions did not permit him to move further than twenty-four hours' march from his point of disembarkation, but the Hanoverian and Hessian troops were on their way to increase the British force to a respectable total of 24,000 and it was clearly necessary for the preservation of the alliance to assist Coburg in the reoccupation of the Austrian Netherlands. The capture of the French frontier fortresses of Lille and Valenciennes would, it was thought in London, compensate the Austrians for Prussian gains in Poland and for the British refusal to agree to the Bavarian exchange. The Duke was therefore permitted to cover Coburg's right flank in his advance on Antwerp and Ghent.

The chronic deficiencies in the administration of the army were swiftly revealed. The King urged an attack on Dunkirk, the capture of which would open a port of supply on the right of the allied army in its attack on the frontier fortresses. The Duke of Richmond, Master General of the Ordnance, warned against allowing the Duke of York to commit his troops to a long Continental campaign. Reminding Pitt that 'our army, cavalry and infantry, consists almost wholly of recruits, no part of which (men or horses) have been raised two months, and the greater part of which are at this moment only raising', he strongly advocated the withdrawal of British troops from Flanders for use in the West Indies.[393] Grenville and Dundas knew nothing about military affairs, and the Secretary-at-War, Sir George Yonge, possessed neither knowledge nor a seat in the Cabinet to lend weight to his ignorance. Pitt, unable to judge the merit of the advice he received, appears to have been the victim of the preposterous optimism that too often blinded him to practical obstacles. He accepted the need to reinforce the Duke of York, the value of an assault on Dunkirk, and the advantages to be gained by the capture of the French West Indies. For good measure he was also prepared to consider suggestions for scattered descents on the French coast—the 'eccentric attacks' so much favoured by his father—and a campaign in the Mediterranean. An army of 20,000, assisted by 13,000 Hanoverians, and 8,000 Hessian mercenaries who had not yet arrived, was not a reassuring agglomeration with which to achieve such widespread ambitions. Cautioning Pitt against simultaneous campaigns in Flanders and the West Indies, Richmond had written, 'To attempt both is to do neither well.' The dilapidation of the army and the inexperience of its commanders made any attempt at anything a scarcely justifiable risk. Half-convinced that the Duke of York's force should be withdrawn from Flanders, Pitt reinforced it with untrained recruits until it numbered 6,500 infantry and cavalry. It was comforting to know that while it acted with the Austrians, though George III would not permit it to come under Coburg's command, the British army might be saved from the blunders of its generals.

By the beginning of May, when Coburg at last began his slow and deliberate advance, the Duke of York had 34,500 men under his command, including the Hanoverians and 15,000 ill-equipped and unenthusiastic Dutch. He was twenty-eight years old, and his apprenticeship with the army of Frederick the Great, in which he had acquired an uncoveted reputation as a stern disciplinarian but none as a soldier, had not prepared him for such a command. His best qualified subordinates were Major-General Sir James Murray, whose ability was stifled by his diffidence, and Major-General Ralph Abercromby. Coburg's army was more than 100,000 strong, and a less pedantic commander might have skirted the French frontier fortresses, none of which was garrisoned in sufficient strength to provide a threat to his lines of communication, and marched on Paris. Had he done so, it is probable that the war would have been won by autumn. The French were in desperate straits: in Paris the Jacobins were struggling for mastery of the Convention; and in Brittany and Vendée the nobility and peasantry, shocked by the attacks on the orthodox Church and the murder of the King, had joined together in arms against the Republic. Proposals for peace had already been sent to London. The Allies, however, moved with stately precision and extreme caution, reaching the fortresses of Condé and Valenciennes at the beginning of June. There they settled down to formal reduction by siege, a laborious and enervating occupation that lasted for two months with little interference from the garrisons and none from outside. The Prussians, who had rejoined the alliance in strength, laid siege, with equal deliberation, to Mainz.

Condé fell on 12 July, Mainz on the 22nd, and Valenciennes on the 28th. The Duke of York's army had played a respectable part, the British regiments of Guards displaying their traditional virtues of discipline and gallantry, but the tedium of the campaign and the insignificance of the Allies' achievements produced a feeling of irritated dissatisfaction in England where a speedy and total victory had been expected.

Not content with squandering an opportunity to end the war, the Allies committed two lamentable errors that did much to prolong it: the garrisons of the captured fortresses were permitted to march away on condition that they did not serve against the Allies for twelve months; and Condé and Valenciennes were taken not in the name of King Louis XVII, held prisoner by the Jacobins, but as additions by conquest to the Austrian Netherlands. By the first, more than 30,000 French troops were released to fight against the insurgent royalists in the Vendée; and by the second, the Austrians, ignoring the protests of the *émigré* princes, made clear their territorial ambitions and stimulated the growth of unity in defence of France against dismemberment. The French were not slow to draw conclusions from the fate of Poland.

France was saved by the inertia and selfishness of the Allies, and by the ruthless energy of the newly formed Committee of Public Safety. The discredited Girondins were replaced and declared traitors by the Jacobins, and two men, Maximilien de Robespierre and Lazare Carnot, both members of the Committee, set about the task of transforming France into an armed camp. Robespierre, by unleashing on the country a reign of terror in which failure and disaffection were rewarded indiscriminately by execution,* created a

* One of the first victims was General 'Moustache' Custine, who was guillotined for his failure to raise the siege of Valenciennes.

compulsory unity that crushed internal dissent. Carnot devised and put into effect the *levée en masse,* a new concept in total war that involved the mobilization of the nation. Internal security and national defence were organized with astonishing rapidity, but even before these great ends could be achieved Carnot was ready to strike back. He understood that the Allies must not be allowed to use the captured fortresses, and their lately secured lines of supply, as springboards for an advance. Early in September he counter-attacked.

The Allies, meanwhile, were hypnotized by the vision of conquest by siege, under the mistaken impression that an advance into the heart of France would promote defensive unity, while a policy of containment and the leisurely acquisition of border fortresses would allow time for the French to defeat themselves by division, terror and anarchy. The Prussians rested. Coburg laid siege to Quesnoy. The Duke of York's force was ordered north to capture Dunkirk. This diversion, against which the Duke and Coburg protested, was the brain-child of the British government. The official object of the detour was to shorten the British expeditionary force's lines of communication and supply, and to destroy the most effective and dangerous base for French privateers. A more cogent, but less openly admitted, object was the capture of some substantial prize that might be used as a bargaining counter at the end of the war. There was a fourth, and pressing, reason for requiring a well-publicized success for British arms. As Dundas wrote to Sir James Murray: '. . . you are well aware that there exists in this country many strong prejudices against continental wars; with many a strong prepossession against the strength of this country being directed in any other channel than that of naval operations. It is extremely essential to meet those prejudices on as strong grounds as possible. The early capture of Dunkirk would operate most essentially in that point of view, and the expedition successfully conducted under the command of a prince of the blood, would give much *éclat* to the commencement of the war.' [394]

Anticipating speedy success, Pitt appointed Sir Gilbert Elliot to act as commissioner for Dunkirk. There was, as Elliot made clear to his wife, no plan to claim the port as a permanent addition to British possessions: 'No further conquests are to be made in that quarter in the name of Great Britain, nor is it intended to retain Dunkirk after the peace.' [395] The implication was that the British, unlike their Allies, were uninterested in conquest; but the moral distinction between retaining a prize in France and exchanging it for another in French colonial territory is too fine for recognition by any but politicians.

The attempt to justify the use of British troops on the Continent and to foster confidence in the leadership and administration of the army was an inglorious failure. Forty-five thousand men under General Jean Houchard drove back the Hanoverian and Hessian force covering the siege, and the Duke of York found his army in danger of being trapped between the relieving army, the garrison, and the sea. He withdrew in haste towards Ostend, abandoning thirty-two siege guns and most of his stores to the French. By doing so he saved his small army from disaster, but his retreat was seen in England as a dismal example of military bungling for which Chatham and the Duke of Richmond were generally blamed. For his failure to follow up his victory and destroy the Duke of York's army, Houchard was recalled and guillotined. He was succeeded in command of the army of the north by Jean Baptiste Jourdan, later to be a marshal of France. On 16 October Jourdan defeated the Austrians, inflicting heavy losses, at Wattignies, relieving Mauberge. On that day, in Paris, Queen Marie Antoinette went to the guillotine.

The campaign in Flanders petered out in mud, and the allied armies withdrew into winter quarters, leaving Carnot to concentrate his armies against the Vendéans. By the end of the year the royalists in the west, who had offered a more serious threat to the Republic than Coburg's Austrians, were reduced to the dispersed tactics of guerrillas. Behind Carnot's armies followed the servants of the Committee of Public Safety, terrorizing the dissident population and leaving whole villages in ashes. The suppression of any form of internal revolt was both essential and urgent. France was surrounded by enemies, and secure interior lines were the prerequisite of survival. Unable to count on the superior arms or training of his troops, Carnot relied for victory upon speed and the concentration of superior numbers. The French nation was regenerated as an army, and the organization, training, formations and tactics of that army were revolutionized to create one of the most formidable military machines ever seen in Europe. In December, having secured his rear, Carnot was ready to turn his attention to Toulon where, to the delighted astonishment of the British government who had neither ordered nor even imagined such an event, Lord Hood's blockading fleet of fourteen ships had taken possession of the town, its arsenal, and twenty-two French ships of the line in the name of Louis XVII.

This remarkable feat had been achieved at the end of August on the invitation of the people of Toulon. It was the outcome of British negotiations for alliances with Naples and Sardinia, and the brutality of French troops in crushing opposition in Marseille. The combined British and Spanish fleets commanded the Mediterranean. In return for modest subsidies, Sardinia and Naples had agreed to provide 20,000 troops for use against France and there appeared to be no obstacle to their joining with the Austrians to support a seaborne British invasion of Provence. This seemed, as Pitt had written in July, 'to offer a fair chance of doing something material in the South, and, if we distress the enemy on more sides than one, while their internal distraction continues, it seems hardly possible that they can long oppose any effectual resistance.' [396]

Hood's Mediterranean fleet arrived off Toulon on 18 July and delivered, under flag of truce, a proposal for an exchange of prisoners. This elicited no definite reply but enabled the Admiral to obtain accurate information about the French fleet in the harbour. There were seventeen ships of the line ready for sea and five fitting out, among them the *Commerce de Marseille* which, as Captain Horatio Nelson aboard *Agamemnon* noted, dwarfed Hood's flagship *Victory*. Failing to tempt the French to battle, Hood drew off towards Nice and returned to search the Golfe du Lion, but could find no enemy ships at sea. At anchor again off Marseille, Hood received commissioners inviting him to take possession of Toulon, with all its naval stores and the fleet in the harbour. His position was precarious. While Pitt and Grenville rejoiced at this turn of events, which Grenville described as 'decisive', Hood made a desperate attempt to obtain troops to hold his unexpected prize. Nelson was dispatched to Naples, where Marie Antoinette's sister, Queen Maria Carolina, might be relied upon to listen to the advice of the British envoy Sir William Hamilton, and her husband's English Prime Minister Sir John Acton; an urgent request for help was sent to the commander of the British garrison at Gibraltar; and a third message was sent to the Spanish fleet, cruising to the west off the coast of Roussillon. Meanwhile, on 27 August, Hood landed 1,500 seamen and marines, taking formal possession of Toulon in trust for the French King until peace should be restored.

Hood's achievement, though widely welcomed, created problems that revealed the inexperience and ineptitude of the government in the conduct of the war. Lacking any overall strategic plan, Pitt and his ministers wavered uncertainly between a number of ideas, none more than half-formed, any one of which would have required the concentration of the entire army's slender resources. Determined to hold Toulon, and to use it as a base for offensive operations in the south of France, Pitt and Dundas were nevertheless reluctant to abandon the projected expedition to the West Indies, and agreed that the army in Flanders must be maintained. They also felt obliged to listen to the entreaties of Burke that assistance be sent to the royalists in Brittany. As he had written to Elliot in September, 'These brave and principled men, with very inadequate means, have struggled, and hitherto victoriously, for upwards of six months, and have . . . done more against the common enemy . . . than all the regular armies of Europe. . . . They amount to about 40,000, though ill-armed and ill-provided. . . . Where can we hope to plant 40,000 men in the heart of the enemy's country at less than a hundred times what the support of that would come to?' [397] Pitt's sanguine imagination conjured up 34,000 troops available for Toulon, but 23,000 of these were to be obtained from Spain, Austria, Sardinia and Naples, and of the remainder all but Hood's 1,500 sailors and marines must be transferred from Gibraltar, Flanders or Ireland. [398] By the end of October nearly 17,000 troops had been assembled at Toulon, but no more than 12,000 were fit for duty, and the British contingent, estimated by Pitt at 6,200 supported by 5,000 Hessians, numbered only 2,114.

Without a force far larger than any that could be spared, Toulon was untenable against an assault from the land. The city lies at the head of an inner harbour dominated at all points but the south-west by hills. The loss of either of the promontories commanding the entrance to the inner harbour would endanger not only the city but also the fleet, making necessary its immediate withdrawal to the outer harbour from where it could give no further support to the army. The Austrian Chancellor, Baron Franz von Thugut, persisted in believing that the forces gathered at Toulon were more than adequate for the city's defence and had no intention of sending the

5,000 men promised from Milan. Pitt was not only relying upon Austrian troops, which he put at 10,000, but hoped for an additional 11,000 from Sardinia, 'possibly also a body of Swiss' which he estimated at '10,000 or 12,000', and, unbelievably, 'in the course of the next summer (if the expedition to the West Indies is successful) about 4,000 or 5,000 British on their return from the Islands.' [399] At the time of his writing this, the expedition to the West Indies had not even set out. Such unfounded optimism was no substitute for planning.

The conduct of the defence and civil administration of Toulon was entrusted to three commissioners: Sir Gilbert Elliot; Lieutenant-General Charles O'Hara, who had brought two regiments from Gibraltar; and Admiral Lord Hood. On 29 November O'Hara was wounded and captured in a skirmish with the French, and command of the polyglot army, in which the British were outnumbered by three to one by the Spanish, fell to Major-General David Dundas, who lost no time in advising the immediate evacuation of the port. On the night of 17 December, the French launched their attack. Twenty-four hours later their artillery was firing down into the city from the heights above the inner harbour. Within three days Toulon had been evacuated. Of the total of forty-five French vessels in the harbour, twenty-two of them ships of the line, eighteen were taken out by the Allies and the remainder were set on fire, though eleven of these were later repaired and rejoined the French fleet. Embarked aboard the British ships were nearly 15,000 royalist refugees, who had flocked to Toulon from all parts of Provence. On Christmas Day, Pitt, who had not received news of the surrender of Toulon, wrote, 'There is still a very good chance of all proving right in that quarter.' [400]

Hood conducted the evacuation with skill, making use of the short time available to inflict the greatest possible damage on French ships and stores that could not be removed, and doing his chivalrous best to save royalist troops and refugee families from the certain murder awaiting those who remained in Toulon, but the scenes of terror on the quayside were horrifying. Some reports estimated that 6,000 screaming refugees, many of them women and children, were left behind; overloaded boats capsized and their occupants drowned; and the Neapolitan troops panicked, deserted their posts and fled to the harbour. Twenty-five years later the Corsican commander of the

287

French artillery that had played a leading part in the defeat of the Allies at Toulon enthralled his captors on the island of St Helena with memories of the ships, fired by the British, exploding in flames in the harbour.

The loss of Toulon was a grievous blow to the prestige of the Allies. After their humiliating retreat in Flanders, this failure gave further proof of the shabbiness of the First Coalition. Underestimating French powers of recovery, the Allies pursued their individual, mean and selfish ends. Too late the Austrians discovered the implications of defeat, to which their inactivity had contributed, at Toulon. The spirit of republicanism was spreading through the Italian States, leaving them willing and almost defenceless victims of French plans for expansion. The royalist cause was seen in France to attract no support: even the small force gathered at Spithead to go to the aid of the royalists in Brittany had waited so long for artillery and stores, which never arrived, that the opportunity had been lost. In eleven months the forces of Prussia, Austria, Holland and Great Britain achieved the capture of four border fortresses and a state of irritated disharmony that heralded rupture. In the same period the French had crushed a rebellion, thrown back an invasion to the north, retrieved Toulon, and reorganized the nation into a force whose political menace was matched by military strength. They had also, though it was to be some years before they realized it, discovered the greatest military genius of modern times.

XX

Strains of Coalition
1794-1795

FOR PITT the first year of war had been one of almost unrelieved failure. Outwardly his spirits remained high. On 8 September, as the Duke of York's army was about to withdraw in haste from Dunkirk, the Prime Minister was at Walmer Castle, where, he told Lord Auckland in a letter agreeing to be godfather to his newly born daughter, Dorabella, 'The occupation of missing partridges has . . . completely consumed all my mornings.' [401] At the end of the month, while Hood was desperately trying to organize the defence of Toulon, Pitt and Addington were invited to dine with the Corporation of Canterbury. As they left for their carriage after dinner, some of the crowd who had gathered to see them displayed signs of 'disapprobation'. 'A pretty story', remarked Pitt, 'will this make in the papers. The Minister and the Speaker dined with the Corporation of Canterbury, got very drunk, and were hissed out of the town.' Addington later recalled that 'The Morning Chronicle . . . acted more leniently. It only stated that the Chancellor of the Exchequer was observed in walking to his carriage, to oscillate like his bills.' [402] Robert Banks Jenkinson ('Young Jenky'), the son of Lord Hawkesbury and one of Pitt's most promising young protégés, noted, however, that 'the first visible effect of Public Affairs upon his Health was in the Autumn of 1793 after the retreat of the British Army before Dunkirk.' [403]

Pitt was drinking heavily, and he was suffering from recurrent and painful attacks of gout. His drinking habits had been noticed as early as 1784 in a popular ballad entitled 'Billy Pitt and the Farmer', and in February 1793 the *Morning Chronicle* published a verse describing Pitt's arrival in the Commons with Dundas:

> I cannot see the Speaker, Hal, can you?
> What! Cannot see the Speaker, I see two!

Such pleasantries might not be remarkable but for the fact that the period was one in which abstemiousness was considered more noteworthy than drunkenness. Wilberforce loyally denied that Pitt drank to excess, and Pretyman that he ever saw him the worse for drink before 1798, but others of his friends were less discreet. Addington, with whom Pitt dined regularly, admitted that 'Mr Pitt liked a glass of wine very well, and a bottle still better.' He remembered many occasions when he had said, 'Now Pitt, you shall not have another drop', but Pitt had insisted on having another bottle brought in, declaring that he would have no more than one glass from it: 'this promise of abstinence', Addington recalled sadly, 'was seldom long remembered'. Young Canning, too, remembered leaving Pitt, after a dinner party where much port had been drunk, 'a little unfit for business', and another dinner in February 1794 when Pitt drunk 'I know not how much Madeira'. Addington noted only one occasion when Pitt was obviously drunk in the House of Commons, but Bland Burges envied 'his possession of faculties when drunk'. [404]

The quantities of wine drunk at Downing Street are not known, but the cellar book for Holwood shows that six bottles of port, four of madeira, and three of claret might be consumed in an evening when Pitt entertained. The number of guests on these occasions was not recorded, but the company for dinner at Holwood seldom numbered as many as six and the disproportionate quantity of port is significant. The same emphasis is notable in Pitt's purchases of wine for the Holwood cellar during the twelve months from 14 July 1784, which included, among the total of 444 dozen bottles, two hundred dozen of port, seventy-one dozen of madeira, forty-eight dozen of claret,

290

and fifteen dozen of burgundy. The figures would be less startling for one who entertained lavishly; but Pitt did not. He preferred the company of one or two intimate friends, and more often than not dined *à deux* with Addington or Dundas. He also owned cellars, which are unlikely to have been any smaller, at Downing Street and at Walmer Castle. His closest drinking companion was Dundas, a connection that Wilberforce considered 'Mr Pitt's great misfortune'. 'Dundas', he added, 'was a loose man, and had been rather a disciple of the Edinburgh School' where hard drinking was commonplace.[405] There can be little doubt that Dundas's influence was harmful, but it is probable that he did no more than provide Pitt with frequent opportunities to enjoy in congenial company a habit already acquired. By 1794 Pitt was showing some dependence upon alcohol and his health was suffering in consequence.

Although the evidence is incomplete, it is clear that Pitt's health deteriorated in periods of extreme stress or disappointment and it seems most likely that the sudden and irregular attacks of gout, and the signs of physical debility noticed by his friends, were brought on by his recourse to alcohol as an anodyne. The first year of the war had failed to bring the swift victory that the Allies had anticipated, but there was still some reason to believe that this could be won in 1794. Pitt was, nevertheless, forced to acknowledge that all his achievements of the past ten years, and his most cherished hopes for the future, were in danger of being annihilated. His painstaking reconstruction of the national economy had given Britain a comparatively firm base from which to finance the costs of war, but he foresaw the destruction of all his work if the war were to be prolonged. He was acutely anxious to hold together, and if possible to invigorate, the palsied First Coalition with Prussia and Austria. To this end he had sent Malmesbury to Berlin. Frederick William was demanding enormous subsidies to pay for his armies. Grenville's instruction to Malmesbury was unequivocal: 'You will state in the most explicit and unreserved terms, that His Majesty never will submit to purchase by a *subsidy* that assistance to which he is entitled by *Treaty*.'[406] The sentiment was reasonable, but Loughborough, who advocated paying a large subsidy rather than risk losing the help, however unreliable, of the Prussian armies, proved to be more realistic than either Pitt or Grenville.

Strongly influenced by Dundas, Pitt continued to ignore what

Windham trenchantly described as 'the danger of running after distant objects, while the great object lies still—of hunting the sheep until you have killed the dog'.[407] In pursuit of sheep, Vice-Admiral Sir John Jervis had sailed on 26 November with 7,000 troops to the West Indies. After a voyage of six weeks they reached Barbados. By the end of May, as a result of remarkable co-operation between Jervis and the army commander, Major-General Sir Charles Grey *, the islands of Martinique, St Lucia, Marie Galantes and Guadeloupe were captured. Tobago had already been taken before their arrival, and, in response to a call from the royalist white settlers of St Domingue, troops from Jamaica had occupied Mole St Nicholas, a fortress on the north-east coast of the island commanding the Windward Passage and often described as the Gibraltar of the Caribbean. Having repulsed an attack by the republicans, who held the capital, Port-au-Prince, the small British expeditionary force began to take over those towns where the royalists could ensure their welcome. This was a promising beginning, and the expedition was reinforced. By the end of 1794 Guadeloupe had been lost and all the conquests of the previous twelve months were threatened.

This transformation was brought about by three forces: the arrival of troops from France to strengthen the republicans on St Domingue; the rebellion of the blacks, granted their liberty and full rights of citizenship by decree of the National Assembly in May 1791; and, most formidable of all, yellow fever, the ghastly 'black vomit', which killed 12,000 British troops in a matter of months and 40,000 in two years †.

In the Mediterranean Sir Gilbert Elliot and Lord Hood had committed Britain to yet another campaign. Corsica, sold to France by Genoa in 1768, offered an ideal base for the navy. As Nelson wrote later, 'After the evacuation of Toulon, where were we to look for shelter for our fleet? . . . All our trade and that of our allies of Italy must all pass close to Corsica . . . all the ships built at Toulon have their sides, beams, decks and straight timbers from this

---

* Father of Charles Grey, the Whig politician, and one of the few thoroughly experienced military commanders in the British army. He had served under Wolfe at Rochefort in 1757, at Minden in 1759, and with distinction in the American war. He was awarded a barony in 1801 and raised to an earldom in 1806.

† A figure that exceeds the total losses of Wellington's army in the five years of the Peninsular War (1809-14).

island.' [408] The island was already in a state of rebellion. Under the leadership of General Pascal Paoli, who, though 'old, very infirm, and pretty heavy', [409] nevertheless had a firm grasp of the political situation and great energy, the Corsicans had driven the republican garrison into the coastal fortresses. Paoli had appealed for British help in the summer of 1793. The presence of Hood's fleet, escorting transports crowded with troops from Toulon, provided the means simultaneously to obtain a safe anchorage for the fleet blockading the French Mediterranean ports and to strike a blow that would compensate for failure at Toulon.

On 7 February, 1,400 troops led by Colonel John Moore landed close to Mortella Bay *. Conquest of the island proved to be a lengthier task than anyone had anticipated. Although everywhere in the interior the British were received with cries of 'Vivano nostri Inglesi', 3,500 French troops occupied strongly fortified positions at Bastia and Calvi, and Lord Hood's overbearing manner and open contempt for the army led to a deplorable, but all too common, lack of cooperation between the two services. General Dundas asked to be relieved of his command and went home. He was succeeded by Colonel Abraham D'Aubant, hurriedly promoted to brigadier-general, whose incapacity was well matched by his self-esteem. He distinguished himself by the pronouncement that he 'was not going to entangle himself in any cooperation'. Moore wrote in his journal, 'It is difficult to speak more nonsense than he does with more gravity and decorum of manner.' [410] D'Aubant refused to lay siege to Bastia, which a detachment from the navy commanded by Nelson undertook without him. In May, after a siege of seven weeks in which the army took no part, Bastia surrendered. D'Aubant went home in dudgeon and was succeeded by Lieutenant-General Charles Stuart, a younger son of the King's boyhood mentor, the Earl of Bute. Relations between the services remained strained to breaking-point, but Stuart was a brave and energetic soldier and Moore was his second-in-command. On 10 August Calvi, the last of the French garrisons, was given up after a long and courageous defence. Both Moore and Nelson were wounded, Nelson losing the sight of his right eye.

---

* The defensive position at Mortella Point was centred about a round tower, later copied for the defence of the south-east coast of England against invasion. The name Mortella was misspelt 'Martello' in Lord Hood's dispatches, and Martello it has remained.

Malaria had taken a greater toll than the French: when Calvi surrendered, little more than three hundred of the besieging troops, sailors and Corsicans were fit to take possession of the town. Corsica was captured, but it was to prove an uneasy conquest. The open feud between the army and navy continued, and it required all Elliot's skill and patience, acting as viceroy, to administer the island and provide an acceptable government for its turbulent people.

In Flanders the Allies prepared for a spring offensive. The army estimates presented to parliament in February made provision for a regular army of 175,000. The defence of Britain would be entrusted to 52,000 embodied Militia, and it was estimated that 34,000 mercenaries would be engaged to augment the army in Europe. Already committed to campaigns in the West Indies and Corsica, the British could not hope to contribute more than auxiliary assistance to the great armies of Prussia and Austria. The most difficult task, however, was to persuade either country to put its armies into the field. Each was acutely suspicious of the other, and it was only by the heroic efforts of Malmesbury in Berlin and Morton Eden in Vienna that Frederick William and his Francophile Foreign Minister, Christian von Haugwitz, were induced to accept a huge subsidy in return for providing an army, and the Emperor Francis II prevailed upon to accept part of this as a charge on Austria. After a series of complicated negotiations, it was finally agreed that the Allies should field armies totalling 340,000, of which 40,000 were to be British or hired German troops. Half of this great force was to contain the French within existing frontiers, securing lines of communication, while an army of 170,000 broke through Flanders to Paris.

In April the advance began. At first the campaign went well for the Allies. The French counter-attack on the right was halted at Courtrai and failed in the centre at Landrecies, but Coburg failed to take advantage of the exhaustion of his enemy and paused to straighten his line. On the right, the 45,000 French troops in the salient driven into the Allied line before Courtrai were vulnerable, and the Duke of York and General Mack persuaded Coburg to concentrate five corps to cut them off. The plan miscarried. Only two of the corps allocated to the task, one of them the Duke of York's, obeyed their orders. On 18 May the British corps, mustering 10,000 was counter-attacked by the French and split in two. The Duke lost touch with both brigades, which fought their way back to the Allied lines, and himself narrowly escaped capture. Early in June the French broke through on the left and invested Charleroi, which fell at the end of the month. The Austrians retreated. The British corps, its left flank exposed, withdrew, abandoning Tournai, Oudenarde and Ghent. The Austrians retreated again, eastward, leaving Brussels undefended and the British unsupported. The Duke of York, who complained bitterly to Coburg that his army had been 'betrayed and sold to the enemy', was forced to fall back to his base at Antwerp. Reinforcements arriving at Ostend escaped immediate defeat and capture by a forced march across the enemy's front to join the rest of the army in its retreat northward. Among them, Lieutenant-Colonel Arthur Wellesley, commanding the 33rd Regiment, was taking part in his first campaign. Later he was to say that it was in Flanders that he learnt how not to fight a battle.

One achievement alone brightened the summer. On 1 June Lord Howe inflicted a decisive defeat on the French battle fleet. The failure of the harvest of 1793 and the blockade of the Channel and Mediterranean ports had faced the French with extreme shortages of food, which, it was clear, would discredit the revolutionary government and lead to dangerous unrest. Grain was purchased by agents in America, and merchantmen chartered to carry it, but there was little chance that this precious cargo could arrive in France without naval escort. In December two ships of the line and three frigates slipped away from Brest, and four months later five more capital ships escaped to join them. At the beginning of May Howe put to sea with the Grand Fleet, which he had withdrawn from its station off the coast of Brittany to winter in harbour. Detaching part of his fleet to escort two large convoys of merchantmen, Howe made for Brest, where he found the French fleet riding quietly at anchor. He then cruised the Atlantic for two weeks, searching without success for the grain convoy. When he returned to Brest on 19 May the harbour was empty. Under the command of Rear-Admiral Louis Villaret de Joyeuse, twenty-six French ships of the line had put to sea three days earlier. The extent of Howe's miscalculation now became plain: not only would the conjunction of the French battle fleet with the squadrons already at sea provide an escort for the grain ships that outnumbered his own reduced fleet, but the squadron he had detached for convoy duty in the Atlantic was outnumbered by five to one.

On 28 May Howe found the French battle fleet about 400 miles west of Ushant and in heavy seas and, over a period of two days and nights, succeeded in cutting out four ships for the loss of one of his own. That night the fleets ran into fog, robbing Howe of battle on equal terms and allowing Villaret de Joyeuse to be reinforced by the five ships of the line which had escaped from Brest in April. As Howe manoeuvred to maintain contact with the French fleet, the convoy of more than a hundred grain ships stole past in the fog. On Sunday 1 June, under a clear sky, Howe defeated the superior French fleet and forced it to run for harbour. He returned to Portsmouth with six captured ships of the line. George III and Queen Charlotte went down to Spithead to greet him, parliament passed a vote of thanks, Howe was presented with a diamond-encrusted sword, and London was illuminated for three nights in succession. In the celebration of victory the real purpose of Howe's mission into the Atlantic, the interception of the essential grain convoy which had been allowed to escape, was forgotten.

Pitt's most valuable achievement of the year was political. In July the Portland Whigs joined the government. During the previous year Pitt had pursued his policy of strengthening his administration at the Opposition's expense. Loughborough had defected; Burke, though infuriated by the government's failure to send aid to the gallant royalists in the Vendée, was converted; the great triumvirate of 'men of business'—Malmesbury, Auckland and Elliot—were working loyally for the ministry; Spencer, after an 'accidental' meeting engineered by Pitt, was tempted by the possibility of succeeding the elderly Lord Camden as Lord President of the Council; and Windham, though loudly critical of the government's conduct of the war, was in frequent contact with both Grenville and Pitt. Few Whigs remained who condemned the war: as Arthur Wellesley's eldest brother, Lord Mornington, who had become a close friend of Pitt's, told Addington, 'The greatest turn of people's minds seems to be to condemn the conduct of the war.' [411] As early as 20 January thirty of the most influential Whigs had met under Portland's leadership 'to consider the means of giving the most effectual support to a vigorous prosecution of the war'. [412]

Fox, whose sense of political mistiming was undiminished by adversity, chose 30 May, less than two weeks after the heavy defeat of the Duke of York's army at Turcoing, to move in the House of

Commons that the war be brought to an end. The proposal received little support. It was common knowledge that Fox rejoiced at the news of Allied defeats, and even his closest friends were unable to escape the conclusion that he was actively hoping for final French victory. The greater the prospect of defeat, however, the more parliament united behind Pitt; and the further Fox removed himself from his party, the more Portland took the party reins into his own hands.

Much of May and June was taken up by inter-party discussions about the repeal of habeas corpus. This drastic proposal was brought about by the continuing activities of the Corresponding and Constitutional Societies. Although there is no doubt that many reports of sedition were grossly exaggerated, and the prosecutions of those accused, the majority of which failed, were damaging to the government,* it is beyond question that a serious attempt was being made to subvert the lower ranks of society and to spread the spirit of revolution. Even more disturbing than the activities of individual societies operating in London, Sheffield, Norwich and other city centres of dissidence, was the proposal to hold a General Convention of the People, to be attended by delegates from all the Societies to co-ordinate action, including the purchase of arms. In May the books and papers of the leading societies in London were seized and examined by a committee of the House of Commons. The report, presented to parliament on 16 May, was described by Pitt as giving proof of 'an enormous torrent of insurrection, which would sweep away all the barriers of government, law and religion, and leave our country a naked waste for usurped authority to range in, uncontrolled and unresisted'.[413] Protesting against the proposal to suspend the Habeas Corpus Act, Fox, Grey and Sheridan could muster only ten supporting votes.

The danger of insurrection was not imaginary, but it was less real than the fear of it. The great majority of the people would have supported the view expressed by Josiah Wedgwood fourteen years earlier: 'I would defend the land of my nativity, my family and

* This was particularly true of the trials held in Scotland, where Lord Braxfield's wanton judgements and Draconic sentences aroused widespread disgust and indignation. Braxfield was responsible for a remarkable definition of sedition as any endeavour to 'create a dissatisfaction in the country' which resulted in 'poisoning the minds of the lieges', though the intention was 'not in the minds of the parties at the time'.

friends against a foreign foe, where conquest and slavery were inseparable, under any leaders . . . rather than rigidly say, I'll be saved in my own way and by people of my own choice, or perish and perish my country with me.' [414]

On 23 May Pitt and Portland met, at the request of the former, to discuss 'the probability of our forming a ministerial arrangement'. The negotiations were lengthy. There was no longer any doubt of Pitt's sincerity in offering coalition, and Portland was as strongly in favour of it as anyone, but the disposal of Cabinet places required careful calculation on both sides. On 3 July the issue was settled. Pitt saw the King and obtained his consent to the Cabinet changes. Earl Fitzwilliam, who was promised the viceroyalty of Ireland but was to take office initially as Lord President of the Council, wrote to his wife of his reservations about the coalition: 'I do not receive this honour (if it is one) with much exultation; on the contrary with a heavy heart. I did not feel great comfort at finding myself at St James surrounded by persons, with whom I had been so many years in political hostility, and without those, I can never think of being separated from.' [415] He was to have even greater cause to regret the arrangement.

Fitzwilliam was not alone in his doubts. In the eight days that elapsed between the settlement and 11 July, when the new ministers received their seals of office, a crisis arose that threatened the new relationship. Windham, whose acceptance of office as Secretary-at-War had been assumed, wrote to Portland refusing the appointment. He feared that Dundas, who was to be Secretary of War, would continue to share the direction of the war with Pitt and Grenville, leaving Windham, although he was to be a member of the Cabinet, without power or responsibility. Tom Grenville succeeded in persuading him to change his mind, but Windham's doubts raised new anxieties in Portland's mind. As Secretary of State for Home Affairs he had expected to exert the influence over the conduct of the war previously exercised by Dundas in that office. Pitt was prepared to offer him the Foreign Office instead, but he would not allow Portland to handle war policy. Portland accepted the Home Office. On 9 July Dundas, who was reluctant to lose the Home Department and offended by Windham's appointment to Cabinet rank, tendered his resignation. Pitt was hurt and astonished. He wrote that Dundas's resignation would leave him 'really completely heartbroken. Had I the smallest idea that it would be the consequence, no consideration would have tempted me to agree to the measure that has led to it.' At his request the King wrote to Dundas to remonstrate with him, and Pitt rode down to Wimbledon to plead with his old friend. Dundas reported that the Prime Minister was 'distract and agitated in a manner to make me very uneasy indeed . . . I begged him to compose himself.' [416] Dundas allowed himself to be overpersuaded. Two days later the coalition government took office.

The new Cabinet was evenly distributed. With Grenville at the Foreign Office and Dundas as Secretary of War, the control of war policy remained unchanged, but the Whigs took five important Cabinet seats: Portland as Home Secretary, Spencer as Lord Privy Seal, Fitzwilliam as Lord President of the Council, Windham as Secretary-at-War, and Lord Mansfield as Minister without Portfolio. Malmesbury, Auckland and Elliot were disappointed, and Buckingham wrote acidly from the secure splendour of Stowe to his brother Grenville that the Cabinet was 'formed from the ranks of the ancient enemy, so nearly complete that it wants only the accession of Mr Fox to render it an efficient administration.' [417] Fox's reaction was one of anguished disillusionment. To his nephew Lord Holland he wrote, 'I have nothing to say for my old friends, nor indeed as *politicians* have they any right to any tenderness from me, but I cannot forget how long I have lived in friendship, with them, nor can I avoid feeling the most severe mortification, when I recollect the certainty I used to entertain that they would never disgrace themselves as I think they have done. . . . I think they have all behaved very ill to me, and for most of them, who certainly owe much more to me, than I do them, I feel nothing but contempt.' [418] His reputation, reduced to a low ebb by factious opposition, seen as disloyalty to his country, was further injured by his acknowledgement of debts amounting to £60,000 which were paid by the subscription of his friends. In September 1795, after a relationship of twelve years standing, he made Elizabeth Armistead his wife; but, for fear of doing more damage to his reputation he made no announcement of his marriage until 1802.*

* Elizabeth Armistead's origins are not known. Two years younger than Fox, she was known to have been associated with 'a notorious establishment in Marlborough Street' and to have been the mistress, variously, of the Duke of Dorset, Lord Derby and Lord Cholmondley. In 1783 the Prince of Wales, who was captivated by her, appears to have shared her favours with Charles Fox. At the time of her marriage to Fox she may have been already bound by another marriage which accounted for the secrecy of their union.

Pitt's political triumph was complete, and his Cabinet strengthened, but he had yet to make any changes that would reform the conduct of the war, which, as Burke had earlier forecast with percipient gloom, was likely to be 'very long . . . and very dangerous'.[419] The situation in Flanders provided ample cause for depression. The Alliance was collapsing. Some slight respite was offered by another upheaval in the government of France. Following a month of mindless butchery, the unprincipled Convention was frightened into striking down the founding fathers of the Terror. Robespierre and his most atrocious associate, Louis Antoine de Saint-Just, went to the guillotine on 28 July. Their removal, marking the end of the Jacobin dictatorship, inaugurated a period of moderate republicanism while the French framed a revised constitution, but the war continued. Without war and the unifying effect of national crisis, which kept the mass of the active population employed far from the cities where their discontent could find expression in riot and rebellion, France was ungovernable.

The divisions among the Allies were too wide to allow them to take advantage of the temporary reprieve. The Prussians, bound by the treaty negotiated by Malmesbury in April to provide 62,400 men in return for subsidies, and a further 20,000 under their separate treaty with Austria, suspended all military action. Neither Malmesbury nor Pitt, who unwisely summoned the Prussian ambassador to Downing Street and accused Prussia of breach of faith, were able to move them. It was clear that Prussia was preparing to repudiate the Alliance. Under the French offensive mounted in September the Austrians retreated beyond the Rhine and the British were driven back behind the Waal. Windham, applying his customary energy to his new duties as Secretary-at-War, visited the army and was appalled by the obvious breakdown of administration. More than 10,000 of the Duke of York's command were unfit for duty, suffering from typhus or gangrenous wounds; the troops were inadequately clothed and fed; the Duke had neither the confidence nor the respect of his men; and there were alarming shortages of artillery and stores. The Dutch, described by Windham as 'brutish, stupid and selfish', contemplated with evident indifference the imminent conquest of their country. The Prince of Orange, whose popularity had sunk to its lowest ebb, drank himself into a state of apathetic stupor and ignored the preparations of the revitalized Patriot Party to welcome the invaders. [420]

In November torrential rains swelled the natural defensive line of the Waal into an impassable flood. Next month, as the rains gave way to petrifying frosts, the Duke of York was recalled. He left behind him a demoralized army of 21,000 troops, more than half of them incapacitated, to defend the United Provinces for which Britain had gone to war. Pitt had wished to replace the Duke some months earlier and the King had agreed to the appointment of Cornwallis, lately returned from India, provided that the Duke retained a command suitable to his rank. At the end of November Pitt wrote to the King, tactfully but firmly requesting that the Duke of York should be recalled. The King was 'very much hurt', observing that considering 'the conduct of Austria, the faithlessness of Prussia, and the cowardice of the Dutch, every failure is easily to be accounted for without laying blame on him who deserved a better fate.' He agreed, however, to Pitt's proposal, adding, 'I shall certainly now not think it safe for him [the Duke] to continue in the command on the Continent, when every one seems to conspire to render his situation hazardous by either propagating unfounded complaints against him or giving credit to them.' [421] A few weeks later Pitt removed his indolent brother Lord Chatham from the Admiralty. He was replaced by Lord Spencer, whose place as Lord Privy Seal Chatham filled.

These changes led to great improvements in the fighting services. The Duke of York, awarded his Field-Marshal's baton and appointed Commander-in-Chief, turned out to be an outstanding administrator; and Lord Spencer, though his experience was not at first equal to his self-confidence, was capable, energetic and resourceful. An even more beneficial change was the resignation, deliberately provoked by Pitt, of the Duke of Richmond. He was succeeded as Master of the Ordnance by Cornwallis, the ablest and most experienced senior officer in the army.

None of these transformations was achieved in time to save the United Provinces. The ageing Duke of Brunswick declined an offer of the command of the Allied armies, the river Waal froze solid, the French attacked across it, and the broken British army retreated in abject disorder and misery to the north. The Prince of Orange fled to England. On 20 January the French entered Amsterdam. Even the Dutch fleet did not escape: French cavalry and artillery captured the greater part of it after an audacious gallop across the ice-packed Zuyder Zee. There was nothing left for the remnants of the British army but a long, humiliating retreat. On 13 April, all but the cavalry and a detachment of artillery, which remained to protect the Electorate of Hanover, embarked at Bremen to return to England. Eight days earlier the Prussians had made a separate peace with the French. In May the new Dutch Republic signed a treaty of alliance with France, the terms of which included the maintenance of a French army in Holland and the employment of the Dutch fleet against Britain. Spain made peace in July. The Prussian treaty, which Malmesbury described as 'one of predatory alliance',[422] was particularly shameful: it provided for Prussia to be compensated for any loss of territory at the expense of Austria and the minor German States. By the end of July 1795 all that remained of the Alliance against France was the association, divided by a continent dominated by the enemy, of Britain with Austria, Piedmont and the Kingdom of the Two Sicilies.

Nor was it only in northern Europe that British hopes had been shattered. In May, in response to the appeals of the royalists and the demands of their Whig supporters, the government had agreed to allow an army of *émigrés* to assemble on the south coast for the invasion of Brittany. No British troops were to be involved, but a supply of arms was provided and the navy could escort the royalists across the Channel and assist their landing. A force of 4,000, put ashore towards the end of June, was welcomed by the peasants of Brittany and on 3 July the fort of Quiberon was captured and 600 republican troops taken prisoner. The government decided to reinforce this success. A frigate was dispatched to Bremen to fetch the comte d'Artois, since the death of the ten-year-old Louis XVII in prison on 8 June the heir presumptive to the throne of France *, and 20,000 British troops were hastily gathered to accompany him to Quiberon. Long before they could sail, republican forces under General Lazare Hoche recaptured the fort and killed or captured the entire royalist garrison. On the orders of the Convention, the prisoners, who had been promised safe conduct, were slaughtered. Meanwhile, the news that the Spanish had made peace, ceding St Domingue to France, made it necessary to send reinforcements to the West Indies. The army intended for the invasion of France was reduced to 5,000 and, after an abortive landing on a tiny island off

* His brother, Louis, comte de Provence, had assumed the title of Louis XVIII.

the Quiberon peninsula that achieved nothing but a premature rising in the Vendée, the expedition was abandoned.

At the end of November 1794 Lord Auckland had written a long letter to Pitt setting down his unfavourable opinion of Britain's allies and advocating a withdrawal from 'all continental exertions and interference'.[423] He proposed concentration on 'the naval war with a great increase in naval strength' and urged Pitt to negotiate for peace. Eight months later, when the First Coalition had disintegrated, the inconsiderable British army had been decimated by typhus in Europe and yellow fever in the West Indies, the belated attempt to support a royalist invasion had failed, and the bright prospect of early victory had turned into the threat of a defeat that foreshadowed the overthrow of the British Constitution, the alternative to negotiation seemed to be destruction. Jane, Duchess of Gordon, was reported to have said that by the end of the war the King would be in possession of every island in the world except Great Britain and Ireland.[424]

Offensive Alliances
1795-1796

THE RAPIDITY OF THE FRENCH ADVANCE in the United Netherlands in January 1795 had threatened the British expeditionary force with destruction. It also narrowly missed robbing Britain of the valuable services of Lord Malmesbury and the more doubtful benefit, which the Prince of Wales would have sacrificed with equanimity, of the future Queen. For some years the King had viewed with disgust and apprehension the discreditable antics of his sons, and in particular of the Prince of Wales, who, past thirty and coarsened by dissipation, showed no inclination to contract a legal marriage and provide an heir to the throne. His corpulence—he weighed 224 pounds in 1789—had moved Amelia Adams, daughter of the American Ambassador, to call him 'the Prince of Whales'. Gillray's superb cartoon of 2 July 1792, entitled *A Voluptuary under the horrors of Digestion*, portrayed the Prince at Carlton House, surrounded by empty wine bottles, decanters of port and brandy, unpaid bills, and well-advertised and clearly labelled remedies 'For the Piles', '. . . for a Stinking Breath', and for venereal diseases.*

On 24 August 1794 George III wrote to Pitt to inform him of the

---

* Velnos Vegetable Syrup, a French potion, and Leake's Pills, a domestic product.

Prince's intention to marry his first cousin, Princess Caroline of Brunswick.[425] The King had expressed his approval, 'provided his plan was to lead a life that would make him appear respectable, and consequently would render the Princess happy.' Lord Malmesbury, whose shrewd judgement, tact, and friendship with the Prince amply qualified him for the mission, was sent to Brunswick to arrange the marriage. Queen Charlotte, who did not share the King's impatience to see their eldest son married without regard to the suitability of the match, had heard disquieting rumours about Princess Caroline: of 'passions . . . so strong that . . . she was not to be allowed even to go from one room to another without her Governess', of 'indecent conversations with men, and . . . indecent behaviour'.[426] It was not Malmesbury's task to discover what truth there might be in these stories but to prepare the Princess for marriage to the heir to the British throne and to escort her back to England.

The Duke and Duchess of Brunswick were enchanted by the prospect of their tiresome and headstrong daughter's brilliant marriage, but they were unable to conceal her deficiencies. The Duke plaintively told Malmesbury, *'Elle n'est pas bête, mais elle n'a pas de jugement.'* This proved to be an understatement. Malmesbury found himself instructing the flighty Princess 'to avoid familiarity, to have no *confidantes,* to avoid giving any opinion . . . to be perfectly silent on politics and party'. He noted with disapproval, 'Princess Caroline talks very much—quite at her ease—too much so.' His doubts were increased by noticing that she appeared 'startled' when he told her 'that anybody who presumed to *love* her was guilty of high treason, and [would be] punished with *death* . . . so also would she.' She was 'very missish', and shocked Lord Malmesbury by sending him a tooth she had drawn—'nasty and indelicate'.[427]

The unhappy envoy was soon obliged to instruct the Princess in a matter of greater delicacy. To his diary, on 18 February, he confided his problem: 'Argument with the Princess about her toilette. She piques herself on dressing quick; I disapprove this. She maintains her point; I however desire Madame Busche to explain to her that the Prince is very delicate, and that he expects a long and very careful *toilette de propreté,* of which she has no idea. On the contrary, she neglects it sadly, and is offensive from the neglect.' The Princess appeared 'the next day well washed *all over'*, but the improvement was not maintained. Two weeks later he returned to the odious subject: 'I had two conversations with the Princess Caroline. One on the toilette, on cleanliness, and on delicacy of speaking. On these points I endeavoured, as far as was possible for a *man*, to indicate the necessity of great and nice attention to every part of dress, as well as what was hid, as to what was seen (I knew she wore coarse petticoats, coarse shifts, and thread stockings, and these were never well washed, or changed often enough). . . . What I could not say myself on this point, I got said through women.' [428]

At last Malmesbury and the Princess set out for England. Passing through Holland on their way to Helvoetsluys, unaware that French cavalry detachments were operating far ahead of the main body of the army, the Princess and her escort were obliged to make a precipitate dash northward to avoid capture. At noon on Sunday 5 April they arrived at Greenwich, where they waited an hour for their carriages. With consummate tactlessness, the Prince, who had discarded Mrs Fitzherbert, had sent his most recent mistress, Lady Jersey, to meet them and she had delayed the departure of the carriages from London. Lady Jersey loudly criticised Princess Caroline's dress, and announced that she would sit beside her for the drive to St James's. This outrageous proposal was firmly rejected by Malmesbury, who was obliged 'to speak rather sharply to her'.

That afternoon they arrived at the Duke of Cumberland's house in Cleveland Row, where the Prince of Wales was introduced by Malmesbury to his bride. The mephitic Princess, as Malmesbury reported, attempted to kneel to the Prince. 'He raised her (gracefully enough), and embraced her, said hardly one word, turned round, retired to a distant part of the apartment, and calling me to him said, "Harris, I am not well; pray fetch me a glass of brandy." I said, "Sir, had you not better have a glass of water?"—upon which he, much out of humour, said with an oath, "No; I will go directly to the Queen," and away he went.' The unfortunate Caroline was no more attracted to her future husband than he was to her: '*Mon Dieu!*' she cried, '*est ce que le Prince est toujours comme cela? Je le trouve très gros, et nullement aussi beau que son portrait.*' Dinner that evening was wretched: the Princess 'flippant, rattling', and the Prince 'evidently disgusted'. The marriage of this ill-matched and reluctant pair was solemnized late in the evening of Wednesday 8 April 1795 at St James's Chapel Royal. The Prince 'had manifestly had recourse to wine or spirits'. That night he slept with his bride. It was generally believed that he never did so again. Nine months after this single encounter, Princess Caroline was delivered of 'an immense girl', the King's first legitimate grandchild.[429]

Pitt's part in this cheerless farce was important but indirect. The Prince's debts, for the payment of which he had already received, since 1783, nearly £500,000 in addition to his official income, were estimated by Pitt in October to amount to £550,000. Between them, the King and Pitt concocted a plan to rescue the Prince from bankruptcy by increasing his allowance to £125,000 a year on condition that the revenues of the Duchy of Cornwall and one fifth of the new grant, a total of £38,000 a year, be used to satisfy his creditors. The King indiscreetly informed his son of this arrangement before parliament had been consulted. To his embarrassment, Pitt found that he was unlikely to be able to carry the proposal in the House of Commons. The Whigs, friends and champions of the Prince of Wales when he was the centre of Opposition and during the long period of the King's illness when both loyalty and sycophancy might be expected to gain rich rewards, expressed almost uniform hostility. Fox, who had been a member of the Prince's most intimate circle, suggested that the Prince should sell the Duchy of Cornwall. Pitt and Loughborough proposed an amended figure of £78,000 a year to be set aside for the payment of debts, and, although the King refused to go back on the original intention to which he had pledged his support, the Prince agreed.

The marriage, the price paid by the Prince for his increased settlement, was a squalid disaster. Within the year he had made a will leaving his wife one shilling and the greater part of his possessions to Maria Fitzherbert, his 'true and real wife'; he continued his association with Lady Jersey, who remained, at his insistence, a lady-in-waiting to Princess Caroline; and by June 1796 he was pleading for an official separation. His behaviour contributed to the gradual widening of the rift between the King, who liked his daughter-in-law and was prepared to ignore her faults, and the Queen, who loathed her. The public generally took Caroline's part, cheering her whenever she appeared in public and hissing Lady Jersey. It was not long before Caroline set up a separate establishment in Blackheath where she consoled herself with numerous lovers.

Pitt's sympathetic handling of the Prince's financial difficulties had not greatly improved his relationship with the heir to the throne, but he had provided further evidence of his desire to oblige the King whenever it was possible to do so without compromising his own principles. In the formulation of war policy George III was not to be treated as a cipher, and, in spite of Pitt's strengthened political position, the King's confidence and co-operation were essential to him. As a war minister Pitt had displayed none of the vigour and understanding of priorities that had distinguished his father's policies. On the contrary, he had squandered the slender resources at his disposal. Buffeted by the conflicting influences of the King, Dundas, Grenville, Richmond and the Portland Whigs, deluded by his own natural optimism, and ignorant of the limitations and deficiencies of the armed services, he had, by attempting everything at once, achieved very little.

It is, nevertheless, easier to criticize Pitt's policy than to find one which, in the circumstances facing him, would have produced a more favourable result. The concentration of the inadequate and malad-ministered British army in Flanders would not in any way have altered the self-interest, greed, indolence and treachery of the Allies, though there is little reason to suppose that its token presence there postponed or alleviated the divisions between them. It is doubtful if a larger army in the West Indies would have achieved more than the small forces, reinforced piecemeal, that operated there in 1794-5, and its losses from disease would have been proportionately greater. The one design that might have ended the war was an invasion of France in support of the Vendéan rebellion; but this could have been effective only in conjunction with a powerful and co-ordinated offensive by Austria and Prussia in northern Europe, which, if it had ever been forthcoming, would have been sufficient in itself to be decisive. If it is plain that Pitt and his ministers displayed woeful ignorance and lack of strategic judgement, it is also, and more effectively, sure that nothing they could have done would have transformed the tenuous First Coalition into a victorious alliance. The lessons of the first thirty months of war were clear: that the French, having escaped defeat when they could have done little to defend themselves, had become the most powerful military force in Europe and required continuing success in battle to sustain the republican government; that the selfishness and divided interest of the Allies could never be reconciled unless they found themselves, as France had been, united by fear of a common enemy; and that until Britain could field a substantial army that was competently administered, trained and led, her role in the war must be confined to diplomacy and the offensive use of the navy. These lessons were not yet understood.

By the end of 1795 it seemed that peace might be attainable upon terms that would not dishonour Britain. The French offensive into Germany, launched in September, went well. Mannheim was taken, and the minor German States, deserted by Prussia, prepared to be overrun prior to the French advance on Vienna. The force of the offensive was, however, already spent. At the end of November the Austrians counter-attacked, recaptured Mannheim, Mainz and Frankfurt, and drove the French back beyond the Rhine. The cause of the French defeat was more political than military. The corruption of the administration had at last drained the strength of the army. Supplies of arms, ammunition, food and clothing were contracted for but not delivered. The new rulers of France were revealed as cynical profiteers. A rising in Paris was suppressed with the aid of the young Corsican artillery officer who had played an important part in the recapture of Toulon: Captain Napoleon Bonaparte was promoted to the rank of brigadier.

France was bankrupt, her people dissatisfied and restless, and her armies showing signs of demoralization. It might be supposed that the Convention would welcome a period of peace while trade and the national economy were restored and at a time when the Allies were in no position to insist upon the restoration of conquered territories. The British had every reason to want peace. The Alliance had disintegrated, all attempts at military intervention had failed, the West Indian conquests were jeopardized by yellow fever and black rebellion, and the disastrous harvests of 1794 and 1795 had resulted in an acute shortage of grain, the rising cost of bread, and widespread riots. Pitt was being pressed by many of those close to him to sue for peace. In a letter marked 'Most Private', George Rose had written to Bishop Pretyman of the terrible cost and consequences of the war; 'it is heart-breaking that they should go on without a rational Hope in the Mind of a human Being of the smallest possible Advantage to the Country in the Cause it is embarked in.' [430] In the autumn, Auckland had drawn up and published, with Pitt's approval, a pamphlet advocating negotiation with France. He sent a copy to Burke, who replied, '[It] has filled me with a degree of grief and dismay which I cannot find words to express . . . nothing can be the consequence but utter and irretrievable ruin.' Pitt wrote to Auckland, 'I return Burke's letter, which is like other rhapsodies from the same pen, in which there is much to admire, and nothing to agree with.' [431]

Pitt's decision to negotiate was not taken lightly. He understood that many of his Whig associates, including some of those in the Cabinet, would not support peace moves. Windham had written of 'the cry of Peace which is beginning to be heard from all parts, the result partly of the base interested spirit which seems to have got possession of this country through the medium of its trade and its wealth, and partly of the wicked Jacobin spirit which we have drawn from the common reservoir of France. At the head of this cry is the wicked little fanatical imp W—— [Wilberforce] who . . . is acting against Pitt under the forms of friendship.' [432] More serious than lack of support from the Whigs was the opposition of the King and of Grenville. George III not only believed that the war should be continued as a defence against the destruction of the monarchies of Europe and all established constitutional government, but he appears to have been almost alone in understanding that the French would regard peace as a threat to the unstable foundations of republican government. Confident that overtures for peace, on terms that would be acceptable to him or to parliament, would be rejected by France, he allowed Pitt to negotiate.

The first offers, made through Switzerland, were rebuffed without discussion. In the autumn of 1796 another attempt was made. Lord Malmesbury was selected to go to Paris as Minister Plenipotentiary to negotiate with the Directory.* He was instructed to express an 'anxious desire to terminate the war by a just and honourable peace',[433] but 'this peace must be negotiated and concluded with the consent of, and conjointly with, our ally the Emperor of Austria, and this condition to be a sine qua non.' Burke commented with asperity that Malmesbury's journey to Paris was slow because he went the whole way on his knees. Malmesbury's best efforts were doomed to failure. The circumstances had changed. Neither the French nor the Austrians wanted peace: both were waiting for the outcome of the campaign in Lombardy. There Napoleon, having burst through the

---

* The executive of France from August 1795 to November 1799. The five Directors, of whom the most important were Carnot and Paul Barras (whose discarded mistress, Joséphine de Beauharnais, married Napoleon Bonaparte), were jointly responsible for the conduct of affairs.

passes of the Maritime Alps, forcing peace on Piedmont and taking Milan, was laying siege to Mantua. Moreover, the French had attracted a powerful new ally. Since the accession of Charles IV in 1788, Spain had been ruled by his Queen, Maria Luisa, and her lover, Manuel de Godoy, whom she had made chief minister in 1792. It was Godoy's influence that had brought Spain to make peace with France, and it was he who, on 5 October 1796, handed the British minister to the Court of Charles IV the Spanish declaration of war against Britain. The bribe that Godoy had accepted as the price of Spanish co-operation was joint control of the Mediterranean and assistance in the conquest of Portugal. Prussia, meanwhile, had begun negotiations to form a northern confederation, which, though non-belligerent, would favour France.

Malmesbury remained in Paris, hopeless, obliged for his personal safety to sport the revolutionary tricolour cockade, and reporting such intelligence as he was able to gather. Pitt wrote to him on 5 November, 'I own I am quite at a loss to judge whether they [the French] feel most the *necessity of peace* . . . or the impossibility of maintaining their power after peace shall have been made.' [434] He was beginning to understand that for the French the war was no longer a matter of principle but a necessity to sustain the government. A week later Malmesbury reported the presence at Brest of eleven ships of the line and between 15,000 and 20,000 troops, thought to be assembled for the invasion of Ireland. He returned to London on Thursday 29 December and dined with Pitt. Two days before he left Paris, the French invasion fleet—forty-three vessels, including seventeen ships of the line, carrying some 15,000 troops commanded by Lazare Hoche—sailed from Brest.

The failure of the French expedition was not due to the vigilance and energetic action of the blockading squadron off Brest, nor of the Channel fleet commanded by Lord Bridport, but to providential storms, the inexperience and indiscipline of the French naval officers, and the audacity of Captain Sir Edward Pellew commanding a lonely frigate, the *Indefatigable*. Gales had blown the British blockading squadron far out into the Atlantic, and the Channel fleet was sheltering in harbour at Portsmouth. The *Indefatigable* alone sighted the convoy, and in a gathering storm attacked it at night with so much vigour that the French, imagining themselves assailed by a powerful fleet, dispersed in disorder. One ship of the line sank and others collided in the panic to escape. While Pellew crammed on all sail to take the news to Falmouth, the ships of the scattered convoy made their way to their destination in Bantry Bay. On 21 December they gathered off the Irish coast. Eight ships were missing; one of them, the frigate *Fraternité*, was carrying the Admiral and General Hoche. Within twenty-four hours a storm had sprung up, which prevented the convoy from entering the Bay. On Christmas Day, gales and driving snow from the east drove the ships to sea. The expedition was abandoned and the convoy returned to Brest, where, on 14 January, it was rejoined by the *Fraternité*. The British Channel fleet sailed too late to intercept the French. It was again Pellew who, with two frigates, caught and drove aground a French battleship, the 80-gun *Droits de l'Homme*, on the coast of Brittany.

Had the French landed 15,000 troops in Bantry Bay, it is almost certain they would have conquered Ireland. A significant part of the population would have welcomed them, and Ireland was defended by an ill-trained and inexperienced force of 12,000, of which the greater number were newly recruited. The combined French and Spanish fleets would have made the reinforcement of Ireland hazardous if not impossible, and could also have cut the trade route across the Atlantic. The fact that the French had come so near to success, and that they had been robbed of it principally by misfortune, underlined once more Pitt's failure to frame or co-ordinate any recognizable war policy. It also drew attention to serious weaknesses in the command of the navy. The resources of the navy were overstrained by the government's scattered military adventures, but the custom of withdrawing the great Channel fleet to Portsmouth to preserve it from the rigours of winter at sea—a custom that had been responsible for the escape of the French fleet to protect the grain convoy in 1794, and the failure to intercept the invasion fleet bound for Ireland—was more damaging. If Britain could not retain command of the sea, the outcome of the war could not be seriously in doubt.

Apparently untroubled by such anxieties, Dundas continued to produce plans for widespread military operations. In 1795 he had been responsible for seizing the opportunity to snatch the Cape of Good Hope * and Ceylon from the Dutch; but he was also

* The Prince of Orange had given his permission for the colony to be occupied by the British, but the Dutch garrison resisted the landing. A Dutch naval expedition to repossess the Cape in 1796 was destroyed by the British fleet.

responsible for the continuous drain of reinforcements sent to die in the West Indies, for the failure to defend Ireland, for a lunatic plan to land two battalions in Holland during the winter of 1796, and for a scarcely less idiotic attack on Puerto Rico. His remarkable visions of conquest in South America were mercifully frustrated by lack of troops. Corsica, the last Mediterranean harbour open to the British fleet, had been evacuated in October. The decision had been made in August, when it appeared that Austria might withdraw from the war, and was revoked, too late, after the Spanish declaration of war in October. The island was occupied by the French, and the British fleet left the Mediterranean.

In November Napoleon defeated the Austrian army sent to the relief of Mantua. Three months later, after crushing the Austrians at Rivoli, he took Mantua. His campaign in Lombardy, which had given the French virtual control of Italy, forcing Sardinia to abandon her tentative alliance and the Kingdom of the Two Sicilies to sue for peace, put an end to any hope that the First Coalition might be sustained and revitalized. It could be only a matter of months before Austria, too, negotiated a separate peace.

Two events served to brighten the dismal aspect of the first months of 1797. The first, a great naval victory, removed the immediate threat of co-operation between the French and Spanish fleets. On the last day of January the Spanish Grand Fleet, twenty-seven ships of the line—including the four-decker, 136-gun, *Santissima Trinidad*, the largest battleship afloat, and twelve frigates—sailed from Cartagena to join the French fleet at Brest. Commodore Nelson, who had been evacuating troops and stores from Elba, sighted the Spaniards off Gibraltar. He sailed calmly through them, pausing only to pick up one of his men who had fallen overboard, and rejoined Sir John Jervis, cruising with his battle fleet off Cape St Vincent. On St Valentine's Day, Jervis, whose fleet was outnumbered by almost two to one and who had only two ships carrying 100 guns against the Spaniard's seven of 112 guns or more, forced an engagement. By a mixture of audacity and superior tactics he succeeded in dividing the enemy fleet and inflicting on it a heavy defeat. Nelson, whose disregard of written orders was to become habitual, broke away from the line of battle to prevent the junction of the divided enemy fleet, fought the monster *Santissima Trinidad* with his 74-gun *Captain*, and subsequently boarded and captured both the 80-gun *San Nicolas* and the 112-gun *San Josef*.

313

Severely mauled, the Spanish fleet withdrew that night to Cadiz. Jervis gathered up his four prizes, which included two first-rates, and sailed for Lagos. Don José de Cordoba, the Spanish Admiral, and his surviving rear-admiral and six captains were court martialled and dismissed from the Spanish navy. Jervis was awarded the earldom of St Vincent and a pension of £3,000 a year. The Admiral's despatches were accompanied to London by Sir Gilbert Elliot, who had sailed with Nelson from Elba and witnessed the battle from a frigate. At the request of Nelson, who did not believe he could afford the expenses of the baronetcy he would be offered, Elliot used his influence to obtain for him a knighthood. Rear-Admiral Sir Horatio Nelson KB chose for his crest the stern of a Spanish man-of-war proper, inscribed 'San Josef'. It may be doubted if there was ever a time in history when the British so urgently needed a naval victory. A conjunction of the French and Spanish fleets would have put into the Channel a force far larger than any the British could muster; and the British navy was on the point of mutiny.

The second glimmer of hope was shed by an abortive and farcical attempt by the French to land a raiding party in England. A band of 1,400 ruffians drawn from the French gaols and promised a free pardon landed at Ilfracombe and burnt a farmhouse. Hearing that the North Devon Volunteers were approaching, they retreated in haste and sailed to Fishguard. There they surrendered to an inferior force of mixed Militia. The affair was ludicrous and intrinsically unimportant, but it provided heartening evidence of the British people's determination to defend their island. There was, however, a serious postscript. Fear of invasion, and well-founded rumours of national bankruptcy, caused a run on the banks. On 26 February the Cabinet authorized the suspension of cash payments. Following a meeting of the Privy Council, paper currency of small denominations was declared legal tender*, and on the 27th a formal statement declaring the solvency of the Bank of England quelled the panic. It was a measure of the size and frequency of Pitt's loans to the Allies, and particularly to Austria, that the Bank of England should have been brought to defend itself in this manner, and he was savagely attacked in the House of Commons for his handling of the national finances.

* The Bank of England had previously issued no notes for less than £5.

British failures abroad, which included the West Indies, where far larger colonial gains would not have compensated for the appalling losses of the army, were accompanied by increasing difficulties at home. On 29 October 1795 the King, driving in his state coach from Buckingham House to Westminster, was hissed and jeered by a large crowd who shouted 'Bread!', 'No War!', 'No Famine!', and 'Down with Pitt!' As he arrived at the entrance to the House of Commons a stone or bullet * broke the window of his coach. Entering the House of Lords, the King remarked quietly to Loughborough, 'My Lord, I have been shot at', and went on to read his speech from the throne with perfect composure. His carriage was attacked again on his return to St James's Palace, and his escort of Guards was hard pressed to protect him from the mob. This incident followed two days after a meeting of the London Corresponding Society at Islington at which a crowd estimated to number 150,000 demanded universal suffrage and an end to the war.

These demonstrations were symptomatic of renewed and widespread unrest. The acute shortage and high price of bread was the cause of general discontent, fertile ground for the seeds of republicanism and revolution. The pamphlets of the popular Societies were deliberately inflammatory, and some openly called for insurrection. With the King's approval the government framed further repressive measures. On 10 November, Pitt introduced the Seditious Meetings Bill in the Commons, while Grenville, in the Lords, moved the treasonable Practices Bill. These banned meetings of more than fifty people without permission of the magistrates, empowered a magistrate to put an end to any meeting and arrest the speaker, and imposed heavy penalties on any who spoke or wrote against the constitution, attempted to coerce parliament, or gave aid to the nation's enemies. There is reason to believe that Pitt, who made an unspirited defence of his Bill against Fox's violent attack, was less than happy with his measures, but he was ably supported by Wilberforce and it was passed by 167 votes to 22. The two extremes of Whig opinion were summarized by Sheridan, who wrote to the Duchess of Devonshire, 'it were better to recruit for Bonaparte, for England is not worth preserving'; and by Mrs Crewe,

---

* There is some doubt whether the window was broken by a pebble or the pellet from an air gun. The Earl of Westmorland, who was in the royal carriage, and other witnesses were convinced that the missile was a bullet.[435]

who wrote to the Duke of Portland, 'Charles Fox seems determined we should have a civil war.' [436]

Protest meetings were held, the largest being in Marylebone Fields, in London, and in York, where Wilberforce harangued a large and disorderly mob, but the support for radicalism fell away. The King, attending the opera the night after his rough treatment by the crowd, had been greeted with vociferous enthusiasm and five repetitions of the National Anthem. Fox accused the government of despotism and the suppression of freedom of speech, [437] but as usual he overstated his case. Mass meetings, where skilful speakers could inflame the mob to violence, were banned, but the press remained unfettered by the laws which restrain expression and discussion in present-day newspapers, and the freedom of parliamentary opposition was untouched. When the survival of a nation is threatened, it is not unreasonable that the freedom of dissident minorities should be curtailed or temporarily suspended for the protection of the majority. It has been suggested that the collapse of the revolutionary movements proved that Pitt's repressive legislation was unnecessary; that no deep-rooted plant could have been plucked up so easily; and that radicalism would, anyway, have died of inanition. Even if this is so, and it could never be proved, radicalism might have been a long time dying, and time was the concession that Pitt could not afford. The defence of Britain required the suppression of any organization or activity that endangered internal security. The Societies withered, though whether as the result of Pitt's legislation or of the growing fear of invasion and defeat is not clear. By the end of 1796 the London Corresponding Society's membership had dwindled to insignificance and it was in debt. Two years later it debated a motion to recruit a corps of Loyal Volunteers.

The most deplorable victim of national crisis and the renunciation of reform was the movement for abolition of the slave trade. French agents had infiltrated the British West Indies, inciting blacks to rebellion. This threat to British settlers, to property, to essential trade, and to British policy, eliminated much of the support Wilberforce had attracted in the Commons and set back the cause for ten years.

On 15 May 1796 Nelson had written to Elliot: 'I very much believe that England, who commenced war with all Europe for her allies, will finish it by having nearly all Europe against her.' [438] By the end of

February next year it was becoming frighteningly apparent that Britain must stand alone against France, and that the navy, the one bulwark of defence against invasion and the springboard of all offensive operations, must withstand the combined assault of the French, Spanish and Dutch fleets. During the following six months it was, ironically, not the might of the enemy that came close to destroying Britain's defences, but the British navy itself.

XXII

The Virgin Minister
1796-1799

AFTER THIRTEEN YEARS as Prime Minister, the last four of them as leader of a nation at war, Pitt was showing signs of strain. For several years he had suffered from gout, intermittent sickness and severe headaches, and his voice was noticed to be hoarse. In 1795 he consulted Dr Walter Farquhar, an ex-army surgeon probably recommended to him by Dundas. Farquhar's report was not, at the time, considered disquieting. 'I found him', he wrote,

> in a state of general debility—the functions of the stomach greatly impaired & the Bowels very irregular—much of which I attributed to the excess of public business & the unremitting attention upon subjects of anxiety and interest. . . . I thought myself called upon to urge the necessity of some relaxation from the arduous Duties of Office, in order to regain strength & afford the natural functions time & opportunity to rally. This Mr Pitt stated to be impossible. There appeared at this time to be little or no constitutional mischief done, but the symptoms of debility with a gouty tendency, which Dr Addington (as Mr Pitt mentioned to me) had always remarked from his infancy, were likely to become formidable if neglected.

During the following years Farquhar, who was awarded a baronetcy on his appointment to be physician in ordinary to the Prince of Wales in 1796, continued to advocate 'relaxation from business', advice that Pitt was quite unable to follow. Farquhar also directed his patient to pay particular attention to 'the stomach & bowels, & to strengthen & aid them by gentle bitters & mild medicines'. This last advice may have been his cautious and tactful way of suggesting that Pitt should drink less toxic alcohol. If so, it was as near as Farquhar ever came to mentioning it. [439]

Sir Walter Farquhar continued to see Pitt regularly and noted that his health was 'variable' and 'much affected by the change of seasons and of situation'. In February 1797 the Archbishop of Canterbury * told Lord Auckland, 'The Premier seems to live much out of sight, and is always *rêveur*—seems to be hoarse, and at a late council his face appeared to be much swollen and not like health.' [440]

Pitt's health, it is clear, varied in direct relation to the pressures of public affairs and of his private life. At times of national crisis or disaster he succeeded in maintaining an appearance of cheerfulness. 'Young Jenky' wrote· of him: 'I never saw any Public Man who appeared so little desponding or who bore up so firmly against misfortunes. He had particularly the faculty of laying his cares aside, of amusing himself with an idle book, or a comparatively trivial conversation, at the time he was engaged in the most important business, & I have heard him say that no anxiety nor calamity had ever seriously attacked his sleep.' [441] Wilberforce, who believed that he knew him more intimately than any one of his friends, having seen him 'in every situation and in his most unreserved moments', remembered Pitt's self-confidence when he first took office: 'Yet though then not five-and-twenty I do not believe that the anxiety of his situation ever kept him awake for a single minute, or ever appeared to sadden or cast gloom over his hours of relaxation'; but he wrote also of his 'sanguine temper', his 'great natural courage and fortitude', and that 'his inward emotions never appeared to cloud his spirits'. As the years passed and the stresses of life became greater, 'his temper was not so entirely free from those approaches to fretfulness'. The 'good-humour', the 'wit and playfulness', and 'facetiousness' that had enchanted his close friends faded; though he

* John Moore, Archbishop of Canterbury 1783-1805, throughout all but a few months of Pitt's political life.

was still able to revive them, particularly in the company of young people. Increasingly, the mask of comedy that he wore for his friends required alcohol to sustain it.[442]

The strain on his health was visible. His friends and Cabinet colleagues noticed the swollen flesh of his face, and a yellowing of his complexion; his bouts of sickness became more frequent, and his headaches and attacks of gout more violent. The burdens of office were heavy, but Pitt was able to share them, to some extent, with Dundas and Grenville. His private anxieties, however, remained private. With the possible exception of Wilberforce, he seems to have had no one with whom he could share them. He did not lack friends, but he remained essentially solitary. He never shared his life in the comforting intimacy of marriage, and it is plain that he had no desire to do so.

In the eighties Pitt's name had been linked with that of Jane, Duchess of Gordon, but there was no prospect of marriage between them. It appears, on the contrary, that the Duchess intended him for her eldest daughter, Charlotte, who subsequently married Colonel Charles Lennox.* Alexander, 4th Duke of Gordon, was one of the richest men in Britain, and one of the most powerful. His Duchess was headstrong, witty and unconventional. Handsome, intelligent, and active in politics, she had few feminine virtues: she rode hard † and indulged in a coarseness of expression better suited to the stable than the dinner table. As a contemporary wrote:

> The Duchess triumphs in her manly mien
> Loud is her accent and her phrase obscene.[443]

Some ten years older than Pitt, she was, from 1784, the most gregarious and influential of the society hostesses who supported the government, and young members of parliament who shared her allegiance gathered nightly at her house in Pall Mall. For several years, after the death of Pitt's sister Harriot, Jane Gordon acted as hostess for his large dinners at Downing Street, but their friendship waned and she ceased to be a regular visitor to 'Bachelor Hall', as she

---

* Later 4th Duke of Richmond. Pitt was believed to have taken an important part in arranging the match.

† She once rode a pig bareback down the street in Edinburgh, but generally chose more conventional mounts.

described Pitt's official residence. When they met again, after a long interval, she greeted him with 'Well, Mr Pitt, do you talk as much nonsense now as you used to do when you lived with me?' He replied, 'I do not know, madam, whether I talk so much nonsense, I certainly do not hear so much.' [444]

In 1796 Pitt's name was more closely linked with that of Eleanor Eden, the eldest daughter of Lord Auckland, and this time it was rumoured that he was intending marriage. Pitt had visited Eden Farm, the home of the Aucklands near Beckenham, several times during the autumn of 1796, on at least one occasion with Lord Loughborough and young Canning, who wrote that 'It was a whole holiday—spent entirely in the country—riding, and rambling about with Lord Auckland, the Chancellor and Pitt all the morning—and in playing all sorts of tricks, follies and fooleries with the same persons and with the addition and assistance of all the Edens from dinner-time to bed-time.' [445] Eleanor Eden was twenty years old, beautiful, vivacious and mature. Pitt evidently found her charming, and although there is no evidence that his attentions to her were ever more than courteously affectionate it is plain that she was flattered by them and captivated by his brilliance, wit and youthful zest for buffoonery.

On 6 December the Countess von Brühl * wrote to Auckland, 'I have letter after letter to say how pleased everybody is with the intended marriage of our minister to your chère fille.' [446] This letter must have caused Auckland considerable embarrassment and it is unlikely that it was the only one of its kind he received. On 22 December he wrote to his old friend, the Irish statesman John Beresford, in a vain attempt to stifle the rumour:

We are all well here, and I will take the occasion to add a few words of a private and confidential kind. You may probably have seen, or heard by letters, a report of an intended marriage between Mr Pitt and my eldest daughter. You know me too well to suppose that, if it were so, I should have remained silent. The truth is, she is handsome, and possessed of sense far superior to

---

* Maria, daughter of General Christopher Chowne, and second wife of John Maurice, Count von Brühl. Brühl, an eminent astronomer, was Saxon ambassador extraordinary to the Court of St James's from 1764 and remained in England, apart from one visit to his homeland in 1785, until his death in 1809.

321

the ordinary proportion of the world. They see much of each other, they converse much together, and I really believe they have sentiments of mutual esteem; but I have no reason to think that it goes further on the part of either, nor do I suppose it is likely ever to go further.[447]

The letter is significant as showing Auckland's realization that the relationship between his daughter and Pitt might not lead to marriage. Beresford was a trusted friend, but even to him Auckland felt obliged to exercise caution. It is clear from his later letters that he desired the match. It is also clear that his motives were not selfless.

By the middle of January 1797 Pitt was aware that his frequent visits to the Aucklands were creating speculation that might be damaging to Eleanor Eden's reputation and drawing him into a net from which he might be unable to escape. On the 20th he wrote from Downing Street a long and 'Most Private' letter to Auckland, which, taken with a second written two days later, is the most revealing of any that have been preserved:

My dear Lord,
Altho' the anxious expectation of public business would at all events have made it difficult for me to leave town during the last ten days, you may perhaps have begun to think that it cannot have been the only reason which has kept me so long from Beckenham. The truth is that I have really felt it impossible to allow myself to yield to the temptation of returning thither without having (as far as might depend upon me) formed a decision on a point which I am sensible has remained in suspense too long already. Having at length done so, I should feel myself inexcusable if (painful as the task is) any consideration prevented me from opening myself to you without reserve. It can hardly, I think, be necessary to say that the time I have passed among your family has led to my forming sentiments of very real attachment towards them all, and of much more than attachment towards one whom I need not name. Nor should I do justice to my own feelings, or explain myself as frankly as I think I ought to do, if I did not own that every hour of my acquaintance with the person to whom you will

322

easily conceive I refer has served to augment and confirm that impression; in short, has convinced me that whoever may have the good fortune ever to be united with her is destined to more than his share of human happiness.

Whether, at any rate, I could have had any ground to hope that such might have been my lot, I am in no degree entitled to guess. I have to reproach myself for having ever indulged the idea on my own part as far as I have done without asking myself carefully and early enough what were the difficulties in the way of its being realized. I have suffered myself to overlook them too long, but, having now at length reflected as fully and as calmly as I am able on every circumstance that ought to come under my consideration (at least as much for her sake as my own), I am compelled to say that I find the obstacle to it decisive and insurmountable. In thus conveying to you, my dear Lord, what has been passing in my mind, and its painful but unavoidable result, I have felt it impossible to say less. And yet it would be almost a consolation to me to know that even what I have said is superfluous, and that the idea which I have entertained has been confined solely to myself. If this should be the case, I am sure this communication will be buried in silence and oblivion. On any other supposition I know that I but consult the feelings of those who must be most in my thoughts by confiding it to your discretion. And in doing so I have every reason to rely on your prudence and kindness, and on those sentiments of mutual friendship which I hope will not be affected by any change which may at present be unavoidable in what have lately been the habits of our intercourse. For myself, allow me only to add that, separated as I must be for a time from those among whom I have passed many of my happiest moments, the recollection of that period will long be present in my mind. The greatest pleasure and best consolation I can receive will be if I am ever enabled to prove how deep an interest I must always take in whatever may concern them.

They will not, I am sure, be less dear to me through life than they would have had a right to expect from the nearest and closest connection.

Believe me, my dear Lord, under all circumstances,
   Ever sincerely and faithfully yours,
     W. Pitt [448]

Auckland replied the following day, making no effort to disguise his distress. 'It has been', he wrote, 'impossible for Ly. Auckland & for me not to remark that you entertained the partiality which you describe; and it has been for several weeks the happiest subject of conversation that we have had thro' the course of a very happy life, to consider it in every point of view. We had from an early period every reason to believe that the sentiments formed were *most cordially* mutual: and we saw with delight that they were ripening into an attachment which might lay the foundation of a system of most perfect happiness, for the two persons for whom we were so much concerned.' After describing his daughter's virtues and accomplishments, and the shock and disappointment felt by his wife and daughter, he went on to invite Pitt's confidence about the 'decisive and insurmountable' obstacles:

We presume that the obstacles alluded to are those of circumstances. (If there are any others we hope you will confide them to us.) I do not mean circumstances of Office & of the Public; they might create a temporary suspension, but could create no permanent difficulty. As to circumstances of fortune, I may be imprudent in the idea, but I cannot think that they ought in such a case to create an hour's interruption in an intercourse essentially sought & loved by us all; still less that they ought to affect the ultimate result, tho' they may impede it. I am sure that the person alluded to has steadiness of mind to wait any indefinite period of Time for that difficulty if possible to be got over. I am sure also that it would be happiness to her, as it has often been to her mother, to share such difficulties, & to endeavour also to lessen them. I only regret that my own position puts it out of my power to remove the difficulties. I have about 2000£ belonging to her from a legacy, & what I owe to the others will not allow me to add much to it.

He ended by suggesting that Pitt should return 'as soon as convenient' to Eden Farm to 'talk about the whole at leisure & again & again'.

Pitt replied at once, in a letter that left no room for any misunderstanding of his intentions:

My dear Lord,

If I felt much more than I could express in writing to you yesterday you will guess that these feelings are all, if possible, heightened by the nature of your answer. I will not attempt to describe the sense I have of your kindness and Lady Auckland's, much less how much my mind is affected by what you tell me of the sentiments of another person, unhappily too nearly interested in the subject in question. I can only say (but it is saying everything) that consideration now adds to my unavailing regret as much as under different circumstances it might have contributed to the joy and happiness of my life.

Indeed, my dear Lord, I did not bring myself to the step I have taken without having, as far as I am able, again and again considered every point which must finally govern my conduct. I should deceive you and everyone concerned, as well as myself, if I flattered myself with the hope that such an interval as you suggest would remove the obstacles I have felt, or vary the ground of my opinion.

It is impossible for me, and would be useless, to state them at large. The circumstances of every man's private and personal situation can often, on various accounts, be fully known and fairly judged by no one but himself, even where, as in the present case, others may be equally interested in the result. On the present occasion I have had too many temptations in the opposite scale to distrust my own decision. I certainly had to contend with sentiments in my own mind such as must naturally be produced by a near observation of the qualities and endowments you have described, with those of affectionate attachment, of real admiration, and of cordial esteem and confidence.

If anything collateral could add strength to those sentiments, they would have derived it (as you know from what I have said already) from every circumstance, with respect to all parts of your family, which could tend to render such a connection dear and valuable to my mind. Believe me, I have not lightly or easily sacrificed my best hopes and earnest wishes to my conviction and judgement. Believe me, also, that further explanation or discussion can answer no good purpose. And let me entreat you to spare me and yourself the pain of urging it further. It could only lead to prolonged suspense and increased anxiety, without the possibility of its producing any ultimate advantage.

Feeling this impression thus strongly and unalterably on my mind, I have felt it a trying but indispensable duty, for the sake of all who are concerned, to state it (whatever it may cost me to do so) as distinctly and explicitly as I have done. Having done so, I have only to hope that reading this letter will nowhere be attended with half the pain I felt in writing it.

I remain, my dear Lord,
    Ever sincerely and affectionately yours,
      W. Pitt

Although obliged to accept Pitt's decision, Auckland was perturbed about the public effect of a final denial. 'I doubt,' he wrote on 23 January, 'whether you are in any degree aware how much this business has been observed and discussed in societies, correspondences, and newspapers.' His wife and daughter, he added, were too distressed to leave their rooms or to see their friends. He proposed a form of answer, to be used by both parties, to any questioning. Auckland was, it seemed, equally concerned to make certain that he forfeited neither Pitt's friendship nor influence. Lord Mansfield's death had left vacant the Lord Presidency of the Council, to which he had succeeded on Fitzwilliam's appointment to Ireland. Pitt had given the office to his brother in September 1796, thus leaving vacant his position as Lord Privy Seal. Auckland chose this inauspicious moment to ask Pitt for the appointment. The office was held in commission for a further twelve months on the pretext that a promise had been made to Lord Mornington, but the true reasons for Pitt's refusal to give the office to Auckland were resentment at his importunity at a time when he believed Pitt to be vulnerable to personal pressure, and the King's opposition. Auckland had stressed too strongly his desire for office: 'To me and to mine it is essential *now*. . . . It would not perhaps be too much to add that if deferred now it ought never to be renewed.' The offer was not made. If Auckland chose to believe that it was deferred he was mistaken.

Auckland had stated his intention of writing to a number of close friends and relations to inform them that all thoughts of an engagement had been abandoned. Pitt unburdened himself to Addington, who, as both an intimate friend and Speaker of the

House of Commons, was in a position to understand his predicament and to help to quell rumours among their political colleagues. Referring to Auckland's letters, Pitt wrote:

> The first answer indeed which I received on Saturday, tho' thoroughly kind, was the most embarrassing possible, as it stated the sentiments entertained to be mutual and pressed for explanation and discussion, proposing at the same time any interval of delay in order to take the chance of overcoming the difficulties and desiring me to continue coming in the interval as if nothing had happened. I had then nothing left but to convey in my answer quite explicitly tho' with as much tenderness as I could, that the decision I had felt myself obliged to take was final and that further discussion could only produce increased anxiety and could lead to no good. This was understood and received as I meant it should; and the answer I received last night, considers the thing as over, and proposes to contradict the reports gradually.

Of Auckland's ambitions Pitt told Addington little, merely mentioning in passing Auckland's assurance that he would not be 'wanting either to the calls of public duty or to what yet remains to me of the private relations of life'.

Pitt's withdrawal has never been satisfactorily explained. Auckland's assumption that it was caused by 'circumstances of fortune', as he delicately described Pitt's financial difficulties, has been generally accepted [449], but it is singularly unconvincing. There is no evidence that Pitt showed any great anxiety about his financial disorder before 1800 and he certainly made no attempt whatever at economy or retrenchment. His difficulties could, in fact, have been overcome by good management and the sale of Holwood, or the acceptance of help, substantial and frequently offered, from friends and admirers. His private resources were negligible and his earnings were not lavish, but they could have been sufficient. His debts were small in comparison with many of his contemporaries. The confusion of his finances and almost total lack of management of his affairs were due to his indifference to money and his extravagance. His debts had never prevented him from acquiring anything he had wanted, and there is no reason to suppose that he ever considered them, except perhaps as a convenient excuse, any obstacle to marriage.

327

An alternative possible reason for his decision to remain single might have been anxiety about his health. His mention to Addington of 'what remains to me of the private relations of life' might be interpreted as an indication that he expected his life to be cut short; but if this was so, he gave no hint of it to anyone else, and his doctor did not believe that his gout, or the recurrent headaches and vomiting, posed any threat to his life.

It is far more likely that the obstacles that he found 'decisive and insurmountable', and which were 'impossible' and 'useless' for him to discuss, were raised by sexual incapacity or deviation. For the greater part of his adult life his obvious indifference to women had been the subject of merciless and often libellous comment in widely circulated news-sheets and pamphlets. The majority of these lampoons taunted him with impotence, but others hinted, without much evasion, that he was homosexual. In February 1784, in the House of Commons, Sheridan spoke of Pitt as a King's minion and compared him with James I's Duke of Buckingham *.[450] This innuendo, the nearest to an open accusation of homosexuality possible in parliamentary debate, was later taken up by Macaulay, who wrote that Pitt's influence with George III was as great as that of Carr † or Villiers.[451]

The wittiest and most scurrilous of lampoons appeared in *The Rolliad*.[452] Two, in particular, drew attention to Pitt's relationship with Tom Steele, with whom he shared a number of short holidays in Brighton. The first compares the manly taste of Fox for beef and porter with Pitt's for tea.

> Pure as himself; add sugar too and cream,
> Sweet as his temper, bland as flows the stream
> Of his smooth eloquence; then crisply nice
> The muffin toast, or bread and butter slice,
> Thin as his arguments, that mock the mind,
> Gone, ere you taste, —no relish left behind.
> Where beauteous Brighton overlooks the sea,
> These be his joys: and STEELE shall make the Tea.

How neat! How delicate! and how unexpected is the allusion in the last couplet! These two lines alone include the substance of

* George Villiers, 1st Duke of Buckingham, most notorious of James I's favourites.
† Robert Carr, Earl of Somerset, supplanted in the King's favours by Villiers.

whole columns, in the ministerial papers of last summer, on the sober, the chaste, the virtuous, the edifying manner in which the Immaculate Young Man passed the recess from public business; not in riot and debauchery, not in gaming, not in attendance on ladies, either modest or immodest, but in drinking tea with Mr Steele, at the Castle in Brighthelmstone. Let future ages read and admire!

The second, entitled *ROSE, or the Complaint,* draws a similar picture in which the insinuation, bolstered by imaginative ambiguity, becomes a plain accusation:

None more than ROSE, amid the courtly ring
Lov'd BILLY, joy of JENKY and the KING.
But vain his hope to shine in BILLY's eyes;
Vain all his votes, his speeches, and his lies.
STEELE's happier claims the boy's regard engage;
Alike their studies, nor unlike their age:
With STEELE, companion of his vacant hours,
Oft would he seek Brighthelmstone's sea-girt tow'rs;
For STEELE, relinquish Beauty's trifling talk,
With STEELE, each morning ride, each evening walk;
Or in full tea-cups drowning cares of state,
On gentler topics urge the mock debate
On coffee now the previous question move;
Now rise a surplusage of cream to prove;
But with the love-lorne beauties, whom I mark
Thin and more thin, parading in the park,
I yet remain; and ply my busy feet
From DUKE-STREET hither, hence to DOWNING-STREET;
In vain!—while far from this deserted scene,
With happier STEELE you saunter on the Steine.

The references to Pitt's taste for tea, though now obscure, would not have been lost upon eighteenth-century readers accustomed to thinking of tea-drinking as an occupation for ladies, and are explained in *Satan's Harvest Home,* an anonymous publication of 1749. In the second part, uncompromisingly titled *Reasons for the Growth of Sodomy,* blame is laid on the domination of women in the education

329

of boys during childhood, the cultivation of effeminate habits, 'foppish attire, continental manners *, indolence, and tea-drinking.' [453]

Other malicious verses, *Epigrams on the Immaculate Boy*, cast doubt more briefly on Pitt's virility:

> 'Tis true, indeed, we oft abuse him,
> Because he bends to no man;
> But Slander's self dare not accuse him
> Of stiffness to a woman.
>
> 'No! no! for my virginity,
> 'When I lose that,' quoth Pitt, 'I'll die;'
> Cries WILBERFORCE, 'If not till then,
> 'By G—d you must outlive all men.'
> Though PITT have to women told somethings, no doubt;
> Yet his private affairs have they never found out.

An even more indelicate sketch of the Prime Minister appeared in a bawdy song written by the popular ballad-maker of the Beefsteak Society†, Captain Charles Morris, an officer of the Life Guards who was a frequent guest at entertainments given by the Prince of Wales at Carlton House:

> 'The Virgin Minister'
>
> Come then, be silent
> And join in my ballad.
> A better you never saw
> Pinned on a wall.
> Oh, the subject won't hurt
> Any Lady's nice palate,
> Because it ne'er meddles
> With ladies at all.

---

* Temporary fashion not withstanding, *le vice Anglais* was not, as is generally supposed, sodomy, but flagellation. 'The English malady' was depression, evidenced by the high rate of suicide.

† Founded by John Rich, manager of Covent Garden Theatre, in 1735. Its members included David Garrick, John Wilkes and, from 1785, the Prince of Wales.

It is all of a sweet pretty
Well-spoken gentleman,
Come to delude this
Lewd world and its wife;
Oh, by c——t, he's so chaste
He won't trust his p——le, man
Out of his hand
To save Venus's life.
Troth, and it's right
That the tool of a Minister
Ne'er should be managed
By hands but his own:
Then, though his labour's
By dexter or sinister,
Still it's all one
While he's working alone. . . .[454]

The intention of this piece of bawdy was not as harmless as it now appears. Masturbation—the subject of a comprehensive and fearsome literature, and believed to be the cause of impotence, sterility, 'diseased semen, incurable trembling & the draining of spinal fluid' [455]—was considered more vicious than homosexuality and was the more reprehended.

During the first sixty years of the eighteenth century the British attitude to deviant sex was generally permissive. Sodomy had been punishable by death since 1533, but there were few eighteenth-century convictions for homosexuality before 1763 and, although some unfortunates died of injuries sustained in the pillory, no one convicted was sentenced to death until 1807. In *Roderick Random* *, Tobias Smollett makes Strutwell say that homosexuality 'gains ground apace and in all possibility will become in a short time a more fashionable device than fornication', and Dudley Ryder noted in his diary that at Oxford University 'among the chief men of the colleges sodomy is very usual . . . it is dangerous sending a young man who is beautiful to Oxford.' [456] The laws, nevertheless, remained on the statute books, applied infrequently and with unequal severity according to the social position of those accused of offences.

* Published in 1748.

Public opinion was, however, changing. One of George III's first acts after his accession in 1760 was to issue a royal proclamation against 'vice, profaneness, and immorality', and a second proclamation was issued, at Wilberforce's instigation in June 1787, when he founded a society to implement it. In the eighties, too, there appears to have been a semi-official campaign against homosexuality, and two alleged sodomite groups were uncovered in Exeter and London. An unfortunate coachman, arrested and convicted with a friend in 1780, was stoned to death in the pillory. Gentlemen from the upper classes, if arrested, were seldom charged, and their names were withheld by the newspapers. By the end of the century public opinion was moving swiftly towards the repressive puritan attitudes associated with the reign of Victoria. J. W. von Archenholtz, a visitor to England, commented in 1797 on the British loathing of homosexuality: 'The English women are so beautiful, the desire of being agreeable to them so ardent, and general, that unnatural pleasures are held in great abhorrence with the men. In no country are such infamous pleasures spoken of with greater detestation.' [457]

There is no direct evidence that Pitt was homosexual, but there are strong inferences that cannot be ignored. Except for his mother and sister, and his brief entanglement with Eleanor Eden, from which he escaped as soon as it appeared that he was expected to offer her marriage, he never in his life showed interest in or affection for any woman. He told his niece Lady Hester Stanhope, 'I must remain a single man,' and she wrote 'Oh! how Sheridan used to make me laugh, when he pretended to marry Mr Pitt to different women!' [458] On the other hand his preference for male company was obvious to all his contemporaries, and with his accession to power he showed a growing tendency to seek the company of younger men, to some of whom he gave political patronage. His early friendships with Steele, and even with Pretyman, were the subject of much gossip and ribaldry, and his affection for Robert Banks Jenkinson ('Young Jenky') and George Canning, both eleven years his junior, was instrumental in furthering their careers. Later, at Walmer, he chose to entertain junior officers of the regiments stationed nearby to dinners at which Hester Stanhope was the only woman present, and his relationship with her step-brothers, James and Charles, and with the 'dazzling' William Napier, was one of remarkable familiarity that denied a twenty-five-year difference in age.

Homosexual inclinations would help to account, too, for his shyness and apparent coldness to strangers, and may have been responsible for his dependence on alcohol. As D. J. West has written, 'Psychiatrists have long recognized flight into alcoholism as the one way in which homosexuals seek escape from their conflicts . . . drinking enables men to enjoy intimate male companionship without provoking comment and so affords a particularly attractive outlet for the latent homosexual.' [459] Voluntary or compulsory abstinence from any physical expression of homosexual desires may lead to neurosis, irritability and depression, but 'when strong-minded persons make a deliberate choice to live celibately they sometimes succeed without visible harm. The task becomes less difficult if the individual is fortified by a strong sense of purpose behind his sacrifice . . . or if he can immerse himself in some cause or activity.' [460]

If Pitt's inclinations were homosexual he would have found it obligatory, for the sake of his political ambition if not for his social position, to suppress them. Had he not done so he would have been condemned by society at large, deserted by his political supporters, and ostracized by the King. In sharing holidays with Steele at Brighton, he took risks which the pamphleteers were quick to advertise. He did not repeat them. His lack of interest in women, his marked preference for exclusively male company, his patronage of and friendship with personable young men to whom he showed the most attractive side of his personality, his shyness in mixed or unfamiliar company, and his growing dependence on alcohol, all strongly support the theory that he was homosexual; but if he was he suppressed his desires well enough to leave no positive evidence of the fact. Whatever the heat of the fire, there was remarkably little smoke.

XXIII

Mutiny and Rebellion
1797-1800

TOWARDS THE END OF 1794 Sir Gilbert Elliot wrote to Dundas, 'I am sorry to say that there is throughout the fleet a strong sense of the discouraging prospect for us.' [461] Two and a half years later the prospect was bleaker than ever. Howe's victory of the Glorious First of June 1794, and Sir John Jervis's at Cape St Vincent on 14 February 1797, had inspired confidence in a few senior commanders and revealed the quality of some of their young captains, but it was a sombre fact that the combined might of the French, Spanish and Dutch fleets left the British hopelessly outnumbered. Command of the sea alone kept Britain safe from invasion and secured British colonial conquests and essential trade.

Unlike the army, which was regarded with fear and suspicion, the navy, upon which so much depended, was an object of national pride, admiration and affection; but its administration, in spite of the efforts of Sir Charles Middleton, was inefficient and corrupt, and its men neglected. For a century and a half the pay of an ordinary seaman had remained at nineteen shillings a month and, as it was not paid anywhere but in the port of commission, it was always in arrears. Merchant sailors, who were able to sell their services at the market price, earned four times as much and under conditions of less severity and danger. At the beginning of March 1797 men of the Channel fleet petitioned Lord Howe for redress of their grievances. Howe, crippled with gout at Bath and on the point of retirement, forwarded the petitions, which were both reasonable and respectfully worded, to the Admiralty, where they were ignored.

On 16 April, when Lord Bridport, who had succeeded Howe at Spithead, hoisted the signal to his fleet to weigh anchor, the crew of the flagship *Queen Charlotte* manned the shrouds and gave three cheers. This was a signal of defiance to the rest of the ships' crews to follow suit and refuse to put to sea. Bridport, who was shrewd, experienced and respected, ordered his captains not to resist the mutiny but to call their crews together and listen to their complaints. Delegates from the sixteen ships were appointed to meet aboard the *Queen Charlotte*, where they drew up regulations for the fleet. These differed little from those already in force: Bridport and his officers retained their commands, and all indiscipline was to be punished in the usual way; but, unless the French sailed, the men would not weigh anchor until their demands had been satisfied. Never was a mutiny so peaceful, so disciplined, or so well justified.

Spencer, the First Lord of the Admiralty, reacted to the shocking news with admirable speed and restraint. After consulting Pitt he left at once for Portsmouth where he set up a commission to examine the sailors' grievances. To their demands for better pay, regular leave and the fairer distribution of prize money, they had added others for improved rations and care of the wounded, and leave to go ashore when in harbour. On the 20th, Frederick, Prince of Württemberg, arrived at Portsmouth on his way to marry Charlotte Augusta, the Princess Royal. Lord Spencer conducted him round the fleet and he was greeted by cheers and salutes as if there were nothing amiss; but the next day, when it seemed that an agreement had been reached, the men declared that the King's pardon must be granted before they would put an end to the mutiny. Vice-Admiral Sir Allan Gardner lost his temper and seized one of the delegates by the collar. In the ensuing riot Gardner was lucky to escape with his life. The officers were put ashore or confined to their cabins, and the red flag of piracy was flown by the whole fleet.

Spencer returned to London that night. With Pitt and Loughborough he travelled to Windsor, where Grenville joined them for a Privy Council. The King signed a royal proclamation pardoning the mutinous crews on condition that they resumed their duties, and a special messenger galloped through the night to Portsmouth, where, on the 24th, Bridport read it aloud to the crew of his flagship while copies were circulated round the fleet. Even before the arrival of the King's pardon the good humour of the crews had been restored and the ships' delegates had apologized to Bridport and invited him, as their 'father and friend', to resume command. The fleet prepared for sea. On 26 April Pitt made use of a budget debate to make public his promise to increase the pay of all seamen and marines.

It seemed that the crisis was over, but the Opposition deliberately stirred up the affair by accusing Pitt, barely a week after his announcement in the House of Commons, of unnecessary delay in introducing a Bill to give effect to his promise. Rumours that the government intended to repudiate the agreement and arrest the ringleaders among the mutineers led to a second revolt of the Channel fleet and isolated acts of violence. On 9 May Pitt moved a resolution increasing naval pay and allowances and it was passed, though not without censure from Fox and Sheridan, in a single day. Pitt wisely decided to send Lord Howe, the most respected of admirals, to Portsmouth to reassure the men. Suffering agonies of gout, the seventy-four-year-old Admiral had himself rowed round the fleet visiting each ship in turn. On 15 May 'Black Dick' was landed and carried shoulder-high to the port governor's house, where the exhausted hero and Lady Howe entertained the ships' delegates to dinner. Two days later Bridport's Channel fleet put to sea.

Meanwhile, the mutiny had spread to Plymouth, Weymouth, and Yarmouth, where the giant Admiral Adam Duncan commanded the North Sea fleet, and to the Nore. At Yarmouth, Duncan, who was loved by his men, temporarily quelled the revolt by sheer force of personality, and the troubles at Plymouth and Weymouth were soon settled. At the Nore, however, the mutiny was led by Richard Parker, a fanatical ex-schoolmaster once court martialled as a midshipman for insubordination, whose gifts as a rabble-rouser were more than equal to those of Vice-Admiral Charles Buckner as peacemaker. Some of Parker's demands were fair, and there has always been a temptation to regard him as a martyr for liberty; but the truth is that he was self-satisfied and self-seeking, an embittered, hysterical and vainglorious popinjay who styled himself 'President' and 'Vice-Admiral' and insisted upon observation of the honours due to his assumed dignity. Later he was to write of the men he had led as 'cowardly, selfish and ungrateful', but he was prepared to use them for his own aggrandizement.

Parker and his militant subordinates refused to discuss their grievances with anyone but the First Lord, and meanwhile paraded in Sheerness, seizing eight gun-boats in the harbour, and sent agitators to Yarmouth to urge the men of Duncan's fleet to mutiny. There, news had been received of troops embarking aboard the Dutch fleet for an invasion of Ireland. Duncan ordered the North Sea fleet to sail for the Texel, but one by one his ships deserted him and returned home. Accompanied only by the *Adamant*, Duncan sailed in his flagship the *Venerable* to the Texel, where, from 1 June to 4 June, he blockaded an invasion fleet of ninety-three Dutch vessels, including fifteen ships of the line, by busily signalling to an imaginary battle fleet over the horizon.

On 28 May Spencer arrived at Sheerness, carrying a second royal pardon, but he found on his arrival that, although joined by the greater part of Duncan's fleet, the mutineers at the Nore were by no means united under Parker's leadership. Spencer therefore declined to receive the seamen's delegation and when Parker refused to moderate any of his most unreasonable demands, which included the right of ships' crews to dismiss their officers, returned to London to put in hand stringent measures to suppress the revolt. The loyalty of the army was secured by immediate increases in pay; the death penalty was introduced for anyone found to be aiding and abetting the mutineers; supplies to the Nore fleet were cut off; and troops were called out to guard the coast and prevent sailors from landing. Within two weeks the mutiny collapsed. By seizing all vessels entering the Thames, Parker had united the people of London against him. By giving the order, on 9 June, for the fleet to put to sea to join the enemy, he destroyed his own authority. Not one ship obeyed him, but two—the *Leopard* and the *Repulse*—allowed their officers to regain command and sail their ships out of danger. Three days earlier the government had formally offered to pardon all but the ringleaders of the mutiny, but Parker did not publish the offer to his followers. One after another the crews surrendered their ships to their officers. On 15 June Parker was given up to the authorities by his own men. At the end of the month he and twenty-eight others of the ringleaders were hanged. Three hundred of the most prominent mutineers were pardoned.

The mutinies, which had left Britain almost defenceless, achieved lasting benefits for the armed services. Attempts to spread revolt to the army, resulting in a brief mutiny among the Horse Artillery at Woolwich on 25 May, had failed, but rumours of impending revolt among some of the proudest regiments, including the Guards, had been loud enough to awaken the government to the urgency of reform. It was to be many years before conditions in either the navy or the army were sufficiently improved to attract any but the unemployed to their ranks, but the reform and reorganization of both services during the following fifty years owed much to the mutineers at Spithead and the Nore.

The spirit of rebellion, which had showed itself alarmingly enough in England and Scotland, was even more threatening in Ireland, where the embers kindled by tyranny and corruption had been fanned into flame by the inspiring example of the Revolution in France. Pitt had not forgotten the advice of Chief Secretary Thomas Orde: 'act towards Ireland with the utmost liberality consistent with your own safety, it must in the long run be the wisest policy.' * The failure of his plans for a settlement in 1785 had taught him much about the intractability of the Irish, the prejudices and greed of the English, and the obstinacy of the King. The obstacles to the imposition of fundamental principles of justice upon the Irish government were formidable, and, although Pitt had turned aside from the problem while he wrestled with the threats of national bankruptcy and later of war, he provided ample proof that he had not forgotten it. In 1791 and 1793 he had forced upon the reluctant Viceroy, the Earl of Westmorland, and the Protestant parliament in Dublin, measures to grant Catholics the right of public worship, parliamentary suffrage and the freedom to build schools. It is clear that he was moving towards the admission of Catholics to parliament, but it is also clear that he knew that such a reform would encounter the most violent opposition in England and Ireland, and involve a direct clash with the King. There was no possibility that any attempt

* See p. 152.

at so radical a change could succeed while Ireland retained a separate parliament.

The accession of the Whigs to the Cabinet in July 1794 brought Irish affairs under the direct control of the Duke of Portland as Home Secretary. Pitt had agreed to the appointment of Fitzwilliam to the Viceroyalty as soon as suitable employment could be found for Westmorland. This proved to be no easy task, and it was four months before the post of Master of the Horse was accepted by him. During this interval Fitzwilliam, whose probity and good intentions were no compensation for his lack of experience, capacity or caution, broadcast the news of his impending succession and details of his proposals for radical change. His correspondence with Henry Grattan, the great Irish patriot, and the influential Ponsonby brothers * raised hopes among them and their followers that he intended to remove from office all those who had shown loyalty to Pitt's administration during the Regency crisis of 1789, when the Opposition to Ireland had called for the immediate succession of the Prince of Wales, and to support Catholic claims to membership of the Irish parliament. In September Grattan and the Ponsonbys arrived in London to discuss these plans.

Warned by the Attorney-General Sir Richard Pepper Arden, Pitt at first took little notice of the danger and foolishly allowed Loughborough to intervene in the transactions. By the middle of October Pitt was confronted by two equally disagreeable courses of action: either to fulfil his promise of the Viceroyalty to Fitzwilliam and face consequences that would prove disastrous to loyal friends in Ireland and his relationship with the King; or to break his promise and accept the resignation, already threatened, of the Portland Whigs from his Cabinet. Either alternative was likely to be ruinous to Ireland and to his own position. He was prepared to negotiate. He dined with Grattan and the Ponsonbys at Portland's house, he consulted Windham, Spencer and Grenville, and finally decided to allow Fitzwilliam's appointment to go forward on condition that his powers were limited by his acceptance of government instructions.

---

* William Brabazon (1744-1806) and George (1755-1817), sons of John Ponsonby, Speaker of the Irish House of Commons from 1756 to 1771. William had been joint Postmaster-General of Ireland from 1784 to 1789, and George Chancellor of the Exchequer under the Viceroyalty of Portland in 1782. Both were staunch Whigs and adherents of Charles James Fox.

In December Pitt, Portland, Grenville, Spencer, Fitzwilliam and Windham held a formal meeting, of which Grenville left a detailed description, to formulate a policy to which the new Lord-Lieutenant must adhere.[462] In the light of later historians' attempts to excuse Fitzwilliam's actions as due to a misunderstanding, and the opprobrium heaped upon Pitt for his failure to make the government's instructions clear to him, it is necessary to note that Grenville's memorandum of the meeting, written in March 1795 and agreed by all the ministers present, leaves little room for misapprehension. Fitzwilliam's proposal to appoint William Ponsonby Secretary of State and George Ponsonby Attorney-General was rejected, though it was agreed that William might be offered the minor post of Keeper of the Signet and that George might be appointed Solicitor-General whenever some suitable arrangement could be made for John Toler, who had held that office since 1789. No mention was made of any intention to remove John Beresford from his position as First Commissioner of Revenue. On the subject of Catholic emancipation, 'a strong opinion was stated that Lord Fitzwilliam should, if possible, prevent the agitation of the question at all during the present Session.' Fitzwilliam's proposal to replace the Irish Lord Chancellor, Lord Fitzgibbon, was strongly objected to as appearing 'to give too much countenance to the apprehension of an intended change of system in Ireland . . . and the same principle was stated . . . as applying to the removal of the old servants of the Government, and to any other measure which could have the appearance either of introducing a new system *or* of casting imputations on the conduct of former Governments in Ireland . . . the most explicit assurances were given by Lord Fitzwilliam that he had not in view the establishment of any new system in Ireland, but that he was desirous of strengthening his Government by the accession of Mr Ponsonby and his friends, and the support of Mr Grattan.' Finally, 'At the close of the conversation, Lord Fitzwilliam, who had brought to the meeting a memorandum of the matters to be talked of, was repeatedly asked whether there were any other points to be discussed, or any new measures to be proposed. The answer was that he knew of none.'

Later, Fitzwilliam was to declare that he had spoken of his wish to dismiss Beresford, and that he had taken Pitt's answering silence to signify agreement. It is scarcely credible that Fitzwilliam should have omitted, at this important meeting, to declare his intention to dismiss the man commonly called 'The King of Ireland'; but it is even less credible that, Fitzwilliam having declared his intention, neither Grenville nor any other of the ministers present should have any recollection of it.

Pitt's predicament was one of exceptional delicacy: not only was he threatened by the resignation of all the Whig ministers so recently drawn into government, but he was also gradually moving towards liberal reforms similar to those favoured by the Whigs and incautiously proclaimed by Fitzwilliam. He disapproved entirely of Fitzwilliam's proposal to replace by ardent Whigs all the office-holders loyal to the King. This was politically unacceptable and an uncomfortable reminder of the jobbery that had distinguished Portland's term as Lord-Lieutenant. Reform of the Irish parliament by the full emancipation of the Catholics was, on the other hand, a target on which he had set his own sights many years before, but he was almost alone in having any accurate understanding of the strength of the King's objections. Pitt knew that he must move slowly and with caution, using peaceful settlement and gradual change to convince the Catholics of his sincerity, and using the evidence of their moderation thus secured to persuade the King of their fitness, as the majority, for full rights of citizenship.

To this slowly maturing design, the work of twelve years of patience and persuasion in the face of vigorous opposition, Fitzwilliam brought all the qualities of ignorance, insensitivity, blind prejudice, lack of judgement and imprudence. On 11 January 1795 he landed in Ireland. Three days later he sent a message to Beresford requiring his resignation, and on the 15th he wrote to Grenville informing him that Beresford had agreed without complaint. This was demonstrably untrue: on the contrary Beresford had written at once to Lord Auckland to ask him to use his influence with Pitt, and a week later, after receiving final notice of his dismissal and the offer of a compensatory pension, he set out for London to present his case in person. Undeterred by Beresford's disobliging refusal to comply with his wishes, Fitzwilliam sacked the two Under Secretaries and warned both Senior Law Officers of his intention to replace them. For good measure he wrote to Portland stressing the urgency of the Catholic question and his inability to deal with unrest in Ireland without a just settlement.

The crisis was genuine, but it was largely of his own making. Since the reforms of 1791 and 1793 there had been little agitation of the Catholic question in Ireland until Fitzwilliam had improvidently broadcast his intentions to Grattan and the Ponsonbys in the previous autumn. Foul weather delayed the mails between Dublin and London and, receiving no immediate reply to his letters to Portland, Fitzwilliam interpreted silence as acquiescence. With his approval Grattan brought in a Bill for the repeal of all laws that militated against Catholics. As Fitzgibbon pointed out to Beresford, royal assent to the Bill would involve the King in violation of his coronation oath. Predictably, Loughborough, the friend of Fitzwilliam and Grattan, was safeguarding his interests by giving George III the same advice.[463]

Fitzwilliam's actions, however well intentioned, could not be countenanced by the British government. They were unacceptable to the King and in flagrant contravention of his instructions. It is charitable to assume that his blunders were due more to stubborn incomprehension than to any active intention to aggravate dissensions that were already dangerously inflamed; but he was as vain as he was foolish, and his determination to place Whig supporters in all the highest offices is an indication of his ambition, with Portland's approval, to rule Ireland without interference from Britain or the government to whom he was responsible. Pitt cannot be exonerated from blame. The instructions were clear enough, but Pitt seems to have made no attempt to take Fitzwilliam into his confidence about his own intentions and sympathies, or to explain that the Irish fuse, already dangerously short, required only the smallest spark to set it alight. Pitt agreed to the appointment of Fitzwilliam against his better judgement and in deference to the Portland Whigs. Believing that Fitzwilliam was unsuited to the office, he did nothing to ensure that he was properly informed and forewarned, and nothing to prevent his falling under the influence of the Ponsonbys and Grattan.

In February Fitzwilliam told Portland, in answer to a letter of stern reproof, that he would not postpone the proposals for Catholic emancipation. To Pitt he wrote that the government must choose between him and Beresford. Pitt's reply was polite but definite: his choice was Beresford. Fitzwilliam was recalled. His behaviour after his dismissal shed little lustre on his reputation. He made the occasion of his leaving Dublin a full-dress viceregal function, and

342

published, in a letter of self-justification in which he also accused Beresford of peculation, part of a confidential dispatch from Portland. Beresford challenged him to a duel, which was stopped by a magistrate when the parties met in July. Fitzwilliam's apology was accepted. At breakfast with Pretyman, Pitt told him that Fitzwilliam 'had been guilty of a greater breach of official secrecy . . . than he ever knew any man before, & he ought to be hanged.' [464]

Fitzwilliam's wilful stupidity and the publication of his letter of defence and accusation, to which the government was unable to reply without revealing details of the agreement made before his departure for Dublin, did irreparable damage to the people he had sought to help. By publicly accusing Pitt and Portland of breach of faith he crushed the hopes, that he had so precipitately raised, of Catholic Irishmen; and by his premature assertion of the rights of Catholics to representation in parliament he laid Pitt's plans for reform in ruins by closing the King's mind finally against emancipation. In a letter to Pitt George III declared that the proposal to admit Catholics to the Irish parliament was 'contrary to the conduct of every European government, and . . . to that of every state on the globe'.[465] He cited the example of Germany, where 'each respective state has but one church establishment, to which the states of the country and those holding any civil employment must be conformists'. The King accused Fitzwilliam of 'overturning the fabric that the wisdom of our forefathers thought necessary, and which the laws of our country have directed' and, 'after no longer stay than three weeks in Ireland,' of 'venturing to condemn the labour of ages'. He concluded by stating firmly, 'the subject is beyond the discussion of any Cabinet of Ministers . . . without previous concert with the leading men of every order in the state.' To George III religious toleration was appropriate and even desirable: religious equality, which he considered irreconcilable with his coronation oath, was not. Nothing but dedication to principle, or incurable optimism, could have persuaded Pitt to raise the question again.

The actions and recall of Fitzwilliam did not lead directly to rebellion, but they made a major contribution to its causes. Grattan and his moderate followers were swamped by the rising tide of Irish disappointment and anger. It was not the principle of representation that roused the Catholics: the revolutionary William James McNevin, a delegate from the United Irishmen sent to Paris to concert plans for a French landing in 1797, agreed that the mass of the people did not care a 'drop of ink' for parliamentary reform or Catholic emancipation; and his fellow United Irishman, Thomas Addis Emmet * echoed this opinion. The peasant population cared only that the tithes and rents paid to Protestant landlords robbed them of a living. The destruction of hopes raised by Fitzwilliam served to inflame the continuous resentment against British oppression. To Wolfe Tone, founder with Napper Tandy and Thomas Russell of the United Irishmen, most of whose leaders were Protestants, 'the connection between Ireland and Great Britain' was 'the curse of the Irish nation'. Nothing but separation would satisfy them.[466]

Pitt offered the Lord-Lieutenancy of Ireland to his old friend from Cambridge days, John Pratt, who had succeeded his father in 1794 as 2nd Earl Camden. Never a position of ease or security, and seldom attractive to anyone who knew Ireland or the Irish, the Lord-Lieutenancy had become the least desirable of all senior offices under the Crown. The soil of Ireland has been fertilized by the decomposition of British political reputations. George Rose wrote to Bishop Pretyman early in March 1795, 'the Situation . . . is really frightful, & that is the true Reason why Lord Camden will not go there.' [467] Camden was persuaded, later in the month, to accept; but, although loyal to the government and obedient to his instructions, he was little better suited to the post than Fitzwilliam.

Camden was ordered to 'moderate, soothe, conciliate'. His first experience of the Irish people was not reassuring. His swearing-in ceremony was made the occasion for a riot in which the mob attacked the Speaker's house and the carriages of the Lord Chancellor and the Primate. The most immediate threat to British rule came, however, not from the Catholic south but from Ulster, where the Presbyterian population suffered under the same tithes and similar disabilities. Republican gospel spread by the agents of revolutionary France found there a far more fertile breeding ground among educated radical Dissenters than among devout Catholic peasantry appalled by the blasphemies of Jacobinism. The French invasion attempt of 1796 was greeted in the south with indifference or alarm; but in Ulster it created wild hope and enthusiasm.

* Elder brother of Robert Emmet, arrested and executed in 1803.

Camden decided upon repressive measures while there was yet time to carry them out, but the forces at his disposal were inadequate and the move was made too late. The army sent to disarm Ulster was obliged to call upon the assistance of the Yeomanry whose volunteers were drawn from the Protestant landowning class. They, and some of the regular regiments employed, behaved with an undisciplined brutality that helped to convert an embryonic republican revolution into a full-scale rebellion in which religion became the main motive force. The Presbyterian revolt was still-born, and the Catholics of the north were driven south, where their tales of rape and pillage under the persecution of the army reawakened all the ancient hatreds. As the Orangemen of the north joined in the destruction of Catholic property in Ulster, the centre of rebellion shifted south, where the Club of United Irishmen, founded by Protestants, was taken over by the Catholic majority who, with their own organization, the Defenders, looked in desperation to France for aid.

In October 1797 the Dutch fleet put to sea with the intention of crippling Duncan's North Sea fleet and opening the way for an invasion. On the 11th, at the battle of Camperdown, Duncan, who only four months earlier had been unable to persuade his crews to follow him to the Texel, pulverized the slightly superior enemy, capturing seven battered ships of the line and effectively eliminating the Dutch navy from the war. Pitt, again ill at Walmer, recovered sufficiently to celebrate the victory with Duncan, who had been rewarded with a viscountcy, at Dover on his triumphant return.

The victory at Camperdown, and Camden's coercion of Ulster, postponed the Irish rebellion until the following year. By then the United Irishmen, seeing their northern organization crushed and fearing that similar measures in the south would extinguish all hope, determined to act without waiting for help from France. In February 1798 the discovery of a plot led to the arrest of fourteen ringleaders, but the movement had gained too much momentum to be halted. Fear of savage military 'pacification' modelled on the methods used in Ulster acted as a spur to Irish impatience. The fear was not groundless: plans had already been laid to pacify Leinster. General Ralph Abercromby, who had reluctantly agreed to take command of the army in Ireland, had issued a general order declaring that 'the frequency of courts martial, and the many complaints of irregularities in the conduct of the troops in this Kingdom . . . proved the army to be in a state of licentiousness which must render it formidable to everyone but the enemy',[468] and forbade officers to use military force without the approval of a magistrate. Reprimanded by Portland, Abercromby resigned. With his going faded the last hope of moderation and justice in the suppression of rebellion.

On 19 May, just four days before the fruition of an audacious plan to seize Dublin, Lord Edward Fitzgerald, the son of the Duke of Leinster, and known to Pitt as an officer who had served with distinction in America, was captured. Fitzgerald, converted to revolution by the harshness of Camden's methods, had become one of the most active and popular of patriot leaders and had been negotiating personally with the French for the invasion of Ireland. When arrested he fought like a tiger, stabbing both his captors before he was overpowered. He died of his own wound, which had not been considered serious, on 4 June. His loss was crucial. Without him the Dublin plot, the pivot of the rebellion, collapsed. During May and June the insurrection spread, but it lacked organization, and the serious risings against the government were scattered and unconcerted. Ulster remained quiet. Republican feeling there had been destroyed, and the Protestants had little enthusiasm for a rebellion to benefit the Catholic majority in the south. It lasted barely a month. The French—900 troops under General Joseph Humbert, landed in County Mayo on 22 August—came too late and were soon defeated. By then Cornwallis had replaced Camden as Viceroy and the rebellion had been stamped out. Wolfe Tone, captured with the squadron that brought him back to his own shores from France, cut his throat.

The horrors of the brief rebellion, terrible as they were, did not compare with the atrocities of the civil conflict, the undeclared war between Protestant and Catholic which spread from Ulster to the south, that preceded it. In the minds of Irishmen, however, the two struggles came to be identified as one in which the people of Ireland united to fight for their freedom. It was plain that there could be no just settlement while the corrupt and wholly Protestant parliament, which resisted or rejected every attempt at reform, continued to rule Ireland. If admission of Catholics to the Irish parliament raised too great a fear of a Catholic majority, the one remaining alternative seemed to be to admit them, as representatives, to the British parliament where their minority might be permanently assured. The

346

system by which an unrepresentative executive in London, responsible to the British parliament, sought to govern an even more unrepresentative parliament in Dublin, to which it owed no responsibility, had been shown to be inefficient, inequitable, and unworkable by any means but wholesale corruption. Pitt, who had long favoured the union of the two parliaments, determined to force through the necessary legislation. He was aware of the strength of the opposition in Ireland, and of the squalid methods he must employ to overcome it. The end, which would include the final emancipation of a suppressed majority, would justify them.

Pitt chose, as his instruments for change, the new Viceroy, Lord Cornwallis, and his Chief Secretary, Lord Castlereagh. Robert Stewart, Viscount Castlereagh, ten years Pitt's junior, had been acting Chief Secretary since 1797.* He was a dedicated supporter of Catholic emancipation for which he was prepared to sacrifice scruples, advantage, and popularity. Cornwallis, although he deplored the use of disgraceful but expedient methods, was in no doubt about the justice of the policy: 'until', he told Pitt, 'the Catholics are admitted into a general participation of rights (which when incorporated with the British Government they cannot abuse) there will be no peace or safety in Ireland.' [469]

Pitt consulted a number of eminent Irishmen, including the Lord Chancellor, the Earl of Clare†, and the Speaker, John Foster. It was obvious that Pitt's proposals would receive a hostile reception among the Protestant landowners, and they could expect to attract little support in the Irish House of Commons, but his decision was made. On 21 December 1798, at a meeting of the Cabinet attended also by the Earl of Liverpool ‡ and Lord Camden, the policy was agreed. Grenville's minute of the resolution leaves no doubt of the government's determination to impose its will:

That the Lord Lieutenant of Ireland should be instructed to state without delay to all persons with whom he may have communica-

---

* He was the first Irishman to hold office. Cornwallis overcame the King's objections by replying that Castlereagh was 'so very unlike an Irishman' that he could be relied upon to carry out his duties.

† John, Viscount Fitzgibbon, had been created Earl of Clare in 1795.

‡ Charles Jenkinson (father of 'Young Jenky'), 1st Baron Hawkesbury, had been raised to the Earldom of Liverpool in 1796.

tion on this subject, that His Majesty's Government is decided to pass the measure of an Union as essential to the well-being of both countries and particularly to the security and peace of Ireland as dependent on its connection with Great Britain: that this subject will now be urged to the utmost, and will even in the case (if it should happen) of any present failure, be renewed on every occasion till it succeed; and that the conduct of individuals on this subject will be considered as the test of their disposition to support the King's Government.[470]

Details of the plan were made public in Dublin in January 1799. Twenty-eight peers and four Protestant bishops would become members of the British Upper House; the cities of Dublin and Cork would elect two members to the House of Commons at Westminster, all other counties and towns returning one member; of the 108 smaller boroughs, one half would return members at the next election, and the other half at the election following; all restrictions on Irish trade and commerce would be removed and all duties equalized, with the single exception that the Irish linen manufacturers would retain their protective privileges. In abolishing the corrupt Dublin parliament Pitt was taking another step towards the sort of electoral reform he had long wished to introduce in Britain. By reducing the power of the borough-mongers he intended to hold out renewed hope to the Catholics who, since the extension of the franchise in 1793, were already able to influence the elections in the counties and open boroughs in the south. They were not yet permitted to elect Catholic representatives, but they could often ensure that the Protestants returned were not irreconcilably anti-Catholic.

In Ireland Pitt's proposals attracted general support from the Catholics, but it was evident that members of the Irish parliament would never vote for the extinction of their own vested interests without compensation. The corrupt system could be destroyed only by corruption. While Cornwallis courted the Catholics, the government resorted to wholesale bribery of the Protestants. In 1799 the Irish parliament rejected the proposals for Union. On 6 February 1800 the resolution was passed by 158 votes to 115. The victory was bought at the cost of £1,260,000 paid in compensation to the owners of 'close' boroughs, valued at £15,000 apiece, the creation of twenty new Irish peerages, sixteen promotions in the peerage, and the reward of British titles to four Irish peers. Twelve substantial pensions were awarded, and there were also significant appointments in the Church and promotions in the legal profession. This was corruption on the grand scale, but it was not specially shocking by the lamentable standards of the Irish parliament. Nor was bribery the exclusive prerogative of those who favoured the Union. Both Cornwallis [471] and Clare had evidence that the Opposition was buying support in parliament at £5,000 a vote.

At Westminster the Union was approved, in spite of violent opposition from Sheridan and Grey, by 236 votes to 30. To those who supported it, the real cost of the Union was not yet discernible. Throughout the negotiations in Ireland it had been assumed that Union was the necessary precursor of Catholic emancipation. It was the assumption that this reform would not be long delayed after the achievement of Union that moved the Catholic majority to support the proposal for government from Westminster. Pitt had never given any undertaking to this effect, but his sympathies were well-known and his speech in the House of Commons on 31 January 1799 gave a clear indication of his intentions. 'On the other hand,' he declared,

Without anticipating the discussion, or the propriety of agitating the question, or saying how soon or how late it may be fit to discuss it, two propositions are indisputable; first, when the conduct of the Catholics shall be such as to make it safe for the Government to admit them to the participation of the privileges granted to those of the established religion, and when the temper of the times shall be favourable to such a measure—when these events take place, it is obvious that such a question may be agitated in an United Imperial Parliament with much greater safety, than it could be in a separate Legislature. In the second place, I think it certain that, even for whatever period it may be thought necessary after the Union to withhold from the Catholics the enjoyment of those advantages, many of the objections which at present arise out of their situation would be removed, if the Protestant Legislature were no longer separate and local, but general and Imperial: and the Catholics themselves would at once feel a mitigation of the most goading and irritating of their present causes of complaint. [472]

Although he had made no promise of Catholic emancipation, Pitt felt a moral commitment to the principle. He knew the King's views on the subject, but he knew also that the Union, which the King and his government were united in believing to be the only method by which the Irish could be prevented from destroying themselves and threatening the security of Britain, could not be achieved without offering the Catholic majority in Ireland the definite prospect of reform. For this principle he was ready to tax his power to the limit. He measured and understood the consequences of failure, and, when the time came, he accepted them.

XXIV

Danger With Honour
1797-1798

IN THE SUMMER OF 1797 Pitt tried once more to negotiate peace with France. Again he chose as his emissary the 'White Lion', Lord Malmesbury. Grenville, Portland, Spencer and Windham opposed the move, but Britain's desperate situation, aggravated by the certainty that the Austrians would make a separate peace that left Britain without an effective ally in Europe, persuaded Pitt to overrule them in the Cabinet. The King, too, deplored the peace mission and made it plain that he thought it ignominious. Burke, the most eloquent advocate of perseverance in a war which he considered a crusade, was no longer able to make his protests heard. The great Irishman was dying in Bath. Sir Gilbert Elliot wrote of his physical deterioration: 'He is emaciated to the greatest degree, has lost entirely his powers of digestion. He considers his own case quite desperate and is rather irritated than flattered by the supposition of his recovery being possible.' [473] Burke died at Beaconsfield on 9 July, proclaiming to the last his defiant hatred of the regicide French, and exhorting his few remaining followers never to sheathe the sword until France was defeated.

As intemperate intellectually as Fox was physically, Burke's passionate denunciation of the evils that he discovered in others

351

made him many enemies. His vindictive persecution of Warren Hastings appalled even his closest friends and inspired Sir Robert Dallas, one of the two defence counsel, to compose a cruel epitaph:

> Oft have I wondered why on Irish ground
> No poisonous reptile yet was found;
> Reveal'd the secret stands of Nature's work—
> She saved her venom to create a Burke.[474]

The premature death of his son, and the failure of either his own party or the government to which he attached himself to listen to his prophecies of doom, embittered Burke's last years. His spirit was soured by loneliness and the knowledge that his gifts had been used, by him and by others, to little advantage. As he told Philip Francis, 'If a man is disabled from rendering any essential service to his principles or to his party, he ought at least to contrive to make his conversation as little disagreeable as he can to the society which his friends may still be indulgent enough to hold with him.' [475]

Malmesbury left for France on 30 June. The negotiations with three delegates from the Directory were held at Lille. From the start Malmesbury was instructed to offer terms so generous that, in order to prevent speculation in the City or any possible leak of information to those who would excite opposition to them, his dispatches were seen only by Pitt and Grenville. Separate dispatches were edited and handwritten by George Hammond, senior Under-Secretary at the War Office, for perusal by the Cabinet. As Hammond's script was almost indecipherable, security was of an unusually high standard. Malmesbury was authorized to offer recognition of the French conquests of the Austrian Netherlands and Savoy and the return of all colonial prizes except Trinidad, the Cape of Good Hope and Ceylon, the last being reserved for exchange. Pitt's anxiety for peace is made plain by Malmesbury's record of a conversation with him at Bath five years later.[476] Pitt told him, Malmesbury remembered, 'That I must recollect, on my leaving England for Lisle [sic], he had . . . in confidence told me his ideas (this is strictly true) but that, besides him and me, perhaps no one knows that, *rather than break off this treaty, we should have given way either on the Cape or Ceylon*. That Lord Grenville, from the beginning had declared he would *never consent* to any concession on *either of these points* . . .

but had the negotiation gone on, and depended on this particular point, he, or Lord Grenville, *must* have gone out; and he added, *it would have been Lord Grenville.'*

At first the mission looked promising. Although three of the five members of the Directory, led by Barras, were determined to continue the war, the moderates were in the majority in the legislative councils, and recent elections had shown the overwhelming desire of the French people for peace. The Directors played for time, privately urging Malmesbury to be patient while publicly they demanded compensation for the ships destroyed at Toulon. As the months dragged by, the French were secretly negotiating peace with Austria and with Britain's last remaining ally, Portugal. On 10 August the Portuguese minister signed a treaty in Paris, the provisions of which, including the exclusion of British ships from Portuguese ports and supplies, contravened existing Anglo-Portuguese treaties. Malmesbury, cunning and unruffled, suggested that if the Portuguese could not safely repudiate the treaty with France the British should violate it, leaving Portugal to complain with insincere anger to the French that they were unable to enforce it. Pressure was nevertheless applied to Lisbon, where the Court refused to ratify the treaty.

On 4 September a *coup d'état*, directed by Barras and supported by the army, threw out the moderates and restored the Jacobins to unchallenged supremacy. The French plenipotentiaries at Lille were replaced, and their terms altered to include the return of all British conquests since the Revolution to France and to her allies the Spanish and the Dutch. Malmesbury was officially informed of a decree by the Directory that if he lacked the necessary powers to accept these terms he should return within twenty-four hours to London to obtain them. He left Lille on 18 September. Two days later he saw Grenville and Canning. Although the French plenipotentiaries remained at Lille there could be no question of Malmesbury's return. Shortly afterwards an approach was made through an intermediary, offering French acceptance of British terms in return for the private bribe to Barras and his friends of two million pounds sterling. Pitt took the proposal seriously and, after consulting the King, made a counter-offer of £450,000. This remarkable overture was at first known only to the King and senior members of the Cabinet, but Pitt later informed the Speaker. Addington replied, 'I believe the state of the country as to its interior to be so bad that we cannot, in strict duty, venture to reject the offer, which may at least give us some interval of rest for doing what we have to do at home— an interval longer or shorter as events may happen but long it cannot be.' [477] Nothing more was heard of the French suggestion. The war continued.

Pitt was unable to meet Malmesbury on his return from Lille. His health had been poor and on 20 September, the day of Malmesbury's arrival in London, he received news of the premature death of his friend and brother-in-law, Edward Eliot, at the age of thirty-nine. George Rose, who was with Pitt, told Pretyman, '. . . the Effect produced by the Event on him is not to be described; the suddenness of the Blow aggravated the Misfortune.' Two days earlier Pitt had complained of 'a Head Ach [sic] which had tormented him for a fortnight, some degree of Cold, & a loss of Appetite.' He was persuaded to see Sir Walter Farquhar, but on the 22nd, as Rose reported, 'Towards the Evening he grew Sick & reached violently, after which he was better; Sir Walter came to him about 9,—he says he is quite clear about the Case & is sure he can do his Patient effectual Good, that there is much gout in it.' [478] The next day Pitt improved, but it was clear to his friends that he was still far from well and the news of Eliot's death had prostrated him. On 11 October he wrote to Addington that Farquhar's treatment and the air of Walmer had helped his recovery, but three days later Mornington wrote to the Speaker, after a visit to Pitt, 'I found him just as you had described him to me, and still more depressed by the death of poor Eliot. He did not disguise the state of his health, and I contributed to prevail upon him to see Farquhar, who put him on a course of medicine from which he has derived much benefit.' [479]

At about this time Pitt seriously contemplated resignation in favour of Addington. [480] He was aware that he had become, to the French, the hated symbol of British arrogance, intrigue and suppression, and he believed that another Prime Minister might have more chance of success in negotiating peace. He was also concerned about his failing health, though there was then little sign that his powers were impaired. He would not, however, have wished to entrust to Addington the handling of the Irish problem, which had already been revived in bloodshed in Ulster. Nor, after the failure of the talks at Lille, would he have felt justified in making Addington responsible for the conduct of the war, the suppression of the Irish rebellion, or the delicate progress towards Union. He believed, and without conceit, that he alone must bear responsibility for the direction of the war, and that none but he would have any chance of succeeding with his plan for Catholic emancipation.

Far from creating gloom, dissatisfaction or fear, the failure of the negotiations at Lille, and the realization that the aim of the French revolutionary government was no longer freedom from tyranny but unlimited conquest, aroused in Britain a general spirit of defiance and unanimity. Announcing in the House of Commons that the French had rejected the latest offers of peace, Pitt made a stirring appeal for national courage and unity of purpose:

> . . . there is not a man, whose stake is so great in the country, that he ought to hesitate a moment in sacrificing any portion of it to oppose the violence of the enemy; nor is there, I trust, a man in this happy and free nation, whose stake is so small, that would not be ready to sacrifice his life in the same cause. If we look at it with a view to safety, this would be our conduct; but if we look at it upon the principle of true honour, of the character which we have to support, of the example which we have to set to the other nations of Europe, gratitude to that Providence should inspire us to make every effort in such a cause. There may be danger; but on the one side there is danger accompanied with honour, on the other side there is danger with indelible shame and disgrace. Upon such an alternative Englishmen will not hesitate. . . . There is one great resource, which I trust will never abandon us. It has shone forth in the English character, by which we have preserved our existence and fame as a nation, which I trust we shall join hand and heart in the solemn pledge that is proposed to us, and declare to His Majesty, that we know great exertions are wanting, that we are prepared to make them, and at all events determined to stand or fall by the laws, liberties and religion of our country.[481]

More controversial than this appeal to the general spirit of patriotism was Pitt's proposal that the greater part of the enormous costs of the war should be met by unprecedented rises in taxation instead of by the more conventional method of raising loans for long-term repayment. 'We ought to consider', he said on 24 November, 'how far the efforts we shall exert to preserve the blessings we enjoy will enable us to transmit the inheritance to posterity unencumbered with those burdens which would cripple their vigour and prevent them from asserting that rank in the scale of nations which their ancestors so long and so gloriously maintained.' [482]

His intentions, which included the introduction of a graduated tax on all incomes over £60 a year, raised a storm of protest throughout the country, and most particularly in parliament and the City, but the Finance Bill was passed in January 1798 by large majorities in both Houses. In addition, Addington had proposed that voluntary gifts of one-fifth or one-tenth of income might be made by all patriotic Englishmen in lieu of assessed taxes. This tactful suggestion had been accepted, and £2,862,000 was raised by these contributions. The King subscribed £20,000 a year from the Privy Purse, though he confided to his Prime Minister that he was not a rich man and could ill afford so great a sum; Pitt, already heavily in debt, gave £2,000, as did Addington, Dundas and Loughborough; the City, and Robert Peel, a calico-printer from Lancashire whose son was to be Prime Minister, each gave £10,000; the men of HMS *Argonaut* each subscribed ten shillings; and the Duke of Bedford, who did not suffer from the financial difficulties experienced by his King or his country, gave £100,000. [483] Addington wrote in high satisfaction to his brother Hiley: 'I am thoroughly convinced that a sense of the real situation in this country is now excited, and that a disposition to exertion, both personal and pecuniary, is rapidly spreading, which will carry us through all our difficulties.' [484]

Wilberforce, who persisted in offering unsolicited advice upon subjects about which he knew little, differed with Pitt about certain of the proposed taxes and was 'much cut and angry' at Pitt's rejection of his suggestions. He nevertheless forgave Pitt and noted piously that he could 'well bear with his faults towards God'. [485] Wilberforce had chosen the autumn of 1797 to try to convince Pitt that the drilling and exercise of volunteers on a Sunday was offensive to their religion. He was to return, with renewed fervour, to this argument during the following years of Britain's greatest peril from invasion, and it is a tribute to Pitt's forbearance and affection for him that he continued to listen patiently to the demands of Wilberforce's inconvenient conscience.

The new tax on incomes, graduated from twopence in the pound for incomes between £60 and £65 and rising to two shillings in the pound for incomes over £200, was accompanied by the trebling of assessed taxes on houses and windows, male servants, horses, carriages and other possessions of the propertied class. Fox, who had been absent from the Commons for several months, returned to lead the Opposition to the imposition of these drastic levies on wealth, declaring that they would ruin the country, destroying property, trade and employment. On his return from St Paul's, on 20 December, where he had attended a service of thanksgiving for the victory of Camperdown, Pitt was cheered, but a hired gang tried to attack his carriage and he was escorted to Downing Street by a troop of volunteer cavalry. Shocked as they were by the weight of the new burdens, the wealthier classes understood the need for them and there was little support for Fox's demand that the costs of war should be shifted onto future generations.

As Britain's fortunes declined and the danger of invasion and defeat increased, the spirit of the nation revived. The British people, who regarded all foreigners as unlikeable, untrustworthy and inferior, heard of the treaty of Campo Formio, by which the Austrians made a separate peace in October 1797, with the same indifference they had shown towards all involvement in the war in Europe. A direct threat to the security of their own island was altogether different: it bred a stubborn patriotism, a willing acceptance of burdens and sacrifices, and an invincible refusal to recognize the possibility of defeat. The growth of this revival of national spirit was cultivated by the publication of a new weekly review, the *Anti-Jacobin*, described by Canning, who conceived the idea of it with Pitt at Walmer in October, as 'full of sound reasoning, good principles, and good jokes to set the mind of the people right upon every subject'.[486]

Within a week of the signing of the treaty of Campo Formio, by which France extended her recognized frontier to the Rhine, gained the Austrian Netherlands, Savoy and the Ionian Islands, and retained control of the United Provinces and the greater part of Italy, 'Citizen General' Bonaparte was appointed by the Directory commander of the 'Army of England'. His appointment, and the preparation of an invasion fleet, accompanied by fanfares of publicity to strike terror into the hearts of Englishmen, served only to strengthen the swell of defiant patriotism. The army in Britain, depleted by commitments in the West Indies, Ireland and India, and

357

by the heavy losses, caused principally by disease, in the campaigns of previous years, numbered less than 32,000 regular troops and some 25,000 Militia. Answering a call to arms—a commodity even less readily available than men—the most unlikely recruits flocked to join the corps of Volunteers raised for the country's defence. Eight companies were raised from clerks of the Bank of England, the servants of the Prince of Wales and the tenants of the Duke of Northumberland were enrolled by their masters, and even the once-devout republican Robert Burns donned the uniform of the patriot. Speaker Addington accepted command of a troop of horse known as the 'Woodley Cavalry', which was reviewed next year by the King, accompanied by most of the royal family.

Fox, who had almost given up attending the House of Commons, where he no longer commanded support, chose another method to make his dissent known. At a banquet held at the Crown and Anchor to celebrate his birthday on 24 January, a toast was proposed by the Duke of Norfolk to 'The Sovereign majesty of the People'. For this he was deprived of the Lord-Lieutenancy of the West Riding of Yorkshire and dismissed from command of a Militia regiment. Fox repeated the toast in May, at a meeting of the Whig Club, during the worst of the crisis in Ireland. This was the petulant action of a man maddened by the frustration of his ambition more than a deliberate attempt to incite others to sedition, but Pitt was justly furious and contemplated a prosecution or the expulsion of Fox from the House of Commons. 'We might', he wrote to Wilberforce, 'send him to the Tower', but he feared that 'at the end of three weeks he might be led home in procession, and have the glory of breaking windows.' [487] It was finally decided that Fox's name should be struck from the Privy Council. This was done, without obvious regret, by the King on 9 May.

More dangerous in its possible consequences was Pitt's quarrel with the radical member of parliament for Southwark, George Tierney. They had clashed in the House of Commons on several occasions, notably in the debate on the new taxation proposals on 24 November, when Pitt had contemptuously crushed Tierney's arguments. On 25 May Pitt brought in a Bill for the more effective manning of the navy, declaring that the urgency of the measure required its passage through the House in one day. Tierney strongly

358

opposed this 'precipitate' legislation. In reply Pitt accused him of 'a desire to obstruct the defence of the country'. Tierney appealed to the Speaker, who, instead of ruling the expression as unparliamentary and requiring its withdrawal, confined himself to remarking tamely that it was so and inviting Pitt's explanation. Pitt submitted his remark to the judgement of the House and added, 'I will neither retract from, nor further explain, my former expressions.' Tierney left the House and, later that evening, sent Pitt a challenge which was immediately accepted. As Speaker, Addington, who should have prevented such a lamentable conclusion, could have intervened to prevent the meeting; but as Pitt's personal friend he would have been thought to be acting on Pitt's behalf, and therefore felt unable to do so. Among their parliamentary friends there was some facetious comment about the inequality of the contest and, indeed, Tierney's short, corpulent body presented an easier target than Pitt's thin and angular figure. It was suggested that Pitt's outline might be chalked onto Tierney and that no shots outside it should be allowed to score. Pitt took the matter more seriously and made his will.

The two men met on Whit Sunday, 27 May, near Kingston Vale with their seconds, Dudley Ryder for Pitt and General George Walpole for Tierney, who made a last but unavailing attempt to prevent the duel. Pitt and Tierney then took up positions twelve paces apart and both fired without effect. After a brief pause for the loading of pistols, both fired again, Pitt deliberately discharging his pistol into the air. Their seconds then insisted that honour was satisfied on both sides. Next day Pitt wrote to reassure his mother: 'You will be glad, I know, to hear from myself on a subject in which I know how much you will feel interested, and am very happy that I have nothing to tell that is not perfectly agreeable. . . . The business terminated without anything unpleasant to either party, and in a way which left me perfectly satisfied with myself and my antagonist, who behaved with great propriety.' [488]

Two people who were anything but satisfied with Pitt's behaviour were George III and Wilberforce. The King, in a state of such nervous irritation that he misdated his letter by a whole year, wrote in stern rebuke, 'I trust what has happened will never be repeated. . . . Public characters have no right to weigh alone what they owe to themselves; they must consider also what is due to their country.' [489] Wilberforce was outraged. He disapproved profoundly of duelling.* That the Prime Minister, his most valued friend, should have fought a duel on a Sunday was more than he could bear. He was 'more shocked than almost ever' and 'resolved to do something if possible'. He bustled up to London on 30 May, bristling with morality and good intentions, and 'gave notice of a motion in the House of Commons against the principle of duels'. [490]

Late that night Pitt wrote a letter that illustrates admirably his mastery of the art of mixing admonition with affection, and pressure with persuasion:

My dear Wilberforce,

I am not the person to argue with you on a subject in which I am a good deal concerned. I hope too that I am incapable of doubting your kindness to me (however mistaken I may think it) if you let any sentiment of that sort actuate you on the present occasion. I must suppose that some such feeling has inadvertently operated upon you, because whatever may be your *general* sentiments on subjects of this nature, they can have acquired no new tone or additional argument from anything that has passed in this transaction. You must be supposed to bring this forward in reference to the individual case.

In doing so, you will be accessory in loading one of the parties with unfair and unmerited obloquy. With respect to the other party, myself, I feel it a real duty to say to you frankly that your motion is one for my removal. If any step on the subject is proposed in parliament and agreed to, I shall feel from that moment that I can be of more use out of office than in it, for in it, according to the feelings I entertain, I could be of none. I state to you, as I think I ought, distinctly and explicitly what I feel. I hope I need not repeat what I always feel personally to yourself.

Yours ever,
William Pitt. [491]

Wilberforce, after giving 'most serious and impartial consideration

---

* Political duels were not rare: Fox was wounded in a duel with William Adam; Sheridan twice fought 'Captain' Mathews; and even Thurlow duelled with Andrew Stuart in 1773. Later, in 1809, Canning fought Castlereagh.

to the question', and although his opinion of the propriety of the motion remained unaltered, decided that 'it would probably rather impair than advance the credit of that great principle which I wish chiefly to keep in view (I mean the duty of obeying the Supreme Being, and cultivating His favour).' He could not resist adding, 'I will only hint the pain you have been the reason of my suffering' and his fervent wish that Pitt might 'at length partake of a more solid and durable happiness and honour than this world can bestow.' Pitt replied briefly, thanking Wilberforce for his 'cordial friendship and kindness on all occasions, as well where we differ as where we agree.' The gift of Wilberforce's friendship could be a severe strain.[492]

Just five months after signing the treaty of Campo Formio, Baron Franz von Thugut reopened negotiations with Britain. He rightly feared that the French would use the treaty as a springboard for further conquest. Already, in February, they had broken their pledge by sacking Rome and plundering the Papal treasury. In March they invaded Switzerland, proclaimed a republic, and re-warded themselves with sixteen million francs in gold. The Austrian ambassador in London was instructed to ask whether the British would be prepared to co-operate against the French Republic, 'irrevocably determined on the total subversion of Europe', and to suggest that a British fleet should return to the Mediterranean. This suggestion was reinforced by the urgent entreaties of Naples, where Ferdinand IV and Maria Carolina, whose daughter was married to the Emperor Francis II, were under continuous pressure from the French.

Pitt was anxious to begin the task of building a second coalition against France. Prussia was not yet ready to renew the fight, though there was much consolation to be found for Britain in the death in 1797 of Frederick William II and the succession of his son, who had married the niece *, of Queen Charlotte. In Russia, too, there had been a welcome change: in 1796 Paul I had succeeded his mother, Catherine the Great, and it was known that he viewed the rapid expansion of France with growing hostility. If Britain could provide a convincing demonstration of the will and the ability to repel a French invasion, there was a fair chance that the old Coalition might be reconstructed with the invaluable addition of Russia.

* Louise, daughter of Prince Charles of Mecklenburg-Strelitz.

In reply to Pitt's inquiry whether a fleet could be assembled for the Mediterranean, Spencer provided, on 6 April, figures that showed conclusively that no adequate fleet could be spared without jeopardizing the protection of the British Isles. St Vincent was already blockading a superior Spanish fleet of thirty battleships at Cadiz; thirty French ships of the line were at Brest; and seven Dutch battleships were at the Helder. Spencer estimated that a further ten French battleships were at Toulon and six at Corfu. The defence of the Channel and the coast of Ireland could not be entrusted to a fleet of less than thirty-five capital ships. The entire disposable fleet numbered fifty-eight, though eleven others were fitting-out or nearing completion, and there would therefore be no more than twenty-three battleships available to watch Cadiz and regain the Mediterranean. The navy, moreover, lacked 8,000 men to complete the crews of the ships available.

Spencer advocated keeping the Channel fleet for defence and sending St Vincent to undertake a single sweep of the Mediterranean to do whatever damage he might to the French navy. If the Spanish left Cadiz and came north, the Channel fleet would deal with them; if they followed St Vincent into the Mediterranean, Spencer was confident that St Vincent would be more than equal to the challenge. It was a logical and bold proposal. Pitt rejected it in favour of one still bolder. He decided, in spite of Admiralty opposition but with the energetic support of Grenville, that a presence in the Mediterranean was essential in order to satisfy the Austrians of British determination to offer all practicable aid against France. The risk was great: any weakening of the Channel fleet or of St Vincent's blockade might result in the escape of the French fleets from Brest and Toulon or of the Spanish fleet from Cadiz, challenging British command of the North Sea and endangering the West Indies. Moreover, if the Spanish broke out from Cadiz, their fleet would be across the lines of communication of the Mediterranean squadron, which might be trapped and destroyed. Pitt resolved that the risk must be taken. This turned out to be one of the most fortunate decisions of his life.

Early in February Napoleon had been at the northern Channel ports supervising the building of flat-bottomed boats and the movement of troops in preparation for an invasion of England. By the end of the month he was back in Paris reporting to the Directory that an invasion could not succeed while the British navy retained command of the Channel. A direct assault was too dangerous, and failure might rouse the monarchs of Europe to renew the war against the Republic. He proposed, instead, an attack on Britain's overseas wealth and trade, the confiscation of which would simultaneously provide essential plunder to restore the shattered economy of France and face Britain with certain ruin. The hazardous invasion would then become unnecessary. In March he completed plans for an expedition to Egypt. A month later, while French agents in Alexandria collected intelligence about desert routes and the navigation of the Red Sea, others were in India, Napoleon's ultimate goal, negotiating with Tipu Sultan, Hyder Ali's successor as ruler of Mysore.

On 1 June Dundas learned that the French expedition, preparing since March at Toulon, had sailed; and it was he who first guessed its destination. By then, Nelson, commanding a small reconnaissance squadron, was already in the Mediterranean under orders to gather information. His flagship, the *Vanguard*, was dismasted in a storm, valuable days were lost in repairs, and the five frigates sailing with his ships of the line were dispersed and returned to Gibraltar. On 6 June Nelson was joined by ten battleships, sent from Cadiz by St Vincent, and received his commission to lead this powerful squadron in pursuit of the Toulon fleet, which he was to attack and destroy. He was given no clue as to the destination of the French armada, and having lost his frigates he was without his 'eyes'.

Napoleon had left Toulon on 19 May. With thirteen battleships, eight frigates and nearly three hundred transports carrying 40,000 troops, artillery and stores, he made for Malta, destroying every ship that sighted his fleet in order to prevent news of its movements being carried to the enemy. Nelson followed, learning on his way that the French had captured Malta and left on 16 June. Risking the possibility that the enemy had veered westward to escape into the Atlantic, Nelson sailed on to Alexandria. His information was wrong. The French had not left Malta until the 19th. On the 22nd the two fleets passed almost within sight of one another. Napoleon and many of the greatest commanders of the *Grande Armée* * escaped. If

---

* Among those later to be generals and marshals of France were Jean Bassières, Louis Davout, Louis Desaix, Andoche Junot, Jean Kléber, Jean Launes, Auguste Marmont and Joachim Murat.

Nelson had not been without his frigates, the war might have been shortened by seventeen years.

Nelson arrived at Alexandria to find the harbour empty. Two days later, as the British squadron sailed for Constantinople, Napoleon landed in Egypt and stormed Alexandria. On 22 July he entered Cairo. George Rose wrote to Bishop Pretyman on 12 September: 'Sir Horatio Nelson's having twice passed Bonaparte in a narrow Sea, considering how very large a Fleet of Men of War and Transports the latter had . . . is beyond all . . . the most extraordinary Instance of the kind I believe in the Naval History of the World. . . . The Consequences of the Escape of the Miscreants, unless they shall be afflicted with the Plague or some other great Calamity, will be worse I fear, infinitely worse, than any Misfortune we have experienced in this eventful war.' [493]

Two weeks later the news arrived in London that Nelson's failure had been redeemed by a magnificent victory. On 11 August he had at last found the French fleet in line of battle in Aboukir Bay, fifteen miles to the east of Alexandria. Nelson's squadron fell upon it and overwhelmed it. In an action lasting eleven hours, nine French battleships were captured and two more destroyed. Of the entire fleet, two ships of the line and two frigates escaped. Three thousand five hundred French sailors were taken prisoner, fifteen hundred of them wounded, and two thousand more were killed. Nelson, wounded early in the engagement, was unable to exercise control over it, but such was the training of his captains that they fought and won the battle without need of his somewhat erratic signals. Later, he told Lord Howe, 'I had the happiness to command a Band of Brothers.' [494]

News of the battle of the Nile, delayed by the capture of the *Leander* carrying dispatches, was celebrated all over England. It was the greatest British naval victory for more than two hundred years and its consequences were far-reaching. The annihilation of the Toulon fleet restored to Britain command of the Mediterranean. This deprived Napoleon's army, trapped in Egypt, of reinforcements and supplies, and crippled his plan to attack India. It also made possible the recapture of French conquests in the Mediterranean and the Adriatic, and revived the spirit of resistance to France in Europe. The Tsar Paul of Russia had already signed a military compact with Austria, and the British ambassador in St Petersburg reported that, in return for a subsidy, Russia was prepared to provide an army of 60,000 to co-operate in restoring peace if Austria re-entered the war.[495] In September the Sultan of Turkey declared war on the French Republic. Next month, the Turkish and Russian fleets, in unlikely alliance, attacked the French in the Ionian Islands. In November, a British force under Sir Charles Stuart captured Minorca.

Throughout the summer Pitt has been in failing health. Auckland found him 'very ill' in June, and Pitt admitted to Pretyman that he was feeling the effects of 'so long making Exertions beyond my real Strength'. In July Pretyman told his wife that Pitt had gone to Court to 'show the Country that he is better—he complains that he cannot be ill quietly'. The *Courier* published a report insinuating that Pitt was insane, a calumny that Auckland was sure originated from 'Messrs Grey and Co'. On 24 October Pitt was able to tell Pretyman, 'Farquhar's Regimen (aided probably by our Victories and the State of the Revenue) has succeeded so well that . . . I have great hopes of being equal to the Busy Scene that is approaching.' [496] He was, in truth, little better. Victory revived his spirits and lent him temporary strength, but he was drawing on reserves that could not be replaced. His health was already damaged beyond repair.

The Second Coalition
1799-1800

IN JANUARY 1799 Sir Gilbert Elliot, 1st Baron Minto *, considered that Europe was 'ripe, or rather rotten for destruction.[497] Pitt, Grenville and Dundas shared this opinion, and it was this fear that, without British intervention, the Allies of the First Coalition might be coerced from neutrality into new alliances with France, that persuaded them to review their strategy.

Between 1795 and 1797 the alternatives—insular withdrawal from Europe combined with negotiable acquisitions in the West Indies, or the use of subsidies and minimal military involvement to support counter-revolution in France and the armies of the Allies—depended upon British command of the Channel, the North Sea and the Mediterranean. Unable to make a clear choice between the two policies, the government had attempted both. The defeat and desertion of the Allies and the consequent threat of invasion not only underlined the inadequacy of the army but also strained the resources of the navy. By the end of 1798 it was clear that French ambitions were unlimited: national bankruptcy and the instability of successive governments could be tolerated only when they were

* Elliot had been raised to the peerage early in October 1797.

disguised or balanced by victory, conquest and plunder, or the urgent demands of home defence. The failure of all attempts to negotiate peace with France convinced the British government that its strategy must be directed towards the overthrow of the militant republican government and its replacement by a stable, moderate administration. This aim could be achieved only by the French people, who must be provided with the necessary incentives of defeat, poverty and hunger.

British foreign policy was therefore turned once more towards the construction of an alliance strong enough to contain the French within existing frontiers, preventing further conquest, and then gradually to force them back. The prospect was not unpromising. The Austrians and the Russians were already showing signs of anxiety and a willingness to join a second coalition. There was, however, a serious obstacle: both the King and Grenville were strongly in favour of a treaty with Prussia and against placing any faith in Austria. The King believed that Austria would 'as usual fail us when we least expect it', though it had been the Prussians whose devious and self-seeking behaviour had been more directly responsible for the failure of the First Coalition. Grenville's reasons were financial. Between 1795 and 1797 the Austrians had raised loans in Britain, guaranteed by Pitt's government, totalling more than one and a half million pounds. The capital and interest payments having fallen into arrears, the Austrians had negotiated by treaty a further loan, approved by parliament, conditional upon the repayment of the earlier debts. Having obtained the new loan, the Austrian government spent the money but declined to ratify the treaty. Grenville was bitterly opposed to the conclusion of any alliance with Austria until the sums obtained under false pretences should have been repaid. His objections were overruled when, in February 1799, Tom Grenville's negotiations in Berlin failed and it became clear that Austria was again being drawn into the war. The Russians had already, at the end of December, signed a treaty of alliance with Britain, agreeing to supply an army of 45,000 in return for a subsidy of £75,000 a month. Although the Cabinet rejected the terms of the treaty, signed by the British Ambassador without prior consultation, it seemed certain, when French troops crossed the Rhine on 1 March, that both Prussia and Russia must join a new coalition.

Austria declared war on France on 11 March, but Frederick

William of Prussia still refused to fight. Within three months the French were facing their greatest peril since 1793. The army, which had crossed the Rhine in March, suffered a series of heavy defeats at the hands of the reorganized Austrians. In northern Italy a Russian army under the brilliant and eccentric Marshal Aleksandr Suvórov* drove the French before it, capturing Milan on 29 March. Two months later Suvórov took Turin. In Egypt Bonaparte had taken the offensive, marching across the eastern desert and along the coast through Gaza to Jaffa; but at Acre, barring the road to Damascus, he was unexpectedly halted. The small Turkish garrison had been reinforced, and the feeble defences strengthened. The reinforcements had come from a squadron of two battleships and three frigates commanded by the dashing and unreliable Captain Sidney Smith. Having captured Napoleon's siege train, which was being brought up the coast in gunboats, Smith and 3,000 ragged but determined Turks settled down with ludicrous confidence to the task of preventing a French army of 40,000 led by the greatest living military commander from advancing through Syria. Unable to take the shabby little fort by storm, Bonaparte was obliged to waste time in a formal siege.

In India, too, French hopes had been shattered. Lord Mornington, Pitt's personal choice, had succeeded Sir John Shore as Governor-General.† Writing to him on 18 June 1798, Dundas made the government's instructions plain: 'If Tipu has made preparations of a hostile nature, or if the Proclamation of Tipu inviting the French was his own, do not wait for hostilities on his part . . . attack him.' [499] Mornington needed little encouragement. He was determined to pursue an aggressive policy of expansion. Since the extension of British territory was expressly forbidden by Pitt's India Act of 1784, Mornington substituted the permanent cession of land for the subscriptions in cash paid by Indian allies in return for military aid and protection, and looked eagerly for any act of provocation that

* Minto, unlike many of his contemporaries, was not impressed by the Russian hero. He described him as 'the most perfect Bedlamite that ever was allowed to be at large . . . stark mad, and . . . contemptible in every respect . . . a little shrivelled old creature . . . the most ignorant and incapable officer in the world.' He attributed Suvórov's success in Italy to 'the excellent Austrian officers who served under him. . . . In difficulty and danger he totally loses his head . . . the danger over, he begins to vapour and take all the honour . . . a mad mountebank.' [498]

† Lord Cornwallis refused to return to India and finally accepted, instead, the far less rewarding Viceroyalty of Ireland.

might justify war. He professed a belief that the acquisition of territory provided essential buffers to secure British possessions, but in fact he knew that every extension of frontiers brought him up against a new enemy who threatened the security he aimed to preserve, conveniently forcing him into another war for conquest. Pitt and Grenville, fully occupied with Europe, took little interest in India, leaving the direction of policy to Dundas. Although the policies of Dundas and Mornington appeared to be in harmony, they were almost diametrically opposite. Dundas was not in favour of individual settlement in India, he believed that those who served the Company should trade and leave, and for this reason he opposed the founding of educational establishments for British children. Mornington was intent on creating a new empire. He was right in believing that a policy of non-intervention was unworkable and dangerous, and he therefore embarked on a policy of expansion through pre-emptive and officially defensive war.

The danger from Tipu Sultan was, in truth, small. He was, in spite of his appeals to the French, unlikely to attack the British unless provoked and to defend his territory. Mornington provided the provocation and therefore the justification for an attack on Mysore. In February 1799 a British force of 5,000 with 16,000 sepoys crossed into Mysore, where it was joined by 16,000 Indian troops sent by the Nizam of Hyderabad and commanded by Mornington's brother, Colonel Arthur Wellesley. Tipu's army of 50,000 was driven back to the fortress of Seringapatam, which was successfully stormed on 4 May. Tipu was killed, and his country divided between Hyderabad and the East India Company.

Three weeks later, having failed in all his attempts to take Acre, Bonaparte abandoned the siege and led his mutinous and plague-ridden army in a ghastly retreat, abandoning his artillery and leaving behind him a trail of dead and dying soldiers. With the French armies everywhere in retreat, the royalists in the west of France took up arms once more against the hated Directory. It seemed that the time had come for the British army to take the field again in Europe. This was Grenville's policy. In opposition to Dundas he believed that France must be conquered by the Allies, and not contained while the French people destroyed themselves. He was also convinced that the campaigns in the West Indies, which had cost the army 10,000 men in five years, were wasteful and made no effective contribution to winning the war. He wrote to his brother Tom on 17 May 1799, 'If I have learnt anything by the disagreeable lessons of the war, it is that success in military operations wholly depends on acting *en masse* on one or two chosen points, and in avoiding to distract your force by multiplying your points of attack.' [500] Irreconcilably opposed to any further subsidies in Austria, which he knew would be misused for selfish ends, he supported the policy of subsidizing the Russians to act on the Austrian front. While the Prussians remained reluctant to join the Coalition, the armies of Austria must bear the greatest burden of the Allied offensive. To sustain them, the Russians must be mobilized and the French must be weakened by an assault on an unprotected flank. Lord Minto was sent to Vienna, replacing Sir Morton Eden *, to make clear to the Emperor and Chancellor Haugwitz the vigour and sincerity of British intentions.

Two possible plans presented themselves: an attack on the United Netherlands, supported by a Dutch rebellion; or a series of landings in northern Italy, covered by the Mediterranean fleet, to strike at the southern flank of armies already hard pressed by Suvórov. A campaign in Italy, however promising, involved unacceptable risks. The use, at such a distance, of an army that might be needed for home defence, and the problems of transporting it with all the necessary armament and supplies, were sufficient reasons for rejecting the plan; but the dangers had been multiplied by the escape in April of the French fleet from Brest. Fortunately for the dispersed and vulnerable British squadrons in the Mediterranean, the French did not attempt to lift the blockade of Cadiz or to regain control of the Mediterranean, but made for Toulon. This unambitious manoeuvre gave St Vincent time to unite his command with the blockading fleet from Cadiz and to take station between Minorca and Barcelona, where he lay in wait to prevent the junction of the enemy fleets. At this critical time St Vincent's health broke down. His successor, Lord Keith, in his anxiety to protect Minorca, allowed the French and Spanish fleets to meet at Cartagena and escape again through the Straits of Gibraltar to Brest. This concentration of the enemy's strength created a new threat to British naval supremacy, but it also gave the Royal Navy an unusual opportunity. A successful

* Younger brother of Lord Auckland; created Baron Henley in 1799.

blockade of Brest would prevent the French from interfering with British amphibious operations.

The choice of Holland as the area for the British attack was determined also by the hope of a Dutch rising and the co-operation that might be expected from both Russia and Prussia. By the end of April the decision had been made, but all plans for an expedition were complicated by the endless dithering of Prussia. The Tsar Paul was ready to co-operate in a seaborne invasion of Holland, relying upon the British navy to transport his army; but Frederick William III, asked to provide 60,000 men, responded with an offer of 230,000 to be subsidized by Britain. He was unwilling to field a smaller force in case the Austrians should make a separate peace. The provision of such an army from Prussia would make a reduction of the Russian contribution desirable, but there could be no guarantee that the Prussians would arrive. Pitt and Grenville decided to ask parliament for a credit of three million pounds to finance the unnecessarily enormous Prussian army in the hope that the combined might of the Allies would crush the French, enforce a swift end to the war, and so justify the cost.

The plan was part of a larger strategic design that provided for a major offensive through Switzerland by Suvórov (transferred from Italy, which was to be left to the Austrians) and a campaign along the lower reaches of the Rhine by an Austrian army under the Archduke Charles.* Its success relied upon a rebellion of the Dutch people, hopes for which were based upon the extensive spoliation of the Dutch economy by the French, and the disasters that had overtaken Dutch colonies and shipping since they had been forced into war against Britain. These hopes, however, ignored the consideration that, to the Dutch, there was little to choose between dominance by France and dominance by Britain, which appeared to be the alternative. The despised Stadtholder William V had already permitted the British to occupy Ceylon and the Cape of Good Hope, and there appeared to be little prospect of these valuable possessions ever being returned. Comfortably installed at Greenwich, he was more interested in the conquest of servant-girls than in any effort to re-possess himself of his country. If the House of Orange could be

---

* Charles Louis, son of Emperor Leopold II and younger brother of Francis II.

prevailed upon to offer any lead to the Dutch people, the leader must be the energetic and belligerent Hereditary Prince William.

On 22 June a treaty was signed at St Petersburg. In return for subsidies of £88,000 on mobilization and £44,000 a month during service, the Russians undertook to supply 17,500 troops for a campaign in Holland. Britain would provide horses for the cavalry and a further £19,500 a month for the hire of Russian transports. The plan of attack was formed without consulting any of the military commanders who were to take part in the operation, but it was agreed that Abercromby should lead the British contingent while the supreme command was reserved for the Duke of York.

Abercromby's army was hastily assembled. The four battalions of Foot Guards were in fine fettle, but the twelve battalions of the line had to be made up to strength by volunteers from other regiments, and the reinforcements were composed of skeleton units filled from the Militia. Cornwallis, whose valuable advice had not been sought, viewed the prospect with gloom: 'If', he wrote 'the new army which we have miraculously raised should be utterly destroyed by next Christmas, which I think highly probable, we shall then be fairly at the end of our offensive resources.' [501] Abercromby was provided with insufficient transports and assault craft, and the vanguard of his army, estimated at 12,000, numbered less than 9,000.

On 1 August Pitt received news that the Prussians had renounced their proposed treaty with Britain and Russia and had opened negotiations with France. He was staying with Dundas near Maidstone and was advised by the army commanders to postpone the expedition against Holland. From Dropmore, Grenville, who had refused to join Pitt in Kent, urged him to overrule the generals. On 3 August, orders were given to Abercromby to embark, and that day Pitt sailed, in brilliant sunshine, through the assembled fleet. He wrote confidently to Grenville, 'The decision being finally taken, I have no doubt it will be acted upon with alacrity, and that we shall now hear no more of difficulties.' [502] The assault troops sailed on the 13th.

At the end of the month Pitt and Dundas rode over to Barham Down to review the reinforcements assembled there and to celebrate Abercromby's landing in Holland. They found an army quite unfit for service. The Militia had spent their bounty money in the taverns of Canterbury, and the ragged *feu de joie* was fired with frightening inaccuracy by men who could scarcely stand. The ceremonial march past was cancelled to avoid embarrassment.

Abercromby landed on 27 August and stormed the forts at the Helder. Three days later Admiral Andrew Mitchell captured the remaining effective Dutch fleet of ten battleships and eighteen smaller vessels. Pitt was jubilant, and such was Grenville's ignorance of military affairs that he believed the campaign to be over: 'The Dutch army', he wrote, 'having been beat, I consider the business as compleat.' [503] He was already contemplating a far more ambitious scheme to make an amphibious assault on Brest to capture or destroy the combined French and Spanish fleets. Abercromby's position was in fact precarious. His victorious vanguard was small and exposed on the dunes without shelter or adequate provisions. He decided to halt and entrench on the line of the Zijpe canal. His orders were to seize 'such a position . . . as might afford a safe rendezvous for the expected reinforcements and a favourable position for carrying on the future operations of the campaign.' [504] He has been much criticized for carrying them out. It is easy in retrospect to assume that a more energetic commander would have pressed on at once to Alkmaar, and it is true that Abercromby was not a general famous for natural optimism; but the strength of the enemy was not accurately known, there was no sign of any disposition on the part of Dutch troops to join his liberating army, and a defeat might, as Cornwallis had feared, rob the British army of 'all the uniformed regiments' and put an end to the campaign.

A French attack on 10 September was easily repulsed, and three days later the Duke of York arrived. He was followed by 8,000 British reinforcements and 12,000 savage-looking Russians who smelt frightful, buttered their bread with grease supplied for lubricating gun-barrels, and were viewed with deepest suspicion by their Allies. Only the Hussars from the Tsar's bodyguard, tall and splendid in unsuitable white uniforms, looked like soldiers.

The Duke of York commanded a force of some 40,000 men, and his subordinate generals included Prince William of Gloucester, Prince William of Orange, and the Earl of Chatham. The Russians were led by General Hermann, and it was stipulated that no major operation must be undertaken without a council of war. An attempted breakthrough at Bergen on 19 September was a failure. General Hermann and his second-in-command were captured, and a fatal lack of communication between commanders resulted in heavy Russian casualties and a deepening of the distrust and suspicion among the Allies. A second offensive two weeks later was more successful, but although the French were pushed back their line remained unbroken. A third engagement on 6 October was equally indecisive and much worse mismanaged. In six weeks, while the French received reinforcements, the British lost nearly 5,000 men and the Russians about half their total force. On 8 October the Duke of York retreated to the positions occupied by Abercromby in September, four days after his landing. Six days later the decision was made to abandon the campaign. The Duke of York, forced to accept humiliating terms * in order to make a peaceful withdrawal, saved his army, his artillery and most of his horses. He estimated that an evacuation of his force under attack would have cost 6,000 men. The capture of the Dutch fleet within three days of Abercromby's landing was the single achievement of the enterprise.

The expedition, a costly failure shamefully mishandled at every stage of its planning and operation, taught the government valuable lessons. Sheridan, in a brilliant imitation of Pitt's most Olympian manner, listed them as the startling knowledge that the Prime Minister's understanding of human nature was defective; that Holland was a country of dykes and canals; and that the weather in October was less clement than the weather in June. The government discovered others more useful for future operations. The preparations had been rushed, the provision of transports and supplies neglected, and too much reliance had been placed on a Dutch rising in support of the invasion. The Hereditary Prince, whose presence with the army had been calculated to animate his people, was described by Abercromby as 'the most ungracious weak prince in Europe . . . he knows as little of the country as if [he] had been bred in Sweden.' [505] Three major-generals emerged with credit—Harry Burrard, Eyre Coote† and John Moore—and in the following year Abercromby made the suggestion that led to Moore's creation of the training camp at Shorncliffe and the founding of one of the most effective of all British army units, the Light Infantry Brigade.

---

* They included the repatriation of 8,000 French prisoners of war held in England.

† Nephew of General Sir Eyre Coote, celebrated for his victories in India between 1757 and 1781. See p. 113.

While the British searched for consoling reasons for their failure, the Second Coalition was collapsing. The general post of the Allied armies and commanders had provided the French with opportunities that they did not neglect. While the Archduke Charles withdrew from Switzerland on orders from Vienna, and before Suvórov could battle his way through the St Gothard Pass to rescue them, the Russians had been surrounded at Zürich. They fought their way out of the trap, but at the cost of leaving Suvórov's exhausted army to face the French army under Masséna. Suvórov, defeated for the first time in his life, lost 13,000 men. The Russians, already at loggerheads with the Austrians, withdrew. They had had enough.

On 23 July, writing to Mornington in India, Dundas had declared, 'Our public situation is most brilliant in every respect and I don't conceive it possible that the French monster can live much longer.' [506] After describing the liberation of Italy by the Russians, the imminent deliverance of Switzerland, the forthcoming embarkation of the expeditionary force to free Holland 'and probably ultimately the Netherlands', and the consequent accession to the Coalition of Prussia, he added, 'We have now forgot Bonaparte, who before this time is probably totally ruined.' Even as he wrote, Napoleon had turned on a force of 15,000 Turks at Aboukir and annihilated it. On 9 October, as the Duke of York's army entrenched for the second time behind the Zijpe, Bonaparte, having eluded the British Mediterranean squadrons, landed at Fréjus on the Côte d'Azur midway between Nice and Toulon. A month later, after the *coup d'état* of Brumaire, Bonaparte was named First Consul *. Windham wrote to Pitt: 'A Government such as the present, dropt from the clouds or rather starting from underneath the ground, is in no state to offer anything. It cannot answer for its own existence for the next four-and-twenty hours.' [507] He shared with Dundas the capacity for making forecasts that brilliantly combined confidence with inaccuracy.

On Christmas Day 1799 Bonaparte wrote personal letters to

---

* Three Consuls were named—Bonaparte, Emmanuel (abbé) Sieyès, and Pierre Ducos—but although the constitutional form of the triple Consulate was devised by Sieyès to prevent Bonaparte from seizing power as a dictator, the Second and Third Consuls were, from the first, mere subordinates. It was Sieyès who, when asked what he had done during the Terror, replied, 'J'ai survécu' ('I stayed alive').

George III and the Emperor Francis II proposing an end to the war. His approach to Britain was treated with contempt. The King described the letter as 'much below my attention' and ordered Grenville to reply in a formal memorandum to Talleyrand rejecting the offer. Grenville was instructed to state His Majesty's readiness to negotiate peace with security, the plainest guarantee of which would be the restoration of the French monarchy. Wilberforce, who had at first viewed the rejection of the French offer with sorrowful disapproval, changed his mind after a conversation with Pitt, but he justly deplored the tone of Grenville's memorandum. The insistence upon the restoration of the monarchy left the French with no practicable alternative to continuing the war. Both Pitt and Thugut believed that Bonaparte was playing for time, and that his sudden appearance as a peacemaker was designed to cloak his intention to divide the Allies and consolidate his power in preparation for further conquest.

On 3 February 1800 Pitt defended his policy in the House of Commons in a long and vigorous speech.[508] He accused the French of 'perfidy, which nothing can bind, which no tie of treaty, no sense of the principles generally received among nations, no obligation, human or divine, can restrain'. He recounted the history of French aggression since the Revolution, of their repudiation of treaties and rejection of peace moves, and of the methods by which Bonaparte had risen to power. He laid stress on the instability of all French governments since 1793, and the lack of security inherent in any negotiation with the new First Consul, whom he described disdainfully as 'this last adventurer in the lottery of revolutions'. He believed that there were signs that the French could not long resist the combined forces of Europe: 'But supposing the confederacy of Europe prematurely dissolved, supposing our armies disbanded, our fleets laid up in our harbours, our exertions relaxed, and our means of precaution and defence relinquished, do we believe', he asked, 'that the revolutionary power, with this rest and breathing-time given it to recover from the pressure under which it is now sinking . . . will not again prove formidable to Europe? . . . And with these considerations before us, can we hesitate whether we have the best prospect of permanent peace, the best security for the independence of Europe, from the restoration of the lawful Government, or from the continuance of revolutionary power in the hands of Bonaparte?'

The war must be continued because to make peace with Napoleon would be to court final defeat. 'As a sincere lover of peace,' he declared, 'I will not sacrifice it by grasping at the shadow, when the reality is not substantially within my reach—*Cur igitur nolo! Quia infida est, quia periculosa, quia esse non potest.**'

The House of Commons approved the government's statement of policy by a majority of more than two hundred. It was, no doubt, gratifying to Pitt and his ministers to know that their intention to prosecute the war had the overwhelming support of parliament, but the Cabinet was more deeply divided than ever about the means to be employed. Dundas, bitterly resentful of Grenville's growing influence and at odds with Windham and Spencer, wished to give up his position as Secretary of War and concentrate on affairs in India, to which he was already devoting much of his time. He was dissuaded, but at the cost of perpetuating the most serious division in Pitt's Cabinet. No clear policy emerged. It was generally felt that the army must be employed, but confidence in its ability to achieve anything useful had been shattered by failure in Holland, and there was little unanimity about the choice of a theatre for military operations. The result was a year of ill-considered, dispersed and futile effort, in which the army was held responsible for failures that were the consequences of Cabinet divisions and indecision.

A decision on Sir Charles Stuart's suggestion for a landing on the Genoese coast to cut the communications of the French army, driven westward by the Austrians, with Toulon, was delayed so long that by the time the troops arrived at Minorca the campaign had already been lost. An attempt to capture Belle Ile, in response to Windham's insistence that aid be sent to the royalists in Brittany, was a fiasco: the island was too strongly garrisoned and no landing was made. Landings at Quiberon and Ferrol were equally fruitless. In desperation the Cabinet decided to send an army under Abercromby into the Mediterranean to seize Cadiz, one of the most strongly fortified ports in all Europe. This remarkable design was frustrated by storms that blew the fleet out to sea and led Abercromby to make the wise decision to abandon the project. Lord Cornwallis wrote in disgust: 'Twenty-two thousand men floating round the greater part of

---

* 'Why, then do I refuse peace? Because it is deceptive, because it is dangerous, because it cannot be.' (Cicero *Philippics VII*, 3.)

Europe, the scorn and laughing stock of friends and foes.' [509] The single British success was the capture of Malta, after a siege and blockade lasting two years, by a small British force commanded by Colonel Thomas Graham*.

While the best of the British army cruised round the Mediterranean pursued by confused and often conflicting instructions from the Cabinet, the last hopes of preserving the dying Second Coalition were extinguished. The Austrians in Italy had driven Masséna's army into Genoa where, on 5 June, it surrendered; but six weeks earlier the French had won an important victory over the Austrians in southern Germany, and by the third week of May Bonaparte had crossed the Great St Bernard Pass with 50,000 men. On the day of Masséna's surrender, Bonaparte entered Milan, and nine days later he inflicted a decisive defeat on the Austrians at Marengo. In Germany General Jean Victor Moreau defeated the Austrians at Ulm and entered Munich. Bonaparte returned to Paris where he began a series of diplomatic negotiations designed to isolate Britain. By the end of the year this aim had been achieved.

Bonaparte's diplomatic offensive, began in July, hinged upon a temporary armistice with Austria. When it expired on 28 November the Austrian army, from the command of which the Archduke Charles had been removed, was crushed at Hohenlinden. Thugut resigned and the Emperor Francis II accepted the terms of Campo Formio as the preliminary basis of a new peace treaty. Russia, the second object of Bonaparte's attentions, was offered Malta in exchange for neutrality. The Tsar Paul, already disillusioned by what he regarded as the selfishness and cowardice of his Allies and the churlish refusal of the British to exchange French prisoners in England for Russians held in France, was prepared to listen to any proposal that offered both compensation and an opportunity to relieve his country of burdensome and profitless alliances. News of the British capture of Malta in September confirmed him in his intention to withdraw from the Coalition.

While he was cutting away the corner-stones of the Coalition, Bonaparte was also undermining the foundations of British trade. Reversing the policy of the Directorate, he opened the ports of

---

* Later distinguished as one of Wellington's most trusted generals in the Peninsular War, and created Baron Lynedoch.

France, renouncing the right of search and confiscation previously applied to neutral shipping suspected of carrying British goods. The British, on the other hand, continued to assert the right of blockade, and to enforce it. Neutral nations were excluded from direct commerce with any country hostile to Britain. In spite of this regulation of trade, the war in Europe had benefited the United States, which had become a serious rival for the carrying trade of the world [510]; but to other countries the British insistence on the right to stop and search any ship on the high seas, and the denial of direct commerce with France, her allies or possessions, became increasingly damaging as the French extended their frontiers. Encouraged by Bonaparte's conciliatory policy the northern powers decided to regenerate the confederation, the 'Armed Neutrality', formed in 1780 to secure the rights of neutral shipping during the American Revolution. In November the Tsar Paul, infuriated by the rejection of his demand that Malta should be handed over to Russia, placed an embargo on all British ships. Next month he concluded a treaty of alliance with Sweden, binding both countries to the terms of the Armed Neutrality. Before the end of the year the northern league had been joined by Prussia and Denmark.

The French alliance with Spain, which had shown every sign of crumbling, was revived by Bonaparte's promise of an Italian crown for Charles IV's son-in-law and the hint of rich rewards in return for Godoy's co-operation. In October, by the secret treaty of Ildefonso, Charles IV agreed to exchange the Louisiana Territory, ceded to Spain in 1762, for Tuscany. The treaty was accompanied by a clear stipulation, formally confirmed eighteen months later, that France would not sell or otherwise alienate the territory without first offering to return it to Spain. To deprive Britain of her last ally, and of the harbours and supplies essential to the Mediterranean fleet, Charles IV agreed to invade Portugal.

To those mounting dangers to Britain presented by Bonaparte's brilliant diplomatic successes there had been added renewed unrest at home. The failure of the harvest in 1799 had resulted in an alarming increase in the price of wheat, which had more than tripled since the beginning of the war. In 1800 a dry summer was followed by torrential rains which again ruined the crops at harvest-time. Lady Malmesbury wrote to her sister, 'Riots are going on all over the country,' and Matthew Boulton, the great silversmith, told his wife,

379

'Birmingham looks like a garrison town with troops parading the streets night and day . . . poor people are nearly starving for want of employment and the big price of food.' [511]

The government reacted swiftly to the situation. While riots were ruthlessly suppressed, special bounties were awarded for imported wheat. Grenville was opposed to any government subsidies. 'I am confident', he wrote to Pitt on 24 October, 'that provisions, like every other article of commerce, if left to themselves, will and must find their level; and that every attempt to disturb the level by artificial contrivances has a necessary tendency to increase the evil it seeks to remedy.' [512] Others, he supposed, might 'assume that the price is undue . . . that it is more than would be produced by the natural operation of demand and supply counteracting each other. Now I know of no other standard of price than this.' Pitt's reply was given in parliament: 'I recognize the freedom of trade in its full extent; but I do not mean to deny that some regulation may be necessary in the present situation of the country.' [513] Imports of grain in 1800 reached an unprecedented figure. A series of Acts of parliament imposed regulations for economy and heavy penalties for speculation in the price of wheat; but still the people went hungry. The loss of shipments from the Baltic aggravated the shortage.

The Armed Neutrality also threatened the navy. Not only would the Baltic fleets of Russia, Sweden and Denmark be used to carry provisions to France, but the essential imported masts and timber, more than eighty per cent of which came from the Baltic countries, would be denied to Britain and supplied instead to the French navy. Pitt, oppressed by ill-health and deepening depression, wrote to Addington of 'the growing evils and dangers of which I own I see no adequate remedy'. [514]

XXVI

Resignation
1800-1801

THE SUCCESSES of the Allies in Germany, Italy, Egypt and India in 1799 revived Pitt's natural optimism and brought about a temporary improvement in his health. He had found time for several visits to Princess Caroline at Blackheath. His first journey there in February had been made with considerable reluctance, and he had told Auckland that he hoped he would not be required to pay his 'homages' there again for some time. By August, however, he had become a popular guest at Montague House. Lady Minto described a dinner party which included Loughborough, Pitt, Dundas, Canning, Bartle Frere, Mrs Crewe with her daughter Emma, Dudley Long and Lady Charlotte North:

> . . . we *did* play at musical magic. Mr Dundas was made, by the power of harmony, to kiss Miss Emma's hand, on his knees. Lady Charlotte was to present the Queen of Prussia's bust to Mr Pitt, and make him kiss it, which, after some difficulty, he performed. The Princess was to tie Mr Long and Mr Frere together, and make each nurse a bolster as a baby . . . the most charming part of all was that of Mr Dundas. I do not think he could be tipsy . . . but he squeezed the Princess's hand in the tenderest manner possible,

called her angel repeatedly, and said he hoped no one but himself would know how much he loved her. What can the old thing mean? . . . he is in high favour, and the Princess dines with him on Saturday to meet the Premier. He [Pitt] was charming on Sunday, and Lady Cholmondeley and Miss Garth *, to whom he was beau, were captivated. When Blindman's Buff was proposed to him (not in earnest, I believe), he said, 'I will endeavour to shut my eyes all I can, but cannot promise the rest of the world will do the same.'

He dined there again, with Addington, Dundas and Windham in October.[515]

Canning's visits to Blackheath were frequent enough to invite scandal. Princess Caroline was understood to enjoy a healthy appetite for sexual activity and it was generally believed that she was consoling herself for the Prince's neglect by an undiscriminating distribution of her favours.† She was later to admit without embarrassment, 'I have a bedfellow whenever I like. Nothing is more wholesome.' Her footman was even more explicit.[516] Canning's behaviour was indiscreet and he must have been aware that it might damage his political career. He was thirty years old, clever, ambitious, and the protégé of a brilliant Prime Minister to whom he was devoted. He was conscious of the fact that many men of less talent and without such powerful connections had held higher positions at the same age. Late in the summer of 1800 he paid one of his many regular visits to Holwood, where Pitt offered him a post, evidently of some considerable prestige but without senior responsibility. He had already worked with Grenville, whom he disliked, at the Foreign Office, and although flattered by the offer, the details of which are not known, he declined it. He could not accept 'an office of mere emolument, which giving neither the means to form nor the right to declare any opinion upon the measures of government, would yet bind me implicitly to the acts of persons in whose judgement and talents (without meaning anything unkind to them) one may fairly say one does not have implicit confidence.' [517] Having

* Charlotte, wife of 1st Marquess of Cholmondeley, Chamberlain to the Prince of Wales; and Frances Garth, sub-governess to the Princess Charlotte.
† Her lovers were reputed to include Canning, Sidney Smith, Captain Thomas Manby, and the portrait-painter Thomas Lawrence.

expressed his feelings, he was immediately anxious that he might have offended Pitt by his candour, and wrote several times to him asking for reassurance that their friendship was unimpaired. Pitt, accustomed to the burdens of affection and admiration, and perhaps recognizing something of himself in his brilliant disciple, replied with gentle patience that it was.

Two months earlier Canning had married Joan Scott. Pitt had played matchmaker, inviting both of them to join a party at Walmer Castle, and appointing Canning to the office of Joint Paymaster-General, which brought him into the Privy Council and provided him with a house suitable to his marriage with an heiress. The couple were married on 8 July 1800. According to Hookham Frere *, Pitt was so moved by the ceremony that he was unable to sign the register.[518] Pitt's 'nervousness' may have been due to sentiment, but he was also faltering under the strain of office, made all the heavier by anxiety. The reverses suffered by the Allied armies coincided, as usual, with a marked deterioration in his health, and it is probable that this was due to his use of alcohol to revive his failing spirits. George Rose told Pretyman on 30 July that Pitt was unwell. On 10 October he reported that Pitt was suffering from a return of his 'old Complaint in the Bowels, Loss of Appetite, & is a good deal shook; he cannot carry a Glass of Beer to his Mouth without the aid of his second Hand.' [519]

Sir Walter Farquhar urged Pitt to rest at Bath, or at least to go to Cheltenham for a change of air, but his suggestions were rejected. Pitt could not, he said, 'leave his Anxiety behind him'. He proposed, instead, to stay at Woodley as the guest of the Speaker. Addington wrote to his brother Hiley on 19 October, 'Pitt is now here. It is to me most gratifying that his wishes anticipated mine, and led him to think of Woodley before I proposed it to him. It is, of course, desirable that his indisposition should not be talked of. He is certainly better, but I am still very far from being at ease about him. Sir W Farquhar is to be here on Tuesday and it will then be determined whether he is to remain here or proceed to Bath or Cheltenham. . . . He wants rest and consolation.' A week later he reported Pitt as being 'recovered beyond my expectations, and

* Diplomat, writer, the friend of Canning and a contributor to the *Anti-Jacobin;* Under-Secretary at the Foreign Office in 1799; later envoy and plenipotentiary at Lisbon. Eldest brother of Bartholomew ('Bartle') Frere.

greatly beyond those of Sir W Farquhar'.[520] With Addington's help Farquhar had imposed severe restrictions on Pitt's drinking.

On 5 November Pitt returned to Downing Street. He was rested, but the breakdown of his health had shaken him and he faced problems as great as any he had experienced in his political career. Among the most pressing and formidable of them was that of Catholic emancipation. The Act of Union with Ireland, passed by both Houses of Parliament in May and confirmed by the Dublin parliament in June, was to take effect in January 1801. Pitt's personal commitment was strengthened by the need, made all the more urgent by the resurgence of French military power under Bonaparte, to provide a permanent settlement that would unite the Irish people and make possible the withdrawal of regular troops for service elsewhere. On 25 September he had written to the Lord Chancellor, then with the King at Weymouth, asking him to return to London for a Cabinet meeting at which the chief points for discussion, 'besides the great question on the general state of the Catholics, relate to some arrangement about tithes, and a provision for the Catholic and Dissenting Clergy'.[521]

Loughborough, whose definition of loyalty to the Crown accorded, on this occasion, with his congenital inability to resist political intrigue, showed the letter to the King.[522] Though he was later to deny it to George Rose, Loughborough had played a double game in 1795.[523] Knowing that Fitzwilliam was determined to introduce measures for Catholic emancipation, Loughborough had nevertheless urged in the Cabinet his appointment as Viceroy while, secretly, he had advised the King that any concessions of the kind would violate his coronation oath. In December, after attending Cabinet meetings at which Pitt's plans were outlined, Loughborough composed a memorandum to the King. Others suspected of attempting to influence the King against Pitt's proposals were Lord Auckland, and his brother-in-law Dr John Moore, Archbishop of Canterbury. The evidence to support this is slight,[524] but whatever the truth of the matter it is unlikely that influence from any direction would have moved the King, whose mind was closed on the matter. He had made his opinion clear six years earlier and had neglected no opportunity to reaffirm it. In June 1798 he had written to Pitt, 'No further indulgences must be granted to Roman Catholics, as no country can be governed where there is more than one established

384

religion', and six months later he had directed that the Lord-Lieutenant of Ireland be instructed 'to use the greatest efforts to prevent an emancipation of the Roman Catholics'.[525]

Pitt was well aware not only of the strength of the King's opposition but also that his Cabinet was divided on the question. He had the support of Grenville, Dundas, Windham, Spencer and Camden, but Loughborough, Portland, Westmorland, Liverpool and Chatham were opposed. Pitt's failure to consult, or even to inform, George III must be ascribed to his reluctance to confront him with the outline of measures not yet decided in detail and not approved by so many influential members of his government. His decision not to confide in the King until he had firm proposals, agreed on by a majority of the Cabinet, to put before him was neither improper nor unusual, but he does not appear to have considered the possibility that confidential Cabinet discussions would be leaked to the King.

By the end of January 1801 George III had lost patience. Knowing that Castlereagh, the Irish Chief Secretary, had visited London to attend a Cabinet meeting, the King approached Dundas at a levee on 28 January and loudly demanded, 'What is this that this young Lord has brought over that they are going to throw at my head? . . . I shall reckon any man my personal enemy who proposes any such measure—the most Jacobinical thing I ever heard of.' [526] To Dundas, and to others who heard what passed, the King's words were ominously reminiscent of those he had used to Lord Temple in 1783 when he was about to rid himself of the Fox–North coalition. Next day the King wrote to Addington,

. . . the most mischievous measure is in contemplation . . . this is no less than the placing the Roman Catholics of the Kingdom in an equal state of right to sit in both houses of parliament, and hold offices of trust and emolument, with those of the Established Church. It is suggested by those best informed that Mr Pitt favours this opinion. That Lord Grenville and Mr Dundas do, I have the fullest proof . . . no consideration could ever make me give my consent to what I look upon as the destruction of the Established Church; which, by the wisdom of parliament, I, as well as my predecessors, have been obliged to take an oath at our coronations to support.[527]

He urged Addington to 'open Mr Pitt's eyes on the danger arising from agitating this improper question, which may prevent his ever speaking to me on a subject on which I can scarcely keep my temper.'

It is probable that Addington showed George III's letter to Pitt. It is certain that he told him details of its content for, two days later, Pitt wrote a long and reasoned letter in which he explained to the King 'the general grounds of his opinion'.[528] His argument was expressed with clarity and with proper deference, and the customary references to Pitt's 'duty, gratitude, and attachment', and genuflexions towards His Majesty's graciousness and condescension were not neglected; but there was an undertone of cold intent that belied the formal humilities. Pitt argued that 'the admission of the Catholics to Parliament . . . would under certain conditions to be specified, be highly advisable, with a view to the tranquillity and improvement of Ireland, and to the general interest of the United Kingdom.' This opinion was 'unalterably fixed in his mind' and must guide his political conduct. If, after an interval for consideration, the King's objections should not be 'removed or sufficiently diminished' to permit his full concurrence with the proposed measures, 'it must be personally Mr Pitt's first wish to be released from a situation which he is conscious that under such circumstances, he could not continue to fill but with the greatest disadvantage'. During the interval Pitt undertook not to 'importune' the King, and to refrain from 'all agitation of the subject in Parliament'. If the King could not agree to his proposals, Pitt was willing to continue in office until some 'new arrangement' could be made. Characteristically, he ended his letter with a rebuke for the King's outburst at the levee, entreating the King's pardon for troubling him but 'taking the liberty of most respectfully, but explicitly submitting to your Majesty the indispensable necessity of effectively discountenancing, in the whole of this interval, all attempts to make use of your Majesty's name, or to influence the opinion of any individual or descriptions of men, on any part of this subject.'

George III replied next day with commendable kindness and restraint.[529] He wrote of his 'cordial affection' for Pitt and of his 'high opinion of his talents and integrity', but declared that the oath he had taken at his coronation, 'enforced by the obligation of instantly following it in the course of the ceremony with taking the holy sacrament', bound him to maintain the Established Church. 'The principle of duty', he wrote, 'must therefore prevent me from discussing any proposition tending to destroy the groundwork of our happy Constitution, and much more so that now mentioned by Mr Pitt which is no less than the complete overthrow of the whole fabric.' If Pitt would abstain from further discussion of the subject, he too would keep silent. He added a last appeal to his Prime Minister: 'I shall still hope his sense of duty will prevent his retiring from his present situation to the end of my life, for I can with great truth assert that I shall, from public as well as private considerations, feel great regret if I shall ever find myself obliged at any time, from a sense of religious and political duty, to yield to his entreaties of retiring from his seat at the Board of Treasury.' Two days later Pitt asked ' to be released as soon as possible'.[530]

Pitt's resignation was not made public until 14 February but it could not be kept secret. He had written to inform a number of his friends, including Rose who expressed his surprise in a letter dated 6 February to Pretyman. In the circumstances he considered Pitt's resignation 'unavoidable', but added with unusual perception, 'I doubt very much whether he will be able to bring to public Notice his Justification'. He was shocked to hear that Pitt's successor was to be Addington: 'The speaker to my utter astonishment takes Mr Pitt's situation—to what Length will Vanity not carry a Man? amiable & good in private life, & I am persuaded honestly attached to Mr Pitt, he is no more equal to what he has undertaken than a Child.' Lady Malmesbury described the choice of Addington as *a farce*, adding, 'it is impossible that Mr Pitt's friend and creature should be his real successor, or more than a *stop-gap* till matters are settled and he may come again.' Of the King's opposition to Catholic relief she wrote, 'if he considers it a point of conscience, no power on earth will make him yield . . . Lord Auckland and the Archbishop of Cant (that is the right spelling you know) have been at him.' Lord Minto, declaring that he had 'long looked on Pitt as the Atlas of our reeling globe', reported the 'despondency and alarm' created in Vienna by the news of Pitt's resignation, and asked to be replaced.[531]

By 13 February rumours were already being ventilated that Pitt's resignation was due to reasons that had not been revealed. Lady

Wellesley wrote to her husband * in India, 'Time will explain this mass of falsehood and intrigue—but when religion is mixed with politics, only misfortune can be expected.' Grenville, who with Spencer, Dundas, Camden and Windham had decided to resign with their leader, wrote to Minto: 'Report and speculation will perhaps also have conveyed to you other supposed motives for this resolution; but I do not fear your thinking so meanly of us as to suppose us capable of assigning other reasons for our conduct on so great and trying an occasion than those by which, and by which alone, it was really actuated. . . . But there was no alternative except that of taking this step or of agreeing to the disguise or dereliction of this opinion on one of the most important questions in the whole range of our domestic policy.' The speculation nevertheless continued. Malmesbury reported the circulation of 'all sort of idle conjectures as to the real cause of his [Pitt's] going, and every fanciful one credited, in preference to the plain and simple one.' Addington himself confirmed that 'the Catholic question was the real, and he believed the sole cause of Pitt's resignation'; but Dundas prophesied that 'the motives which I and my colleagues have assigned for our resignation, drawn from the Popery question, no historian will believe.'

The suspicions about Pitt's, and to a lesser extent George III's, motives have persisted. The ineptitude of Pitt's handling of this crucial situation, and his determination to sacrifice office for principle, have seemed out of character. It is known that George III was becoming increasingly irritated by the authoritarian behaviour of Pitt, Grenville and Dundas. He found himself too frequently in disagreement with his ministers. He acknowledged, however, the impossibility of any stable alternative government being formed without Pitt's support. The doubts raised by these considerations have been aggravated by Pitt's subsequent behaviour.

On 5 February Addington had accepted George III's invitation to form an administration, and five days later, after his resignation as Speaker, he was warmly embraced by his sovereign and told, 'My

* Lord Mornington, who had been created Baron Wellesley in the English peerage in 1797, had been awarded an Irish Marquessate in 1799. He was bitterly disappointed, having set his heart on a promotion in the English peerage. He told Dundas that he looked upon his new dignity as a mark of deprecation rather than of honour; to Pitt he wrote, 'I was confident there had been nothing *Irish* or *Pinchbeck* in my conduct, or in its result, I felt an equal confidence that I should find nothing *Irish* or *Pinchbeck* in my reward.' [532]

dear Addington, you have saved your country.' On the 16th the King wrote to him apologizing for 'writing so ill, for I am in bed with a severe chill'. Dr Thomas Gisborne * was called, and the King was also visited by the Reverend Thomas Willis. Next day he was noticeably agitated, and on the 19th Pitt told Rose that 'His Majesty's mind was not in a proper state.' Dr Henry Reynolds was summoned and Thomas Willis called again. The King said earnestly to him, 'I have prayed to God all night that I might die, or that he would spare my reason . . . for God's sake keep me from your father and a regency.' Dr Francis Willis was then eighty-three and too old to be consulted, but his sons John and Robert arrived to take charge of the royal patient. During the following five weeks the Willis family assumed extraordinary powers and exercised a totally unconstitutional control over affairs of State. They acted as intermediaries between the King and his ministers, discussing confidential policies, examining State papers, and delivering documents to the King for signature without other witnesses.[534]

The situation was one of extreme delicacy. The King was seriously ill. His mind was deranged, and on 2 March he was in a coma and hourly expected to die. Meanwhile, his ministers, who had resigned in February, had been unable to deliver up their Seals of office. On 14 March the King was well enough to receive the Seals from Pitt, showing him 'the utmost possible kindness both in words and manner'.[535] Three days later he presided at a Privy Council, but his recovery was not complete and the Willis family feared a relapse. At the end of the month they were told to pack their bags and go, but they merely kept out of his way and suggested that he be moved from Windsor to Kew. Early in the morning of 17 April, after dismissing his doctors, the King took it into his head to ride over to Blackheath to see the Princess of Wales and the five-year-old Princess Charlotte. The Queen, weighed down by fear and anxiety, consulted Addington and asked the Willis brothers to return. By an act unparalleled in British history and probably treasonable, they kidnapped the King on his way to Kew and held him prisoner in the Prince of Wales's house there until 19 May. In desperation the King refused to sign any official papers unless he was allowed to leave the

* Gisborne had become senior physician to the King after the death of Sir George Baker in 1797. Dr Warren had died in the same year and Anthony Addington in 1790.

house and see the Queen and his family. On 21 May the Willis brothers were finally dismissed, and five weeks later the King left to convalesce in Weymouth.

George III's illness faced Pitt with a personal crisis. On 6 March the King had instructed Thomas Willis to convey a message to Pitt: 'Tell him', he said, 'that I am now quite well—quite recovered from my illness; but what has *he* not to answer for who is the cause of my having been ill at all?' He had already used similar words to Lord Chatham: 'As to my cold, that is well enough; but what else I have I owe to your brother.' Pitt was so overcome with distress that he sent a reply, again through Willis, that he would never again, during the reign, 'aggravate the Catholic Question, that is, whether *in* office or *out* of office.' Willis delivered this assurance to the King: 'I stated to him what you wished . . . and after saying the kindest things of you, he exclaimed "Now my mind will be at ease." ' Pitt's promise, witnessed by Addington, was given in a moment of genuine distress. It was a generous and spontaneous gesture of real concern and affection. It was also a declaration of his belief that he was to blame for the recurrence of the King's illness. Overwhelmed by anxiety and remorse, he abandoned, in a single act of allegiance, the principle for which he had already sacrificed his political career.[536]

Because Pitt's renunciation of principle was also the repudiation of a promise, understood but never stated, and the desertion of an oppressed people, it was misrepresented in his own time and has been generally condemned since. He has been accused of servility, self-interest, and a breach of faith, revealing the hypocrisy that lay beneath the veneer of integrity. These accusations are based on the assumption that his ambition had remained undiminished by seventeen years in office, that his health was unimpaired, and that his declaration of support for Addington's new ministry was as false as the reason he had given for his resignation. The simple explanation is that he had been led by his often untrustworthy optimism into an extraordinary error of judgement. Knowing the strength of George III's opposition to Catholic emancipation, Pitt had nevertheless believed that he could be persuaded by reasoned argument and by the weight of support for the proposal in parliament. Conflict in the Cabinet gave him pause and decided him against informing the King until he could be sure of majority approval for an official Cabinet Minute. Challenged by the King, he was obliged prematurely to present a case that must fail. He was soon to understand that although all the greatest politicians of the period—Fox, Sheridan, Windham, Canning, Grey, Castlereagh, Wilberforce, Grenville, Dundas—would speak in favour, even the active support of the King might not be sufficient to force the Bill through both Houses of parliament. The great mass of the people, a majority of the House of Lords, and probably a majority in the Commons were determinedly anti-Catholic.

The Revolution of 1688 had been the revolt of an overwhelmingly Protestant people against a Catholic King. The Hanoverian succession was founded upon the determination of the British people to put aside political divisions in order to retain the Established Church, and this fact determined the religion of the monarch. Neither George III nor his people had forgotten that their predecessors had been obliged to fight against Catholic-led Jacobite rebellions, and the horrors of the Gordon riots were still fresh in men's minds. Politically it made good sense to abandon a proposal that could not be carried by parliament. Far more important to Pitt was the principle of commitment to a course of action which he believed combined justice with service to the best interests of both countries. It is unlikely that anything but his devotion to the Constitution could have persuaded him to relinquish it.

It was plain that George III's illness was a recurrence of the malady that had precipitated the Regency Crisis, and Pitt, like everyone else, accepted the medical opinion that during the winter of 1788-9 the King had been insane. If the King's reason, and thus his reign, were to be saved, all causes of agitation and stress must be removed. For Pitt the security and prosperity of the nation, to which he had devoted his life, depended upon the preservation of constitutional monarchy as represented by George III. He was willing to hand over the government to Addington, with his support. He was not prepared to entrust the nation to the Prince of Wales and Fox. This was the principle for which he would sacrifice all others.

The delay, imposed by the King's illness, in surrendering the Seals raised hopes that Addington might yield his position. Pitt roundly declared that he thought this proposal 'utterly improper, and that he should hold no intercourse with those who would not concur in a strenuous support of the New Administration; nor should he think those persons friends to himself who croaked about their instability.' [537] From the moment of his resignation he did his utmost to persuade his followers to stay in office. Portland, Westmorland, Chatham, and the elderly Earl of Liverpool were willing, as were Pitt's friends Dudley Ryder and Steele; but Cornwallis, Canning, Castlereagh, Long and Rose all resigned, and Addington was left to form his government from what Malmesbury described as 'very nothingy men'. [538]

Canning's resignation in particular troubled Pitt. There was more than a hint of hysteria in Canning's jealous loyalty to his chief. This showed itself in his adamant refusal to submit to Pitt's instruction, and in an irresponsible display of animosity towards Addington. Pitt was obliged to extract from him an undertaking that he would moderate his behaviour, a promise that Canning was incapable of keeping. Addington, meanwhile, cobbled up an administration that presented the appearance of a truncated torso of which the most prominent feature was the rump. His own talents were slight. His nomination as Speaker had been criticized on the ground that he was not an aristocrat. His appointment to be Prime Minister aroused even louder condemnation for the same reason. He was patronizingly dubbed 'the Doctor', a sobriquet which, in view of his shortcomings as an orator, suited him at least as well as his previous title of 'Mr Speaker'. To a parliament and a country accustomed to the personality and glittering authority of William Pitt, Henry Addington was a fustian nonentity, a provincial *locum tenens* who could make no decisions without the approval of his temporarily absent master. It was generally agreed that Addington's ministry could not stand without Pitt's active support and that its reign would be short-lived.

Pitt, meanwhile, was beset by troubles of his own. His health was poor, and for the first time in his life he was showing anxiety about the shocking state of his private finances. During the previous October Rose had written to Pretyman of 'A History of Debts and Distresses as actually sickened me . . . there is an immediate Danger of an Execution or something as bad for about £600, & of an unpleasant expose [*sic*] for about £400; for these some expedient *must* be found . . . but the Evil is much deeper, & a Cure should be attempted without delay.' He added accurately, 'Holwood is, & while he has it, must be, the Sink of Expence.' In July 1801 he estimated Pitt's debts at £46,000. Holwood, valued at about £16,000, was to be sold, but 'the Sale of everything he has in the world . . . would not clear him of Debt.' [539]

The King had offered to pay Pitt's debts, but the memory of the £20,000 that George III had given to Lord North in 1782—assistance that had put North in the position of King's pensioner—was enough to make Pitt decline. For much the same reason he refused an offer of £100,000 from the City bankers and merchants, or the suggestion of a public subscription; but he reluctantly agreed to allow his friends to organize a private fund, which eventually raised £11,700, on condition that he should not know the names of the subscribers. If the names were unknown to him, he could not be tempted to use his political influence to repay the friends who had helped him; nor could he be accused of doing so. Lord Camden, Lord Carrington *, Pretyman, Rose, Steele and Dundas each gave £1,000. The sale of Holwood did not take place until the autumn of 1802, when it realized £15,000 at auction, but Pitt's creditors were satisfied, for the time being, with the money raised by subscription and £4,000 from 'the sale of Gold Boxes with Diamonds which Mr Pitt had rec'd from foreign Powers as presents.' [540]

Pitt's refusal to accept help from the King, or from anyone outside his immediate circle of friends, was another proof of the obstinate determination to retain his independence that he confused with integrity. He does not appear to have considered the burden that such purity imposed on the generosity of his friends. He had a rare capacity to inspire affection, admiration, and even reverence, which often went unrewarded. Wilberforce, who gave £500 to the fund to relieve Pitt's debts, wrote: 'I really love him for his public qualities and his private ones, though there too he is much misunderstood. But how can I expect that he should love me much, who have been so long rendering myself vexatious to him?' Poor Rose, whose doggy devotion was not reciprocated, poured out his pathetic disappointment to Pretyman in a series of lengthy missives filled with anxiety and unrequited longing for recognition. 'I am persuaded', he wrote in September, 'I never had his Affection, & for many Years I have doubted much if I had his Esteem . . . My Attachment to him as a *public* & a *private* Man has been warm & strong, never varying . . . that Mr Pitt should prefer the Society of others to mine I can easily understand—many of his private friends are more nearly of his own age, have been educated with him, & had infinitely superior Talents to make them companionable.' [541]

* Bob Smith, rewarded by Pitt with a barony in 1796.

The upheaval caused by Pitt's resignation in March was confined to political circles. Less than four months later William Wellesley-Pole wrote to his brother, Lord Wellesley, 'It would surprise you to see Pitt lounging about the streets in a morning, generally by himself, and seeming not to have anything to do. . . . It is surprising how little sensation his going out has made in the country, nobody speaks of him, no address, no subscriptions, no stir of any kind anywhere.' [542] Addington's government was pedestrian, but no more incompetent than many that had gone before. It lacked skill in parliamentary debate, but among the 'nothingy men' in the Cabinet there were three who were later to be capable Prime Ministers *, and, contrary to expectation, the ministry appeared to command support both in parliament and in the country. The King was charmed with the administration, which he regarded as his own cleverly constructed toy: it lacked, perhaps, some of the colour and brilliance of the one he had broken, but he had no doubt that it would work quite as well. It would, indeed, for so long as Pitt chose to sustain it.

* The Duke of Portland, Lord Hawkesbury ('Young Jenky') and Spencer Perceval.

XXVII

An Interval of Peace
1801-1803

ADDINGTON's wartime administration began with two brilliant
successes, both of which he owed to the planning of Pitt and
Grenville. In January, in response to the revival of the Armed
Neutrality, the Cabinet imposed an embargo on all ships of the
League. Letters of marque issued for the seizure of all Danish,
Swedish and Russian vessels found at sea produced a rich harvest of
merchantmen. Later in the month orders were given for a secret
naval expedition to be assembled at Yarmouth. Command was
entrusted to Admiral Sir Hyde Parker, a brave but hesitant sixty-
two-year-old known to the navy as 'Old Vinegar'. As second-in-
command the Admiralty appointed Vice-Admiral Lord Nelson. On
12 March, two days before Pitt surrendered his Seals of office, the
fleet of eighteen battleships and thirty-five smaller vessels sailed for
the Baltic. Nineteen days later, after the rejection of an ultimatum,
Nelson led twelve of the lighter battleships into the narrow King's
Channel at Copenhagen and battered the Danish fleet into submission.* In return for Nelson's promise not to bombard the city, the

* It was in the heat of this engagement that Nelson, putting his telescope to his blind eye,
pretended not to see Hyde Parker's signal to break off the attack.

395

Danes agreed to suspend their alliance with Sweden and Russia. Six weeks later Russia lifted the embargo on British ships and the League of Armed Neutrality collapsed.

The second victory was won by the army. In October 1800 orders had been issued to Abercromby to end his army's prolonged and unproductive Mediterranean cruise and to co-operate with Turkish troops and British forces from India and the Cape of Good Hope in an attempt to destroy the French army in Egypt. It was a bold and imaginative stroke at a time when the Second Coalition was disintegrating, and its success owed little to accurate planning. Abercromby's ill-equipped army of 15,000 infantry was hopelessly out-numbered by the French, who were securely established in a country whose climate and terrain were unfamiliar to the British.

On 2 March Lord Keith's Mediterranean fleet, escorting the expeditionary force, anchored in Aboukir Bay. Six days later, led by Major-General John Moore, the first wave of assault troops landed. In less than an hour the British lost 600 men, but the French defences were broken and a precarious bridgehead established. On 21 March Abercromby's army, in position some three miles to the east of Alexandria, was attacked by the French under General Jacques Menou, who had succeeded to the command after the death of Kléber in 1800. After a furious battle the defeated French withdrew behind the fortifications of the city. Abercromby died of his wounds; but at the end of June his successor, General John Hely-Hutchinson, entered Cairo and accepted the surrender of 13,000 French troops. Bonaparte's ambitions for conquest in the Middle East were shattered beyond repair.

The Austrians had made peace with France at Lunéville in February. Minto, in a dispatch written at the beginning of January, reported their troops as 'literally disabled by fatigue, want, and hardship of every sort'. The Archduke Charles had told him that 'there was no remedy for the disorders of the army'. Later Minto wrote of the 'lamentable and ignominious peace' and declared 'all descriptions of people . . . are heartily ashamed of it.' The French, as he was quick to notice, 'observed their treaty with their usual good faith; that is to say they have required the strict execution of all that is favourable to themselves without the slightest observance of those limitations which are favourable to the other party. They have begun to exact and lay on contributions by their authority in the countries which their troops occupy.' Britain was, once more, alone but for the unwavering loyalty of Portugal, whose exposed position was an additional cause of anxiety. The murder of the Tsar Paul promised some hope for the future. It was, as Lady Malmesbury told her sister, 'quite a virtuous act to kill him'. The new Tsar, Alexander I, had 'written a most conciliatory letter to the King'.[543]

It seemed, nevertheless, that Britain's best hope of survival lay in peace, however temporary. In June 1800 the King had written to Pitt, 'No disaster can make me think the treating for peace either wise or safe whilst the French principles subsist . . . for no confidence can be placed in the present French Government. My opinion is formed on principle, not on events, and therefore is not open to challenge.'[544] A year later he was no more enthusiastic, but he understood that the country needed a period of recuperation and that Nelson's victory at Copenhagen and Abercromby's successful landing in Egypt would strengthen the government's hand in the negotiations for a treaty. Addington had already made a tentative overture in March. This had been rebuffed, but by the summer Bonaparte was ready to propose peace terms. He was, in fact, anxious to conclude a treaty on his terms before the defeat of his army in Egypt became known in Europe.

From the British point of view the terms were not attractive. Britain must surrender to France, Spain and the Dutch Republic all colonial conquests except Trinidad and Ceylon. Malta must be restored to the suzerainty of the Knights of St John. In return, France agreed to recognize the integrity of the Turkish Empire and Portugal, promised an indemnity to the House of Orange, and undertook to evacuate all troops from Egypt and Naples. George III wrote to Lord Hawkesbury, Grenville's successor as Foreign Secretary: 'The King has received the Minute of the Cabinet on the proposed peace with France. To repeat his doubts whether any confidence can be placed in any agreement to be made with that country till it has a settled Government would be in reality a stop to all negotiation. He will not oppose the concluding peace, though he cannot place any reliance on its duration, but trusts such a peace establishment will be kept up as may keep this country on a respectable footing, without which our situation would be most deplorable.'[545]

The Preliminaries were signed on 1 October. Pitt, who was

erroneously thought by Malmesbury to have 'counselled, and, of course, directed the whole',[546] publicly supported the terms and defended them in the House of Commons. None of the senior Cabinet ministers who had resigned with him could find anything good to say of them. Windham wrote in disgust to Addington, 'the country has received its death blow'; Grenville declared, 'All confidence in the present Government is completely and irretrievably destroyed'; and Dundas told Pitt, 'the only wise and friendly thing I can do is to impose upon myself silence.' In spite of his increasing doubts about Addington's abilities as Prime Minister, Pitt remained true to his promise to sustain the new government. Wilberforce described his loyalty as 'one of the noblest instances of true magnanimity that was ever exhibited to the admiration and imitation of mankind'. George III was reported to have said to Addington, 'I do not think you right, but I have now made up my mind to your peace and I'll support you like a man.' [547]

After six months of negotiation at Amiens, confirming his worst fears of Bonaparte's untrustworthiness, the elderly Lord Cornwallis was at last presented with a final peace treaty. It was signed on 27 March 1802. The French had used the interval, while British seapower was held in check by the armistice, to reinterpret or repudiate some of the most important conditions of the Treaty of Lunéville by which Bonaparte had agreed to recognize and respect the independence of the Swiss, Dutch, Ligurian * and Cisalpine † Republics. In January Bonaparte had accepted the Presidency of the Cisalpine Republic which French troops continued to occupy. British protests were thrust aside on the grounds that Bonaparte's treaty with Austria was of no concern to Britain. By private agreement with Spain, France had gained the Louisiana Territory, Elba and the Duchy of Parma. Meanwhile, an army of 25,000 sailed from Brest, escorted by twenty-two battleships, to reconquer St Domingue. Lastly, it was proposed that the integrity of Malta under the decadent and powerless order of the Knights of St John should be guaranteed not by the Tsar, as had been agreed, but by the King of Naples, who was so vulnerable to French threats as to be unable to

---

* The old Republic of Genoa.
 † Formed in 1797 from the greater part of northern Italy and comprising Lombardy, Mantua, Brescia, Verona, Cremona, Rovigo, Modena, Carrara, Massa, Romano, Ferrara and Bologna.

guarantee the independence of his own territory. It was finally accepted that the British garrison should be withdrawn within three months, leaving the island's independence and neutrality to be secured by the principal powers of Europe, all of which were either too remote from Malta to implement the guarantee or under the influence of France and therefore unwilling to do so. This arrangement invited annexation of the island by Bonaparte, a violation of the treaty of Amiens that could be prevented only by the British navy. Addington's Cabinet awoke belatedly to the realization that control of the Mediterranean depended upon possession of a naval base; that no other base but Malta was available; and that Britain was therefore bound by treaty not only to the evacuation of Malta but also to a withdrawal from the Mediterranean. This, in turn, reopened to Bonaparte the gateway to Egypt and India. Fox, trapped between the hinges of Addington's ministry, which he despised, and the opposition to the treaty led by Grenville, whom he loathed, abandoned all pretence of patriotism. On 22 October he wrote to Grey, 'The triumph of the French Government over the English does in fact afford me a degree of pleasure that it is difficult to disguise.' [548]

Long before the signing of the Treaty of Amiens there had been agitation to restore Pitt to office. Indeed, it had arisen as soon as it became known that Addington was to succeed him, and Pitt's determined support of the government and adamant refusal to countenance any talk of his return had not put an end to it. Among the leaders were Canning and Rose, whose dogged endeavours to dislodge Pitt from his chosen position as the unshakeable buttress of Addington's ministry were encouraged by the belief that the King's faith in Pitt was undiminished. In June 1801, just three months after Pitt's surrender of the Seals, Rose wrote to Pretyman, 'The King *certainly* thinks as highly of Pitt as ever, & I verily believe would be glad to have him back again: but how that is to be affected [*sic*] I protest I cannot yet conjecture.' [549] In spite of the King's cordiality towards Pitt whenever they met, there was no good reason to believe anything of the kind. On the contrary, there was ample evidence of the King's satisfaction with his new ministers and it would have been a far stupider king than George III who failed to realize that a pliable Prime Minister who had the counsel and support of Pitt was far less aggravating than Pitt himself.

Although they were known to have Pitt's approval, the terms of the peace strengthened opposition to the new government but without a proportionate increase in the demand for Pitt's return. Addington's position was also weakened by his evident incompetence in financial matters. Rose reported to Pretyman that Pitt had 'a grand Plan of Finance which he has given to Mr A but I fear the latter will hardly be made to understand it'; and Pretyman wrote that Addington's reputation stood 'very low in the City, having shown himself to be utterly ignorant of Finance'. It was unfortunate for Addington that he was most obviously inadequate in a department in which Pitt had excelled.[550]

Most damaging of all to Addington's reputation was the widespread suspicion, fomented by Canning and Rose, that Pitt's loyalty was being repaid with backstairs denigration. Rose in a flurry of partisanship and capitals declared, 'Ignorance, Timidity, Cunning, Artifice & Treachery, triumph over Talents, Courage, Openness, Liberalty & Fair-dealing.'[551] He had no doubt that Addington was personally involved in trying to discredit Pitt with George III, and early in December he took the opportunity offered by a long ride with the King to contradict some of the rumours that had been spread concerning Pitt's reasons for resigning. Pretyman told his wife of a conversation with Pitt early in 1802: 'Mr Pitt feels his situation is a very difficult one. He certainly does not think the present Ministers suited to the circumstances of the country, and he knows that all his private Friends are dissatisfied with what is going on . . . he is very anxious for the Country, and I am confident that he will support as long as he possibly can consistently with the Good of the Public.'[552]

Pitt was being fed by his supporters with stories of Addington's perfidy, and in February their friendship, already under severe strain, showed the first sign of attrition. In a debate in the House of Commons, Tierney accused Pitt, in his absence, of having held back expenses of the war 'until peace, by which he had thrown a burthen upon his successor, who had now the odium of applying for four or five millions of money to provide for expenses which his predecessor had incurred.'[553] Tom Steele made a spirited defence of Pitt, but Addington, who had already spoken in the debate, merely denied in a single sentence that any expenditure had been concealed or withheld 'with a sinister or deceptious view'. This was accepted by the House as a vindication of Pitt's conduct but the incident was misleadingly reported in the newspapers and it is possible that Canning or some other well-wisher seized the chance to stir the embers of animosity. Pitt wrote to Addington on 10 February from Walmer. 'I know how little newspapers can be trusted for the exactness of their reports. . . . But if the substance of what passed is anything like what is represented, I . . . own to you that I think I have much to wonder at and to complain of, and that what is due to my own character will not suffer me to leave the matter without further explanation.' [554] Addington replied at once in evident alarm that he had asked Tom Steele to give Pitt a full account of the debate. A week later, after seeing Steele and Charles Long, Pitt somewhat grudgingly declared himself satisfied. They met and were reconciled, but both knew that their friendship had sustained permanent damage.

The relationship between Pitt and Addington deteriorated steadily during the following twelve months, but they found themselves briefly in agreement in May, when Auckland, who was Postmaster-General in the new administration, made an unheralded attack on the terms of the Treaty of Amiens. Addington wrote him a minatory letter of rebuke. Finding himself stung by a hornet that he had identified as a gnat, Auckland was obliged to make an abject apology in order to avoid dismissal. Pitt who had quarrelled with Auckland over the Catholic question, and had suffered from his declaration in the House of Lords that the resignation of the previous government was a mystery obscured by a veil through which the eye could not penetrate, could not resist congratulating Addington. Such opportunities for the exchange of mutual compliments were becoming rare.

On 28 May a banquet was held at Merchant Taylors' Hall to celebrate Pitt's forty-third birthday. It was organized by Canning in such a manner as to make it seem to arise from 'the spontaneous attachment of the citizens of London'. Pitt, who would not have approved, was neither informed nor invited. *The Times* later reported that 975 people had attended. The evening was chiefly distinguished for the performance, by Charles Dignum, a tenor from the Drury Lane Theatre, of a song said to have been written by a certain Claude Sprott. No one present had any difficulty in identifying Canning as the author. The last verse was destined to become famous:

> And Oh! if again the rude whirlwind should rise
> The dawnings of peace should fresh darkness deform,
> The regrets of the good and the fears of the wise
> Shall turn to the Pilot that weathered the Storm.*

The song was repeated and the last verse sung a third time before Lord Spencer called for a toast to 'The Pilot that weathered the Storm'. It was drunk to loud applause and hammering of hands on the tables. This festivity was the first and most public of Canning's broadsides in his own renewed offensive against Addington. It was not long before another of his rhymes was as famous and popular as his song: 'Pitt is to Addington as London is to Paddington' was the sort of comparison that even members of the Cabinet found convincing.

Any hopes of Pitt's early return to the government were dashed by his illness. Minto wrote in June: 'Pitt has been *very* ill, and so gone to Walmer for his health, where, though better, people are uneasy about him. It seemed like a return of his old complaint. Dundas says that he persists in forswearing public life.' Farquhar left a telling account of his patient's condition:

> Whether owing to the particular state of the mind or the sudden change of habit & employment cannot be exactly ascertained, his stomach became more seriously affected, and after restless nights he was seized with vomitings almost every morning. The dislike of all kinds of nourishment increased; a spare breakfast was made; & the sight of dinner always brought on Retching,—consequently the weakened Constitution received no support. Having devoted my attention chiefly to his diet, & employed the most approved remedies without effect, I recommended him to try the effect of

---

* In the original the last two lines were less tactful:
>   While we turn to thy hopeless retirement our eyes
>   We shall long for the Pilot that weathered the Storm.
They were presumably changed when it was known that friends of Pitt's who were in Addington's government were to attend. One of them, Hawkesbury, took his dinner into another room to avoid embarrassment.

the sea air at Walmer Castle. The success was not equal to my expectations, even aided by a steady perseverance in the Stomach Medicines.[555]

Early in September Pitt's health worsened. He wrote to Farquhar complaining of 'severe morning sickness, & absolute dislike to all food, with all the unpleasant symptoms of aggravated debility'. Farquhar went down to Walmer and stayed there for a week. He wrote later,

I found the Stomach rejecting everything, & the bowels obstinately refusing their office—the nerves seriously affected— the habit [bodily constitution] wasted—& the whole system deranged. These distressing and discouraging Symptoms con- tinuing for some days unabated in spite of the most powerful remedies. Mr. Pitt expressed himself with his usual good humour, that he believed he had at last baffled the art of Medicine, and that the Expedients to rescue him were at an end. . . . A tepid Bath was ordered, & afterwards a volatile fetid Night Draught. I then retired under his promise to send for me in the event of any change during the night. In less than an hour a servant came into my room to say that his Master felt himself wonderfully relieved, & wished to see me. . . . From this time the severe & threatening symptoms gave way, and the stomach recovered in some degree its powers. . . . A mild and restorative Plan was ordered . . . which succeeded, and was apparently followed by progressive amend- ment which continued for some time.

On 22 September Pitt was able to write, with his usual optimism, to Wilberforce, 'My complaint has entirely left me, I am recovering strength every day, and I have no doubt of being in a very short time as well as I was before the attack.' Farquhar, more cautiously, strongly recommended rest and a course of the remedial waters at Bath. Pretyman, too, was anxious about the effects of Pitt's illness: 'His mind', he wrote, 'had lost part of its natural strength and energy.' It was common gossip at the time that, since his retirement from office, Pitt had been drinking heavily, and Farquhar's prescrip- tion of a 'volatile fetid Night Draught', which would certainly have contained alcohol, is significant as an example of small quantities of

403

alcohol being used to calm and ease an alcoholic patient and to help restore his appetite. Farquhar also recognized the symptoms of acute gout, and it seems to have been at about this time that he became seriously concerned about Pitt's condition.[556]

While Pitt lay ill at Walmer, the armed services were drastically reduced and British visitors jostled one another across the Channel to gape at Paris under the First Consul. While St Vincent at the Admiralty cut naval personnel from 130,000 to 70,000, and the ships of the line in commission from more than a hundred to forty, British tourists exclaimed in admiration at the sight of the new Caesar, mounted on a 'stately, prancing' white charger, reviewing his troops. British artists flocked to Paris to gaze in astonishment at the plundered riches of Italian art reposing in the Louvre.*

Pitt left Walmer for Bath towards the end of October. By then it was already plain that Bonaparte had no intention of abiding by the terms made at Lunéville and Amiens. In August Bonaparte was declared First Consul for life and, in anticipation of an imperial title, chose to style himself Napoleon. That month his army, taking advantage of a French-inspired insurrection, crossed the frontiers into Switzerland. This provoked an exchange of letters, felicitously described by Fox as couched in terms of 'reciprocal Billingsgate', between the governments of Britain and France, but the French occupied and subjugated Switzerland without further opposition. When at last it became clear that Napoleon was rebuilding his battle fleet and making preparations for another invasion of Egypt, Addington gave orders that Malta should be retained, in contravention of the Treaty of Amiens, as a naval base. This belated recognition of the strategic importance of Malta, combined with the continuing reductions in the strength of the navy, which St Vincent seemed to be hell-bent on destroying, did little to inspire confidence in Addington's ministry. As the prospect darkened, St Vincent threatened to resign if the government went to war, and Minto was shocked to discover that the majority of the navy's ships were 'so much out of repair as to be unfit for service'.[557]

Pitt, who had already concluded that Addington was 'a stupider fellow than he thought him,' nevertheless felt himself bound by his

* Among the artists who visited Paris in August were John Flaxman, Henry Fuseli, John Hoppner, John Opie, Martin Archer Shee and J. M. W. Turner. The looted pictures returned to the Pitti Palace in 1815 included eight Raphaels, two Titians, a Giorgione and a Rembrandt.

promise to support the government. The precise terms of the pledge are not known. Canning, reporting a conversation with Pitt in September or October, while he was staying at Walmer, quoted Pitt as stating that the promise was 'solemnly binding, not redeemable by any lapse of time, nor ever to be cancelled without the *express consent* of Mr Addington.' Pitt had admitted that he had 'in the first instance, gone too far, and pledged himself too deeply', but added: 'I will not affect a childish modesty; but recollect what I have just said—I stand pledged: I make no scruple of owning that I am ambitious—but my ambition is *character*, not office. I may have engaged myself inconsiderately, but I am irrecoverably engaged.'[558]

In order to excuse Pitt's later actions, his biographers have tended to dismiss Canning's evidence as unreliable.[559] It is certainly extraordinary that any politician of such experience should have engaged himself to so one-sided a contract and without regard to changing circumstances or the future needs of his country, but Canning's account was written within four weeks of his conversation with Pitt, and it has the ring of authenticity. This was, indeed, the kind of promise wrung from Pitt by the emotion of the moment. One of his most attractive attributes was his impulsive generosity; and his loyalty to his country, to the King as the symbol of the Constitution, and to his closest friends, was never questioned by the basest of his enemies. At the time of George III's illness, when he gave his promise never again to raise the question of Catholic relief during the King's reign, it would have been no more extraordinary to give Addington a promise of support that would enable him to govern, to make peace with France and to revive the national economy.

Throughout the autumn of 1802 Pitt was bombarded by the exhortations and admonitions of his friends. Finding that they could not move him to oppose the government, Malmesbury and Canning, who were particularly importunate, conspired to persuade him to stay at Bath where he could not actively support it. They told him ceaselessly 'how very dangerously he committed himself by allowing himself to be consulted *partially*, and by giving advice on some isolated measure, while the great system, of which this was only part, was kept secret from him.' Pitt at last agreed that while he remained at Bath 'he would decline giving any advice at all'. He deplored the canvassing that had been undertaken on his behalf and irritably told his advisers that 'the zeal, schemes, or interests of officious and

405

selfish people disgusted and soured him, by their too eager and too indiscreet exhortations.' [560]

Pitt was nonetheless becoming increasingly uneasy about the obvious ineptitude of Addington's government and embarrassed by his pledge not to oppose it. In July he had urged Castlereagh to accept the offered appointment of President of the Board of Control, but he had been unable to persuade any other of his supporters to strengthen the administration by joining it. He had, once more, given evidence of his integrity by refusing the Clerkship of the Pells, worth £3,000 a year, when it became vacant on the death of Barré.* When Tom Steele also refused it, Addington bestowed it on his own sixteen-year-old son. Dundas, on the other hand, accepted the titles of Viscount Melville and Baron Dunira. The King expressed the hope that 'it would keep that gentleman quiet, and that he would not enter into that captious opposition that did no credit to some members of the House of Lords.' [561] Pitt was 'beyond measure surprised'.[562] He was even more astonished and displeased when Lord Melville became Addington's emissary in March of the following year to persuade Pitt to return to office in a ministry headed by Addington.

Pitt's retirement at Bath came to an end in December, when he paid a series of visits to the Marquess of Bath at Longleat, his mother at Burton Pynsent, George Rose at Cuffnall's, Grenville at Dropmore, and Malmesbury at Park Place. He was in excellent spirits, 'full of energy and vigour, determined to shrink from nothing'. In October Pitt had told Canning that he would return to office at Addington's request, at the King's command, or by public demand for a change of government. Grenville, who had strongly opposed the peace terms approved by Pitt, had nevertheless declared, 'in the most express terms, that whenever Pitt would assume the lead in the King's councils, he was ready to support him most strenuously and invariably', and he had promised the same for his brother Tom. At the end of December Pitt took Malmesbury into his confidence: 'Mr. Pitt said that he had revolved the great question of his *coming forward* again and again in his mind, and that the result of his most serious deliberation was, that it was not yet time.' The government had recently shown an energy, vigour and spirit, which, in spite of his misgivings about its competence, persuaded him to wait. He

* See p. 126.

could not act 'from what he supposed to be the character and intentions of the Ministers' but must judge from their actions. Any other course would be 'a dereliction of character, and . . . a breach of faith.' Pitt would not return 'till he saw that either the audacity of Bonaparte, or a relapse to concession and yielding' made it his 'most bounden duty' to do so. He repeated to Malmesbury the opinion he had given during a conversation in the previous April, that he must differentiate 'between maritime and Continental power'. The Continent being 'at least for the moment, beyond the reach of our interference', Britain must concentrate on resisting any attempt by Napoleon to erode British naval strength: 'all and every act that tends to his maritime aggrandizement, in whatever shape it appears . . . we *must* protect against, and if that will not do, *act*. By this I mean any attempt to take possession of Holland and its Colonies, or of Portugal, and above all, any attempt to break in upon our power and establishments in India.' [563]

Pitt's long absence from Westminster, and his more recent retirement from his appointed position as counsellor emeritus, appeared to leave a vacuum that political gossips were quick to fill. There was talk of a coalition between Fox and Addington, and of a new ministry to be led by Grenville; but both ideas were impracticable. Pitt had exchanged his position of Prime Minister in retirement for one of Prime Minister in waiting. Addington's government could not be expected to survive for long without Pitt, and, while he lived, no alternative government could stand. Even Sheridan, in a speech in May condemning Pitt for increasing the power of the Crown and injuring the privileges of the Constitution and the people, had admitted, 'If ever there was a man formed and fitted by nature to benefit his country and to give it lustre, he is such a man.' [564] Addington was not, however, anxious to relinquish power. Suspicions that he had been personally involved in a campaign to malign Pitt had been strengthened by a scurrilous attack that appeared in *The Times* on 2 December. This was generally supposed to have been inspired, if not written, by Hiley Addington in revenge for a stream of invective against the Prime Minister issued by Canning. Under such assaults from their most devoted supporters, the lifelong friendship between Pitt and Addington was crushed.

In January 1803, in response to repeated requests, Pitt met Addington twice in Richmond. With some hesitancy and evident embarrassment, Addington broached the subject of Pitt's return to office. Pitt replied that in the event of it being thought necessary that he should do so, he would first require to know the King's wishes. A few days later he retired to Walmer. Within a month he was again ill, suffering from 'a bilious attack and gout'. Fox, lacking any worthy opponent at Westminster, wrote to his nephew, 'Pitt is ill with his gout at Walmer—I believe *really*, but half the world says *sham*. There seems to be a sort of deadness in the house of commons, worse even than in the worst times in the House of Lords.' [565]

Pitt, meanwhile, was having difficulty in holding his supporters in check. He had already warned Rose against attacking the government on his behalf. In February he was subjected to an eight-page letter from Canning, described by Malmesbury as '*fortiter in re*, but not *suaviter in modo;* too admonitory, and too fault-finding for even Pitt's very good-humoured mind to bear.' [566] Pitt did not reply. He remained at Walmer, the victim of intermittent bilious attacks and gout.

On 19 March Lord Melville arrived at Walmer armed with Addington's proposals. They were simple to the point of imbecility: Pitt should join the government as Chancellor of the Exchequer; Addington would step down to be Secretary of State for Home Affairs; and Pitt's elder brother, the 'late' Lord Chatham, should become First Lord of the Treasury and Prime Minister. If Addington supposed that fraternal devotion would be enough to persuade Pitt to accept this remarkable concoction as suitable medicine for the nation's ills, he was to be swiftly corrected. Pitt was under no illusions about his brother's capabilities: Chatham was not entirely incompetent but he was incurably indolent. Pitt replied coolly that the Prime Minister must control the Cabinet and the national finances; he must also enjoy the confidence of the King. He would return, at the command of the King, as Prime Minister, or he would not return at all.

Three weeks later Pitt and Addington met at Charles Long's house in Bromley. Their negotiations, which were carried on for five days, came to nothing. Pitt repeated that he was willing to form a new administration if requested to do so by the King and with Addington's agreement, but declined to commit himself to a government that would exclude Grenville, Windham, and Spencer, to whom Addington objected. Addington wrote to Pitt that his Cabinet colleagues could not agree 'to restore to a place in their councils all those persons whose opinions they considered to be hostile to the interests and peace of the country.' Pitt replied in two sentences: 'I have received your letter of the 13th. It requires nothing but a simple acknowledgement.' The next day he relented, and explained his position in greater detail; but not, as he said, to reopen discussion, which he considered closed, but 'to have an *exact record* of what has passed . . . that there should exist an authentic document which could leave no room for doubt.' After stating that he had given no authority to Addington to discuss any formal proposal with his Cabinet, he set down his recollection of their conversation. 'The subject', he wrote, 'originally began by your having intimated to me a wish that I would resume the part I had before held in His Majesty's Councils (I would not become a member of them in any other). . . . To this I replied, that if called upon by His Majesty, and in that case only, I was ready to resume the office I had held. . . . I distinctly said that till I was made acquainted with the King's pleasure I could say nothing binding, nothing *officially* communicable; this I repeated, and that what I might say to you was as from friend to friend.' He stressed again his refusal to discuss names or appointments, and that he would not do so until he knew the King's wishes.[567]

This account did not accord with Addington's.[568] He insisted that as early as January Pitt had shown a readiness to return to office; and that they had discussed in detail the disposal of offices, Pitt insisting upon the restoration of Grenville, Spencer and Windham to their previous positions. On 20 April Addington gave his own account of the affair to the King, who expressed resentment against the high-handed manner of his former Prime Minister. Pitt repeatedly asked Addington to show his own letter to the King. This Addington did on the 27th. George III brushed it aside and refused to read it. Addington's last hope of strengthening his administration was ended, and, while he was struggling to exclude from office all those who had opposed the Treaty of Amiens, his own government was being driven inexorably into repudiating it.

On 18 May Britain declared war on France.

Passive Opposition
1803-1805

NAPOLEON was not ready for war. With the new year had come news from St Domingue. Toussaint L'Ouverture, the leader of the island's blacks, had set up a constitutional government, declaring himself president for life. He had been captured by treachery and sent to France, where he died in prison, but the Haitian climate had taken an appalling revenge. While the blacks hid in the mountains, the French army was decimated by famine and fever. Among the 25,000 dead was their commander, Napoleon's brother-in-law, General Charles Leclerc*. While the greater part of his naval strength was occupied in the Caribbean, Napoleon was not anxious to be drawn into a renewal of a maritime war. On the other hand, the removal of the British from Malta was essential to his plans for a second assault against Egypt and the conquest of India. His attempts to achieve this aim by enlisting the aid of the Tsar Alexander having failed, he resorted to bombast and bluff. He deliberately made known his intentions towards Egypt, insulted and threatened Lord Whitworth, the British Ambassador in Paris, and demanded that the British press, which almost daily published offensive articles about him,

---

* He had married Maria Paulina (Carlotta) Bonaparte in 1797. Soon after his death she married Prince Camillo Borghese.

should be censored. Nothing could have been better calculated to unite the British people behind the government's resistance to Napoleon's demands.

At the end of February the Cabinet's instructions to Whitworth reflected a stubborn determination not to evacuate Malta until the island's independence was secured, the integrity of the Turkish empire guaranteed, and restitution made for the violations of the Treaties of Lunéville and Amiens. Napoleon had never admitted that British acceptance of the terms of the Treaty of Amiens had been founded on the assumption that he would abide by those of Lunéville. To the British government, violation of one automatically violated the other. Napoleon affected to believe that the two treaties were separate and unrelated agreements concluded with different adversaries, and that the affairs of Europe were no concern of Britain's. The immediate cause of the war was the British refusal to leave Malta, but the true cause was the dawning realization in England that Napoleon's definition of peace was conquest without war.

Napoleon wished to avoid war with Britain until his preparations were completed and the French fleet could be withdrawn from the Caribbean, but above all he was determined that, if there must be war, it should be against Britain alone. His acquisition of the Louisiana Territory from Spain in 1800 had offered a serious threat to American trade passing down the Mississippi through the great port of New Orleans. Robert Livingstone, the United States minister to France, made no secret of his government's alarm at the prospect of the French becoming masters of Louisiana and the Floridas, and there were signs that the Americans were preparing to ally themselves with Britain in defence of their trade. Napoleon hurriedly solved this problem by selling the territory, more than one million square miles of land, for the derisory price of £15,000,000. This transaction, in direct contravention of the Treaty of Ildefonso, released Napoleon from an obligation to defend territory that, without strong French bases in the West Indies, would be indefensible against either the Americans on land or a British invasion supported by superior naval strength. It was a masterly strategic stroke that simultaneously rid France of a liability and removed the threat of an Anglo-American alliance.

In a last bid to gain time, Napoleon obtained agreement from the

411

Tsar that Russia would mediate over Malta, but the offer came too late. In spite of the reluctance of the British to offend the one great power that might help them in a war in Europe, Whitworth was recalled. 'It appears', Lord Malmesbury wrote, 'that Russia has been gained over—won by France by corruption and flattery—lost by us by indolence, incapacity and ignorance. It is the manner in which Russia has declared herself favourable to France that has terminated the discussion on war. Had Russia been neutral or passive Bonaparte would have given way.' [569] If Malmesbury was right, the British government's mistake was a fortunate one. There could be little doubt that war with France was inevitable, and any postponement was to Britain's disadvantage. In spite of St Vincent's stringent economies the Royal Navy was still the greatest power at sea. When war was declared on 18 May the French had only two seaworthy ships of the line in harbour at Brest, and the squadrons at Toulon and Rochefort were in little better shape. While the French fleet was dispersed across the Atlantic, the British regained command of the Channel, the North Sea and the Mediterranean.

On 20 May Pitt returned to the House of Commons. The Whig member of parliament and diarist Thomas Creevey wrote in disgust, 'This damned fellow Pitt has taken his seat and is here.' Next day he added with glee, 'I really think Pitt is done: his face is no longer red, but yellow; his looks are dejected; his countenance I think much changed and fallen, and every now and then he gives a hollow cough. Upon my soul, hating him as I do, I am almost moved to pity to see his fallen greatness.' Rose described him as 'perfectly well and in good spirits', but Pitt told Pretyman, 'I came to Town a good deal unwell, and not very equal to the Fatigue of anxious discussions in the House.' [570]

He had suffered another bereavement. Hester, Dowager Countess of Chatham, had died on 3 April at Burton Pynsent. The funeral was held at Westminster Abbey, where her body was buried beside that of her husband. Pitt had seen little of his mother during the previous few years, and he was a poor correspondent, but there is no doubt of his attachment to her and he talked of his grief to Rose, who was staying with him at Walmer when he received the news. Soon after his return to London, where he had taken a modest house in York Place, 'care, fatigue and anxiety . . . brought on a renewal of the former unpleasant Symptoms.' Farquhar was distressed to find that

'He could retain nothing on his stomach, nor could he sit down to dinner without being sick.' Pitt's attendance in the House of Commons, and the irregularity of his meals, aggravated the symptoms and Farquhar prescribed 'a hot luncheon with 1 or 2 glasses of good brisk Ale' every day at two o'clock. Remembering old Addington's prohibition against ale, Pitt objected to this diet, but 'with his usual good nature he consented to make the trial'. The use of mild alcohol to ease physical symptoms of alcohol poisoning was again palliative.[571]

On 23 May the House of Commons debated the declaration of war. Addington, who had chosen to make his appearance in the full fig of commander of the Woodley Cavalry, was greeted with shouts of derisive laughter. Pitt's speech, his first for a year, and delivered from his place in the third row behind the government front bench, was aimed, as Canning remarked, to be fired over the government's heads. He was cheered when he rose to speak, and when he sat down eighty minutes later there was loud and prolonged applause. His speech was, as Malmesbury reported, 'strong in support of war, but . . . silent as to Ministers, and his silence either as to blame or praise was naturally construed into negative censure.' Creevey was appalled: 'Then came the great fiend himself—Pitt—who, in the elevation of his tone of mind and composition, in the infinite energy of his style, the miraculous perspicuity and fluency of his periods outdid (as it was thought) all former performances of his. Never, to be sure, was there such an exhibition: its effect was dreadful.' Little remains of this speech, which, unlike Fox's, was scarcely reported. Fox, condemning the government and the declaration of war, made what was generally agreed to be the greatest speech of his life, but the Opposition, supported by Wilberforce, could muster only 67 votes against 398 for the government. More than two hundred of the members had never heard Pitt before, and he treated them to a display of all his dazzling ability. Sheridan wrote to Lady Bessborough, 'Detesting the Dog as I do, I cannot withdraw this just tribute to the Scoundrel's talents.'[572]

Pitt's speech was a great performance, but for all his resolution he was unable to disguise the effects of his illness. John Ward wrote in distress, 'His physical powers are, I am seriously concerned to remark, perceptibly impaired. He exhibits strong marks of bad health. Though his voice has not lost any of its depth and harmony, his lungs seem to labour in those prodigious sentences which he once thundered forth without effort.' [573] The strain of office was also beginning to affect Addington. He had never imagined himself as leader of a wartime government without Pitt's participation and support and he was conscious of the general opinion, expressed in the *Morning Chronicle* of 1 June, that 'so many great and able men' should not be out of office in a time of crisis when the government was in the hands of men 'neither recommended by connexion, abilities, nor experience'. He was reported to be drinking as much as twenty glasses of wine at dinner to fortify himself for the conflict of parliamentary debate. [574]

Pitt remained in London for the greater part of June and took part in the budget debate opened on the 13th. Having abolished Pitt's income tax in 1802, Addington found himself without sufficient funds to meet the expenses of war and was obliged to reintroduce it. In doing so he made an important amendment to the methods of collection. Tax-payers were no longer invited to make their own assessments—in Addington's words, they no longer had to 'decide between their interest and their duty'—but income was, wherever possible, taxed at source. Tax was set at one shilling in the pound, with the first £150 of income exempt, and raised more than Pitt's had produced at double that rate. Addington lacked Pitt's mastery of financial affairs but he was the true author of the modern system of income tax.

In July Pitt withdrew to Walmer and remained there until October. As Lord Warden of the Cinque Ports he had raised a corps of 3,000 volunteers, which he drilled and exercised tirelessly. His health improved and, although he wore one boot larger than the other to accommodate his gouty foot, he took his duties as colonel as seriously as he had taken his political life, and played an active part in all the manoeuvres. Major-General John Moore, with whom he was on terms of some familiarity, visited him in October from Shorncliffe. Pitt said to him, 'On the very first alarm I shall march to aid you, with my Cinque Port regiments, and you have never told me where you will place us.' Moore, whose faith in irregular troops had not been strengthened by his experience of the reinforcements sent to Abercromby's command in Holland, replied, 'Do you see that hill? You and yours shall be drawn up on it, where you will make a most formidable appearance to the enemy, while I with the soldiers, shall be fighting on the beach.' [575] Pitt's reaction to this instruction is not recorded.

Towards the end of the summer Pitt's life at Walmer was transformed by the arrival of his niece, Lady Hester Stanhope. Charles, Lord Mahon * had succeeded his father as 3rd Earl Stanhope in 1786. In the same year the friendship between the brothers-in-law had cooled when Stanhope opposed Pitt's proposals for a Sinking Fund. His active support of the French Revolution had led to a permanent estrangement, and during the following years Stanhope's behaviour had become increasingly unpredictable and peculiar. His children were terrified of him and escaped from his control at the earliest opportunity. Believing in manual labor, he had apprenticed two of his sons to a blacksmith and a shoemaker, and his daughter Hester was regularly dismissed from the great house at Chevening to tend turkeys on the common. For some years Hester had taken refuge with her grandmother, the Dowager Countess of Chatham, at Burton Pynsent. After Lady Chatham's death she was homeless. Pitt surprised himself and dumbfounded his friends by inviting her to make her home at Walmer Castle.

It was an extraordinary gesture. Some years earlier he had told Hester's brother, 'Under no circumstances could I offer her a home in my own house',[576] and he had good reason for finding such a suggestion disagreeable. The presence of any woman in his house was unwelcome, implying a total change in his way of life; but Hester would be a particularly tiresome distraction. At twenty-seven she was tall, handsome and headstrong. She held firm opinions, and possessed a sharp tongue and inexhaustible energy. It was generally assumed that Pitt's spontaneous generosity had, once again, driven him into ill-considered action that he would soon regret. To everyone's astonishment the arrangement turned out to be an unqualified success. Hester was generous and tender-hearted; and she was also intelligent, witty, vivacious, eloquent and an excellent mimic. She became devoted to her uncle. She enjoyed the almost exclusively male company at Walmer, and succeeded, as few women could have done, in being accepted as part of it. 'There are', she wrote in November, 'generally three or four men staying in the house, and we dine eight or ten almost every other day. Military and

* Married to Pitt's sister, Lady Hester Pitt, in 1774, see p. 47.

naval characters are constantly *welcome* here; women are not, I suppose, because they do not form any part of our society.' [577] Specially welcome at Walmer were General John Moore, for whom Hester shared her uncle's admiration, her step-brothers Charles and James, and their closest friend, William Napier.

While Pitt, at Walmer, went through 'the fatigue of a *drill-sergeant* . . . parade after parade, at fifteen or twenty miles distant from each other', [578] Addington was enthusiastically raising an army to repel the expected invasion. The Military Service Bill, passed in July, provided for the enrollment and training of volunteers between the ages of seventeen and fifty-five. The appeal was embarrassingly successful. By the first week in September, in what Addington described as 'an insurrection of loyalty' [579] more than 350,000 recruits had swelled the ranks of the Militia. There were no arms for more than a small fraction of them. Recruitment in several counties had to be forbidden, and many patriotic volunteers were made to feel importunate and superfluous. The appeal, made without sufficient thought or preparation, was a public blunder that cast even graver doubts on Addington's competence as a war leader.

Addington's strategy was one of inaction. While Napoleon's invincible armies controlled Europe and Britain's navy commanded the seas, there was, he believed, little to be done but wait. Britain needed allies, but the ambassador of the most sympathetic European nation, Austria, had told him, 'We are a giant, but a giant exhausted; and we require time to regain our strength.' [580] Napoleon could not defeat Britain without invasion, and it seemed that Britain's survival depended upon his making the attempt. Addington hoped to destroy the best of the French army in the Channel or on the beaches. Meanwhile, he put in hand plans for the re-conquest of French possessions in the West Indies.

Throughout the summer and autumn of 1803, while Addington's government struggled to disentangle the chaos caused by the Military Service Act, Napoleon directed his energies towards the building and assembly of his invasion fleet. Roads were constructed; a chain of gun batteries was erected along the coast to protect the landing craft being brought from building yards all over France to the main point of assembly at Boulogne, where the harbour had to be enlarged to accommodate them; subsidiary anchorages were created; and troops were massed at selected Channel ports. Napoleon planned to embark 160,000 troops in 3,000 barges, and the best intelligence indicated that he would make his assault in the third week of October. In retrospect it seems incredible that the greatest military genius of his time should have believed that keelless shallow-draught barges, helpless against adverse winds and tides, could cross the Channel, even in fog, under the guns of the Royal Navy. St Vincent, hastily reconstructing the navy he had decimated by premature economies, proclaimed his confidence that they could not: 'I do not say the French cannot come. I only say they cannot come by water.' [581] Part of the French fleet was immobilized under the blockade of Brest, L'Orient, Rochefort and Toulon. The rest, withdrawn from the West Indies, had been unable to reach French harbours and were bottled up in neutral Spanish ports. Nothing could be achieved by the French until at least one of the blockaded squadrons was able to escape and help to release the others.

Pitt remained at Walmer, refusing to leave his post while wind and tide favoured invasion, until December, when he made his appearance in the House of Commons to criticize the government's military preparations. Many of his suggestions for the improvement of recruitment and training were accepted, and he returned to Kent for Christmas. He was still not ready to join the Opposition, but he was concerned and irritated by Addington's supine defensive attitude, and he was subjected to growing pressure from the discreditable campaigns managed by Canning on the one side and Hiley Addington on the other. On 5 January 1804 he wrote in confidence to Wilberforce, 'it will be necessary for me pretty soon to make up my mind on the line to pursue . . . before I form any final decision, I shall much wish to consult yourself and a few others whose opinions I most value.' [582] He held discussions with Grenville, but could not be persuaded to use his power to defeat the government. Grenville, incredibly, allied himself with Fox and took Windham with him.

In February the King again fell ill, showing the familiar and disturbing signs of agitation and mental derangement. Acting on their promise, given to their father after his previous illness, the Dukes of Kent and Cumberland refused to allow the Willis brothers to see him. George III was treated by Dr Samuel Foart Simmons, physician to St Luke's Hospital for Lunatics. In attendance were also Sir Lucas Pepys, Sir Francis Milman, Dr Henry Reynolds and Dr William Heberden Jnr. Although a bulletin was issued on 17

February announcing that the King was out of danger, he suffered from frequent relapses, probably exacerbated by Simmons's treatment, which included daily confinement in a straitjacket, and his recovery was delayed until August. On 19 February Malmesbury called on Pitt and discussed with him the dangers of invasion and the threat to national security posed by the King's illness and the renewed prospect of a Regency under the Prince of Wales. Pitt made it clear that he would hold 'no communication, no discourse whatever, with the present Administration', and that he would continue his constructive criticism, but he declined to make the removal of the government the primary object of his endeavours.[583]

Three weeks later, as the Fox and Grenville parties drew together, Pitt gave his word that if he were called upon to form a new administration he would name Fox for senior office; but he added fair warning that he expected the King to proscribe Fox and that he must yield to the King's decision. At the end of March Pitt made up his mind. He wrote to Melville of his conviction that every week that Addington's government was protracted increased the dangers to the country.[584] His refusal to take the lead in active opposition could no longer be justified. He cannot have been unaware that the coalition of Fox and Grenville was coming to be recognized as the alternative government, although the King would not accept it and, without Pitt's support, it could not command a satisfactory majority. If he were not to give up all thoughts of returning to office, he could not afford to delay his return to regular attendance at Westminster, and in open opposition.

Addington could govern with Pitt's support; he was even prepared to do so without it; but he could not stand up against Pitt, Fox and Grenville in opposition. Under pressure he soon wilted, becoming indecisive, mistrustful and neurotic, scenting treachery and persecution on every side. His Cabinet colleagues floundered between loyalty and the desire to escape from a failing ministry. As his majorities in the House of Commons dwindled, Addington's grip on the Cabinet weakened. On 19 April he advised George III to commission Lord Eldon *, who had become Lord Chancellor after the dismissal of Loughborough in 1801, to consult with Pitt. Four days later, in a debate on the army, Pitt led the Opposition in a

* Sir John Scott, created Baron Eldon in 1799.

merciless attack on government policies. Addington's majority sank to thirty-seven and he resigned.

Meanwhile, Pitt's negotiations with the King had failed to produce any solution satisfactory to either of them. He had written a well reasoned and temperate letter, explaining his actions and making plain his hope of being permitted to form an administration that would unite 'as large a proportion as possible of the weights and talents and connections, drawn without exception from parties of all descriptions, and without reference to former differences and divisions'. For this purpose he proposed to consult Fox and Grenville. The tone of the King's reply was far from conciliatory. He deplored Pitt's antipathy towards Addington, who had 'the greatest claim to approbation from his King and Country for . . . handsomely coming forward . . . when the most ill-digested and dangerous proposition was brought forward by the enemies of the Established Church.' He required 'strong assurances' that Pitt would give unconditional support to the Test Act, 'the palladian of our Church Establishment'. He also expressed his astonishment that Pitt 'should for one moment harbour the thought of bringing such a man' as Fox to his notice. If he persisted in this determination to offer office to Fox and Grenville, the King could not 'avail himself of the ability of Mr Pitt'. Pitt loyally defended Grenville and affirmed his belief in the 'propriety and rectitude' of his proposals for Catholic Emancipation but he accepted that he was bound by 'both a personal and public duty to abstain from pressing that measure'. He requested a private audience at which he might have the opportunity to explain his planned administration. He was determined to attempt to overcome the King's objections to Fox and Grenville. If the King would not receive him, he wrote, 'I cannot retain any hope that my feeble services can be employed in any manner advantageous to your Majesty's affairs or satisfactory to my own mind.' [585]

Pitt was granted his audience on 7 May. Although he had seen the King on several occasions at levees, it was three years since they had met in private and Pitt was concerned to know from the physicians whether their patient's health might be endangered by this encounter. Having obtained satisfactory assurances from them, he was received by the King and spent three hours with him. Later, Pitt told Rose that he had congratulated George III on looking better than at the time of his recovery in 1801. [586] 'That', the King replied, 'is

419

not to be wondered at. I was then on the point of parting with an old friend; I am now about to regain one.' He was not yet fully recovered from his latest illness but he was rational and as obstinate as ever. He agreed to accept the Grenvilles and even Fox's friends, but nothing would persuade him to admit Fox. Pitt's plan for a government uniting the talents of all parties was thus checked by George III, but it was Grenville who destroyed it. Fox received the news of his exclusion with resignation and generosity, and undertook not to use his influence to prevent his friends from joining the new administration. Grenville, on the other hand, refused to join any government from which Fox was excluded, and he was followed by Windham and Spencer. The party that had united in the national interest in 1794 was split, at a time of even greater national crisis, into three groups led by Pitt, Grenville and Addington. Pitt was left to patch up a Cabinet from the remaining fragments. It was not the ministry he had hoped for, but it was, in spite of its weaknesses, superior to the one it replaced. On 18 May, the day Pitt returned to office, Napoleon had himself crowned Emperor in Paris.

Grenville's rejection of office was deplorable. Fox had expected the King's refusal to employ him, and Grenville cannot have been surprised at it. If it hurt his pride to know that Pitt had had to plead with George III for the inclusion of the Grenvilles, it might also have been obvious to him that his own refusal would hurt Pitt more than the King and that the interests of the country would not be best served if neither he, nor Spencer nor Windham, served in the government. He seems to have believed that if Pitt had refused to form an administration without Fox the King would have yielded, but George III was not prepared to admit Fox while any other alternative remained. He still retained a touching faith in Addington and would certainly have used all his influence to support him in preference to any government that included Fox. There is no justification for the charge that Pitt made no attempt to persuade the King. On the contrary, he abandoned the attempt only when he realized that it could not succeed. Pitt's decision was, as usual, dictated by the national interest, in which a crucial consideration was the King's health. Although he was able to conduct business, it was reported as late as 13 June that the King's mind was still easily agitated and 'nothing that can affect his prejudices or private feelings is proposed to Him'.[587]

The government that took office in May was not, by any stretch of the imagination, the powerful coalition that was needed, and it was led by a Prime Minister who was the enfeebled shadow of former greatness. Pitt's health had benefited from the long rest, but the improvement was superficial and temporary. It was not long before the strain of office, his anxiety for the country, and the opposition of the factions led by Fox, Grenville and Addington, drove him to fight dejection and fatigue in the only way he knew. Young William Napier, a frequent guest at Pitt's house in the autumn, wrote that Pitt would 'return to dinner exhausted and seemed to require wine, port, of which he generally drank a bottle, or nearly so, in a rapid succession of glasses'.[588]

In contrast to Addington's, Pitt's war policy was aggressive. He was convinced that a long-term defensive attitude merely enabled the enemy to forge the weapons of victory and choose the ground on which it was to be won. His first priority was the defence of Britain against invasion. His second was the revival of alliances, without which the British army was powerless to act in Europe. In both of these purposes he was severely hampered by the irrational behaviour of the King, who meddled with arrangements that he had already approved, issued orders which he had not discussed with his ministers, and succeeded, in his confusion of mind, in creating an atmosphere of general muddle, uncertainty and irritation. The ailing monarch's unpredictable conduct, exasperating to Pitt and his Cabinet, also discouraged the formation of alliances. The Tsar and the Emperor were disinclined to attach their countries by treaty to one which might, at any time, fall under the rule of a dissolute prince and his Francophile friends.

Pitt's most urgent task was to revitalize the army and navy. By a series of measures devised to attract men into the regular army from the overstrength Militia, he tried to reverse the trend set by Addington's incompetence. At the Admiralty, Melville applied himself to making good the shortages resulting from St Vincent's economies. He made no secret of his opinion that the navy was in a deplorable state, and Minto thought him 'as likely to repair the evil by despatch and activity as any man that could have been placed at the head of the Admiralty'. Grenville described him contemptuously as 'learning the conduct of the navy by studying the manoeuvres of the bathing machines at Worthing'.[589]

Throughout the year Napoleon had made desperate attempts to extricate his scattered naval squadrons from British blockades at Brest, Rochefort, Cadiz, Toulon, the Texel and Ferrol, but the British commanders were too experienced to be drawn away from their stations, and the French fleet remained dispersed and impotent. Sure of his success, Napoleon had caused a medal to be struck to commemorate the *Descente en Angleterre*. With a fine imperial disregard for accuracy it was inscribed '*Frappé à Londres en 1804*'. The threat of invasion remained real, but it could not be carried out while the Royal Navy controlled the Channel. Napoleon determined to strengthen the fleets at his disposal by forcing Spain back into the war. Under duress the reluctant Charles IV agreed to pay France an annual subsidy of 72,000,000 francs (a sum one-fifth greater than the price paid by the United States for the Louisiana Territory), to coerce Portugal, and to allow French crews to travel overland to man the French ships blockaded at Ferrol. The Spanish response to British complaints was rearmament. It appeared that Charles IV and Godoy were about to abandon the last pretence of neutrality by offering France the co-operation of the Spanish fleet.

Pitt determined to offer some discouragement to this unwelcome alliance. The British Ambassador at Madrid, Hookham Frere, was instructed to demand the demobilization of the Spanish fleet. Meanwhile, the blockade of Ferrol was tightened to prevent the sailing of either French or Spanish ships, and four frigates were detached to seize the treasure fleet returning from Mexico to Cadiz laden with silver to finance the equipment of the Spanish fleet. The escorts fought, one of the ships blew up, and 300 Spaniards were killed. On 12 December Spain declared war on Britain. The attempt at coercion had failed, but there was some compensation to be found in war against Spain. It was less complicated than a formal diplomatic minuet with a nation which claimed the protection of neutrality while its treasury and fleet were at the disposal of the enemy.

There were further compensations in the changing attitudes of Russia and Austria. By the autumn the Tsar Alexander was ready to sign a treaty to enforce a French withdrawal from Italy, Holland and North Germany. By the end of the year the Austrians had agreed to join in imposing a reasonable peace. These alliances were tenuous and there was no immediate prospect of their being translated into a co-ordinated military plan, but Pitt was content to lay the foundations, confident that Napoleon's impatient appetite for empire would complete the work.

While he strengthened Britain's defences and began the slow construction of new alliances, Pitt received frequent and uncomfortable reminders of the instability of his administration. Divided, the power of Grenville, Fox and Addington was formidable; but their united opposition threatened the government's survival. If the ministry could not be strengthened by the accession of Grenville or Fox, the Opposition must be weakened by the removal of Addington, who commanded a personal following of 68 votes. In December Pitt arranged a reconciliation. In spite of his reluctance to leave the House of Commons,* Addington was persuaded in January 1805 to accept the title of Viscount Sidmouth and the office of Lord President of the Council. This appointment restored Pitt's sagging majorities but it did nothing to make good the serious deficiencies of the Cabinet, and disgusted some of his most loyal friends, notably Canning and Rose. Canning offered his resignation from his place as Treasurer of the Navy but finally allowed himself to be persuaded. Walking with Wilberforce in the park, Pitt said, 'I am sure that you are glad to hear that Addington and I are at one again. . . . I think they are a little hard on us in finding fault at our making it up again, when we have been friends from our childhood, and our fathers were so before us, while they say nothing to Grenville for uniting with Fox, though they have been fighting all their lives.' [590]

Sheridan expressed his frustration and anger in the House of Commons. 'The Right Honourable Gentleman', he declared, 'went into office alone;—but lest the government should become too full of vigour from his support, he thought it proper to beckon some of the weakness of the former administration. He, I suppose, thought that the Ministry became, from his support, like spirits above proof, and required to be diluted; that like gold refined to a certain degree, it would be unfit for use without a certain mixture of alloy; that the administration would be too brilliant and dazzle the House, unless

---

* Addington had been pressed by George III to accept a profusion of peerages—Earl of Banbury, Viscount Wallingford and Baron Reading—but he had declined them all, accepting only the tenancy of White Lodge, Richmond Park, which the King had bestowed on him in 1801, and a cumbersome royal portrait by Sir William Beechey.

he called back a certain part of the mist and fog of the last administration to render it tolerable to the eye.' [591] Henry Addington, said Canning, was like the measles: everyone had him once. The disappointment of the Opposition served only to underline the adroitness of Pitt's manoeuvre. His powers, with his health, were failing; but as a master of practical politics he still had no equal.

XXIX

The Third Coalition
1805

IN JANUARY 1805 two men whose influence with the King had contributed to Pitt's resignation made their own final exits—Lord Loughborough, created Earl of Rosslyn as a reward for a life of scheming ambition, died at Windsor. The King pronounced a fitting epitaph: 'He has not left a greater knave behind him in all my dominions.' [592] The death of John Moore, Archbishop of Canterbury, created a vacancy that Pitt was determined to secure for his own nominee. Two years earlier Bishop Pretyman had inherited an estate on condition that he assumed the name of his benefactor, and it was George Pretyman Tomline, Bishop of Lincoln, that Pitt recommended to succeed Dr Moore as Primate of All England. The King rejected this proposal out of hand and, after a furious argument, appointed Dr Charles Manners-Sutton. Pitt contemplated resigning. Tomline, whose natural pomposity was in no way diminished by the knowledge that he owed his elevation to the bishopric of Lincoln to his pupil, wrote to Rose: '. . . this defeat may be of serious mischief upon public grounds. And indeed I know persons of great consequence who will consider Mr Pitt's acquiescence as very uncreditable to him.' [593]

There were probably far more who rejoiced. Tomline had an

unenviable reputation for sanctimonious self-esteem and casuistry, and his long intimacy with Pitt had been the subject of uncharitable speculation. A contemporary described him as 'the thin figure of emaciated divinity, divided between religion and decorum; anxious to produce some truths, and conceal others; at once concerned for *fundamental* points of various kinds; ever at the *bottom* of *things*.' [594] Pitt's display of peevishness at the King's refusal to translate Tomline to the See of Canterbury earned him a rebuke from John Villiers *, Comptroller of the Royal Household. 'You hardly know', he wrote on 10 February, 'the degree of frustration these Contests [with the King] produce. Depend upon it, the present system of little personal schemes on his part, of occasional contested concessions on yrs., will overset his health.' [595]

Pitt's loyalty to his friends was more severely tried when the report of an inquiry into the administration of the navy, instigated by St Vincent during Addington's ministry, was published in February. The evidence showed that Alexander Trotter, Paymaster of the Navy, had speculated in public funds. These speculations, which had involved sums as large as £1,000,000 at a time, covered a period of more than ten years. All the transactions had been successful, and the Commissioners stated fairly that they had caused no loss to the government since the accounts of the navy had been regularly balanced by the repayment of borrowings. The Treasurer of the Navy from 1782 to 1801 had been Henry Dundas, now Lord Melville and First Lord of the Admiralty. The report of the Commissioners contained thinly veiled accusations that he had been a party to Trotter's speculation and had profited from it. In evidence, Melville had admitted to having borrowed money from Trotter. The sums he borrowed were represented as being small, but the largest was alleged to have been £30,000. He had also diverted funds intended for the navy to other uses, and refused, for reasons of security, to specify how they had been spent.

The evidence against Melville was inconclusive. It was clear that he had been culpably negligent in his supervision of the navy accounts, but he was not alone in being notoriously careless of money and, during the long period of his Treasurership, he had held other more senior appointments, including those of Home Secretary and

* Succeeded his elder brother as 3rd Earl of Clarendon in 1824.

Secretary of War, which left him little time for the detailed supervision of smaller departments. The office of Treasurer was effectually a sinecure involving little commerce with the Paymaster apart from occasional conferences. There was no evidence adduced that Melville had, at any time, known the source of the moneys he had borrowed from Trotter, and it was obvious that the funds diverted to other public services, for which he was unable or unwilling to produce proper accounts, had been used to finance the secret service.

On 8 April Samuel Whitbread, the radical Whig son of a nonconformist brewer, moved eleven resolutions of censure against Lord Melville, charging him with malversation. Pitt, urged to abandon Melville to his fate, flatly refused to do so. He knew that a successful vote of censure would damage his own reputation and that of his government, but Melville was one of his oldest friends and he was convinced of his innocence. Advised by his Cabinet that there was no possibility of obtaining a majority for outright rejection of the charges, Pitt agreed to move for a Select Committee of Inquiry. No other course, Sidmouth informed him, would secure the essential votes of the Addington group, without which Melville's impeachment was inevitable. Whitbread introduced his censure motion in a speech lasting three hours. Pitt did not attempt to defend Melville in detail, but declared firmly that the evidence was too flimsy to warrant a vote of censure, and moved for a Select Committee. He was ably supported by Canning, Spencer Perceval and Castlereagh, but Fox, George Ponsonby and Lord Henry Petty * spoke strongly against Melville and it was evident that the verdict of the House would be determined by the votes of the independent members. When Wilberforce rose to speak, Pitt leaned forward on the Treasury Bench to catch his eye. In his first sentence Wilberforce declared his support for Whitbread's motion. The integrity of his conscience was unchallenged, and on a moral issue no speaker was more influential. When the House divided, the votes cast for and against the motion were found to be equal. The Speaker, Charles Abbott, gave his casting vote in favour of censure.

This triumph for the Opposition caused an uproar. A fox-hunting

* Son of Pitt's old political chief, the Marquess of Lansdowne (Lord Shelburne). Lansdowne, who had for some years allied himself with Fox, died a month later at the age of sixty-eight.

427

member gave the 'view-halloo' and there were loud shouts for the Prime Minister's resignation. Malmesbury's son, Lord Fitzharris, left a vivid, if not altogether accurate description of Pitt's reaction:

> I sat wedged close to Pitt himself the night when we were 216 to 216; and the Speaker, Abbott (after looking as white as a sheet, and pausing for ten minutes) gave the casting vote against us. Pitt immediately put on the little cocked hat that he was in the habit of wearing, when dressed for the evening, and jammed it deeply over his forehead, and I definitely saw the *tears trickling down his cheeks*. We heard one or two, such as Colonel Wardle . . . say, they would see 'how Billy looked after it'. A few young ardent followers of Pitt, with myself, locked their arms together, and formed a circle, in which he moved, I believe, *unconsciously* out of the House.[596]

Melville resigned at once from the Admiralty and on 5 May he wrote to Pitt advising him to yield to the Opposition's demands that his name be struck from the list of Privy Councillors. Whitbread's move for impeachment was rejected on 11 June, but two weeks later a second motion to this effect was carried. Nearly a year later, after a trial lasting twelve days, Melville was acquitted on all charges, but the confirmation of his innocence came too late to be of any consolation to Pitt.

The loss of Melville, who withdrew in dignified silence to Scotland, was a grievous blow to Pitt. Although their friendship had cooled in recent years, Melville had remained one of his staunchest personal allies, and his untiring efforts at the Admiralty had done much to restore the strength of the navy. Napoleon reacted characteristically to the news of Melville's downfall. '*Faites faire*', he wrote to his Minister of Finance, '*un petit pamphlet sur l'affaire Melville pour montrer l'immoralité du gouvernement Anglais.*'[597]

To the consternation of Sidmouth, who wished to promote one of his own followers to make room in the Cabinet for another, Pitt appointed Admiral Sir Charles Middleton to be First Lord of the Admiralty with the title of Lord Barham. It was a bold decision which displeased the King and risked an immediate rift in the Cabinet. On 22 April Sidmouth wrote to Pitt, 'I deplore the choice you have made. It will, I fear, have the effect of weakening and lowering the

Government, at a time when it is peculiarly important to give it additional strength, and to raise its character.' [598] The elevation of the government's character that he had in mind was the promotion of his vicious brother Hiley, or of his brother-in-law Charles Bragge Bathurst, both of whom had taken leading parts in vilifying Melville. He offered his resignation, but was persuaded to withdraw it by Pitt's assurance that the appointment of Middleton, in his eightieth year, must be considered temporary. Pitt's choice was not made from perversity or the desire to exclude Sidmouth's adherents from senior office. For many years the ex-Comptroller of the Navy had acted as personal adviser to Pitt and to the First Lord of the Admiralty. As Admiral Sir Charles Middleton he had been known as a fine sailor, a loyal champion of abolition of the slave trade, a leading agriculturalist, and an outstandingly capable naval administrator. As Lord Barham, he displayed the full range of his talents as a strategist and became the architect of the most important naval victory in British history. Creevey, with more acid than judgement, described him as a 'superannuated Methodist'.

While Pitt was struggling to maintain the uneasy coalition that formed his government, he was redoubling his efforts to kindle the damp twigs of European alliance so laboriously assembled during the previous twelve months. It was a measure of his success that Napoleon once more offered to negotiate. On 2 January he wrote to George III, addressing him in the brotherly terms of one emperor to another, proposing peace terms. The King, who regarded French revolutionary liberty as licence, and had no desire to be on terms of either equality or fraternity with Napoleon, left it to Pitt to compose a frigid reply. It was, as Pitt had hoped, Napoleon who set alight the Third Coalition against France. In May he annexed the Ligurian Republic and had himself crowned King of Italy. Frightened and affronted, the Austrians renounced their policy of armed mediation. Three months later they joined the Anglo-Russian alliance. Pitt had already won his first victory. Threatened by the armies of Russia and Austria, Napoleon was obliged to postpone his plans for the invasion of Britain.

As late as the first week in August he had hoped to achieve this object. The British fleet, dispersed in blockading squadrons off Brest, Rochefort, Toulon, Ferrol and Cadiz, battered by winter gales and forced to put in to distant friendly ports for water and provisions, was unable to confine the French. On 11 January a powerful French squadron carrying 3,500 troops had escaped in a snowstorm from Rochefort and sailed to the West Indies. A week later Admiral Pierre Charles de Villeneuve took his fleet of eleven battleships and nine cruisers out of Toulon but was forced back again by storms and the fear of encountering Nelson's fleet in the Mediterranean. Napoleon revised his strategy. In March he issued new instructions: the two most powerful fleets, at Brest and Toulon, were to break out, put to sea without a fight, relieve the blockades of Ferrol and Cadiz, and concentrate in the West Indies, where they would attack the British garrisons. Having drawn the British navy after them, the combined fleet of more than forty ships of the line would return to take control of the Channel, releasing any ships still blockaded in port, and providing an invincible escort for the invasion fleet of 2,000 transports ready to sail from Boulogne.

His plan failed because it took no account of the essential differences in experience and command structure between the French and British navies. The French navy took its instructions from the Emperor, who had no professional understanding of ships or the sea. There was little opportunity for the exercise of individual initiative, and the lapse of time between the issuing of orders and their receipt often nullified their effect. British Admirals, on the other hand, received their instructions from a supreme naval strategist, Lord Barham, and they were expected to interpret and act upon them in the light of experience and local circumstances. British Admirals pursued the enemy, acting on their own understanding of his policy and intentions; they took individual risks that affected the Admiralty's grand strategy; and in time of danger they concentrated their fleets, as if by instinct, at the approaches to the Channel.

Villeneuve broke out from Toulon at the end of March, lifted the blockade of Cadiz, and disappeared with his combined fleet into the Atlantic; but the Brest fleet was held in harbour, the Rochefort fleet returned to port from the West Indies, and the blockade of Ferrol was maintained. Nelson pursued Villeneuve to the West Indies where, finding neither the Brest nor the Rochefort fleets to reinforce him, the French Admiral decided to run for home. On 22 July Villeneuve's fleet was intercepted off Cape Finisterre by fifteen British battleships under Rear-Admiral Sir Robert Calder, but the opportunity to cripple the combined fleet was lost and by the middle of August it was back, with little loss, in harbour at Ferrol.

These manoeuvres of the French fleets achieved nothing of value. From the Admiralty Barham issued clear instructions to counter any move the French might make. Villeneuve's escape nevertheless caused great anxiety. The Allies of the Third Coalition had at last agreed upon a plan of action, and Pitt had not waited for Austria to enter the war to put part of it into effect. On 17 April a fleet of forty-five transports carrying 7,000 troops and escorted by only two battleships had sailed for Malta as part of a plan, co-ordinated with Russia, to secure Sicily and attack the southern mainland while an Austrian army operated in the north of Italy. The British expedition ran the gauntlet of no less than five enemy fleets, two of which were already at sea.

These attacks on the enemy's southern flank were to be orchestrated with a combined Anglo-Russian offensive in northern Europe while a second Austrian army of 70,000 reinforced by 50,000 Russians barred the way to Vienna. The strategy suffered from fatal flaws: it involved offensives on widely separated fronts, inviting Napoleon, working on interior lines, to exploit the advantages of concentration and mobility; it relied heavily on the co-operation of Prussia; and it left the heart of Austria protected by an army that was inadequate for the task until the Russian reinforcements could arrive. It was particularly unfortunate that command of the weakest sector should have been given to General Mack. Without waiting for his Russian allies, Mack moved forward into Bavaria.

Napoleon had already decided to strike at the weak centre of the arc of attack developing in the north, the east and the south. The effectiveness of his campaign depended upon speed and involved great risks. He must force the Austrians to sue for peace before the offensives in north Germany and Italy gained momentum; and he must balance the chance that a violation of the Prussian territory of Ansbach—unavoidable if he were to concentrate his armies fast enough to carry out his plan—would precipitate war with Prussia, against the hope that a crushing defeat of the Austrian army would deter the Prussians from joining the Allies. Keeping open negotiations with Vienna, he instructed his minister in Berlin to bribe the Prussian King with the offer of Hanover. Meanwhile the 'army of

431

England' was on the march from Boulogne, and two more, from Holland and Hanover, were on their way to join it. Before Mikhail Kutusov's Russians could reach it, Mack's army had been encircled and routed at Elchingen by French armies numbering more than 200,000. On 20 October Mack surrendered. The road to Vienna lay open to the French.

In one lightning campaign Napoleon had torn a gaping hole in the main fabric of the Alliance. The offensive in northern Italy was abandoned while the Archduke Charles withdrew his army in a vain attempt to save the Austrian capital. By the end of October the Third Coalition had become defensive. The single success of the Alliance was won by the British navy. In August Villeneuve had put to sea again, pursued by Calder. By the end of the month the combined French and Spanish fleets were once more in Cadiz. This was the opportunity for which Barham had hoped. Villeneuve could not remain in Cadiz, where he would soon run short of supplies, and it could be only a matter of weeks before he was ordered to challenge British control of the Mediterranean and obstruct British and Russian operations in the south of Italy.

Nelson was at home at Merton when he received orders to report to the Admiralty. There he saw Lord Barham, who appointed him to command of the Mediterranean fleet. Later he had three meetings with Pitt at Downing Street and explained his conviction that victory over the enemy fleet was not enough: nothing short of annihilation could win the war at sea. At the end of the last of these meetings, on 6 September, Pitt escorted Nelson to his carriage, a mark of respect, as the Admiral noted with pride, that he might not have extended to a royal prince. Six days later, while waiting in an anteroom to see Castlereagh, Nelson met Major-General Sir Arthur Wellesley, lately returned from India and a series of triumphant victories in the Maratha war. Nearly thirty years later the Duke of Wellington remembered his first impression of Nelson's 'light and trivial character', of a style 'vain and silly'; [599] but by the end of their conversation he had changed his opinion. Nelson 'talked like an officer and a statesman . . . he was really a very superior person'. On 14 September Nelson was in Portsmouth, where Canning and George Rose had joined a great crowd to see him leave. On the 16th he set sail in the Victory.

On 20 October, while General Mack surrendered with 30,000

Austrian troops to Napoleon at Ulm, Villeneuve's fleet of thirty-three ships of the line was at sea. Nelson, having deliberately allowed his enemy to clear the harbour and set sail for the Straits of Gibraltar, attacked on the 21st off Cape Trafalgar. In an action lasting nearly five hours the combined French and Spanish fleets were, as he had promised, annihilated. All but eleven ships of the line were destroyed or captured, and of those that escaped to Cadiz none could be repaired to fight again. The first report of the disaster at Ulm reached London on 2 November. Pitt refused to believe it, but next day Malmesbury translated for him a full account that had appeared in a Dutch newspaper. Four days later came the news of Trafalgar. It was greeted in London with relief and gratitude, but the death of Nelson made any public celebration seem inappropriate. 'Great and important as the victory is,' wrote Lord Minto, 'it is bought too dearly . . . we shall want more victories yet, and to whom can we look for them?' [600]

On Saturday 9 November Pitt attended the Lord Mayor's banquet at Guildhall. During the past four years his popularity had waned, but on that day, for the last time, he was welcomed by cheering crowds who unhitched the horses and drew his carriage along Cheapside. In reply to the toast to him as 'The Saviour of Europe', Pitt made one of the shortest and most eloquent speeches of his life: 'I return you many thanks for the honour you have done me; but Europe is not to be saved by any single man. England has saved herself by her exertions, and will, I trust, save Europe by her example.' [601] Courage and hope had not deserted him, but his face bore the marks of stress and exhaustion.

His optimism was genuine. He still believed that Frederick William III might be persuaded to join the Third Coalition, and Napoleon's recent violation of Ansbach had raised hope into expectation. The British expeditionary force to North Germany was on its way and a Russian army was marching to join it. By the end of the year 60,000 British troops were committed to this adventure. Buckingham wrote to Grenville, 'What madness is this if the Ministers are not sure of Prussian co-operation.' [602] It was, indeed, madness. Frederick William's price for his help was Hanover, already occupied by the French. It was unthinkable that any British government should barter George III's heritage for any alliance, and Pitt, aware of the King's precarious health and sanity, could never have considered such a proposal. For Britain the price was too great. The French could buy Prussian neutrality with a promise. Frederick William hesitated just long enough to provide the British with scope for another military disaster.

It would be difficult to overestimate the burden of responsibility and anxiety borne by Pitt. His government was weak, and it was under constant attack in the House of Commons from an Opposition that included Fox, Sheridan, Grey and Windham. In the Lords, too, his position had been weakened. In July Sidmouth had resigned again, and the support of the old Addington group could no longer be relied upon. With few exceptions Pitt's colleagues lacked experience or outstanding ability, and he was obliged to take over much of the business of the Foreign Office and War Office, in addition to his own work as Prime Minister and Chancellor of the Exchequer. Hester Stanhope later described the pace of his life:

> . . . in town, during the sitting of parliament, what a life was his! Roused from sleep (for he was a good sleeper) with a dispatch . . . then down to Windsor; then if he had half an hour to spare, trying to swallow something:—Mr. Adams * with a paper, Mr. Long with another; then Mr. Rose; then, with a little bottle of cordial confection in his pocket, off to the House until three or four in the morning; then home to a hot supper for two or three hours more, to talk over what was to be done next day: and wine, and wine! Scarcely up next morning, when tat-tat-tat—twenty or thirty people one after another. . . . It was enough to kill a man.[603]

A younger man, in prime health and the early summer of his life, might have found the strain intolerable; but Pitt was prematurely aged by exhaustion and disease. He was forcing his mind and his body to peaks of activity that they could no longer support without the aid of alcohol and drugs. Rose wrote of his uneasiness 'for some time past at Sir Walter [Farquhar] drugging him constantly without being quite sure of the Seat of the Complaint'.[604] Farquhar was not entirely to blame. The powerful stimulants prescribed by him were intended to 'prop him up for certain particular occasions . . . not to

---

* William Dacre Adams, Pitt's secretary.

be used *habitually* or *frequently* as their effect wd be prejudicial.' [605] Pitt disregarded the warning.

On 7 December, yielding at last to the urgent and repeated advice of his physician and his friends, Pitt set out for Bath. He was suffering from gout which gave him great pain, 'excessive weakness, and a total debility of digestion'.[606] He hoped that a course of the famous waters would repair his digestion and develop the 'fit' of gout thought to be the necessary preliminary to recovery. He was not, however, able to enjoy the rest and freedom from anxiety that he needed. People crowded to see him *, and he received a stream of visitors bringing State papers and dispatches. He remained cheerful, although he reported that the gout continued 'pretty smartly' and of 'a feverish pulse', and declined Farquhar's offer to attend him at Bath. He was confidently waiting to hear that Prussia had joined the Third Coalition, and that the main Austrian and Russian armies had re-grouped to halt the French, who had entered Vienna on 13 November, in Moravia.

On 19 December the first rumours arrived of a great battle near Olmutz seventeen days earlier. There seemed to be reason to believe that the Allies had won a splendid victory, and successive reports from Amsterdam tended to confirm this. It was not until the 29th that the truth became known. On 2 December Napoleon had crushed the Austrian and Russian armies at Austerlitz. More than 30,000 Allied troops had been killed or taken prisoner, the defeated remnants of both armies were retreating in confusion, and the Austrians had asked for an armistice. The Third Coalition had collapsed. Nothing but the intervention of Prussia could revive it. If Prussia came to terms with France, the British expeditionary force in Hanover might be destroyed.

Pitt's reaction to this appalling news is not known. Wilberforce described him as wearing thereafter 'the Austerlitz look', but he never saw Pitt after the news of the battle had been confirmed. There is the legendary story that Pitt pointed to a map of Europe and said, 'Roll up that map: it will not be wanted these ten years,' but the evidence for it is slight. The reports of Austerlitz trickled through to England slowly and the official dispatches from Austria, which did

---

* One man came 139 miles by a coach to see him and having been gratified immediately returned home.' [607]

435

not reach him until 3 January, represented the battle as a reverse, not a shattering defeat. As late as the second week in January, Pitt still nursed the hope that negotiations with Prussia might succeed and the Third Coalition might yet be saved. He could remain at Bath no longer. On 9 January he set out to travel by easy stages to Bowling Green House on Putney Heath which he had leased in 1803. It was to be his last journey home.

XXX

The Last Journey
1806

WHEN PITT left Bath on 9 January, he had just two weeks to live. He had written to Castlereagh about the negotiations still being pursued in Berlin, and ended, 'My second attack of gout is now subsiding, and I hope to recover from it quicker than the former; but I am sorry to say I have more ground to gain, before I am fit for anything, than I can almost hope to accomplish within a fortnight. Bath is no longer thought of use, and I shall move as soon as I can.'[608] Farquhar, who had joined him at Bath on 4 January, was 'very much shocked at his appearance. He was much emaciated, very weak, feeble and low. He attempted to join the Dinner Table, which at length he did with great difficulty. He eat [sic] very little, but drank some Madeira and Water.' In consultation with Dr John Haygarth, Farquhar decided that the natural waters of Bath should be given up and prescribed five grains of rhubarb, thirty drops of 'Paregoric Elixir' and infusions of Cascarilla.* The gout in Pitt's left foot subsided, and asses' milk, which had proved efficacious on prior occasions, was added to his diet. Farquhar called in Dr William Falconer, physician to Bath

---

* Paregoric Elixir was a camphorated tincture of opium used to relieve pain; Cascarilla, more popularly known as 'bark', is a bitter tonic obtained from the bark of the plant *Croton Eleuteria*.

437

Hospital, who agreed that, although the waters were having a beneficial effect on the gout, Pitt's general state of debility would be best treated by a change of air and his return home. Pitt's own anxiety to do so strongly influenced the doctors in their decision. [609]

On the 8th Falconer and Haygarth 'took the opportunity also of feeling the Stomach and Bowels very particularly; and they certainly afforded Mr Pitt much comfort by the assurance that they could discover no organic mischief. He indeed appeared better.' In spite of these assurances Farquhar remained deeply concerned about his patient's condition: 'his appearance at this time was of a man much worn out. One day his eyes were almost lifeless, and another his voice hollow and weak, while his pulse was remarkably weak, and generally from 100 to 120. After the arrival of Dispatches these Symptoms were always considerably increased. It was remarkable however that when in bed the Pulse ranged from 70 to 84 with a soft skin and without heat.' Any solid food brought on spasms of vomiting, and the only nourishment Pitt could take was an egg beaten up with a teaspoonful of brandy three times a day. At two o'clock in the afternoon of Thursday 9 January, Pitt walked slowly to his carriage, leaning on the arms of his nephew, Captain Charles Stanhope, and General Edmund Phipps*. Farquhar had proposed that they should spend five days on the journey, but Pitt was impatient to be home and, after two nights spent at Marlborough and Reading, and a couple of hours' rest at Lord Camden's House, he reached Putney on Saturday evening. At Bowling Green House, Hester was waiting anxiously at the top of the stairs to receive him: 'The first thing I heard was a voice so changed, that I said to myself, "It is all over with him." He was supported by the arms of two people, and had a stick, or two sticks, in his hands, and as he came up, panting for breath . . . I retreated, little by little, not to put him to the pain of making a bow to me, or of speaking.' [610]

Pitt had complained of peculiar pain in his stomach, and on Sunday, at Farquhar's insistence, Dr Matthew Baillie, an eminent morbid anatomist, and Dr Henry Reynolds were summoned to make another physical examination. 'They were apprehensive that some of the principal organs abt. The Liver or Stomach were in a diseased

* The Hon. Edmund Phipps, younger brother of Lord Mulgrave, Foreign Secretary in Pitt's administration.

state.' Baillie and Reynolds confirmed the opinion of Haygarth and Falconer that there was no organic damage and, later that day, while Farquhar went to fetch Tomline from Fulham where he was staying with the Bishop of London, Pitt went out for a drive in his carriage. Next day, apparently satisfied that his patient was making good progress, Farquhar left Bowling Green House. When he returned on Tuesday afternoon, he found Pitt much worse: 'he complained of his sensations. I hoped it might be some slight accession from cold, and not immediately connected with his complaints—but his account of himself soon convinced me that it was of a more serious nature. "Sir Walter," said he, "I have been compelled to disobey your injunctions—I have done too much. When in conversation with persons upon important business, I felt suddenly as if I had been cut in two." ' [611]

Farquhar had obtained Pitt's promise that he would open no letters nor attempt to attend any public business, and it had been arranged that Tomline, whose discretion could be relied upon, should attend to all Pitt's correspondence for him. Farquhar was horrified to discover that both Castlereagh and Hawkesbury had held long discussions with Pitt in his room on Monday. Canning had also called to see him: 'The change since Bath dreadful!' he wrote, 'and his appearance such as I shall never forget. He was very, very kind and seemed to have something on his mind that he wished to say to me but could not.' Charles Stanhope went with Tomline to Pitt's room that evening. They found him 'very unwell. He said . . . "I am very shabby indeed tonight"; he complained of fatigue from the long conversation with Lord C and Lord H and said he was more ill than usual . . . soon after he took his Brandy and Water and went to bed almost immediately.' During the day he had complained of a sore throat and had gargled several times to relieve it. Early on the morning of Tuesday 14th, Tomline, whose room was next to Pitt's, heard him coughing, and he was later told by a manservant that Pitt had 'had retchings before he got out of bed and a great propensity for sickness: however he kept it off'. That afternoon he was sufficiently recovered to go for a short drive with Hester, but he was exhausted when he returned and 'got upstairs with great difficulty'. Chatham, Canning, Mulgrave and Wellesley came to see him, but only Chatham and Wellesley were admitted to his room. That evening young Stanhope found him 'thoughtful and low', but when Tomline saw him at ten o'clock Pitt said he was 'better, much'. An hour later Tomline heard him coughing and retching. 'From this period, the 14th January', Farquhar wrote, 'the Symptoms became truly and immediately alarming. I took up my residence at Putney Heath, and summoned Drs Reynolds and Baillie to join me on the following morning, and to continue in daily attendance.' [612]

Lord Wellesley had recently returned from India after handing over the office of Governor-General to Cornwallis, and Pitt had looked forward eagerly to his arrival in England. Pitt needed Wellesley's strength, abilities and loyalty in his Cabinet. As soon as he heard of his homecoming he invited him to Putney. 'I am', he wrote on 12 January, 'recovering rather slowly from a series of stomach complaints, followed by severe attacks of gout, but I believe I am now in the way of real amendment.' This comforting account did nothing to prepare Wellesley for the shock awaiting him two days later at Bowling Green House. Pitt made a determined attempt to disguise the gravity of his illness but Wellesley was not deceived: 'Notwithstanding Mr Pitt's kindness and cheerfulness', he wrote later, 'I saw that the hand of death was fixed upon him.' The effort was too much for Pitt, who fainted when his guest had left him. Wellesley was astonished to find that neither Pitt's doctors nor his friends realized that he was dying. Chatham was characteristically wrapped up in his own affairs and insensitive to his brother's danger. He, too, saw him on the 14th and 'accosted him in a manner and tone as if he had been sitting in Downing Street'. Wellesley warned Grenville, who 'received the fatal intelligence with the utmost feeling in an agony of tears, and immediately determined that all hostility in parliament should be suspended'. [613]

Farquhar persevered in his belief that Pitt's condition was not due to any organic injury and concentrated on attempts to relieve the symptoms of 'general debility' by the free use of opiates. Pitt was pathetically weak and suffering from a 'low fever' with a pulse rate of 130 to 140. He was fed asses' milk, chicken broth, and yolk of egg beaten up with brandy and sugar, but he could digest nothing and vomited painfully after every meal. 'I wonder', said the footman who prepared this invalid food, 'that they persist in giving him the egg; for he brings it up every time.' Farquhar was not alone in recognizing the distressing fact that his patient was growing daily weaker from lack of nourishment. 'His stomach will bear nothing,' Tomline wrote, 'how then is he to recover strength?' Although his physicians did not consider Pitt's life to be in any immediate danger, it was evident that his recovery would be slow, and it was doubtful whether he would ever again be strong enough to bear the burdens of political office. Meanwhile, as he lay ill at Putney, unable to deal with any public business, his government was deprived of the only strength it possessed. Tomline told his wife, 'The act of resigning would certainly be very painful to him on many accounts; but still unless some favourable change should soon take place what good can he do by continuing in office? It appears to me better for his Dignity and Character, and perhaps better also for the Country, that he should retire before anything unpleasant or awkward is said or takes place in Parliament and some at least of his political Friends are decidedly of that opinion.' [614]

On the 15th Pitt saw no one but Rose, who tried to hide his shock and distress at finding his idol so weak and emaciated. Next day Tomline wrote to his wife and to Rose that Pitt seemed better: 'He thinks so himself and says he feels something like a desire for food.' Pitt's valet, John Pursler, 'an excellent and attentive man', also thought there was a noticeable improvement. During the next three days Pitt's condition was described as 'stationary' and the doctors were more hopeful. On the 17th Tomline was encouraged to hope that Pitt might have 'turned the corner'. He was moved to a larger room, his own bedroom being 'small and close', but 'his weakness was so great it alarmed Sir Walter prodigiously. The pulse were 130 or 140 . . . Mr Pitt was quite hysterical and fainting and only supported by Madeira.' Next morning he was 'materially worse'. Dr Baillie described the symptoms as the 'Low Fever of an Exhausted Constitution'. For the first time, it seemed, since they had attended him regularly, Pitt's doctors were afraid that he might not recover. [615]

That day James Stanhope arrived at Bowling Green House. He was greeted at the gate by George Rose, who told him with tears in his eyes, 'I fear there is danger.' There was a continuous procession of visitors to the house—the Dukes of Cumberland and Cambridge, Canning, Hawkesbury, Tom Steele, Sidmouth and Wilberforce among them—but Pitt was not allowed to see even his brother or the devoted Hester. George III's eyesight was failing and he was no longer able to write his own letters, but he sent a number of messages by his secretary, Colonel Herbert Taylor. Tomline, who had been Pitt's closest companion since his arrival, curtailed his visits to Pitt's room: as he told his wife, 'By rarely going to him myself I can better keep other people from him . . . speaking is painful to him.' On Monday 20th hope was fading, though Tomline said 'Sir Walter does not despair'.[616]

Two days later he had the unhappy task of telling Pitt that the end was near. His account of the meeting, which appears in a letter written to his wife a few hours later, is transparently accurate:

> I went to him this morning about eight—he knew me, though he had been very rambling and confused in the night. I proposed to pray with him: he objected; but spoke of himself with the greatest Humility and foremost Trust in the Mercy of God, observing that his objections arose not from want of Religious Feeling, but from an opinion of the inefficacy of Prayer in the last moment. I told him that his mind was exactly in a State in which Prayers ought to be used, and pressed the point; he complied and I read the Prayers in the Liturgy for the visitation of the Sick.

Tomline told Rose that morning that Pitt had refused the Sacrament, saying that he had not the strength to go through it, and that he had said, 'I have, as I fear is the case with many others, neglected prayer too much to allow me to hope that it can be very efficacious now.' When their prayers were ended Pitt tried to write his will, but succeeded in scratching less than one barely legible line before he became too exhausted to continue. He therefore dictated it to Tomline, who read it back to him. Pitt then signed it at the end of each of its three clauses, and his signature was witnessed by Tomline, Farquhar and Pursler.[617]

Pitt's will acknowledged a professional debt of one thousand guineas to Farquhar dated from October 1805, and left £12,000 with interest from October 1801 to be divided among Charles Long, Tom Steele, Lords Carrington and Camden, and Joseph Smith in repayment of the subscription raised for him. He also required 'if money can be found for it' that each of his servants should be paid a sum equal to twice their wages, and charged his brother and Tomline with the care of his papers. He added sadly, 'I owe more than I can leave behind me.' When his will had been witnessed, Pitt asked to be left alone, and he remained quiet and apparently asleep for two or three hours.[618]

James Stanhope remained with him all that day and through the following night, though, as he wrote three days later, 'I did not allow him to see me, as I felt myself unequal to the dreadful scene of parting with him, and feared (although he was given over) that the exertion on his part might hasten the dreadful event which now appeared inevitable.' Hester, who had been refused permission to see her uncle, crept into his bedroom while Sir Walter Farquhar was at dinner. Pitt was feverish and his mind was rambling, but he recognized her, expressed his fond hopes for her future happiness, and gently bade her farewell. After she had gone he continued to speak of her, repeating several times, 'Where is Hester? Is Hester gone?' In the evening Farquhar gave him some champagne, but he had difficulty in swallowing it. Sir Walter apologized: 'I am sorry, Sir, to give you pain. Do not take it unkind.' Pitt replied mildly, 'I never take anything unkind that is meant for my good.' Later his mind wandered and he spoke his confused thoughts aloud. To the seventeen-year-old James Stanhope, who watched alone by his bed as Tomline, Farquhar, Charles and Hester rested exhausted in their rooms, he seemed to be waiting anxiously for a messenger from Berlin, and sometimes he called 'Hear, hear', as if he were in the Houses of Parliament. Often he cried out in pain.[619]

At one o'clock in the morning of 23 January the household was disturbed by the arrival of a certain Mr South, who had driven from London with vial of hartshorn oil which, he insisted, had been known to 'recover people in the last agonies'. Farquhar, knowing that there was nothing more he could do, finally yielded to South's entreaties and poured two spoonfuls of the oil down Pitt's throat. 'It produced no effect but a little convulsive cough.' At half past two Pitt became quieter, but James had noticed that his hands and feet were becoming very cold. A little later Pitt cried out in a strong, clear voice, 'Oh my country; how I love my country.' He did not speak again. At half past four on the morning of 23 January he died, quietly and without a struggle, 'like a candle burning out'. It was the twenty-fifth anniversary of the day on which he had taken his seat in the House of Commons as the newly elected member of parliament for Appleby.[620]

Pitt's illness and death have been variously ascribed to overwork, anxiety and depression caused by news of Austerlitz and the fall of Lord Melville. It is true that at forty-six he was physically exhausted, but his rapid decline was due less to over-exertion than to advanced disease. It is a curious fact that eighteenth-century physicians knew more about the symptoms of gout than of almost any other affliction, and there can be little doubt that the diagnosis in Pitt's case was accurate. They were less well equipped to recognize the symptoms of gout crystallized in the kidneys, leading to renal failure, or of cirrhosis of the liver. Nor were they familiar with the methods of treatment for either disease.

From an early age Pitt had shown a liking for alcohol, and old Dr Addington's prescription of port was undoubtedly influential in determining Pitt's preference, shown by the cellar books for Holwood,* for the most toxic of wines. The burdens and anxieties of his political life, probably aggravated by frustration and the suppression of his emotions, swelled a harmless appetite into a lethal hunger. By 1793 he was already showing the first signs of uraemia, a symptom of inherited gout, and eight years later his jaundiced complexion was a clear warning of approaching renal failure. A weak pulse-rate is one of the marks of alcoholism and it is significant that those of Farquhar's prescriptions that contained solutions of alcohol were effective in easing Pitt's discomfort. From the account left by Farquhar, who attended Pitt regularly for the last ten years of his life, and from the observations of contemporaries, it is possible to diagnose his disease with some accuracy. Pitt suffered from gout, crystallized in the kidneys, and alcoholism, and his death was due to renal failure, probably accompanied by cirrhosis of the liver. Farquhar, who doubted whether retirement 'attended by the contemplation of the misfortunes of his Country' would have prolonged Pitt's life, recognized that his debility was caused by 'the early habit of the too free use of wine'. General Phipps, who had seen much of Pitt at Bath, was close to the truth when he gave it as his opinion that 'Mr Pitt's constitution was worn out by gouty dispositions, and by the habit of taking too strong stimulants—Care of mind, which always affects the stomach, must have had a bad effect upon him.' [621]

Within an hour of Pitt's death, young James Stanhope was on his way to Downing Street, where he and William Dacre Adams sealed up all books and papers. Both Tomline and his wife were oppressed by the responsibility of protecting Pitt's possessions, and most particularly his private correspondence, from creditors. His debts

* See p. 290.

were estimated at £55,000. Tomline was bewildered: 'I have heard much unfeeling things, besides all sorts of embarrassment and difficulty and management and contrivance. Mortgages, Bonds upon Bonds, jointly and separately, Annuities &c., &c. All this from . . . Coutts.' Mrs Tomline wrote to him of 'the transcendent character *you* are *appointed* to *guard* from *misrepresentations*'. She confessed herself to be 'tormented with fear of what some Creditors may do if doubts arise about the payment of Mr Pitt's debts. . . . Papers have been seized in such cases.' She urged her husband to 'remove the Papers *immediately*' from Pitt's houses. There was already a move to pay Pitt's debts again by subscription, but on the 27th notice was given in the House of Commons of a resolution for their settlement from public funds. [622]

On that day, too, Henry Lascelles * brought forward his motion for an Address to the Crown 'that His Majesty will be graciously pleased to give directions that the remains of the Right Hon. William Pitt be interred at public charge; and that a monument be erected in the collegiate church at St. Peter, Westminster, to the memory of that excellent statesman, with an inscription expressive of the public sense of so great and irreparable a loss and to assure His Majesty that this House will make good the expenses attending the same.' The words were chosen with care: they were precisely those used in the motion passed by the House twenty-eight years earlier to honour Pitt's father. Fox and Windham objected to the description of Pitt as an 'excellent statesman'. 'It cannot be expected,' Fox declared, 'that I should so forget the principles I have uniformly expressed as to subscribe to the Condemnation of those principles by agreeing to the motion.' Windham's opposition, which was deplored by his political chief, Lord Grenville, was even less generous. In spite of them, the House passed the motion by the overwhelming majority of 258 votes to 89. The Common Council of the City of London passed a resolution to erect a monument to Pitt by the narrow margin of 77 votes to 71. The disasters of Ulm and Austerlitz had overshadowed the triumph of Trafalgar and reduced Pitt's popularity to a low ebb. A week later the House voted £40,000 for the payment of Pitt's debts, and pensions of £1,200 a year to Hester Stanhope and £600 a year for each of her sisters.

Pitt's body lay in state in the painted chamber of Westminster Hall

---

* MP for Yorkshire; succeeded his father as 2nd Earl of Harewood in 1820.

through 20 and 21 February. On Saturday 22nd, at twelve-thirty, the long funeral procession formed for the last journey to the Abbey. More than three thousand tickets for the Abbey had been issued to 'Gentlemen and Esquires', and by order of the Garter King of Arms 'Round Hats' were worn by all who attended the service, 'The Nobility and Gentry in Mourning, without Weepers, and with Mourning Swords'. Wellesley and Grenville were Assistant Mourners, and the Dukes of York, Cambridge and Cumberland were among those who followed the coffin. Thomas Hughes, a Prebend of Westminster Abbey, reported that 'many of the Noblemen and Gentlemen who attended were afflicted to shedding tears. Lord Mulgrave was so much so as scarcely to be able to support himself.' After a service lasting about twenty-five minutes conducted by the Bishop of London, Pitt's remains were interred in the family vault close to his father and mother.[623]

Canning's grief at Pitt's death had been 'dreadful; he could not cry or speak'. After the funeral he wrote to his wife, 'It is all over, dearest love, I have seen poor Pitt laid in his grave, and I feel somehow, a feeling of loneliness and dismay which I have never felt half so strongly before.' The Duke of York was reported to be 'more affected than any person there'. Wellesley, acknowledging Tomline's letter informing him of Pitt's death, had written: 'In him I have lost the great object of my respect and affection; nor can I yet estimate the public misfortune, while my memory is entirely occupied with the recollection of his private virtues, of the warmth of his friendship, and the generosity and tenderness of his heart. In every view his loss is indeed, irreparable, nor is it profitable to contemplate its probable consequences without grief and dismay.'[624]

The prospect for Britain was, indeed, bleak. The day before Pitt's death Grenville had written to Minto: 'What is to be done in consequence of this misfortune few people can even guess; but the prevailing opinion seems to be that there is to be an attempt to patch together the poor remnants of this present government. If so we are indeed a nation destined to destruction.'[625] George III made a half-hearted attempt to encourage Hawkesbury to take Pitt's place, but 'Young Jenky' knew that the ministry had become a headless corpse: it might twitch briefly but it would never again be capable of co-ordinated movement. For the first time in more than twenty years the King found himself without a choice of government. He was obliged to send for Grenville, and to accept with him Fox, and Fox's friends.

The new administration came to be known as 'The Ministry of all the Talents', but it included none of Pitt's followers, and the exclusion of Canning and Castlereagh gave the lie to the description. Receiving Fox in the Closet for the first time after his appointment as Foreign Secretary, the King said to him, 'Mr Fox, I little thought you and I should ever meet again in this place. But I have no desire to look back on old grievances, and you may rest assured I shall never remind you of them.' Fox replied, 'My deeds, and not my words, shall commend me to your Majesty.' The reconciliation was short-lived. The day after Pitt's death had been Fox's fifty-seventh birthday. He had said that the loss of Pitt would 'render every debate flat and uninteresting', and added, 'I hate going to the House. I think I shall pair off with Pitt.' Within six months he was enduring all the unavailing and painful punishments prescribed by his physicians as a cure for dropsy. On 7 August he was tapped of five gallons of fluid but, while his face and the upper part of his body were thinned to emaciation, his legs swelled again. At twenty minutes to six in the evening of Saturday 13 September he died. On 10 October, he, too, was buried in Westminster Abbey.[626]

Grenville's government lasted little more than a year. The deaths of Pitt and Fox had removed from parliament the only leaders of sufficient political stature to command unity and loyalty from men whose abilities and ambitions drove them into mutual conflict. The ghost of Pitt cast a long shadow but it lacked substance. His young disciples—Canning, Castlereagh, Hawkesbury—did not lack talent, but they could not agree upon a leader. Their feelings towards Grenville were ambivalent: although they opposed his government, they looked upon him as the natural head of their party. Sidmouth, who had been regarded until 1801 as Pitt's puppet, spent the last thirty-eight years of his life looking over his shoulder to the opinions of his missing master, like a toy forever fixed in a gesture left uncompleted when the clockwork mechanism wound down. Canning made it clear that he would never serve with him in any administration. He would work with Castlereagh, Hawkesbury and Spencer Perceval, and did so in Portland's Ministry from 1807 to 1809, but he would not work for any of them. When Perceval became Prime Minister in 1809, Canning refused to serve. Pitt's death had left a vacuum, and the most brilliant of his disciples could find no one but himself qualified to fill it.

Pitt knew little about the use of armies and he is generally regarded as having been a poor strategist. He once admitted ruefully, 'I distrust extremely any ideas of my own on military matters.' [627] His successors were little better. The war against France was not so much won by the armies of the Fourth Coalition, or by Wellington in the Peninsula, as lost by Napoleon's seizure of the Spanish throne and his invasion of Russia. It was, however, Canning, as Foreign Secretary, who saw the opportunity offered by the revolution in Spain in 1808 and sent an army under Sir Arthur Wellesley to Portugal; and of the twelve members of the Cabinet led by Lord Liverpool (Hawkesbury) during the last three years of the war, eight had served in Pitt's last administration.

In 1815, after twenty years of endurance, Britain emerged victorious, the most powerful nation in the world. The foundations of that power were laid by Pitt during his first ten years in office. His achievements were four-fold: the revival of the national finances, the implementation of important long-term administrative reforms, the reorganization of British imperial commitments, and the rehabilitation of Britain in Europe. The central focus of all his policies was trade, and it was the preservation and expansion of trade during Pitt's nineteen years as Prime Minister that enabled his successors to take advantage of the energy and inventiveness of the British people.

Pitt's political life spanned twenty-five years of a period of upheaval throughout Europe, America and India. At the end of it Britain was transformed and, in spite of the loss of the American colonies, strengthened. By 1806, when Pitt died, Britain had withstood the dual revolutionary shocks presented by industry and insurrection, and there was growing confidence that future changes in the structure of government and society would be made within the law. The British Revolution was accomplished without bloodshed, and this achievement owed much to the stabilizing influence of Pitt's long tenure of office. His work was incomplete, and much of it was destroyed in his lifetime, but the foundations were sound and his heirs built upon them with certainty.

Pitt's claim to statesmanship may be arguable; it may rest upon definition; but his supreme skill as a politician is beyond question. He based his behaviour and actions on the conviction that his politics

448

must be practicable. Further, he understood better than any of his contemporaries (except perhaps, Lord North) that success in politics depends upon an accurate valuation of priorities and the recognition of immovable obstacles. Faced by such an obstacle, Pitt turned away from it. Fox spent his talents and his energies in the pursuit of aims that were, in his time, manifestly unattainable. Fox claimed to be the voice of the people, crying for individual liberty and the freedom of parliament against the Crown; but he was not a man of the people, and his principles were never egalitarian. Nor, while his wagon remained hitched to that tarnished star, George, Prince of Wales, could he be said to be anti-monarchist. Pitt aspired to a hero's laurels, not to a martyr's crown. He was prepared to compromise and to acknowledge and live with failure. His compromises, however reluctant, were genuine. Fox's were not, and he was seldom able to disguise the fact that, although his political stance had shifted, his personal opinion remained unaltered.

Pitt was truly a man of principle, of one single principle that transcended all others and on which no compromise was possible. The welfare of his country, with which he associated the preservation of the Constitution and loyalty to the Crown, was the mainspring of his life, and for it he was ready to sacrifice cherished causes, personal advantage, and even his own reputation for integrity. This dedication was absolute. His reserve and iron self-discipline subdued all open expression of gaiety or emotion. The 'very hearty, *salutation-giving, shake handy* sort of person',[628] whose kindness, wit, brilliant mimicry and bad jokes charmed his friends, has been obscured by the proud, cool and aloof manner he presented on public occasions. The contrast with Fox's disorderly genius and uninhibited warmth has been sharpened by the passage of years. Both men failed in much of what they had set out to accomplish. Fox failed because he wore responsibility like a cloak to be shrugged off at will. When Pitt failed he fastened it about him to ward off the chill of disappointment. Both men had great gifts, but Pitt alone possessed the qualities of integrity and endurance necessary to inspire confidence and courage. To his successors he left an example of leadership, fortitude and self-denial. To his country he bequeathed the priceless legacy of hope.

Notes and References

CHAPTER I

1   Christie's Catalogue 7 May 1789. Copy in Kent County Archives, Maidstone (Till MSS U468, Q5/1)
2   Addington to Chatham, 30 October 1773. Chatham Papers, PRO 30/8/15
3   *Chatham Correspondence*, Vol. IV, p. 363
4   Quoted J. Holland Rose: *Pitt and the National Revival* (London 1911) p. 44
5   Fox Papers, BM Add MSS 47593
6   J. Johnson (ed.): *Memoirs of William Hayley* (London 1823) Vol. II, p. 27 See also Cuthbert Headlam (ed.): *The Letters of Lady Harriot Eliot 1766-1786* (Edinburgh 1914) pp 2-3
7   Quoted Sir George Pretyman Tomline: *Memoirs of the Life of William Pitt* (London 1821) Vol. I, pp 3-4
8   J. Holland Rose: *Pitt and the National Revival*, p. 46
9   Evidence of Henry Addington, who saw a later performance at Hayes. Hon. George Pellew: *The Life and Correspondence of the Rt. Hon. Henry Addington First Viscount Sidmouth* (London 1847) Vol. I, p. 28
10 Lord Ashbourne: *Pitt: some Chapters of his Life and Times* (London 1898) pp 7-8
11 Chatham to Joseph Turner, Fellow of Pembroke, 3 October 1773. Quoted Lord Rosebery: *Pitt* (London 1891) p. 8
12 *Chatham Correspondence*, Vol. IV, p. 289

13 Wilson to Lady Chatham, 15 December 1773. Chatham Papers, PRO 30/8/67

14 The date of Addington's description is not clear, but it is almost certain that it was given at this period. See notes of Mrs Pretyman's recollections for October and November 1801. (Chevening, Stanhope MSS 'Mr Pitt' II) and Addington to Lady Chatham, Chatham Papers, PRO 30/8/15

15 Pitt to Lady Chatham, 28 June 1779. Chatham Papers, PRO 30/8/12

16 Tomline: *Memoirs of the Life of William Pitt*, Vol. I, p. 7

17 Ibid. pp 7-8

18 A. M. Wilberforce: *The Private Papers of William Wilberforce* (London 1897) Vol. I, p. 68

19 Thomas Gisborne to William Smith, 15 April 1834, Wrangham MSS. Quoted Robin Furneaux: *William Wilberforce* (London 1974) p. 11

20 R. I. and S. Wilberforce: *The Life of William Wilberforce* (London 1838) Vol. I, p. 11

CHAPTER II

21 BM Add MSS 32684 f. 121

22 See Ida Macalpine and Richard Hunter: *George III and the Mad Business* (London 1969)

23 Lord E. Fitzmaurice: *Life of William, Earl of Shelburne* (London 1875-6) Vol. I, pp 110-11

24 Sir Nathaniel Wraxhall: *The Historical and the Posthumous Memoirs* (1772-1784) Vol. I, p. 328

25 J. Greig (ed.): *Diaries of a Duchess 1752-74* (London 1926)

26 Quoted J. Steven Watson: *The Reign of George III* (Oxford 1960) p. 98

27 John Hughes for Pennsylvania and Jared Ingersoll for Connecticut

28 Sir William Anson (ed.): *The Autobiographical and Political Correspondence of Augustus Henry, 3rd Duke of Grafton* (London 1898) p. 110, 'Lord Chatham did never open to us, or to the Cabinet in general, what was his real and fixed plan.'

29 Fitzmaurice: *Life of William, Earl of Shelburne*, Vol. I, p. 382

30 Lord Chesterfield: *Letters to his Son* (4th edition London 1912) Vol. II, p. 353

31 Ibid. p. 360

32 Anson: *Correspondence of the 3rd Duke of Grafton*, p. 137

CHAPTER III

33 Memorandum dated 9 October 1768. *Chatham Correspondence*, Vol. III, p. 337n.

34 Ibid. Vol. III, p. 338

35 Ibid. Vol. III, p. 343

36 See J. W. Fortescue (ed.): *Correspondence of King George III from 1760 to December 1783* (London 1927-8) Vol. II, p. 58

37 *Annual Register*, May 1768, p. 86

38 The riots 'still continued almost every night from the 29th March to ye 12th or 13th May.' Guildhall Library MS 3724

39 Anson: *Correspondence of the 3rd Duke of Grafton*

40 Quoted Sir Tresham Lever: *The House of Pitt* (London 1947) p. 173

41 Wraxhall: *Historical and Posthumous Memoirs*, Vol. I, p. 366

42 Horace Walpole: *The Last Journals* (London 1910) Vol. I, p. 83

43 Fortescue: *Correspondence of George III*, Vol. II, p. 126

44 Annual Register, 1769, p. 84

45 *Address of the Corporation of the City of London* (London 1865) p. 17

46 *Chatham Correspondence*, Vol. III, p. 469

47 L. G. Wickham Legg (ed.): *British Diplomatic Instructions 1689-1789*, Vol. VII, France, Part IV 1745-1789 (Royal Historical Society, London 1934) pp 117-18

48 *Chatham Correspondence*, Vol. IV, pp 239 and 298

49 Fortescue: *Correspondence of George III*, Vol. III, p. 241

50 *Chatham Correspondence*, Vol. IV, p. 186

51 Fortescue: *Correspondence of George III*, Vol. II, p. 325

52 BM Bridport Papers II. Quoted Dorothy Hood: *The Admirals Hood* (Oxford 1967) p. 35

CHAPTER IV

53 *Chatham Correspondence*, Vol. IV, p. 331

54 Ibid.

55 Walpole: *Last Journals*, Vol. I, p. 349

56 Ibid. p. 350

57 Bridport Papers BM Add MSS 35192

58 *Virginia Gazette*, 5 May 1774

59 Walpole: *Last Journals*, Vol. I, p. 433

60 Palmerston MSS C31 (Broadlands). Quoted Brian Connell: *Portrait of a Whig Peer* (London 1957) p. 119

61 Quoted Lever: *House of Pitt*, p. 200

62 Hood Papers. Quoted D. Hood: *The Admirals Hood*, p. 37

63 Quoted Pellew: *First Viscount Sidmouth*, Vol. I, p. 6

64 Quoted Lever: *House of Pitt*, p. 201

65 Fortescue: *Correspondence of George III*, Vol. III, p. 449

66 Quoted John Brooke: *George III* (London 1972) pp 303-4

67 Fortescue: *Correspondence of George III*, Vol. IV, p. 59

68 Ibid. Vol. IV, p. 92

69 John Almon: *Anecdotes of the Life of the Right Honourable William Pitt, Earl of Chatham* (London 1793) Vol. II, pp 511-12

70 Wedgwood to Bentley, 11 April 1778. Wedgwood Archives, Barlaston
71 *Chatham Correspondence*, Vol. IV, p. 177n.
72 Quoted Pellew: *First Viscount Sidmouth*, Vol. I, p. 8
73 Pretyman MSS, East Suffolk Record Office, Ipswich T99/14
74 Holland Rose: *Pitt and the National Revival*, p. 62
75 Almon: *Anecdotes of the Life of the Earl of Chatham*, Vol. III, Appendix Z, pp 308-12
76 Holland Rose: *Pitt and the National Revival*, p. 62

CHAPTER V

77 Earl Stanhope: *Life of the Right Honourable William Pitt* (London 1861-2) Vol. I, p. 25
78 Headlam: *Letters of Lady Harriot Eliot*, p. 30
79 Walpole: *Last Journals*, Vol. II, p. 237
80 Ibid. Vol. II, pp 247-8
81 Pretyman MSS T108/39
82 Holland Rose: *Pitt and the National Revival*, p. 66
83 Stanhope: *Life of William Pitt*, Vol. I, p. 38
84 Pretyman MSS 435 T108/39
85 *The Speech of the Hon. Charles James Fox delivered at Westminster February 2, 1780* (London n.d.)
86 C. J. Fox: *Speeches of the Right Honourable Charles James Fox in the House of Commons* (London 1815) Vol. I, p. 245
87 Abergavenny MSS Historical Manuscripts Commission (1887) p. 29
88 Wraxhall: *Historical and Posthumous Memoirs*, pp 232-45
89 Stanhope: *Life of William Pitt*, Vol. I, pp 41-2
90 Ibid. p. 41
91 J. Godechot: *The Taking of the Bastille, July 14th, 1789* (London 1970) p. 5 *et seq*.
92 Wraxhall: *Historical and Posthumous Memoirs*, Vol. I, p. 255
93 *Morning Chronicle*, 5 June 1780
94 C. P. Moritz: *Journeys of a German in England in 1782*, translated and edited by Reginald Nettel (London 1965) p. 36
95 Stanhope: *Life of William Pitt*, Vol. I, pp 41-2
96 *Wilberforce Correspondence*, Vol. I, p. 244
97 James Hatton (ed.): *Selections from the Letters and Correspondence of Sir James Bland Burges, Bart*. (London 1885) pp 60-61. This anecdote has been challenged (especially in the biography of Gibbon by J. M. Robertson and D. M. Low) as improbable. No satisfactory evidence, however, has been adduced to refute it. Burges's memoir, although not written until some forty years after the event (he died in 1824) does not read like invention and it is certainly not inconsistent with what is known of Pitt's character and behaviour, or, indeed, of Gibbon's. The

453

allegation of improbability rests on the assumption that Gibbon could not have been worsted in argument by the twenty-one-year-old Pitt.

 98 Letter and notes from Joseph Jekyll to Bishop Pretyman Tomline, 4 and 6 May 1820. Pretyman MSS HA 119/562.
 99 Stanhope: *Life of William Pitt*, Vol. I, p. 45
100 Chatham Papers, PRO 30/8/12
101 Quoted Pellew: *First Viscount Sidmouth*, Vol. I, p. 28

CHAPTER VI

102 Moritz: *Journeys of a German*
103 *Nottingham Journal*, 3 April 1784
104 J. H. Jesse: *George Selwyn and his Contemporaries* (Boston 1843) Vol. IV, p. 380
105 BM Add MSS ff 325-6
106 Joseph Farington: *The Farington Diary*, edited by James Greig (London 1923-7) Vol. II, p. 283 and Vol. III, p. 162
107 *Parliamentary Register* 1781, p. 17
108 E. S. Roscoe and Helen Clergue (eds): *George Selwyn, his Letters and his Life* (London 1899) p. 131
109 Stanhope: *Life of William Pitt*, Vol. I, p. 57
110 *Parliamentary Register* 1781, p. 571
111 Stanhope: *Life of William Pitt*, Vol. I, p. 48 dates this letter December 1780, but the original manuscript (Pretyman MSS T108/42) is dated 7 February 1781 from Burton Pynsent. James had died on 13 November.
112 Bridport Papers III. Quoted D. Hood: *The Admirals Hood*, p. 58
113 Fortescue: *Correspondence of George III*, Vol. V, 3566 and 3567
114 Fitzmaurice: *Life of William, Earl of Shelburne*, Vol. III, p. 131
115 Wraxhall: *Historical and Posthumous Memoirs*, Vol. II, p. 249
116 C. Matheson: *The Life of Henry Dundas, 1st Viscount Melville 1742-1811* (London 1933) p. 79
117 *Parliamentary Register*, Vol. VI, p. 412
118 Ibid. Vol. III, pp 120-26
119 Lord John Russell (ed.): *Memorials and Correspondence of Charles James Fox* (London 1853-7) Vol. I, p. 322

CHAPTER VII

120 Russell: *Memorials and Correspondence of Fox*, Vol. I, pp 446-7
121 *Considerations on the Provisional Treaty with America, and the Preliminary Articles of Peace with France and Spain* (London 1783). Thought to have been written by Andrew Kippis DD, FRS, a nonconformist minister and part-editor of *Biographica Britannica*, but directed by Shelburne to publish his proposals.
122 Duke of Buckingham and Chandos (ed.): *Memoirs of the Court and Cabinets of George III* (London 1853-5) Vol. I, p. 148

123 Russell: *Memorials and Correspondence of Fox*, Vol. II, p. 33; Tomline: *Memoirs of the Life of William Pitt*, Vol. I, p. 89

124 Fox: *Speeches*, Vol. II, pp 122-3

125 R. Pares: *King George III and the Politicians* (Oxford 1953) p. 122n. 3

126 Stanhope: *Life of William Pitt*, Vol. I, p. 98

127 Ibid.

128 Wilberforce: *Life of William Wilberforce*, Vol. I, p. 26

129 *Parliamentary History*, Vol. XXIII, pp 543-50

130 Stanhope: *Life of William Pitt*, Vol. I, pp 105-6

131 Ibid. Vol. I, p. 107

132 Holland Rose: *Pitt and the National Revival*, p. 126

133 Bathurst MSS. Historical Manuscripts Commission 1923

134 Fitzmaurice: *Life of William, Earl of Shelburne*, Vol. III, p. 375. Lord Ashburton's report of an interview with George III on 9 March 1783

135 Stanhope: *Life of William Pitt*, Vol. I, Appendix, pp iii-iv

136 Ibid. Appendix p. iv

137 Buckingham: *Courts and Cabinets of George III*, Vol. I, p. 219

138 A. M. W. Stirling: *Coke of Norfolk and His Friends* (London n.d.) Vol. I, p. 212; Russell: *Memoirs and Correspondence of Fox*, Vol. II, p. 20; the *Public Advertiser*, April 1783; Lord North to his father, 18 February 1783, quoted Stanley Ayling: *George the Third* (1972) p. 297

139 *Parliamentary History*, Vol. XXIII, p. 945

140 Russell: *Memorials and Correspondence of Fox*, Vol. II, p. 114

CHAPTER VIII

141 Walpole: *Last Journals*, Vol. I, p. 7

142 Wilberforce: *Life of William Wilberforce*, Vol. I, p. 18; Tomline: *Memoirs of the Life of William Pitt*, Vol. I, p. 43n.

143 Bishop Jebb's description. J. C. Colquhoun: *William Wilberforce, His Friends and His Times* (London 1866) p. 172

144 Wilberforce: *Life of William Wilberforce*, Vol. I, pp 25, 28-9

145 Lansdowne MSS. Quoted J. Ehrman: *The Younger Pitt: The Years of Acclaim* (London 1969) p. 108

146 Sir Herbert Maxwell (ed.): *The Creevey Papers* (2nd edition, London 1804) Vol. I, p. 61

147 BM Add MSS 38213 ff 79-80

148 Countess of Minto (ed.): *Life and Letters of Sir Gilbert Elliot, First Earl of Minto from 1751-1806* (London 1874), Vol. I, p. 275

149 Earl Stanhope: *Miscellanies, Second Series* (London 1872) pp 25-6

150 Stanhope: *Life of William Pitt*, Vol. I, p. 127.

151 Pretyman MSS T108/39

152 Ibid.

153 Apart from the references quoted from Pitt's letters, the account of the visit to France is taken from Wilberforce's recollections printed in Wilberforce: *Life of William Wilberforce*, Vol. I, pp 36-44

154 Stanhope: *Life of William Pitt*, Vol. I, p. 131

155 Pitt to Lady Chatham from Hotel de Grande Bretagne, Paris, 15 October 1783. Stanhope: *Life of William Pitt*, Vol. I, p. 132

156 Le Vicomte d'Haussonville: *Le Salon de Madame Necker* (Paris 1882) Vol. II, pp. 50-57

157 Minto: *Sir Gilbert Elliot*, Vol. II, pp 125-6

158 Palmerston MSS B1. Quoted Connell: *Portrait of a Whig Peer*, p. 245

159 Russell: *Memorials and Correspondence of Fox*, Vol. II, p. 208

160 Burke: *Works* (Bohn edition 1882) Vol. II, pp 246-7

161 Buckingham: *Court and Cabinets of George III*, Vol. I, pp 288-9

162 Ibid. Vol. I, p. 285

163 Fortescue: *Correspondence of George III*, Vol. IV, p. 476

164 Stanhope: *Life of William Pitt*, Vol. I, p. 155

CHAPTER IX

165 Some confusion has arisen concerning the date of Temple's resignation. Pretyman states that it was 'determined upon at a late hour in the evening of the 21st' (Tomline: *Memoirs of the Life of William Pitt*, Vol. I, p. 233); Holland Rose *(Pitt and the National Revival)* concludes that it must be dated after Pitt's friendly letters to his cousin written on the 23rd. Wilberforce mentions it in his diary as common knowledge on the 22nd, and it is clear that it was announced by Grenville in the House of Commons on that date, after Pitt had spent a sleepless night contemplating its implications.

166 Tomline: *Memoirs of the Life of William Pitt*, Vol. I, p. 233

167 Minto: *Sir Gilbert Elliot*, Vol. I, p. 91; Wilberforce: *Life of William Wilberforce*, p. 48; *Reminiscences of Charles Butler Esq. of Lincoln's Inn* (London 1822) Vol. I, p. 161; Russell: *Memorials and Correspondence of Fox*, Vol. II, p. 221

168 Stanhope: *Life of William Pitt*, Vol. I, p. 168

169 Farington: *Diary*, Vol. II, p. 262

170 Moritz: *Journeys of a German*, p. 52; Wraxhall: *Historical and Posthumous Memoirs*, Vol. II, pp 1-3; Walpole: *Last Journals*, Vol. II, p. 496

171 Fox to Richard Fitzpatrick, 22 September 1767. Fox papers BM Add MSS 47580, f. 3

172 Ibid. 23 July 1768, BM Add MSS 47580, f. 4

173 Palmerston MSS B1. Quoted Connell: *Portrait of a Whig Peer*, p. 393

174 Farington: *Diary*, Vol. III, p. 260

175 T. W. Copeland (ed.): *Correspondence of Edmund Burke* (London 1958) Vol. III, p. 385

176 Fox: *Speeches*, Vol. I, pp 13-14

177 Wraxhall: *Historical and Posthumous Memoirs*, Vol. IV, p. 633 and Vol. I, p. 370

178 Richard Porson, BM Add MSS 47590

179 Wilberforce: *Life of William Wilberforce*, Vol. I, p. 49

180 Pretyman MSS HA 119/562

181 Stanhope: *Life of William Pitt*, Vol. I, p. 198

182 Wilberforce: *Life of William Wilberforce*, Vol. II, p. 133

183 Ibid. Vol. I, p. 63

CHAPTER X

184 Verbatim report of Pitt's speech in the House of Commons, 8 June 1784. Tomline: *Memoirs of the Life of William Pitt*, Vol. I, p. 549

185 See B. R. Mitchell and Phyllis Deane: *Abstract of British Historical Statistics* (London 1962) especially Chapter XIV

186 See Pitt Papers, PRO 30/8/283, 30/8/293-4; *Reports from Committees of the House of Commons 1715-1801* (London 1803) Vol. XI, p. 284

187 *Parliamentary Register*, Vol. XV, p. 277

188 R. Price: *An Appeal to the Public, on the Subject of the National Debt* (London 1772) p. 19

189 R. I. and S. Wilberforce: *The Correspondence of William Wilberforce*, Vol. I, p. 9

190 Pitt Papers PRO 30/8/275

191 Auckland Papers BM Add MSS 34419, f. 385

192 Adam Smith: *Wealth of Nations* (London 1776) Vol. IV, Chapter III

193 Robert John, 3rd Baron Auckland (Bishop of Bath and Wells) (ed.): *The Journal and Correspondence of William, Lord Auckland* (London 1862) Vol. I, pp 163-5; Melville MSS, Eskbank, quoted Holden Furber: *Henry Dundas First Viscount Melville 1742-1811* (Oxford 1931) p. 68

194 Fox: *Speeches*, Vol. III, p. 273

195 Ibid. Vol. III, p. 258

196 Auckland: *Journal and Correspondence*, Vol. I, p. 127

CHAPTER XI

197 *English Historical Documents*, Vol. X 1714-1783, edited by D. B. Horn and Mary Ransome. (London 1957) p. 703

198 Russell: *Memorials and Correspondence of Fox*, Vol. I, p. 407

199 Fortescue: *Correspondence of George III*, Vol. IV, 2449

200 Ibid. Vol. IV, 2726-8

201 Ashbourne: *Pitt: some Chapters of his Life and Times*, p. 73

202 Stanhope: *Life of William Pitt*, p. 72
203 Ashbourne: *Pitt: some Chapters of his Life and Times*, p. 72
204 Fox to Fitzpatrick, April 1782. Russell: *Memorials and Correspondence of Fox*, Vol. I, p. 412
205 Ashbourne: *Pitt: some Chapters of his Life and Times*, p. 73
206 Ibid. pp 83-4
207 Ibid. p. 90n
208 Bolton MSS, quoted Ashbourne: *Pitt: some Chapters of his Life and Times*, pp. 85-90
209 Ibid.
210 *Correspondence between William Pitt and Charles, Duke of Rutland* (London 1890) pp 71-2
211 Bolton MSS. Quoted Ashbourne: *Pitt: some Chapters of his Life and Times*, p. 108
212 Evidence given to the Committee of Trade by the Manchester Cotton Delegation. Quoted Vincent T. Harlow: *The Founding of the Second British Empire 1763-1793* (London 1952) Vol. I, p. 595
213 Bolton MSS. Quoted Ashbourne: *Pitt: some Chapters of his Life and Times*, pp 116-8
214 Josiah Wedgwood's evidence given in the Council Chamber, Whitehall, 19 February 1785. Quoted Eliza Meteyard: *Life of Josiah Wedgwood* (London 1865) Vol. II, p. 538-9
215 Wedgwood to Bolton, 1 May 1785. Wedgwood Archives (Liverpool MSS 3244, f. 4)
216 Mayer MSS. Quoted Meteyard: *Josiah Wedgwood*, Vol. II, p. 544
217 Quoted George Savage and Anne Finer: *The Selected Letters of Josiah Wedgwood* (London 1965) pp 282-3
218 Fox: *Speeches*, Vol. III, p. 78; *Parliamentary History*, Vol. XXV, p. 778
219 *Correspondence between Pitt and Rutland*, pp 65-6
220 Quoted Savage and Finer: *Selected Letters of Wedgwood*, p. 285
221 Stanhope: *Life of William Pitt*, Vol. I, pp 286-7
222 Auckland Papers. BM Add MSS 34420, f. 106v

CHAPTER XII

223 Stanhope: *Miscellanies, Second Series*, p. 26
224 Ibid. pp 25-6
225 Rev. Christopher Wyvill: *Political Papers* (London 1794-1804) Vol. IV, p. 119
226 Quoted D. G. Barnes: *George III and William Pitt 1783-1806* (Oxford 1939)
227 *Correspondence between Pitt and Rutland*, p. 111
228 Walter Sichel: *Sheridan* (London 1909) Vol. II, p. 75

229 Stanhope: *Life of William Pitt*, Vol. I, p. 236
230 Quoted Ehrman: *The Younger Pitt: the Years of Acclaim*, p. 582
231 Stanhope: *Life of William Pitt*, Vol. I, p. 229
232 Ibid. Vol. I, p. 231
233 The evidence of this transaction is incomplete. There is no doubt that the loan was raised (Pretyman MSS 50/3/182) but proof is lacking that it was paid to Hester, Countess of Chatham. Pretyman told George Rose that he believed this to be so.
234 *Quarterly Review* 1836; Rev. Leveson Harcourt (ed.): *The Diaries and Correspondence of the Right Hon. George Rose* (London 1860) Vol. II, p. 293
235 *Wilberforce Correspondence*, Vol. I, p. 9
236 Ibid. Vol. I, pp 21-4
237 Chatham Papers. PRO 30/8/219
238 Ibid. PRO 30/8/204-5
239 Headlam: *Letters of Lady Harriot Eliot*, p. 116
240 Stanhope: *Life of William Pitt*, Vol. I, p. 278
241 Headlam: *Letters of Lady Harriot Eliot*, pp 117 and 120-21
242 Stanhope: *Life of William Pitt*, Vol. I, p. 275
243 Fitzmaurice: *Life of William, Earl of Shelburne*, Vol. III, p. 422
244 *Wilberforce Correspondence*, Vol. I, p. 246
245 *Pitt and Wilberforce* (Anon. Edinburgh 1899) pp 16-17
246 Headlam: *Letters of Lady Harriot Eliot*, p. 135
247 Ibid. pp 150-52; *Pitt and Wilberforce*, pp 38-9; Holland Rose: *Pitt and the National Revival*, p. 290; Lever: *House of Pitt*, p. 155
248 Headlam: *Letters of Lady Harriot Eliot*, p. 155; *Pitt and Wilberforce*, pp 38-9
249 Wilberforce: *Life of William Wilberforce*, Vol. I, pp 89 and 103; Lord David Cecil: *Melbourne* (combined edition London 1955) p. 168
250 Wilberforce: *Life of William Wilberforce*, Vol. I, pp 94-5; Wilberforce: *Private Papers*, pp 12-15
251 Ibid. pp 72-3
252 Chatham to Pitt, no date but probably December 1785. Quoted Holland Rose: *Pitt and the National Revival*, pp 397-8; Minto: *Sir Gilbert Elliot*, Vol. I, p. 98; Russell: *Memorials and Correspondence of Fox*, Vol. II, pp 283-4
253 C. F. Barrett (ed.): *The Diary and Letters of Madame D'Arblay* (1904 edition, London) pp 357-8
254 Earl of Malmesbury: *Letters of the Earl of Malmesbury, His Family and Friends* (London 1870) Vol. II, pp 124-30

CHAPTER XIII

255 Sir William Gordon to Alexander Carlyle, June 1780. University of

459

Edinburgh MSS Carlyle Letters No. 104; Wraxhall: *Historical and Posthumous Memoirs*, Vol. I, p. 425. Quoted Furber: *First Viscount Melville*, p. 291; Minto: *Sir Gilbert Elliot*, Vol. III, p. 349

256 HMC Abergavenny, Appendix VI, p. 50, no. 440; *Parliamentary History*, Vol. XVII, p. 496

257 *The Rolliad and Political Miscellanies* (revised edition, London 1795) *Criticisms*, p. 13

258 Historical Manuscripts Commission Dropmore MSS (1892-1927), Vol. I, p. 240; Melville MSS (Furber Collection) Furber: *First Viscount Melville*, pp 38-9

259 Pretyman MSS (copy) HA/119/T108/17

260 Private Accounts of Warren Hastings. BM Add MSS 29, 229

261 Pitt in the House of Commons, 2 March 1787. *Parliamentary Register*, Vol. XXI, pp 367-8

262 *Parliamentary History*, Vol. XXV, pp 1094-5

263 Auckland: *Journal and Correspondence*, Vol. I, p. 127

264 *Parliamentary Register*, Vol. XX, pp 373-4

265 Wilberforce: *Life of William Wilberforce*, Vol. V, p. 341

266 Quoted Keith Feiling: *Warren Hastings* (London 1954) p. 348

267 Wilberforce: *Life of William Wilberforce*, Vol. V, pp 340-41

268 Stanhope: *Life of William Pitt*, Vol. I, Appendix p. xix

269 Hastings Papers, April 1791. BM Add MSS 29,172

270 Quoted Feiling: *Warren Hastings*, p. 353

271 Minto: *Sir Gilbert Elliot*, Vol. I, pp 204-18; J. E. Norton (ed.): *Letters of Edward Gibbon* (London 1956) Vol. II, p. 172

272 Quoted Feiling: *Warren Hastings*, p. 360; Pellew: *First Viscount Sidmouth*, Vol. I, p. 41

CHAPTER XIV

273 Lady Ilchester and Viscount Stavordale (eds): *Life and Letters of Lady Sarah Lennox* (London 1901) Vol. I, p. 67

274 Wraxhall: *Historical and Posthumous Memoirs*, Vol. I, p. 295

275 E. W. Harcourt (ed.): *The Harcourt Papers: Memoirs of the years 1788-9 by Elizabeth Countess of Harcourt, Lady of the Bedchamber to the Queen* (Oxford 1880) Vol. IV, p. 2

276 Stanhope: *Life of William Pitt*, Vol. II, Appendix p. ii

277 Barrett: *Madame D'Arblay*, Vol. IV, p. 160

278 Chatham Papers. PRO 30/8/103, pt 2

279 Stanhope: *Life of William Pitt*, Vol. II. Appendix pp v-vi

280 Harcourt: Harcourt Papers, Vol. IV, p. 28

281 Buckingham: *Court and Cabinets of George III*, Vol. II, pp 6-7

282 Ibid. Vol. I, pp 444-5

283 Pretyman MSS T108/42

284 Buckingham: *Court and Cabinets of George III*, Vol. II, p. 21

285 Lord Palmerston's Journal. Quoted Connell: *Portrait of a Whig Peer*, p. 182

286 Ibid. pp 183-4

287 A. Aspinall (ed.): *The Correspondence of George, Prince of Wales* (London 1963-71) Vol. I, p. 388

288 Minto: *Sir Gilbert Elliot*, pp 237-9

289 Auckland: *Journal and Correspondence*, Vol. II, pp 256-7; F. Blaydon: *The Diaries of Colonel the Hon. Robert Fulke Greville* (London 1930) pp 107-11 and 119; Malmesbury: *Letters*, Vol. IV, pp 317-8

290 *Report from the Committee appointed to examine the physicians who have attended his Majesty during his illness, touching the state of his Majesty's health* (London 1788)

291 *Parliamentary History*, Vol. XXVII, p. 706

292 Thomas Moore: *Memoirs of the Life of the Right Honourable Richard Brinsley Sheridan* (London 1825) Vol. II, p. 38

293 *Parliamentary History*, Vol. XXVII, pp 709-10

294 *Parliamentary Register*, Vol. XXV, p. 45

295 Stanhope: *Life of William Pitt*, Vol. II, p. 10

296 Aspinall: *Correspondence of George, Prince of Wales*, Vol. I, p. 355

297 Pretyman MSS (copy) T108/42

298 Minto: *Sir Gilbert Elliot*, Vol. I, p. 248

299 Auckland: *Journal and Correspondence*, Vol. II, p. 252

300 This diagnosis is the pioneer work of two psychiatrists who are also historians of medicine: Doctors Ida Macalpine and Richard Hunter, authors of *The 'Insanity' of George III: A Classic Case of Porphyria (British Medical Journal* 8 January 1966) and *George III and the Mad Business* (London 1969). Their article, together with others by Professor Abe Goldburg and John Brooke, was reprinted in the British Medical Association's publication *Porphyria—A Royal Malady* (London 1968). For a different, but less convincing, opinion see M. Guttmacher: *America's Last King, An Interpretation of the Madness of George III* (1941), and Charles Chenevix Trench: *The Royal Malady* (London 1964). The disease was first defined by J. Waldenstrom in 1937

301 Macalpine and Hunter: *George III and the Mad Business*, p. 173

302 Blaydon: *Diaries of Fulke Greville*, p. 133

303 Minto: *Sir Gilbert Elliot*, Vol. I, pp 254-5

304 Sichel: *Sheridan*, Vol II, pp 424-5

305 Auckland: *Journal and Correspondence*, Vol. II, p. 269

306 J. Stockdale: *The History and proceedings of the Lords and Commons*

of Great Britain . . . with regard to the Regency (London 1789) pp 456-8

307 Wraxhall: *Historical and Posthumous Memoirs*, Vol. III, p. 69-70; Minto: *Sir Gilbert Elliot*, Vol. I, p. 281; Palmerston's Record Book of political anecdotes F23, quoted Connell: *Portrait of a Whig Peer*, p. 198

308 Minto: *Sir Gilbert Elliot*, Vol. I, pp 303-5; Chatham Papers PRO 30/8/59; Buckingham: *Court and Cabinets of George III*, Vol. II, pp 149-52

309 Harriot G. Mundy (ed.): *The Journal of Mary Frampton* (London 1885) p. 21; *The Times*, 24 April 1789

310 Minto: *Sir Gilbert Elliot*, Vol. I, pp 293-5

311 Ibid. Vol. I, p. 320

312 Barrett: *Madame D'Arblay*, Vol. V, p. 36

CHAPTER XV

313 Albert Sorel: *L'Europe et la Révolution française* (1885) Vol. I, p. 346; C. Ross (ed.): *Correspondence of Charles, First Marquess Cornwallis* (1859) Vol. I, pp 203-4

314 Harris to Joseph Ewart (Secretary to British Mission at Berlin) 15 March 1785. Malmesbury: *Letters*, Vol. II, p. 113

315 Comte de Mirabeau: *La Cour de Berlin* (1788) Vol. II, p. 13

316 A. Cobban: *Ambassadors and Secret Agents* (London 1954) pp 123-4

317 Malmesbury: *Letters*, Vol. II, p. 80

318 Harris to Carmarthen, 2 February 1785, and 'Inclosure A: Considerations upon the State of Europe in 1785'; Malmesbury: *Letters*, Vol. II, p. 103

319 B. M. Egerton MSS 3498; Stanhope: *Life of William Pitt*, Vol. I, Appendix p. xix

320 Holland Rose: *Pitt and the National Revival*, p. 319

321 *Public Advertiser*, 13 December 1786

322 Malmesbury: *Letters*, Vol. II, p. 245

323 Circular dispatch to all ambassadors, 21 September 1787. Quoted Holland Rose: *Pitt and the National Revival*, p. 377

324 Malmesbury: *Letters*, Vol. II, p. 254

325 Holland Rose: *Pitt and the National Revival*, p. 509

326 *Parliamentary Register*, Vol XXVII, pp 564-5

327 8 March 1739. *Parliamentary History*, Vol. X

328 BM Add MSS 34436; Auckland: *Journal and Correspondence*, Vol. II, pp 382 and 392-3

329 Quoted Sichel: *Sheridan*, Vol. II, Appendix 4, p. 432

330 Fox: *Speeches*, Vol. IV, pp 178 and 198-9

331 Holland Rose: *Pitt and the National Revival*, p. 614
332 Ewart MSS. Quoted Holland Rose: *Pitt and the National Revival*, p. 617
333 Count Herzberg to Marchese di Lucchesini, 7 May 1791. Quoted Holland Rose: *Pitt and the National Revival*, p. 628
334 Moore: *Sheridan*, Vol. II, pp 134-5

CHAPTER XVI

335 Russell: *Memorials and Correspondence of Fox*, Vol. II, p. 361
336 Stanhope: *Life of William Pitt*, Vol. II, p. 38
337 Wedgwood to J. Barker, Geneva, 29 August 1789. Quoted Savage and Finer: *Selected Letters of Wedgwood*, p. 319
338 Quoted D. B. Horn: *Great Britain and Europe in the Eighteenth Century* (Oxford 1967) p. 25
339 Quoted G. Rudé: *Europe in the Eighteenth Century* (London 1972) p. 268
340 The debate is reported in *Parliamentary History*, Vol. XXVIII, pp 334-72
341 Minto: *Sir Gilbert Elliot*, pp 350-51; quoted Horn: *Great Britain and Europe in the Eighteenth Century* (Oxford 1967)
342 *Parliamentary History*, Vol. XXVIII, pp 503 and 627
343 Ibid. Vol. XXIX, pp 248-9
344 The debate is reported in *Parliamentary History*, Vol. XXIX, pp 364-401
345 Ibid. pp 379-80 and 403
346 Paine to Burke, 17 January 1790. Northumberland Record Office A IV 73a (copy). Printed in *The Durham University Journal* 1951, Vol. XLIII, pp 50-54
347 *Parliamentary History*, Vol. XXIX, p. 826
348 BM Add MSS 34, 438
349 Minto: *Sir Gilbert Elliot*, Vol. II, p. 2
350 *Parliamentary History*, Vol. XXIX, pp 1300-41

CHAPTER XVII

351 Wilberforce: *Life of William Wilberforce*, Vol. V, p. 241
352 Ibid. Vol. I, pp 150-51
353 Wraxhall: *Historical and Posthumous Memoirs*, Vol. V, p. 149
354 Wilberforce: *Private Papers*, p. 20
355 Quoted Furneaux: *Wilberforce*, p. 93
356 Hansard, Vol. 28, p: 68; Fox: *Speeches*, Vol. IV, p. 16
357 Wilberforce: *Life of William Wilberforce*, pp 340-44
358 This famous story rests on the sole authority of Stanhope (*Life of William Pitt*, Vol. I, pp 145-6) who stated that he had heard it from

members of parliament present at the debate. An incomplete account of the debate appears in *Parliamentary History*, Vol. XXIX, pp 1133-58

359 Wilberforce: *Conversational Memoranda*, quoted Furneaux: *William Wilberforce*, p. 111; Minto: *Sir Gilbert Elliot*, Vol. II, pp 5-6

360 Stanhope: *Life of William Pitt*, Vol. I, pp 375-6

361 Buckingham: *Court and Cabinets of George III*, Vol. I, p. 385

362 Stanhope: *Life of William Pitt*, Vol. II, p. 77

363 Ibid. Appendix, p. xiii

364 Ibid. Vol. II, pp 75-80

365 Wilberforce: *Life of William Wilberforce*, Vol. I, p. 391; *Correspondence between Pitt and Rutland*, pp 150-51; Rose: *Diaries and Correspondence*, Vol. II, p. 260

366 Stanhope: *Life of William Pitt*, Appendix, pp xiii and xv

367 HMC Dropmore, Vol. I, p. 534; Malmesbury: *Letters*, Vol. III, p. 592; Rosebery: *Pitt*, p. 67; Cornwallis-West: *Life and Letters of Admiral Cornwallis* (London 1827) p. 427

368 Stanhope: *Life of William Pitt*, Vol. II, pp 148-50

369 Declaration by the Sheffield Society, May 1792. Quoted Holland Rose: *Pitt and the Great War* (London 1911) p. 25

370 PRO Home Office 102-5. Quoted Meikle: *Scotland and the French Revolution* (Glasgow 1912) p. 82. See also the same author's 'The King's Birthday Riot in Edinburgh, 1792', *Scottish Historical Review*, Vol. VII, pp 21-8

CHAPTER XVIII

371 See F. O'Gorman: *The Whig Party and the French Revolution* (London 1967), p. 94

372 PRO Chatham Papers 30/8/168

373 Malmesbury: *Letters*, Vol. II, pp 454-61

374 Ibid. pp 462-6

375 HMC Carlisle, pp 696-7

376 HMC Dropmore, Vol. II, p. 142

377 Minto: *Sir Gilbert Elliot*, Vol. II, p. 65

378 Headlam: *Letters of Lady Harriot Eliot*, pp 85-7

379 Fox Papers. BM Add MSS 47571, ff 16, 18; and 47570, ff 189-90

380 Minto: *Sir Gilbert Elliot*, Vol. I, p. 389

381 Fox Papers. BM Add MSS 47561, ff 133-4

382 Malmesbury: *Letters*, Vol. II, pp 474-5

383 Minto: *Sir Gilbert Elliot*, Vol. II, pp 71-2, 82-5

384 Ibid. pp 92-6

385 *Parliamentary History*, Vol. XVII, pp 149-50

386 See O'Gorman: *The Whig Party and the French Revolution*, Appendix, pp 2-4

387 Malmesbury: *Letters*, Vol. II, p. 506

CHAPTER XIX

388 For a detailed account see Holland Rose: *Great War*, pp 85-117
389 Quoted Moore: *Sheridan*, Vol. II, p. 198
390 Bridport Papers IV. Quoted Hood: *The Admirals Hood*, p. 100
391 The family name, originally Wellesley, was abbreviated to Wesley in the seventeenth century, and the 1st Duke of Wellington was born Arthur Wesley. His brother Richard, 2nd Earl of Mornington, changed the family name back to Wellesley in 1798.
392 Minto: *Sir Gilbert Elliot*, Vol. II, pp 118-9
393 Pretyman MSS. Quoted Holland Rose: *Great War*, p. 131
394 Dundas to Sir James Murray, 16 April 1793. Auckland: *Journals and Correspondence*, Vol. III, p. 24
395 Minto: *Sir Gilbert Elliot*, Vol. II, p. 159
396 Holland Rose: *Great War*, p. 144
397 Minto: *Sir Gilbert Elliot*, Vol. II, pp 170-73
398 Holland Rose: *Great War*, p. 151
399 Ibid. p. 152
400 George Rose: *Diaries and Correspondence*, Vol. I, p. 132

CHAPTER XX

401 Auckland: *Journal and Correspondence*, Vol. III, p. 114
402 Pellew: *First Viscount Sidmouth*, Vol. I, p. 91
403 Lord Rosebery (ed.): *Letters relating to the Love Episode of William Pitt together with an account of his health by his physician Sir Walter Farquhar* (London 1900) p. 49
404 Wilberforce: *Correspondence*, Vol. II, p. 298; Stanhope MSS 'Mr Pitt II': Pellew: *First Viscount Sidmouth*, pp 152-3; Canning: *Journal*, Harewood MSS, quoted W. Hinde: *George Canning* (London 1973) p. 35
405 'Holwood Cellar Book', PRO 30/8/203; PRO 30/8/219; Wilberforce: *Life of William Wilberforce*, Vol. III, p. 219
406 Malmesbury: *Letters*, Vol. III, p. 3
407 Minto: *Sir Gilbert Elliot*, Vol. II, p. 96
408 Quoted Ibid. Vol. II, pp 278-9n.
409 Ibid. Vol. II, p. 257
410 Quoted C. Oman: *Sir John Moore* (London 1953) p. 104
411 Mornington to Addington, 8 November 1793. Quoted Pellew: *First Viscount Sidmouth*, Vol. I, p. 112
412 Portland to Burke, 19 January 1794. Wentworth Woodhouse MSS, Burke Letters I

413 *Parliamentary History*, Vol. XXXI, pp 497-505
414 Wedgwood to Bentley, 9 August 1779. Wedgwood Archives
415 Northamptonshire County Record Office, Fitzwilliam MSS X512/5/1
416 Scottish Record Office Melville Castle MSS GD51 1/17/24/2; Arniston MSS Arniston Letter Book No. 91
417 HMC Dropmore, Vol. II, p. 597-8
418 Fox Papers, BM Add 47571, ff 143-6
419 Wilberforce: *Life of William Wilberforce*, Vol. II, p. 391
420 E. Verney (ed.): *The Journals and Correspondence of Sir Henry Calvert* (London 1853) pp 338-60; L. S. Benjamin (ed.): *The Windham Papers* (London 1913) Vol. I, pp 220-26
421 Stanhope: *Life of William Pitt*, Vol. II, Appendix, pp xxi-xxii
422 Malmesbury: *Letters*, Vol. III, p. 250
423 Auckland: *Journal and Correspondence*, Vol. III, pp 266-75
424 Ibid. p. 233

CHAPTER XXI

425 Stanhope: *Life of William Pitt*, Vol. II, Appendix, p. xx
426 Aspinall: *Correspondence of George, Prince of Wales*, Vol. III, p. 9
427 Malmesbury: *Letters*, pp 164-201
428 Ibid. pp 207-11
429 Ibid. pp 219-20
430 Pretyman MSS T108/44
431 Auckland: *Journal and Correspondence*, Vol. III, pp 319-20
432 Minto: *Sir Gilbert Elliot*, Vol. II, p. 385
433 Malmesbury: *Letters*, Vol. III, pp 259-60
434 Ibid. p. 259
435 See Palmerston MSS B1 (quoted Connell: *Portrait of a Whig Peer*, p. 326)
436 Quoted D. M. Stuart: *Dearest Bess* (London 1955) p. 78; Portland MSS, University Library, Nottingham PWF 3177; A. Aspinall: *The Later Correspondence of George III* (Cambridge 1962-3) Vol. II, p. 560
437 *Parliamentary History*, Vol. XXXII, pp 409-22
438 Minto: *Sir Gilbert Elliot*, Vol. II, p. 346

CHAPTER XXII

439 Rosebery: *Love Episode*, pp 31-2
440 Ibid. p. 32; Auckland: *Journal and Correspondence*, Vol. III, pp 378-9
441 Rosebery: *Love Episode*, p. 49
442 *Pitt and Wilberforce*, pp 13-20
443 *The Female Jockey Club* (1794)

444 Rosebery (ed.): *Bishop Tomline's Estimate of Pitt*, p. 33n
445 Canning to Rev. William Leigh, 4 October 1796. Harewood MSS. Quoted Hinde: *Canning*, p. 56
446 Auckland: *Journal and Correspondence*, Vol. III, p. 367
447 Ibid. p. 369
448 The correspondence between Pitt and Auckland escaped Pretyman who, inheriting Pitt's papers, destroyed everything of a personal or compromising nature, because Auckland's letters were returned to him by Pitt. They were, however, suppressed for many years, being published in full for the first time by Lord Rosebery (*Love Episode*, pp 1-30) more than a century after they were written. Pitt's letter to Addington is in the Sidmouth MSS and is quoted in Philip Ziegler: *Addington* (London 1965) pp 83-4. Dundas also destroyed all personal letters written to him by Pitt.
449 See Holland Rose: *Great War*, p. 303
450 See Sichel: *Sheridan*, Vol. II, p. 58
451 Lord Macaulay: Essay on Pitt (*Works*, London 1882-5, p. 417)
452 The quotations that follow are all taken from *The Rolliad* (*Criticisms, Political Eclogues, Political Miscellanies,* and *Epigrams on the IM-MACULATE BOY*). Revised edition London 1795
453 D. J. West: *Homosexuality* (London 1955, Pelican edition 1960) p. 25
454 Quoted John Wardroper: *Kings, Lords and Wicked Libellers, Satire and Protest 1760-1837* (London 1973) pp 108-9
455 G. Cheyne: *The Natural Method of Cureing the Diseases of the Body and the Disorders of the Mind depending on the Body* (London 1742) p. 283. See also S. Solomon: *A Guide to Health or Advice to both Sexes* (n.d.) pp 99-105; and W. Brodum: *A Guide for Old Age, or a Cure for the Indiscretions of Youth* (London 1795) pp 49-65
456 W. Matthews (ed.): *The Diary of Dudley Ryder* (London 1939) p. 143
457 J. W. Archenholtz: *A Picture of England* (London 1797) p. 309
458 C. L. Meryon: *Memoirs of Lady Hester Stanhope* (London 1845) pp 178-9 and 58-9
459 West: *Homosexuality*, p. 150
460 Ibid. p. 169

CHAPTER XXIII

461 Minto: *Sir Gilbert Elliot*, Vol. II, pp 278-80
462 Pelham Papers. BM Add MSS 3118, f. 268
463 Rt. Hon. W. Beresford (ed.): *The Correspondence of the Right Hon. John Beresford* (London 1854) Vol. II, p. 75; 'Thoughts on the Emancipation of the Roman Catholics in Ireland, and dangers from granting them'. Quoted John, Lord Campbell: *Lives of the Lord*

Chancellors (London 1845-68) Vol. III, p. 172

464 Pretyman MSS. Quoted Ashbourne: *Pitt: some Chapters of his Life and Times*, pp 204-5; HMC Carlisle (1897) p. 703 *et seq.* and Appendix Pt 6; Pretyman MSS T108/45

465 Stanhope: *Life of William Pitt*, Vol. II, Appendix, pp xxiii–xxv

466 *The Report of the Secret Committee of the House of Commons and the House of Lords August 1798* (London 1893): B. O'Brien (ed.): *Autobiography of Wolfe Tone* (London 1893) Vol. II, p. 235

467 Pretyman MSS T 108/44

468 Holland Rose: *Great War*, p. 235; Watson: *Reign of George III*, p. 372

469 Quoted Watson: *Reign of George III*, p. 399

470 Pretyman MSS. Quoted Holland Rose: *Great War*, pp 406-7

471 Ross: *Cornwallis Correspondence*, Vol. III, p. 84

472 Quoted Holland Rose: *Great War*, pp 414-5

CHAPTER XXIV

473 Minto: *Sir Gilbert Elliot*, Vol. II, p. 415

474 Quoted Farington: *Diary*, Vol. II, p. 102n.

475 J. Parkes and H. Merrivale (eds): *Memoirs of Sir Philip Francis* (London 1867) Vol. II, p. 246

476 Malmesbury: *Letters*, Vol. IV, p. 128

477 Sidmouth MSS. Quoted Ziegler: *Addington*, p. 77

478 Pretyman MSS T108/44

479 Stanhope: *Life of William Pitt*, Vol. III, p. 66; Pellew: *First Viscount Sidmouth*, Vol. I, p. 196

480 See Tomline: *Memoirs of the Life of William Pitt*, Vol. IV, p. 101

481 *The War Speeches of William Pitt the Younger*, selected by R. Coupland (3rd edition Oxford 1940) pp 228-9

482 Ibid. p. 234

483 See *Parliamentary Papers* (1806) Vol. III, p. 205

484 Pellew: *First Viscount Sidmouth*, Vol. I, p. 200

485 Wilberforce Journal. Quoted Furneaux: *Wilberforce*, p. 175

486 Harewood MSS 62. Quoted Hinde: *Canning*, p. 58

487 Duke MSS Wilberforce Papers. Quoted Furneaux: *Wilberforce*, p. 182; see also Pitt to Dundas, 5 May 1798, Stanhope: *Life of William Pitt*, Vol. III, p. 132

488 Stanhope: *Life of William Pitt*, Vol. III, p. 132

489 Ibid. Appendix, p. xiv

490 Wilberforce's diary, 27-30 May 1798, quoted Furneaux: *Wilberforce*, p. 183

491 Wilberforce: *Life of William Wilberforce*, Vol. II, pp 281-2

492 Ibid. Vol. II, pp 283-4

493 Pretyman MSS T108/44

494 Quoted Oliver Warner: *A Portrait of Lord Nelson* (London 1958) p. 128

495 PRO Foreign Office 65/40

496 Auckland: *Journal and Correspondence,* Vol. IV, pp 11, 35 and 40; Pretyman MSS T108/42

CHAPTER XXV

497 Minto: *Sir Gilbert Elliot,* Vol. III, p. 49

498 Ibid. pp 107-9

499 Quoted C. H. Philips: *The East India Company 1784-1834* (Manchester University 1961) p. 103

500 Stowe Papers, Box 312. Quoted Mackesy: *Statesman at War: The Strategy of Overthrow 1788-9* (London 1974) p. 79

501 Ross: *Cornwallis Correspondence,* Vol. III, p. 123

502 HMC Dropmore, Vol. V, p. 232

503 Stowe papers ST5, Vol. II, p. 331. Quoted Mackesy: *Statesman at War,* p. 204

504 PRO War Office 6/20 p. 139

505 Dundas Papers, Scottish Record Office, Melville Castle Muniments GD/51/1/703/11

506 Quoted Edward Ingram (ed.): *Two Views of British India* (Bath 1970) pp 166-7

507 Benjamin: *Windham Papers,* Vol. II, p. 143

508 *War Speeches,* pp 246-87; *Parliamentary History,* XXXIV, pp 1303-97

509 Quoted Fortescue: *Correspondence of George III,* Vol. IV, p. 798

510 As late as 1804 James Monroe wrote from London, 'Our commerce was never so much favoured in time of war'. American State Papers, Foreign Relations Vol. III, p. 98 (Washington 1832-3)

511 Minto: *Sir Gilbert Elliot,* Vol. III, p. 145; quoted Eric Delieb and Michael Roberts: *The Great Silver Manufactory* (London 1971) p. 119

512 Stanhope: *Life of William Pitt,* Vol. III, pp 247-50

513 *Parliamentary History,* Vol. XXXV, p. 793

514 Quoted Pellew: *First Viscount Sidmouth,* Vol. I, p. 263

CHAPTER XXVI

515 Auckland: *Journal and Correspondence,* Vol. IV, p. 88; Minto: *Sir Gilbert Elliot,* Vol. III, pp 61-2

516 Queen Caroline's evidence before the Commission of Inquiry 1806. Quoted C. Hibbert: *George IV, Prince of Wales* (London 1972) p. 209. Her footman, Roberts, is reported to have said of her that she was 'very fond of fucking'.

517 Harewood MSS 30. Quoted Hinde: *Canning*, p. 91

518 G. Festing: *John Hookham Frere and his Friends* (London 1899) p. 31

519 Pretyman MSS T108/44

520 Addington to Hiley Addington, 19 October and 30 October. Quoted Pellew: *First Viscount Sidmouth*, Vol. I, pp 266-7

521 Stanhope: *Life of William Pitt*, Vol. III, p. 268

522 In view of the King's later expressions of astonishment at Pitt's behaviour, some doubt has been cast on the truth of this story. The proof of it is contained in a letter of self-justification written by Loughborough and circulated to his friends in the spring of 1801. (Campbell: *Lord Chancellors*, Vol. VI, p. 326)

523 G. Rose: *Diaries and Correspondence*, Vol. I, pp 289-303

524 Malmesbury accused Auckland of using his influence 'indirectly, through the Archbishop of Canterbury and the Bishop of London, to raise an alarm in the King's mind, and to indispose and exasperate him against the framers of this measure' (Malmesbury: *Letters*, Vol. IV, p. 3)—an accusation strenuously denied by the Bishop of Bath and Wells, editor of the Auckland correspondence (Auckland: *Journals and Correspondence*, Vol. IV, pp 113-5)

525 G. Rose: *Diaries and Correspondence*, Vol. II, p. 244. Quoted D. G. Barnes: *George III and William Pitt*, p. 362

526 *Diary and Correspondence of Charles Abbot, Lord Colchester* (London 1861) Vol. I, p. 232

527 Pellew: *First Viscount Sidmouth*, Vol. I, p. 286

528 *English Historical Documents*, Vol. XI, no. 3, pp 159-62

529 PRO Chatham Papers 104

530 Stanhope: *Life of William Pitt*, Vol. III, Appendix, p. xxx

531 Pretyman MSS T108/44; Minto: *Sir Gilbert Elliot*, Vol. III, pp 192-4 and 198-9

532 Ingram: *British India*, p. 259; PRO 30/8/188, f. 109

533 Carver Papers. Quoted: Iris Butler: *The Eldest Brother* (London 1973) p. 260; Malmesbury: *Letters*, Vol. IV, p. 9; Minto: *Sir Gilbert Elliot*, Vol. III, pp 190-91; L. Jennings (ed.): *The Croker Papers* (London 1884) Vol. II, p. 339; *Life of Sir James Mackintosh* (London 1836) p. 171

534 Aspinall: *Later Correspondence of George III*, Vol. III, pp 502 and 508. Willis MSS BM Add MSS 41692-3

535 G. Rose: *Diaries and Correspondence*, Vol. I, p. 335

536 Stanhope: *Life of William Pitt*, Vol. III, pp 302-5

537 Quoted Ziegler: *Addington*, pp 106-7

538 Malmesbury: *Letters*, Vol. IV, p. 36

539 Pretyman MSS T108/44

540 Ibid. T108/45

541 Wilberforce: *Life of William Wilberforce,* Vol. II, p. 270; Pretyman MSS T108/44

542 Wellesley Papers BM Add MSS 37308

CHAPTER XXVII

543 Minto: *Sir Gilbert Elliot,* Vol. III, pp 186, 208-11 and 216

544 PRO Chatham Papers 104

545 BM Add MSS 38190, f. 2

546 Malmesbury: *Letters,* Vol. IV, p. 59

547 Windham Papers. Quoted Ziegler: *Addington,* p. 125; Dacres Adams MSS PRO 30/58; Henry Holland: *Memoirs of the Whig Party* (London 1852) Vol. I, p. 185

548 Stanhope: *Life of William Pitt,* Vol. III, p. 357

549 Pretyman MSS T108/44

550 Minto: *Sir Gilbert Elliot,* Vol. III, pp 227-8; Pretyman MSS T108/44, 45

551 Pretyman MSS T108/44

552 Ibid. T108/45

553 Stanhope: *Life of William Pitt,* Vol. III, p. 368

554 Pellew: *First Viscount Sidmouth,* Vol. I, pp 489-91

555 Minto: *Sir Gilbert Elliot,* Vol. III, p 251; Rosebery: *Love Episode,* pp 52-3

556 Rosebery: *Love Episode,* pp 34-5; *Pitt and Wilberforce,* p. 52; Farington: *Diary,* Vol. II, p. 63; Pretyman MSS T108/44

557 Minto: *Sir Gilbert Elliot,* Vol. III, p. 259

558 Pretyman MSS T108/44; Malmesbury: *Letters,* Vol. IV, pp 75-8

559 See Stanhope: *Life of William Pitt,* Vol. III, pp 394-5

560 Malmesbury: *Letters,* Vol. IV, pp 110 and 121

561 Jennings: *Croker Papers,* Vol. II, p. 339

562 Stanhope: *Life of William Pitt,* Vol. III, p. 426

563 Malmesbury: *Letters,* Vol. IV, pp 78-80, 147-9 and 152-7

564 Sheridan in the House of Commons, 14 May 1802. Quoted Sichel: *Sheridan,* Vol. II, p. 308

565 Rosebery: *Love Episode,* p. 35; Fox Papers BM Add MSS 57575, f. 23

566 Malmesbury: *Letters,* Vol. IV, p. 164

567 Ibid. pp 180-83

568 Ibid. pp 184-7

CHAPTER XXVIII

569 Malmesbury: *Letters,* Vol. IV, p. 253

570 Maxwell: *Creevey Papers*, pp 14-15; Pretyman MSS T108/44, T108/42
571 Stanhope: *Life of William Pitt*, Vol. IV, p. 31; Rosebery: *Love Episode*, pp 35-6
572 Malmesbury: *Letters*, Vol. IV, p. 256; Maxwell: *Creevey Papers*, p. 15; C. Price (ed.): *The Letters of Richard Brinsley Sheridan* (Oxford 1966) Vol. II, p. 196
573 Hon. John William Ward to Rev. E. Copleston, 30 May 1803. Stanhope: *Life of William Pitt*, Vol. IV, pp 48-50
574 Farington: *Diary*, Vol. II, p. 100
575 J. C. Moore: *The Life of Lieutenant-General Sir John Moore K.B.* (London 1834) Vol. II, pp 8-9
576 Duchess of Cleveland: *The Life and Letters of Lady Hester Stanhope* (London 1897) p. 38
577 Ibid. p. 42 (Misdated 1802 for 1803)
578 Ibid. p. 44
579 Sidmouth MSS. Quoted Ziegler: *Addington*, p. 200
580 Pellew: *First Viscount Sidmouth*, Vol. II, p. 310
581 Quoted Sir Arthur Bryant: *Years of Victory 1802-1812* (London 1944) p. 85
582 *Pitt and Wilberforce*, p. 54
583 Malmesbury: *Letters*, Vol. IV, pp 288-90
584 Stanhope: *Life of William Pitt*, Vol. IV, pp 139-44
585 Ibid. Appendix p. iv; PRO Chatham 104; Pretyman MSS T108/45 (n.d. but franked 1804 and later endorsed '6th May')
586 G. Rose: *Diaries and Correspondence*, Vol. II, p. 121
587 Farington: *Diary*, Vol. II, p. 252
588 P. Napier: *The Sword Dance: Lady Sarah Lennox and the Napiers* (London 1971) p. 30
589 Minto: *Sir Gilbert Elliot*, Vol. III, p. 349; HMC Dropmore, Vol. VII, p. 230
590 Wilberforce: *Conversational Memoranda*, quoted Furneaux: *Wilberforce*, p. 228; Wilberforce: *Life of William Wilberforce*, Vol. III, p. 211
591 Moore: *Sheridan*, Vol. II, p. 330

CHAPTER XXIX

592 Campbell: *Lord Chancellors*, Vol. II, Stanhope: *Life of William Pitt*, Vol. IV, p. 251
593 Stanhope: *Life of William Pitt*, Vol. IV, p. 252
594 *Rolliad Criticisms*, pp 21-2
595 Pretyman MSS T108/42

596 Lord Fitzwilliam's Notebook. Malmesbury: *Letters,* Vol. IV, p. 347n. This account has been generally accepted as authentic, but it contains at least one error: Lieutenant-Colonel Gwyllym Lloyd Wardle was not elected to parliament as member for Okehampton until 1807 and can therefore have had no part in the scene. If Pitt was helped from the House 'unconsciously', he must have recovered sufficiently to return to the Chamber. The record of proceedings shows that he spoke three times after the vote was taken. Creevey, however, confirms Pitt's 'fallen crest' and 'dolorous air' in the House of Commons. (Maxwell: *Creevey Papers,* p. 34)

597 Quoted J. A. Lovat-Fraser: *Henry Dundas Viscount Melville* (London 1916) p. 96

598 Stanhope: *Life of William Pitt,* Vol. IV, pp 288-9

599 Jennings: *Croker Papers,* Vol. II, p. 233

600 Minto: *Sir Gilbert Elliot,* Vol. III, pp 373-4

601 Holland Rose: *Great War,* p. 538; Stanhope: *Life of William Pitt,* Vol. IV, pp 346-7

602 Harewood MSS 30. Quoted Hinde: *Canning,* p. 137

603 Meryon: *Lady Hester Stanhope,* Vol. II, pp 65-6

604 Pretyman MSS T108/44

605 Farington: *Diary,* Vol. III, p. 176

606 Malmesbury: *Letters,* Vol. IV, p. 343

607 Farington: *Diary,* Vol. III, p. 140

CHAPTER XXX

608 Stanhope: *Life of William Pitt,* Vol. IV, pp 367-8

609 Rosebery: *Love Episode,* pp 40-42

610 Ibid. pp 43-5; Meryon: *Lady Hester Stanhope,* Vol II, p. 79

611 Pretyman MSS HA T99/27; Rosebery: *Love Episode,* pp 44-6; Farington: *Diary,* Vol. III, p. 291

612 Rosebery: *Love Episode,* pp 46-8; Canning's Diary, Harewood MSS 29D; Pretyman MSS T99/26

613 Pretyman MSS T109/27; Meryon: *Lady Hester Stanhope,* Vol. III, pp 165-6

614 Wellesley Papers, BM Add MSS 37309; Stanhope: *Life of William Pitt,* Vol. IV, pp 373-6; Pretyman MSS T99/26; *Quarterly Review,* Vol. LVII, quoted Butler: *Eldest Brother,* p. 371

615 Pretyman MSS T99/27; James Stanhope gives the valet's name as Parslow (Stanhope: *Life of William Pitt,* Vol. IV, p. 380) but the name John Pursler occurs in the list of servants compiled in 1821 by James Knox, Solicitors, 44 Bedford Square, showing the wages owing in satisfaction of Pitt's will (Pretyman MSS HA119/562)

616 James Stanhope's account, Stanhope: *Life of William Pitt*, Vol. IV, pp 378-82; Pretyman MSS T99/27

617 James Stanhope's account (Stanhope: *Life of William Pitt*); Pretyman MSS T99/27; G. Rose: *Diaries and Correspondence*, Vol. II, p. 230 and cf. p. 254

618 The Pretyman MSS T108/45 contain a photographed facsimile of Pitt's will, taken by permission of Sir James Hannen, Judge of the Court of Probate, and legally attested in 1873. This comprises three clauses only and is clearly the will described by Rose, who saw it 'with the ink hardly dry . . . subscribed by Mr Pitt in three places', (G. Rose: *Diaries and Correspondence*, Vol. II, p. 232). Another 'copy' in Tomline's hand (Pretyman MSS HA119/503) includes a fourth clause bequeathing 'a thousand or fifteen hundred pounds a year' to each of Pitt's nieces, and £1,000 a year each to Charles and James Stanhope. This clause appears to have been dictated separately and at a moment when Pitt's mind was confused for he knew no such sum was available for these annuities.

619 James Stanhope's account (Stanhope: *Life of William Pitt*); Cleveland: *Lady Hester Stanhope*, p. 56

620 James Stanhope's account (Stanhope: *Life of William Pitt*). Pitt's last words are quoted by Cleveland (*Lady Hester Stanhope*, p. 55), using James Stanhope's account, as: 'Oh, my country! how I *leave* my country!' Earl Stanhope (*Life of William Pitt*, Vol. IV, p. 382) was, however, quoting from his uncle James Stanhope's original manuscript, obtained from the Duke of Bedford in 1860, and this version must be preferred, although Cleveland's appears to have been more widely accepted. Canning thought the words 'wholly unlike Pitt's usual simplicity of character' and substituted, on Tomline's authority, the cumbersome and much less simple sentence, 'I am sorry to leave the country in such a situation' (Granville: *Correspondence*, Vol. II, p. 169). As Tomline was asleep when Pitt spoke for the last time, and had not seen him since the previous morning, this pompous and incredible version may be dismissed. Disraeli's charming and popular story that Pitt's dying words were to ask for one of Bellamy's pork pies owes its origin to an ancient door-keeper at the House of Commons, who 'remembered' it many years after Pitt's death. If Pitt ever made such a request, he must have done so long before he died, at a time when he was still able to swallow solid food.

621 Rosebery: *Love Episode*, pp. 48-50; Farington: *Diary*, Vol. III, p. 141; For this diagnosis of Pitt's condition I am indebted to Dr Philip Cole MD of New Orleans

622 Pretyman MSS T99/27

623 Stanhope: *Life of William Pitt*, Vol. IV, pp 392-3; Pretyman MSS T99/15; Farington: *Diary*, Vol. III, p. 166

624 Countess Granville (ed.): *Private Correspondence of Earl Granville* (London 1916) Vol. II, p. 162; quoted Hinde: *Canning*, p. 141; Pretyman MSS T108/42 and T99/26

625 Minto: *Sir Gilbert Elliot*, Vol. IV, p. 376

626 Princess Augusta's account, quoted J. H. Jesse: *Memoirs of the Life and Reign of George III* (London 1867) Vol. III, pp 473-4; Stuart: *Dearest Bess*, p. 134

627 Benjamin: *Windham Papers*, Vol. II, p. 246

628 Quoted Hinde: *Canning*, p. 81

Select Bibliography

Subsidiary sources quoted are detailed under *Notes and References*.

1 MANUSCRIPT SOURCES

British Museum and Library
Auckland Papers
Bridport Papers
Chatham Papers
Fox Papers
Grenville Papers
Hardwicke Papers
Hastings Papers
Melville MSS
Pelham Papers
Rose MSS
Wellesley Papers
Willis Papers
Windham Papers

Buckinghamshire County Record Office
Grenville Correspondence

Cambridge University, Pembroke College
Pretyman Papers

476

Chevening
Stanhope MSS, Pitt Papers

East Suffolk Record Office
Pretyman MSS

Exeter County Archives
Sidmouth Papers

Leeds City Libraries, Archives Department (Sheepscar Library)
Harewood MSS

National Army Museum, London
Coote Papers

National Library of Scotland, Edinburgh
Dundas Papers

Northamptonshire County Record Office
Burke Letters
Fitzwilliam MSS

Nottingham University Library
Portland MSS

Public Record Office
William Dacres Adams MSS
Chatham Papers
Colchester Papers

Scottish Record Office
Melville Castle Muniments

Sheffield Public Library
Burke Letters
Wentworth Woodhouse MSS

2 PUBLISHED SOURCES

Abbott, C. (ed.): *The Diary and Correspondence of Charles Abbott, Lord Colchester,* 3 Vols, London 1861
Adams, C. F. (ed.): *The Works of John Adams,* 10 Vols, Boston 1856
Adams, E. D.: *The Influence of Grenville on Pitt's Foreign Policy, 1787-1798,* Washington 1904
Albemarle, Duke of: *Memoirs of the Marquis of Rockingham and his Contemporaries,* 2 Vols, London 1852

Almon, John: *Anecdotes of the Life of the Right Honourable William Pitt, Earl of Chatham*, 3 Vols, London 1793

Annual Register

Anon.: *Satan's Harvest Home*, London 1749

Anson, Sir William R. (ed.): *Autobiographical and Political Correspondence of Augustus Henry, third Duke of Grafton*, London 1898

Archenholtz, J. W. von: *A View of the British Constitution and of the Manners and Customs of the People of England*, London 1794

A Picture of England, London 1797

Ashbourne, Rt. Hon. E. G., Lord: *Pitt: Some Chapters of his Life and Times*, London 1898

Ashton, T. S.: *An Economic History of England: The Eighteenth Century*, London 1955

Aspinall, A.: *Politics and the Press c. 1780-1850*, London 1949

(ed.): *The Later Correspondence of George III*, 8 Vols, Cambridge 1962-3

(ed.): *The Correspondence of George, Prince of Wales*, 5 Vols, London 1963-71

and Smith, E. A. (eds): *English Historical Documents*, Vol. XI, Oxford 1959

Auckland, Robert John, 3rd Baron, Bishop of Bath and Wells (ed.): *The Journal and Correspondence of William, Lord Auckland*, 4 Vols, London 1862

Ayling, Stanley: *George the Third*, London 1972

Bagot, J. F.: *George Canning and his Friends*, 2 Vols, London 1909

Baring, Mrs H. (ed.): *Diary of the Rt. Hon. William Windham*, 2 Vols, London 1866

Barnes, D. G.: *George III and William Pitt 1783-1806*, Stanford & Oxford 1939

Barrett, C. F. (ed.): *Diary and Letters of Madame D'Arblay*, 6 Vols, London 1904-5

Benjamin, L. S. (ed.): *The Windham Papers*, 2 Vols, London 1913

Beresford, Rt. Hon. W. (ed.): *The Correspondence of the Right Honourable John Beresford*, 2 Vols, London 1854

Bessborough, Earl of: *Georgiana: Extracts from the Correspondence of Georgiana, Duchess of Devonshire*, London 1955

and Aspinall, A. (eds): *Lady Bessborough and her Family Circle*, London 1940

Bickley, F. (ed.): *Diaries of Sylvester Douglas, Lord Glenbervie*, 2 Vols, London 1928

Blaydon, F. M. (ed.): *The Diaries of Colonel the Hon. Robert Fulke Greville*, London 1930

Bloch, I.: *Sexual Life in England, Past and Present*, London 1938

Briggs, Asa: *The Age of Improvement 1783-1867*, London 1959

Brooke, John: *George III*, Collins 1972/Panther 1974

Brown, P. D.: *The Chathamites: A Study in the Relationship between Personalities and Ideas in the second half of the Eighteenth Century*, London 1967

Browning, O. (ed.): *The Political Memoranda of Francis, Duke of Leeds*, London 1884

Bruce, H. A. (ed.): *Life of General Sir William Napier KCB*, 2 Vols, London 1864

Bryant, Sir Arthur: *The Years of Endurance*, London 1942

The Years of Victory, London 1944

Buckingham & Chandos, Duke of (ed.): *Memoirs of the Court and Cabinets of George III*, 4 Vols, London 1853-5

Bunbury, Sir Henry: *Narratives of Some Passages in the Great War with France 1799-1810*, London 1927

Burke, Edmund: *The Works of the Right Hon. Edmund Burke*, 2 Vols, London 1834

Butler, Iris: *The Eldest Brother*, London 1973

Butterfield, Sir Herbert: *George III and the Historians*, London 1957

Campbell, John, Lord: *Lives of the Lord Chancellors*, 8 Vols, London 1845-68

Camperdown, 3rd Earl of: *Admiral Duncan*, London 1898

Carey, C. S. (ed.): *Letters written by Lord Chesterfield to his Son*, 4th edition, 2 Vols, London 1912

Cecil, Lord David: *The Young Melbourne*, London 1939

Christie, I. R.: *The End of Lord North's Ministry*, London 1958

Wilkes, Wyvill and Reform, London 1962

Cleveland, Duchess of: *The Life and Letters of Lady Hester Stanhope*, London 1897

Colquhoun, J. C.: *William Wilberforce, His Friends and his Times*, London 1866

Connell, Brian: *Portrait of a Whig Peer*, London 1957

Copeland, T. W.: *Edmund Burke*, London 1950

& others (ed.): *The Correspondence of Edmund Burke*, 9 Vols, London 1958-70

Corbett, J. S., & Richard, H. W. (eds): *The Private Papers of George, Second Earl Spencer*, 4 Vols, London 1913-24

Curzon of Kedleston, Marquess: *British Government in India*, 2 Vols, London 1925

Derry, John W.: *Charles James Fox*, London 1972

The Regency Crisis and the Whigs, Cambridge 1963

de Tocqueville, A.: *The Ancien Régime and the French Revolution*, Oxford 1937

d'Haussonville, Le vicomte: *Le Salon de Madame Necker*, translated by H. M. Trollope, 2 Vols, London 1882

Dorchester, Lady (ed.): John Cam Hobhouse, Lord Broughton: *Recollections of a Long Life*, 6 Vols, London 1909-11

Dunfermline, J. A. Abercromby, Lord: *Lieutenant-General Sir Ralph Abercromby KB, 1793-1801: A memoir by his son*, London 1861

Dutens, L.: *An History of the late important period; from the beginning of his Majesty's illness, to the . . . period of his Majesty's reappearance in the House of Lords*, London 1789

Ehrman, John: *The Younger Pitt: the Years of Acclaim*, London 1969

Ellis, Kenneth: *The Post Office in the Eighteenth Century*, London 1969

Eyck, E.: *Pitt versus Fox: Father and Son*, London 1950

Farnsworth, A.: *Addington, Author of the Modern Income Tax*, London 1951

Feiling, Keith: *Warren Hastings*, London 1954

Festing, G.: *John Hookham Frere & his Friends*, London 1899

Fitzmaurice, Lord E.: *Life of William Earl of Shelburne*, 3 Vols, London 1875-6

Fitzpatrick, W. J.: *Secret Service under Pitt*, London 1892

Fitzwilliam, Earl, & Burke, Sir R. (eds): *Correspondence of Edmund Burke*, 4 Vols, London 1844

Flugel, J. C.: *Man, Morals and Society*, London 1945

Forrest, G. W. (ed.): *Selections from the State Papers of the Governors-General of India: Lord Cornwallis*, 2 Vols, Oxford 1926

Fortescue, Sir J. W.: *History of the British Army*, 13 Vols, London 1910-1930
(ed.): *Correspondence of George III from 1760 to December 1783*, 6 Vols, London 1927-8

Foster, Sir W.: *John Company*, London 1926

Fothergill, Brian: *The Mitred Earl, An Eighteenth Century Eccentric*, London 1974

Fox, C. J.: *Speeches of the Right Honourable Charles James Fox in the House of Commons*, 6 Vols, London 1815

Furber, Holden: *Henry Dundas, First Viscount Melville 1742-1811*, Oxford 1931

Furneaux, Robin: *William Wilberforce*, London 1974

George, M. D.: *English Political Caricature*, 2 Vols, Oxford 1959
London Life in the Eighteenth Century, London 1965

Godechot, J.: *The Taking of the Bastille July 14th 1789*, translated by J. Steward, London 1970

Gore-Browne, R.: *Chancellor Thurlow*, London 1953

Gottschalk, Louis (ed.): *Letters of Lafayette to Washington*, New York 1944

Granville, Castalia, Countess (ed.): *Private Correspondence of Granville Leveson-Gower, First Earl Granville 1781-1821*, 2 Vols, London 1916

Grattan, Henry (ed.): *Memoirs of the Life and Times of the Rt. Hon. Henry Grattan*, 5 Vols, London 1841

Greig, J. (ed.): *Diaries of a Duchess*, London 1926
(ed.): *The Farington Diary*, 7 Vols, London 1923-7

Gwynn, John: *London and Westminster Improved*, London 1766

Gwynn, S.: *Henry Grattan and his Times*, London 1939

Halévy, Elie: *England in 1815*, translated by E. I. Watkin and D. A. Barker. Revised edition, London 1949

Hansard. See *Parliamentary Debates*

Harcourt, E. W. (ed.): *The Harcourt Papers*, 14 Vols, Oxford 1880-1905

Harcourt, Rev. L. V. (ed.): *The Diaries and Correspondence of the Right Hon. George Rose*, 2 Vols, London 1860

Harlow, Vincent, T.: *The Founding of the Second British Empire 1763-1793*, 2 Vols, London 1952-64

Hathaway, W. S. (ed.): *The Speeches of the Right Honourable William Pitt, in the House of Commons*, 4 Vols, London 1806

Hatton, James (ed.): *Selections from the Letters and Correspondence of Sir James Bland Burges Bart*, London 1885

Hayley, William: *Memoirs of the Life and Writings of Hayley, by himself*, 2 Vols, London 1823

Headlam, Cuthbert (ed.): *The Letters of Lady Harriot Eliot 1766-1786*, Edinburgh 1914

Hibbert, Christopher: *George IV, Prince of Wales*, London 1972
  King Mob, London 1953
Hill, Draper: *Mr. Gillray, The Caricaturist*, London 1965
Hinde, Wendy: *George Canning*, London 1973
Historical Manuscripts Commission: Abergavenny MSS
                                   Bathurst MSS
                                   Carlisle MSS
                                   Dropmore MSS
                                   Lonsdale MSS
                                   Rutland MSS
Hobhouse, C.: *Fox*, 2nd edition, London 1947
Hobsbawm, E. J.: *The Age of Revolution*, London 1962
Holland, Henry, Lord (ed.): *Memoirs of the Whig Party*, 2 Vols, London 1852-4
Hood, Dorothy: *The Admirals Hood*, London 1941
Horn, D. B.: *Great Britain and Europe in the Eighteenth Century*, Oxford 1967
  & Ransome, Mary (eds): *English Historical Documents*, Vol. X, London 1957
House of Commons. *Reports from Select Committees of the House of Commons 1715-1801*, 15 Vols, London 1803
Huish, Robert: *Memoirs of George IV*, 2 Vols, London 1831

Ilchester, Lady, and Stavordale, Lord, (eds): *Lady Sarah Lennox: The Life and Letters*, 2 Vols, London 1901
Ingram, Edward (ed.): *Two Views of British India: The Private Correspondence of Mr. Dundas and Lord Wellesley: 1798-1801*, Bath 1970

Jennings, L. J. (ed.): *The Croker Papers 1808-1857*, 3 Vols, London 1844
Jesse, J. H.: *George Selwyn and His Contemporaries*, 4 Vols, Boston 1843
  Memoirs of the Life and Reign of George III, 3 Vols, London 1867

La Combe, F.: *Tableau de Londres*, London 1784
Laughton, J. K. (ed.): *Letters and Papers of Charles, Lord Barham*, 3 Vols, 1907-11
Lecky, W. E. H.: *A History of England in the Eighteenth Century*, 8 Vols, London 1891-1904
Leigh, Ione: *Life of Castlereagh*, London 1851
Lever, Sir Tresham: *The House of Pitt*, London 1947
Leveson-Gower, F. (ed.): *Letters of Harriet, Countess Granville 1810-1845*, London 1894
Lewis, W. S.: *The Yale Edition of Horace Walpole's Correspondence*, 34 Vols, Oxford 1937-65
Three Tours through London in the Years 1748, 1776, 1797, New Haven 1941
Londonderry, Marquess of (ed.): *Memoirs and Correspondence of Viscount Castlereagh*, 12 Vols, London 1848-53
Lopez, Claude-Anne: *Mon Cher Papa, Franklin and the Ladies of Paris*, Yale 1966
Lovat-Fraser, J. A.: *Henry Dundas, Viscount Melville*, London 1916

Macalpine, Ida, and Hunter, Richard: *George III and the Mad Business*, London 1969

Macaulay, T. B., Lord: *Works*, 4 Vols, London 1882-5

Mackesy, Piers G.: *Statesmen at War: The Strategy of Overthrow*, London 1974

Mahan, A. T.: *The Influence of Sea Power upon the French Revolution and Empire 1793-1812*, 2 Vols, London 1892

Malmesbury, Earl of, (ed.): *Diaries and Correspondence of James Harris, First Earl of Malmesbury*, 4 Vols, London 1844

(ed.): *Letters of the Earl of Malmesbury, His Family and Friends*, 2 Vols, London 1870

Manwaring, G. E., and Dobrée, B.: *The Floating Republic*, London 1935

Marshall, Dorothy: *Eighteenth Century England*, London 1962

Matheson, C.: *Life of Henry Dundas, 1st Viscount Melville 1742-1811*, London 1933

Matthews, W. (ed.): *The Diary of Dudley Ryder*, London 1939

Maurice, Sir J. F. (ed.): *Diary of Sir John Moore*, 2 Vols, London 1904

Maxwell, Sir H. (ed.): *The Creevey Papers*, 2nd edition, 2 Vols, London 1904

Meikle, H. W.: *Scotland and the French Revolution*, Glasgow 1912

Meryon, Dr C. L.: *Memoirs of Lady Hester Stanhope as related by herself in conversations with her physician*, 3 Vols, London 1845

Mill, James: *History of British India*, 9 Vols, London 1818

Minto, Nina, Countess of (ed.): *Life and Letters of Sir Gilbert Elliot, First Earl of Minto from 1751-1806*, 3 Vols, London 1874

Mitchell, L. B.: *Charles James Fox and the Disintegration of the Whig Party*, Oxford 1971

Moon, E. P.: *Warren Hastings and British India*, London 1947

Moore, James C.: *The Life of Lieutenant-General Sir John Moore K.B.*, 2 Vols, London 1834

Moore, Thomas: *Memoirs of the Life of The Right Honourable Richard Brinsley Sheridan*, 2 Vols, London 1825

Mundy, Harriot G. (ed.): *The Journal of Mary Frampton*, London 1885

Murray, R. H.: *Edmund Burke*, Oxford 1931

Namier, Sir Lewis: *England in the Age of the American Revolution*, Oxford 1930

The Structure of Politics at the Accession of George III, Oxford 1957

Napier, Priscilla: *The Sword Dance: Lady Sarah Lennox and the Napiers*, London 1971

Nettel, Reginald, (ed. & trans.): *Carl Philip Moritz: Journeys of a German in England in 1782*, London 1965

Newspapers: *Argus, Courier, English Chronicle, Morning Chronicle, Morning Herald, Morning Post, Public Advertiser, Star, Sun, The Times, True Briton*

Norris, John: *Shelburne and Reform*, London 1963

Norton, J. E. (ed.): *The Letters of Edward Gibbon*, 3 Vols, London 1956

O'Brien, R. B. (ed.): *Autobiography of Wolfe Tone*, 2 Vols, London 1893

O'Gorman, F.: *The Rise of Party in England: The Rockingham Whigs 1760-82*, London 1975

The Whig Party and the French Revolution, London 1967

Oldfield, T. H. B.: *Representative History of Great Britain and Ireland*, 6 Vols, London 1816

Oliver, J. W.: *Life of William Beckford*, London 1932

Oman, Carola: *Sir John Moore*, London 1953

Omond, G. W. T. (ed.): *Arniston Memoirs 1571-1838*, 1887

Pakenham, Thomas: *The Year of Liberty*, London 1969

Pares, Richard: *King George III and the Politicians*, Oxford 1953

Parkes, J. and Merrivale, H. (eds): *Memoirs of Sir Philip Francis*, 2 Vols, London 1867

Parliamentary Debates, ed. W. Cobbett (later *Hansard's Parliamentary Debates*) Series I, 41 Vols, 1812-20

The Parliamentary History of England, 36 Vols, 1806-20

The Parliamentary Register

Pearce, R. R.: *Memoirs and Correspondence of the Most Noble Richard Marquess Wellesley*, 3 Vols, London 1846

Pellew, Hon. George: *The Life and Correspondence of the Rt. Hon. Henry Addington, First Viscount Sidmouth*, 3 Vols, London 1847

Philips, C. H.: *The East India Company 1784-1834*, Manchester 1940

Pitt and Wilberforce (privately printed by Lord Rosebery) Edinburgh 1899

Pitt: *The War Speeches of William Pitt the Younger*, selected by R. Coupland, 3rd edition Oxford 1940

Plumb, J. H.: *England in the Eighteenth Century*, London 1950

Price, Cecil (ed.): *The Letters of Richard Brinsley Sheridan*, 3 Vols, Oxford 1966

Reid, Loren: *Charles James Fox*, London 1969

Report from the Committee appointed to examine the physicians who have attended his Majesty, during his illness, touching the state of his Majesty's health, London 1788

Roberts, W.: *Memoirs of the Life and Correspondence of Mrs. Hannah More*, 4 Vols, 3rd edition London 1835

Roscoe, E. S. and Clergue, Helen (eds): *George Selwyn, his Letters and his life*, London 1899

Rose, J. Holland: *Pitt and the National Revival*, London 1911
Pitt and the Great War, London 1911
Pitt and Napoleon, Essays and Letters, London 1912

Rosebery, Lord: *Pitt*, London 1892
(ed.): *Bishop Tomline's Estimate of Pitt together with Chapter XXVII from the Unpublished Fourth Volume of the Life*, London 1903
(ed.): *Letters relating to the Love Episode of William Pitt together with an account of his health by his physician Sir Walter Farquhar*, London 1900

Ross, Charles (ed.): *Correspondence of Charles, First Marquess Cornwallis*, 3 Vols, 1854

Rudé, George: *Europe in the Eighteenth Century*, London 1972
Hanoverian London 1714-1808, London 1971

Wilkes and Liberty, Oxford 1962

Russell, Lord John (ed.): *Memoirs, Journal and Correspondence of Thomas Moore*, London 1860

(ed.): *Memorials and Correspondence of Charles James Fox*, 4 Vols, London 1853-7

(ed.): *The Life and Times of Charles James Fox*, 3 Vols, London 1859

Rutland, Duke of: *Correspondence between the Right Honble. William Pitt and Charles, Duke of Rutland . . . 1781-87*, London 1890

Sichel, Walter: *Sheridan*, 2 Vols, London 1909

Smith, Adam: *Wealth of Nations*, London 1776

Sorel, Albert: *L'Europe et la Révolution française*, 1885-1911

Southey, Robert: *Letters from England*, London 1807

Stanhope, Earl: *Life of the Right Honourable William Pitt*, 4 Vols, London 1861-2 *Miscellanies*, Second Series, London 1872

(ed.): *Secret Correspondence in connection with Pitt's Return to Office 1804 from MSS at Melville Castle*, London 1852

Stapleton, A. G.: *George Canning and His Times*, London 1859

Stavordale, G. Fox-Strangways, Lord (ed.): *Further Memoirs of the Whig Party*, London 1905

Stephens, A.: *Memoirs of John Horne Tooke*, 2 Vols, London 1813

Steuart, A. Frances (ed.): Horace Walpole: *The Last Journals*, 2 Vols, London/New York 1910

Stirling, A. M. W.: *Coke of Norfolk and His Friends*, London n.d.

Stockdale, J.: *The history and proceedings of the Lords and Commons of Great Britain . . . with regard to the Regency*, London 1789

Stuart, Dorothy M.: *Dearest Bess*, London 1955

Summerson, Sir John: *Georgian London*, revised edition London 1970

Sutherland, Lucy: *The East India Company in Eighteenth Century Politics*, Oxford 1952

Taylor, G. Rattray: *Sex in History*, London 1953

Taylor W. S. and Pringle J. (eds): *Correspondence of William Pitt, Earl of Chatham*, 4 Vols, London 1838-40

Tomline, Sir George Pretyman: *Memoirs of the Life of William Pitt*, 3 Vols, London 1821 (fourth volume privately printed London 1903)

Trevelyan, Sir G. O.: *The Early History of Charles James Fox*, London 1881

Trotter, J. B.: *Memoirs of the Latter Years of the Right Honourable Charles James Fox*, London 1811

Tucker, J. S.: *Memoirs of Admiral the Right Hon. The Earl of St. Vincent*, 2 Vols, London 1844

Tunstall, Brian: *William Pitt Earl of Chatham*, London 1958

Twiss, H.: *Life of Lord Eldon*, 3 Vols, London 1844

United Service Journal 1836

Verney, E. (ed.): *The Journals and Correspondence of Sir Harry Calvert*, London 1853

Walpole, Horace: *Memoirs of the Reign of George III*, 4 Vols, London 1845
Watson, J. S.: *The Reign of George III 1760-1815*, Oxford 1960
West, D. J.: *Homosexuality*, Pelican edition, London 1960
Western, J. R.: *The English Militia in the Eighteenth Century*, London 1965
Wheatley, Henry B. (ed.): Sir Nathaniel William Wraxhall: *The Historical and the Posthumous Memoirs 1772-1784*, 5 Vols, London 1884
Wickham, W. (ed.): *Correspondence of the Rt. Hon. William Wickham*, 2 Vols, London 1870
Wilberforce, A. M.: *The Private Papers of William Wilberforce*, London 1897
Wilberforce, Robert Isaac and Samuel: *The Correspondence of William Wilberforce*, 2 Vols, London 1840
The Life of William Wilberforce, 5 Vols, London 1838
Williams, Basil: *William Pitt, Earl of Chatham*, 2 Vols, 1912
The Whig Supremacy 1714-60, Oxford 1962
Woodruff, Philip: *The Men who ruled India*, 2 Vols, London 1953
Wyvill, Rev. Christopher: *Political Papers . . . chiefly respecting a Reformation of the Parliament of Great Britain*, 6 Vols, London 1794-1804

Ziegler, Philip: *Addington*, London 1965

Index

489

491

495

Pitt, William *(cont'd.)*
French Republic, 271-72; and
French Revolution, 234, 236-37, 239,
241-42, 243, 244, 245-47, 248-49;
funeral, 445-46; and George III, 193,
194, 390-91, 427-28; Gibbon's debate
with, 67-68; and Gordon riots, 60,
64-65, 67; government threatened by
Fox-North Coalition, 127-28; and
Hastings impreachment, 180-81, 185,
187-89, 192, 239; Holwood House
purchase, 166-67; and House of
Lords, 256-59; illness, 10-11, 318-20,
328, 354, 365, 383-84, 402-4, 412-13,
434-35, 437-43; income tax proposal,
355-57; and India, 116, 117, 118,
126, 127, 134-35; 178-79, 368-69;
invited to form government after
Shelburne's resignation, 95-97; and
Irish question, 149, 150, 151, 152-61,
338-42, 343, 345, 346-50, 354-55,
384-91; joins Fox and Grenville vs
Addington, 418-19; joins Western
Circuit, 69; Lincoln's Inn rooms,
55-56; loans to Allies, 314; maiden
speech in parliament, 77-79; and
mail coach controversy, 139-40; and
marriage of Prince of Wales, 304-5,
307-8; on mob attack of Palliser
house, 57; monument to, 445; and
mother's death, 412-13; and mother's
finances, 165; vs Napoleon, 412-16,
417, 421; natural shyness of, 169; and
navy, 275-77; and navy mutinies,
335-36; niece Hester shares home
with, 415-16; and Nootka Sound
incident, 226-29; and Ochakov debate, 229-33; optimism and popularity of, 164-65; parliamentary
reform disavowed by, 245-46, 248-49;
parliamentary reform proposals,
82-84, 99, 104-5, 163-64; peace negotiations with France, 309-11, 351,
352-55; preparation for parliament,
58-60; and Princess Caroline, 381-82;
promises George III to drop Catholic

emancipation idea, 390-91; and Prussia's attack on Belgium, 225-26;
records of speeches, 78n; reduction
of government expenditures, 138-39;
and Regency crisis, 195, 196-99, 200,
201-2, 203-4, 205-7, 208, 209-10,
211; repeal of habeas corpus, 297;
resignation, 391-92, 394; return to
House after resignation, 412; and rift
between Fox and Burke, 241-42; and
rift in Whigs, 262-66, 269, 273; and
second coalition vs France, 371,
372-73, 374, 375, 376-77; and Seditious Meetings Bill, 315-16; sexual
inclinations, 328-33; and sister Harriot, 165, 168-70; and slave trade
issue, 249, 250, 251-56, 316; social
life, 101-3; speech on American war,
79; support of Addington's government, 404-6; support of Melville in
Trotter scandal, 426, 427-29; takes
office after Addington's resignation,
419-24; tax proposals, 136-38, 140,
355-57; and theft of Great Seal, 130;
and third coalition vs France, 429,
431, 432, 433-34, 435-36; Thurlow
asks for aid vs Fox-North government, 104-5; and Thurlow's dismissal, 256, 260; and trade, 142; trip
abroad, 106-9; and Triple Alliance
(first coalition vs France), 223-24,
278, 281, 283-84, 285; and war with
France, 281, 283-84, 285, 286-87,
289, 291-92, 300-1, 303, 308-11, 312,
395, 397-98; wheat price increases,
380; Whigs join in coalition government with, 296-300; and Wilberforce's conversion, 170-74
Pompadour, Madame de, 19
Ponsonby, George, 339, 339n, 340,
342, 427
Ponsonby, John, 339n
Ponsonby, William Brabazon, 339,
339n, 340, 342
Porson, Richard, 126
Portland, Duke of, 76, 82, 86, 87, 92,

498